Contemporary Authors®
Autobiography Series

ISSN 0748-0636

Contemporary
Authors

Autobiography Series

Shelly Andrews
Editor

volume **27**

GALE

DETROIT · NEW YORK · TORONTO · LONDON

EDITORIAL STAFF

Shelly Andrews, *Editor and Desktop Publisher*
Linda Andres, *Contributing Editor*
Motoko Fujishiro Huthwaite, *Associate Editor*
Marilyn O'Connell Allen, *Assistant Editor and Graphics Manager*
Cindy Buck, Sheryl Ciccarelli, Charity Anne Dorgan, Mary Gillis, Heidi Hagen,
Alan Hedblad, Laurie C. Hillstrom, Carolyn C. March, Tom McMahon, Adele Sarkissian,
Mark Schafer, Gary Senick, and Diane Telgen, *Contributing Copyeditors*

Victoria B. Cariappa, *Research Manager*
Corporate Research Information Service

Hal May, *Publisher*
Joyce Nakamura, *Managing Editor, Children's and Young Adult Literature*

Mary Beth Trimper, *Production Director*
Deborah Milliken, *Production Assistant*

Barbara Yarrow, *Graphic Services Manager*
Randy A. Bassett, *Imaging Supervisor*
Robert Duncan, *Imaging Specialist*

Theresa Rocklin, *Manager, Technical Support Services*

Gale Research
835 Penobscot Building
645 Griswold Street
Detroit, MI 48226-4094

Library of Congress Catalog Card Number 86-641293
ISBN 0-7876-1142-5
ISSN 0748-0636

Printed in the United States of America

10   9   8   7   6   5   4   3   2   1

Contents

Special Thanks

We wish to acknowledge our special gratitude to each of the authors in this volume. They all have been most kind and cooperative in contributing not only their talents but their enthusiasm and encouragement to this project.

We also would like to thank past, current, and future contributors and other individuals who have taken the time to provide feedback and make recommendations for this series.

Ivan Argüelles	Marvin R. Hiemstra
Bob and Susan Arnold	Fanny Howe
Jake Berry	Hank Lazer
Michael Bishop	Jim Leftwich
Dorothy Bryant	Russell Leong
Josephine Carson	Leza Lowitz
Neeli Cherkovski	Sarah Menefee
Cid Corman	Alice Notley
Ruth Daigon	Harry Polkinhorn
Vincent Ferrini	Judith Roeke
Jack Foley	Mark Schafer
Edward Foster	Julia Vinograd
Reginald Gibbons	Lisa Zeidner

We encourage our readers to explore the whole *CAAS* series. Please write and tell us if we can make *CAAS* more helpful to you. Direct your comments and suggestions to the editor:

MAIL: Editor, *Contemporary Authors Autobiography Series*
Gale Research
835 Penobscot Bldg.
645 Griswold St.
Detroit, MI 48226-4094

TELEPHONE: (800) 347-GALE

FAX: (313) 961-6599

Preface

A Unique Collection of Essays

Each volume in the *Contemporary Authors Autobiography Series (CAAS)* presents an original collection of autobiographical essays written especially for the series by noted writers.

CA Autobiography Series is designed to be a meeting place for writers and readers—a place where writers can present themselves, on their own terms, to their audience; and a place where general readers, students of contemporary literature, teachers and librarians, even aspiring writers can become better acquainted with familiar authors and meet others for the first time.

This is an opportunity for writers who may never write a full-length autobiography to let their readers know how they see themselves and their work, what brought them to this time and place.

Even for those authors who have already published full-length autobiographies, there is the opportunity in *CAAS* to bring their readers "up to date" or perhaps to take a different approach in the essay format. In some instances, previously published material may be reprinted or expanded upon; this fact is always noted at the end of such an essay. Individually, the essays in this series can enhance the reader's understanding of a writer's work; collectively, they are lessons in the creative process and in the discovery of its roots.

CAAS makes no attempt to give a comprehensive overview of authors and their works. That outlook is already well represented in biographies, reviews, and critiques published in a wide variety of sources. Instead, *CAAS* complements that perspective and presents what no other ongoing reference source does: the view of contemporary writers that is shaped by their own choice of materials and their own manner of storytelling.

Who Is Covered?

Like its parent series, *Contemporary Authors,* the *CA Autobiography Series* sets out to meet the needs and interests of a wide range of readers. Each volume includes essays by writers in all genres whose work is being read today. We consider it extraordinary that so many busy authors from throughout the world are able to interrupt their existing writing, teaching, speaking, traveling, and other schedules to converge on a given deadline for any one volume. So it is not always possible that all genres can be equally and uniformly represented from volume to volume, although we strive to include writers working in a variety of categories, including fiction, nonfiction, and poetry. As only a few writers specialize in a single area, the breadth of writings by authors in this volume also encompasses drama, translation, and criticism as well as work for movies, television, radio, newspapers, and journals.

What Each Essay Includes

Authors who contribute to *CAAS* are invited to write a "mini-autobiography" of approximately 10,000 words. In order to give the writer's imagination free rein, we suggest no guidelines or pattern for the essay.

We only ask that each writer tell his or her story in the manner and to the extent that feels most natural and appropriate. In addition, writers are asked to supply a selection of personal photographs showing themselves at various ages, as well as important people and special moments in their lives. Our contributors have responded generously, sharing with us some of their most treasured mementoes. The result is a special blend of text and photographs that will attract even the casual browser. Other features include:

Bibliography at the end of each essay, listing book-length works in chronological order of publication. Each bibliography in this volume was compiled by members of the *CAAS* editorial staff and submitted to the author for review.

Cumulative index in each volume, which cites all the essayists in the series as well as the subjects presented in the essays: personal names, titles of works, geographical names, schools of writing, etc. To ensure ease of use for these cumulating references, the name of the essayist is given before the volume and page number(s) for every reference that appears in more than one essay. In the following example, the entry in the index allows the user to identify the essay writers by name:

> Auden, W.H.
>   Allen **6:**18, 24
>   Ashby **6:**36, 39
>   Bowles **1:**86
>   etc.

For references that appear in only one essay, the volume and page number(s) are given but the name of the essayist is omitted. For example:

> Stieglitz, Alfred **1:**104, 109, 110

CAAS is something more than the sum of its individual essays. At many points the essays touch common ground, and from these intersections emerge new patterns of information and impressions. The index is an important guide to these interconnections.

For Additional Information

For detailed information on awards won, adaptations of works, critical reviews of works, and more, readers are encouraged to consult Gale's *Contemporary Authors* cumulative index for authors' listings in other Gale sources. These include, among others, *Contemporary Authors, Contemporary Authors New Revision Series, Dictionary of Literary Biography,* and *Contemporary Literary Criticism.* For autobiographical entries written by children and young adult authors see *Something about the Author Autobiography Series.*

A Brief Sampler

Each essay in the series has a special character and point of view that sets it apart from its companions. A small sampler of anecdotes and musings from the essays in this volume hint at the unique perspective of these life stories.

Juvenal Acosta: "I go to teach, and I have in front of me all these young faces, all these eyes, all these hidden talents. What do they expect from me? Poetry cannot be taught. . . . Some of them have read too little, and some have read too much. They want to be poets. Who will get an A? who will get a C? I cannot grade anxieties or sadness, cannot grade an honest image. I will say, and I do say, be honest, stay awake, open your eyes, listen to the music of the end of the century, search whatever truth you want to find, write as if a demon had possessed you, love without fear, walk the streets in order to face possible epiphanies, stay up until dawn so you can understand, quit your job, hate me if you have to, but write and write and write. Your heart will show you the way."

Albert Cook: "I loved that house with its screened-in porch of seemingly endless length, its screened-in small summer house between it and the general store my grandfather had once run, its large, fragrant woodshed now become a garage, stacked high with wood for the winter, its henhouse out back towards the woods that stood across a field behind, its large kitchen around the giant black all-purpose stove where the beans were slow-baked unfailingly every Saturday, its bins for the dry beans and for flour, its large dining room where the family's early-nineteenth-century sampler (now owned by my half sister) hung over the giant rolltop desk that held all the records of the town. There my grandfather would now and then closet himself with some townsperson. Beyond the sunny dining room was the large living room, opening on the wraparound porch through a vestibule. It was organized around the console radio where my grandparents would settle down to hear favorite serials. Visiting the Robert Frost place a couple of years ago, I was surprised to see that on a slightly smaller scale the house where Frost set his first New England poems matched my grandparents' point for point: large stove, dining room, living room, woodshed, henhouse, woods across a field behind."

Edward Field: "As I write this, my world is on the verge of extinction. Everything is different now and I may be an anomaly, but I still feel that the Left, whatever its errors and ideological faults, generally has the best orientation for a livable society. The major theme in my poetry has been speaking up for the poor, the unwanted, the underdog, and by extension, the 'lower' functions of the body. True to my Jewish traditions, I write from the heart, though that is unfashionable in our increasingly selfish, market-oriented universe. When I started writing, I wanted my poetry to save the world. I saw myself standing up in the marketplace and speaking to the people. Later, I desperately believed, against the world, that poetry could save me. In spite of the evident truth that poetry can change nothing, I trust the instincts of the young and why they are attracted to poetry, as if it actually could overcome injustice. It has to do with an idealism that gets lost as you get older, especially as you get involved in the poetry world with its factions and power struggles. It has to do with poetry as magic, the magic of words. I still believe it's a kind of magic."

Fanny Howe: "There were many women like me—born into white privilege but with no financial security; given a good education but no training for survival. Some of us ended up in cults, some in jail, some in far-out marriages. The daughters of white activists tended to become more engaged than even their fathers were, and like certain Greek heroines, they drove themselves to madness and incarceration in carrying to the nth degree their fathers' progressive positions. Because my family (academic, artistic) had no extra money, there was no cushion for the crash from a comfortable home into the literal cold streets. Somehow Carl and I did manage to carve a niche for ourselves—through marriage and new jobs luckily acquired—just off the streets. We were both somewhat conservative in our habits. No drugs, no rock-and-roll. Crossing the racial divide was the only radical ingredient in what we were doing. Basically we were in hiding when we weren't working."

Mary Mackey: "My parents read to me almost every night before bedtime; and during the day, I read everything I could get my hands on from the Oz Books (which I adored) to my father's medical texts (which included horrendous accounts of fetal deformities). Because I read so much, I came to school armed with a huge vocabulary of words I could barely pronounce. I did well enough in every subject (except math) to be branded a teacher's pet; but at the same time I talked out in class, interrupted the other students, and argued with the teacher. I can remember stubbornly holding to the proposition that the shortest distance between two points was *not* a straight line if there happened to be a mountain in the way, and no amount of reasoning or threatening could persuade me otherwise."

Len Roberts: "Two stories my mother used to tell us when we were young typify, I think, her younger years. The first one went like this: On a typically cold, upstate New York winter night, she had gone to bed with her sisters. It was freezing, as usual, she would tell us, so cold that she sometimes felt numb. Well, early the next morning, while it was still dark, she woke to her sister screaming and thrashing in the bed beside her. When the light was turned on, she saw a large muskrat in the corner of the room and then, at the foot of their bed, blood. The muskrat, which had evidently crawled up from the canal in front of their row house, had bitten her sister's foot while she slept. My mother could never sleep soundly in that bed again, she would tell us, and we, as children, knew exactly what she meant. The second story was less dramatic but still shed a good deal of light upon her youth. One night when she was almost asleep she heard some movement downstairs. Her parents were asleep, she thought, so she crept down the stairs to see what was making the noise. There, at the kitchen table, she would whisper to us, were her mother and father eating cake. *Cake,* she would hiss, that they would not share with their children, and which her wages had helped to buy. Whether or not my grandparents were such people, I never knew, but my mother often held that incident up as one she felt most represented her early life: poor, naive, and betrayed."

These brief examples only suggest what lies ahead in this volume. The essays will speak differently to different readers; but they are certain to speak best, and most eloquently, for themselves.

Acknowledgments

Grateful acknowledgment is made to those publishers, photographers, and artists whose works appear with these authors' essays.

Photographs/Art

Juvenal Acosta: pp. 1, 9, 13, Bettina Larroudé; p. 4, Antonio Sandoval; p. 6, TEO Number 6; p. 7, Juvenal Acosta; p. 8, Laurd Hernández; p. 11, Ed Fitzgerald; p. 15, Eugenio Castro; p. 16, Bia Wouk.

Gregory Benford: p. 22, Club Photo "Eddy."

Albert Cook: p. 63, Brown Studio; p. 76, Hank Kranzler.

Frank Davey: p. 83, Linda Davey; p. 90, David Robinson; p. 95, Michael Christopher; p. 98, Michael Ondaatje; pp. 102, 105, George Bowering; p. 107, Elizabeth Humphrey; p. 111, Alex Smith.

Fanny Howe: p. 135, Laurence Scott.

Arthur Winfield Knight: pp. 153, 170, Rob Martel; pp. 156, 167, Bob Brunner; p. 157, Margaret Fisher; p. 161, John Chan; pp. 164, 165, Robert Turney; p. 166, Arthur Knight; p. 168, Perry Gaskill.

Hank Lazer: p. 185, cover of *Doublespace: Poems 1971–1989*, Segue Books, 1992, reprinted by permission of Segue Books; p. 191, cover of *3 of 10*, from a painting by Jess, Chax Press, 1996, reprinted by permission of Jess Collins.

Mary Mackey: p. 199, Heather Hafleigh; p. 213, Lynda Koolish; p. 217, Angus Wright.

Alice Notley: p. 224, Rudy Burckhardt; p. 227, Pietro Gigli; p. 232, Ann Charters; p. 235, Edmund Berrigan; p. 237, Katy Lederer; p. 238, Janet Collins.

Douglas Oliver: p. 241, Marc Atkins © 1996; p. 253, J. B. Diederich.

Leonard Roberts: p. 263, Steve Beseris.

Floyd Salas: pp. 316, 320, Floyd Salas; p. 319, Ginny Staley.

Text

Albert Cook: Poem "In Memory of My Grandfather" and excerpt from poem "Coming Along," from *Progressions*, by Albert Cook. University of Arizona Press, 1963. Copyright

Contemporary Authors ®

Autobiography Series

Juvenal Acosta

1961-

NOTES OF A FOREIGN SON

*For Gustavo Ramos Rivera,
a foreign son*

I am not a James Baldwin scholar. I came upon his books so recently that I felt somehow guilty when I had the idea of acting on the inspiration that Baldwin gave me for some aspects concerning the writing of my own notes. But after studying his bittersweet style and being repeatedly struck by the lightning of his noble rage, I couldn't avoid feeling not the right as much as the need to write my own notes in that spirit. A renegade's American spirit. These are, therefore, the notes of the bastard son from a foreign country who became the unwanted son of this elusive and unwilling "America."

*

When James Baldwin's *Notes of a Native Son* was first published in 1955, I was not even born for my date with my North American destiny. Around that time another important book was being written in California, perhaps in this same town where I've been lucky enough to sit and watch the decay of my decade from the comfort provided by the shadow of these Berkeley pine trees. This other book gave— not only to Mexicans but to people from many different national, racial, and cultural backgrounds—important clues for the search of their own identities: *The Labyrinth of Solitude* by the Mexican poet Octavio Paz. It is not by chance— I hope—that I arrive at these two works. They are important pieces of the intellectual machinery that went into building part of the modern consciousness of our neighboring countries at a time when I need to search for answers to my dilemmas of identity in this California limbo.

*

*Juvenal Acosta (left) with his friend,
the painter, Gustavo Ramos Rivera, 1994*

Notes of a Native Son and *The Labyrinth of Solitude* converge in many surprising ways. At first sight one could be shocked at the idea that two writers from such different, and perhaps opposite, backgrounds and experiences could have something in common. But it is not in the land of the obvious where these two giants meet. What I find striking is the hidden dialogue that is established between the quiet, elegant, and eloquent Baldwin, who poses fundamental questions as he invites us to see his

1

scarred back, and the privileged and sophisticated Paz, who tries to deal with questions for which there has been no possible answer for centuries—answers just as questions are always timely. What they share is more profound where silence occupies the always elusive place of words and tells us who we, perhaps, are: citizens of doubt. Both writers are complementary sides of a tossed coin that is still in the air. Their reflections on the nature itself of identity and the issues that burn us when we think of these bastard sons of the northern portion of our continent, the Black and the Mexican, enable us to further the quest for answers at the end of yet another fistful of years we call millennium.

*

While thousands of my fellow Mexicans cross the frontier between Mexico and the United States—that border that separates hope from desperation, to fulfill their wetback destinies (and demonstrating, by doing so, that the border is a painful and not too imaginary open wound that desire and need do not respect)—I sit and think that what really separates our countries is not an iron fence and not even a language, but a different awareness of ourselves regarding our attitudes towards life and the degree of confidence we have about our destinies.

I did not cross that line "illegally." There were times when I wished I had, but that is the romantic and somehow stupid thought of someone who feels guilty for having had the luck of avoiding misery. Since I arrived as a guest to teach in California, am I entitled to speak about that border that I didn't have to suffer? To put it in a way that Baldwin himself might have put it, I say, of course I qualify: I am a Mexican.

*

In my eleven years since my arrival, I have had two radically different experiences of life in this country: that of the intellectual and that of the laboring worker. But what is remarkable in the first place is that I actually came to the United States, a country I had been taught to distrust, a country I had learned to despise.

*

I grew up in a middle-class family of the Mexico City suburbs where no one ever considered relocating to even another city within Mexico. Our background was deeply nationalistic, leftist, not very religious, and, of course, anti-yanqui. Our shelves at home were filled with books, some of which could have sent my parents to jail had we lived in the United States during the fifties: Mao Tse-tung, Marx, Paulo Freire, the diaries of "el Ché" Guevara, and a decent selection of our Mexican and Latin American talents: Fuentes, Vargas Llosa, Paz, and Borges, to name a few. There was no Bible on those shelves until I got one from my grandfather who rediscovered God (just in case) towards the end of his life.

Mexico during the sixties and a good part of the seventies was an entirely different country. At the time, outsiders saw us as an upbeat young nation with nothing but future in our hands and a rising economy ready to back up all predictions of prosperity. I was born in 1961, and by the time I was five my very young parents had managed to buy the house they still live in; they had the car, the white picket fence, two kids, and a couple of nice vacations every year. Does it sound familiar? I was raised (despite all nationalisms) on Kellogg's Corn Flakes and ketchup, "The Addams Family" and Mickey Mouse. In a way, I was a North American child, born south of the border.

*

My father was some sort of immigrant himself. He had come from rural Mexico to the big city, the *Capital*, and was "lucky" enough to marry my mother, who was the daughter of an established Mexico City family. My mother's sisters, four of them, hated my father. He had what middle-class people call bad manners; he looked provincial, was poorly dressed, and didn't fit the profile most middle-class urban girls from Mexico City looked for in a man: He wasn't white; he didn't have a recognizable last name, and he wasn't a doctor. He was not even a college professor, but a schoolteacher. Even after thirty-five years my father's bitterness shows on his face when he remembers how one of my aunts brought home a white, blue-eyed young man, who eventually became her husband and who in no time at all got the attention and considerations my father didn't get until many years later. His bitterness haunts me once in awhile when I face a mirror: I look very much like him.

*

Racism is not exclusive to Anglo-dominated cultures. I can witness to that. What was denied to my father when he married my mother was in turn denied to me. I didn't understand the detachment of my grandmother and my aunts until many years later. My father and I weren't white enough; therefore, we were not good enough. The only exception was my grandfather. He was just like us. He had come from rural Mexico and was lucky enough to marry someone's daughter. Like my father and me, he had dark Indian features, was a school teacher, and didn't give a damn about the petty bourgeois preoccupations of his wife and daughters. Grandfather Hernández was a painter and had a studio on the third floor of the house, and that is where I would go when we visited. He used to receive the most fascinating visitors at his upstairs refuge. There were times I wasn't allowed to be there for too long, since he would be busy with all the people who dropped by (in Mexico no one makes appointments to see friends). With the exception of my mother, the women of the family considered grandfather some sort of a drunken bohemian; he was considered a good-for-nothing who always disregarded the pseudo-aristocratic ways of his wife and daughters.

*

My grandfather became serious about painting when he retired from teaching, and then he simply died when he got bored after more than twenty years of increasing deafness. The day he died in 1989 I got a call from my mother asking me to come home because it was time for him to go. From Berkeley, I sped to the San Francisco Airport and made it to the hospital in Mexico City six hours later, just in time to see him before he died. He liked me so much that he decided to die twice that day just so he could see me. When I arrived at the hospital his youngest son was outside in the hallway, pale and shaking. He told me Grandpa had been resuscitated just a couple of minutes before my arrival. He had died, but he came back the moment I arrived. I saw him and told him very important things I had not been able to tell him since I had left for the United States three years before that day.

*

I'm a Mexican writer living at the end of a wonderful and terrible century. Last week I "celebrated" my eleventh year of self-imposed exile in the United States, a country that most Mexicans don't like but need.

The journey that led me to this morning of uncertain California spring began when I was eighteen years old. Young Mexicans don't leave their parents' house the way young Americans do. But I slammed that door behind me and took off in desperate anguish and solitude. Many North Americans can relate to the void in which a person lives when growing up in the suburbs. But a Mexican suburb is probably worse. What made sense in the United States didn't in Mexico City. I didn't know it back then. It took me years to be able to phrase that anguish. I left barely on time; my brains had not died.

When I left I had in mind a lot of unclear questions and a specific project: to become a writer. I had no means of any kind in order to conduct my search, but I had innocence and doubts, which are a valuable tool for any young artist.

For three years I wandered around Mexico City, going back and forth between my parents' house and empty apartments, drinking, falling in and out of love. I mastered the art of surviving without any money. I tried to get laid as much as I could and used poetry as a way of meeting women, usually older than I, usually sadder. I registered at three different colleges and dropped out of all three of them. I was at war with my parents and drank daily. My body was skinny and unhealthy; love was out of sight, and the city had become a nightmare, its unsizable solitude overwhelming.

So I left the city and went to Morelia. Five of my poems had been taken by a little magazine, and by the time I got to Morelia I had copies of it in my backpack to back up my literary background. I arrived in Morelia as a

"Mexico City poet" and was befriended by the young artists and intellectuals of that town. It was a very important time in my life. I would just sit for hours in the city's coffeehouses, drinking *café fuerte* and talking Artaud and Rauschenberg, discussing Revueltas and Paz with my new friends. I went to philosophy school at the state university and became some kind of student leader. My life as a full-time young poet and bohemian lasted for two years.

*

I had come to the United States for twenty days in 1986 to teach some poetry workshops, but I liked Berkeley and San Francisco so much that I decided to stay a little longer, and then a little longer yet, though it didn't make sense to any of my friends or family that I should be here. Then I met a woman and life took over.

*

What is it like to come to Berkeley from Mexico City? Well, let me tell you: I woke up after the shock of seeing the night before a huge Hell's Angel riding his hog very politely as I crossed the Bay Bridge from San Francisco towards the East Bay—the radio was playing "Hotel California" as I discovered for the first time the breathtaking sight of the city's Embarcadero. Then I went for a walk, and as I made it to downtown Berkeley I saw about a thousand delirious Deadheads hanging out at a park, a multicolored, dancing, pot-smoking, patchouli-smelling crowd waiting for a concert of the Grateful Dead to start.

*

Only ten years ago Berkeley was a very different town, and California and the United States were very different places. Life within the boundaries of the United States creates an illusion of self-sufficiency that isolates us: our relations with the rest of the world are always distant. We lack points of reference in time and space. Berkeley during the eighties lived some of its last bohemian years that gave it the glory that still attracts new students and nostalgic tourists

"*My parents, Laura and Juvenal,*" 1988

in search of long-gone hippie or beatnik radicalism. But today, Telegraph Avenue is no longer that extension of the Haight-Ashbury of San Francisco; it has become a business battleground where the Gap and Ben and Jerry's dispute with the local small merchants for the right to own a piece of the marijuana dream that has turned into a yuppie nightmare. No poets will you find nor flower children, but nineteen-year-old Republicans majoring in computer science. They watch with distrust the homeless who stand on the sidewalks, leftovers of a generation mostly gone bizarre and Birkenstock or Berzerkeley with or without Noah's bagels with cream cheese and lox. People's Park, the piece of land that witnessed the micro-revolution that Ronald Reagan had the dubious honor of putting out with rubber bullets and one death, is the perfect site for small drug dealing and future parking lots. Berkeley has gone to hell by going yuppie style.

*

Yes, I came as a poet but "a pen is not a spoon," as a South American writer once said. Berkeley gave me cappuccino dreams, blond love, and pizza by the slice—but no money for my words. In a period of less than a year, I became a failed apprentice of several trades: cookie maker, dishwasher, gas-station attendant, waiter, espresso jockey, house painter, and babysitter.

And finally I became a carpenter, an occupation that would become my trade for the years to come. I learned to swing the hammer with the best and found a part of me that I never suspected could exist. I gave Berkeley many retaining walls, foundations, and sheared walls. My being from a city in which ground tends to shake, I understood the ways in which California tends to swing.

*

Manual labor is very much out of the question for a Mexican or Latin American artist or intellectual. As such, you just are not supposed to do those things; by rejecting manual labor the writers and artists of Latin America don't know what they are missing as protégés of the state who make a living of teaching or working for the cultural institutions sponsored by the government: the Zen of the backbreaking work. But that doesn't mean that the transition from spoiled poet to carpenter is an easy one: the day I found myself immersed in the hard survival game immigrants play in the land of the free, where absolutely nothing or nobody is really free, I felt lost. I couldn't speak the language and didn't know the rules. But I wrote a lot of poetry.

*

I am a poet from another culture in a foreign country, which—despite its geographic closeness to Mexico—doesn't really know a lot about my culture. This ignorance, however, is well balanced by the ignorance Mexicans have regarding American culture. I have found myself often complaining about the stereotypes that prevail in the United States about my country. (Please, don't talk to me anymore about that weekend you spend in Tijuana!) But what we Mexicans know about the United States is not very much, really.

Because a poet is a "member of the royalty" in my city (a poor—though well-respected—royalty), once in here, I wanted to be acknowledged as a poet rather than as just another Mexican washing your dishes after you had your polenta, but that of course didn't happen. If most Americans cannot name at least one of their Pulitzer Prize winners, why should they

care about my privileged but lost status and my own literary traditions?

In 1987, running out of money and between jobs, I was forced to sell some of the books I had brought with me from Mexico. I took works written by some of the most famous writers from Mexico to the Berkeley bookstores that had sections of Spanish literature. But nobody knew who these authors were. They hadn't heard their names. They said they were sorry but refused to buy. I was shocked: these Mexican talents were nobodies outside their own country. I got to keep my books, bitterly happy.

*

In one of his most popular poems, the poet Paul Celan said, "Death is the master of Germany." Solitude, not death, is the master of America. I have seen how America has decided to make of the foreigner its most frightening enemy. I speak about this as America's foreign son. As the unwanted son who inspires not affection but fear.

*

For Americans, identity has become a crucial question as they discover their own solitude in a world that grows increasingly apart and distant from their own destiny. In an era of information and alleged immediate communication, we paradoxically isolate ourselves more and more everyday.

My attachment to this land that has become my home grants me the right of being critical of its failures. I love California and the San Francisco Bay Area. I have found myself or, at least, a part of myself in the midst of this foggy coast. Every time I go away I miss something very concrete: a walk around the Berkeley Hills looking at the windy city across the Bay, a cup of coffee at Peet's, a cigarette with cappuccino at North Beach's Enrico's after going by City Lights.

My love for California gives me the right to worry about its future. Back home, in my chaotic and terribly beautiful Mexico City, future is a question without answer. Economic disaster has destroyed almost all remaining dreams. But California is that portion of Mexico that we can still keep alive. I have not come to California like Rulfo's Pedro Paramo went to Comala, looking for his father. I have come to California to perhaps encounter myself. I have come to try to look at myself from the mirror of distance. If the United States will decide that its foreign sons are not to be trusted, then my future and the futures of my unborn children are uncertain. When James Baldwin found himself in foreign lands he also found that he was "equal," but this equality came from his bitter discovery of racism outside of his own home: he was equally distrusted, equally unequal. Baldwin, America's native son, offered a solution based on a tremendous sense of dignity: he claimed his rights as a son of this land and did not take a negative answer. The foreign sons and daughters of America have to face the same dilemma and must act based upon that sense of dignity. This sense will be rediscovered once we realize that at some point in our history most of us were foreign sons.

Notebooks

March 1996. Tomorrow I will become an American citizen.

Today I walked from my truck (the only things left from my years as a carpenter are a truck and rough hands) towards the San Francisco State University campus, where I'm teaching poetry, and then I had the clear realization that my body was on fire.

*

I have always understood life as an irresolvable tension between opposite forces: Light and darkness. Good and evil. A dialectic processing of this kind of thinking as understood by anyone with a minimum knowledge of Marxist theory would describe a possible solution to this conflict. I don't see a solution. A tension is to be explored. I could not solve a tension. Given the opportunity to live a tension, I would have

The author in Patagonia, with his wife and their parents:
(from left) Lucho, Laura, Juvenal, Bettina, Juvenal, Sr., and Betty

to go all the way into it—and very likely let it explode. Mine is a dialectic of exploding passions.

*

I go from MTV to François Villon and pause for a minute to reflect on what I'm doing. Books line my walls, and the general view of this side of the house offers an easy conclusion to whoever wonders about my work.

I always wanted to be a writer. And even though being a writer is one of the most stupid decisions a practical person can make nowadays, I couldn't see another option.

*

September 1994. I was born thirty-three years ago. Thirty-three is a magic number. Our foremost poet from the beginning of the century, Ramón López Velarde, died at thirty-three, the age of the "blue Christ," as he once wrote. This is an age for a poet to die; there are other cases in which Mexican poets have died at this age. But my thirty-three years are a beginning, for I have just started to learn how to be alive.

There are many different aspects to my life that I would like to reflect on in order to understand the possible points of departure for the voyage I'm about to take. I'm starting a life where others finished it. When I became infected with the virus of poetry, I didn't know the risks involved in such "profession." Now, after fifteen years of practicing the blues of divine nothingness, I've come to a point where I must jump into life in order to survive.

*

When I think about my origins I have to remember a line in one of my poems: *"Have I got the time to be concerned about the origin of my bones. . . ?"* Yes, I have.

I came from two blood lines that stand opposite to each other. Like most Mexicans, I find in my immediate family the traces of the Indian and the Spanish cultures intertwined in a very complex manner. My features are those of an Indian, but there are probably hundreds

"My wife, Bettina, and our cat Nicolasa Tomasa in our Berkeley apartment," 1992

of years behind me in which no Indian language has been spoken. I regret not speaking one of the many native languages that are still spoken in Mexico today.

*

September 1996. On a certain afternoon of 1969 I was sent by my mother to buy bread at our local bread shop. It must have been the last week of August. In August, the Mexican autumn brings rain to the streets of Mexico City and cleans the air. It is the time of the year when if we are lucky we can see the volcanoes from downtown. I walked out the door with a couple of coins and, as I was approaching the intersection where that street ended, I had to stop. I could not understand it right away. Something had occurred—there was something very different and intense that I somehow felt. It took me a while to see that it had to do with the quality of the light. How long did it take me to see it? I do not know. But I stood right at that corner until I saw *it*. It surrounded my small body and embraced me. I was neither cold nor hot. For the first time in my conscious life I was experiencing a perfect moment. I was being blessed by an epiphany

I had never suspected. At some point I went and got the bread, I suppose, but that I cannot remember. I was not hungry; therefore, I did not care.

This autumn I went back again wanting to find it, and one more time the August rain, like every year, had washed the pretty but scarred face of my old town. I did not really see *it*; I was not able to find it. I was almost disillusioned when this suspicion relieved me: maybe another child was being touched by it at that very moment.

*

It is October 3, 1968, and as every morning, my brother and I are getting ready to be driven to school. We have to shower, get dressed—I have to help my brother with his shoes—and come down to have breakfast. As I go down the stairs, I see my father's face wearing an expression of pain. He is holding the newspaper in his hands and can't believe what he is reading. The day before the Mexican army and the Mexico City police have killed hundreds of students in the sadly famous Massacre of the Plaza de Tlatelolco, also known as the Plaza of the Three Cultures—the Three Cultures of Death—I start to cry, without really knowing why.

*

After the 1985 earthquake, Mexico City found herself broken—like Frida Kahlo's pelvic bone. Like her bones for Frida, the city's broken bones became her obsession. She, my city, had been changed. We all had been broken.

Two years after leaving Mexico City I came back to that navel of the universe. I made it just in time for the moment of the fracture. The city split beneath my feet and broke my heart. I had turned twenty-four only four days before, and my back broke, and my heart broke, and no words could come out of my mouth for shame and rage had taken over.

*

I never liked the suburb where I grew up. The developers of that area of town thought

Acosta (left) with his brother, Luis Enrique, in front of their kindergarten, 1967

that it was time for Mexico to start looking like Los Angeles. Why not? We were not a poor country anymore. The fifties and sixties had brought financial prosperity to Mexico, and we deserved to hope for our own American dream. *Ciudad Satélite* was built, and my parents moved into it. Shame on the Mexican dream. The real Mexico City had been far from my own small dream.

*

My mother wanted to be an actress and for some inexplicable reason wanted her oldest son—me—to be a philosopher. She married my father at twenty. She could have been a model, but my father would not stand for that. My mother stopped playing with her children after seven or eight years of marriage. One day she found me crying. I was seven, and I told her I did not want to grow up because I did not want to suffer. I became a poet, and my mother never became an actress. Had I been a philosopher I could probably explain my life with greater depth.

*

The Mexico City metro gave me the most unexpected present I ever had. I had been back in town for a few days and had a copy of my first book of poems with me. I had recently read a wonderful short story by the Argentine writer Julio Cortazar in which the main character goes into the Paris metro and falls in love with a woman. They play a game in which the reflection of her face in the train's window looks at his face, and he bets that she will leave the train at a certain station. If she leaves before or after he will lose her and play the game with a different woman. He fails to guess, but he falls in love with her and follows her. They have coffee and become lovers. After a while he confesses to her that he has broken the rules, and they decide to look for each other again. The lovers return to the Paris subway.

It wasn't Paris but Mexico City, and I found a woman and fell in love with her. I remember some golden stripes of hair and the year, 1985. I wanted to talk to her, and she was looking at me. I also wanted to respect the rules of the game and avoid the traps of my desire. I told myself that she would leave the train at the same station I would, but as we approached the station's platform, she did not move. I almost panicked. Quickly, I wrote something on my book, and when the doors opened I put it on her lap, looked intensely at her, and rushed away. I was loyal to the rules of the game, but I lost her forever.

I cried all night, got drunk, and wrote a long poem. At the time I was convinced that when it comes to love you cannot play dirty. Every now and then I look for her when I go back to the San Cosme metro station.

*

Poetry does not heal. It helps you understand the wound.

*

March 1996. I am in San Francisco. I am walking in San Francisco, and as I walk I feel how my body slowly starts to burst into flames.

I stop as I did many years before when I saw light for the first time at the intersection on my way to buy bread. I am burning.

"Me, Argentine artist Gaby Fernández, and Gustavo Ramos Rivera," 1997

Maybe because I have to die. Maybe because I have to be born. Raise myself from my shit and my ashes. If I burn, what will be left of my punished body? I burn slowly, and I proceed to walk. Nobody seems to notice that there is a man who is walking as a moving torch. I die.

A couple of hours later I call Michael McClure to ask him whether he's been on flames before. He has not but suggests I should be alone for a while so I can understand the process. Go away to the mountains, he says. My friend, the painter Gustavo Ramos Rivera, tells me about Orozco's mural: the burning man in Guadalajara. Alberto Blanco advises about the symbolic weight of this event.

That night I don't sleep since I want to witness my own birth. Perhaps I should change my name. I write a long letter to McClure. I see the new day, how it caresses the Oakland hills. I am alone in this world but have no fear. I am silent.

*

March 25/26, 1996

Dear Michael:

I called you earlier today, and I just have to believe that it was not a mere coincidence that I *found* you.

(I write this trying to *load*—as much as my English allows me to do so—my words with as much sense as I possibly can.)

I'm rather intrigued by the fact that I "chose" to write the poem I read to you over the phone in English—You know all those things people say about the poem choosing you, and not the other way around.

But going back to bureaucracy and nationalities, it is rather strange that my last poem as a Mexican I happened to write in English.

And now, as the new day arrives in Oakland, comet outside somewhere and me broken as an old dish, I write you a letter to perhaps try to understand the why's and how's of this event.

I knock at the door of my 34, wearing a strange hat, and I find myself fragmented and bruised. My identity shattered by desires and realities.

I called and told you: Michael, I burst up in flames.

I did, indeed.

Then I had to come out of myself and see what had happened.

—This was not supposed to happen, but it did.

I was under the impression that a couple other things were going to occur today. The first one, that I would call Alberto Blanco to just talk with him about my perceptions of this day, as they relate to all the powerful symbols that are brought about by my decision of becoming an American citizen. The second one was the belief that I would sit at a coffee shop somewhere to write a poem (in Spanish) about that as well. But when we think we have things under control, we ourselves can't escape being controlled from beyond and within.

I ended up burning up my skin under the sun and getting a message from the past and the future, and calling you afterwards, instead of calling Alberto.

I've been getting ready for this for a long time and now I'm afraid. I am dying in order to be reborn from my ashes. And I was explaining that to Gustavo ten minutes before you told me exactly the same thing that I had been saying to him.

Of course this whole business of becoming a U.S. citizen is not about the legal implications of changing nationalities. I barely have to tell you this because I know you understand this whole issue very well. Borges used to say that the concept of Nationalism was/is an aberration.

I'd been saying for a while that I wanted not to be Mexican anymore, meaning: I didn't want a nationality.

But I always wanted a language, and mine is that eagle who feeds off snakes. Flying flesh. If I had to quit my language in order to change my civilian identity, it is very likely I would not consider any of this, you know. But that's not the case.

It is the case, however, that I'm changing a skin that does no longer fit my persona. I see in the mirror a blurry face and I don't recognize the stranger: he looks like someone I used to know. He is afraid of me, but not the other way around. So far, anyway.

You wrote something I decided to make mine: *To be alive is to feast in desperation.*

I've been learning the truth of that revelatory line from day one, and I'm about to jump into the real feast. And my appetite is huge, Michael, and the void is made of fire.

Lawrence Ferlinghetti, Neeli Cherkovski, a...
Juvenal Acosta in front of Ferlinghetti's
City Lights Bookstore, San Francisco

I decided I wouldn't go to sleep tonight. Comet somewhere out there announcing the edge. A dictator is about to die. Hopefully the one inside of me.

You asked: How does it feel to burst into flames? To be on fire? I told a friend today that Francisco de Quevedo once said of love: *Es hielo abrasador . . . es fuego helado . . .* is burning ice . . . is chilling fire. . . .

My veins—as if they were in love (were they?)—were full of burning ice and they—they, not me—wanted to scream. Acid gluing my muscles together, glass cutting my optic nerves from within. And above all: thirst. But not for water, Michael, not for water.

I started to have premonitory dreams about my death about six months ago. And, attending to the symbolic side of that announcement, I realized today what my mind was up to all along. (Ironic to think that, even as I write these words, technically speaking, I'm agonizing.)

But my death is just a form.

And I've been so caught up in forms all my life!

Will the creature about to rise from the ashes be free of forms?

Only death is unshaped; only death we don't know.

Is my intention of staying up all night today a weak attempt at preventing death from coming?

Do we write in order to avoid death? We, who are trapped by forms, long for the unknown freedom of the non-existent. We long for life as we imagine it; for life as an intuition. Thresholds are usually portrayed as tenebrous and sinister.

Re-cycle sadness! Welcome back to the origin! You are born naked into deceit, and then you don't even know it. How long does it take to learn to see?

I want to search for clues in my blood.

Go inside it and bathe in its color, dive into my genes.

I want to be ready to translate Kerouac! And this is something most translators do not give a shit about!

I want to taste my self inside of me.

You suggested that I should be with myself and that is where I'm searching, Michael. I am with my self: this is the body I occupy on Earth. This is where I can be found when I'm not to be found elsewhere. I want to see me in here. Knock knock, open the door . . . *it's me.*

Were there other men on fire before me? Orozco went up in flames. Was Pollock ever on fire? Do you know that? I hope he was.

My ancestors used to burn their lands in order to make them fertile. And I do not own other land than my own body. My land of citizenship is my body. My first origin and my final end. Wherever I go I bring my land with me. I am, like José Gorostiza, full of me. Sieged.

The sacred fire signals the end and the beginning. I'm having labor pains. I'm making the century burn. In-from-off me. In front of me.

I burn my body as a sacrifice to the eagle
I have not been able to be
   In order to be fertile I must burn
   and with that fire my files should go up
in flames as well

   In my blood: the history of my nation, the
chronicle of my tribe, the premonition of the
end.
      Fire is not silent. I will burn all of that so
I can rescue it and make it fertile. From fire
a new voice shall come and say: open the door
. . . *it's me*

   The eagle will fly above the burning landscape

      land   fire
      escape   scape

   I want not to have questions, but more than
that: not to give answers
      the city of my body is a new city blessed
by absolute ignorance

      after the earthquake, San Francisco burnt
for days. And when the fire was over *we* rebuilt it from its ashes
      I arrived in here from the devastation of
my own city and I brought her, destroyed, within
me.
      I brought her dead and her unchanged skin,
lacerated and gray from pollution

      now I have to make it burn
      so I can take its remains and make it arise
clean and young outside of me forever

      not be that city who is strangled
      who is the violation of all universal laws
      leave her behind as a mad lover
      as a terrible doubt

      the cycle of the transformations of death
      gives free passports but my ticket ain't one
way man

      I agonize in the midst of the new City
      but this journey into the night is not a
journey into darkness
      for darkness is not always dark

      Dark ness beats subtle in the heart of fire
      as light pulsates in the spinal chord of doubt

We are not the papers we must sign. We
must burn those papers.

   What do you do when you go to open the
door and
      discover that the one who's been knocking
all along is *you?*
      Would you let yourself in, into that house
on fire?

      Knock
      knock

      Calinfierno
      Californo
      Kaliforno
      there is a door
      and nothing lays
      behind it

      End of the century in California:
      the dog next door
      barks at the passing comet

      I want to be born
         = I want to be
               b
               u
               r
               n
               t

      wouldn't you try to rescue
      your self
      from a house on fire?

      You r self

      Truly yours

      y   our   self?

      Our words are at war

      oh! I see. . . .

      nonsense innocence

      scattered ashes on the edge of truth

      my Vesuvio heart trapping me inside its lava
      I must be a continuation

a snake who bit her tail
a blind jaguar
the fallen feather
who falls and can't
lust absolute
timeless link
forgiveness
finally

Your hands are shaped with the shape of fire
look at them

I have to be *their* continuation . . .
Where did the stream of fire begin?

Come on! For god's ache!
Is it safe to be awake?

The stream of consciousness a stream of fire

By discovering fire
Man discovered himself

When we killed the first bison
we didn't know we were committing
suicide

I am the continuation of that killing

I am my bison . . .
god . . .

by finding fire
I find myself

I ≠ ≠ ≠ scar

Quevedo:
polvo serás, mas polvo enamorado . . .
dust you shall be, but dust in love. . . .

chilling fire

　　　　　　*

With the poet Alberto Blanco

　　　　　　　　　2 de abril, 1996

Querido Alberto:

El fuego que está hecho de sombra es más intenso. Tengo una semana de nacido. Y en el corazón del fuego está la duda y en el corazón de la duda la palpitación de ese silencio que marcha apresurado. En el centro de ese bosque de cenizas cuya entrada vigila celosamente el tigre de Blake, ¿encontraré ese fuego sagrado? En el centro del fuego un corazón de sombra. Y entre las preguntas que yo me hago el deseo de no encontrar respuestas, pues la pregunta es suficiente ahora.

Ahora que me habito las necesidades se me acaban. Los deseos son otros. El pan sabe distinto. Y saludo lleno de alegría mi hueso.

Abro lo ojos.

Ah. . . .

Me siento culpable ahora por no sentirme culpable. Pero tal vez estuve agonizando mucho tiempo y me acostumbré a la idea de no ser yo. Mueres, pero qué muerte mayor que no morir, que muerte más severa que la de la agonía. Y yo me venía muriendo desde hace tanto, Alberto. Ahora, me visto en la mañana y me rasuro y, efectivamente, estoy frente al espejo. Un día de estos hasta voy a sonreir.

¿Por qué, el día de mi juramento como nuevo ciudadano de este país, antes de ir a la corte, me detuve con Gustavo a tomarme un café en North Beach y me encontré a una amiga de mi ex-mujer que me dijo que X se había vuelto loca? Ella, la madre de mis miedos.

Y como si este sentimiento de orfandad no fuera suficiente hoy me desperté pensando—me avergüenzo casi por pensarlo—que nuestro poeta padre va a morir muy pronto.

Como si esta ansiedad y esta preocupación por el fin del siglo significaran que absolutamente todo tiene que recomenzarse a partir de cero, y por lo tanto estamos obligados a verdaderamente despojarnos de todo lo pasado, todo lo aprendido y verdaderamente empezar.

Algo está pasando. Lo siento pasar junto a mí este mismo momento. Se detiene. No estoy solo. Se me ocurre pensar que eres tú.

Ahora suena el teléfono y una mujer que va a escribirte una carta y que seguramente recibirás después de ésta, puesto que quiere tu dirección, me empieza a hablar de tu poema "Mala Memoria." Todo tiene sentido. He estado recibiendo avisos y he estado adivinando cosas. Solo el fuego me ha sorprendido.

En él voy a depositar todos los archivos de mi memoria, confiando en que su abrazo es necesario.

¿Cuando algo se quema, se quema como ofrenda o como sacrificio?

Antes—ahora hay un antes—el mundo no estaba lleno de señales. ¡Qué regocijo!

Esta lluvia, por ejemplo. ¿Para apagar este fuego que lleva ardiendo una semana? Siete días ardiendo y ahora llueve. El mes que marca mis diez años de vida fuera de México se inicia con una lluvia torrencial que es capaz de apagar cualquier incendio. Señales en el fuego.

Una gran sed comienza a ser satisfecha. Sin explicación, como las preguntas de los niños.

Parte de este abrir los ojos es darme cuenta de que no estoy solo. Siempre temí la soledad y ahora no temo quedarme solo. Quiero, incluso, estar solo. Porque no lo estoy. No puedo estarlo. Mi miedo obedece a otras razones. Algo va a pasar Alberto y quiero estar despierto para verlo.

Estoy en un estado de Beatitud.

Estoy naciendo.

Pero todo parto es doloroso.

Mi mujer me recuerda mis obligaciones civiles y terrenas y eso significa que no habrá tiempo para parir puesto que hay cosas urgentes que atender. Y yo atiendo.

Ah. . . .

Pasó el día y yo en él hacia esta hora imprecisa donde hay que recuperar lo que el día destrozó—y tratar de darle forma (o quitársela).

El reloj marca una hora irreal. La casa está en silencio. Pido inteligencia.

Paciencia para entrar en el corazón de esta materia que no se entiende con el ojo.

Cuando la realidad te ha derrotado inventa tu propia realidad.

Aun de la traición viene algún entendimiento.

Hay amarguras más altas. Dolores más profundos.

En un cuerpo como el mío, hecho de cicatriz, acostumbrado a ella, aún hay espacio Alberto para mucha cicatriz. Pero si he de ser abierto y tasajeado; si he de verme herido y marcado nuevamente, una y otra vez, que sea una marca fértil la que quede, un tatuaje de luz y no un escupitajo.

Un pacto con el tigre: Devóralo todo, menos este simulacro de alma. Recién comienzo a abrir los ojos y me gusta aun lo que no veo. En mí muere el deseo tal y como lo conozco. Estoy conforme en mi piel, bendigo mi hueso.

Quiero caminar hasta mi casa. Besar la frente de mis padres. Darles mi pésame por su hijo muerto y darle un beso en la frente a mi cadaver. Sentarme a mi lado y meditar en las cosas que hubiera hecho, las palabras que no dije, los hijos que no vi, que no existieron.

Recordar que debo una explicación a alguien, a Esculapio un gallo y una carta. A mí: Un abrazo en mi ataúd de lata y mi perdón.

El camino frente a mí es un camino que me conduce siempre a casa.

Yo me tuve que ir a buscar mi cadaver sucesivo. Y planté con pistas el camino. Pero olvidé o las señales o el lenguaje en que las había escrito. Intenté consolarme con la idea de que el retorno es imposible, pero no descarté la posibilidad de que las señales me encontraran.

En mi costado la costilla fracturada se me clava y me reprocha mi falta de cuidado. Mi irresponsabilidad.

Pero no tengo tiempo más que para estudiar el minuto que tengo frente a mí. El ruido del tren a la distancia es un llamado. Y en la libreta los signos que no he escrito me preguntan y me piden tiempo.

ESTE es el comienzo.

*

The author with Tino Villanueva

In January of 1994, when the Zapatistas started their uprising, I was in Mexico. I did not go to Chiapas out of shame and discretion. It took me more than a year to go there, and it also took an invitation by my friends Elva Macías, the great Chiapaneca poet, and her husband, Eraclio Zepeda, the wonderful teller of short stories and poet. They wanted me to see Chiapas, but I was reluctant for a while: some revolutionary acts were already taking place. I ended up going for a few days, but stayed away from the area of conflict.

I went, however, to San Cristobal de las Casas and to San Juan Chamula. My eyes still hurt from what they saw. I was not used to seeing that kind of poverty, that misery of the human body, that deprived way of life. Is this Mexico? I asked myself. Is this my people, these little kids who never grow, who barely eat? I saw myself in those eyes and ran away, not to the mountains, but to the comfort of the hotel where I threw up until no food was left in my stomach. Aside from feeling disgust for myself, what the fuck am I supposed to do? I can only remember what the great poet from Chiapas,

Jaime Sabines, wrote: "What can I do if I am not a saint, a hero, or a crook?"

Next day I had eggs with chorizo, fresh bread, and lots of coffee. At the table I wrote a stupid, useless poem.

*

September 14, 1994. Very confident, I say: Well . . . Pound said that the *image* is what should be most important in the poem. No! Ginsberg almost shouted. Not the image but the *sound* . . . Like this: and he started reciting one of Kerouac's Choruses from *Mexico City Blues*. You see? He went on: You must pay attention to the way the vowels sound, the pause between the words . . . it's like singing. Kerouac, he explained, learned to say his poems from listening to Billie Holiday and Frank Sinatra, and I did it from listening to Kerouac.

We were drinking *cappuccini* at North Beach's Enrico's, in San Francisco. He and Bob Sharrard, editor at City Lights, the Brazilian novelist João Almino, and I, who was talking in Spanish with Allen. He told me about the time he spent in

Juvenal Acosta with Lawrence Ferlinghetti and João Almino

Mexico. That evening I turned thirty-three and went home to listen to my Kerouac recordings. Driving back to the East Bay I realized that Aztec poets, who believed in poetry as song, shared the same poetics with Ginsberg, who perhaps is the last American bard of the century.

*

Summer 1996. Life's greatest moments: I had been watching with Bettina the surfers for hours, wondering about the lives of relentlessly beautiful people who come from all over the world to Puerto Escondido to ride the Pacific Ocean waves. That evening we had drinks with our friends Bia and João, who were staying in a nicer hotel in the same town on the coast of Oaxaca. Bia is totally adorable: Not only is she a remarkable artist but she is gracious, elegant, sophisticated, rebellious, and iconoclastic. Bettina used to tell me that I was in love with her. And of course I'm in love with her. Who wouldn't? Bia said: "All of those guys waiting all day long for the perfect wave!" And I say: "Yeah, what a waste of time."

The next day I got up, drank coffee, and went to the beach. I rented a surfboard and decided to devote the rest of the day to the waves until I got it down. The extremely unpleasant experience of swallowing ocean water or the pain of getting your skin all messed up from the rough contact with the board couldn't stop me. After long hours I was on top of a wave, and then another. I got it down, somehow. I understood. I told myself: I'm over thirty, but my spiritual age is seventeen: My hair is growing longer; a bead is on my chest; and I can wait all day on the coast of Oaxaca for the perfect wave.

*

God, I'm teaching creative writing. Just a couple of days before the job was offered to me, I was walking on the Oakland hills with McClure. He had been trying for a while to make me understand and appreciate nature, since as a Mexico City-born urbanite, I had always been extremely distrustful of nature. The hills of northern California are the perfect place for a beginner, and Michael is the perfect teacher. Sometimes we go on these walks, and we talk about poetry and trees and people we know or dead people. I said to Michael: "I will never teach creative writing; poetry is something you cannot teach to anybody." He agreed; he teaches English at the California College of Arts and Crafts in Oakland, but will never teach creative writing. Then I call him two days later, and I say, a little bit ashamed, "Michael, I've taken this job." But he is understanding, probably more than I am.

Anyway, I go to teach, and I have in front of me all these young faces, all these eyes, all these hidden talents. What do they expect from me? Poetry cannot be taught. I can tell them how to write fine lines; I can teach them how to avoid unnecessary adjectives, how to give coherence to their thoughts, how to write. But poetry is not there; it does not belong in a classroom. I dropped out of four colleges because poetry was not in the classrooms, and now I have to evaluate their poems, their effort, their images, their obsessions, their desires, and their fears. Some of them have read too little, and some have read too much. They want to be poets. Who will get an A? who will get a C? I cannot grade anxieties or sadness, cannot grade an honest image. I will say, and I do say, be honest, stay awake, open your eyes, listen to the music of the end of the century, search whatever truth you want to find, write as if a demon had possessed you, love without fear, walk the streets in order to face possible epiphanies, stay up until dawn so you can understand, quit your job, hate me if you have to, but write and write and write. Your heart will show you the way.

*

A further memory: I'm eleven months old, and I'm in my cradle trying to stand up. My mother sings as she walks around the house. I follow her with my eyes, and I'm so happy that she is singing that I want to follow her and be in her arms. I couldn't suspect that one day she would stop her singing.

*

Every time I'm asked to read my poetry at a literary event or every time I have a book presentation at a bookstore or college in the United States, I'm faced with a welcoming crowd that has, conscious or unconsciously, some degree of expectations due to my national origin, my race, my physical appearance. It is not rare that those expectations translate into a silent demand that goes beyond the nature itself of my work as a poet: be "Mexican." Give us some "Mexican" poetry. Give us a notion of your world as we understand it. As we want it to be?

*

As a Mexican intellectual, my status in the United States is that of solitude.

Coming from a city that is obscenely populated by twenty million desperate souls, it is easy to miss the enormous possibilities of selecting from a great variety of people, radio stations, TV channels, movie theaters, newspapers, coffee shops, and bookstores—all of those things that are vital to writers. But these goods we all take for granted in our own land are very scarce once we step out of its borders.

In California, the "labyrinth of solitude" of the Mexicans, who for many reasons live here, is more painful and intricate than that of our fellow Mexicans south of the border.

*

In *Black and Red* by Stendhal, one of the characters is heard saying: I cannot be forced to believe in what I said yesterday; I'm not a slave of my own opinions. I go by that rule. My work, therefore, is a living monument to doubt. I have been working for many years trying to find an accurate way to express inaccurate feelings and obsessions about three worlds: the outside world, my own inner world, and my interpretation of both within the context of language.

*

My particular situation for the last years as a poet who chose self-exile has brought about a whole different spectrum of considerations to the process of reflecting on my writing. My native tongue, Spanish, started to be insufficient to express a whole different set of rules and realities that were exclusive to a different culture. I started to dream in English, and then I felt the need to write about my everyday life in the language that I was exposed to on a daily basis. This started to happen after seven years of living in the United States.

Just as the Portuguese poet Fernando Pessoa, I had to invent a different persona ("Pessoa" in Portuguese means "persona") who wrote poetry in a substantially different way. Pessoa "invented" many different poets with different poetics and styles, even different lives. I didn't go that far. The invention of this poet who writes in another language is not as sophisticated, but it is somehow complex. On the other hand I do not consider myself proficient in the writing of English the way I do in Spanish, therefore I am limited to whatever I can grasp while trying to be a poet who writes in this language. But reality and word, reality and language depend strongly on one another. We build words according to our experience of the exterior world. We build poems according to our perceptions of what the world is like as it passes through the filter of our understanding. We try to express it with words that allude to that experience.

Poetry is a tool for understanding. We must try at least to understand our most primal instincts and motivations despite the crude fact that we are not allowed anymore to function based on the dictate of our instincts.

*

I keep in a drawer of my desk the maps of the cities that I love. Not only those cities that I know, but also the one metropolis—should I say cosmopolis?—that I have constructed with the bits of cities that I know. Here I have the map of that impossible city.

We all have the novel that we want to write, but have not managed to. In this novel boy meets girl in that imaginary city. It happens on the avenue Rio Branco in Rio de Janeiro. I'm there looking for Alan Riding, whom I don't know, but he is a friend of a friend and at the time he is reporting for the *New York Times* from Brazil. As I walk looking for the numbers on the buildings, I step on the shit of a Carioca dog and the woman who walks towards me in the opposite direction laughs that laugh

that only Brazilian women have. I stop her, for my heart itself has stopped, and we go to Mario's on the corner of Union and Columbus for cappuccino and those excellent focaccia sandwiches made with eggplant that are absolutely the best of San Francisco. Yes, we are now in San Francisco and, therefore, I cannot find Mr. Riding. But who wants to see Mr. Riding when the company of my newly found friend could have made Columbus forget about discovering the Americas? Love happens, and we take a cab that goes from Washington Square—the one in San Francisco—to my apartment in Palermo. Not Italy, of course, but the neighborhood Palermo in Buenos Aires. We make love for hours and hours, and we read poems written by Sabines and Nathaniel Tarn, separately of course—the writing of the poems, not our reading of them. A long night is ahead of us, and I want to marry her the next day, but at 5:00 A.M. she starts to get dressed, and I cannot believe my eyes. Don't leave, please, don't ever leave. She has to take a plane. Cannot postpone it. My muttering heart falls from my lips. She goes away. I look at the coming daylight through the window as it awakes the people of Manhattan, and no poem I write can serve as consolation. It's cold, despite the fact that most people think of Mexico as a place that is always hot. She is as imaginary as this city. She is as imaginary as my words.

BIBLIOGRAPHY

Poetry:

Diciendo unas palabras negras, Comite Editorial del Gobierno de Michoacan, 1985.

Paper of Live Flesh, Brighton Press, 1991.

Tango of the Scar, Ediciones Tarumba, 1996.

Editor:

Light from a Nearby Window (poetry anthology), City Lights Books, 1994.

Alberto Blanco, *Dawn of the Senses* (poetry), City Lights Books, 1997.

Translator:

Juvenal Acosta has translated into Spanish the work of many contemporary poets from the United States, such as Jack Spicer, Bob Kaufman, Michael McClure, W. S. Merwin, Jack Kerouac, and Charles Bukowski. His poetry and literary criticism has been published in Mexico and the U.S.

Gregory Benford

1941-

Science does not know its debt to imagination.

—Ralph Waldo Emerson

*Back from the war: Greg (right), his dad,
and twin brother Jim, 1945*

Southerners feel their difference from the beginning. Though I have written fiction about abstruse physics and the people who care about such abstractions, all quite urban delights, I have always been aware that I come from a far distant culture.

I grew up in rural Alabama, in the small towns of Robertsdale and Fairhope, across the bay from Mobile. From my birth as an identical twin in 1941 until my father took us to Japan in 1948, I lived a simple and probably idyllic life, amid a Huck Finn world of sluggish heat, muddy rivers, infinite pine forests, and abundant creatures. E. O. Wilson relates in *Naturalist* how the same land made him into a biologist a decade before and only a dozen miles away. Somehow, despite a lifelong fascination with the myriad complexities of the natural world, I became a physicist.

I also learned something of storytelling. My stepgrandfather, universally called Mr. Fred, even by my grandmother, told tales beside a crackling fire in the tin-roofed house on stilts beside the Fish River. I listened to the cadences and swerves of dense, Southern spinning, and found it marvelous. Decades later I found a recording of Faulkner, one of my favorite authors, and heard my grandfather's identical accent telling stories that seemed to flow from some unfathomed wellspring, and knew that I came from some roots that ran deep.

My brother and I quickly became Us against the pervasive Them of rural Alabama. Aware of a larger world out there, the narrow hardscrabble life did not appeal even to Huck and his buddy.

We were mischievous, of course. Confronted in the kitchen with a breakfast item we did not like, we stashed it behind the stove when Mom wasn't looking. Lacking foresight, we six-year-olds did not realize that a week later the smell would unmask the trick. We were hellions, independent minded, a pattern that took us through twenty-five years as we attended the same schools and universities, both getting doctorates in physics from the University of California at San Diego, I in 1967, Jim in 1969.

Nobody glimpsed such a future for us in the 1940s, including us. Jim and I grew up among farmers and laborers, mostly from my mother's family of Nelsons. My mother taught English and my father taught agriculture in Robertsdale High, except for his three years fighting in The War. He was a forward observer in field artillery, fighting across France, the Bulge, and through Germany to Austria. I believe he was the only beginning forward observer in his battalion to survive the war, and suspect that his farmboy field-smarts made the difference. In 1945 he returned to teaching, developing an agriculture training program for the whole state, and then in 1948 the Cold War called him with a Regular Army appointment which he seized as a way up into a world he had glimpsed in the war. With him we went, first to his training in Oklahoma at Fort Sill (where in 1967 he retired as commandant), then to Japan for 1949–51. My father served on MacArthur's general staff and we saw the range of Japanese life, hard and strange, with communists rioting in the streets and farmers working the rice paddies only miles away, in a fashion unchanged by millennia. With my brother I lay in bed at night in our compound housing and listened to marines firing at communists trying to get inside, and realized that the world was a lot bigger and tougher and darker than sunny Alabama knew.

I came upon an oddly fascinating book in the Narimasu school library, *Rocket Ship Galileo* by Robert Heinlein. My mother, an excellent teacher, encouraged reading and Jim and I went through the usual series: Hardy Boys, Tom Swift, historicals and action stories and fairy tales. But Heinlein was different. I ventured all my savings, about two dollars, on his *Farmer in the Sky* the moment I saw it in a PX. I still have it, minus the jacket, and eventually wrote a prequel, *Jupiter Project.* I came to read a great deal of fiction, lots of it science fiction, as the Cold War deepened and its chill winds blew the Benfords to Atlanta in 1952, Germany in 1954, and Dallas in 1957. Somehow the whirl of strange cultures combined with the siren call of the fantastic, pulling me toward science fiction.

Along the way I was a good but unexceptional student, more interested in hobbies than studies. Science and sf appealed to me equally. I had seen reviews of fanzines in such down-market sf magazines as *Imagination,* and with Jim began publishing one in 1954. At first a pale product from a hectograph, *Void* eventually came to be a major fanzine of the now-revered Golden Age, acquiring as co-editors Ted White and Terry Carr.

Greg (center) with his parents and brother, Jim, Japan, 1950

Not until 1958 did my future take shape, mostly because a battery of tests, the Iowa Exams, showed me to rank in the 99th percentile of ability, with Jim a point behind—genetic determinism at work, perhaps. Our high school in Dallas immediately placed us in advanced classes, but the major propelling factor was the chance reading of *Atoms in the Family* by Laura Fermi, her loving autobiography of her great physicist husband, Enrico. This vision of a life spent pursuing deep aspects of reality, with the implicit self-criticism and checking basic to science, entranced me. I took advanced physics and math in my senior high school year and was off. A scholarship sent me and Jim to the University of Oklahoma, and in four years we went together for graduate work to the University of California at San Diego.

Fast changes, intense work, expanding perspectives—our horizons grew intellectually, just as they had from our extensive travels. Down the telescoping perspectives of time, these transformations seem swift, but of course to a boy growing into manhood the days often shambled by, unendurably slow. I think the sense of strangeness and isolation flowing through all these years brought, with the shifting, vastly different locales, a feeling for the fragility of human culture. This became for us inextricably bound up with the appeal of science fiction, which played upon those elements. I suspect many sf readers tend to be loners, and writers certainly are. It may seem odd for an identical twin to term himself a loner, but twins are so tightly bound (or at least we were, for so long, even to the point of wearing identical, mother-selected wardrobes into our early twenties) that we adopted an Us/Them posture, and that Us was solitary. Such a posture helped us survive the cross-currents any Southerner faces in an academic life, where most automatically assume that a Southern accent implies a lower IQ.

I quickly noticed that and set about changing my accent in my teenage years, until by the time I had my doctorate in theoretical physics in 1967 I could pass verbally as an ordinary, middle American. At times the flinty-eyed would joke about rednecks and I would smile knowingly and make another about, say, Californians or New Englanders.

This got to be a joke with the New England woman I married in 1967, Joan Abbe, daughter of a deceased Unitarian minister and

Two fanzine editors: Greg (left) and Jim, Germany, 1957

independent-minded, rock-ribbed widow, Lillian. Joan tolerated my oddities, most especially the reawakening of interest in writing fiction which surfaced anew in 1964, smack in the middle of graduate school, after lying dormant from my high school years. I had always liked writing, and fanzines had stoked that fire, but reading in the middle 1960s brought home to me that my instincts lay with the great writers of genre novels like Raymond Chandler and John D. MacDonald, plus of course the usual Valhalla of Clarke, Asimov, Heinlein, Bradbury and the like.

I published my fourth short story in 1965 and kept writing a few stories a year until 1969, while taking up my career as a physicist. (The interconnections between sf and science are myriad. I explored them somewhat in an autobiographical essay in *New Legends,* edited by Greg Bear, in 1995.) I felt a tension between my imagination and the severely constrained sort of physics I was doing then. By 1969, when I contracted for my first novel, I knew I was destined to pursue a two-pronged career, forever balancing science against its apparent opposite, fiction.

For my doctorate I had begun as an experimenter in solid-state physics, studying the relaxation of electron and nuclear spins in low temperatures. A fellow student discovered a strange effect about the time I became bored with the tedium of experiment. I was also getting tired of being a student; here was my chance at a relatively quick liberation, if I could also do theory. I was not at all confident that I could; my mathematics was sound but not inspired, and I had a more intuitive feel for physics than an analytical one. Somewhat timidly, I switched professors and attacked that strange effect with an arsenal of theoretical approaches. Most of these failed but led to interesting calculations in themselves, which I eventually thriftily published. After more than a year I did find a plausible explanation, which alas still awaits the technical capability to test it. This got me my doctorate in four years, the first in my class to finish, and for the first time relieving a sense of inferiority I had felt all the way through my academic career. I had always been acutely conscious of coming from a small Southern town, of going to Oklahoma University instead of MIT or a similar Big Name School, though I realized my first year at UCSD that I had gotten quite a good education at OU.

From 1967 to 1971 I lived a life divided between two difficult masters, fiction and physics. The Lawrence Radiation Laboratory at Livermore was a prime fusion research center and I entered into its projects exploring, trying several fields—rarefied, mathematical solid-state physics; plasma stability theory; intense, relativistic plasma beams—in the hope that something would announce that here was my life's work.

Nothing did. I carried through a lot of calculations but found my interest in fusion flagging, as I came to doubt that any of the approved methods—machines with names like Astron, Magnetic Mirror, and Tokomak—would truly produce a practical reactor generating electrical power. (And twenty-five years later, this has proved true, with many billions spent and the program in retreat.) I moved most enthusiastically into the study of relativistic electron beams, a hot new area where much theory beckoned. My brother moved in the same direction, geographically and intellectually, and we have worked together ever since, albeit at some distance.

In 1971 my daughter Alyson was born, my father suffered a near-fatal heart attack, and my disagreements with the leadership of the plasma physics theory group came to a head, all in the same month, January. Within half a year I had found a position as an assistant professor at the newest UC campus in Irvine and we were moving to Laguna Beach, where we have lived ever since.

Thus settled, I began a long research career which has had some success: grants, the-

Marriage to Joan Abbe, Boston, 1967

sis students, even the Lord Foundation Award in 1995 for my work in theoretical astrophysics. Moving into astronomical subjects came as a natural outgrowth of my growing career as a writer, principally of science fiction, which escaped the constraints of science while evoking its power and promise.

I began attempting novels with a brooding, reflective space opera called *Deeper Than the Darkness* (1970; rewritten as *The Stars in Shroud*, 1978), then in a young-adult homage to Robert Heinlein, *Jupiter Project* (1975). Only then did I feel accomplished enough to attempt heftier work, beginning with *If the Stars Are Gods* (with Gordon Eklund), then *In the Ocean of Night*. By this time my research was well funded and we traveled extensively, taking sabbaticals in Cambridge, England, in 1976 and Italy in 1979 and 1982. I worked on jets of matter from energetic galactic centers, black holes, and pulsars, as well as assembling a laboratory group at UCI to study relativistic plasma dynamics in highly energetic experiments.

Life was rich, my family growing; my attention turned to the ground between science and science fiction. I began work on *Timescape*, finally finishing the manuscript in spring, 1979, quite sure that this novel was quirky, self-indulgent, and bound to have a marginal audience at best. I poured in historical detail, oddments of observation, and intricate scenes of scientists at work; the novel is more than a bit autobiographical.

I did not think such matters interested many readers. Certainly I didn't expect that, since the novel would inevitably be released as science fiction, the usual science fiction audience would find in it the fare they relished. In truth, I am still rather surprised at the popularity of the book. It now has over a million copies in print, and won a fistful of awards when it appeared in 1980. Yet to me it seems the most private of my novels (with the possible exception of *Against Infinity,* written just after *Timescape*). I spun it out of fifteen years of thought and experience.

The novel began as a short story, "3:02 P.M., Oxford," published in *If* in September 1970. I've never had the courage to reread this fledgling effort, concerned with an English laboratory where a time communicator is built. I never consulted it while writing the novel, but the basic notions are there—time and England. I tried another tack with "Cambridge, 1:58 A.M.," published in *Epoch* in 1975. Here some of the novel's major characters appeared and the English motif sprang full-blown into my mind as I wrote the story (by dictation; I was building an addition to my house and had little time). Only then did I have the scheme in full, and slugged away at the book for four more years, often with the help of my sister-in-law, Hilary Benford. David Hartwell later contributed excellent editing.

The underpinning of it all was a scientific paper on tachyons, particles that travel faster than light, which I wrote with William Newcomb and David Book in 1970 ("The Tachyonic Antitelephone," *Physical Review*, D2, p. 263). This idea and its causal problems intrigued me greatly and still do.

I remember thinking one day, *Well, suppose we did detect tachyons?* It wasn't a totally idle question, because an Australian cosmic ray experiment in 1972 reported a highly energetic particle moving above twice light speed. The observation hasn't been confirmed, but it did excite the scientific community for a while. Okay, what if? I tried to envision how working physicists would proceed. Build a time machine? Nonsense!—test the ideas and paradoxes first; one step at a time. That's what I kept in mind while I wrote.

Still, when I finished the manuscript it seemed to me a dense work, filled with knotty philosophical problems and lots of facets of the scientific mind, as I had observed. Not a fast-moving, gripping thriller, no. It played on what (C. P.) Snow called *Two* Cultures—the abyss that separates the scientific and humanist persuasions. I used my sabbatical leave experiences at Cambridge for color. As well I drew on my years as a graduate student in La Jolla—in fact, my identical twin and I appear as characters in the novel at just the point where we began graduate work. I also used a lot of my own life history in constructing Gregory Markham, who sometimes reflects my views in the text itself.

In the years of labor I had layered several other themes into the novel, lapidary imagery such as the varied use of waves in time, in oceans, in human affairs. I jockeyed the chapters about to achieve a symmetry: the action cycles between 1962 and 1998, and the novel was published in 1980, halfway between these two worlds. That was because I felt we were already halfway between these contrasting lands of light and darkness, but also for a further effect—the present acts like a lens in the novel, focusing events at the opposite time in a different fashion. And, as with a true lens, the image is inverted from the original.

But I wonder if readers truly care about such matters; these are authors' satisfactions, after all. I've gotten many letters about the book, often asking me to write a similar novel. Perhaps someday I shall, though I suppose I did write a similar one in *Artifact,* whose interests are archeology and physics. In *Timescape* I discovered how easily the realistic novelist can construct his realm. You simply observe closely and report back; much of the real-world context does your work for you in overcoming the reader's disbelief. But few science fiction works can so rigorously make use of this method, and even fewer have enough science in them to invoke the power of deep scientific imagery.

Finally, the characters in *Timescape* seem to stay with me, like people you knew in college and every now and then wonder how they turned out. My subconscious has already supplied detailed stories of what happened after the novel, and in fact I cut from the manuscript an alternative ending which continued their lives further. So to me *Timescape* is a continuing story, given life as well by the fact that new readers still encounter it and bring their own freshness to that world. I'm quite grateful for that.

Perhaps I should have stuck to such near-future novels of scientists at work, but my imagination was not to be chained. As a fan, I had always loved the sweeping sagas of space and time from sf's Golden Age: the Foundation novels, Heinlein's Future History, Anderson's savvy tales of galactic trading and intrigue. Slowly, I began thinking of writing my own, never guessing that I was embarking not on a project but a voyage.

I did not set out to write a series of interconnected novels over a span of twenty-five years. The project grew on me, and I made plenty of mistakes bringing it to fruition.

I could describe here my inner struggles alone, the endless interior workings one performs before the blank page—but external events proved just as important. I suspect this happens more often than most of us would like.

In 1977 I had published my fourth novel, *In the Ocean of Night,* concerning an irritable astronaut who discovers evidence of a galaxy-spanning network of intelligent machines. It was nominated for a Nebula and I went about my normal profession as a professor of physics at the University of California, Irvine. But my subconscious would not let me alone. I kept thinking of what such ideas implied, and by 1982 wrote *Across the Sea of Suns,* with the same character exploring nearby stars. Here the physicist collided with the writer. I had been doing research in astrophysics since 1974, and noticed that our own galactic center was abrim with intriguing new observations. In the core, within a few light years of the exact center, there are a *million* stars within a single light year. On average, the nearer stars are only a hundredth of a light year away, ten thousand times the distance from the Earth to the sun. Imagine having several stars so close they outshone the moon.

As one might expect, this is bad news for solar systems around such stars. Close collisions between all these stars occur in about a hundred thousand years, scrambling up planetary orbits, raining down comets upon them as well.

The galactic center is the conspicuous Times Square of the galaxy—and far more deadly than the comfortable suburbs like ours. Joel Davis's *Journey to the Center of Our Galaxy* details how horrific it is, pointing out that the survival time for an unshielded human within even a hundred light years of the core is probably only hours.

In the Ocean of Night explored the discovery that computer-based life seemed dominant throughout the galaxy. The British astronaut, Nigel Walmsley, had uncovered the implication that "evolved adding machines," as he put it, had inherited the ruins of earlier, naturally derived alien societies.

Working with Walmsley set tough problems. I had picked a British point-of-view character because he was an outsider in a space program usually run by Americans. I had a feeling for the Brits from my sabbatical there in 1976, though I'd been writing stories which I incorporated into the first novel as early as 1972. Further, while one novel can trace the core events of a character over years, perhaps a life, still I did not know how Walmsley would change over the considerable span of Book #2.

I finished that book in a mental muddle. My subconscious had begun to present me, uninvited, with events beyond the end of the book. In the first version of #2, a Simon & Schuster hardcover, I ended on a note of difficulty and defiance.

Then publishing intervened. *Timescape Books* collapsed and Pocket Books held hostage several books, seeking to extract their investment. Pocket's publisher-in-chief told my agent (none of them would speak to a mere author) they would not publish the paperback of *Across the Sea of Suns* and wanted $80,000—yes, $10,000 more than they had paid me—for the rights. I refused and the book went into stasis for several years. I eventually escaped by paying $10,000, as I remember.

All this while scenes, ideas, and characters popped into my head as I worked on other books. By this time I had learned to follow my subconscious. If I didn't, I stalled on other projects. Slowly I realized that a larger series of novels yawned before me.

Bad news, I knew immediately. Series novels must each have a sense of an ending, while foreshadowing more. I hadn't done this in the first two books. Or had I? Book #1 closed with an expansive embracing, and #2 hadn't reached most of its audience yet.

When Lou Aronica at Bantam offered to publish the whole series, I took the plunge. I added more to the ending of #2 and Lou remarked at the voice of the new material, which he said echoed the rest of the novel well. I blinked; I hadn't even thought of rereading *Across the Sea of Suns.* The ambience had simply been sitting there, still fresh. Reas-

Jim, Robert Silverberg as Pope Sextus the Sixth, and Greg, Halloween, 1978

sured, I set out writing #3—and hit a snag straightaway.

A series treats the arc of a figure's life, but the galaxy-spanning novel covers so much space and time, I couldn't get Walmsley around to see and live enough.

Worse, the galactic center was the obvious place for machines to seek. By the early 1980s we knew that there is a virulent gamma ray flux there, hot clouds, and enormously energetic processes. Most of this we gathered from the radio emissions, which penetrate dust clouds and revealed the crackling activity at the center for the first time. Infrared astronomy soon caught up, unmasking the hot, tangled regions.

By the time I finished *Across the Sea of Suns* in 1983, I realized that I could do some research myself on the galactic center. I had by that time written papers on pulsars and galactic jets, accumulating both expertise and curiosity. Strikingly, mysterious features appeared in the galactic center radio maps. In 1984 I was giving a talk on galactic jets at UC Los Angeles, and my host was Mark Morris, a radio astronomer.

"Explain this," he challenged, slapping down a radio map he had just made at the Very Large Array in New Mexico.

My first reaction was "Is this a joke?" The glossy print showed a feature I immediately called the Claw, but which Mark more learnedly termed the Arch: a bright, curved prominence made up of slender fibers. Though the Arch is over a hundred light years long, these filaments are only about a light year wide, curving upward from the galactic plane, like arcs of great circles which center near the galactic core, which lies several hundred light years away. These intricate filaments shine by energetic (in fact, relativistic) electrons, radiating in strong magnetic fields, which are aligned along the filaments.

My first intuition, seeing the radio map of the Arch was "This looks artificial." Astronomy reflexively assumes that everything in the night sky is natural. The sf writer in me immediately explored the opposite. I decided to extend the Walmsley books by at least one more, set at galactic center.

I worked on a theory for those thin filaments which glow by electron luminosity, a hundred times longer than they were wide. I thought of neon lights, which are glow discharges sustained by electric currents in slender tubes. Could these fibers be a sort of slow-motion lightning, taking perhaps hundreds of thousands of years to discharge?

Those hunches became the kernel of several papers on the center, a model which has become generally accepted—for now, pending more data. While I was mulling over maps and jotting equations, I kept on writing fiction. Over years, the writing fed the physics, and vice versa.

Intriguing setting is essential in a series of novels, or else a sense of sameness creeps in. I used all the gaudy color and striking effects I could muster in #3 of what came to be called the "Galactic Series" (by my publisher, Bantam), *Great Sky River*—a reference to the ancient Indian name for the Milky Way.

I focused on the inner few light years, for dramatic effects, even though I knew the sheer particle and energy flux there made humans quite vulnerable. To protect them I made them huge and armored. The central figure was a man named Killeen, who flees across a ruined landscape dominated by the black hole, which his people call the Eater of All Things—though they don't quite know why.

This ravaged panorama seemed an ample stage to act out my main theme, the superiority of machines in much of the galaxy. I also got to spring their size as a twist at the very end of the series, when they meet Walmsley, whom they take to be a dwarf.

By then, measures of the orbital velocities of stars very close to the true galactic center, called Sagittarius A, suggested that a point mass of about a million stellar masses lurks there, giving off very little light.

Much controversy surrounds these observations, though, with some holding that the data could mean only a thousand stellar masses is needed. I opted for a million, because then a ship could fly through the ergosphere, the very rim of the black hole, and not be crushed by the tidal forces. This would be crucial to the last volume, #5—I thought.

The profligate energetics of the center would draw sentient machines, I felt. The black hole would intrigue any inquisitive life form, their struggles surging across a virulent territory. Humans would be part of it all, but certainly not the major players.

How to put humans in this mix? I collided here with the classic hard sf dilemma: humans versus the immense landscape. How to make them seem significant? How to simply make it plausible that they could survive? One could invoke miracles, of course, in the form

With James Gunn at the Jet Propulsion Lab, 1980

of magic materials or offstage events which just happen to put people where you need them. I wasn't willing to do that. Picky, perhaps, especially in a time when fantasy novels unbounded by visible constraint began dominating the marketplace, and hard sf held little sway on the bestseller lists. But I couldn't make myself take a simpler path, and this proved a significant slower of my work. I pondered and time slid by.

After stalling yet again on my "Galactic Series," slowly I went back to fundamentals. I began envisioning what it might be like at stage center, where the diet of particles and photons is rich and varied. Only hard, tough machines could survive for long there.

In the fourth novel, *Tides of Light,* I drew out these contrasts. Hard work, but fun. I devised "photovores" and "metallovores" as adaptations to special evolutionary niches. After all, machines that can reproduce themselves would, inevitably, fall under the laws of natural selection, and adapt to use local resources. The entire panoply of ecology would recapitulate: parasites, predators, prey.

How to envision this? I prepare for novels by writing descriptive passages of places and characters. In spare moments I began working up snapshots of possible life forms and their survival styles.

Years before I had found a technique to deal with "obstructions"—a better word than the fearsome "block," and to me it meant something rather more subtle. At times I simply couldn't get my subconscious to flower forth with free material along the lines of the novel.

So I pretended that I was working on another story entirely and wrote that. Sometimes

I found I was right—it really didn't connect with the novel. Most times, with some tuning, it did. I made a policy of following through, publishing the work independently if possible, out of an almost superstitious belief that my subconscious would catch on. So far it hasn't . . . I think.

That's why occasionally pieces of my novels appear first as short stories. I often don't know whether they fit the novel, sometimes until years later. This trick I had to use again and again, because my subconscious proved lazy and headstrong. I'd planned to rap out three novels and be done by 1989, but #3 appeared in 1987, #4 in 1989 . . . and then I got interested in another novel, wrote it in three tough years, and ground to a halt. The pesky subconscious just wouldn't cooperate with my game plans. This cost me considerably, for the series' momentum broke and undoubtedly some readers lost the thread.

In 1990 I had to start from scratch again, thinking through the overarching logic of the series. Slowly it dawned that some part of me had shied away from doing the last novel because I couldn't reconcile the many forces within the narrative. I realized with a sinking feeling that one more book wouldn't be enough, either.

Intelligent machines would build atop the galactic center ferment a society we could scarcely fathom—but we would try. Much of #5, *Furious Gulf* was about that—the gulf around a black hole, and the gulf between intelligences born of different realms.

For years I had enjoyed long conversations with a friend, noted artificial intelligence theorist Marvin Minsky, about the possible lines of evolution of purely machine intelligence. Marvin views our concern with mortality and individualism as a feature of biological creatures, unnecessary among intelligences which have never had to pass through our Darwinnowing filter.

If we can copy ourselves indefinitely, why worry about a particular copy? What kind of society would emerge from such origins? What would it think of us—the Naturals, still hobbled by biological destiny?

A Saturn 5 booster lying dead in Houston: (from left) Greg Benford, Fred Pohl, James Gunn, Brian Aldiss, and Jack Williamson

The author's wife, Joan, with their children, Alyson and Mark,
while working in Japan on the TV series

Through books #3, 4, and 5 I had used the viewpoint of humans hammered down by superior machines. This got around the Walmsley lifetime problem, but demanded that I portray people enormously different from us. They had to seem strange, yet understandable—a classic sf quandary.

A slowly emerging theme in the novels, then, was how intelligence depended on the substrate, whether in evolved humans or adaptive machines—both embodying intelligence, but with wildly different styles.

By the time I reached the last volume, in 1992, I had spent over twenty years slowly building up my ideas about machine intelligence, guided by friends like Marvin Minsky. I had also published several papers on the galactic center and eagerly read each issue of *Astrophysical Journal* for further clues.

I finished the last novel, *Sailing Bright Eternity,* in summer 1994. It had been twenty-five years since I started on *In the Ocean of Night* and our view of the galactic center had changed enormously. Some parts of the first two books,

especially, are not representative of current thinking. Error goes with the territory.

I had taken many imaginative leaps in putting together a working "ecology" for the center. I included outre ideas, such as constructions made by forcing space-time itself into compressed forms, which in turn act like mass itself: reversing Einstein's intuition, that matter curved space-time.

All this was great fun, requiring a lot of time to think. I let my subconscious do most of the work, if possible—an easier way to write, but it stretches out projects, too.

Long-suffering readers wrote asking when the next volume would appear and I felt badly about it, but I knew the writing could not be rushed. I had not anticipated that each volume would demand so much thought, and still less that I would need an extra novel to do the job. In the end, all six books comprise about three quarters of a million words.

My published physical model of the galactic center is done in what I call the "cartoon approximation"—good enough for a first cut, maybe, but doomed to fail somewhere. Sf works in this approximation, necessarily. I had assayed a grand theme, how Mind relates to Nature.

In any case, models are like art, matters of taste. Nobody expects a French Impressionist painting to look much like a real cow; instead, it suggests ways of looking at cows. Sf should do that.

I learned a lot of tricks along the way, many of them embarrassingly obvious. In 1969 I never outlined, though that year I had sold my first novel with a three-page description and ten thousand words of a novelette. By 1992 I kept notes by subheadings—INCIDENTS, NOTIONS, TECH, TIMELINE, CHARACTER, BITS O' BUSINESS, etc.—in a three-hole binder and on computer, so I could lift and insert.

More important, I had grasped that the climaxes of each book should resemble a stairway. Each should play for higher stakes which do not undercut the resolutions of the earlier novels. Each should open the philosophical canvas at least a bit, particularly in a galactic, hard sf novel sequence such as mine. Each should explain mysterious elements of the past novels, but leave some shadows to shed a glow into for the future. Each should tell us something deeper about the lead figure. Each figure should move through a defining moment of his life.

This last point may be crucial. I used two central figures, Walmsley and Killeen, neither particularly likeable. This may be a quirk of mine, but I've never enjoyed trotting around in the head of a bright-eyed, perpetual optimist; this may reveal more about me than I wish, but there it is.

Each of these men had to learn and grow, but not abandon themselves to the cosmic perspectives. As Gary Wolfe remarked in reviewing the last novel, "This is the classic problem of hard sf, of course: a rhetoric of action and human drama must be juggled with a rhetoric of science and philosophy in a way that must be made to appear seamless . . . (often) writers either give us cardboard characters against a spectacular backdrop, or fudge the science in order to make the plot work out."

I felt the pressure of keeping these guys human more and more as the novels waxed on. So I gave them vices, irksome habits, troubles with their women, faults—big ones, including bad tempers and emotional isolation. (Even Einstein picked his nose, remember.) Yet each

figure made progress, or at least came to understand himself better.

I didn't actually figure all this out clearly—in fact, some of the above paragraphs have made these points clear to me only while I was writing them. (This is a common experience for me, too. I don't know what I think until I express it. That old subconscious, again.)

I had always intended to make the series Stapledonian, recalling *Star Maker,* but squeezed through the aperture of a modern, rounded novel. I used talks with aliens, with machines, with disembodied intelligences lodged in magnetic configurations, with archly amused denizens of the far future—anything to avoid the overweening narrative voice; though I used that, too.

This single decision—more aesthetic than craftsmanly, and made unconsciously as well—created more work for me than anything else in the sequence. It is my preferred method overall, even outside the "Galactic Series," but it imposes great constraints. That fits with my own feeling about hard sf—that it works best because of its self-imposed restrictions, in the fashion that a sonnet does. Constraints improve.

Would I write a series again? Maybe, but not right away.

Do it this way again? Nope—I hope I'd avoid some of the traps.

Most important, I fathomed my own limitations, and how little my subconscious could be bossed around. It's useful to know who really does most of the heavy lifting.

Along the way I had taken excursions. I published two volumes of short stories, their origins best discussed in my notes in *In Alien Flesh* and *Matter's End.* I wrote the scientific suspense novel *Artifact,* based on Greek archeology. This attempt to reach a larger audience failed when the publisher refused to treat it as anything other than a Benford sf novel. I tried again, more ambitiously, with *Chiller,* published under the pseudonym Sterling Blake in 1993. Its cryonics theme sprang from my discovery that a solid organization, Alcor, existed to freeze people in hopes of eventual revival by future technology—fruitful ground, I thought, for a scientific suspense novel, whereas other treatments had all been horror novels.

Alas, as with *Timescape,* I found that when your publisher is not really behind a book, little else matters. *Chiller*'s Blake was supposed to get treatment as a new scientific suspense novelist, but the editor who bought it, Lou Aronica, had departed, so the novel was simply dumped with no advertising or real promotion beyond issuing a lot of bound galleys. It got no reviews in major places (much like *Timescape,* which the *New York Times Review of Books* ignored) and when word of Blake's identity leaked, I discarded the pseudonym, though Blake did one short story, and an essay on *Chiller's* topic, the modern cryonics movement.

By the middle 1990s I had come full circle, finished a long series and seen my children grow to adulthood. Time to look back, assess the path followed. I was still happily married and doing research, though I had folded my experimental program in the funding crunch of 1994; maintaining a lab was simply too much work. We had found a lot of new physical effects, but money was ebbing in such fundamental areas, so I reverted to doing only theory—principally in astrophysical plasmas. By 1997 I had written about 150 scientific papers, held many grants, and became aware of the transient nature of even scientific discovery. Much work is read by but a few, and soon forgotten.

After reflection, I changed vectors again. I agreed to write a novel set in Isaac Asimov's Foundation universe. *Foundation's Fear* is just out as I write this, spring 1997, and seems very successful. I have also finished a new novel, *Cosm,* which returns to my attempts to unite sf and modern suspenseful narrative. As with *Chiller,* I felt there had to be a way of using science in fiction which did not rely upon scaring the audience or raising unfounded apprehensions about the science which fascinates them.

I had thought about this unitary goal long and hard. Sf is seldom best viewed as a laboratory for the construction of a better world. Precisely when fiction becomes programmatic, focused on a commanding agenda, does it lose its ability to engender life in the mysterious labyrinths of words. The terrible truth is that writing is hard and will stay that way; that the correct attitude won't help you get under the skin of characters and produce work which will outlive yesterday's newspapers; that what is worth listening to in a writer is his individuality, his quirky reflection in his prose; and that you betray him or her if you seek to reduce writers to a set of positions. Tories can be masters and revolutionaries can be sods, and vice versa, of course.

I have worked through decades when sf was overtaken by events and by the visual media. TV and film have pilfered many sf ideas and approaches, usually without attribution, and without the informing vision surrounding the effects it lifts. I had my own engagement with TV and learned much from it. I'll devote some attention to it here, for it dominated several years and illuminated much of the troubles scientists have communicating in our time.

Of all areas I've worked in, TV took the prize for roller coaster living. In the late 1980s Japanese National Broadcasting (NHK) approached me about a project they had in early planning stages. It was to be a big series show on modern science, stressing the astronomical connections.

I consulted for them, reviewed memos, went to innumerable dinners with passing squads of producers, directors, and scriptwriters. Eventually they asked me to help outline the show and I gave it a working title which stuck: *A Galactic Odyssey.*

They wanted to take a very different approach to the problem of popularizing—using elements of drama alongside straight expositions, interviews, graphics, and the like. What kind of frame could do that? Intriguing, I thought. I worked up a plan to shape the shows around the voyage of the starship *Helios,* on the first flight beyond our solar system.

Most of the airtime would be in documentary format. In the sf frame, we would follow the adventures of the *Helios* crew of six as they visited sites in the Milky Way. The first ninety-minute-long introductory segment was straight documentary. The next seven were hour-long shows, each with three dramatic scenes, at opening, middle, and close, totaling about twenty minutes.

Halfway into outlining the show, they asked me to write the fictional frames. I had my misgivings. A year before I had written a TV script which did get shot, but emerged mystifyingly different from my vision. This was standard for the business. Since I wanted to learn more about scriptwriting, I took the job.

By now the show was behind schedule. I wasn't surprised, since NHK had spent a year and a half planning and fidgeting and re-planning. So when I received a visit about doing the scripts, they saved for last the fact that I had only a month in which to do them.

I learned something about writing under pressure. In TV writing, you must keep it simple, be direct, use sights instead of talk. I made the deadline, with two hours and twenty minutes of (estimated) drama screen time.

Writing such compact drama scripts was an education in brevity. I began to long for the elbow room of novels. There were compensations, though, in the freedom to let the audience *see* what you mean.

Using sf at all in the solemn format of upscale, top-ticket documentaries implies that science fictional devices are becoming commonplace vehicles. Still, I was somewhat surprised that NHK cheerfully accepted sf ideas; they saw that showing *people* visiting exotic sites was far more immediate than merely doing better computer graphics of them.

So I indulged myself. I stretched the physics a bit and had *Helios* fly by a star just as it goes supernova. Pretty unlikely, even though they had selected the star because it was close to that point. Great graphics, but how could they survive? I let them narrowly escape, using a trick: they used a Jovian-sized planet for a shield, speeding radially outward in its shadow.

This was a cheat, actually. The neutrino flux alone would have killed them, even with the Jovian trick. So I gave them a neutrino shield. Physics knows of nothing that can absorb neutrinos effectively, but there have been some theoretical speculations . . . so I yielded to temptation. A slight crack in my realism armor, perhaps, a step down the road that leads to the "wantum mechanics" of such shows as *Star Trek*—you wantum, you gettum. Anything you want, boss, and consistency from show to show be damned. Drama, y'know.

Midway through the writing, NHK came visiting again. They had never decided how to handle the connecting up of all these elements. Perhaps it would be best to have an occasional on-camera commentator? Well, I said, that was one approach, sure. They looked pleased. And . . . would I please consider being this commentator?

This was much more than I had bargained for. My imagination was fixed on the blithe abstractions of writing. Actual work in front of a camera was a decidedly daunting prospect. Still . . .

The starship *Helios* loomed large, a clean white sphere sprouting antennas. It glided away

With Arthur C. Clarke in London, 1987

from a barren desert planet, heading into serene deep space . . .

DISSOLVE TO: Traffic. Horns. Gasoline stench. Gaudy neon.

Well, I thought, we wanted a jarring cut for the opener, and this certainly fit the bill.

I was a minute into the take when the bag lady came shuffling into my field of view. If she just moved across the camera angle and kept going, I thought, maybe things would be all right. I kept on talking about alien life forms, a topic carefully selected for this location—a traffic island smack in the middle of Times Square.

"The sorts of aliens we could discover with our current approach bear a striking resemblance to the radio astronomers themselves—curious, devoted to the night sky, with lots of technology and energy. We—"

The bag lady swerved toward me and called jerkily, "Hey! Somebody's trying to start a war between us and Germany."

Well, maybe the mike wouldn't pick her up. I kept talking and got through the next sentence. If she would please just keep moving—

"Don't you care? Somebody's trying to start a war between the United States and Germany!"

I shrugged. "Actually, lady, it's been done. Twice."

One of the cameramen came trotting across the traffic lanes. He waved the bag lady away, but since he spoke only Japanese, they got into a tangle of angry incomprehension.

After she had wandered off, and after a gang of Puerto Rican teenagers tried to persuade us to make them famous by letting them do their dance routine behind me, we did five more takes—seventeen in all. By that time I was feeling pretty alien myself.

Location shooting, I learned, is fraught with weirdness and accident. I had to shoot about thirty locations in six months for the series, which was running further and further behind schedule.

This meant, for example, standing in the rotor wash of the camera helicopter as it lifted from the floor of Meteor Crater, Arizona, smiling numbly for five takes, as the sub-zero wind blew my hair around and turned my lips blue. I was clad in a sports jacket and light slacks, for the sake of clothes continuity with the preceding shot, which had been two months before and thirty degrees warmer.

Location shooting also meant trying to keep the script straight in my head atop Mauna Kea, Hawaii, at 13,700 feet. After a few hours of walking about, cold was the least of my problems. I found that oxygen deprivation kept snatching away bits of my memory. I would hit the end of a sentence and hang there, with no idea of what came next.

Oddly enough, it was fun.

The NHK producers were quite happy to spend, say, $300,000 creating a flyby of the black hole at the galactic center, complete with burnt-orange accretion disk and silvery jets. They even wanted me to talk about my own novels set there. Pulsars, neutron stars—anything astronomical was OK, fit for the computer graphics budget of several million dollars. This was big time TV, yes.

But aliens . . . Well, maybe Godzilla had spooked them.

They wanted a whole hour about life in the galaxy, but refused to ever show aliens. My entire script about planets as potential life sites was rewritten, by a director, to treat only dead worlds. So the crew spent its time in Death Valley digging holes for the camera.

Why? I asked. Prospecting for life, the director said.

Any biologist could have told them that the atmosphere, observed by *Helios* from space, would reveal signs of life. Chemical cycles for any gas-breathing life are constrained to a fairly narrow range. This argument had been used by James Lovelock to predict that Mars would reveal no life, back in the early 1970s.

Such arguments got waved away. People could understand prospecting for life—it was just like digging for gold, see? I shook my head. Cultural mismatch.

While there is no detail whatever about how *Helios* worked, I did get away with basing the last hour show, "The Anvil of Time," on relativity. No super-duper faster-than-light space drive for we hardnosed types—so we got some pretty special effects of *Helios* zooming by stars at near-light speed. The crew used Einstein's time dilation to span the galaxy, so they had to pay the price.

We spent months debating whether the crew, seeing that thousands of years had passed Earthside, would return. People took rather fierce positions, some holding that the *Helios* crew would fly ever onward, drawn by mysteries. I made them return; an Odyssey has to come home. But then the directors refused to show

Sailing, 1988

the Earth or solar system altered after millennia. No orbital colonies, no signs of humans visible from space.

Why? I asked. They frowned.

Anti-ecological. Tampering with the natural solar system. Bad vibes. "Such changes are disturbing." An enigmatic smile. The cultural thing again.

The Japanese took an aesthetic approach to much traditional scientific material. We opened the series with a shot of leafy glades and the line, "We love natural beauty, but what does it imply?"—then cut to a rocket, the planets, and stars.

NHK spent huge sums developing a new type of camera, capable of shooting in mere moonlight. It gave high quality, fully colored pictures, so that while I walked by an observatory in Chile, you could see my red tie and also make out the bright colors of stars overhead, including Alpha Centauri, the nearest star system.

In that shot the director laughed out loud at the Carl Sagan reference when I said, "There aren't merely billions and billions of stars in our galaxy; there are a good fraction of a trillion—and maybe more."

His laugh loused up the first take, which would've been perfect. On the other hand, on a later take they caught a meteor that flashed in startling yellow overhead as a punctuation, as I finished the last line.

It helped in dealing with the producers that I could switch from sf writer to scientist at the drop of a metaphor. I was scientific advisor, host, and drama script writer. When the drama director wrote in a scene in which the *Helios* engines failed, he didn't know that devising a wholly new kind of drive on the spot was both unlikely and a genre cliche.

Merely saying so didn't dissuade him, of course. So I pointed out that the big scene, in which they reach their difficult destination by withstanding 3-g acceleration for a full minute, would take *Helios* only a few more kilometers.

Even a director could see that wasn't much on a galactic scale. So we tinkered, cut, made it not quite so askew.

The best thing about making a grueling show is the people you meet. I spent a day with Stephen Hawking, the first time I had seen him in years. He had prepared a long response to some questions I'd sent. We discussed on camera the philosophical implications of modern cosmology, and he remarked on the "argument from design" resurrected by Freeman Dyson and others of note. (They have used observations that the crucial numbers which govern natural laws, such as nuclear binding energies, seem extraordinarily finely tuned to the values which make life and intelligence possible. Maybe even suspiciously so.)

Hawking was skeptical. He remarked that this might provide solace for some, "but only for belief in a distant, cool, and indifferent God."

The working scientists were always a pleasure. The interminable delays for setup of lighting and cameras were great times to get caught up on shoptalk.

Astronomy and physics are now thoroughly worldwide activities, threaded through with sf fans. I found Aldiss and Anderson paperbacks stashed for a dull moment in the control room of the big telescope at Las Campanas, atop the Andes Mountains of Chile.

The woman director of the Mount Wilson Observatory took me on a tour of the undergalleries of the 100 inch scope, where Hubble measured his plates and discovered the expansion of the universe. I got to do a shot sitting in the same rickety chair Hubble used for decades to discover the expansion of the universe. That was thrilling, as was the fifteen-foot plunge only inches away. Hubble had never fallen off; I came quite close twice in a single hour.

The director took all this for granted, of course. She then asked me if I knew Hal Clement or Joe Haldeman. What were they like?

We did a shot with me standing on the Bonneville salt flats, playing on the fact that in winter they look like a snow field. This was to suggest the freezing out of our atmosphere if the Earth were a bit farther from the sun. Then we switched to the opposite possibility, that a nearer sun would evaporate away our oceans, leaving meters-deep salt plains.

"Very fantastic," the director said happily.

A park ranger with us said skeptically, "Sounds like science fiction to me."

The director looked shocked and countered, "Oh, but it is! Of the very best kind—it is true!"

The most imaginative element NHK would allow in the documentary was a series of paintings by Bill Hartmann, the astronomer-artist at Kitt Peak Observatory, a most pleasant fellow.

We worked out a water-world sporting only minor islands, and sea life just beginning to discover simple technology. A gloomy city loomed in the background of his undersea painting. We shot a discussion between Bill and myself of the possibilities available in odd planets. A tide-locked world with a thin, life-supporting twilight zone. Twin inhabited planets—one with an oxygen atmosphere, the other still methane-dominated. An inhabited moon. The documentary director wanted all these discussed, but the drama director would have no part of them in *his* show . . .

I learned a lot about how science and sf interact. The Los Angeles public television station, KCET, was producing a rival show, *The Astronomers,* to air in fall 1990. I saw rushes from it, then the final show. While its desire to show the life of scientists was commendable, I was reminded that from the outside, watching us work is remarkably like a long, close scrutiny of paint drying. Still, the speculations of scientists are just as wild as anything we sf writers do; theirs are merely government-funded.

It's an unnerving experience, standing in a Los Angeles studio and watching actors play out scenes you've written, word for word. Quite solid and quite uncanny, like walking into one of your own dreams. It took far longer to shoot a script than it did to write one.

It's even stranger to turn from the set and look into the synthesizing eye of the monitors, where the set image was superimposed on the graphics, in real time. I could see beyond the *Helios* crew the swirling, technicolor disk of a monstrous black hole.

This ability to place frail human figures against the immensity of creation is powerful, and is only beginning to be dramatically realized. In counterpoint to all this techno razzledazzle, I had to underline in the closing comments that our goal in understanding nature is in part to fathom ourselves, our uniquely human place in nature.

I found it doubly striking that the churn and dazzle of warped space-time is still an *idea* of ours—a metaphor, if you will—not yet truly confirmed by observation. Increasingly, the objects of high science are fictions toward which reason and inference lead us. They will remain unseen, glimpsed only with the lens of scrupulous deduction—and with the telescope of our imaginations.

I ended the entire series with the only real indulgence the mass of producers and directors allowed. The NHK method was a sort of corporate mentality gone mad—each hour had a separate authority, with whom I negotiated the script. This is how I tried to sum it all up, with my own personal flavor:

I hope that the interwoven strands of the sciences can lead to a philosophy for our century which will be of one piece, reflecting the seamless connection we have to this world that came out of nothingness and into something so vast and various.

A great astronomer, Harold Shapley, once said "we are the brothers of boulders, the companions of clouds." Astronomers know that we are also the sons of the stars.

Yet the stars are mortal, just as we. Our galaxy is the stage for a drama of worlds being born and dying, while even mighty galaxies collide, shatter, and merge. In grand diversity the action continues.

Biology teaches us that if somewhere along the way evolution had made a small change in the script, we humans would not be here. We are fragile—but so, in the long run, is the universe.

The galaxy is still young, only ten billion years old. Within twenty billion more the stars which nurtured life will ebb, growing cooler, redder. The giant blue stars will be gone forever. The galaxy will dim as black holes grow. There will be fewer warm spots for life. The Milky Way will witness the final act, a long twilight struggle, and if life remains anchored to planets, it is doomed.

I take a brighter view of the far future. Just as astrology once said that the stars rule the affairs of men, I believe, as Arthur Clarke put it, that the time will come when men rule the affairs of stars.

Life's greatest challenge will be survival after the stars are gone. As Shakespeare said,

Now entertain conjecture of a time
when creeping murmur and the poring dark
fills the wide vessel of the universe.
Life—that is, mind—arose out of matter.

The grandest philosophical question is, will all life's struggles come to nought? Can we survive the gathering cold and dark? Will the universe slow, contract, and collapse, reversing the big bang? Astronomers' quest for the shadowy dark matter will perhaps answer this question.

The Killer B's, 1997: (from left) David Brin, Greg Bear, and Greg Benford

I believe that life will persist through the dimming of the galaxy, the growth of monstrous black holes, even through the eventual decay of matter itself into nothing more than electrons, their anti-particles, and light. I hope there will always be a role in the galaxy's evolution for beings capable of knowing joy. As the poet T. S. Eliot put it, "We are the music, while the music lasts."

We shot all that, but when the final editing got done, only about half got through. Still, NHK wedged a lot into the series, and it aired repeatedly in Japan, its first venue, in 1990 through 1991.

It won the Japanese version of the Emmy for Best General Program. It showed in 1991 in Europe, in translation. NHK published a five-book series, full of gorgeous color photography, graphics, and with short introductions by myself. They sold well.

Then nothing happened. The show had ended up costing over $6 million, the biggest budget overrun NHK had ever had, and they needed to sell it in the U.S. market.

But the NHK structure took nearly all support money away from the program as soon as the final cut came out. Negotiations with U.S. networks were cordial, but the program needed editing. The Japanese style is alternately leisurely, with long panning shots, and then jerky. But there was no money for re-editing.

So the entire project fell into a corporate hole, one step short of the major market that could make the whole enterprise profitable. KCET's *The Astronomers* had fallen on its face in the market, with less than 10 percent of the audience that Sagan's *Cosmos* had garnered a decade earlier. The word was out that astronomy shows didn't work.

This tendency of TV and films to ride on conventional wisdom about the market is notorious, and amusing. Once I saw a letter written on luxurious stationery by a studio maven about buying an option on a novel of mine about Greek archeology, *Artifact*. "Nobody goes to movies about archeology," he said. "Too intellectual and dry." This was a year after the release of *Raiders of the Lost Ark*.

And nothing kept on happening.

So *A Galactic Odyssey* never showed in the U.S. The Carnegie Institute did re-edit the first episode for brief showings, but not the series. NHK broke up the entire team and the project is now solely in the hands of marketing, which means no creative people involved. They have shown it around and it is reasonably well received, I hear. But it would need reworking for the more sophisticated American market, and there's nobody around any longer to do that delicate job.

Gregory Benford, while shooting the TV series, Kitt Peak, Arizona, 1990

People ask me about it, and I just shake my head. What did I learn from an involvement of fully three years, finally?

First, novelists don't fit well in intensely committee-dominated projects. Decisions about showing aliens, or even categorizing civilizations by their energy consumption (somehow not an ecologically virtuous point of view), were made by faceless executives—most of whom had no scientific training whatever. And they don't think that it is important.

Novelists think in larger chunks. Hard sf novelists probably don't make the best diplomats, either, about scientific facts. Or at least, *this* novelist didn't.

Second, don't let the scientific content get compromised for schedule or convenience. Realize that just about nobody has the same commitment to the material that scientists do—but apply pressure at the essential points.

Third, use a particular rhythm in presenting science, to draw out its human aspects. This rhythm runs

philosophy —> *science* —> *philosophy*

Begin with a grand overview, posing certain human or social problems as they relate to science. Then go to the science, the technical true grit, that can then lead back to those deep philosophical issues. Offer a response, maybe even a solution, on the basis of the scientific content just detailed.

This rhythm opens the sciences, imbuing large human issues with the flagrant excitement of the new, the fresh, the real. You can even yield to calls for a new vision or morality, speaking from the solidity of a scientific pulpit.

In both visual and print media, this has been the style of the best broad scientific popularizations of the last few decades. Recall Steven Weinberg's *The First Three Minutes*, Douglas Hofstader's *Godel, Escher, Bach*, Sagan's *Cosmos*, E. O. Wilson's *On Human Nature*, and many others.

Lastly, have some input in editing. Much of *A Galactic Odyssey* got rearranged, slanted, and cut by people who knew little or nothing of the technical material. Such power is hard to get, but essential.

A minor point: never do location shooting without firm guidelines. Otherwise, you are the tool of the lighting, camera, and sound crews. I waited atop Mount Wilson from 9 P.M. until 2 A.M. for the crews to set up. It was a chilly January night and after rehearsing, there wasn't much to do. Then I had to do moving-and-speaking shots over precarious walkways outside the big dome of the observatory, while worn out. We finished at 4 A.M. I looked pretty awful on camera, too, and nearly went off a hundred foot drop, but the lighting was perfect . . .

Science is hard to popularize; its material is arcane, dense, and, for many, forbidding, even frightening. But scientists themselves must keep trying. Of course, much of the process of popularizing is, for the scientific mind, disagreeable.

But what's the alternative?

For the moment I have resolved to try again with *Cosm*, my latest novel, to speak to the larger, mainstream culture which fears science as often as it enshrines the technology science engenders. I shall then write at least one nonfiction work, *Deep Time*, and reconsider fiction thereafter. I am less convinced that science fiction can communicate directly to the mainstream audience; instead, more often our inventions are filtered by the hacks like Crichton and Cook, who know how to thrill the large audience, and to deftly pickpocket the genre. Sf as the literature of ideas unfortunately implies that its central concerns and methods can be detached from the works themselves and pirated by those who neither know nor respect the field. These screenwriters and pop novelists end up conveying sf to the public more effectively than we genre novelists do, alas.

So here I am in 1997, still charting a career which I've given up trying to predict. The comforts of writing are many, as are those of physics. The two worlds rub against each other uneasily in my life. I shall probably always cycle between them, seeking the ideas and experiences that lend a vibrancy to life. The richness of science opens to an informed writer, while the imagination in fiction can fuel that of the scientist.

To be continued, I hope.

Copyright © 1997 by Abbenford Associates

BIBLIOGRAPHY

Science fiction:

Deeper Than the Darkness, Ace Books, 1970, revised edition published as *The Stars in Shroud,* Putnam, 1978.

Jupiter Project (for young adults), T. Nelson (Nashville, Tennessee), 1975, 2nd edition, 1980.

(With Gordon Eklund) *If the Stars Are Gods* (based on Benford's novella of the same title), Putnam, 1977.

In the Ocean of Night: A Novel, Dial, 1977.

(With Gordon Eklund) *Find the Changeling,* Dell, 1980.

(With William Rotsler) *Shiva Descending,* Avon, 1980.

Against Infinity, Timescape Books, 1983.

Time's Rub, Cheap Street (New Castle, Virginia), 1984.

Artifact, T. Doherty Associates, 1985.

Of Space-Time and the River, illustrated by Judy King-Rieniets, Cheap Street, 1985.

In Alien Flesh, T. Doherty Associates, 1986.

(With David Brin) *Heart of the Comet,* Bantam, 1986.

(With others) *Under the Wheel,* Baen, 1987.

(Editor, with Martin H. Greenberg) *Hitler Victorious: Eleven Stories of the German Victory in World War II,* Berkley Publishing, 1987.

We Could Do Worse, Abbenford Associates, 1988.

Sail the Frozen Star, Bantam, 1988.

(With Arthur C. Clarke) *Beyond the Fall of Night,* Putnam, 1990.

Centigrade 233, Cheap Street, 1990.

(Editor with Martin H. Greenberg and author of introduction) *What Might Have Been Volume 4: Alternate Americas* (anthology), Bantam, 1992.

(Under pseudonym Sterling Blake) *Chiller,* Bantam, 1993.

Matter's End (short stories), limited edition, Cheap Street, 1991, reprinted with illustrations by Judy J. King, Bantam, 1994.

(Editor) *Far Futures,* Tor, 1995.

Foundation's Fear, HarperPrism, 1997.

"Galactic" series:

Timescape, Book #1, Simon & Schuster, 1980.

Across the Sea of Suns, Book #2, Timescape Books, 1984.

Great Sky River, Book #3, Bantam, 1987.

Tides of Light, Book #4, Bantam, 1989.

Furious Gulf, Book #5, Bantam, 1994.

Sailing Bright Eternity, Book #6, Bantam, 1995.

Scientific advisor, host, and drama script writer, for *A Galactic Odyssey,* television series (limited), Japanese National Broadcasting (NHK), 1990–91. Contributed a novella to Robert Silverberg's *Threads of Time: Three Original Novellas of Science fiction, by Gregory Benford, Clifford D. Simak, Norman Spinrad,* T. Nelson, 1974; an autobiographical essay to *New Legends,* edited by Greg Bear, 1995; author of foreword to Olaf Stapledon's *Last and First Men: A Story of the Near and Far Future,* J. P. Tarcher (Los Angeles), 1988; contributed introduction to *Look Away,* by George Alec Effinger, illustrated by Donna Gordon, Axolotl Press (Eugene, Oregon), 1990.

Contributor to anthologies, including *Again, Dangerous Visions,* edited by Harlan Ellison, Doubleday, 1972; *Universe 4,* Random House, 1974, *Universe 8,* Doubleday, 1978, and *Universe 9,* Doubleday, 1979, all edited by Terry Carr; and *New Dimensions 5,* edited by Robert Silverberg, Harper, 1975. Author of numerous research papers on astrophysics, plasma physics, and solid-state physics. Contributor of articles and stories to magazines, including *Magazine of Fantasy and Science Fiction, Natural History, Omni,* and *Smithsonian.*

Lennart Bruce

1919-

I first saw him outside the pompous Order of Carpenters' building (a charitable institution) in the center of Stockholm. In front of it was a fountain big enough for kids to sail their toy boats. He was crouching at its edge, a sailboat in his hand, pushing it across the water. The wind tugged at the white sail, steading its course toward the other side of the pond. I was holding a small tin boat; I inserted a white rectangular combustion tablet into it, ignited it with a match, and it rattled across the water next to his yacht.

His two-years-younger brother was at his side. Their heads were crew-cut in the manner of poor kids, but he boasted that they were sailing with their father on his big yacht far out in the Stockholm archipelago. He further told me that his dad had two automobiles, a mansion just outside the capital, and a hunting lodge on Rödlöga, a string of islands facing the open waters of the Baltic Sea.

His name was Per-Olof, and he too had passed the tests to enter the secondary Swedish grammar school, the New Elementary and High, behind the Fish & Meat market next to the Stockholm Concert Hall.

I was proud of my new school cap. Per-Olof, nicknamed Pelle, hadn't had the time to buy one yet. The cap had a shiny visor attached to a black-velvet-covered band. Attached to it in turn was a crown of silk which had to be thrust backward for elegant swankiness. Its inside had a blue and yellow lining: the colors of the Swedish flag. In the center of the velvet-covered band there was a laurel of golden metal around two torches aflame with a star in between, symbolizing the wisdom of learning. The leather facing had my initials embossed: my identification. Thus my cap became my first sign of social distinction. I had been put to the test because my parents happened to have the money to pay for my education. But all around the poor kids roamed the streets calling us names.

Lennart Bruce

We moved up through the grades, became buddies. When together we thumbed through the only porno mag in Sweden at the time, *Parisian,* where the daring illustrations had been toned down a shade of explicitness for the yet puritan market, unintentionally adding to their illicit enticement. I asked, "What do you like best, their breasts or their asses?" He blushed and answered, "Their breasts." "Their asses," I stated.

The spring semester had just come to an end. The sky was blue, here and there hidden behind white summer clouds. We glanced up into it, the paradise instant, pure, unsoiled expectation without walls in any direction. Sunlight between tree shadows, flowers, warm air, scent of resin, friendly birds and insects, the unlimited instant, in the way of animals. . . . We ran. "How can you run on such a hot day?!" said a friendly grownup.

We ended up together at the examination ending our twelve years of Swedish schooling, each reading a couple of sentences about a bear in French. I had to give an account of French history from the days of the Sun King on. He recapitulated the most important sections of the Swedish constitution. We had both made the choice of Russian instead if Latin and read from a novel of Chekhov in the original language. . . .

We made it and stood in line to shake our teachers' hands that up till then only had slapped us. We put on our new white-crowned caps signifying the end of school and ran out as if fleeing for our lives.

Heading toward the Rödlöga islands we took a swig of aquavit once we had passed the most treacherous shoals. We passed islands somber with firs on our way to the outer fringe on the yet distant horizon with their low vegetation, dwarfed fruit trees, heather, and lilies of the valley in the crevices between the rocks. In the coves facing the open sea there was an abundance of fish, sea-bass and pike which always put up a fight when caught on your lure. You could choose their color. In the shallows they were silver-gray and further out among the seaweed and kelp, gold-shimmering. If you happened to get one of the old big ones on your bait, it tore the line as the barber cut a strand of hair to test the sharpness of his blade. . . .

We were partners now. I had just returned home to Sweden after my business sojourn in South America with an Argentine movie, *La Guerra Gaucha.* We sold it to Sandrew, the Swedish movie tycoon. We brushed past young Ingmar Bergman on our way into his office. We were offered coffee and Danish. Sandrew, who was of working-class stock, drank from his cup's saucer. It was the first Argentine film ever shown in Sweden. It opened at Sandrew's most prestigious movie house, the Grand. There was a preshow at another of his theaters, the Astoria, with cocktails and snacks offered by the Foreign Office. I had been asked to make the inaugural address in two languages.

We bought the next movie in France. It was called *Clochemerle* and had been banned there

because it made fun of the Catholic church. In one of the scenes, the radicals erected a urinal right in front of the cathedral. It was a smash hit, ran for sold-out houses: the ingredients, wit, and the right proportion of obscenities before violence had taken over. We then invested our profit in other French films, among them *The Lovers in Verona,* about Romeo and Juliet, with Anouk Aimée as Juliet, beautiful but sad and not the slightest obscene. What we had gained on *Clochemerle* we lost.

Again we were heading out to the open sea, movies left behind us, but with expectations without limits, our friendship intact in spite of business together. And our closeness would never be ravaged by that spoiler of sincere relationships. But he had a hot temper paired with his boundless generosity. Late one night he slammed the door and sailed straight out to the Svenska Högarna, a lighthouse outpost in the Baltic.

He drowned out there. His mother cursed at his grave site because he lay behind the headstones of the fishermen. "He can't see the sea even," she wept. But around it still stand the woods, not at all somber. The church behind the few graves blends inconspicuously into the nature around.

I lost my best friend; a tie with the homeland had been severed.

"My friend Per-Olof shortly before his drowning"

My mother was pretty and impulsive, a truthsayer. That gained her both friends and enemies, but she mostly won back the latter with her warmth and generosity.

We spent one summer in western Sweden, on an island facing the North Sea. It stormed and rained incessantly. Mother almost lost her mind, especially as Father remained in Stockholm tending his business. The only time Mother laughed that summer was when in answer to her question: "Why do you want to run barefoot in the ice cold rain?" I said, "To spare the soles of my shoes!" She thought that was very funny coming from the mouth of a three-year-old.

Father was dark-haired for a Swede, and two of his brothers were redheads, giving some credence to Grandmother's wild tale of a Scottish origin in tune with our surname. She maintained that our ancestor was a forester who fell in love with a Swedish lass and pursued her to Sweden. He was already married in Scotland but that didn't prevent him from marrying the Swedish woman, thus committing bigamy. A cousin of mine who married into nobility went chasing our ancestral origin all through Sweden on bicycle, probably in the hopes of catching up with his well-born wife. Unfortunately he found only blacksmiths, peasants, and burnt-down churches with their records lost. Once as a teenager, I was confronted with a Swedish count by the name of Hamilton, who asked me if I, like him, was of Scotch descent. I lied to him, straight in the face: "Yes, descendant of King Robert the Bruce." "Is your genealogy fully documented?" he asked with a malicious smile.

Father was laid off from his work at a candle factory when electricity was introduced. He then started his own business together with an inventor. Among their far-flung projects were the Catacombs of Stockholm, a funeral home, and the eternal shoe-sole. When that business folded he entered into partnership with two brothers of some means. They financed his journey overseas. In Canada he secured the agency of Purity, a flour. On his return he bought out the brothers, married my mother, and ventured into the most volatile of all trades, the importation of fresh fruit, joining the gang with its sky-jumping mentality: just before hitting the ground one released the parachute. "Nothing to it," one said.

But then Father got a simple although genial idea: that in the Southern hemisphere the

"My parents, Johan and Agda Bruce, at the time of their marriage," 1910

fruits from his point of view literally grew upside down, that is, they ripened and were harvested in our springtime. He chartered a ship and filled it with apples, pears, and grapes. One chilly April morning it sneaked into the harbor of Stockholm. His competitors gasped: "How come we didn't think of that?!" His fortune was made, and we moved up to a more affluent neighborhood.

Mother loved moving, choosing the new places. Father always asked her advice on important matters. When her opinion differed from his and, in the end, turned out to be correct, he mumbled, "damned thing, that you should always be right."

The bananas killed Father. The ruthless United Fruit people held a monopoly using the brand name Jamaica Bananas. But they didn't come from that island, something Father soon took to heart. He promptly went there, secured the exclusive agency, and began marketing the true Jamaica bananas. A fierce competition began. Father and his assistant, an opera singer who had lost his voice, worked day and night.

Lennart with sister Ingegerd and mother, early 1920s

One morning after having settled a workers' strike, instead of going home to sleep off his fatigue, he went to the sauna, dozed for hours in the heat, then took an ice-cold shower on his head and got a stroke. He was only forty-eight years old when he died.

The man who took over the management after Father's death was more the accountant type—and a good one at that—but he didn't have Father's free-flying imagination. Our firm lost the banana account. The competitors took over and sat down at a table freshly laid.

After the tragic drowning of my close friend, ending our movie business, Mother wanted me to join the family company. There was one problem, though, my father's successor didn't like the idea at all.

Then World War II flared up, and military service intervened. I was drafted. Sweden balanced on the brink of war, as expressed by the Swedish poet Karl Ragnar Gierow in his "Evening News: The sudden media bomb shells hit our living rooms, each blast inching closer / every day / protecting ourselves underneath the skirts of Mother Sweden / against the glare of searchlights / we rise heavily from our chairs / our legs leaden from centuries of peace."

Mother worried: "If there is a war, son, drop your gun and run," she said, mother's love and Swedish neutrality entwined in her embrace of good-bye when I left for my regiment.

Sergeant Johansson and I became friends. The night before it happened, the two of us had been to Skara, a nearby town. We got a little drunk at the local tavern, and he threw himself on his bunk with his clothes on and fell asleep. At dawn I was wakened by a noise, heard cautious steps, but turned in bed without paying further attention.

Suddenly, I heard the sound of a distant shot. When I looked down into his lower bunk, it was empty. Somebody came running: "The sergeant shot himself!" When the captain of our unit got the news he sat up in bed only to fall back again with a whimper, slipping back into sleep. He thought he had had a bad dream; such an unlikely early casualty of World War II in neutral Sweden where people died in peacetime only for personal reasons. There was an investigation by the local police, and the day after, Johansson was brought into the depot behind the barracks. I went there to say farewell. He lay resting so quietly, pale as a figure of wax, head bandaged hiding the shot wound and its secret in there. Toward evening his family, a little group of people in dark clothes, came and took him away in silence.

Hitler's rampage through Europe swiftly conquered Poland, Denmark, and Norway. He demanded transit of troops and material through Sweden. The Swedish government refused. Hitler was furious. Eventually, under intense pressure, he got his way on the condition that only unarmed men on or returning from leave were allowed passage. Hitler rumbled that he would take care of Sweden later, for now he had more important matters on his agenda: the campaign against Holland, Belgium, and France.

I was summoned to the office of the company commander and ordered to report for duty on the transit trains. I don't know if it was because of my comparatively good grade in German at school or simply because he wanted to get rid of me. . . .

This day, there were rumors of something special in the offing as we were meeting the ferry from Sassnitz in Germany to Trelleborg on the Swedish shore of the Baltic. We, that is, a sergeant and I, under the command of a lieutenant, were commissioned to guard the train on its journey through Sweden. Our little group was the ultimate guarantor that our country's neutrality was respected while we supervised almost a thousand German soldiers. Every night two to three thousand travelled through Sweden. One contingent on a straight course south-north, destined for Narvik in Norway, and then back the same way. Our train had a shorter route, crossing in a northwestern direction and then back. Although officially controls were said to be strict, there was no custom's inspection of the men or their baggage. Their suitcases could very well have hidden light automatic weapons. Nothing would have prevented them from marching off the train and occupying one or several of the cities or towns we passed, except, that is, for our patrol.

Slowly the ferry appeared through the fog. We were on the dock waiting beside the railway tracks and the train we were to guard. Today, also waiting for the ferry, was an engine with only three cars on a side track. One was a dining car, and I took a peep through its window. Tables were laid, decorated with German and Swedish flags. It came as a shock to see them together: the black swastika, so ominous, and ours with its bright yellow cross on blue, evoking visions of the Stockholm skerries, flags snapping in the wind at the sterns of leisure boats in summer.

The ferry touched alongside the quay. A gangway was lowered. Two tall German officers in long leather coats appeared. They took position before the gangway, facing each other, making the "Heil, Hitler" salute, arms high in the air. And there he came, a little limping man, Goebbels. His dark head on its thin neck under the huge uniform cap gave the impression of a magpie chick. On short notice, the Swedes had not been able to muster anything better in his honor than a detachment of old reserve vets. One of them hollered: "Attention!" The men shuffled into position somewhat individually. Majestically slowly the little man walked down the gangway lifting his hand laxly into the same position as a waiter carrying a tray, but without the tray, no feast offered, although the Swedish crew on board the ship received a tip of fifty reichsmark each.

Without delay Goebbels, his entourage, and the Swedish officers entrusted with guarding him boarded the special train. When the last man lifted his foot from the platform, it started rolling.

Then, the soldiers we were supposed to be in charge of began disembarking. We shared the responsibility with a German patrol, also three men—an officer and two sergeants. Attached to the train was a car of civilians, Norwegians. We tossed a coin to decide who was going to collect their passports; a nasty job. This time it fell on me. As soon as the train picked up speed, I left our compartment for the civilian car. My orders were to stay in the doorway because of the risk of attack. I had a list from which I called the passengers' names. The Norwegians loathed the Germans, but they hated us with a vengeance. They regarded us as traitors, although, officially at least, our job was to supervise the Germans.

There were bomb threats, and indirectly we were kept informed about imminent crises and threats of war when Swedish officers came running to the train on its few stops. In nervous agitation they whispered: "Be on your guard tonight, this is it!"

But it never happened. Only one train with supplies was blown up, with no casualties. A couple of times we saw someone sneak off the train at a station and vanish into the dark. We didn't report it—strictly against the rules, as was any communication with the soldier passengers or the German military patrol.

"Now we'll throw them off their guard, get some top secret information out of them," said our lieutenant as we headed for their compartment.

We exchanged rarities in wartime rationing. They offered Simon Artzt cigarettes, thick as cigars, the fine white paper wrapped around the Turkish tobacco burning like incense. We responded by offering chocolate and Swedish arrack liqueur. Our coffee substitute was largely made from old figs—with worms crawling in them it was rumored—and was as bad as theirs, but their beer was better. Our lieutenant talked most of the time, didn't give the Germans much chance to reveal any secrets. After a couple of toasts, uniform collars were unbuttoned. The Germans seemed pretty much like us, besides they were Austrians. When they got a chance, they told jokes ridiculing Hitler, Göring, the whole Nazi hierarchy. We got drunk, and the Streife Führer, head of their patrol, stumbled down on his knees and pinned all his decorations onto my chest. "Worthless," he said, "inflation in the butcher trade. In the old days you had to lose a leg or an arm to get 'das Kreuz,' today it's enough to get your little finger blown off!"

Our lodgings up north were on the Norwegian side of the border. We were forced to share quarters with the German SS, their black uniforms ornamented with death's-heads, awkward looking when they played table tennis as a pastime. When Hitler raged in his speeches, they sat before the radio quiet and awed.

One day, desperate to escape the sordid surroundings, I ventured outdoors on skis. As I passed, the Norwegians spat at me. Those inside their houses pulled their blinds to be spared the sight of me. Thus I was forced out into the woods and fields. A foolhardy excursion, as I realized later, when I learned that I had been reported from three different Swedish border outposts as "solitary soldier in Swedish uniform proceeding from foreign territory crossing the Swedish-Norwegian border three times."

I shudder when I think of the guns trained on me not only from the Swedish side.

Our infantry regiment was to be transformed and integrated into a tank division. Most of us guys took the bait: immediate leave, and then, when called back at the earliest in six months, tank training rather than crawling in the mud.

I was one of the few who didn't swallow it, however. After my stint on the transit trains, I was sent on a land mine course. That's where the scraps wound up. In the case of war we were supposed to advance before the main troops to locate and dismantle mines. Average life length statistically under the circumstances could be counted in minutes or hours, at best. But at last, after the mine training, I was honorably discharged.

Two of my uncles, Ernst and Algot, had emigrated to America. The former went to South America and established himself as Don Ernesto, successful businessman in Uruguay and Swedish consul general. Uncle Algot also went south, crossing the border into Mexico, where he joined Pancho Villa's army. He had a bullet lodged in his nape but survived and ultimately wound up as a state park ranger in California. His last address was "Dead End," fitting for an old soldier.

Rather than staying cooped up in Sweden in a renewed struggle with Axel Almberg, the head of the family company, I wanted to travel,

and South America was practically the only destination for a neutral Swede in wartime. I dropped Don Ernesto a letter asking for a job. He got me one in Buenos Aires with a firm owned by Norwegians, Kierulf & Gravdal.

My girlfriend Harriet and I married after clearing our papers with the Swedish authorities, as well as with the combatant powers for safe conduct. We sailed on the M/S *Ecuador,* a freighter, from Gothenburg to Buenos Aires. We left port on June 6, 1944, D day.

Even neutral ships had been torpedoed by the Germans. Once we were outside the Gothenburg archipelago, we passengers had our lifeboat drill. Quite tiny on deck, our vessel grew, assuming the size of a galley almost, as it hit the waves. It was equally heavy to move with our limp attempts at rowing. Out of step we splashed the long oars in the heavy sea. Behind the dripping oar blades opened the endless ocean, gray, with mines and torpedoes, drowning and death.

Back on deck of our ship we now began our awkward honeymoon under strict prohibition to undress at night because of the hazards of war.

We were on a northerly course in a wide half circle. Before leaving the Norwegian fiords behind, the German coastguard boarded our ship for inspection. When Norway had sunk behind the horizon, the English came aboard from a torpedo boat in the open sea. From then on we were seemingly on our own. It was ominously calm, all military action converging on the beaches of France. We saw the swastika against the sky on the wings of a solitary reconnaissance plane and the British insignia on another aircraft, luckily unaware if we were scrutinized from submarine periscopes. Here and there our constant watch pointed out mines heaving heavily in the waves.

"We never knew what happened to the *Brasilia,*" said the first mate when we were having aquavit and beer in his cabin, "she just vanished with men and all, no trace of her, not even a buoy. . . ."

Eventually the Faeroes appeared, fog-swept, treeless but green, a bastion of dream rising from the reality of ocean.

We only remained in Torshavn harbour a couple of hours to refuel. The beauty of the islands was stunning as we passed on our way out between them, the open ocean frothing through the sounds, battering the green steepness of the sparse land, smudges in the vast eye of the sea. The screams of birds followed us, reminding me strangely of the shriek that escaped from deep down my sister's throat when she was told of Father's death—a longing—"a tyranny of umbilical chords . . . with their ever tender ache," to quote the Swedish poet Artur Lundkvist.

After weeks on the open sea, another bastion rose out of the ocean off the Brasilian coast outside Cabo de São Roque, the islands of Fernando de Noronha. Eventually, the Argentina coast started haunting us with its flatness, the mirage of the pampas and the scarce clumps of trees suspended above, as though without roots in the quivering air of an optical illusion.

We lay in roads overnight outside our destination, Buenos Aires. After five weeks at sea the captain invited us passengers to a farewell dinner. All through the voyage he had been a sullen recluse. Now he opened up with a sudden unexpected extravagancy, apparently relieved to get rid of us who for so long had intruded upon his domain, the one of the sea, in his mind totally distanced from the one ashore. The following morning we steered into Río de la Plata, and Harriet's and my strange honeymoon, sleeping with one eye open on the alert for disaster, came to an end.

At the office of Kierulf & Gravdal sentences in Spanish burst into my confused brain as the boss of my department, Slaughterhouse Byproducts, dictated to me as I typed. But to take down telephone messages in the foreign language, with no lips to follow for guidance, was even worse. Although wonderful were my excursions to Mercado de Abasto. "Aqui se come bien"—"Here you eat well," every cab driver assured me. One of them told me how he had been lassoed in the bush, how the whites gave him clothes and taught him to drive a car. I never had a better driver.

Mercado de Abasto is part of Buenos Aires' stomach, like the old Halles de Paris. But here only the flora is represented, the fauna is marketed elsewhere. Everything thrived in this fertile land. I already had gained fifteen pounds since landing three months before, lean after years of European rationing. Behind the splendid wholesale displays business was brisk: oranges, apples, pears, apricots, peaches, lettuce, parsley, onions, garlic. . . . The wheels of the carts turned in a mush of fruit salad.

General Edelmiro Farrell was president after a military coup. But one of his young ambitious colonels, Juan Domingo Perón, soon took over.

There was some shooting. Two big movie houses on Avenida Corrientes got their windowpanes pierced by bullets. The small caliber holes were left for the wind to whistle through.

"Perón, Perón!" Los descamisados—the shirtless ones or the poor—shouted as they roamed the avenues and streets of the city hoping for improvement in their dismal living conditions.

There were those who said Perón was of Swedish descent, that his family name once was Person, but that his ancestors had swallowed the "s." But that must have been long ago judging from his black hair, sleekly following his scalp. I met him once at a party thrown by the Swedish envoy. Tall and smiling he beamed, that ever seducing combination of courteous attention and power. He was a colonel and strongman then, walking the "Parque de Palermo" with Eva Duarte, an enamored couple.

I had experienced something similar once before when meeting Alexandra Kolontay, friend of Lenin and member of the inner Bolshevik circle. I met her in a roundabout way through my studies of the Russian language. It was during the war when even Americans and English flocked around a Soviet ambassador. She was said to never forget a face or a name, a feeling I got when shaking her hand.

I received a letter from my sister Ingegerd. She stated that she intended to come for a visit, didn't know how long she would stay. It made me worried. Since Father's death she had had a history of mental illness. Her singular beauty seems to have been a drawback, exposing her to hazards of all kinds.

I went to meet her. She stood on the deck of the *Ecuador*—the same ship that Harriet and I had arrived on—her makeup slightly overdone. There was an ominous glow in her eyes from deep inside, lending an unusual shade to their blue. She had had another of her harrowing experiences. In Stockholm she had done something very unpopular even in neutral Sweden. She had had an affair with Hans Thomsen, the German ambassador to Sweden and former German consul general in New York. He was a career diplomat of an old Hamburg family.

Thus she was branded a Nazi, and where could she go but to Argentina, where she happened to have a brother and an uncle next door! She had no idea of politics, however. In Stockholm she had worked at the Museum of Egyptology. She disliked Wagner, and her favorite literature was the Russian classics. Later she married two Englishmen, one after the other. She lived in London then. Later she died at a mental hospital in Malta.

There were other fugitives in Buenos Aires. I had met one of them at a party, Starhemberg, a stately Austrian prince, his nose like the beak of an eagle. One day my sister and I bumped into him in the street. He invited us for dinner at the home of his magnate friend Fritz Mandl, who supported Perón financially. In Austria Mandl had married the Hungarian actress Hedy Lamarr and had tried to buy up all the copies of the movie *Ecstasy,* where she ran naked through the woods. Starhemberg and Mandl had fled Europe together. Somehow they had landed on the wrong side of Hitler. Mandl was known for his lavish parties, and we accepted.

In my sister, Fritz Mandl saw a blond Hedy Lamarr and launched a frantic courtship although he was married to Hertha, a Valkyrie straight out of Wagner.

The perfect setting for a disaster. All my worries had been confirmed. I had to get my sister out of Buenos Aires. Harriet and I were going south on a mission to buy fruit for export, and we talked her into coming along. But Mandl, a man with a grasshopper's square jaw, exuded powerful energy. In the course of our journey he bombarded her with pleas to return. At the stations where our train stopped, there were telegrams waiting for her, pleading her to return. The chorus of his insistence was deafening. Finally she said, "I have to go back." Harriet and I couldn't dissuade her. We parted, and Harriet and I continued alone to buy Argentinean and Chilean fruit for Europe from growers along our route.

As soon as we got to Santiago de Chile I phoned my sister. At first I thought she sounded alright, but then as we went on talking there was an undertone that scared me. "Are you sure everything is alright?" I asked, "Can you make it on your own until we're back?" "Yes, yes," she said. "How is Mandl?" I asked. She answered with a laughter, went on laughing, couldn't stop. I tried frantically to interrupt her, and when I said, "Why didn't you come with us instead of going back?" she said, "Yes,

"My sister Ingegerd," 1936

I suppose that was a stupid thing to do." Harriet and I decided to return to Buenos Aires without delay.

We were gliding into the shaded light of the station. I tore at the leather strap to open the window, leaned out looking for Ingegerd, couldn't see her. But . . . there was Fritz Mandl. Something must have happened. I waved to him. He waved back. His smile seemed strained. When I got out of the car, to my surprise he took my arm and led me down the platform. I resisted, stiffly tagging along, swaying at his pace as we walked, arms hooked, Harriet left behind. I felt embarrassed, ridiculous. How on earth did I wind up walking arm in arm with this man?! I tried to tear loose, but he tightened his grip.

"I've seen to it that she gets the best possible care, yes, she couldn't get a better physician anywhere in the world," he assured me.

"What happened to her?" "A nervous breakdown," he answered, "she probably had too much to drink, an alcohol problem."

I was speechless. He went on talking: "She became abnormally agitated. I moved her to a hotel, the best in town, best room, top floor. One day she took all her money and threw it to the people in the street below, scattering bills like confetti—a lot of money." He went on, "She had asked me for a considerable sum the day before and under the circumstances I didn't want to argue. Now everything went out of her windows. People threw themselves at the bills, got into fights, traffic jammed, the police came. The hotel manager phoned me. I was at an important meeting but had to rush over. The police broke into her room. She had to be put under medical supervision. As you understand, I saw to it that she got the best possible care," he reassured me over and over again. But somehow he never got to the core of what really happened. He took me home in his limousine, and in a daze I pondered what might have happened. After all she was quite normal when we parted; even if we knew that she had weak nerves, this seemed too sudden.

Later I got through to him on the telephone. He agreed to pick me up and take me to the hospital. He talked about visiting her every day, but I got a strong feeling that from now on he wanted me to take over. Neither was he any longer trying to soften the blow by hiding the seriousness of her condition.

When we arrived, we were received by her doctor without delay, and he took us to her. Through some kind of garden we advanced to a solitary building within the hospital compound. I heard somebody howling. We passed into the isolation section of the building, stopped in front of a door. A nurse unlocked it and we entered.

The sight was devastating. My sister lay in some kind of a box, more like a coffin than a bed, in a straitjacket, all tied up, its long flaps winding around her body, fastened with metal clips. She had been doped, was totally helpless. I had a feeling she recognized me, but the contact faded. The room was a cell with a bare minimum of furniture, windows barred. I turned and walked out.

"Do you have to keep her like this?" I asked the doctor. "It's only for her own good," he assured me, "when she is hallucinating she rushes around terrified of snakes, eagles, what have you. . . . Her physical strength is then tenfold. Nobody is strong enough to hold her, and she could hurt herself seriously."

It was hard for me to argue. Everything can be explained in a mental institution, pa-

tients have no rights. Never mind the exorbitant charges. . . . Mandl started talking frantically, that is, as frantically as he could in the foreign language. He mixed up nouns, verbs, pronouns in his embarrassed agitation, calling her "he." He went on with a harangue about how she had had too many dry martinis (his favorite drink), about how poisonous the mixture of gin and vermouth was . . . "Don't you think it might have been the olive?" I asked.

Eventually Ingegerd recovered, was released from the hospital, and Harriet and I went with her to the countryside, Ascochinga, in Provincia de Cordoba. Finally, we got a coherent account of what had happened. Hertha had terrorized her with obscene phone calls, even threatening her life, and assaulted her physically on Plaza San Martin in Buenos Aires' most high-class shopping district. It must have been quite a sight with the two women clawing at each other, banging purses on each other's heads, on their knees beneath the statue of South America's great liberator.

With the Mandl incident behind us we booked passage back to Sweden. If for no other reason than just to get a change, we asked to get a ship other than the *Ecuador* among the about a dozen ships of the Johnson Line that sailed between Sweden and South America, but due to a last minute rescheduling there she was again for us to board, the *Ecuador*—she seemed to follow us. The sea voyage was relaxing. To my surprise the freighter had quite a library. I read mysteries, but also Melville's *Moby Dick,* Tolstoy's *War and Peace,* and some poetry, some I didn't quite understand, but that didn't bother me too much; on the contrary, poetry presented a challenge, and I realized that it was necessary to learn how to read, cooperate with the poem, letting it invoke your whole being, not only your brain.

Back in Stockholm I started to work in the family company. The tension grew between Axel Almberg and me. In South America I had learned to work relatively independently with some measure of responsibility, but now I was cut off from everything essential that was going on. I was assigned the typing of invoices and envelopes. I didn't want to confront the man. In a way I understood him. He looked upon me as some upstart, threatening his position dutifully gained. He had run the company fairly successfully since Father's death, and there I was, kind of an heir with no other qualifications than my birthright.

On the way to my headquarters for renegade activities, installed in the attic of our office facilities, I had to pass through the room where the old man was sitting. He never said good morning, pretended to be too busy. When old family business friends from father's days, who had been invited into our home and I consequently knew well, came visiting the office, he slammed the door in my face as I tried to join. One day, however, I did the unthinkable: I stopped in front of his desk and said, "How are you today?" He lifted his head and looked at me in utter astonishment. "I mean, what kind of mood are you in today?" I went on.

"Out of my room," he roared. "I have as much right to be here as you," I said. He rose, purple in his face, and dodged out of the room without another word.

The next morning I found a note on my desk signed Axel Almberg: "Because of the insult I have been subjected to by the Bruce family, I will not come to the office until further notice. I will only be available in my home for consultation."

He expected "the family Bruce" to appear at his home desperately begging for help. He had fallen for that illusion so common: believing oneself irreplaceable.

Sure, the situation was critical, but that was the idea.

Father had directed our activities solely overseas, now classified as hard currency markets and totally restricted. The effect was disastrous for our company. Its activities were simply closed down, except for our importation from Israel and Cyprus, totally inadequate to cover our overall expenses.

On one of my visits to the port, I happened to kick over a wooden box. The Swedish lumber industry was in bad shape, laying off workers. What about exporting the slats to our U.S. fruit suppliers for assembly into wooden fruit boxes? They would fill them with fruit and send them back to us on the condition that the dollars generated by the sale of timber be used for the import of fruit! The authorities accepted my proposition. My competitors found to their surprise that there was overseas fruit on the market again.

But I soon saturated my fruit suppliers' needs for crating material, and the arrangement was limping: the fruit was considerably more expensive than the packing. I had to find another barter object. I literally needed boxes as big as houses. The swap of packing material against fruit gave a handsome profit, though, which I used to make trial shipments of prefabricated houses to Texas and California. In exchange for my effort, I convinced the authorities to give me a license to utilize some of the currency thus brought into the country for the import of fruit. I had no idea what I was getting into when I exaggerated the possibilities of exports into thousands of houses. But I presented the project to the authorities seemingly without loose ends. In reality it was more of a dream, a pure gamble. But I thought perhaps the timing was right. The Korean War had just come to an end with a red blot in the protocol, the death of Stalin; and by the efforts of Eisenhower, now elected president.

But I had badly underestimated the difficulties on the U.S. side. There was really no market for prefabricated houses, especially not foreign ones, and my efforts to get my fruit suppliers to accept them as housing for transient labor also failed. Through my sending houses on trial to the United States I had practically depleted our cash reserves, and the situation was now really desperate.

It was the time of the year when the Israel marketing board travelled through Europe to sell their crop. This year the Rokach-Isacson-Chorin team, old friends from Father's days, couldn't make it to Sweden, but they sent a deputy, a man I had never met. It was the old routine: take the representative out for dinner at a posh Stockholm restaurant.

After ordering our dinner we sat sipping our drinks and chatting. I told him of my houses in the United States and my futile search for a buyer there. We agreed on the irony that Israel could use any amount of housing for refugees pouring in from everywhere in the aftermath of the war and its devastation. But Israel was without funds, and banks were reluctant to extend credit because of the war with the Arabs.

"Don't you have an organization in the U.S.?" I asked, mostly to break the silence after a pause in our waning conversation. "Sure, the Jewish Agency of New York, our main source of income." "In dollars?" "Certainly," he answered, "but also that income is pledged, there's no cash, Israel can only pay in promissory notes."

"Inspecting Hood River fruit, which arrived in Stockholm Freeport as a result of my triangular Sweden/USA/Israel transaction"

"But they are in dollars?" I asked. "Sure," he confirmed.

That's when I got my idea! A humming brightness vibrated me: the feeling of the coin inserted in the slot machine releasing all its contents. That's it! I would sell my Swedish prefabs to the Jewish Agency of New York for shipment to Israel against payment in dollar promissory notes. Those in turn I would use instead of cash to pay my U.S. suppliers of fruit. They had to see the advantage of accepting them for the chance of exporting to an otherwise closed market, now opened by my financial scheme. I would sell the American fruit in Sweden, transforming it into cash that I would use to pay for the houses, then shipped to Israel. I felt jubilant, a chance derailment in my brain, a benevolent catastrophe! The Swedes, I imagined, couldn't very well object to the switch; the Swedish lumber industry would get a healthy injection, and homeless refugees would get a roof over their heads in their new country, Israel.

I bought my plane ticket to the United States for immediate departure to place the credit with my suppliers and hopefully the banks. I understood it would involve a loan, extended over four, five years at least, but I felt confident I could swing the deal.

On my travels I read a lot, business journals, etc. But as a counterweight I always brought with me poetry. I figured that it was the densest information from an opposite sphere. I had learned of its existence essentially thanks to the best thing that can happen to anyone: a formidable teacher.

According to us students in junior high, the most dreary subjects on the curriculum were religion (we had more of that than any other subject, glorifying Christianity and not a word was said about other religions, such as Buddhism, Hinduism, or Islam) and then literature.

Then one day at the beginning of the semester, a man in his early thirties stormed into our classroom. As through magic he made literature come to life. His name was Bernard Tarschys. He started discussions, often alone against us thirty students, arranged for us to make individual writing compositions beyond the scope of grading's straitjacket. He awarded our achievements with prizes, valuable books, paid for out of his own pocket. He encouraged me personally when I confessed my admiration for the nineteenth-century Swedish poet Stagnelius, whom my previous teacher had declared muddled and mediocre. How many times my thoughts have gone to that man with the deepest gratitude! Years later, when he had published several books, and I myself had started to write, I paid him a visit in his office at the Stockholm Royal Library. He had every reason to be skeptical but received me with the utmost courtesy. And above everything, when I sent him my translation into English of the Swedish classic Vilhelm Ekelund, he thanked me with a letter in spite of severe illness. It was signed, "your colleague Bernard."

The strain of recent events made my senses swirl, almost gave me a feeling of free suspension as I sank back in my four-engined hammock, the plane. Tolerably relaxed after a drink and a glass of wine, I opened my *Poeta en Nueva York* by Garcia Lorca. That's where I'm on my way, I thought. I didn't understand everything, but it didn't matter. Somehow I almost preferred the challenge of Lorca and, for example, Saint-John Perse. Their music gave a sense that their works were guided by a more all-inclusive force than that of the brain alone.

Eventually, I laid aside the book and fell asleep to the humming of the engines. Ahead of me a telegraphic message had already crossed the Atlantic destined to a former boyfriend of my sister, a Dutch emigré, a busybody who had to be booked in advance.

I was showed to his desk in the mezzanine hall of the Bankers Trust, where the president of the international department had divided up the world among his executive vice presidents. The big room without partitions was filled with the subdued hum of money being turned over.

"I have talked with Hammer, the head of the Jewish Agency of New York," he said. "We have a lot of business with him, quite a financial czar. I told him about your scheme. He didn't think he would be interested; too many promissory notes floating around. But we can always pay him a visit to hear what he has to say." Then he turned to the question of the credit. "What are the terms of the loan, a million over a year, eh?" "No, it's a multimillion-dollar deal over four to five years." He leaned back in his chair, his back against its posh leather back, and looked at me as if I were insane. "You are crazy. If we were talking about the Bank of England or at least the Riksbank of Sweden as a lien! . . ."

I blushed while defending myself. "The war is still only cold, but if it should develop into a shooting hot one, there probably wouldn't be much left of the Bank of England nor of the Riksbank after some nuclear blasts. But try to target the world Jewry; like using cannons against a spider's web. Hitler tried . . ." He interrupted my flow of eloquence. "Do you want me to arrange a meeting with Hammer?" "Sure, but he might insist on even longer terms?" "Then tell him to jump in the lake!" he said with a newly acquired Americanism, sounding somewhat out of place with its Dutch accent tilting slightly toward the German.

Gottlieb Hammer was a stocky man with the somber look of someone who handles a lot of money. The banker introduced me. Hammer greeted us at his desk underneath a huge photo of himself shaking hands with Albert Einstein. "I might consider a loan over five, six years, but I won't sign any note under $100,000." "It's impossible to arrange shipments

at even numbers. The total determines the figure," I argued. "That's your problem, not mine," he said.

I wouldn't dispute him at this stage. "I'll see what I can do," I said, "you will hear from me." I didn't feel too bad. After all I didn't get an outright no. When we left I asked the banker, "How much credit would your bank pick up?" "Preferably none, and certainly nothing longer than six months." I felt pushed against the wall.

Thus figuratively my Canossa wandering toward the goal of peddling promissory notes for the Jewish Agency had begun. First stop Washington D.C., the Department of Agriculture. But they weren't set up for schemes like mine. Then on to California. There I got the runaround between my supplier, Sunkist, and the Bank of America, and so on through Sacramento and all the way up to Seattle. There was one chance left, the Apple Growers' Association in Hood River, Oregon, our main supplier of apples and pears. The man I knew there, Arvo Hukari, an

"Inaugurating the first computer brought by me from the USA to Sweden," 1956

American of Finnish descent, was an old friend of the family since Father's days.

To my surprise he met me at the airport. He had driven all the way from Hood River. Leaving Seattle, the turning point of my journey had felt like a recognition of defeat. But at the sight of Arvo's smiling face my depression dispersed. He wasn't only a grower and businessman. After the death of his wife he became judge in a juvenile court. It was said that he would drive a hundred miles, even at night, to help a youth in trouble.

He invited me to stay at his house, a welcome change from hotel rooms. Before sunset we walked through his orchard adjacent to the house. After our walk we sat and talked. It got dark, we went on talking without putting on the lights. I told him everything about my simple idea with its random components added, picked up here and there. "That's right," he said, "that's right."

What a relief! Together with him my uncertainties, and the lies to cover them up on my way, somehow turned into truths as I unfolded my scheme. There was something indescribable about Arvo. How had he survived in the fierce world of business? Somehow his openness and warmth bent back into strength.

That night I slept well without dreams haunting me. In the morning after breakfast we drove to the head office for a meeting with the management and the other growers of the cooperative.

Arvo sat silent while I presented my case. When I had finished he said, "I'll accept that paper in payment for my fruit, and on arrival at destination."

That meant quite a deviation from the customary payment by letter of credit. The others hesitated. But Arvo was one of the largest growers. Then another big grower joined. He was of Japanese descent and had been sent to a detention camp during World War II in spite of being an American citizen. He knew the life of an outcast, a refugee. Then another who liked gambling went along. Then several substantial growers came in, and then there was a landslide, everybody joined. The battle was won, really thanks to Arvo.

Had I acted irresponsibly, pulling them along? The outcome would decide. Each link of the chain had to be forged separately to then be joined: still a long way to go. But now my idea had been given birth, started to move

outside my head. A bastard? But that wasn't its fault. Now it had to be nursed with love and care. But what had I done? On the verge of bankruptcy I had taken on commitments of millions. And should it end in a disaster, the amounts involved were so staggering that I would vaporize in their friction, a shooting star.

Now I asked Jim Klahre, the president of the company, "Would you do me a favor? Call the head of Sunkist and tell them that you're in on the deal." He did, and then handed the receiver to me. "The ships are filling up, you'll have to decide quickly if you want to join," I said. And so we went on through the other suppliers. It worked. They called urgent board meetings, and that same day I had their decisions, all favorable.

With the bulk of the credit placed, Hammer agreed to a tenure of only four years, and Bankers Trust took the full first year. Thus, as the generals say, there were only mopping-up operations left. With some difficulties the Swedish authorities accepted the switch from the United States to Israel. That in turn opened up the deal to include all exports from Sweden to that country. Including both sides, proceeds of industry as well as fruits and later cotton, the amounts involved, counted in today's money, approached two hundred million dollars. With that kind of turnover, I was made an instant millionaire.

This made me dizzy. I went on a buying spree. I bought supermarkets in Stockholm and brought the first computer from the United States to Sweden in the mid-fifties. I was offered a transport concession in Liberia, West Africa. I started the first bus company there. That in turn led to the installation and running of cold storages and markets in Monrovia and Buchanan. My constant travelling put a strain on our marriage. Harriet and I divorced. She married again. Our two children stayed with her. And I had fallen in love with and married my closest coworker, Sonja. We established our home in West Africa. It would be hard to find an environment more distanced from Sweden, and we worked arduously to adapt.

We grew very fond of our African coworkers. And the African names: Opera, Trouble, Moses One, Moses Two, Laffey (for Lafayette), Princie (for Bwagwant Sigh Bhukkar), Mammadou, Mammadi, John Policeman, and then Mr. Remember. When I asked him for his last name, he looked down and answered timidly, "A-Little-Better." He was our night watch on the lookout for thieves in a land where the destitute stole with a certain legitimacy—because they were starving. He also protected us from troublemakers in a more general sense. Once when I was on the porch and Mr. Remember was preparing for his night watch, we came to talk about the devil. Half mockingly, with a touch of superiority, I asked if he believed in him, and he answered, "Yes, the devil is always there waiting to jump into you if you give him the chance." He was a wise man, no matter that I once caught him holding the book he was reading upside down.

One night he pounded my window to wake me! The Honorable Secretary of Public Works and Utilities was on his way downhill from a party at the Ducor Palace Hotel, swaying from one side to the other on Broad Street, where we lived. He ran the hood of his limousine into the rear of our truck. When I got out of bed he had already managed to back away and was turning the corner of the street below after his rape in steel. But Mr. Remember was sure of the identity of the man and volunteered as a witness.

In the morning I went over to the office of our bus company (named Fulintonguer after the fastest deer in the country) to file a complaint. Our counselor, Charles L. Simpson, Sr., a man in his sixties, had once been the vice president of the republic. His grandfather was born in Florida, one of the first freed slaves: they saw their dreams fade when reaching the coast of their ancestral homeland. After hostilities and endless difficulties they eventually struck a deal with King Peter, a chief on the mainland. They paid him twelve rifles, six muskets, some barrels of gunpowder, clothes, and provisions, altogether worth perhaps three hundred dollars in 1820 currency. . . . Simpson promptly wrote the secretary asking for indemnities. He ended his letter: "We trust that you are in pretty good form this morning, doing nicely and taking good care of your vast responsibilities. Yours sincerely, C. L. Simpson."

I learned a lot from Mr. Remember. Only his name inspired afterthought. He was addressed with the honorable title "old man." The first time I, in my mid-forties, was titled thus, I took it for criticism or irony, coming as I did from a youth-oriented society. But in a country where people rarely got over forty, each

year above was looked upon as a gift from God, and one was worthy of honor. "Old" was also close to the concept "wise." Remember, as the most venerable elderly, was head of a family with several hundred members in this land of polygamy. He had officiated at many funerals. He told me about all the flowers and wreaths, about the wake, the mourners crowding the house of sorrow. Everybody willingly paid for the arrangements, even beyond their means, to celebrate the deceased, who lay meticulously prepared surrounded by flowers, resting peacefully, more so than in life. Everybody waited their turn to sit beside the deceased to talk with him or her, sometimes for hours, offering a toast for the well-being on the other side. Then the loudly wailing women proceeded the funeral march to the beach, where the grave was dug. The dead was lowered into it, the sand thrown back on top, a mound the only marker, lasting perhaps a couple of weeks depending on weather or wind. The mourners stepped forward one at a time, some on swaying legs, to stick their emptied bottles in the sand. The grave thus ringed, the headdress of the deceased, looking forlorn without a head, was thrown on top of the mound to the accompaniment of the breakers' thunderous music. Behind, the crowns of the palm trees stood, roses in the sky.

My investments required more and more money. I had to take substantial loans from my Swedish bankers.

Unfortunately, they didn't share our enthusiasm for our new country, and after three years of hard but, as we felt, inspiring work they foreclosed on me. I had pledged everything I had in Sweden as well as in Africa. Accordingly, after our swing through the world of finance we were back to zero, even far below that, in short, ruined, weighed down with liabilities beyond our capacities.

I had balanced on a knife's edge of financial adventure, where success lay on one side, disaster on the other. Eventually I was "cast off," plunging into the abyss except for Sonja's and my love. It was a bad spot to go broke, and I slipped into a deep depression. I got violently ill, probably malaria, as I had neglected my quinine tablets. Sonja helped me to survive. She took over the running of a bakery and an ice cream parlor we still owned because they had happened to wind up in her name.

Recalling those days, I still feel the ominous danger that surrounded us, the fecund heat, the thunderstorms, and the torrential rains, clouds seeming to rest on one's eyebrows. I had high fever and began hallucinating. It was as though my whole life had risen in phantasms around me in a huge wave that wouldn't break. I was terrified, but at the same time I couldn't help but be fascinated by the visions. They revealed a new dimension of my psyche that I had been unaware of until my subconscious feverishly, in the true sense of the word, began exploring its different layers.

As I tried to focus, the shapes of the grotesqueries lodged in my memory, they seemed to lead me toward a new beginning, a fresh and changed concept of the world. In this I was helped by a mentor other than my teacher Tarschys, the Swedish classic writer of mainly aphoristic prose, Vilhelm Ekelund, whose writings I had encountered by chance during my earlier literary excursions.

One of his sentences stood before me: "Don't forget those for whom a sudden terrible experience became the key to the richness of life and spiritual vision—don't forget them! The boundless happy inner expansion that takes place when the doors to the outer world of desires have to be closed—don't forget! And in addition to this (if one draws on the future) always to live! Thus being relieved of all anguish of vanity and pride." And then: "You are never any higher than at the beginning—better to crawl than to swell." This admirably suited the state of mind that I had been forced into, and his words made me rebound in the direction of survival, in a sense touched by his hands, cool enough to carry their treasure to me while I was suffering from the burns inflicted in the heat of tropical Africa. "Light. The light puts out all pain. Light is the coolest of all." (Vilhelm Ekelund) His enduring words made me think of the granite cobblestones brought from my native Sweden to cover the streets in the outskirts of Buenos Aires, that I walked once. They proved to be as hardy, even if as difficult to tread. Under his influence I wrote one of my very first poems:

> Litmus—to be filtered
> through the gift, the
> living litmus paper,
> toward the changed eyes
> of an expanded
> vision.

Finally, I got out of bed and started to work in the bakery. At first I loathed it. Up at four a.m. I hated the heat of the oven; as if it weren't hot enough in Equatorial Africa! I had a tendency to feel unjustly treated, to feel sorry for myself. But then Ekelund's words made me see everything in a larger context. That whatever meaning there was, you had to create yourself. The shadow that had engulfed me? There was only one remedy: to move out of it.

Ekelund had given me new eyes, created a bridge between my depression and the refreshing of my senses. They were sharpened. I started to like the bakery rather than hate it. The oven with its fire, the black Africans moving around it with their chores, the kneading and the shaping of the dough. I saw a rite of creation in the rising of the bread. The bakery became its own cosmos, its ingredients the secret recipe, the magic yeast, the water, the salt, the fat, the sugar, the fire that didn't burn, only made the bread rise under the supervision of Takini, the Italian foreman, white like a ghost, covered from head to toe by flour dust, its fine particles becoming visible like stars at night when hit by the light from the oven's fire.

We tried to make what remained of our business profitable, even brought a pastry baker from Denmark, but to no avail. Without the turnover of our main food companies, we couldn't utilize their larger buying discounts.

The management of the Swedish bank had new people take over our activities. One might say it was a hostile takeover in the true sense of the word. When we protested, the bank said, "Unless you do as we say we will crush you for life." They worked at doing just that.

Finally, Sonja and I gave up. "Let's leave." Where to? was the question. "To somewhere big where we can disappear and start a new life." "I suppose you don't mean Russia," said Sonja. "That leaves America."

We sold whatever we had in our home and booked passage on the freighter M/S *Brooksville*, bound for Savannah, Georgia, its cargo rubber and our old Volvo.

We had our, as one might say, last supper in the house of our former employees. Our food and booze still left was heaped at the end of the table to be shared with our friends. In every nook of the room was the sadness of the goodbye. We finished our meal, toasted a dubious future, and carried our bags on board ship. In the glaring light of the ship's corridor we tried to be cheerful, but the tenseness of our farewell was almost unbearable, and we were relieved when at last a member of the crew announced: "All visitors ashore!" Engines started hammering. Slowly we detached from the quay, stood waving as we slipped away on top of the rubber cargo through the narrow opening between the piers. The scattered lights from the shore faded and vanished. The coast looked ominously dark, as it hid the fate of our African friends.

In spite of all, I couldn't believe I wouldn't come back someday. But that return would never happen. In the coup d'état of 1980 after we left, thirteen Liberians previously in power were seized by sergeant Samuel K. Doe, the instigator of the coup and then, at the age of twenty-eight, Africa's youngest strongman. The thirteen were condemned, without proper legal proceedings, by a military tribunal and found guilty of "high treason, rampant corruption and violations of human rights." They were sentenced to die. Three among them were friends of ours. Cecil Dennis had been our lawyer, and we had become quite close with the family. When Cecil's wife Agnes gave birth to a daughter, she was christened Sonja. He was an ambitious man and eventually became secretary of state, the highest position in the government next to the president. Among the condemned were also Jim Phillips, my former partner at the Philbruce supermarket, and Clarence Parker, who played the piano so beautifully. He was condemned in his capacity of treasurer of the ousted True Wig Party.

From hearsay and media reports, including the gruesome photos that were awarded the Pulitzer prize that year, we were able to put together what had ensued. The condemned were taken in minibuses to the beach where Sonja and I used to walk. Sometimes we had seen soldiers there, in full uniform but strangely barefoot, conducting their manoeuvres in the sand.

The condemned were tied to heavy poles driven into the sand. It proved too much of a

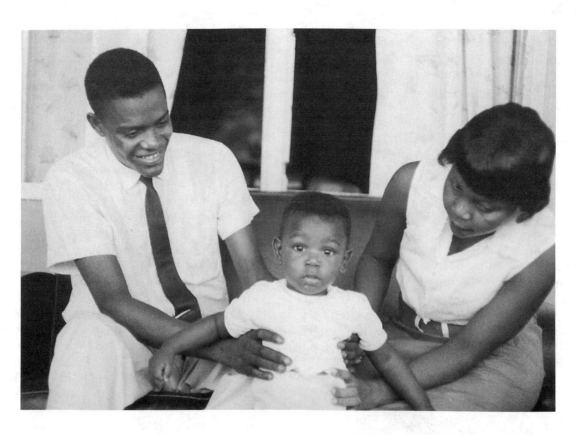

Cecil Dennis with his wife, Agnes, and daughter, Sonja;
"he was executed as a result of the coup"

chore for the soldiers to erect thirteen poles. The crew gave up after the ninth. From the minibus the last four victims had to watch what would also become their fate. The men were stripped down to the waist. Some had their pants and shoes torn off. They were tied with one long rope running from pole to pole. They faced their executioners without blindfolds, their backs to the sea. Soldiers milled around them, taunting and cursing them. It took well over half an hour to get the firing squad in line, one soldier in front of each pole. The two oldest men collapsed and hung unconscious, doubled over the rope, showing no sign of life even before they were finished off. Cecil remained calm, didn't even blink when his shoes were torn off. He mumbled a prayer. A soldier shouted at him. "Liar, you know no God!"

And then the command: "Fire!"

Cecil was only wounded. His eyes showed dazed astonishment at still being alive, until a barrage of bullets through his head killed him. Jim Phillips begged for mercy to the very end. As he was led out, Clarence Parker waved to some friends among those invited by Doe to watch the gruesome spectacle. He smiled even in death. For several minutes the automatic weapons rattled their rounds before the bodies were eventually cut loose from the rope and left bleeding in the sand.

I still see before me Jim's and Clarence's smiling faces when they were visiting us in Sweden. It was summer. We went fishing in the archipelago at Pelle's Rödlöga. We were lucky with the weather, one of those heat waves so rare in the cool Nordic summer. Clarence and Jim had slept late after the long journey, and when they appeared for a belated breakfast served in the shade outdoors, Clarence exclaimed that it was just like Africa. Strawberries were on the table, and Jim told the story about his first strawberry, how its deep red had made him think it was all sweet and then it was so sour.

Cecil Dennis had been respected all over Africa for his work in international affairs. Pleas from all over the world to save his and the others' lives went unheeded. Cecil had also visited us in Sweden. He was impressed by the function of our ombudsman. We had discussed capital punishment and our argument that justice and revenge didn't go well together. It stands out as beyond imagination that it would be demonstrated to him in this horrible way.

The coup was the beginning of Liberia's grisly civil war. Violence breeds violence. After ten years of repressive reign Doe was threatened by rebel forces invading Liberia from the north under the command of a previous member of Doe's government, Charles Taylor. Getting as far as Monrovia the rebels split into two factions, and the conflict developed into tribal war. Taylor dominated the interior and declared himself president. His renegade opponent, Prince Johnson, occupied parts of the capital Monrovia, now under siege. Johnson also declared himself president. He managed to capture Doe, who was tortured and mutilated, his body pushed around the city in a wheelbarrow.

The country plunged into chaos, and over a million Liberians were forced to flee across the borders; 150,000 were killed, mostly civilians, including five American nuns, over the years, not counting deaths among the estimated 300,000 starving.

When we lived there, Tubman, then president, declared in his annual message:

> The gracious and beneficent pinions of the All-wise and Almighty Providence have extended guidance . . . Let our deliberations, Gentlemen, continue to be selfless, politic, patriotic and spiritual, and may the God of our fathers continue to keep, preserve and prosper the State . . .

Once on an informal occasion he had offered me Johnnie Walker Black Label, his favorite drink. He started out as a preacher but chose to be president so he could go on drinking— at least according to one of his favorite jokes.

M/S *Brooksville* made good speed. We crossed the Atlantic in barely a week. We spent most of our time looking back across the sea toward Africa, and then in the opposite direction toward an unknown future with that mixture of hope and anxiety felt by immigrants.

We slid into the port of Savannah. We passed customs, a routine inspection. Our entry papers were checked; no problem. Immigration quotas still had a clear racist tendency. People from northern Europe were favored, and Sweden had a huge quota open. That would soon be changed by J. F. Kennedy, giving preference to skills not easily found in the United States and to close relatives of legal residents and American citizens. We got down on the

A recent photo of Lennart and Sonja Bruce

dock waiting for our car to be unloaded. Once on terra firma the car was scrutinized by an official from the Department of Agriculture. It was before the plague of drugs, but the inspector was thorough. He crawled underneath the vehicle with his flashlight. What strange bugs might hide inside this contraption, a bastard strain, a new race of bugs, pale Swedes and black Africans, the Viking Africanus bug, gnawing at the roots of U.S. agriculture.

I went job hunting, constantly on the move for meetings that only lasted a couple of minutes while consuming a whole day in travel time. But everybody checked back to Sweden and eventually wound up with the bank, and there they got the ice-cold shoulder that was to be expected. We soon left the East Coast for the West, where I had all my acquaintances from the old fruit business days. But now things were different. Everybody knew I didn't have any money—wealth, a kind of genderless sex that makes one attractive.

When we got to the West Coast, we were pretty low on cash. On our spare time we browsed the bookstores, a pleasant surprise in

America, much more hospitable than their European counterparts. Some were open until midnight, with tables and chairs where one could sit and read. Some served coffee and no need to buy a book even. This was about the only entertainment we could afford. We had rented a furnished apartment with a slanting floor. Before the meal it was uphill, but after, fortunately, it was downhill for the washing of dishes.

We spent a lot of time in City Lights bookstore, owned by Ferlinghetti, on Columbus Avenue, reading down in the basement, once part of a church we were told. I continued my habit of reading poetry, and Robert Creeley's work appealed a lot to me. I had started some attempts at what was then called the sullen art. As a result I sent him some of my scribbling with the words "is this worthwhile?" Almost to my surprise he answered. He wrote that my question really was my own problem. But then he encouraged me by giving me good advice about what to read and by saying that I could both feel and think, the main prerequisites for an aspiring poet.

You get a lot of time on your hands when you are waiting for replies to job applications. For me the most difficult time was doing nothing. "Having nothing better to do," was a phrase that grew upon me from glibly negative to positive after careful pondering. As time passed, it seemed impossible to find something better to do than the dialogue between reading and writing. This was especially the case when learning to write in another language. The one you're "born with" seems like a gift from above encircling one's head, not unlike an aura. Using it seems almost unfairly easy when one turns to writing in another idiom. The acquired language becomes almost visual, like a cherished tool that one painstakingly learns to use. Handling it fills one with joy and pride. The secret is how to know one's limitations, as in so many ways of life. I slowly discovered that writing in two languages was a gratifying method. When working as I do with two parallel versions, one in each language, sparks of association, rhythmic waves, flow between them, enriching both.

BIBLIOGRAPHY

USA

Poetry:

Making the Rounds, Kayak (San Francisco), 1967.

Observations, Kayak, 1968.

Moments of Doubt, Cloud Marauder (San Francisco), 1969.

The Mullioned Window, Kayak, 1970.

Exposure, Cloud Marauder, 1972.

Letter of Credit, Kayak, 1973.

Subpoemas, Panjandrum (Los Angeles), 1974.

The Broker, Panjandrum, 1984.

Fiction:

The Robot Failure, Cloud Marauder, 1971.

Translator:

Fernando Alegría, *Instructions for Undressing the Human Race* (translator from Spanish, with Matthew Zion), Kayak, 1968.

Vilhelm Ekelund, *Agenda* (translator from Swedish), Cloud Marauder, 1976.

Vilhelm Ekelund, *The Second Light* (translator from Swedish, also editor), North Point (San Francisco), 1986.

Speak to Me (an anthology of Swedish-language women poets; translator from Swedish, with Sonja Bruce), The Spirit That Moves Us Press (New York), 1989.

Claes Andersson, *Poems in Our Absence* (translator from Swedish, with Sonja Bruce), Bonne Chance Press (Cleveland, South Carolina), 1994.

SWEDEN

Poetry:

Utan Synbar Anledning (title means "For No Apparent Reason"), Norstedt (Stockholm), 1988.

Förskingringen (title means "Misappropriations"), Symposion (Stockholm), 1990.

Fiction:

En Nasares Gång (title means "Ways of a Carpet Bagger"), Symposion, 1993.

Kafferepet (title means "The Coffee Break"), Symposion, 1995.

Other:

En Sannsaga (autobiography; title means "A True Fairy Tale"), Tiden (Stockholm), 1982.

Det Andra Ljuset (anthology; title means "The Second Light"; Vilhelm Ekelund's aphoristic prose), Symposion, 1993.

Contributor of numerous poems to periodicals including *Chelsea, Choice, City Lights, Green Flag, Massachusetts Review, The Nation, New American Review, New Mexico Quarterly, Rolling Stone, Saturday Review, Sumac,* and *Tennessee Poetry Journal.*

Albert Cook

1925-

*Albert Cook, Wakefield, Massachusetts,
about 1927*

It was my mother who fostered me and bolstered me from the beginning. She grew up in an Ohio village as the second eldest in a dirt-poor family of eight children. When she was sixteen in her tiny high school she was given the army alpha intelligence test, and she got a score higher than all but seven men of the entire World War I U.S. Army. She was immediately hailed as a prodigy, graduated, sent off to Ohio State, and pulled into the swirl of life around campus. There she encountered my father, a salesman traveling from New England for Lever Brothers. She dropped out of school, married, and deferred her education for forty years.

My father, the pampered youngest son of his family, was the first to graduate from college. He trained briefly for the First World War, further delayed his degree by easy living, but then settled down into the staid, reserved life of a conservative executive. Already officially engaged to an entirely appropriate fellow Yankee when he arrived in Columbus, he startled everyone by making the mistake of breaking it off and marrying my mother. She gave birth to me at the age of nineteen in the hospital of Exeter, New Hampshire, the nearest one to the village where my grandfather had settled as a cooper. Eventually he had become the town clerk there, holding the office for decades. His wife ran their large house for summer boarders, and she, my grandmother, seems to have been the only member of the family who treated my disoriented mother decently. We drove the distance there for ceremonial stays from wherever we happened to be living. They saved the comic sections of the Boston Sunday papers in a pile for me by the stove, and I rushed to them at each arrival after the long drive.

I loved that house with its screened-in porch of seemingly endless length, its screened-in small summer house between it and the general store my grandfather had once run, its large, fragrant woodshed now become a garage, stacked high with wood for the winter, its henhouse out back towards the woods that stood across a field behind, its large kitchen around the giant black all-purpose stove where the beans were slow-baked unfailingly every Saturday, its bins for the dry beans and for flour, its large dining room where the family's early-nineteenth-century sampler (now owned by my half sister) hung over the giant rolltop desk that held all the records of the town. There my grandfather would now and then closet himself with some townsperson. Beyond the sunny dining room was the large living room, opening on the wraparound porch through a vestibule. It was organized around the console radio where

61

my grandparents would settle down to hear favorite serials. Visiting the Robert Frost place a couple of years ago, I was surprised to see that on a slightly smaller scale the house where Frost set his first New England poems matched my grandparents' point for point: large stove, dining room, living room, woodshed, henhouse, woods across a field behind.

The poorer house of my Ohio grandparents was smaller and far shabbier: simple furniture, next to nothing on the cracked walls, faded wallpaper, a pervasive smell of mold, and, as I remember from my first visit, an outhouse. Behind it ran a muddy stream, the Scioto River, where small freshwater crabs could be found floating under rocks. They were used for bait by my grandfather on fishing expeditions. I tried to capture him later in a poem my mother framed and passed around to the family under a photograph of him holding a fishing pole over his shoulder:

In the river where you went fishing, crayfish
Trailed foetal white at the edge of the brown
    sluggish current.
Behind the iron railing trees grew too dense
    for deep shade.
You used doughballs for bait, crayfish lacking,
    and were gone all afternoon,
Returning, often as not, laden with carp,
Your eyes unladen. Such was your decline.

Your eyes affirmed that the burden of eight
    children
Constrained but did not depress the
    unwizened
Indeterminate set, scarce darkened by age,
Of their steel gray answer to grandchildren
    and strangers.
Sent into the world too young by your
    father's drink,

You avoided drink, from that Tennessee
    moved north,
Had a family, and ended up papering houses,
Then lived out the long rest of your life on a
    pension,
Fishing, or in the back room of the poolhall,
    over cards.
You dealt, it was dealt, unbearably equally.
Yet your gray coevals told at a Reunion
How once, when young, in the forest, you
    found a honey tree. . . .

Who was bugler at the full military funeral
The Legion gave you? Or was there a bugler?
Your war was over, bugler, before you got to it.
Back home, still, you lived decades on the
    memory of bugling,
On the government pittance for it, and taught
    me to bugle
As Memorial Day you bugled in the same
    town graveyard
Where veterans of a war without bugles have
    borne you, your survivors.

When I was five, breaking the move from Springfield to Albany, we rented a camp for the whole summer on Crooked Lake, staying into October. I learned to swim there, pushing off our dock in my linen water wings for many weeks till the great moment when I could leave them behind. We returned for the following three summers, and during the last I swam all the way across the lake, followed in our rowboat by my Uncle Dave, one of my mother's brothers.

In our first Albany house we lived on the edge of the city. At the end of our short block was a woods where I loved to wander. One path led, after what I remember as most of a mile, to a large amusement park where I would stroll and watch the crowds, occasionally feeding a penny into the glassed machine where a mechanical gypsy would dip down and pick up with a claw hand a random prize to deliver through a small chute. The other path led to a steep hill off the main street, issuing behind a Catholic school. That first Albany house was far enough out that there was still a large farm with horses on my walk in towards town to school. Do I really remember hearing the terrified neighings of the trapped horses as the barn burned down? I did see the charred remains on my walks.

Literature was all around me, pervasive and elusive. At the time when I was drawn to a book of Greek myths at the front of my first-grade classroom, my Uncle Paul arrived out of his Ohio high school into our household in the teeth of the Depression. He sold door to door off of a tray slung from his neck the pies my mother baked, waited for the job with Protection Company, where my father was a salesman, and studied by lamplight in his attic room the manuals that would make him a lieutenant in the Citizens Military Training Corps, a supply major in Australia during the war,

Albert (left) with his younger brother, Richard, Springfield, Massachusetts, 1929

and, it all counting, an early-retired Cape Canaveral technical writer turned real estate agent. Back then he also wanted to write and won contests from *Black Mask* magazine, writing in his off-hours from the Protection private police force.

Of all my many cousins, the only writer of the lot published in his youth a play with French's. After the war he settled down for life as an itinerant high school class photographer in the country and mill towns become fringe exurbs, not far from the farms of my father's ancestors. A recent visitor to those farms is my much younger half sister, a journalist who aspires to write fiction.

My mother, a lifelong would-be writer, spoke anxiously in her final months about the unread books of poems on her shelf. They stood behind her flights, at long-spaced moments of stress, into conventional verse. My radio-announcer younger brother, when he broke away from the big time, wanted also to break into being a writer via the tape recorder, which was to give private shape to what he kept so suc-

cessfully uttering in public. In that new mode he sailed to a dream of Tahiti; there he married for good a mute, obsessive Polynesian, his fourth wife, his widow now.

When we moved from Albany to Utica my parents sent me for three entire summers to the Albany Y camp, where I improved my swimming and learned to develop pictures in the camp darkroom. There I practiced the bugle that my Ohio grandfather had begun teaching me, becoming one of the camp buglers my last summer, when I was twelve.

My father was transferred from city to city. And within the cities we would move as well. Our second Albany house, further in toward the city, also abutted a wood, one that was later leveled to make room for the campus of SUNY Albany. The third was an apartment most of the way downtown. In Utica, too, our first house was even further out, on the actual property of a farm. My walk to school led through part of a wood, along railroad tracks, and across an open field. That field was later leveled for a playground where I played paddleball, tennis, basketball, and pickup football. Still later the playground was leveled to build a GE plant where my future brother-in-law would find the employment that freed him from the family business. And still later the GE plant was abandoned.

Starting in Albany, my father soon showed his unhappiness with my mother by staying away from our house longer and longer, even on days when he was not traveling. Typically he would make us wait in the car for sometimes over an hour while he completed some errand, and even when I was in my teens on ceremonial father-son fishing expeditions he would park me on a rock and disappear for hours upstream where the fish really were, returning with his full creel to me and my empty pole. He loved to drive, and we spent Sundays those years exploring the terrain north, south, east, and west of the city where we happened to be living.

Our second house in Utica was a flat on the main street near an orphanage; our third one was up a hill on the best street in town. Behind the houses across the street a wooded ravine fed down into a sewer running a mile or so underground, roofed high enough to permit surreptitious expeditions through it to the other side of our district. And a mile or so out the railroad tracks into another neighborhood stood a movie theater, the James, where every Saturday afternoon I could see two films, serials, cartoons, and an amateur show, while munching complimentary popcorn, all for a dime. Later the theater was converted to a synagogue in honor of a schoolmate who died early. I had many friends, and I was included as a possible though ungifted player in the seasonal sports, baseball, football, and basketball, the seasons changing as if by magic when one day on the impromptu field as we were playing baseball a couple of boys would be passing a football off in the wings, and within a week everybody would be playing football.

A confident and exploratory twelve-year-old, I delivered magazines on a weekly route, swam on the seventh-grade team, sang as a soprano in the paid choir of the downtown Episcopal church, and worked quickly up the ranks as a Boy Scout in my own Congregational church. When our scoutmaster resigned, I took it on myself to ring the doorbell of a neighbor I hardly knew and asked him to assume the post (which he did). I learned hypnotism out of a pamphlet ordered from a novelty company and succeeded in hypnotizing my brother and some of my friends. Word got around: on the school playground some unknown kid from another class would come up, blurt out, "Hypnotize me!" and dash away.

Just before my thirteenth birthday we got the news that this idyll was over. My father had been promoted by a transfer back to the home office in Boston. In the new school I was refused admission to the college entrance track because I had not had the others' opportunity to start French in seventh grade. I offered to try to catch up ("I'll try very hard. I already know a few French words; I'm a stamp collector"). But I was placed in the shop program, on a metal lathe, where I turned out a metal rock hammer that I put to use in my rock-collecting expeditions on the wooded hills up from our new house. This spell in the shop program recalled my experience in the new school on our second Albany move when I was nine and found myself in a class where strangely no other child in the room could answer any questions. That lasted only a couple of weeks till I was transferred from the bottom track to the top track.

And then later that Boston year we moved again, this time to an apartment on the edge of a fancy suburb where the new school, full of the affluent (five of the twenty boys in that eighth grade were later in my Harvard class), threw me off balance. By May it was announced that by this school's assessment I was failing in all subjects. If my mother had not stormed in to protest, I would have had to repeat the grade. They decided to let me graduate. The school gave me the role of bugler at commencement, and then abruptly withdrew the invitation when some teacher remembered that the offspring of a legendary Brahmin family (who died that summer in a hunting accident) had taken a few trumpet lessons and so was a more appropriate bugler—just as when I won a spelling bee against the offspring of another legendary family, the star of the school (later a marshal of my Harvard class and a renowned lawyer), the teacher declared a mismatch and started over.

All that year I had noticed widening cracks in the family unity, though I can recall no open arguments, simply absences on my father's part and anger on my mother's. It was announced over the summer that they were separating. We drove back towards Utica to reinstall my mother, my brother, and myself; then my father returned to Boston. Newspapers all along our route announced the German invasion of Poland.

Our new house in Utica was not on the best street in town this time; it was a rooming house my mother set up on the main street. She took a job as a clerk in a downtown hotel. Many of her old friends snubbed her; we were now déclassé. Very soon a strange man appeared on our porch looking for me. My mother had set up an interview with the supervisor of routes for the local newspaper. I was to deliver papers to set aside money for college. My schedule abruptly changed. I delivered papers every day for four years in all weathers, getting up at 5:45 to pick up my bundle that had been dumped on a nearby corner.

Walking the route alone those early mornings I began composing poems in my head again, writing them down and revising them at home.

My brother became increasingly unmanageable and soon was sent away, first to a prep school that expelled him for stealing apples in a nearby orchard, then on back to my grandmother in the Ohio village, to the very high school my mother had attended. He stayed there and graduated when I was in college.

In my solitary independence I taught myself to play chess from a book. Soon tiring of feeble games with my contemporaries, I ran a news item in the local paper that a meeting of the (nonexistent) Mohawk Valley Chess Club was to take place that month and prospective members should phone me. This notice flushed out a local physician from a suburb, who phoned to ask whether a group of professionals who met at his house monthly to play chess might join our club. On my confession, he invited me to their next meeting, and I improved my chess through the winter. I subscribed to the main chess monthly and bicycled one summer down to Colgate for the day to observe some of the best players in the country at the New York State chess championships. Later, at a war-depleted Harvard, I was the shaky eighth board on an eight-man Harvard chess team.

In ninth grade I became editor of the school magazine where I had published in sixth grade a poem that had already appeared in a newspaper column for children's writing. I began to read poetry widely, and fiction, and philosophy—at first in popular introductions and compendia and then, as I got into tenth grade, in full treatises, some of which I dimly understood. I realized that if I really wanted to read Plato I would have to know Greek. By then I was in the high school downtown, where an earlier enlightened superintendent of schools had hired as his heads of departments men who were already teaching in college. One of these, a Ph.D. in classics, was still there. I approached him to teach me Greek, and I had daily sessions with him for the rest of my high school career, along with the more usual Latin courses.

I was also ranging free, often away from the larger rooming house my mother was running closer to downtown. I intended to become a writer; I bought a typewriter and a manual and taught myself to type, typing up stories and poems I never showed anywhere.

I was also becoming contestatory. Thrown out of the senior honors English class for ostentatiously refusing to read an assigned trashy novel, and for arguing with the sacrosanct *Atlantic Monthly*'s wartime putdown of Spengler, I became the first person ever from our school to win publication in that magazine's national prep school contest; in their student prize fascicle the *Atlantic* editors printed my sonnet sequence epigraphed with a quotation in Greek from Xenophanes, and they singled out for their prose honor list my rhapsodic essay on the novels of Thomas Wolfe.

My sophomore year I was chosen with two others in a school assembly contest to represent the city for a station in Schenectady that ran a Sunday program modeled on *Quiz Kids*. The alcoholic speech teacher, with whom I had never studied, chose me to represent the school at a statewide youth congress in Syracuse. And in my senior year, for the local radio station on which my brother was to become an announcer some years later, I was the male half of a duo hosting a children's program, *The Wizard and the Witch*.

At the suggestion of another English teacher I called on the city's one Rhodes scholar, a man who had been fired from Hamilton during the Depression for a mild socialism, then failed to take hold as a high school Latin teacher in spite of sponsorship from the head of the Latin department, my mentor. He was reduced to a job as night watchman in the milk plant owned by one of his own classmates, the father of my earlier hypnotism cronies up on the hill. Random nights I listened in his living room to his disquisitions about history and politics, walking home late.

Through the local bike shop, where I had used my newspaper earnings to buy one of the town's few English bicycles, I met the local checkers players, a different stratum, reaching down into factory workers and retirees like my Ohio grandfather, who had taught me pointers about the game. One of the articulate regulars around the stove in the bike shop turned out to be the Congregational minister who had been imported from Scotland a few years earlier to the church where I was a Boy Scout, and then fired for having an affair with a parishioner. He was now estranged from her and working as a printer.

The owner of the bike shop organized daylong rides through the nearby communities, of ninety miles or so out and back, on the then lightly used highways. And I went on forays of my own: one to Lake Champlain, from which my companion and I took the train back; one to visit my cousins in Michigan; and one which started out north to Watertown and became on an impulse we voiced as we crossed the bridge over the Thousand Islands a 650-mile circuit of Lake Ontario, lasting a week and taking us, in late September 1941, through

College graduation,
Cambridge, Massachusetts, 1946

a Canada that was already at war. I was written up in the newspaper and dressed down by the high school guidance counselor. I bicycled all over the routes surrounding the city, at random, or on expeditions to collect rocks. (I found garnets on one, a glacier-scraped piece of shale on another.)

Summers I hung around the tennis courts, meeting there a fellow aspiring poet, who later became a published one, a colleague and lifelong friend. I also hung around the bowling alleys, where I made another friend who distinguished himself in our elective course on European history, later a CIA man and library administrator who in his retirement has become a cabinetmaker, working on refinishing some cabinet doors for us as I write.

My parents were still only separated. The summer before my senior year I joined my father in Boston, taking a room in an apartment building next door to the building where he had a room. We met every night for supper. I got a job in the Boston ballparks hawking pop and hotdogs. In the locker room un-

der the stadiums I was roughed up and ostracized by the clannish townies who had bullied me on the streets when I was in eighth grade. That summer fueled both my fears and my aspirations. And the aspirations, if nourished, I felt, could provide an escape from what I feared, the world of rough survival in which the company of other hawkers jostled. Another place beckoned, Harvard Yard and the Harvard library. I dropped into the Widener reading room and scrutinized its shelves of books on reserve for English courses. And on the steps of the Fogg Museum I heard a sentence that still rings in my mind. It epitomized the cultural speculation I sought: "So it's simple, James, the more decadent the society, the more flamboyant the architecture." Indeed, given the approximate age of the speaker and the itself flamboyant British accent in which the sentence was uttered, I fancy I can identify him, though I have never met him, nor have I ever heard him since.

Writers everywhere. In Utica generations before my time of growing up there a pre-Civil War banker had held forth about a crude symbolic logic worked out during his off-hours and presented before the Utica Lyceum; he turned it into a book that was buried nearly a century till its resurrection and republication by a symbolic logician at Berkeley while I was teaching there in the early fifties. Harold Frederic, whom I first heard of from a Berkeley colleague, surveyed in Utica the stresses and limitations of Methodist bureaucracy and Catholic sophistication. An imperious woman led him to transplant all this to the Sussex of Henry James (whose grandfather laid out the streets of Utica) and of Stephen Crane, who had studied at nearby Syracuse University. Having made his name with an evocative story about a victimized prostitute, Crane had married a trapped, devoted madam. Frederic would have found there a context for his own personal, powerful maturation of those relevant sexual sympathies; and, indeed, comparable considerations had already been sketched out in the pamphlets, bearing a Utica imprint, of the Oneida Community, located between Utica and Syracuse. Another local writer, Thomas Jones, Jr., most persistent and perdurable of sonneteers, was published first by the Thomas Bird Mosher who early gave Pound a cold shoulder, and ultimately by one of the major publishers, who had done likewise. Jones was a crony of the busy poetaster Clinton Scollard, who taught at Hamilton College, where Pound briefly studied and graduated, in what is now a suburb of Utica. I gathered these two poets, and others, into an anthology of Utica poets I compiled when I was in high school, seeing myself as on the way to becoming one of their number. On my newspaper route, living in a large, single, first-floor room in a run-down mansion of the main, elm-shaded street, was the retired Hamilton professor who had taught Pound Provençal. That tradition must have provided some of the books for the glassed-in bookcase he warned me away from as I approached it in the business of collecting on my newspaper rounds. Nor did he recognize me when he came by around midnight Saturdays to the Kewpee, the hamburger joint where I worked on the weekend night shift. He sat quietly over his pie and coffee when the Roller Drome crowd after its closing flooded in for giant burgers and frosted malteds.

Then there was my high school hitchhiking crony, picked up by a local Communist because he published a fantasy story in the high school literary magazine about a Soviet soldier kissing the Russian earth. Much later in life he paid to put into print the careful fruits of metaphysical, social, and religious meditation, including some measured comment on the Soviets, his balance riding the crest of desperation in both (if not all) instances. Retired now, he toys with the bad idea of giving a bad novel he has written another vanity publication.

A few miles north in nearby Talcotville intermittently the pastoralizing, patronizing, crude, and urbane critic Edmund Wilson, who by implication allows for little of this, was writing away at his own local impressions and investigations. Within easy drive was the friendly anthropologist-bureaucrat of Albany, who gave him the data for the book he would write about the local aborigines. The anthropologist was based at the state museum that I used to love to visit when I lived in Albany as a child, returning with fascination to its exhibit of crystals and phosphorescent minerals, before I began collecting rocks myself. It was to Utica this quasi-mandarin was summoned to pay his back taxes, giving himself away by writing to justify his peculation after the fact in a book that attacks public military spending. Evasions and concentrations canceled each other out, as they always threaten to do.

Soon after my rearrival in Utica in ninth grade I discovered that in one of the buildings of the Cultural Institute near downtown anyone could listen on request to rolls played on the old player organ:

I, having
heard the player organ
reel out Rachmaninoff's
"Stone Island,"
was some years
later driven across
that island on a Soviet bus,
not knowing of Pushkin's
death at that spot (the site
on the itinerary) in a
foul duel anything beyond the sense
of passion I began
to undergo, knowing
still how it drove me on
under huge trees at night
from the endowed mansion
containing the organ.

The following year I heard that in the building next door the Institute offered to all comers all day long the choice of music selections played on its massive Capehart from a collection that completely lined the walls below the windows of the large salon. This room became a meeting place for the culturally inclined at the high school, my poet-tennis friend, the history buff, the local piano prodigy, my hitchhiking crony, a theater enthusiast who was to become my college roommate and later a psychoanalyst, the still younger parochial school student who had begun reading Proust and Joyce under his eighth-grade desk (later my collaborator in an anthology of Greek tragedy)—and, among many others, Carol, the girl who was later to become my sweetheart and my wife. We went there almost every afternoon after school, rushed home for supper, and rushed back, staying till the Institute closed at 10:00 P.M. We would file our music requests with the attendant, sit and talk in low tones or play chess or read the current copy of *Poetry* magazine and other books too advanced for the local library, like T. S. Eliot's translation of Perse's *Anabase.* Over three years we outgrew Tchaikovsky's symphonies, progressing gradually to Beethoven's quartets—and to Couperin's *Les Ténèbres,* a title we overheard the Hamilton College intellectuals choosing one afternoon and forthwith made a favorite of our own. The Institute held one winter a free evening course on Renaissance painting by an émigré professor of art history at Hamilton, from which I also took an extension course on philosophy. I had begun going in ninth grade to the movies the Institute brought up once a week all winter from the Museum of Modern Art; in four years we saw much of the history of film.

At our high school graduation picnic, while others were playing baseball, Carol and I sat on the grass in a long conversation that resulted in our agreeing to write one another when I went off in a few weeks to Harvard for the wartime-accelerated beginning of my freshman year.

My first week there I found a note pinned to my freshman theme inviting me around to the rooms of a sophomore who had studied with John Berryman the year before. After about five minutes he said, "I'm homosexual. I can see you're not. That's okay." He continued, "As Kenneth Burke says, . . ." I had read very widely by then, seeing Eliot and Pound as the acme of the modern, but this was a new name. When I said, "Who's he?" my host expressed surprise and lent me *Counter-Statement.* We had the same exchange over *Partisan Review, The Castle,* and some other books as well. I walked out of his rooms with my future in my arms and returned all through the semester to the weekly literary salon he held, till he was expelled for homosexuality. Frequenting those literary nights were ex-members of the temporarily defunct *Harvard Advocate* and others like myself, including an aspiring poet who was to become the novelist John Hawkes.

I had entered a large world, where my classmate who had won the Westinghouse national science contest (later a physicist for Westinghouse) was abashed at being outclassed by a promising physicist who went on to the Princeton Institute and then to a post at Berkeley. (Later he and I were fellow Fulbright professors in Vienna.) Living in a wing of our residence house was the pre-Hitler chancellor of Germany, Heinrich Brüning, and Gaetano Salvemini, a famed opponent of Mussolini now a professor of history, lived a couple of floors up in the entry where a hospitable, crippled French tutor welcomed all and sundry. I heard news about the philosophy of history from a budding comparatist who was dating the daughter of Bertrand Russell.

I took five courses instead of the regulation four, and I audited three more, doing all the reading. I was thus busy night and day. In the Latin course I audited was a prospective Latin teacher who was to become the poet Robert Creeley. I soon learned why none of the people whose criticism I admired were teaching me, though nearly all were on university faculties. There were records of Pound reading the *Cantos* in the Poetry Room, Eliot had given Norton lectures eleven years before, and one professor was writing a book on Eliot, yet the official poet, the Boylston Professor, sneered at Pound and Eliot and everything modern. Even the charismatic young professor who was the author of a book on Joyce, when I encountered him later, sneered at Faulkner, William Carlos Williams, the later Stevens, and many others. The expert on the seventeenth century liked to get a laugh from his classes by referring to "a tale told by an Eliot, full of Pound and fury." There was still much intellectual direction and stimulation to be had, from the classicists Arthur Darby Nock and John Finley and Werner Jaeger in my field, and in many quarters elsewhere too. With the last of the "Humanists" I studied seventeenth-century French literature; I took courses from a theoretician of the "psychology of language" and from a theoretical sociologist. For the rest we educated each other.

Not having twenty-twenty vision, I was ineligible for the naval officer training program that my qualified classmates could enter. I enlisted in the army so as not to be drafted out of my second semester, and I entered active service that winter. While still at the reception center I got a three-day pass to attend my mother's divorce hearing in Boston. One evening at the YMCA there I met a uniformed Canadian who for me embodied all the purpose of the war. Converted to communism when he was a graduate student of economics and saw the hordes of strikers massed in his plains city, he had enlisted to join the Spanish Loyalist forces overseas; captured and imprisoned a long time in a Fascist jail, he found himself released in time to reenlist for World War II. He had given most of a decade to this, but I was to give little more than six months. Devoted as I was to the war effort, by the time I finished infantry basic training I had become subject to splitting headaches. Instead of being shipped as a replacement for the still unexpected Battle of the Bulge, I was discharged at a moment in September 1944 when it was assessed that the war would be over before winter and all doubtful cases should be released. Hating the army, and especially professional soldiers as death-dealers, I felt immense relief, and at the same time immense guilt for abandoning the cause of the century.

Carol wrote me faithfully during my time in the army, and we grew deeply close as she went off to Antioch College, having worked a year to earn some of her fees.

I had begun *Finnegans Wake* in Utica. Now back at Harvard I joined a *Finnegans Wake* reading group of four or five, organized by a freshman who kept massive notebooks on each paragraph of the text. The group met evenings all through the winter after my army discharge. It included a member of the faculty and a Canadian graduate student who would join my department at Buffalo twenty years later. The freshman, after a spell in the family business on graduation, went to graduate school and became a renowned sociolinguist. I also lifted weights weekly the same winter in the rooms of a classmate and ran with him mornings, long before "jogging" became popular, in a loop around the bridges over the Charles. This man had abandoned his home at fourteen or fifteen, sent himself to a cram school, got into and got free of West Point, and was now gung-ho for a business career, boasting of the wealthy fiancée he had cultivated and acquired for her father's high-level connections. His dorm room was hung with ticker tape, and his portfolio of holdings was swelling. But then he had a change of heart. "If I had ten lives," he said, "I might spend one of them making money." He precipitously gave up all that for religion, philosophy, and literature. He spent a summer in the Ozarks trying to write a novel, but it didn't pan out. He then went back more quietly to business and married the no-nonsense physical education girlfriend whom he had courted after breaking with the other.

I had already won as a freshman the undergraduate poetry award, the Garrison Prize, and on my return to Harvard I made some new literary friends. Lou was already writing accomplished poems. He was soon to take a part in a film by another who was in the process of launching himself as a filmmaker. Dipping in and out of school, when he graduated

Lou buried his poems and attended to his career in advertising. But he surfaced as a poet again thanks to a long, near-mortal brush with Hodgkin's disease. Lou was an enthusiast of sports car rallies, till fear of dying suddenly turned him ahead on his own clock, if then back to the fold of poets. He stuck to his desk on weekends out in the space of an elegant colonial town distant from his workaday city, till his death did come—but not before he had broken the record for lines of verse published in the *New Yorker* and been presented a medal in Widener Library.

Norm, another avid would-be writer, kept maniacally dreaming up Wagnerian projects. *Guetteur mélancholique,* he cycled into repeated breakdowns. Fired as a young advertising copywriter after one breakdown, he got a job as a comic-book editor and was then fired after another breakdown. He had already formulated a couple of years out of the never-finished college how the pop writer, too, must give his all and square the depth of his past.

He fulfilled his prophecy a score of years later, surviving the legal troubles sometimes occasioned by his outbursts in the advanced breakdowns. He shaded from promising playwright into first the punch-loaded film writer of a collaboration between a gun-maniac worker (as from the Detroit of his childhood) and a jaded, gutsy ad man (as of his own stormy, silent twenty years); then the honest draftsman of a film about the one honest policeman; then the high-credit screenwriter of a black slave stud in the Old South, his own ingrained forthrightness repackaging the nightmare of interracial sex. His biggest hit celebrates the emergence into wider aspirations of an honest, avid dancer who follows his partner out of a metropolitan Italian enclave (*Saturday Night Fever*). Here and there the script echoes my haunted friend's own stresses and aspirations. He was following the prediction he had uttered in the form of a denial: he had turned out to be giving commercial writing his lifeblood. The money that showered in only fueled his movie phases.

The gloss and hurly-burly of his life spelled the lifelong sacrifice. Early on his star-blasted eyes were burning, as all but foreseeing his acclaim, his Herculean breakdown cycles, his prosperity.

Still, these were single literary friendships. I remained unconnected to the official college literary groups. What I published in one group magazine, *Wake,* I submitted in the dead of night under a pseudonym that encapsulated the contradictions of my self-image: Charles Hamilton Sorley, a minor British poet who died in World War I. I kept the barrier-bridge of my absorption in classics between myself and my more insistent preoccupations, and the further barrier-bridge of my focus on French and other literatures. I refused to join the poetry workshop into which the kindly head of the Poetry Room invited me. Constantly auditing English courses, the only ones I took for credit then or ever were Chaucer, Anglo-Saxon, and a graduate seminar on the critical literature of neoclassicism. I saw myself as a loner while being treated well by an officialdom my anti-authoritarian self scorned. In this, indeed, I was one of a generational group of self-styled loners, as I gradually discovered, learning later that many of my schoolmates felt the same way. And even in centralized, hierarchical France, as I have recently come to learn, some of the most famous and best-placed thinkers of our time saw themselves in their youth as isolated loners, at least six of them having publicly testified to that effect.[1]

The following summer I spent in New York, sharing with my mother a small Village apartment and working as a typist-receptionist at the American-Scandinavian Foundation. Carol was in Manhattan too on a co-op job from Antioch, and we were constantly together all over the city, now secretly engaged. That summer we joined the throngs at Times Square on V-J Day. One of our favorite places was the old Museum of Non-Objective Painting with its gray carpets and velvet-covered walls, mellowing piped-in baroque music. The attendant on the second floor turned out to become Mrs. Delmore Schwartz, recognizable when she opened the door of their apartment some years later, to which I had been invited on the heels of his accepting my double sestina for the *Partisan Review.*

The contrast of confidence and isolation came once again to a head at my early graduation in 1946, where I was the Latin orator, choosing as my topic "On Joy for War's End and Concern for Its Imminence" (De Belli Gaudio Finiti et Imminentis Sollicitudine). Eisenhower was the commencement speaker, and the whole

assemblage rose in homage to him. Still smarting from my army experience, and determined not to honor any professional soldier, I sat planted resolutely in my front-row seat, resisting the efforts of those next to me to drag me to my feet. Eisenhower on his way down off the platform shook my hand. The next day my scandalized tutor in advanced Latin composition, who had been an officer in a unit preserving art monuments in Italy, argued with me vigorously. Still, however scandalously I acted, and however simplistically (I had no notion of Eisenhower's later demonstrated commitment to peace), those responsible for assessing me always rated my intellectual performance equitably—a rare advantage it took me years to appreciate.

I wanted badly to live for a while in a French-speaking milieu, but limited funds and the recent war and my desire not to be too far from Carol kept me from France itself. I settled that summer for French Canada. Staking myself with my savings from prize moneys, I went to the library and from a map picked a village that looked to be far enough away from Montreal to be wholly French-speaking but close enough so that I could bicycle in to a university library once a week or so. I flew to Montreal, took a bus to Sainte Rose, found almost at once down the main street a sign *Chambre à louer,* and rented the room. For the next two months I ate at the communal table of this farm family (the farm a distance from the village), spoke French all day, wrote poetry and the draft of a verse play and a long story, and evolved out of a central notion in my undergraduate thesis the schema for what the next summer would become my first critical book, *The Dark Voyage and the Golden Mean.* And then I joined Carol in Boston.

The agnosticism of my adolescence was being tempered by my war-sharpened sense of the pervasive sinfulness of the world and of the redemptive possibilities that beckoned at the same time. These stirrings, transmuted and fortified by a yearlong study of theological writings and Dante, brought me to the threshold of the Church. The role of the Roman Church in the war, and much else, put me off from it. A friend who hoped to become—and did become—an Anglican priest kept up an ongoing dialogue with me. Finally I was ready for conversion. He took me to the Anglican monastery of St. John the Evangelist in Cambridge

---

[1]Jacques Derrida, Michel Serres, Louis Althusser, Michel Foucault, Pierre Bourdieu, and Claude Lévi-Strauss.

for instruction, after which I was received into the Episcopal Church, of which I am still a communicant. For a while later I joined the lay order to which Dante belonged, the Third Order of Saint Francis.

The stimulation towards thinking about Greece that John Finley triggered was supplemented in graduate school by Eric Havelock, who communicated the excitement of his evolving ideas to the seminar in the pre-Socratics I took my first semester, along with Dante in Italian, beginning Sanskrit, and a private reading course on Thucydides. Present in all three of these group courses was a man whose fourth course turned out to be an advanced course in physics. For his war service he had published a book-length treatise on the mathematics of supersonic flight. He was a member of the Society of Fellows, of which I had vaguely heard before and now hoped to enter, since it provided three supported years for writing. (He, too, was eventually converted to Episcopalianism. He became a priest, editor of a series of intellectual magazines and books, author of studies of Near Eastern thought and of a trenchant meditative diary, and a professor of Old Testament at the Church Divinity School of the Pacific until he was fired for leading a protest against the entry of official military weapons into the San Francisco Cathedral during the Vietnam War.)

In my independence I was already too far along, being now a graduate student, to join the traditional magazines at school, and so I founded my own, with my Utica poet friend and others:

> The vital advances are being made in theoretical works like those of Kenneth Burke and others. We applaud this tendency. For literary criticism, focusing as it does the most abstruse problems of ontology, ethics, the theory of knowledge, and their interrelations, is the chamber music of philosophy.

So I wrote in the manifesto for *Halcyon,* a magazine that was to bring fiction and poetry together with criticism in the vigorous continuing mode of the time. We published Wallace Stevens, James Merrill, Allen Ginsberg (as a reviewer), e. e. cummings, and many others, including ourselves.

A year earlier as an undergraduate I had written my first, and almost my only, fan letter to Kenneth Burke, congratulating him on

The Grammar of Motives. I did not meet him till nearly thirty-five years later when we coincided as visiting lecturers at the SUNY Buffalo English Department. This was more than a decade after my three-year tenure there as its chairman, when I reshaped it along principles still partly based on the *Halcyon* manifesto.

My literary aspirations included playwriting. Presenting myself that fall to the forming theater group at Harvard, I was sidetracked into typing up multiple copies of a section of a windy, self-indulgent British play they were mounting. I soon withdrew. Not long afterwards I presented myself to the Tributary Theater of Boston, where I was taken on as a stage manager for *Peer Gynt, Ghosts, King Lear,* and *Measure for Measure.* Wanting to produce an *Oedipus Rex,* they commissioned me to prepare a verse version that would be stageworthy. They produced it, and in its revised form it is still in print.

My contrast of confidence and isolation was brought to a head by my election to the Society of Fellows, an honor which I owed, as I owed intellectual stimulation and much else, including the publication of my first book, to the sponsorship of John Finley, the mentor who directed my undergraduate thesis and stuck with me through all the vagaries of my purposes. As an aspiring writer and self-directed thinker I was refusing to take the Ph.D., abetted for that purpose by the official posture, though not the actual practice, of the Society of Fellows. It had been founded on the principle of sidestepping the Ph.D., though of the eight people elected my year, I was the only one who did not already have that degree.

Then, and for decades afterwards, I gathered myself to write fiction, trying to model myself on a range of commanding virtuosi in my own language, and beyond them on Flaubert, and on Proust, whom I had already begun to imitate in high school from the florid English version of the time. (I had soon plunged into the old, badly printed first French edition and have since been reading him steadily all my life.) My own style differed from the outset. I published stories at very long intervals, beginning early with one in *Partisan Review.*

Swept after our long wait into the joy of marriage, Carol and I entrained to New York for a few days in a borrowed Brooklyn Heights apartment, then back up the Hudson on the Hudson River Day Line, proceeding to the isolated hunter's cabin in the Adirondacks where we spent the summer with our cold well, ice chest, and kerosene lamps, rowing together on the lake:

> Yes yes, love claims us, our several marriages
> Rescued from war. On a train to the same
> City, bemused bride, we took our common
>   flight,
>
> You in the yellow dress of a mere ten years
>   gone by.
> In that world we dipped, out again by waters
>   of a river—
> Fed lake, high. And we are brunted to be
>   courting
> Responsibilities of labyrinthine energy, alive.

(Curiously the same poem, written in Cleveland, places along with three of our earlier cities of residence another two that I had no way of knowing or guessing would one day take up the major time of our lives: "Letters this past year snowed in from New York/Buffalo, Vienna, Berkeley, Providence.")

At our return from the Adirondack summer I entered upon my appointment to the Society of Fellows, threw in the wastebasket the paper attesting to my loyalty to the State of Massachusetts (I never heard another word about it), and once again took up success-in-isolation, burying myself not mainly in critical writing but in poetry and fiction—at the same time reading vastly for what would become a few years later the critical writing of my second book, *The Meaning of Fiction.* I wrote an essay that would be incorporated as part of a chapter in *History/Writing* and another that I would collect in *Soundings,* both after almost forty years. And, under the inspiration of a keen young historian of art and architecture in the group (he to abandon that for a career as a college president), I drafted a few pages that would turn out to be the germ of my four books on art.

Carol was soon pregnant, and we moved up our planned trip to France. We settled for four months in a hotel room right in the center of Saint Germain des Prés recommended by the already famous young poet in the Society. We plunged into exploring, viewing, and reading. Another poet, who was readying to found his own magazine, greeted us and showed us around. In the cheap restaurant much fre-

Marriage to Carol, June 19, 1948

quented by other Americans we met over a copy of *Partisan Review* a couple who became our close friends. He was a painter, she a writer. (He was already ill and died five years later; she then married a writer and became a painter herself.) They introduced us to an indigent Israeli painter and his wife, who also became our friends.

Earlier I had had our friend Ken mail me from his teaching post in Dijon Sartre's *L'Etre et le néant,* which I spent much of the summer of 1948 studying through, during our honeymoon in the Adirondacks. Following this line during my later sojourns to France, I attended Merleau-Ponty's inaugural course at the Collège de France in 1952, Lévi-Strauss's course in the winter of 1963–64, and Lacan's lectures in the late sixties and early seventies.

David was born on our return. During that summer Carol was stricken in the polio epidemic of 1949, and our apartment became a rehabilitation watch once she was returned from a month at Massachusetts General Hospital, which luckily stood just at the foot of our street. She could not come to the party for my first book at the Gotham Book Mart (attended by, among others, James Merrill, Hayden Carruth, Paul Goodman, and Oscar Williams). It was not till January that she could go out on crutches. Her first outing was to attend Dylan Thomas's inaugural reading in America, which bowled us both over, as during our courtship we had read in rapture together his poem "A Winter's Tale."

We spent the whole following summer with the infant David in a cottage overlooking the Bay of Fundy, and three more entire summers, the last one after my first Buffalo year, David now fifteen, Daniel twelve, and Jonathan ten. Huge tides, misty fog every morning, water and headlands out our window, strawberries in the field beyond the garden out back, fresh eggs from the farm next door, fresh fish from a delivery truck. We kept busy building wood fires in our stove and fireplace, invigorated by swimming in the icy water, clamming, fishing, and taking excursions to town with our generous landlord's family, ranging further afield in the summers afterwards when we had a car. I wrote in a tiny space on the second floor of our cabin.

> Then we lived in an old
> Man's house by the sea shore.
> On the slope to the bay
> He let pink and purple
> Lupine grow and grow wild.
> His wife sowed them, and more.
> In us the fronds stipple
> A thousand miles away.
>
> Back we went once again.
> Love keeps gathering head
> To strength not before known.
> Time acts as its leaven.
> All lights: a broken fan
> Of peacock plumes, tail-eyed,
> Hung over clouds, given
> A shining not their own.

It was my deep conviction that a devotion to writing meant I should not teach. "The professor's preoccupation with the past as a scholar and with the future as a teacher could only confuse the presentness of the writer's self-set concerns." Some such were the words I wrote to the Society as I left it not for an academic job but for the fortunes of what I could pick up otherwise, unaware that these words contained an affirmation in the form of a denial. Carol loyally backed me in this troublesome venture. We were to have another child six

months hence—Daniel—when we moved to New York. A flurry of vain job searches left me as a salesman on the exploited staff of the commission-only force of *Encyclopedia Britannica*. Briefly I did motivational interviews on car selection for a psychologically oriented market research firm. Next I was typing lists for an executive employment agency that masked itself as a self-help cooperative. I supervised my two associates, a minister losing his faith who disappeared mysteriously every morning for what was probably an analytic hour, and a young Romanian diplomat who had defected and then come to the end of a stipulated support from Radio Free Europe—with which I had interviewed myself. (He had been to art school and found his way to a successful career as an illustrator of children's books.) I wrote every evening, or tried to. Fired from this job along with most of the staff—the organization was subjected to a pseudo-dissolution—I landed through a member of my church a post as accountant for the Brooklyn Museum Art School, from which I was ultimately fired after unsuccessfully blowing the

With Carol and the author's mother who is holding David, Boston, 1949

whistle on the sweetheart deal of the major supplier to the school's art store. I ended up as the technical editor for a trade journal of the commercial fishing industry, my longest job during that year. I knew nothing about motors and simply paraphrased my monthly column out of a manual issued by Shell. Soon Shell phoned me to hire me away, but by summer I knew I was to have a student Fulbright to France; during my last weeks on the job I watched with relief and anticipation out the window of my office as the transatlantic liners moved in and out of their berths on the Hudson piers.

France this time was hard for our two children, and for us. We traded our New York apartment for a large but primitive apartment in the Paris suburb Clamart, where downstairs lived a modiste and her ex-Wehrmacht officer-husband. Upstairs there arrived a painter already deep in gastronomy who became a famous writer on food. We shared an icebox with him in the hall, and he painted David's portrait (never in our possession). The semiautomatic toilet for everyone was on the first floor.

We had one coal stove in the living room and one small wood stove in the children's bedroom. In our unheated bedroom days I wrapped several layers of clothing around myself to write poems, a verse play, and a long monograph on Balzac, reading through all of *La Comédie humaine* in the process (I vividly appreciated his characters' attention to domestic heating). I later condensed what I had written for the Balzac chapter of *The Meaning of Fiction.*

Carol and I would get a baby-sitter once a week, or sometimes oftener, and go into Paris for the day, visiting our painter friends from the earlier sojourn, wandering about the city, and attending the theater, returning either on the last metro and bus out from the Porte de Versailles or on the train at half-past midnight from the Gare Montparnasse, which obliged us to walk home a couple of miles up the hill through the dark. Clamart was a Communist suburb and an old White Russian enclave. Opposite our front window was a walled estate owned by a prosperous pre-Revolutionary family that ran a small wire factory on the pre-

Albert and Carol Cook, with sons Jonathan, Daniel, and David, and Albert's brother Richard, Tilden Park, Berkeley, 1954

mises and had a whole entourage, complete with private chapel and priest. On their wall across the street, facing our apartment, was painted in big letters: American Go Home. It was the time of the Rosenberg trial, and one poster showed a smiling Eisenhower, every tooth an electric chair. Another poster said, "Don't send your sons to fight under Nazi officers for the Bank of Indo-China." (It was France's Vietnam war, and at that time ex-Nazis did predominate in the Foreign Legion.)

Before returning we managed to spend the summer in England, with the help of the British Fulbright Commission, which arranged to have us share a house in Chiswick. We shepherded over as we flew the daughter of a friend of our Israeli painter (the friend's husband had been executed as a resistant by the Nazis). The family we joined ran a nursery school downstairs in which we enrolled David; their presence allowed us to leave overnight, as we did for a trip up the Thames as far as Henley, and on to Oxford. The family became our friends. He was an oil chemist turned teacher of candy chemistry whose father had been a leader in the British Communist Party. As a Boy Scout he had been entrusted with funds, which he concealed in his backpack, for the German Communists beleaguered under Hitler. They arranged a visit—I hitchhiked—to the communal colony in the Shropshire countryside where her brother was a teacher. We kept in touch for years after their emigration to Australia.

Having practiced the experimental method, as one wry Harvard philosopher put it, I was ready to propose myself for teaching jobs. I was interviewed in Florence by a Berkeley professor whom I had impressed when he dined at the Society of Fellows, and I was hired. It was right after the Berkeley oath controversy, and as part of my appointment I was obliged to sign the university's oath and have it notarized, which I did, at the Clamart town hall. Back in America we took the train across the country and sublet a small house on the Berkeley flats for the year, not having the funds to buy a car, let alone a house. My sponsor hinted that his own house in the hills might be for sale, in a part of that community so expensive I could have afforded it at no time in my life. He had misapprehensions about me, and soon other misapprehensions developed. While I felt I had done well in my teaching,

With Carol, Cleveland, 1959

after my first year I was told that I had not, that my second critical book, of which they had seen one hundred pages, was so unintelligible I would never be able to publish it, and that my creative writing was uncertain. All this was delivered by the chairman, in the presence of my "sponsor," as a bill of particulars in the process of firing me and preemptively denying me a second three-year term, as I believe they had not done to any of the forty or so assistant professors passing through that rank over the decade. I was also, I believe, the only one with a book behind him and a publishing career firmly under way. Another of the charges against me was that I had exhibited dilettantism when I submitted myself to a course, complete with examinations, in Hebrew. I was doing this for both devotional and intellectual reasons, preparing myself to write what would later appear as my studies of Job and the Song of Songs (*The Root of the Thing*) and the Hebrew prophets (*The Burden of Prophecy*).

My two lame-duck years at Berkeley were pleasant but uncomfortable. I forged ahead with my writing, and with Hebrew. By the end of the first of those years I had completed *The Meaning of Fiction*. I took the two huge black binders of the manuscript in to my former sponsor and reached up to hand them over, asking him to read them, but he held up his hands in front of him and said he did not have time.

Luckily I got a research Fulbright professorship to the University of Munich, where I

At the Center for Advanced Study,
Palo Alto, 1967

deepened my immersion in recent German poetry, expanded my own poetry, and began my books *The Classic Line* and *Prisms*. We met a German art critic who had known Rilke, and I had brief ceremonial encounters with a couple of professors. Our closest friends were the family of an art historian on a Guggenheim who had abandoned the house we rented after a quarrel with the difficult resident landlady. Our first new car, a Volkswagen, took us on many expeditions to as close as the nearby Starnbergersee and as far as Vienna. I audited a course on Pascal given by Romano Guardini, and we went to many concerts.

Toward summer that year, still jobless, we took off for Rimini on the Adriatic, stopping off at the Pound Castle in the Tyrol above Merano, having been introduced to Pound's daughter Mary by Eva Hesse, our new Munich friend, Pound's translator. It was August before my cliffhanging attempts at a job search elicited a telegram from Western Reserve in Cleveland offering a one-year post. My new chairman, puzzled, later asked the Berkeley eighteenth-century specialist, my ex-sponsor's close friend, why they had fired me. "He was not one of us," he replied.

I stayed for six years and was allowed a role I could not have exercised at Berkeley as the university's main exponent of modern literature. Within a month I was asked at a neighboring school to take part in a panel on *Endgame*. Because Reserve had appointed leanly for years, the younger staff was sparse in number, and we formed a vivid social milieu of mutual support and encouragement. The best literary students there flowed into my courses. While writing *The Classic Line* and finding no satisfactory version of the *Odyssey* from which to quote, I did some renderings of my own and found them an ideal means of loosening my poetic style. I proceeded systematically to carry through with translating the entire poem.

In the middle of my time there I accepted a teaching Fulbright to Vienna, where I renewed and fortified my German, met some poets, polished the *Odyssey,* and reveled with Carol in the rich musical life of the city. In persistence and stubbornness I was still trying to find my way into writing fiction, redrafting earlier work and scrapping it while inventing larger structures that would direct and contain what I might produce. The harvest yield of withdrawal to a foreign country was diminishing, and yet for my poems it still functioned. I broke into writing haiku. The boys' isolation was compensated for, as it had been in Munich, by the ski excursions they loved to the mountains an hour or so south. They became very fond of our friend Ken, now the Dutch uncle of a group of expatriate students of psychiatry. Having foundered or floundered in America, he had come to Vienna for affordable psychoanalysis, staying on since before our Munich days. He had visited us there. Here, down on his luck, he became almost part of the family. He was still in touch with the writer, a fellow Irish-American, who had broken into fame for *The Ginger Man,* a novel that chronicled Ken's Dijon days as a sidelight on their Dublin experience. He was to cast Ken as the protagonist of a Vienna novel too. Ken was beginning to work part-time—as he would, on his return to America, a while full-time—for another American Dublin friend who had gained renown as the most creative Jungian of his generation. Ken was the link when we ourselves met this psychiatrist during his years in Zurich, where we had visited him from Munich, and again at intervals, usually with Ken.

Ken joined us as far as Bern in our ample Peugeot (he would split off from there to Zurich), through our youth hostel trek across Europe on our way to a London summer. There we rented the Hampstead cottage of our Cleveland subtenant. I read my poems at the poetry festival of the Mermaid Theater. On the liner home, knowing I was to be teaching some Russian poets in my modern poetry course, I began the study of Russian and kept it up for another decade, until I got a fellowship to Moscow on the senior scholar exchange to write what would become the Russian chapters of *Thresholds.* I also steeped myself in Russian poetry, and I began to translate some poems which especially drew me, an enterprise that took its final form as my collaborative book *The Burden of Sufferance: Women Poets of Russia.*

For my plays I developed a style for dialogue and a strategy of stage presentation. They stayed in verse for over a decade: one of these was staged in Cleveland, another broadcast over

With his grandson Nicholas, 1996

With grandson Paul, Buffalo, 1987

WBAI–New York and KPFA–San Francisco. Then I evolved an idiom that was neither verse nor prose but something between the two, for plays that were semiallegorical in conception. I have continued to write them over the years, publishing one and having small productions of others.

I had submitted some poems to the *Arizona Quarterly,* which wrote back asking to see more. Soon after I sent those I got another letter: the University of Arizona Press would like to do a book! It had been ten years since the editor of a major publishing house had phoned me at night to announce that a book of poems had been accepted for publication, an acceptance that after many twists mutated into a rejection. Now delighted, I put together *Progressions,* and Arizona brought it out, complete with illustrations.

I ruminate constantly working towards a poem. When a new music pulls at my ears it tends to be a sign that the poem will be a long one, first *Midway,* and then a decade later, for more than a decade itself, finally *Modes,* which I thought of as the last of this series employing the "syllabic module" and at one time came to think would last me my whole life, on the model of Pound or Olson (or for that matter, Whitman). My way turned out to be different, thankfully, and lo, along, slowly, came "Prophecies," and then "Dooms and Inclinations," and then "Transfers." I still don't know of a nascent poem at first even when it will turn out to be only epigram-length, or only a haiku; most of my many haiku start out headed for more expansive expression. As I perpetually do too. In the inch as in the mile.

What are my purposes as a poet? Do these poems cohere into a unity other than retrospective—or crucially prospective as I keep trying to forge ahead? The very expatiations of my bulky critical commentary on poetry, which I have always thought of as an endless prolegomenon to my own poems (whatever else they have been), tend to displace the integrative center of my purpose. My masters are themselves a large and various chorus whose voices I try to blend with my own.

My salary as a full professor at Reserve was almost exactly at the official federal figure defining the poverty level for a family of five. Poorly paid, my colleagues and I were involved in frequent contestation against bad policies in the university. When I heard about the chairmanship opening at Buffalo, at first I passed it over; I had never wanted to administer anything, and I had sent from Vienna a brief "No" to a Big Ten university that had asked me to be a candidate for its chairmanship. Buffalo was rated far lower. But Buffalo had become a state school with the promise of massive infusions of state money. English had fifty staff members with a prospect then of growing to seventy; twenty-five on the staff were in a low, temporary rank, and there were only three full professors, all scheduled soon to retire. Carol urged that if I took university policies seriously, this was my chance to put my money where my mouth was. My old Utica poet friend was on the staff and guided me through preparing my interviews; I was hired. At once I found myself both prosperous and dynamically at the center of gratifying, empowered professional fulfillment.

I took the job only on condition that I not have to keep regular office hours, and I intended to give it, as I did, just the three years of the initial term. During that time I bureaucratized the department and organized our considerable hiring not on the hackneyed principle of covering century fields, but rather of looking for the best people we could find and then letting them carry on or develop as they might. Instead of having a single poet in residence I established poetry on a par with other activities, and we hired several poets, while others whom we hired blossomed into poets. Much activity was soon generated; it drew marvelous graduate students and an unpredictable range of keen thinkers to the staff.

I was able to taper out of my chairmanship under the auspices of a fellowship at the Center for the Advanced Study of the Behavioral Sciences. There, instead of any isolation, I found an intellectual continuum of stimulation. Everyone in the redwood studies, each facing through a glass wall into greenery, operated effectively all day on the high, even plane produced by meeting at the outset the three minimum requirements—intelligence, commitment, and good work habits. Over Christmas we drove the whole family the twenty-five hundred miles to Mexico City in our Volkswagen camper, stopping off on the way at the Poet's House of the University of Arizona and visiting my old classmate who was a priest there. Mexico was a revelation to all of us. Crossing into Mexico, we were enchanted by the mix of Spanish, nineteenth-century French, and modern buildings set in the context of indigenous civilizations. We celebrated Christmas in the Cathedral of Guadalajara and swam at Mazatlán, reveling when we reached Mexico City in the light-strung trees of the Alameda.

All the Buffalo developments took place in the toils of an oath controversy, and of the Vietnam War. On my arrival nine of the ten non-signers of the oath in the entire state of New York belonged to my department. Only one of these was a writer. "You have many writers on the staff here," said a visiting art critic to the president's wife. "Yes," she said, "and they're all under investigation." Having signed the oath myself, I did everything I could to aid the non-signers. The president had begun calling me by my first name within a month after my arrival. Within another month he reverted permanently to my title. His successor fostered me, but the next in succession was an administrator I had had trouble with from the

Albert and Carol Cook in Egypt, 1996

beginning. He was installed as president for his role of student-suppressor as a leader of the faculty faction favoring the Vietnam War, against which I had been involved in active protest virtually since my arrival. Though our rich intellectual and social life continued, the last several years of that administration worked to erode my confidence in the collective decision making. I was searching for another job. Then out of the blue I got a phone call from Brown inviting me to apply for a slot in its Comparative Literature Department.

The arrangements were quickly concluded. Before leaving Buffalo I was asked to do an interview with the main local paper, and I agreed. The interviewer turned out once to have been the editor of the student paper that groaned under this president's policies, and she was delighted when I assailed his administration. The interview, to my surprise, was printed under a headline on the front page of the Sunday paper. "My wife comes from Buffalo," the president of Brown said on my arrival, with a genial twinkle in his eye, "and her family sends her the newspapers from there."

Brown fulfilled exactly my expectations. It provided, though in a somewhat austere community, a range of enriching possibilities for my professional expansion. I lived for the next decade, as I have for nearly another decade since my retirement, in an ambience where I could flourish in the confidence of enlightened encouragement. It persists, as I have too.

BIBLIOGRAPHY

Nonfiction:

The Dark Voyage and the Golden Mean: A Philosophy of Comedy, Harvard University Press, 1949.

The Meaning of Fiction, Wayne State University Press, 1960.

Oedipus Rex: A Mirror for Greek Drama, Wadsworth, 1963.

The Classic Line: A Study of Epic Poetry, Indiana University Press, 1967.

Prisms: Studies in Modern Literature, Indiana University Press, 1967.

The Root of the Thing: A Study of Job and the Song of Songs, Indiana University Press, 1968.

Enactment: Greek Tragedy, Swallow, 1971.

The Odyssey: A Critical Edition, Norton, 1972.

(With Edwin Dolin), *Plays for the Greek Theater,* Bobbs-Merrill, 1972, reprinted as *Greek Tragedy: An Anthology,* expanded edition (also see below), Wayne State University Press, forthcoming.

Shakespeare's Enactment, Swallow, 1976.

Myth and Language, Indiana University Press, 1980.

French Tragedy: The Power of Enactment, Swallow, 1981.

Changing the Signs: The Fifteenth-Century Breakthrough, University of Nebraska Press, 1985.

Figural Choice in Poetry and Art, University Press of New England, 1985.

Thresholds: Studies in the Romantic Experience, University of Wisconsin Press, 1985.

History/Writing, Cambridge University Press, 1988.

Dimensions of the Sign in Art, University Press of New England, 1989.

Soundings: On Shakespeare, Modern Poetry, Plato, and Other Subjects, Wayne State University Press, 1991.

Temporalizing Space: The Triumphant Strategies of Piero della Francesca, Peter Lang, 1992.

Canons and Wisdoms, University of Pennsylvania Press, 1993.

The Reach of Poetry, Purdue University Press, 1995.

The Burden of Prophecy, Southern Illinois University Press, 1996.

The Stance of Plato, Littlefield, Adams, 1996.

Poetry:

Progressions, University of Arizona Press, 1963.

The Charges, Swallow, 1970.

Adapt the Living, Swallow, 1981.

Delayed Answers, Edwin Mellen Poetry Press, 1992.

Modulars, Edwin Mellen Poetry Press, 1992.

Modes, Edwin Mellen Poetry Press, 1993.

Affability Blues, Edwin Mellen Poetry Press, 1994.

Reasons for Waking, Edwin Mellen Poetry Press, 1996.

The Future Invests, Edwin Mellen Poetry Press, 1997.

Haiku, Edwin Mellen Poetry Press, 1997.

Play published:

The Death of Trotsky, in *Theater and Drama* (spring 1971).

Plays produced:

Double Exposure, Eldred Theater, Cleveland, 1958.

Night Guard, broadcast by WBAI–New York and KPFA–San Francisco, 1962.

Big Blow, Chamber Theater, Buffalo, 1964.

Check, Chamber Theater, Buffalo, 1966.

Pan Is Dead, First Stage (Boston), 1984.

Recall, produced at Brown University, 1987.

Translator:

Oedipus Rex by Sophocles, in *Ten Greek Plays,* Houghton Mifflin, 1957, reprinted in *Greek Tragedy: An Anthology,* expanded edition, edited by Albert Cook and Edwin Dolin, Wayne State University Press, 1996.

The Odyssey of Homer, Norton, 1967.

(With Pamela Perkins), *The Burden of Sufferance: Women Poets of Russia,* Garland, 1993.

Other:

Criticism published in *Accent, American Journal of Philology, American Poetry, American Poetry Re-*

view, *Arethusa, Arion, Arizona Quarterly, Audit, Boundary 2, Bucknell Review, Canadian Journal of Italian Studies, Carleton Germanic Papers, Centennial Review, Clio, College English, Comparative Literature, Comparative Literature Studies, Costerus, Criticism, Dada and Surrealism, Essays in Criticism, Exemplaria, Explicator, French Review, Hebrew University Studies in Literature and the Arts, Helios, Hellas, Illinois Classical Studies, Iowa Review, Journal for the Study of the Old Testament, Journal of Aesthetics and Art Criticism, Journal of Religion, Kenyon Review, Maia, Milton Studies, Modern Fiction Studies, Modern Language Notes, Modern Language Quarterly, New Literary History, Niagara Frontier Review, Nineteenth-Century Fiction, Novel, Oud Holland, Quaderni Urbinati di Cultura Classica, Sagetrieb, Stanford French Review, Stanford Italian Review, Stanford Literary Review, Symploke, University of Toronto Quarterly, Western Review,* and *Word and Image.*

Translations published of Venantius Fortunatus, Paul Celan, Osip Mandelstam, Anna Akhmatova, and Andrei Vosnezensky. Poetry published in more than forty periodicals, and stories published in *Elephants and Other Gods, Partisan Review,* and *Spring.* Full bibliographical information on article publications can be found in *The Scope of Words: In Honor of Albert S. Cook,* edited by Peter Baker, Sarah Webster Goodwin, and Gary Handwerk, Peter Lang Publishing, 1991.

Frank Davey

1940–

WRITING A LIFE

WEEDS (1970)

In the bush below the house there are no weeds or else every tree and bush and plant is a weed. Weeds are both biography and not biography. You can't get all the weeds into one life or one garden. A life can begin with "W" for war but the weeds are here first, as unselected as a newborn child. As war is selection. A crude selecting as the planes or guns or rockets rain bombs or Agent Orange on people and plants that have abruptly become weeds.

WAR POEMS (1979)

A cool sunny day. A child is sitting in a pram outside the Abbotsford village real estate office. On his head is a green hand-knit cap embroidered in red with his name. The billy goat that is tethered beside the office to trim the grass leans in and eats the cap.

The wearer of the cap was born nearby in Vancouver, B.C., April of 1940, but began thinking of himself as I much later. "Frank wants," he would say. And he really did. He does not remember the billy goat. He remembers Frank. Yet he was already I when I sees his father, just come in from work in his rough jacket and trousers, upset beside the back door, and his mother then upset, and his father has just brought the newspaper from the porch, and they are upset about ships that have sunk. "Those damn Japs," his father is saying. And there are photos, and the ships are the *Repulse* and the *Prince of Wales*.

"What's your name?" "Frank," the child replied. "Hank, your name is Hank?" "Frank!" the child replied, or thought he had replied. "Hank?" He remembers his mother's story about his hat and about the billy goat but does not remember the billy goat.

Frank Davey in Santorini, Greece, 1989

Sometime later his mother and father are upset again, and I is a lot more I, and his father has again just brought in the newspaper, and across the top in four-inch black letters is the word "DIEPPE." In both scenes I is a small pair of eyes near the doorway from the dining room looking down the length of the kitchen over the worn linoleum to the back door where his mother and her mother are gathered around my father and the newspaper. From the child's point of view there is a major problem of context, although there are also letters arriving from his grandmother's sisters-in-law, letters which his grandmother reads aloud to my mother and that tell of houses crushed by bombs and the miraculous escapes of children hidden beneath staircases and dining room tables.

I lie on my back on our front lawn beside my father and look up at the blue sky. That's a Halifax, he says. A Lancaster. Those are B-17s, Liberators. That's a Mitchell. Much of identity and identification is memory, and memory flashes pictures of a young man in soiled work clothes holding a newspaper by the back door, of my grandmother reading small cramped pages of letters, of Commonwealth Air Training Program planes droning in orderly formations toward the mountains.

Tish (1961)

Tish is where all the words began and for many where they ended.

bp said that for anthologists and historians there could be only one *Tish*-poet and that until Daphne and Fred stopped being *Tish* poets and started being some other kinds of poet that needed representation they would not be in many anthologies. That's bpNichol, Daphne Marlatt, Fred Wah. For a long time bp was the anthologists' pick for representative concrete poet, but now anthologists no longer represent concrete poetry.

The story goes that a bunch of us student writers kept meeting in (Professor, but none of us called him that) Warren Tallman's living room, on evenings and Sunday afternoons to discuss poetry and poetics whether he wanted us there or not. He usually did. The story goes that we collected money so Robert Duncan could come to Vancouver and give a week of lectures in Warren's basement on modernist poetics, and he came up on a bus from San Francisco because that was the only fare we could afford, and talked for four or five nights and days in and out of Warren's basement. Warren was more impressed with us than we were and so arranged for us to give a reading to Duncan and others in a room at the university. After, we are all sitting around again in Warren's living room and someone, probably Warren, says we should start a magazine, and some of us were still thinking about Duncan's story of Carl Sauer's figuring out when rice was domesticated in the Amazon basin by

examining fossilized human feces, and of how Charles Olson had interpreted that story in *The Maximus Poem*, and so one of us said we could call it "shit." Duncan, who had encouraged us in our interest in phonetics, said no, how about "Tish?" We have all told this story so often that it must be true, and it probably is.

Once when I was in high school a bunch of us got together to form a club and had a secret ballot to choose a president and I got all the votes. I was so happy to be president and so humiliated to have everyone know I had voted for myself. When the five of us chose one of us to be managing editor of *Tish*, I was happy we did not have a secret ballot. Everybody wanted me to be the managing editor, god knows why, and I did not have to say that I did too.

Nineteen months and nineteen mimeographed issues of *Tish* later, the five of us—

*"With my mother and father
at White Rock, B.C.,"* 1944

myself, George Bowering, Fred Wah, James Reid, and David Dawson—who got together to edit, print, and distribute a magazine were famous. Well, semi-famous, wherever four or five poets gathered together in Toronto, New York, Montreal, Vancouver, or San Francisco.

In the nineteenth issue we all wrote something about the most important thing about *Tish*. Some of us have done this several times since in other magazines or books. The most important thing about *Tish* I should have said was that it made us enact ourselves as writers. Made us write poems every day because there was an issue coming up that needed them. At the end of the nineteenth issue we each had a bookful. No, maybe that wasn't the most important thing. Maybe it was our opting out of the whole circuit of sending poems off to other people's magazines in Toronto and Montreal and asking to have them legitimated. Asserting our own legitimacy. Publishing ourselves over and over and over. As Peter Quartermain wrote of *Tish*, "If a man says 'It's all rubbish!' once, you shrug. But when he says it once a month for a year and a half, when he says it for 409 pages, you begin to pay attention."

No, there was another most important thing. There were the friendships, that continue so far, closely with George, Fred, and Lionel Kearns, and more distantly, and with more interruptions, with David, Jamie, and Daphne. These were the first close friendships I made that kept enduring despite separation and slowly diverging interests. We made these friendships in part because George, Lionel (even though he had declined to be a *Tish* editor), Fred, David, Jamie and I lived virtually as siblings for nineteen months. As teaching assistants, George and I had coincidentally been assigned by the University of British Columbia's English department to a large common office in an old World War II army hut (the third person in the office—demonstrating the coincidence—was not another writer but W. H. (Bill) New, later to be editor of *Canadian Literature*). George and I bellied our two desks up against one another in the middle of the room, and for those nineteen months exchanged poems, bad puns, shouts of outrage, and reflections on poetics. We made the room, despite Bill New, unofficially "The *Tish* Office." Lionel Kearns— another coincidence—had his office across the hall. We wrote pairs of poems for our *Tish*

paired poems page. George and I would spend eight to ten hours a day in the office writing, marking, reading, and editing, and Fred, Jamie, David, and Lionel would also spend one or two of these hours here, reading *Tish* mail, arguing, conferring, gossiping. . . . In a cubicle attached to the office we set up our printing press, first a Dutch-made mimeograph machine and later a secondhand Addressograph-Multigraph Model 80 offset. Fred hung out inside as our official printer.

Most of the issues of *Tish* had a map of B.C. on the cover. We figured we were all outsiders, and so we presented ourselves as regionalists and outsiders. Outsiders to the English department from which we sometimes stole paper. Outsiders to Daphne's parents' middle-class living room, which I could see from the doorway. Outsiders to all the famous mythy poets in Ontario and the social realists at Contact Press, most of whose poems we liked anyway. Before the nineteen issues were all published, other people in Toronto and Vancouver and Montreal were calling us insiders. We had made the inside feel outside and our outside look inside. Later John Guillory would explain what we had done in a book called *Cultural Capital*. We had turned the *Tish*-office into a Canadian cultural capital.

After nineteen issues we all got married and moved to other places—Fred married Pauline and went to Albuquerque, George married Angela and moved to Calgary, I married Helen and moved to Victoria, David married Deena and moved to Seattle, Jamie married Carol and moved to the CPC-ML. These events happened quickly but took a couple of years. But for many people we are still the *Tish* poets and that is all there is to be said about us.

SURVIVING THE PARAPHRASE (1983)

I am of course making this all up. Not making up the events but which ones I tell, how I am telling them, and how they are telling me. Saying something about them by not saying much about them. I'm not much of an authority on most of them, not having paid much attention to many things while I was living them, and not having wanted to remember some things while they were happening. My first year in *Tish* I was still remembering wanting, and wanting, to spend my hours talking with Daphne

Buckle, and she was elsewhere making plans to marry Alan Marlatt. This is difficult to sum up. A lot of the energy I put into getting my *Tish* buddies to publish nineteen issues in nineteen months was more than likely displacement of the energy and anticipation I had felt talking with Daphne about art and writing and life over hours of coffee or tea in Dean's Cafe or the Black Cat Cafe in the winter and early spring of 1961. *Tish* was good for poetry and good for self-esteem. I had also bought myself a TR4 sports car late that June—the car that appears with me, George, Bobby Hogg, and Red Lane on the cover of *The Writing Life,* the first book about *Tish.* Daphne was good for *Tish* and for at least one new car sale. The day after that photo I would set up my typewriter on a picnic table in a nearby campsite and cut the stencils for *Tish*'s first issue.

Over the next decade I would get a reputation as being something of a phenomenologist of poetry and skeptic about what passed for Canadian literary criticism. This was partly because I knew I didn't often understand what was happening to and around me and couldn't see how others could pretend to understand most things about something else. "Art does not seek to describe but to re-enact," Olson had written. This made a whole lot of sense to me about literary criticism as well as art, particularly when the people you care about rarely tell you everything you'd need to know to understand. Or don't know it themselves. Or know that you'd rather not know it.

Not that I was in a hurry to write literary criticism. I submitted a collection of poems as my master's thesis at UBC in 1963, the first of only three such theses to be accepted by the Department of English before the setting-up of the UBC Creative Writing Department in 1964. George and Lionel wrote the others. That summer, while George and Lionel and Fred and Jamie and David were taking part in the legendary-in-1963 Vancouver poetry workshop that Warren Tallman had organized, and where Olson, Duncan, Robert Creeley and Allen Ginsberg were all teaching, and while George and Lionel were each sorting through various teaching offers at universities elsewhere in Canada, I worked at a very junior summer position in the UBC library acquisitions department. Helen and I had married at Christmas of 1962. She was one year from her UBC degree and obliged by degree requirements to complete either on the UBC

campus or at the brand new University of Victoria which had been until 1963 a UBC affiliate. She needed to live during 1963–64 only in Vancouver or Victoria. *For love,* Creeley had written. Midway through the summer a small notice on the English department bulletin board announced a job in English at Royal Roads Military College, in Victoria; I obtained the job, to my surprise, largely on the basis of my now numerous poetry publications: a book, a guest-edited issue of Louis Dudek's *Delta,* and various poems in a dozen journals in three countries.

In Victoria I continued to write poetry, publishing *City of the Gulls and Sea* in 1964, *The Scarred Hull* in 1966, *Four Myths for Sam Perry* in 1970, and writing most of *Weeds* in 1968–69. I began imagining myself as a poet who would need secure university employment to continue writing, but noticed that tenure usually required a Ph.D. I began looking for a doctoral program that might fit with my writing and steal the least time from it. Avoiding grad schools that required a lot of course work, I enrolled in the summer of 1965 at the University of Southern California, doing the course work in the summers of 1965 and 1966, writing the sixteen hours of comps in the winter of 1967, and defending my dissertation in August of 1967. Although I eventually published parts of this work ("Theory and Practice in the Black Mountain Poets") in a chapbook as *Five Readings of Olson's "Maximus"* and as an article in *Boundary 2,* I had little interest in writing criticism until my chair at Royal Roads, Gerald Morgan, urged me to write papers on Canadian poetry for the 1968 and 1969 meetings of the local chapter of the Humanities Association of Canada, of which I think he was president. Gerald and Janka had a cute daughter named Monica, who was studying law. I remember protesting that I knew relatively little about Canadian poetry other than the contemporary, and his replying somewhat irrelevantly "but you write it, don't you?" My 1968 paper on Leonard Cohen and Bob Dylan was soon published by James Reaney's *Alphabet,* and my 1969 paper on the politics of E. J. Pratt's poetry by *Canadian Literature,* and both reprinted in anthologies a few years later. Gerald was a Conrad scholar and before that a master mariner. I used to like to think his wife was Polish. The Cohen/Dylan paper took me to my first meeting of the Association of Canadian

Davey (second from right) with Robert Hogg, George Bowering, Red Lane, and unknown friend of Lane's, in Oliver, B.C., 1961

University Teachers of English (ACUTE) at York University in Toronto in 1969.

A year later I had a tenurable job at York, hired, I came to believe, with Eli Mandel's support, as a poet with a Ph.D. who could teach creative writing, American poetry, and Canadian literature. Clara Thomas, one of the senior York Canadianists, was rumoured to have been skeptical about my appointment because she figured I would soon want to return to British Columbia, but we became friends and co-authors anyway. Also appointed that year at York were William Gairdner, who had just completed a thesis on contemporary French literary theory, and Barbara Godard, who was completing one on Canadian fiction at the Université de Bordeaux. The three of us were thrown together as lecturers to a 12-section 300-student Canadian literature class. It was there in Bill and Barbara's lectures that I began hearing about the European analogues to Olson's phenomenology—Merleau-Ponty, Poulet, Bachelard—and was drawn for the first time to look seriously at structuralism, buying and reading Barthes's *Writing Degree Zero* and *Elements of Semiology* and *On Racine* in 1971, *Mythologies* in 1973 and Jameson's *The Prison House of Language* in 1974. Bill later left York and now writes right-wing tracts about heterosexuality and family life.

The immediate effect of these books was to offer another route to the phenomenologi-

cal text-based poetics I had been developing since the *Tish* period, and to my skepticism about criticism. A poem is itself its only adequate enactment and representation. A poem does not represent something prior to itself but enacts the moment of its own construction. Criticism cannot represent a poem or novel but merely be a new text that enacts a reading of those texts. In the course of my working my way toward such propositions, and of, in a sense, attempting to bridge *Tish* poetics and French structuralism, came the founding meeting of the Association for Canadian and Quebec Literatures (ACQL), at the University of Toronto, at the Learned Societies meetings of May 1974. Thematic criticism, with its source in Frye's *Anatomy of Criticism* and its recent popularization in Canada by D. G. Jones's *Butterfly on Rock* and Margaret Atwood's *Survival*, and its methodology of using bunches of plot summaries to develop general paradigms of one unified Canadian Literature, had within the past five years installed itself as the dominant approach in Canadian literary studies. I took advantage of my invitation to speak at the conference to take apart the assumptions of this criticism, using not Atwood, whom I had already critiqued elsewhere, but Jones as my example of it. Some scholars have called the moment of my lecture a turning point in Canadian criticism. I remember the seats in the amphitheatre were filled and that there were people standing in the aisles and doorways. I remember Miriam Waddington grabbing me as I left the podium and saying "That's good, you're not a structuralist, are you?" Perhaps, like many others, she had mistaken Jones's and Atwood's criticism as structuralism. Then I noticed Doug Jones, and his wife Monique, sitting quietly near the centre. I wished they'd been somewhere else. I wish I hadn't taken advantage. I wished I'd been somewhere else. I wished I hadn't made so many things up.

THE SCARRED HULL (1966)

I wrote *The Scarred Hull* in Victoria in 1964, and my friend George published it the next year in Calgary as an issue of the long-poem magazine *Imago*. It's a fairly simple long poem that juxtaposes accounts of nineteenth-century shipwrecks on the west coast of Vancouver Island with narratives about children whom my first wife, Helen, was teaching in a "special education" class at South Park School, across from Beacon Hill Park in Victoria. It was her first year of teaching. Many of my friends decided to read the poem's ships and children as metaphors, not just for each other, but for my life as well. Warren Tallman had started this kind of reading of me in 1961 in his introduction to my *D-Day and After,* calling its context "the haunted house of the lost object." He was thinking of Daphne. There are many lost objects in the sea. I think of *The Scarred Hull* as a step toward *The Clallam* of 1973, and toward thinking about issues of class, justice, fatality, and power. The lower your class the worse your luck. Although in my memory schools had always been sites of class conflict: working-class children and middle-class teachers and school boards. It was probably more those schools in Abbotsford, my schools, than South Park School in Victoria, that I produce in *The Scarred Hull.*

But when I think about those schools I don't see them right away. I see instead the gravel road between my home and the school, and the kids loitering beside it. My parents' house was on a small lot on the edge of a small village, five blocks from the elementary school, two blocks up a hill from the post office, and four blocks from the B.C. Electric maintenance yard where my father worked. Much of my early life took place on the wooden sidewalk that ran from the brow of the hill to the concrete sidewalk at the bottom. Walking to town with my mother and grandmother on their shopping trips. Walking to school down the hill and across the railway tracks. Walking home and back for lunch. Some boys my age lived further up our road but I met them only when we all began school. We would wander slowly home, throwing rocks into the various empty whisky and rum bottles that reappeared each day in the grass between the sidewalk and the road, and they would tell me about the New York Yankees and Roy Rogers and Hopalong Cassidy. I knew something about the 1930s and something about Passchendaele and Coventry and Northallerton and Southampton, something about George Formby and Gracie Fields, and about my dad's favorite trumpet player, Harry James, but nothing about baseball or cowboys.

When I was five and a half, I won second prize in beginners piano in the Mission City Music Festival, playing "The Blue Bells of Scot-

land." When the adjudicators reported, I was humiliated to be jokingly praised for having counted out loud. During a recess in grade one, I became exasperated with Perry Long and threw a piece of a broken crockery at him and cut him for three stitches over the left eye. When I was in grade two, I won our elementary school's piano talent prize. The school had eight rooms, grades one to eight. When I was in grade three, Patsy Leary, who lived three houses up the lane, got run over by a car but all the wheels missed her and she was unhurt. "I'm dead," she cried, from underneath the car. When I was in grade four, I was elected class president. When I was in grade five, John Piper and I competed in drawing scenes of MIG-15s and F-86s dogfighting. When I was in grade six, Patsy Leary asked me to be her partner in the schottische which our class performed at the Mission Festival. When I was in grade six, I became pretty good at badminton and persuaded a tough guy, Allan Thompson, to be my doubles partner. When I was in grade seven, Allan got Patsy pregnant. When I was in grade eight, I played in the B.C. table tennis championships, and also won second prize in the B.C. Pulp and Paper Association essay contest. Alan and Patsy had just got married and were wheeling their new baby around the village. When I was in grade nine, I got exasperated with Bob Gilberg for jacking around with a football and suckerpunched him in the stomach. Two weeks later he helped me walk off my exhaustion after I placed last in our junior high's half-mile race.

In grade one Miss Chappell, our teacher, who retired the next year, strapped Rennie Harms. My mother and grandmother always spoke respectfully of Miss Chappell. He kept grinning in order to avoid crying, and so she strapped him again. He kept grinning.

READING "KIM" RIGHT (1993)

I've always had a weakness for blonde women but never been involved with one. You can read about this in my "Dead in France" poem about the death of bpNichol, or in "Amber" my poem about visiting the Amber Palace near Jaipur, except there I forgot to mention that the girls and women were blonde. Sometimes I think I have this weakness because my mother was blonde. Sometimes I think it's because I grew up in the years of Monroe, Mansfield, and Diana Dors. Except my blondes usually look more like Doris Day.

Or maybe it's because I grew up during World War II and my father liked to read men's magazines with stories like "Irma, Queen of the Nazi Death Camps" with the predictable drawings of a leggy blonde with black whip and jackboots. A woman as young as your imagination and old as Chaucer's "merciles beaute." A sign of a woman.

Prime-ministerial candidate Kim Campbell, born in Port Alberni, educated at UBC, took me back to the signs and images of my youth and all those beautiful middle-class right-wing co-eds who wouldn't look at a scruffy student poet and were going to marry guys in Law and Commerce. Why would I want them to look at me? Campbell didn't marry anyone in Law or Commerce but a mathematics professor who had written that we should kiss the feet of land developers. Now that's a bad sign. Of course it wasn't just me who had a weakness for this blonde woman in the spring of 1993. Enough Canadians to elect her leader of the Conservatives; enough, the pollsters said, to re-elect that party of businessmen and military spending. All of the above is about the semiotics of some relationships that women have to power, or to male power—marrying it, offering to lead it, enacting its fantasies. All of these enough to make a guy angry, or an angry guy write a book.

READING CANADIAN READING (1988)

One of the problems with me trying to write autobiography is that I've been writing it for a long time. That comes from my starting out as a phenomenological *Tish* poet. And then becoming a self-reflexive *Open Letter* poet. Anybody who wants to know in detail how I have claimed to have spent my childhood should read my *War Poems*. Or how I have pretended to have spent my adolescence should read "In Love with Cindy Jones" in my *Popular Narratives* or "For One of Them" in *D-Day and After*. I had a long adolescence. And anyone who wants long reflective narratives about my writing my early books of criticism—*Earle Birney, From There to Here, Surviving the Paraphrase, Louis Dudek and Raymond Souster,* or *Margaret Atwood: A Feminist Poetics*—should read my *Reading Canadian Read-*

ing, in which I wrote chapters on each of them. My critical life as a critic.

POSTCARD TRANSLATIONS (1988)

Sometimes I've thought that life was a long semiotic adventure. Everything's in code. Everything open to interpretation and translation. Including the cogitating "I" of "I've thought that life was a long semiotic adventure."

I inherited a collection of Edwardian postcards from my maternal grandmother, who had acquired them in rural Yorkshire. Many had been mailed from India by her brother. Postcards are not merely photographs but products of visual construction. Politically, I've often been interested in making subliminal messages liminal, so I began translating the postcard photos into language, and later the postcard photos my wife Linda and I were sending from Florence or Nice or Salamanca. Translation can

"When I was on the staff of Royal Roads Military College," Victoria, B.C., 1964

Frank Davey   *Contemporary Authors Autobiography Series,* **Volume 27**

free a writer from the confessional and the biographical, from the obligations of lyric. Or free a critic from the analytical. I began translating the architecture of Europe and India. Translating my childhood. Translating tanks, armoured cars, field guns, submarines, the Heinkel bomber on the roof of the Frankfurt airport. I translated India and Abbotsford in *The Abbotsford Guide to India.* Translated Camille Claudel in *Popular Narratives.* In May of 1989 Linda, our daughter Sara, and I drove from Thessalonika to Skopje to look for a conference that was supposed to begin the next day at the university. I strolled over to the university the next morning, and was referred by the security guard to the library where there was a book launch. The book being launched was a translation into Macedonian of my *Postcard Translations.* The Canadian Embassy's attempts to send me news of the project had been lost in my temporary translation from being a writer into being a European traveller.

All of the above and the following are of course also "I" translations.

Post-National Arguments: The Politics of the Anglophone-Canadian Novel Since 1967 (1993)

In manuscript I had titled this book *National Arguments,* planning it to be a book about how the arguments within a nation about its cultural choices, together with the discourses in which those arguments are conducted, constitute its nationhood. But so many of the novels which I examined located most of their crucial events and signs outside of Canada that my editors suggested the "post-national" title.

It is difficult for Canadians to distinguish between the post-national and the colonial, just as it is often difficult when travelling outside of North America to distinguish between the multinational and the American. This is the price Canadians pay for having created a country of modest economic and military strength—its cultural productions are modestly regarded and valued, both inside and outside the country. The cultural value of the productions of more powerful nations is inflated by association with the symbolic value of the military and economic power of those nations. Canadian artists who have successfully exported their works have in most cases been marketed in ways that disguise

Davey with Bowering at the latter's home in Vancouver, 1973

their Canadianness: Margaret Atwood's books appear in their US editions to be the work of an American; Ondaatje is often constructed outside of Canada as "Commonwealth" or Sri Lankan.

When I was growing up in the 1940s or '50s, most successful Canadian novels were published in London or New York, and writers often wrote with those cities' publishers in mind. Poets often sent their poems for consideration by British and US journals, although in terms of the book publication of poetry, Canada was virtually a closed field. Canadians could hope only to get book publication in Canada, and only Canadian poets were considered by Canadian publishers. There were eleven books of poetry published in all of Canada in 1961.

In the 1960s and 1970s the establishment of dozens of new publishers and journals, mostly assisted by the Canada Council, changed everything. Novelists began writing only for Canadian readers and publishers. Poets found numerous publishers and numerous review journals, and stopped hoping to receive book reviews abroad. Most of us stopped caring what foreign readers and publishers might think of our writing. Writers who did care, and who did publish abroad, were either thought of as unspeakably commercial, like Janette Turner Hospital, or unspeakably colonial, like Daryll Hine, and indeed few of us spoke or wrote of them. Sometimes a non-Canadian publisher would discover and be impressed by a Canadian text or writer, and publish it—as often happened with bpNichol's poems and with Margaret Atwood's early novels, but these events were much different from the publication of work that Canadians had constructed from the beginning for foreign readerships.

This is the literary field in which I did most of my writing. It was a closed and boundaried field in terms of implied audience, book and periodical distribution, and book promotion, but not a closed field—and could not have been—in terms of intertextual relations.

POPULAR NARRATIVES (1991)

I was sitting just inside the glass patio doors of our villa at Université Canadienne en France at Villefranche-sur-mer, just east of Nice. Linda was there too—she'd taken a month's leave from her law practice to spend October with me. It was warm but dark. I was probably sipping wine. Linda was probably washing Belgian endives or stirring a boeuf bourguignon. There was a hesitant tap at the window—it was "Dean Doug" Parker, dean of this little hilltop campus. He had a telegram from my friend Elizabeth Humphrey, executive assistant to the chair of English at York. She is very restrained, thoughtful, and formal. "Regret to inform you," it read, "that bpNichol has died."

Doug was nervous. He didn't know how well we knew bp. We were astonished. We didn't know Barrie had been ill or had been in any way facing death. He slipped away. We said how can it be, what has happened, what about Ellie and Sarah, how could this happen to him, he was our best friend, end of an era, end of Coach House, end of poetry, and other most predictable things. We kept saying these things for several days.

bp was my best friend in Toronto and unlike many of my other friends also Linda's good

friend. When someone dies who fits into your life and your expectations of what life is going to be, you usually begin reconsidering. I was having to reconsider who I was writing for. Who I was sharing *Open Letter* with. Who I was editing for Coach House Press with. In Toronto I had shown bp almost all my new writing within a week or two of writing it. He would drop by sometime between nine and eleven at night, on his way home from a meeting, or on his way from three or four visits to other friends. He'd have a folder of his new writing, I'd make some Earl Grey tea, he'd read from his folder aloud, then I'd look at it while he looked at mine. I'd been in France since early July. Had begun writing a poem mostly for him on sunny afternoons in Paris, in Père Lachaise cemetery. Sitting near the tombs of Héloise and Abelard— of abbesse Héloise who somehow reminded me of ex-nun Ellie. Not far from the grave of Apollinaire. Quite a ways from Stein's. This fall in Villefranche I had been writing other things that I'd wanted him to see. The story of a medieval barmaid in Augsburg. Of my learning junior high school courtship rituals. Of learning to read the postcard art of European tourism. bp was this kind of reader, of inchoate road signs, maps, people, stories. Now . . .

The most important thing that happened to me that year in Europe was bp's death. I had got food poisoning from a slice of mille-feuille in Beauvais. My seventeen-year-old daughter had played in the violin section of the Cannes Symphony Orchestra in concerts at Antibes, Menton, Cannes, and Nice-Acropolis. I had stood in the same week on the ramparts of Mycenae and Troy. I had looked into the gold eyes of Alexander's father. I had been struck by lightning on the slopes of Mount Parnassus. I had driven past smoldering army vehicles in Kosovo. When I got back to Toronto, Coach House Press was in ruins, *Open Letter* needed new editors, and my living room was empty almost every evening.

OPEN LETTER (1965)

I began the journal *Open Letter* because I missed my *Tish* buddies. In Victoria in 1964 there were a few writers but they got together mostly to impress each other. I imagined a journal which would be a sort of virtual *Tish* office. Each editor—myself, George, Fred Wah, David Dawson—would have a section in which to publish a letter to the others, some writing, and writing or letters they'd gathered from other writers. The big gossip in 1969, the year I left Victoria, was that Robert Sward had punched out Robin Skelton at Ivy's Bookshop. So I opened *Open Letter* to be a virtual *Tish* office, and Daphne Buckle wandered through with curious prose poems. bpNichol dropped by. And Victor Coleman.

The virtual office was working rather well. I learned how to write prose poems by misreading the prose poems Daphne was sending me and *Open Letter* to publish. I could have asked her how to write them—after all she was in grad school studying how to translate French prose poems—but I was too embarrassed to ask. David Dawson wrote so much that the seventh issue became a Dawson book. Each issue cost around $270 to print and $20 to mail.

I saw Victor Coleman for the first time in June of 1969, in Toronto, when Linda and I were scooting across the country in my TR4

"With my wife Linda and our children Michael and Sara," Abbotsford, B.C., 1975

toward Montreal and Sir George Williams University where I was going to be writer-in-residence. George was at the Learned Societies meetings at York University where I was presenting the Cohen/Dylan paper, and took us down to the Huron Street Coach House to meet his publisher. Victor was puzzling because he was always earnest and serious except when he was laughing, so then you began to think his laughter was serious also. A few months later Victor came to Montreal to visit George and saw the prose poems I'd been writing after misreading Daphne's prose poems in *Open Letter.* He and Coach House published them the next fall as *Weeds,* with the text entirely handset by Nelson Adams. By then I was living in Toronto, and Victor suggested that Coach House take on the publishing of *Open Letter* as a much larger journal. I got bpNichol and Victor and later Steve McCaffery to help out as editors. Someday I should thank Victor for all the years I had working on *OL* and other things with bp.

Margaret Atwood (1984)

Not everyone can name one of the minor characters in their lives "Margaret Atwood." All the time George and Lionel and Fred and David and Jamie and I were becoming *Tish* poets, she was scribbling away somewhere in the tree-lined streets of Toronto's Annex the poems that were going to appear with ours in Colombo's anthology *Poetry 64* and change what was the eastern-Canadian poetry we were responding to. We had heard of Victor Coleman and David McFadden who were poets who lived in eastern Canada but were not to our eyes or ears eastern-Canadian poets, but we had not previously heard of "Margaret Atwood." After that we would see and hear about her a lot, and she would become the most famous eastern-Canadian poet ever and inadvertently fill up the borders of many of the pages we had imagined ourselves filling. She was to become our companion in Canadian writing, whether or not we wanted an eastern-Canadian companion. This was not true of John Colombo or Daryll Hine or Alden Nowlan or Roo Borson, whom if we ignored would not become companions.

It became important for me and George and others to write about Margaret Atwood because she had by the mid-1970s shifted the field we were writing in, and many other writers had to re-mark their positions within it. She had shifted its weight back toward Toronto where only some of it but not most of it belonged. She had shifted it toward women, among whom we had not had enough companions in writing. We were subconsciously glad to have her detached and ironic companionship, although it was costing many Canadian writers large parts of their audience. She had also shifted the field back to Frygian thematics and away from language as the ground of culture and politics, even though her own words were precise and complexly political. We could not forgive this superficial structuralism in Frye and its glib generalizations about Canada and we could not forgive them at all when Atwood wrote *Survival* and defined out much of the Canadian culture and writing we valued. This was when I began writing about her writing—a review of *Survival* and *Surfacing* in which I pointed to their tilt toward Frye's and George Grant's Ontarios. Ontarios which they and she called Canada.

After this review she commented to my wife Linda that I must have "female-Hitler evil-stepmother" fantasies about her. Although it might have been amusing to think of Atwood's face on one of the jack-booted Aryan girlie-bodies of my father's deathcamp magazines, I had to remember that it was Atwood who was constructing this image of herself rather than me or my father constructing it. Among the things the remark "said" was how lightly Atwood was taking Canadians' various struggles for cultural power, and how "natural" she thought Ontario Tory dominance of Canadian cultural paradigms to be. Her own assertions of authority were to be seen as just and appropriate; those of others, and their objections to hers, as absurd or neurotic. I could suggest more, particularly about the Hitler reference, but presumably only at the risk of being accused of fantasy.

THE LOUIS RIEL ORGAN & PIANO COMPANY (1985)

One of the conventions about biography is that one is more shaped by events early in life than later in life. I had plastic models of British battleships, the *Rodney* and the *King George V*, to float beside me in the bathtub. What if the source of this convention is the bafflement of a child about a world already underway, sailing and flying in such precise squadrons. I had gun-metal models of a Sterling and a Lancaster. Later events pass with similar precision, but we are accustomed to their passing and our bafflement. I had bright-coloured plastic models of a P-40, a Hurricane, and a Spitfire. Or we imagine our bafflement to be understanding. I had a thick colouring book of jeeps and battleships and half-tracks and bombers and escort cruisers. On my fourth Christmas I received a large clockwork army tank, with guns that were sparked by lighter flints when it clattered across the floor. During dinner preparations on New Year's Day, I was winding it and something happened to its gears and it catapulted itself in two-three large leaps across the kitchen and into my mother's and grandmother's legs. I was in terrible trouble.

*   *   *

At dinner time my father and grandmother would sit across from each other at the kitchen table and argue about politics. My mother sat at the end, near the sawdust stove, that later became an oil stove. I sat on my father's side of the table. I still do. My grandmother always voted Conservative because her father in Yorkshire had voted Conservative and Churchill was a great man. My father always voted CCF and talked about not wanting my mother to cancel his vote. Most of the details of these scenes are lost to me now except for my father's story about rail cars filled with scrap iron passing through Vancouver in the 1930s on their way to the docks and Japan. All the working men, he would say, knew this scrap would be coming back to them as bullets, but the businessmen, they didn't care, as long as they got their bucks. Bucks, he said, not dollars. What I know now about the scene are long stories about how my father and grandmother got to this table. My father's grandfather had come from Devon to southwestern Ontario as an illiterate farm worker in 1849, the last year of the Talbot Colony. Had married a Canadian-born Quaker widow, fathered a son and daughter, and died. My father's father had become a farm worker, a logger in Michigan, a piano and organ tuner in eastern Ontario. Had married a Methodist farm girl from north of Oshawa, moved to Vancouver to work for the B.C. Electric Co., bought a house on Vancouver's working-class east side, fathered sons in 1907 and 1910, driven his wife with his temper and fists from the house in 1913, and divorced her in 1914. My father left school at sixteen to work as a labourer, was nineteen when the stock markets crashed, and twenty-eight when he found his first "steady job" as a laborer with B.C. Electric and married my mother. This is not a biography he ever recounted, except some of the later parts, and these only in anecdote.

My grandmother told her story often, of a Yorkshire childhood in large houses among apple orchards. Her father had owned a brewery or tavern, one of her brothers had managed a tea plantation in Darjeeling, another had been a ship's engineer and sent her postcards from Archangel, Amsterdam, New York, and Singapore. Her husband's family still owned a large farmhouse near Moulton in east Yorkshire, "Kilnsey House." She had trained and worked in Newcastle as a telegrapher before marrying my grandfather, giving birth to my mother, and moving in 1913 to Vancouver, where my grandfather found work as a carpenter at the Rat Portage Mill. Then came the war, and he enlisted in the Duke of Connaught's own, and served, fought, as a machine gunner in the Seventh Canadian Infantry Division at Passchendaele and Mons. Marched into the Rhine in 1919. Returned to a maintenance job with the Vancouver school board. They saved money, bought a house on Vancouver's middle-class west side, bought a car.

My father's family heirlooms were a set of Model-T socket wrenches and an alarm clock, both of which he'd bought himself and smuggled past his angry father when he left home in 1938 to marry. My grandmother's were two oil paintings that had once hung in her father's tavern, three albums of Edwardian postcards, six packing crates hammered together in Yorkshire by her husband and that now served as jam cupboards in our basement, and three large photos of her husband in army uniform, two of which hung in my bedroom. Private Albert F. Brown. The "F" was for Frankland. Frank.

Louis Dudek and Raymond Souster (1981)

One of the tasks of the writer, beyond being a writer, is to shape the literary field that one's writing must fit within. This is partly done by the writing, through the intertexts it invokes and the discourses it reworks, and through the institutions with which it becomes affiliated. But a writer can also intervene as an editor, as Louis Dudek and Raymond Souster did in founding their numerous little magazines, and in founding in 1952, with Irving Layton, Contact Press, or as a critic and theorist as Dudek also did in writing *Literature and the Press* and *Selected Essays.* When we began writing in Vancouver in the 1960s, the field of poetry was dominated ideologically by a modernist theme-based "mythy" poetry written mostly in Ontario linked to the theories of Northrop Frye. This was a poetry that for the most part implied that power resided outside the social—thus masking as "natural" its own socially and materially founded power in the universities and magazines and publishing houses of Central Canada. The largest exceptions to this dominance were Raymond Souster's minimalism and localism, and Louis Dudek's insistences on poetry's connections to history, economics, and technology. Their writing, and that published by Contact Press, and by Dudek's magazine *Delta,* was the Canadian writing that in 1961–63 most engaged us.

No matter what you think of the above story, it still works for me. I continue to regard Louis Dudek as one of the major Canadian poets of the 1950s and 1960s. One whose readership has been limited by literary fashions of Ontario, by his repeated critiques of Frye, and by his insistence—long before Foucault or Bourdieu—on the influence of technological change and institutional power on literary production and critical judgment. Such theories are always resisted by the literary dominants—and Dudek paid the price, being excluded from numerous academic anthologies produced by the major Toronto publishing houses, and ignored by critics like Jones or Atwood. The dominants resist because their own power rests on transparency—on its material ground *not* being visible. In the 1980s I not only published this book on Dudek and Souster but also, with the help of bpNichol, published a special *Open Letter* issue of Dudek's essays, *Texts and Essays,* and through Coach House Press the Dudek poetry collection *Cross Section: Poems 1940–1980.*

King of Swords (1972)

Like many kids, I first became class conscious at grade school, although it took me rather

Davey coming to an agreement with Robert Creeley about the beer, Vancouver, 1979

longer to learn the concept of class consciousness. I first learned about the New York Yankees and Brooklyn Dodgers from boys whose fathers had the leisure to think about baseball. My father never mentioned baseball. Later I would know enough to think that this was because of class and also gender. The same boys knew all about the Carlsbad Caverns and the redwood Trees of Mystery because their parents had cars that could travel to New Mexico or California and the money and time to drive them there. These were the Ford dealer's son, the village policeman's son, the doctor's son. We got our first car in 1948, a '46 Chev that you can read about in *War Poems* and that would safely cover the fifty miles to Vancouver. My subject position was behind my dad in the backseat, and beside my grandmother, who was seated behind my mother. This allowed me to identify with my dad but did weird things to my relationship with my grandmother. On Peak Frean's cookie tins, the king sits beside the queen.

I also had class problems with books. The car dealer's son had a *Book of Knowledge* and

his parents a subscription to *Reader's Digest* condensed books. He could give smart answers at school. I had my father's old Henty books from his own childhood, my grandmother's atlas of the counties of England, and a subscription to a British magazine *Open Roads for Boys*. Later I would realize that mine was a problem in ethnicity as well as class, but by that time class mobility had brought my parents their own subscriptions to *Reader's Digest* and Book-of-the-Month Club.

When my father bought a new 1951 Chev, we began driving in his summer holidays to Banff and Yellowstone and Reno and Salt Lake City and all the places that the car dealer's son had taught me were exotic and important. Except we never got to Carlsbad or California. I persuaded my grandmother that these long distances would be hard on her health and so managed to change my subject position to that of what I thought was a normal kid, between my father and mother in the front seat. I have often felt guilty about what I told my grandmother who had contributed money to buying both the cars and who I know got the message that on these trips she wasn't wanted. A question about kings and princes: how the centre of the front seat has more status than the driver's side of the back seat.

King of Swords is a marriage poem marked by the king's role. By the many-castled England of my grandmother's memories. By the stupid identification with the rich and titled that has sent countless uneducated soldiers to war in defence of their king. The hero sits on a horse or on the driver's side of the front seat. His woman sits in his lap, or clings to him from behind the saddle, or huddles at his right side behind the steering wheel. You can read about the codes that govern the latter in "In Love with Cindy Jones," the opening section of *Popular Narratives.*

What I gave up in persuading my grandmother not to accompany my parents to Yellowstone and beyond was someone to talk to during the travels. The best my mother could do was read travel brochures aloud with my father correcting her pronunciation. My father would talk to me while putting up the tent or lighting the Coleman lantern—about how to put up a tent or light a lantern. He liked to strike up conversations with the other men in the campground. These comments appear to be caricatures but they resemble what I remember.

KARLA'S WEB (1994)

Karla will be remembered as the beautiful blonde young wife from St. Catharines, Ontario, who helped her husband Paul rape and murder slightly younger women, including her little sister, and videotape his raping. I called the book *Karla's Web* because of the web of technology they wove around their crimes and the fans of their murders wove at the internet address alt.fan.karla-homolka, and because Paul used Karla as the reassuring "bait" of normality in luring one of his victims to his car. The question now is to what extent am I or you caught, discursively or otherwise, in Karla's web. This is a big question because it's a huge web. A web of culture that led Karla not to find it unusual that her husband occasionally beat her, like my grandfather beat my grandmother (though she found it unbearable), or raped other women, or one night brought home a fourteen-year-old "sex slave" he had grabbed from her backyard and already raped. It's hard not

to think of women as losers since statistically more of them are poor, more receive low pay, more are unemployed, more are single parents, more get raped, more get murdered by the other sex, more weep in war movies. My grandmother was not a loser, and that may have bothered my father. He always looked after my mother, his "little girl," and kept her from wanting to weep. I was in part a student of my father's practices. Karla also rhymes with the blonde Nazi women in jackboots on the covers of magazines my father used to read in the 1950s. I always wondered if he wanted to save these young women or be their prisoner. Or, if you save these women, do you also become their prisoner? And would they be at all interesting once you'd saved them?

Anyway, those questions may be why for me Karla has remained a signifier—a blonde jackbooted female drawing, or an ominously tranquillized face on a book cover (mine). A signifier that gives one subject positions—above or below, saving, beating, or cringing. Ironically, the historical Karla and Paul also saw themselves as signifiers, preferred to see themselves so—as actors in their own continuing porno/snuff movies.

Now that I think of it, I suspect that my grandmother, my father's mother, was also one of those women, the first, who terrified my father. These are awful things to be putting together. By having walked out on him, his father, and brother. By having worked scrubbing floors in order to own her own house and buy gifts for her sons. By having defied his father by sneaking back to see them. My grandmother was so emphatically not Karla. Did my father ever forgive her?

GRIFFON (1972)

I wrote the short "long poem" *Griffon* in the early 1970s, as part of my looking-around my new home in Southern Ontario. It's a minor poem, a mid-continent analogue to my *The Clallam,* written around the same time, both focussed on ships as vessels of a founding North American capitalism as uncontrolled and as disdainful of life as any form of capitalism we encounter today. Not much of a surprise here, except that people in most "democracies" go on allowing even larger exchanges of life for profit, frightened by possible job and investment losses even more than by possible death. Father Hennepin lamented the loss of the *Griffon* and its cargo but not the loss of the sailors' lives. Our own governments' pension policies push us into retirement plans that invest in companies that may or may not be endangering us in order to enrich us. By 1972 I had purchased for both my children life insurance policies that reinvested various dividends into the stock market.

FROM THERE TO HERE: A GUIDE TO ENGLISH-CANADIAN LITERATURE SINCE *1960* (1974)

In 1985 at York University the English department's search committee asks if I would let myself be nominated as department chair. Historically, the department has usually elected the candidate least likely to change things, so I think that I could stand for office without fear of election. I hadn't had a lot to do with the department. About a third of its members were concentrated around its departmental office, and the rest scattered in various college buildings around the campus. Most of us attended more college meetings and parties than we attended English department meetings. A couple of years before I arrived at York the English department had deposed a chair widely perceived to be autocratic and had re-written its constitution to limit a chair's powers and give most power to the department meeting. Most of the members had been hired when York's primary mandate was undergraduate teaching and everyone was expected to teach first and second year classes. Many thought it was irresponsible to take time away from teaching to write books or articles and to accept pay increases awarded because one had published. One year when the university offered merit pay, the majority of the members voted to give the department's share back to the administration. Another year they voted that its members were all equally meritorious. I'm not sure how I got hired—maybe because I wrote poetry and hadn't yet published any books about writers or literature. Sometimes the department, which also acted as a hiring committee, tried to hire the candidate least likely to be distracted from teaching by books or articles they might want to write.

In 1973 I was recruited by the deans of Arts and Fine Arts to chair a committee that was to attempt to set up an inter-faculty creative writing program. The English department had one introductory creative writing course, now taught in seven sections, but had resisted teaching upper-year creative writing courses because members feared that honours students might take them for degree credit and dilute their degrees. Irving Layton had managed to establish a third-year poetry workshop. In 1975 when our committee tried to create courses in fiction-writing and a second poetry workshop, the English department declined to offer them and so we had to offer them to the Humanities Division, which eagerly accepted. Playwriting and screenwriting were already offered by the Theatre and Film departments in Fine Arts. The next year the dean named me Co-ordinator of the new Creative Writing Program, and the Humanities Division hired Clark Blaise to teach its new fiction-writing courses. Much of my job was to walk between the various buildings that housed the English, Humanities, Fine Arts, and Theatre departments. The Program office was on neutral ground, in my college.

Part of the arrangement I managed to negotiate for the program was that the hiring of part-time instructors for any Creative Writing courses, including the English department's introductory course, would be done outside the union hiring rules and in consultation with the Program coordinator. The English department was thus persuaded to hire bpNichol to teach sections of the introductory course and sometimes Irving Layton's senior course. Because of a shortage of space, part-time teachers often had to share a windowless office with five or six others. I volunteered to share my courtyard-view office with bp, and so twice a week had great conversations with him over lunch and unmarked poems and essays. We made Coach House and *Open Letter* plans and co-authored essay plans. It's a long way from there to here.

I gave up being Coordinator in 1979, after one three-year term. I don't remember why, although the fact that Clark Blaise had resigned after one year because of his wife Bharati Mukherjee's encounters with Toronto racism, and Dave Godfrey, whom Humanities had hired to the same position, resigned also after one year, with the result that the money that funded this position was lost in the recurrent politics of funding cutbacks, may have had something to do with it. I am good at starting or expanding things but am an unenthusiastic caretaker. In 1980 I was briefly acting master of my college. In 1984 I was acting master again. Calumet had been a fine arts and creative writing college for most of the seventies and early eighties and now was being overrun with business students who wanted to close the creative-writing reading room and stop holding concerts and poetry readings in the common room because these disrupted their bridge games. John Bentley Mays and I and others had inadvertently brought these students to Calumet by establishing in 1979 York's first microcomputer room which we thought would inspire writers and visual artists. John Bentley Mays had left Calumet to become Fine Arts reviewer for the *Globe and Mail*. Maybe I was ready to leave Calumet.

Back at the English department the Graduate Program had just received its provincial review and the reviewers had given it only temporary re-certification. Many of the faculty who had been hired as undergraduate teachers and had done little publishing had been teaching regularly in the graduate program. Because of the small size of graduate classes, the teaching of such classes was perceived by the department

to be a bonus which was to be distributed democratically, like merit pay. The review committee threatened to de-certify the program unless all faculty who had published fewer than three articles in the past five years were purged from its faculty. I remember discussing this with Barbara Godard and our both being amused. The purge was done and the program re-certified, and the undergraduate department was left with numerous members unlikely ever to be considered qualified to teach a graduate course.

The main reason I let myself be nominated for department chair was to have the chance to complain indirectly about various policies. Except for the annual grades meeting and the occasional meeting to decide hirings, I hadn't been to more than three or four department meetings since the mid-1970s because everything I suggested got voted down by the democrats.

I took this personally because I considered myself a democrat. After being nominated, I told the department that it needed to hire new members with research records that would enable them to teach almost immediately in the graduate program. This should not have been

"With Victor Coleman at Ron Mann's shooting of Echoes Without Saying,*" Toronto, 1983*

an extraordinary thing to propose but what is extraordinary is of course a consequence of context. I told them I would be a chair who would be visible in the academic and arts communities. I thought saying these things would guarantee my defeat but on the first ballot the first candidate had 19 votes, I had 18 votes, and the third candidate had 5 voters. On the run-off, I was elected 23 to 19. In 1989, while I was in France on sabbatical I was re-elected by a vote of something like 34-3.

Reconsidering all these events makes me sad—sad mostly, I suspect, because of all the people who I worked with through these years who were there and are now elsewhere—not just bp and Eli Mandel who are dead but colleagues and friends from various Calumet, Creative Writing, and English Department committees. Also because of all the people "I" in the name of the department hired during those years and left behind in 1990 when I moved to London. Some people were sad when I left York. They threw me a party. Some felt, I was told, betrayed. The University of Western Ontario, in London, is an old university, founded in 1878, but to many at York a rival for status and grad students. I was tired after twenty years in Canada's largest city. I missed bp. Western offered me research money and additional time from teaching to write things like this autobiography.

FOUR MYTHS FOR SAM PERRY (1970)

We started *Tish* at the beginning of the sixties and had no idea about what was starting. Bobby Hogg used to come into the *Tish* office and squat in the far corner smoking pot, and we had no idea about what was starting. While we were writing poems at our *Tish* desks, the Russian and Yankee Cuban missile boats kept getting closer and closer but the postman kept delivering our copies of *Gramma* and posters of Che Guevara. I remember the issue of *Evergreen Review* that had a tattered Kennedy election poster on the cover. Then I moved to Victoria and Kennedy was shot just before coffee break at Royal Roads Military College. A little later Jack Spicer was dead, and film and acid had joined poetry as the things to do in Vancouver, and Helen and I had a twelve-string guitar, and Blew Ointment and Very Stone House were the new Vancouver publishers to take very seriously. I used to come to

Vancouver from Victoria to go to readings and visit friends and feel very old-fashioned. Maybe I was.

In Los Angeles in 1965 Helen and I lived in an apartment on the Southern Cal campus near Jefferson and 37th Avenue South, and here there was no new or old-fashioned, only people scrambling not to get crushed on the Harbour Freeway or shot down by a fellow-shopper at Pay 'n' Save Drugs. Every day you could be mugged or sunburned. Cars still carried "Goldwater 64" bumper stickers. The morning paper carried yesterday's Vietnam body count in a front page rectangle beside the weather forecast. Helen and I arrived in LA just after dark in my little TR4 and looked for a motel near USC. The motel signs all announced hourly rates and clean sheets. Our second month there the Watts riots began and soon had spread all around the university. We began to hear the first of thirty-seven—I counted—gunshots. On television we could get pictures of our neighbourhood food markets burning. Some of the fraternity boys went up on our roof with rifles but the elderly building manager went up and disarmed them. Our building had no corridors, just exterior walkways overlooking Exposition Boulevard. On the third day the National Guard set up road blocks below and yelled at us and pointed guns whenever we opened our door onto the walkway. To visit a neighbour you had to crawl along the walkway behind the shelter of the concrete railing. People still wonder why I don't like the US. On the fifth day the curfew was lifted and we drove out to the nearest unburned market to get food and as usual we were the only white customers. I always feel relaxed in supermarkets even after riots and was wandering around and browsing while Helen filled our cart. A great big guy grabbed me by the shirt, cocked his right fist, and accused me of stalking his sister—who was nearly as big and had no front teeth. Despite her lack of teeth and the fact I hadn't noticed her, I thought he had some justice on his side. I was pleased he hadn't yet hit me. The obvious thing to say was that his sister was so goddamn ugly that no man would think of stalking her but here the obvious was obviously not useful. I told him we hadn't been introduced. If I were a big black guy and just hours after the Watts riots found myself a middle-size American white guy to punch out, right there in my very own unburned neighbourhood supermarket, I would be so punch happy. He still hasn't hit me and I think this is a good sign. Helen arrives with our cart and asks what's going on? I tell him again that we haven't been introduced. He lowers his fist slightly. He looks puzzled. She looks puzzled.

On the way back from the market we are overtaking a truck full of national guardsmen when a nearby car backfires. All the guardsmen leap up and point their guns in all directions including ours. Later that year the U.S. blows up Amchitka Island in an A-bomb test. In Los Angeles there is a 4.7 earthquake that dumps the books out of our bookcases. Back in Canada Sam Perry, poet, filmmaker, drug explorer, onetime *Tish* editor, shoots himself, November, 1966. The event is one of millions of irrational, apolitical acts that are happening in a world overdosing on war and politics. I am reading, among many other things, John Speirs's book on the non-Chaucerian tradition of medieval poetry, Margaret Murray's *The God of the Witches,* Robert Graves's *The White Goddess,* Alan Watt's *Easter.* A Euro-American community that has brought into being in the U.S. Black Panthers, Weathermen, and Students for a Democratic Society, that in Canada is about to create Rochdale College, and in Europe is about to explode into the demonstrations of 1968, is also producing psychodelia, magic mushrooms, be-ins, and Aquarian astrology. One of the younger *Tish* poets is in New York City, struggling with heroin addiction. Another is rumoured to have joined a Buddhist sect in Tibet—friends are wondering aloud whether this is a sect that requires castration.

I found 1965–75 extremely difficult and exhilarating years. So much was possible and yet so little was being done. So many people imagined that their clothes, their communes, their drugs, their mysticisms, their folk musics, their sit-ins were changing society while, in fact, the only actions that were changing society were ones of raw power: the US Civil Rights demonstrators who risked and courted violence; the gunshots that killed Kennedy, Evers, King, and Malcolm X; the polls that persuaded Lyndon Johnson not to seek re-election; the plots that ended the career of Diefenbaker. When the oil crisis of 1973 raised prices and unemployment, we were back in a society as materialistic as that of the early '60s. Unable to evolve a sustaining internal politics, Rochdale College, with its mysticisms of non-interference and spon-

taneous cooperation, fell to the drug-dealing entrepreneurs who had seized its upper stories and to the banks that foreclosed its mortgage. Students who in 1972 had wanted to write poetry and read Leonard Cohen now wanted to get into business school and read Ayn Rand.

I can remember in 1969 sitting with Clark Blaise and Bharati Mukherjee in their Montreal living room, while Clark recounted how he had come to share Bharati's "Indian" response to a burned-out light bulb. She would walk into a room, notice the bulb burned out, and think "how interesting," he told us, as if the fates had ordained it to be burned out. But it would not occur to her that she had the power to replace it with an unbroken one. Within the various circulating 1960s discourses of mysticism, that story made sense to me in 1969. Today I would be more likely to refer the story to Bharati's upper-class Calcutta childhood, in which burned-out light bulbs would be mysteriously replaced by servants. Or to think of the story, and of the mystical discourses of the 1960s to which it belongs, as a sign of the feelings of political powerlessness so many people experienced even as the US Civil Rights movement and the various anti-Vietnam-war demonstrations were unfolding.

FIVE READINGS OF OLSON'S "MAXIMUS" (1970)

Once several years ago I had a dream in which I was back in my childhood house and having difficulty getting to the main floor. I could get to the dormer rooms of the second floor, where my grandmother had lived, amid the mahogany cabinets and chairs and English bone china she had saved from her Vancouver home, or I could get to the basement where my father kept his Model-T socket wrenches under a work bench he had built for himself out of old cross-arms and scrap lumber from his employer, the BC Electric. The dream, of course, leaves out my mother, sitting silently in between at the end of the kitchen table. It also leaves out her father, my grandfather, the builder of the jam cupboards that are also in this basement, the Frankland, the unheard voice behind the photos in my bedroom. Your grampa Brown was a fine man, my father would often say to me, in tones he did not use for my grandmother. Many of his tools were ones he had inherited from Grampa Brown. This dream, of course, was a classic Freudian dream, but does its Freudianness come from the house, from me, or from my having read Freud long after leaving the house?

*   *   *

There were no photos of my father's family anywhere in our house. There was a thirtieth wedding anniversary photo of my grandmother and Grampa Brown on the mahogany piano. A wedding photo of my mother and father in their bedroom. The largest photos were of Grampa Brown in his Canadian Expeditionary Force uniform in my bedroom.

*   *   *

One of the strongest impressions I have from my childhood is that nothing of much note took place between the year of my birth and the arrival of our first television set from Jimmy Fraser's new TV and Radio store in 1951. Another is that the years before my birth were the years of giant events and people, and that it would be years before my own world caught up. The last new car models made had come out in 1941. The streetcars in Vancouver, and the interurban tram that carried us from the village to Vancouver, had been made in the 1930s. President's Cars. Our big mahogany dining room suite, our tea wagon, our radio, our piano, had all been bought by my grandmother in the twenties and thirties and been brought to our house after my grandfather had died, in the summer of my birth. In White Rock, the seaside town south of Vancouver where my mother and father would take me during the war for a week of seaside holiday, only the hotel-owner's Austin, that picked us up at the bus stop, seemed to be moving. All the other cars were parked, sackcloth wrapped around the tires, waiting for the war to end.

When the war did end, nothing much changed. The new cars that appeared looked like the old cars. In 1948 my father purchased our first car, a 1946 Chevrolet that looked much like a 1940 Chev or a 1948 Chev. When he took us for our first drives around the Fraser Valley or into Vancouver, all the marvellous things that we saw—the Patullo Bridge, the

Vancouver City Hall, the power dams at Ruskin and Stave Falls, the Vedder Canal that had drained Chilliwack Lake and created Sumas Prairie—had been built before the war. Across the border in Washington state there were extravagant concrete bridges and highways with dates from the 1930s embossed into them.

EDWARD & PATRICIA (1984)

In 1975 I had joined the new editorial board of Coach House Press, which had been put together by owner Stan Bevington after Victor Coleman had resigned over his unhappiness with Stan's enthusiastic acquiring of computer typesetting technology. At least once a month the new board—my wife Linda, David Young, Rick/Simon, Michael Ondaatje, bpNichol, Dennis Reid, and Stan—met to select manuscripts and plan advertising strategies. Many of us—myself, bp, Mike, David, and Dennis—were authors who had been published by Coach, and there was a general expectation that we would continue to support the press by publishing some of our best work with it. One of our first new ventures was "Coach House Manuscript Editions," an attempt to publish books that would be stocked in our computers rather than our warehouse and be printed only as orders were received. Most of these were to be works-in-progress, and to be updated from time-to-time by the author, with the new version effectively erasing the older version from the computer. In 1979–80 I published three successive drafts of *War Poems* in this format, Mike Ondaatje published *Claude Glass*, and bpNichol published an early draft of a section of *The Martyrology* Book 5. The new board members worked both collectively and independently, with each able to bring to the press two titles a year, no questions asked, and able in addition to acquire the entitlements of editors who were unable to find suitable titles for a given year. I reminisce lengthily about this process in an essay—"The Beginnings of an End to Coach House Press"—in the spring 1997 issue of *Open Letter*. Collectively, we sorted and evaluated the unsolicited manuscripts and assigned them to individual board members to edit and "see" through production. bp published *The Martyrology* Books 3 & 4, in 1976, *Journal* in 1978, *The Martyrology* Book 5 in 1982, and *Zygal* in 1985. Mike Ondaatje published *Secular Love* in 1984 (after the board had

Explaining to Naim Kattan how to run The Canada Council, Victoria, 1987

collectively talked him out of the title "Raccoon Lighting"). I published *Capitalistic Affection!* in 1982 and *Edward & Patricia* in 1983.

Both bp and I, however, noticed that the sales of our Coach House books were lagging considerably behind the sales of books we had published with other publishers, and that sales of my two books and of his *Journal* and *Zygal* were also lagging behind sales of other Coach House titles. My suspicion was that one or two of the promotion staff regarded our books as suspect, possibly even as vanity titles, and were making few initiatives of their own to promote them. bp went as far as to say the staff didn't take the titles seriously. Was this because the staff were now up to twenty years younger than us? Was this because bp and I were offering fewer initiatives for promoting our own titles than we were making for those we were editing for Coach House by other authors? bp published only one more of his books, *The Martyrology* Book 6, with Coach House before his death in 1989. I stopped bringing books to Coach House, publishing *The Louis Riel Organ & Piano Company* with Turnstone Press in 1985

and *The Abbotsford Guide to India* with Press Porcépic in 1986.

The wonderful thing about publishing a book like *Edward & Patricia* at Coach House was the interest of the production staff. The type was produced from my Apple II computer's electronic file, transferred by modem to the Coach House Unix system. For the cover I purchased two porcelain dogs at a nearby shop on Bloor Street, which Stan Bevington photographed and made part of the cover. Now, as well as the two porcelain dogs, I also have Sigmund Dog, who sleeps beside me on a Belouchi rug as I write this. He is a Great Dane, almost four, and this week in mid-May is the number two ranking Great Dane show dog in Canada. This weekend we will both sleep in my van in the parking lot beside the Kitchener-Waterloo dog show.

EARLE BIRNEY (1971)

When I was young boy I was a boy soprano. No one noticed this fact at home but at elementary school each of six classrooms was configured as a choir and sent to compete at the Mission City music festival across the Fraser River. I always got to sing descant. At the festival I noticed that there were young boy soloists competing who couldn't sing as well as me, and so I asked my parents to arrange private singing lessons. As it happens my godmother, Marie Lobban, was the village singing teacher. She was also the wife of Lyle Lobban, the hard-drinking foreman of my father's B.C. Electric line gang, which was how she'd become my godmother. I probably hadn't seen her since my christening. I walked each week to the Lobban farmhouse on Mackenzie Road, past the barking black Lab chained to a tree in the yard, for my singing lessons. For three years in a row I placed second in the Mission festival to another of her students who later became my brother-in-law. On my fifteenth birthday, long after my voice had "broken," Marie Lobban gave me a gift, *Down the Long Table* by Earle Birney. She had heard about it on CKNW radio. It's the only gift I remember her giving me. This was how I found out about Earle Birney, who lived fifty miles away and was the best-known poet in British Columbia.

I read the novel but didn't think much more about Birney until I was at UBC and he was its famous writer-professor who much of the time was away in South America or Europe or Asia researching or travelling. In my third year he was not away, and I took his senior Chaucer course along with a bunch of graduate students, and he taught as if the prioress and miller and nun's priest were all alive, and at the end gave me an "A" and less than that to some of the grad students. The next time I saw him, eleven years had passed and I was writing a book on the author Earle Birney because I'd gone to my first Toronto literary cocktail party in June 1969 and Gary Geddes had said "You wanna write a book on Earle Birney?" I'd said sure, because I figured it was about time I wrote that kind of book. Now when I want a Toronto book contract, I go there and seek out a literary cocktail party.

After the party I discovered that the more I found out about Earle Birney the author, the more he seemed like Frank Davey. Considering all his conflicts and compromises, this was not necessarily a good thing to discover. I was careful to conclude by declaring him an outstanding poet.

D-DAY AND AFTER (1962)

D-Day and After was my first book, although not my first writing. There was another collection of poems, unpublished, that immediately preceded them in which I had tried to write myself into poetry for a young woman, and before that numerous poems that I wrote to be a writer of poems. For several years those poems took me into the meetings of a student club at the University of British Columbia, The Writers' Workshop, and eventually to the young woman. It was 1960, and poetry could still be a young woman.

I had gone young to university, bored with high school like my son and daughter would be much later, and having completed the last two years of high school in one. It would be two years before I could stop seeing university girls as older women and break the habit of dating high school girls who, as blond and wonderful as they were, and as fond of White Spot hamburgers, knew almost nothing of my university hours or even that I wrote poems and stories so I could be a writer at the Writers' Workshop. Or revealed much of their own other hours. So far so ordinary. I was yet to learn that someone could be much more important to me than I was to them, or that I could be more important to some else. . . .

Nevertheless, the University of British Columbia was a pretty good place in the late 1950s for a kid from a one-high-school dairy-farming town in the Fraser Valley. Because my dad worked on the line gang, I managed to win a B.C. Electric Company special scholarship. UBC was the only university and best university in the province, recently enriched academically, like many Canadian universities of the time, by the flight of American academics from the McCarthy investigations, and from the dominance of cold war ideologies that had followed. (I learned very quickly that among the best Americans are the ones who leave.) There were lots of middle-class kids from Vancouver and Victoria, kids for whom going to UBC was no more momentous than proceeding from grade school to high school. But there were also lots of kids from elsewhere in the province, kids who like me were among the one, two, or three from their high schools to get to university. For some reason it was mostly these who became my friends— among them Gladys Hindmarch from Ladysmith, Carol Johnson (later Carol Bolt) from Fort St.

John, Bob Hogg from Abbotsford and Langley, George Bowering from Oliver, Lionel Kearns and Fred Wah from Nelson. Some of their names may now be widely known, but they were new to me and have kept that newness.

CULTURAL MISCHIEF (1996)

I really wish Greg Curnoe hadn't died. Friendship is sometimes an urgency to listen one to the other. In three days I am going to give a reading from *Cultural Mischief* at the local artists-run gallery, The Forest City, which Greg helped found. I moved here to London, Ontario, on the first of July of 1990. I thought of it as Greg's hometown, although it was also James Reaney's town and Jack Chambers's town, Jamelie Hassan's town and Christopher Dewdney's town. Greg had painted all kinds of abrasive and mischievous work including a public portrait—part of his Montreal/Dorval airport mural—of Lyndon Johnson masturbating as his soldiers died in Vietnam. The day we arrived it was Greg and Sheila's twenty-fifth wedding anniversary and they threw a garden party where we met almost everyone they'd ever known in London. Greg was so skeptical of the US that he always refused to be exhibited there. Now another million dollar's worth of his paintings have been bought by the Art Gallery of Ontario and will never be sold in the US. Almost all the autobiographical propositions I would make about Greg and me are hidden away among the lines of *Cultural Mischief*. Silly little things like helping him dig into the river bank below his house for artifacts from the printers and iron-workers and native peoples who had lived there before him. Like finding near Chatham a house that had bullet holes and a rusty US sword from the War of 1812. Like his taking me to see the childhood homes of Christopher and Jamelie.

If writing or painting isn't mischievous, if it doesn't disarrange the culturally familiar and demand reconsiderations, I'm usually not interested. Most of the poetry written these days is just more boring advertisement for the sensitivity of the writer, who then award each other prizes for sensitivity. Greg would rather have been thought aggressively inquisitive than sensitive. My poetry, thank god, like Greg's paintings doesn't win prizes. He constructed dozens of self-portraits, some with watercolour, some with large rubber stamp letters, painting versions of himself into being the way a writer might write selves into being. He wanted to know who he could be, and how much of him had already been painted long before he breathed or painted.

NOTES ON THE LANGUAGE OF THE CONTEMPORARY CANADIAN LONG POEM (1983)

I cannot remember my grandmother not living with us, but I know that she did not arrive until 1941. She had become chronically ill after Grampa Brown died, and come to believe that she had been told by her doctors that she had one year to live. He had died of a cerebral hemorrhage two months after my birth. My mother called it a cebereal hemorrhage. He was fifty-seven. She said he had died because he had got blood poisoning in the trenches in Flanders and had received a saline injection. A war injury. Six months before he died, he had gone to the army recruiting office to volunteer for World War II, she said. Families are full of biographical self-fashioning.

My grandmother died in 1964, almost two years after my first marriage. So I grew up with two women and a war and a father and the memory of another father, but the precise dynamics of this grouping are slippery. What can I do, my mother once asked my grandmother as she came into the kitchen as dinner was being prepared. Here, boil some water, my grandmother replied. My father and grandmother sat across the kitchen table and argued about politics. My grandmother did the laundry in the basement with our Maytag wringer washer, while my mother carried the wet clothes upstairs and hung them on the line. My grandmother made our Christmas shortbread, mince tarts, and cake, from recipes she had copied from her mother's in Yorkshire. My grandmother supervised my evening prayers and went with me to Sunday school. My father made me a wooden chair and table and sheet-metal blackboard for me to do school work at in the year before I went to school. My mother took me to piano lessons. My grandmother ordered breeches and short pants for me from Eaton's catalog so I could be dressed like an English schoolboy. When grade one began and I refused to keep attending unless I had long pants like the other

"Conspiring with Robert Hogg," Ottawa, 1990

boys, it was my grandmother who took me to a store to find them.

Sometimes I have been told that I had two mothers. Sometimes I've wondered whether my mother was the closest I will ever come to having a sister. When I was ten we walked up the highway together to the fall fair. We had a good time until the horseshow when Ken Turnbull, one of the farmers who was supervising, yelled at us that kids weren't allowed to sit in the stands, and my mother yelled back that he should shut his "shitty mouth." When I was sixteen my father taught me to drive in his brand new Plymouth Belvedere, and she decided she should also learn to drive and so my father enrolled her in a driving school. Shortly after she told my father that she'd heard from a friend that I had rolled the Plymouth but managed to get a body shop to repair it before bringing it back the same evening. When I was eight I disagreed with her about the instructions my piano teacher had written in my book. She slapped my face and I disagreed. She slapped my face with her hand and the stone of her diamond ring, and I disagreed. She called my father and asked him to punish me for calling her a liar and I disagreed. She said I had gone out of my mind and that they were going to take me to the mental hospital in New Westminster, and I disagreed. She sent my father to back the car out of the garage. I don't remember where my grandmother was. I don't remember whether I agreed. All this not remembering is not a good sign. All of this is in *War Poems*, the unfinished book, the book now unfinished for twenty years.

THE CLALLAM; OR OLD GLORY IN JUAN DE FUCA (1973)

The last of my shipwreck poems. So far. I am not anti-American, only a skeptic toward America.

The commercial causes of the *Clallam*'s sinking predict the causes of the Westray mine disaster, the Bre-X gold fraud, the loss of the *Titanic*. It was the captain of the *Clallam*, avoiding the assistance of Canadian ships, insisting on being towed twenty-six miles back to his US port rather than two or three miles to Victoria, who invoked differences between the two countries. And the fatality list, which included all the ship's Canadians.

Abbotsford, the village where I grew up, was two miles from the US border-crossing that led toward Bellingham, Washington. The proximity could make one more rather than less aware of difference. Half of the buildings in Sumas, the US border town, were taverns. Most of the American men seemed to have crew cuts and wear military-style clothing. On Dominion Day in 1950, the US Custom's agent made my dad remove the Canadian flag he had tied to our car's antenna. Most American towns and cities could think of only a few strange names for their streets—Jefferson, Van Buren, Lexington, State. The police wore their guns with the butts and hammers visible. The Highway Patrol wore Stetsons in which I read the possibly random violence of cowboys. They were about to execute Julius and Ethel.

David Robinson was editor at Talonbooks, which was publishing *The Clallam*. He was a fan as well as an editor, and kept after me to send him more manuscripts—*King of Swords* the year before, *The Arches* in 1980. He liked the smartass dimensions of my books, the passages that were formally or rhetorically or socially outrageous, the surprise discursive shifts between pages. I do too—poetry that is the putting together of fragments of language that seem never before to have been juxtaposed. Until he left Talon in the mid-1980s, he kept asking me to let the press publish *War Poems,* which he'd seen parts of in the Coach House manuscript editions of 1979. His partner Karl Siegler, who now owns the press outright, has been similarly supportive of the rhetoric and politics of my books, their various sardonic edges. It was Karl who helped me sharpen the focus of *Reading "KIM" Right* and edited its chapters by return fax in order to get it into print by the opening of the 1993 Canadian federal election campaign, and who helps me produce Talon's New Canadian Criticism series.

CITY OF THE GULLS AND SEA (1964)

The city is Victoria, to which Helen and I moved in 1963. Sunny and cool. On Sundays we would drive around the waterfront because we could think of nothing else to do. If you think this doesn't make sense, it doesn't make sense to me, either. In the evenings, she would sometimes have us drive to the Woolco department store, the only large store that was open, to have something to do. Modernist ennuie. Sometimes we argued, and she would run out of the apartment, get into her Hillman Minx, and drive away aimlessly. I would run after her, jump into my TR4, and follow her until she drove back to the apartment. I don't remember what we argued about.

Our first apartment was on Richardson Street, in Fairfield, close to the downtown but about ten miles from Colwood and my work at Royal Roads Military College. Each morning I would drive out along the Gorge waterway to the college, which was located on Sir James Dunsmuir's old estate of Hatley Park. The main building was the Edwardian "castle" Dunsmuir had built with its ballroom and billiard room, which was now the officers' mess of the college and where the steward, a young enlisted man, would bring me lunch. The Dunsmuir family had made its money at the turn of the century by underpaying Chinese laborers to work its coal mines—most of which money its daughters gambled away in Monaco. The cadets were obliged to salute me anywhere on the grounds. In the classrooms they would sit at attention when I entered, and the class leader would request permission to "relax dress," which meant they wished to be able to loosen their ties. On average they were three to four years younger than me. My tie was one I had recently bought for these occasions. Sometimes I played billiards with the younger officers, who were likeable guys although they seldom had much to say about the ideology of literature.

For Helen the two highlights of the academic year were the Christmas and Graduation balls at the college. For each ball she sewed herself a new gown, determined to present herself more memorably than any of the other faculty or military staff wives. She was young and pretty and this goal, given the possibilities she could identify for herself in this city, delighted her, and why not. There were no women's washrooms in the main classroom block where the ball was held, and so half of the men's washrooms were converted to women's by the insertion of huge sprays of flowers into each urinal. Or so Helen and the other women reported.

Meanwhile, outside the college, the 1960s were unfolding, and male university teachers were discarding their ties and teaching in blue jeans, like I do now in 1997. One of the young officers played a guitar and his wife had subversive records by Peter, Paul, and Mary. I had no close friends, not even the dark-haired Dorothy, a teen-age poet and evening hippie I sometimes secretly took to poetry readings. I washed and polished the TR4 regularly, and kept it supplied with new Pirellis. After our 1965 summer in Los Angeles we moved to an apartment on Boyd Street in James Bay, an apartment that looked much like the one on Richardson. After spending 1966–67 in Los Angeles, we bought a split-level three-bedroom house on Cook Street in Victoria that was decorated much like the two apartments. That year, at the Christmas Ball, I met my present wife, Linda, who was married to a new member of the Royal Roads English Department with whom I shared a telephone. She had stayed in Vancouver rather than move with him to Victoria. The telephone sat in a hole cut in the wall between our two offices.

CAPITALISTIC AFFECTION! (1982)

I think of this as my bpNichol book. I think of this as my last book of the poetry years of the 1960s, which began ending in the mid-70s. bp had a comics collection that filled twenty or more feet of specially-constructed shelves that themselves filled, from floor to ceiling, an entire room of his Toronto house. I used to visit that room and re-read the comics I had more innocently read in the 1940s and early '50s, learning how I had learned to believe many of the things I now believed without wanting to. Sometimes bp would arrive at our house with a new spread of colour comics he had just acquired, and sit reading and chortling. *Maggie and Jiggs. Dick Tracy.*

My favorite comics had been American war-celebrating ones—*Johnny Hazard, Terry and the Pirates, Steve Canyon.* I had thought the geometric rows of rivets on a DC-3 or P-51 were the pinnacle of modernist aesthetics. I had thought the Dragon Lady much more dangerously attractive than I've ever thought Margaret Atwood. So much for Canadian cultural sovereignty. So much for sharing years with a woman.

I think of this as one of my lost books. I wonder if the staff at Coach House Press ever mailed out review copies. I think of it as my most Canadian book, punctuated as it is with quotations from some of my least favorite Canadian critics. I re-read the poems about Dagwood's grief and Narda's ennuie and wonder how sad I must have been there in north Toronto in 1980. Maybe someday a biographer will happen by and tell me.

Davey and his wife Linda at an English department party given in his honour, York University, Toronto, 1990

CANADIAN LITERARY POWER (1994)

Robert Kroetsch said that this book made "possible new understandings of how literature enters into dialogue with politics, economics, and the modes of cultural production in a society . . . we call Canada." Terry Goldie said that here was Frank Davey leaping again "from the expected path, changing and growing like no other critic in Canadian Literature." Frank Davey says he hopes they are right, about the leaps, the understandings. But not about the "no other critic." I need this "no other critic," just like I need the "no other writer," to be the writer I imagine myself being. One comes into being relationally. At the time *Canadian Literary Power* was being released, I was starting a two-year term as president of the Association of Canadian University Teachers of English (ACUTE), and I was not going to do this job alone. The story of my life is a story of a field of people in a small house in Abbotsford, in an old army hut briefly called the *Tish* office, in and around a journal called *Open Letter,* in and around meetings and conferences in Edmonton, Strasbourg, Ottawa, Seattle, Siena, Delhi, and Saskatoon where writers, friends, and colleagues have gathered, in and around a Toronto coach house still known as Coach House Books or Coach House Printing—places where bp and Barbara Godard and my wife Linda and my children Michael and Sara and my other companions and competitors have all in different and incomparable ways offered possibilities of being. *Canadian Literary Power* begins with a remark by bp but opens from there into the Canadian field of writing in which texts and publishers and awards and journals have provided an array of terms and struggles which over forty years have helped make my and others' imaginations of "Frank Davey." Without them I would not have read, imagined, or responded.

BRIDGE FORCE (1965)

Most of the poems in *Bridge Force* were written in the *Tish* office at the University of British Columbia, and published in *Tish* itself, and then included in my MA thesis, although it took two more years for the book to appear. Robert Creeley was one of my thesis supervisors. A crucial stage in my becoming a writer was a move from writing that was occasioned mostly by emotional crisis and urgency to writing that was occasioned mostly by the satisfaction of having created textual meaning. This is a not a simple or binary move. Even writing that arises from emotional desolation and anguish is motivated in part by the pleasure and recompense of giving textual shape to that anguish. Even the creation of an abstract form is somewhere motivated. When I was in my twenties and early thirties, my writing friends and I often talked about other friends who we thought were "crisis poets"—poets who risked their relationships, and sometimes their lives, in order to have crises that would move them to write. I think it was Robert Duncan who first pointed out this problem to us. Most of the poems of *Bridge Force* were written in the aftermath of my (self-induced?) crisis over Daphne Buckle. Although there is also in this book a stepping back, a search for historical or philosophical context, for value beyond the hurtin'-songs of lost love.

I remember getting different advice from Creeley in a Montreal bar in 1970, when he said I wasn't willing to take enough risks for my writing. This, of course, was the man that once wrote that for love he would break open his beloved's skull and put a candle behind her eyes. I was beginning to perceive such desires as problematic. I was both pissed-off by his presumption and amused because of how chaotic and chancy my life had been over the last six months, during which I had secretly written much of the prose-poem book *Weeds,* broken up with Helen, eloped on five-day's notice from Victoria to Montreal with Linda, who then was still married to my ex-Royal Roads-colleague Roger but was now pregnant with our son Michael, and left my job at Roads to live for a year in eastern Canada. I published eight books between 1970 and 1973.

The question of crisis poetry is closely related to the limitations of the lyric and to the repetitiveness of lyric angst. How many times can one fall on the thorns of life, wittily or sensuously bleed, and hope a reader cares? Duncan saw the writing of poetry as a vocation, a calling both into a community of poets and into the much larger community of social concern. The risk to be taken, he wrote in *Tish* 13, is the risk of giving up the personal aggrandisement of "the witty possibilities of political and sexual reference" for "the reality of the City the poets live in." There was another risk that Duncan also urged one take,

Davey giving the keynote address at the Canadian Studies Conference in Jammu, Kashmir, 1996

the risk of breaking with the language forms with which one had become comfortable, of breaking with—as I wrote in *Arcana* in 1970—"poems that reproduce the pages of past living." People have never known quite what to expect when opening a Frank Davey book, which has sometimes been a marketing problem for my publishers but a satisfaction to the writer.

THE ARCHES (1980)

The Arches was my second book of selected poems and was edited by that other publicly apprenticing poet bpNichol. Anyone who has two selected poems published before he is forty, and one of them edited by bpNichol, is very lucky. *The Arches* was titled after a poem by that name that recalled my father, his building of arches out of old hydro poles and cross-arms beside our house, and his singing, *sotto voce,* sexually suggestive lyrics to 1920's songs. "Underneath her arches," he sang, "happiness is there." My father was preoccupied, mystified, by sex and sexually vibrant women. I was finding out. Did he know that his small boy was slowly understanding his small alterations to the song? Later he was terrified and attracted in turn by both my wives—that they seemed to be women while his own wife was, as he called her, a little girl. That they returned his shy innuendos with jokes of their own, and defied his requests to be specially attentive to their mother-in-law. After he died in 1985 I found a tattered French-language cartoon of beach adventures in which the hero's dick sneaked out the side of his bathing suit and underneath the arches of the crotches of delighted young ladies while their boyfriends or parents stood by unsuspecting. My mother had known it was there and seemed to be waiting for me to discover it. He had died suddenly from a metastasized prostate cancer. In my last memory of him, he's in his pajamas walking down the hall to the bathroom to pass more blood, and looks back sheepishly to attempt a wry joke.

My father was always worried about my marriages, worried that I had taken on more woman than was wise. Sometimes I too was worried that I had. Sometimes I thought he was recalling his own mother, that tall and determined Ontario farm girl whom his father had beaten when he couldn't stop her from earning extra money by cleaning the church across the street on East 29th Avenue, who had then left him despite having to leave her sons, had re-married to a meek Cockney man shorter than her, bought a house, and surreptitiously met with her sons despite all his attempts to prevent this. My father had been four, his brother seven. My father adored and feared his mother. When I brought my wives home, I loved to see the fear in his smile.

Arcana (1973)

You write a book in which all of the poems are responses to the cards of the Tarot pack and the last poem denies magic. This is the story, or my story, of the sixties, a struggle for agency. It is one thing to admit one cannot foresee the field of events—the coincidences, aggressions, syntheses that the interactions of agencies produce—another not to know one can change a light bulb. Curiously, in 1969, I pursued my present wife Linda, even when she claimed not to want me to, and not out of any sense of inevitability but because I was fortuitously arrogant enough to believe I could. Mysticism is the opiate of the disappointed. Things are because they were meant to be. The broccoli, I wrote, burns in the pan.

Moving from Montreal to Toronto in the summer of 1970, Linda and I had few understandings of the city, and few connections with it. Those connections—York University, and its English department, which had hired me, and Coach House Press—i.e. Victor Coleman—which was publishing *Weeds* even as we arrived and would publish *Arcana* in 1973, were my connections, and left Linda groping for ways to locate herself. I don't think I understood that, because this particular inequality had never happened to me before. At Coach House I felt partly alienated by my relatively secure job, pension plan, Ph.D. I missed George. I remember Victor and Sarah inviting us to their apartment in Rochdale, us stepping over the various Harley-Davidsons parked in the lobby, feeling like tourists in their apartment. Maybe Victor felt similarly in the house we were buying in north Toronto. I remember later when Victor was living on Ward's Island off the Toronto waterfront, and we visited him one winter Sunday afternoon for dinner. The only way to and from the island was by pedestrian ferry and the hourly island bus. We took ten-month-old Michael with us in his new snow suit. When we left we had to walk about half a mile to the bus which would take us to the ferry. It was about -10 Fahrenheit, with a stiff wind. Linda still hadn't got over the BC habit of wearing light winter clothes. The last hundred yards was across a windy field to the bus shelter. About half way across Linda began stumbling, and then said she couldn't go any further. I ran with Michael to the bus shelter and left him inside it, then ran back to get Linda. When I reached her, I could see the bus approaching. I was very cold too. She got back to her feet and inspired mostly by the bus managed to walk to the shelter and the now waiting bus. Afterward she said she could understand how people could freeze to death in Ontario within sight of assistance. It had been no time to be mystical. By 1976 Linda had enrolled in the very non-mystical Osgoode Hall Law School, and by 1980 was a lawyer on Bay Street. Despite my misgivings, this address did not require her to become a Bay Street lawyer.

L'An Trentiesme: Selected Poems 1961–70 (1972)

Anyone who gets his selected poems published when he is thirty years old is either lucky, unlucky, or precocious. bpNichol and I once reflected that he and I were different from many writers because unlike them we went through our apprenticeships publicly. At thirty years I and these poems had not faded from someone's memory but were being typed up for photo-offset reproduction at the York Street Commune in Vancouver, the city of my birth. There was a sort of direct line from Stan Persky at the commune, who operated Vancouver Community Press, and *Tish,* because he had been its editor in 1969–70 for its last few issues. Then *Tish* segued into Dan MacLeod's alternative newspaper *The Georgia Straight* and became *The Georgia Straight Writing Supplement.* It was a busy year.

1970 was also the year that my son Michael was born, a few weeks after Linda rode in the back seat of a speeding Montreal cab with Allen Ginsberg beside her rubbing her large abdomen through her coat and singing his adaptations of Blake's songs of innocence and experience. The cabbie kept turning around to look. The songs and scores were published soon after in *Tish E.* Linda and I took another Montreal cab from our house to the hospital and sat there playing gin rummy until 2 A.M. and Michael seemed nearly ready to be born. And yet he wasn't ready, Linda later reported. He was born offended, pissed off, enraged by the lights and hard surfaces and other discomforts of the outside world. I could sympathize. Scowling and serious, he reminded me of my father. He is still very serious and fond of women. I remember afterward walking out of the hospital into the cool March night and thinking everything had changed, and of course it had.

ABBOTSFORD GUIDE TO INDIA (1986)

India is where Columbus and Cabot and Cartier all hoped to have been going and now I have been there several times and they have not. I was not born a world traveller. I was not even born in Abbotsford, because my mother and father had moved there only the year before my birth and being a city girl she didn't like the village hospital and rode the interurban tram back to Vancouver to give birth to me. She would not have liked hospitals in India.

Most of my life I have been like my father in wanting to be close to home and to a woman whose presence makes a house home. I think I learned this from my father, and that he learned it in 1914 when he was four years old

and his mother left home and did not return except to visit neighbours where she could secretly touch her children. Except when his work on the BC Electric line gang took him away overnight, he never travelled without my mother. This is not easy to write because I made it up too long ago. It also made travelling difficult because when I was away, like in 1974 when I made a reading tour of the western Canadian arctic, I would pay less attention to where I was than to my desire to be back home.

In the 1960s I used to think that it was class and low income that had kept me from travelling outside North America. And in the 1970s low income and small children. By 1982 I had maybe developed some critical intelligence. The cover of *The Abbotsford Guide to India* shows an Indian woman tourist in a sari relaxing at a shepherds' camp in the Himalayas high above Pahalgam in Kashmir. The horses which have brought her and me there are grazing in the background. When I thought of applying to go to India, I had not thought of riding in Kashmir. The Shastri Indo-Canadian Institute had advertised for four specialists in Canadian Literature to conduct a four-week workshop in the spring of 1982 for junior Indian faculty at a university in central India. I had never been able to get myself to leave North America, so I thought if I could go to India I could go anywhere. In 1961 when I had been graduating from UBC I had applied to CUSO (Canadian University Students Overseas) to go and work on a CUSO aid project in Sarawak, but I must have failed the interview. Instead I stayed in Vancouver and helped start *Tish* and the rest of this "I" is now history.

I can recall wishing many times I was not in India and many times that I was nearer to leaving India, but I can't recall being homesick in India. I was too busy being warm, too busy working to figure out what it might be that I was seeing, too busy hanging onto the back of a scooter, a pony, an elephant. Rosemary Sullivan and I got to Delhi earlier than the other two of our workshop team, and went off to Jaipur to lecture at the university. We spent four days there, most of it in the back of Ravi Das's scooter rickshaw, which I'd persuaded Rosemary we should rent, along with Ravi, early the second morning when we couldn't get seats on the city tour bus. Most of this part of my life lurks somewhere in *The Abbotsford Guide to India.* On the third day Ravi's scooter

"Showing Sigmund, my Great Dane," Sarnia, 1996

had labored, stalling twice, up the hill to the Amber Palace. I remember the dry eroded mountains, Ravi's optimism, the cold Limca sold by the roadside vendors. After the workshop in Dharwad, in northern Karnatika, I stayed another month, travelling slowly, sometimes alone, sometimes with Rosemary, from Bombay to Aurangabad, Udaipur, Srinagar, Khajuraho, Varanasi, and Delhi.

India opened for me onto Yugoslavia, Germany, France, Italy, Turkey, and so on into Europe. A reversal of the Aryan migrations. I was back again in 1988 for a conference in Delhi celebrating the two decades of the Shastri Institute. A small narrative of the conference opens my *Popular Narratives*. I spent four days in Bombay afterward visiting the Canadian Studies Centre of SNDT Women's University. I went around Bombay taking photographs of the Victorian buildings that had been depicted on the postcards my great-uncle Jack Kirkup had sent my grandmother in 1905. I returned for three weeks earlier this year, spending New Year's Eve in Jammu listening to gunfire and won-

dering if it was celebratory or political. Nita Ramaiya at SNDT had translated the *Abbotsford Guide* into Gujarati and published it through the university. I rode the amazingly crowded Bombay suburban trains with new friends at the university. At a reading that Nita arranged, two of my poems were read in each of Gujarati, Bengali, Maharashtri, English, Kanada, Hindi, and Malayalam. I ate chicken biryani from a banana leaf on the train from Bombay to Baroda. I found a ride to the Shore Temple in Mahabalipuram. I stayed for three quiet days in the guesthouse of Professor Narasimhaiah's ashram-like estate, in the countryside west of Mysore. I took an overnight train Madurai, and another one to Trivandrum. On the latter the young Indian man in my compartment was afraid to leave the train at his stop until a soldier who was standing on the semi-dark platform agreed to escort him. I travelled back to Bombay where all one Sunday the men and boys fly kites, from the rooftops, from the bridge over the railway tracks, from the field-hockey grounds, from the cricket grounds. Some kites get caught in strange winds, and dashed to the roofs of seven-story buildings. Some lose their cords and sail purposefully at medium altitude southward across the city.

BIBLIOGRAPHY

Poetry:

The Scarred Hull, Imago (Calgary), 1966.

Weeds, Coach House Press (Toronto), 1970.

King of Swords, Talonbooks (Vancouver), 1972.

The Clallam; or Old Glory in Juan de Fuca, Talonbooks, 1973.

Capitalistic Affection!, Coach House Press, 1982.

Edward & Patricia, Coach House Press, 1984.

The Abbotsford Guide to India, Press Porcepic (Victoria, British Columbia), 1986.

Poetry chapbooks:

City of the Gulls and Sea, privately printed (Victoria), 1964.

Griffon, Masassauga Editions (Toronto), 1972.

War Poems, Coach House Press, 1979.

Postcard Translations, Underwhich Editions (Toronto), 1988.

Poetry collections:

D-Day and After, Tishbooks (Vancouver), 1962.

Bridge Force, Contact Press, 1965.

Four Myths for Sam Perry, Talonbooks, 1970.

L'An Trentiesme: Selected Poems 1961–70, Vancouver Community Press, 1972.

Arcana, Coach House Press, 1973.

The Arches: Selected Poems, edited and introduced by bpNichol, Talonbooks, 1980.

The Louis Riel Organ & Piano Company, Turnstone Press (Winnipeg), 1985.

Popular Narratives, Talonbooks, 1991.

Cultural Mischief: A Practical Guide to Multi-culturalism, Talonbooks, 1996.

Criticism:

Five Readings of Olson's "Maximus," Beaver-Kosmos (Montreal), 1970.

Earle Birney (Studies in Canadian Literature 11), Copp Clark (Toronto), 1971.

From There to Here: A Guide to English-Canadian Literature since 1960 (Our Nature/Our Voices, Vol. 2), Press Porcepic (Erin, Ontario), 1974.

Louis Dudek and Raymond Souster (Studies in Canadian Literature 14), Douglas and McIntyre (Vancouver), 1980.

Notes on the Language of the Contemporary Canadian Long Poem, Island Writing Series (Lantzville, British Columbia), 1983.

Surviving the Paraphrase: Eleven Essays on Canadian Literature, Turnstone Press, 1983.

Margaret Atwood: A Feminist Poetics, Talonbooks, 1984.

Reading Canadian Reading, Turnstone Press, 1988.

Post-National Arguments: The Politics of the Anglophone-Canadian Novel Since 1967, University of Toronto Press, 1993.

Reading "Kim" Right, Talonbooks, 1993.

Canadian Literary Power: Essays on Anglophone-Canadian Literary Conflict, NeWest Press (Edmonton), 1994.

Karla's Web: A Cultural Examination of the Mahaffy-French Murders, Viking/Penguin (Toronto), 1994, revised edition, 1995.

Editor:

Wyndham Lewis, *Mrs. Duke's Million,* Coach House Press, 1977.

(With Jari Brodie) Opal L. Nations, *The Browser's Opal L. Nations,* Coach House Press, 1981.

Judith Fitzgerald, *Given Names: New and Selected Poems, 1972–1985,* Black Moss Press (Windsor, Ontario), 1985.

(With Fred Wah) *The SwiftCurrent Anthology,* The Coach House Press, 1986.

Greg Curnoe, *Deeds/Abstracts: The History of a London Lot,* Brick Books (London, Ontario), 1995.

(With Neal Ferris) Greg Curnoe, *Deeds/Nations,* London Chapter of the Ontario Archaeological Society, 1996.

Contributor to numerous anthologies, including *Poetry/Poesie 64,* edited by John Robert Colombo and Jacques Gobout, Ryerson, 1965; *How Do I Love Thee: Sixty Poets of Canada (and Quebec) Select and Introduce their Favorite Poems,* edited by John Robert Colombo, Hurtig, 1970; *Skookum Wawa,* edited by Gary Geddes, Oxford University Press, 1975; *The Poets of Canada,* edited by John Robert Colombo, Hurtig, 1978; *The Long Poem Anthology,* edited by Michael Ondaatje, Coach House Press, 1979; *The Maple Laugh Forever,* edited by Douglas Barbour and Stephen Scobie, Hurtig, 1981; *The New Oxford Anthology of Canadian Verse,* edited by Margaret Atwood, Oxford University Press, 1982; *An Anthology of Canadian Literature in English,* edited by Donna Bennett and Russell Brown, Oxford University Press, 1983; *The Contemporary Canadian Poem Anthology,* edited by George Bowering, Coach House Press, 1983; *A Walk by the Seine: Canadian Poets on Paris,* edited by Cary Fagan, Black Moss Press, 1995. Contributor of poems, articles, and reviews to numerous magazines, including *Boundary 2, Canadian Literature, The British Journal of Canadian Studies, Paragraph, West Coast Line, Etudes Canadiennes, Rampike,* and *Canadian Poetry.* Editor of *Tish,* 1961–63; *Open Letter,* 1965—; Coach House Press, 1976–96.

Edward Field

1924-

Though I learned poetry from reading modern poets like W. H. Auden and Hart Crane, who took pride in being difficult, my poetry is defiantly easy to understand. But the "moderns" were part of an arts generation that rejected popular culture. Looked at another way, Modern Poetry was always about demonstrating its superiority over the common herd, setting oneself apart from the banalities of the "philistines." In short, it was out to sound different from the daily papers.

I am less interested in that. Even if I too am critical of materialism, capitalism, the conventions, I cannot identify with the snobbishness of many poets. My poetry speaks to ordinary people, aims for common ground. It has grown directly out of what I come from, and, though I've developed and changed in many ways, I've seen little reason to "rise above it." So a detailed examination of my family and childhood is pertinent to my development as a poet, and to an understanding of my poetry.

My parents were simple Jews who emigrated from Eastern Europe. That does not mean they were simple at all. Like most Jews, they were complex people, with a strong sense of Jewishness, compounded of a history of persecution and suffering and a long tradition of literacy and learning. Humor was part of wisdom, crucial to it, in fact, and I could never understand putting "light verse" into a separate category, as if being funny made it less serious. My favorite poet, W. H. Auden, was undeniably serious and got away with ignoring such restrictions.

Though my parents became free thinkers and raised us without religion, I and my five brothers and sisters never forgot we were Jews. The village of Lynbrook, twenty miles by Long Island Railroad from the city, where we spent our childhood after the family moved from Brooklyn where I was born, would not let us forget. In the thirties, Nassau County, where Lynbrook was located, was a center of the German-American Bund and a hotbed of anti-

Edward Field, at eleven years old, with his sister Barbara, two years old

Semitism. I knew I was in trouble when, my first day in school, a teacher came into the classroom and asked sharply if I was the Jew. Even in New York City, then, many occupations were closed to Jews and my father had to change his name from Feldman to Field in order to get a job as a commercial artist in the advertising department of MGM.

But though we now lived in a completely WASP neighborhood, completely American, my upbringing was European. My father was the typical Old World parent, responsible in material ways, but tyrannical. He believed that children must be trained. My mother's slaps and

My mother in 1920

spankings were never in the same class as his, which usually involved the razor strop or belt. I was so cowed that even outside the house, I never could fight back when attacked by other boys. Even with years of therapy, I've never recovered from these humiliations.

Though my parents came out of poverty, they had been influenced by the post-Napoleonic Jewish enlightenment as well as the Eastern European socialist tradition. My mother read Tolstoy and other Russian classics as soon as she learned to read after coming to America as a child. Later, she became a follower of Bernard McFadden and went through a vegetarian stage of feeding us raw vegetables. She was a believer in the benefits of nudism and whenever possible, as on vacations in remote Maine, we all had to take off our bathing suits and run around naked. She also believed in eurythmic dancing, and encouraged us to leap wildly around the room with her, "expressing ourselves," whenever the gypsy music she loved played on the radio—the radio was always tuned to classical music in our house. In fact, by my father's strict rules, we were forbidden to lis-

ten to popular music, or go to the movies like other children, though we were allowed to listen to the radio serials after school.

We were all given music lessons, and while my two older sisters showed aptitude for the violin and piano, I, an undersized child, was saddled with a cello, an instrument as large as I was, which I lugged to school for years, starting in the sixth grade, to play in the high school orchestra. Evenings, our house rocked to the sound of each of us practicing in a different room. Under the direction of Mr. Silverman, my older sister's violin teacher, my sisters and I played trios and performed in local events. For several months when I was a teenager, we had our own radio program of "light classics." "The Field Family Trio and Their Romantic Melodies," the announcer would say, as we launched into our theme song, "Moment Musicale."

In many other ways we were at odds with the values of the neighborhood we lived in. My parents were the rare Democrats in a staunchly Republican town. But even worse was our atheism. If asked our nationality by other children, we were told to say we were American-Jews. But as to religion, we were to declare we were atheists. When we went around innocently announcing this, we were set upon by the other children and beaten up. When we turned to our father for support he would tell us, airily, to reason with them. His only attempt to protect us was a single foray he made to our grammar school to threaten a teacher who had smacked my sisters. On the whole he preferred to ignore the punishment we were taking, feeling that he was giving us the advantages he had never enjoyed in his boyhood shtetl in Russia, and besides, life wasn't easy for Jews anywhere and we'd better get used to it.

Even in a town that mostly ignored world events, I became aware of what was going on, with the German-American Bund meeting in high school auditoriums and swastikas scrawled on telephone poles. My parents occasionally had visitors from New York City who discussed things like socialism, and my mother, thrilled by the "success" of communism, told us that after the revolution in Russia the prisoners were let out of jail and Jews were free to go to Moscow. One night I overheard a conversation of adults around the dining room table discussing whether it would do any good to convert to Christianity to protect the children. Our music teacher had my sisters and I play at a benefit for the Spanish Civil War in New York City, where I remember people with cannisters on the subway and street corners collecting for the Republican cause.

Sex was always a major issue in the family. It wasn't too serious that Ma spanked us when she looked out of the upper windows of our house and saw us playing "dirty stuff" with other children under the sumac bushes in the fields behind the house, where we thought we were shielded from view, but my father was destructively puritanical, intent on controlling our sexuality. Yet, I think we all saw him, rather than my mother, as the sexual center of the family, which was ironic. My younger twin brothers saw his evenings "working late in the city" or "going to sketch class" as evidence of his screwing around. As a believer in modern thought, my mother was concerned that we wouldn't pick up misinformation "on the street," as she did, so she instructed us all where babies came from, though not the crucial point of how daddy's seed got into momma's egg. For all this frank-

My father at his drawing board

ness, one of my sisters was sixteen before she learned the facts of sexual intercourse. Ma also told my sisters about menstruation to prepare them, but I had no guidance about my own development except from the *Boy Scout Handbook* which threatened dire effects from "self abuse." After puberty, I suffered terribly from sexual guilt, unable to control my need to masturbate and having little privacy. It became even worse when I started having sex with men, and the fear of exposure to my family increased, as well as living with the danger of being arrested, beaten up, or blackmailed.

The tyrannical regime of my father weakened over the years, as my parents became Americanized. My mother liberated herself in stages, first fighting for the right to escape, via Greyhound bus, to Miami Beach for a few weeks in the winter, then started defending my sisters' rights to wear makeup and go on dates. All of us children were crazy about popular songs, and even my mother, who had a lovely voice, started to sing them instead of classics. Risking battles with my father, my mother would give in to my twin brothers' constant demands for things that other American children took for granted, like sports equipment, Boy Scout uniforms, a dog. My youngest sister, Barbara, had an almost-normal American bringing up, though she eventually escaped to Europe where she has lived ever since.

The Field Family Trio: Edward, cello; Adele, violin; Alice, piano

When I graduated from high school, my father asked me for the first time if I wanted to go to college. Lynbrook High School, which turned out mostly clerks for insurance companies and banks, had a very small number of students going on to college. Though I took the college preparatory course, no one at school had ever discussed applying and I had never thought about it. In any case, after graduation was a little late to begin. Still, I found it was possible to take late entrance examinations for Columbia University, where my father's bosses at MGM had all gone. But there was a quota for Jews at that time, and my scores were not high enough to jump the barrier, so I went looking for a job.

Much as tourist accommodation were marked "restricted" when my family took summer vacation trips, the want ads in the New York Times were mostly "gentile only." I don't know why I didn't lie, but it never occurred to me to write "Christian" on the employment application forms. But I finally found a job as an office boy in a Jewish-owned advertising agency.

The following winter, 1942, I enrolled in the School of Commerce of New York University. I was the first one in my family ever to go to college, and there was no question of studying something as impractical as liberal arts. Even if I'd been interested in something like engineering, the field was closed to Jews. Likewise, banks and politics, and medical and law schools had quotas. The Second World War, which had started the previous winter, would change all that. My father had suggested I study marketing, since it included advertising, his own field. But by the following fall I admitted to myself that I couldn't tolerate the boredom of my business-oriented courses, and dropped out to enlist in the Air Force.

Though I could never figure out what I wanted to be "when I grew up," the answer came to me in March of 1943. I had finished basic training in Miami Beach and was getting on a troop train for Colorado, where I was to study at a clerk-typist school, when a Red Cross worker handed me a bag of useful items for the journey like toothbrush and comb. Also included was a paperback book, one of Louis Untermeyer's anthologies of great poetry, which I read while crossing the country.

This was a bombshell. I knew immediately that I was going to be a poet. It was something nobody else would want to do, so it must be right for me. It had simply never occurred to me before. I soon started scribbling verses

Field, as an enlisted man, 1943

of the "I was lonely last night" variety, though I also tried a Kiplingesque ballad of an airman, with the refrain, "I'll see you in Kunming."

After I finished the clerk-typist course, I was stationed at Tinker Field in Oklahoma City and working in the regional air command headquarters, when I had a love affair with a tough-talking master-sergeant who occupied one of the non-com rooms in my barracks. Southern and baby-faced, a cigar between his teeth, Glenn spent his free time tying trout flies in his room while carrying on cussing contests with other southerners, which he invariably won. He wasted no time in moving me, a mere corporal, into his barracks room, and briefly it was a romantic, passionate experience. But for no reason that I can think of, love turned to hate, and I longed to escape. It did not occur to me to confess this to him, since I had said the fatal words, "I love you," which could not be withdrawn.

Fortunately, a bulletin came across my desk about the Air Corps' need for flying personnel, so I applied for the Aviation Cadet Program, hoping to be shipped off to pilot training which would solve my predicament over Glenn. This plan was nearly defeated by my weight. Still as skinny as ever, I needed to gain several pounds to pass the physical. So I gorged on bananas and chocolate malteds and barely squeaked by, and succeeded in escaping from the wreckage of love into aviation cadet training. After taking batteries of tests, my fantasy of being a fighter pilot was punctured when, largely due to my high scores in math, I was assigned to navigation school. A year later, I graduated as a navigator with the rank of second lieutenant.

It was a long flight from Lincoln, Nebraska, on a B-17 that my crew was ferrying across the Atlantic to England. We stopped for refueling in Maine, Labrador, Iceland, and on each of our stops I always met up with my best buddy, a fellow navigator, who had gone to Cornell and was cynical about everything. When I confessed that Rupert Brooke was my favorite poet, Dave laughed scornfully and said that the greatest modern poet was T. S. Eliot. But when he showed me "Prufrock" and "The Waste Land," I was mystified. They made no sense.

My real introduction to modern poetry came in England, where I was stationed on an airbase in the Midlands. I was flying bombing missions over Germany and would go to the Officers' Club evenings and drink whiskey sours to unwind. It was at the bar that I met my first poet ever. Coman Leavenworth, a gnomelike young man with a beak of a nose that seemed to reflect his aristocratic Anglo-Saxon origins, had gone to Columbia University and had already published poems in literary magazines like *Poetry Chicago*. As an officer in the ground crew, Coman got into London regularly, and he would tell me about the poets he met at the Gargoyle Club, a hangout for writers, not only the English poets George Barker and Stephen Spender, but the Americans Harry Brown and Dunstan Thompson. Under Coman's influence I bought George Barker's *Noctambules*, a now-forgotten poem that began, thrillingly, "The gay paraders of the esplanade, the wanderers in time's shade . . . ," and a little book of Dylan

The author (front row, third from the left) with his flight crew in England, 1945

Thomas with its bracing lines, "my wine you drink, my bread you snap."

The European war ended just before I completed my tour of duty. I'd helped bomb historic cities on twenty-five missions where five planes had been destroyed by flak under me. Once, we even crashed into the North Sea, as I've described in a poem entitled, "World War II." From England, my squadron was transferred to the south of France where we were to ferry American soldiers to Casablanca on one leg of their homeward journey. We moved into tents on a vast desert of an airbase that the Germans had wrecked before retreating.

If wartime England had seemed grim and damp, France was a paradise. In the picturesque village of Istres near my airbase, I breathed in the smells of Provence. I found a restaurant where I ate my first French meals and drank the local red wine with little white goat cheeses on grape leaves served for dessert. On a pass to Paris, I discovered the gay world, and when I entered Le Boeuf sur le Toit for the first time wearing silver wings on my officer's uniform and a white silk scarf around my neck, every man in the place, most of them members of various armed forces, turned his head to look. It was my first experience in being "popular," so different from my lowly status back in Lynbrook High.

But rather than ferry GIs across to North Africa, I was assigned to fly a courier run to London, and would spend my free time there at The White Room, a gay drinking club in Soho. I had once gone to a play in New York City and hadn't much liked it. Now, hearing other members of the club discussing the theatre, I went to see Gielgud in "Hamlet," "The Circle" by Somerset Maugham, an Ivor Novello musical, a revue with Hermione Gingold and Joyce Grenfell. But it mystifies me that I never had any interest in the British Museum, the National Gallery, the Royal Opera, or even in going around the city to look at the spectacular bomb damage. I hadn't done any sightseeing in Paris either, but took it for granted.

In December 1945, a year after my arrival in England, I returned to America on an aircraft carrier, whose flight deck crumpled under battering North Atlantic gales, and, after three years in the army, was discharged.

One of the first things I did was to contact Dunstan Thompson, whom I had heard about from Coman Leavenworth. We met for drinks at a cocktail lounge in Manhattan called the 1-2-3, where a pianist tickled the keys as a background to the conversations at the tables. The perfect aesthete, Thompson had a wonderful dome of a head with bulging eyes and a minimal chin, and he waved his long delicate fingers expressively, a dead ringer for a drawing of Keats in the National Portrait Gallery in London. I was in awe. He had been a star at Harvard and had a cultural development I couldn't hope to attain, though I made lists of all the subjects I needed to study, the books I must read. His two books of poetry did nothing to disguise the fact that he was homosexual, in fact the high aesthetic pose more than justified it. Shortly after our meeting, he left the United States for good, first travelling through the Middle East to write a book, then settling in England, where he converted to Catholicism and retired from the poetry world. After his death in 1974, I paid tribute to him with a selection of his poems in *Poetry Pilot*, the publication of the Academy of American Poets.

That winter, I reenrolled at New York University, but by the rules of the GI Bill, though I wanted to study liberal arts, I was not allowed to transfer from the School of Commerce and was even forced to take Business English. But I managed to get into classes in Homeric Greek and French at the nearby Washington Square College of Arts & Sciences, where I quickly discovered the literary set in the cafeteria. Learning about existentialism and orgone boxes and socialism became far more exciting than anything in my classes, so my attendance dropped. Though I proclaimed myself a poet, I still wrote little poetry, and what I did was merely instinctive outpourings of a juvenile nature. I think I was accepted by the cafeteria crowd more for my good looks than my knowledge.

After living in a white-only town and the segregated army, I especially enjoyed getting to know black classmates. Wilmer Lucas took me to Harlem clubs, and the flamboyant Lloyd George W. Broadfield III brought me to the Greenwich Village studio of the painter Beauford Delaney and the elegant apartment of scholar Dr. Alain Locke. When Dr. Kinsey was staying at the Astor Hotel on Times Square, Wilmer and I offered ourselves as subjects for his survey on male sexuality. Kinsey divided up his questions into six categories, and having my varied sexual experiences organized and tabulated like that, without the least judgment, seemed to lift a burden from my shoulders and sent me out into the streets elated.

At the NYU cafeteria I also met a person who was later to figure significantly in my life. Alfred Chester was an odd, shapeless youth with Kalmuk eyes in a pale, puffy face, who wore a reddish wig after losing all his hair from a childhood illness. Lacking sideburns or eyebrows or a beard, the wig was unmistakable. He was already a writer, but not having been in the armed services, was much younger than me and I did not take him very seriously at that time.

In 1948, I dropped out of NYU, where my attendance at classes had become spotty to the point of losing me the GI Bill, and went back to France on a converted troopship, determined to make my thousand dollars in savings last a year. Drawn by the magnet of Paris, the cultural capital of the world, I was quite surprised to learn later of the Beat explosion in San Francisco. Why would anyone have wanted to go there? As it turned out, Paris was the right choice for me, as San Francisco was for the Beats, though they too discovered Paris in a few years.

On the ten-day sea voyage, I was lucky enough to meet a remarkable man, the poet Robert Friend, with whom I explored the mysteries of modern poetry. After a summer on the Mediterranean, I settled into a cheap but chilly furnished room on the left bank and spent most of the day in the well-heated Cafe Pergola on Boulevard St. Germain where I worked on my poems, making a café express last as long as I could. Robert Friend often joined me and would show me the poems he was working on. Together we studied the poems in the Oscar Williams anthology of modern verse, puzzling out their obliquities and elisions. The months Friend was in France was the basis of my education in Modern Poetry and in poetry writing. He somehow imparted to me the process, which I'd been unable to discover for myself in my previous attempts to write.

I soon had a poem accepted by *Poetry Quarterly* in London, but I never received a copy and am unsure that it actually appeared. So my official first publication was probably in the glossy quadrilingual quarterly *Botteghe Oscure* which was published in Rome by the Princess Mar-

guerite Caetani. Her nephew Paul Chapin, whom I met in one of the left-bank cafés, showed her my poems and she took a group for her second issue.

Paris was an education for me in many ways, as it has been for so many other Americans. It was the greatest bargain in the world after the war. I could live on two dollars a day, which included eating all my meals in restaurants and going to the theatre and opera. In St. Germain-des-Prés I met people like the young James Baldwin, already a rising star, who took me seriously, and the singer Anita Ellis, who took me to lunch in the Eiffel Tower. I made friends who have stayed with me throughout my life—the poet Ralph Pomeroy, Fred Kuh who later started The Spaghetti Factory in San Francisco where I would stay on my reading tours, and Harry Goldgar, brilliant translator of Yeats into French and the first to publish Jean Genet in English.

On a visit to London that Christmas I met Stephen Spender. I was a great admirer of his poetry, and with the confidence gained from the leap forward in my writing I phoned him. He invited me to his house and we had tea in his study. His hand was on my knee in no time, but even if I had been attracted to him, I could hear his wife, children, and the household staff just beyond the door! Later he took me to a cocktail party given by the novelist Rose MacCauley at the Gargoyle Club (which I had longed to go to during the war), where I met literary people I had only read about. When T. S. Eliot arrived, pushing his roommate, the editor Max Hayward, in a wheelchair, a bright young novelist named Philip Toynbee announced, "Let's introduce the two Americans!" I would have died of embarrassment.

I attracted a lot of attention in those days with my curly hair and vivid complexion, and a man rushed up to me and asked excitedly if I was Catalan. When I said, No, Jewish, he looked horrified and fled. People did not say they were Jews in the genteel literary world back then. It was an affront to good manners, as proclaiming your homosexuality would be. It was a subject about which you kept quiet, were expected to be quietly ashamed. A number of the top poets even felt free to make anti-Semitic remarks in, and outside of, their poems, and there was no way to protest. I later wrote to T. S. Eliot asking him about the anti-Semitic passages in his poetry, and was surprised when he wrote back, claiming he was no more anti-Semitic than anti-Lapp or anti-Eskimo. But of course the evidence is there in the poems. And the implication was that the Jews were as remote from him as Lapps and Eskimos.

In the spring of 1949, faced with returning home, I boldly cashed in my boat ticket and instead went to Greece, which was still in the throes of civil war. I was at home there as in no other place, and started learning the polysyllabic language immediately. Greece was a country where, compared to the oppressive atmosphere in the States, being homosexual was no problem.

Most of the poems in the first section of my first book *Stand Up, Friend, with Me,* were written there. These had begun to emerge in a relaxed conversational style even before Greek friends introduced me to the poetry of Cavafy, which combined the voice of the demotic language with infusions of the more literary tongue. Similarly, I used my parents' Yiddish intonations to soften the literary aspects in my writing. I figured that way to get in the tenderness with which Cavafy always wrote and which Greeks used in speaking, as if addressing the child in each other, so under his influence my poems addressed the child in the reader.

When my money ran out in Athens, I managed to find work as an artists' model to earn a few dollars a day. A famous Greek actress named Marika Kotopouli fed me lunch almost every day, but for dinner I could only afford apples and bread. After six months of spartan existence, I signed on as a deck hand on a freighter and arrived back in the States at the beginning of 1950.

Coming home was a shock, partly because I was faced with supporting myself for the first time in my life. Until then, I'd been a soldier, a student on the GI Bill, then living in Europe on my savings, and here I was in my late twenties without any way of earning a living. I was obsessed with poetry but couldn't see how to survive as a poet. I made that survival more painful and difficult, since according to my bohemian principles, getting a steady job would have meant selling out. I didn't feel comfortable with teaching, with the idea of poetry as part of a university career. Lots of poets, the majority, find shelter in that world, but it is an alien atmosphere for me. Of course, I

didn't have a degree, so I couldn't have taught back then anyway.

I found myself in an America that, compared to the pleasures of France and Greece, seemed unutterably grim to me. There was only a shabby little bohemian band that still hung out at the San Remo in the Village. The fifties was a period of national hysteria against everything human, those years of the witch hunt of leftists and homosexuals, the Rosenberg executions, loyalty oaths, bomb shelters and cold war hysteria, even the imprisonment and death of looney, nonconformist Wilhelm Reich for claiming his orgone boxes could cure cancer. A number of Americans escaped to more hospitable countries abroad, if they were lucky enough to skip out before their passports were lifted. A few, even more courageous, refused to cooperate and either went to jail or became outcasts like my friend, the writer Millen Brand, and were unemployable for years. But many major artists turned state's evidence, swept up in the panic that the United States was being taken over by subversives, or perhaps just protecting their jobs.

Following a tip from the perhaps-crazy poet, Robert Lowell, that Yaddo was a nest of communist conspirators, the FBI swept down in a raid on the artists colony in Saratoga Springs, and terrorized everyone. More than the execution of the Rosenbergs, that assault symbolized the decade for me, when artists were taught such a bitter lesson for social concerns. So it was not surprising when painters retreated to the neutrality of abstract expressionism, poets concentrated on formal subjects like carousels and angels, and psychiatrists tried to make their queer patients straight by talk therapies or shock treatments, even lobotomies. It was against this background that I discovered the eighth-century Chinese poet Tu Fu and breathed in his free spirit. He wrote not only about politics, but was not afraid of being sentimental, both discouraged in American poetry. He felt it was within his competence, indeed his duty as a poet, to advise rulers on how to deal with his country's problems, a country in turmoil, although they listened as little to poets in the eighth century as they do today.

Inspired by my conviction that I should be part of the "working class," a "poet of the people," I haunted the hiring hall of District 65, a left-wing union. But when I did get jobs in factories and warehouses, I didn't stay long in any of them, and it became harder and harder to force myself out of bed. I just didn't see how to go on with my life or my poetry in New York, and there was no way I could return to Paris. In despair, I started in a form of Freudian therapy called Group Analysis that took over my consciousness for several years, and influenced my thinking for years after that.

Though in the long run this turned out to be a destructive experience, early on I went through a critical episode, a remarkable, though unhappily brief, period of what I can only describe as a state of "expansion," and which perhaps could be clinically described as a manic phase of my manic-depressive nature, except that what I felt was almost olympian in its openness and calm. I would like to have remained in that state forever. My poem "A Journey" was a later attempt to describe what happened to me. The title of my first book, *Stand Up, Friend, with Me,* was a line from the first poem (not included in the book) that I wrote after I "stood up."

What happened was very much like the plot of Dostoievsky's novel *A Raw Youth,* in which the illegitimate son is recognized by his natural father and experiences a tremendous exhilaration. I was leaving the house for my therapy group, one afternoon, when out of the blue my father offered me money (money equals love?). As I walked to the Long Island Railroad station in a state of emotional turmoil, holding back the tears, I felt I was coming apart and barely made it to the analyst's. But in the waiting room I realized I was an hour early and that he was still in his office with the previous group. I couldn't hold back any longer and crouched in the corner of the room and started screaming, until he came out and calmed me down.

An hour later when my own group met, I could barely wait for everyone to sit down when I *stood up.* I was shaking as I forced myself to my feet, while the whole group started shouting at me to stop doing that to myself, but even though I was crying and shaking all over, I had to stand up. Perhaps I was crazy, but at the end of that session, I walked out of there healed. It was wonderful to be able to breathe so easily, feel part of other men, where I had always felt separate. I felt sane for the first time in my life. I was perfectly normal.

I started writing like mad, composing a poem called "It Is Dawn and the Cock Is Crowing,"

which I mimeographed, mailed to friends all over, and at the next group meeting high-handedly passed out a copy to everyone in the room, which enraged them further. But I felt very sure of myself by now. Poem after poem flowed out of me during the following weeks. The only one I have kept, including it in my first book, was "Prologue." I still have a tattered original mimeographed copy of "It Is Dawn and the Cock Is Crowing," but have never published it. It has many interesting qualities, but its amalgamation of Marxism and Freudian psychology seems naive and embarrassing, where once, briefly, I thought I was speaking ultimate truth like a prophet.

Critics have interpreted my book's title *Stand Up, Friend, with Me* in different ways. Actually, the "friend" of the title addressed the downtrodden, all the underdogs in the world, inviting them to join me in my new pride in myself, my new-found courage to stand up against all oppressors.

Unfortunately, this wonderful state of being soon faded away, never to return, and I sank into a fearsome depression that the therapy, with its continual attack on my homosexuality only made worse. From there on, it was all downhill. The therapist even urged me to drop poetry, since it could never be the basis for a satisfying life. His own prescription for psychological health was to get a job to be able to afford an apartment and have a girlfriend. There was no question of encouraging me to get a boyfriend, even though I pursued homosexual experiences ever more desperately.

I also persisted in struggling with my writing and published poems in magazines at least, even if my book manuscript kept getting rejected by publishers. One of my difficulties in writing at this time was caused by a phenomenon that often occurred when I sat down to write—the words began to sing. And then no matter what I wrote, it was incredibly beautiful—just anything sounded like great poetry. At that time, what came easily like this was not my idea of poetry, even if I couldn't bear to sit there and work on poems through innumerable drafts, as I once had. What a fool I was not to trust what was coming out! So I remained dissatisfied. It also didn't help that leftist friends found my work decadent and negative.

My poetry has always reflected what I was going through, my psychological grapplings. It was a healing force, as opposed to the misguided psychotherapy that was merely breaking me down. This kind of poetry is often criticized as "just" therapy, which undermines its "purity," whatever that means. But I always saw poetry as a solution to my life problems, something that could rescue me from nothingness, from despair, therefore a therapy, if you want to call it that. I still believe that healing is one of poetry's important functions.

So many of my poems chart psychological insights, snatched from the muddle of the depression that I suffered from for years. They embody a fragment of hope, dearly won, even if transitory. My poems usually represent a rediscovery of my feelings, the opposite of depression, which I experience as not-feeling, a limbo of the feelings.

In 1955, I finally wised up to the destructiveness of my therapy group and quit. By luck this coincided with a two-month fellowship to Yaddo. I was very confused and doing little writing there, when I came across a group of poems by Frank O'Hara in *Poetry Magazine*. Frank's sexy, surrealist poems seemed fresh and funny to me, though when I read them to a group that gathered for drinks at the cocktail hour, they reacted with outrage at their irresponsibility, their flaunting of homosexuality.

When I returned to New York, I looked O'Hara up, and began staying over with him in his ratty apartment on East 58th Street which he shared with the writer, Joe LeSueur. Frank was far more balanced and sophisticated than I, and had made a world of his own in New York, where I could never feel I had a center. Frank's friends seemed to revolve around him, so, that summer, I met a large number of them, the rising stars of the next generation. Most instructive to me was his casual, relaxed attitude toward his poems, writing them at lunch at the museum where he worked, as William Carlos Williams did in his office, in-between patients. Frank's kindness to me, at a time of great uncertainty, boosted my ego tremendously, and with his confidence in himself, served as a good example of a gay man living successfully and apparently guiltlessly. I wasn't in love with him, but I was grateful for his support when I needed it.

The affair ended a few months later, but I had gotten some new ideas about poetry and my own life that over the next years would help me re-orient myself. Frank O'Hara showed me the way. Or gave me the courage to follow my instincts, accept what was happening already— every so often you have to shift gears and start writing differently. It can be a difficult period, and there are sometimes years of uncertainty until you find the new voice/subject matter/direction and move forward again.

One of the sins of my poetic generation was that every poem was supposed to be written and rewritten in the attempt to make it a masterpiece. You couldn't just write your poems, and let them be the poems of their moment, of that impulse. So thanks to Frank O'Hara, I was able to get through my block, caused by my insistence that my poetry should be something that I could no longer make it, be something other than I could do, and get writing again. I stopped making demands that my poetry be anything other than what came out.

I put aside my prejudice against white-collar jobs and began working as a temporary typist, which seemed the easiest way to earn a living at the time. My "View of Jersey" poems were written in an office where I had a view of the Hudson River and the New Jersey shore. I wrote a poem a day over the months I worked there, usually starting with the spectacular view out the window, without demanding that the poems be masterpieces. But each poem was a small victory, a thawing. So it was particularly satisfying that Donald Allen included two of them in his landmark anthology, *The New American Poetry, 1945–1960*.

The country, too, had been in deep freeze for years. But soon the Supreme Court allowed books that used to be banned pornography, like *Lady Chatterley's Lover* and *Ulysses*, to be published. It was like a cracking of the ice in spring.

I had never thought of doing anything but writing poetry, but it was not a full-time occupation, and after the affair with Frank O'Hara ended, with no group meetings to fill up my life, I hardly knew what to do with myself. Elia Braca, an actress who was going with my painter friend, Herman Rose, was playing the lead in *The Heiress* in a small company in the Village, and when I met the director, she suggested I take a part in her next production, *The Imaginary Invalid* by Molière. This experience before an audience was a revelation, and I decided to become an actor.

I started studying the Stanislavsky Method with a shrewd dumpling of a Russian woman,

Vera Soloviova, who had been a member of the Moscow Art Theatre. Suddenly, my life was filled with classes, rehearsals, auditions. Method acting is a kind of therapy in itself, in some ways even an improvement on talk therapy, since it makes you use your body, with the added advantage that you play characters different from yourself, the one you're by now sick of. It was also liberating to study speech and start speaking differently from little Eddie Field with his Brooklyn accent. I remember the nerve it took, the first time I had to open my mouth with my new vowels in front of my family. It announced that I had the right to be separate from them, be my own person. I never "made it" as an actor, but at least I had the experience of playing major roles in summer theatres.

In 1960, I was working in the typing pool of an advertising agency, and the supervisor assigned the typewriter next to me to a new temp, a terrific-looking young man from California named Neil Derrick. It was a case of immediate attraction between WASP and Jew. We started a non-stop conversation, that led the supervisor to switch him to another typewriter rows away from me. But we were soon going out together and in a few weeks I moved into his cold-water flat on West 47th Street in Hell's Kitchen. Neil was several years younger than me, and, though he had always kept a journal, he had never gotten down to writing, but now he started writing fiction.

"The Garden," the last poem in *Stand Up, Friend, with Me*, is a celebration of my finding a companion in life and how it changed everything. Before this, I had only thought of myself as a public person, never private. But when I finally connected with somebody, it meant that I didn't have to live a life of hell anymore, symbolically playing the scapegoat and the voice of mankind, which I was not really suited for anyway. Settling down with Neil, I drifted away from my theatre career and concentrated on my writing again.

After our ad agency jobs ended, Neil landed a permanent half-time job at the front desk of the Museum of Modern Art, which allowed him to do his writing, while I settled into a long-term temporary job at a writing school in Rockefeller Center. It was there in the back room that I met, hunched over a pile of students' assignments, a novelist I had long admired, Millen Brand, the author of *The Out-*

In 1963, when "my first book was published"

ward Room and the screenplay of *The Snakepit*. A saintly idealist, he was blacklisted, banned, and working for pennies per manuscript corrected, with eyes permanently red-rimmed behind his thick glasses from long hours on the job.

A few months after I moved in with Neil, my old friend from the NYU cafeteria, Alfred Chester, returned to New York after a decade in Paris. If he was a callow youth when I last saw him, the years abroad had matured him and given him enormous confidence in himself. He had published widely, won a Guggenheim fellowship, and in spite of his strange appearance, had a long, if stormy, live-in relationship with a handsome Israeli pianist, as well as other romantic affairs. In Paris he had convinced numerous literary Americans, French, and British of his brilliance, and had returned on the strength of receiving $3,000 from *The New Yorker* for a story. At the publication party, when "A War on Salamis" appeared, I met his friends Susan Sontag, Maria Irene Fornes, and Harriet Sohmers who clustered around him adoringly.

He was already a powerful influence on these three striking and talented women.

Alfred and I became fast friends for the next several years, as he became one of the hottest figures on the New York literary scene.

In 1962, I was busy at my clerical job, when I got a call from the Academy of American Poets that I had won the Lamont Award for *Stand Up, Friend, with Me.* This, after it had gotten twenty-four rejections from publishers. By the time the book came out the following year, much had changed in the poetry world and it was generally praised for those very qualities that had made it so difficult to find a publisher, its colloquialism, emotionality, daring subject matter.

Neil and I celebrated by going to Europe. For me it was the first time back since my shattering return to New York in 1950. In the spring, when a Guggenheim fellowship of $4000 came through, we set off from Paris on a tour of Europe. In Berlin, where my sister Barbara lived with her Dutch husband, Ack Van Rooyen, who played trumpet in the radio station orchestra, we bought a second-hand Volkswagen and drove through East Germany, across Switzerland, northern Italy, and the French Mediterranean coast to Spain. We were heading for

Gibraltar to meet Alfred Chester, who was escaping from his New York success as a critic to live in Morocco and write fiction again. After taking the ferry across the Straits to Tangier, the three of us, with Alfred's dogs, arrived by taxi at Paul Bowles' villa in the seaside town of Asilah. Bowles had invited Alfred to stay with him until he could find a house of his own, but, though he was prepared for the dogs, he hadn't expected two friends as well! Nevertheless, he put us up for the night, so we were there for the historic meeting of Alfred and Dris, a Moroccan Alfred was to live with for several years.

At sundown, Paul led us down to the beach where the fishing boats had come in with the day's catch, now spread out on the beach for sale to the townsfolk. Suddenly a tall, ruggedly handsome young fisherman came toward us across the sand with a large fish dangling from his fist, and Paul introduced him to Alfred. After Neil and I returned to Paris and at the end of the summer to New York, we got fascinating letters from Alfred describing his life with Dris that I have since collected and edited, under the title *Voyage to Destruction.* Two years later Alfred Chester cracked up and never recovered.

Back in New York in the fall of '63, I found myself a minor celebrity. My book was receiving marvelous reviews and the edition of 1,000 quickly sold out, with the Gotham Book Mart offering copies at five times the cover price. Grove Press brought out a paperback edition that went through several more printings. With all the attention I was getting, it was not easy for Neil. The phone rang constantly, and whenever he answered, it was invariably for me. When we entered a room, he was ignored as people rushed up to me. But he accepted this with good grace, and escaped to his job at the front desk of the Museum of Modern Art where he got plenty of attention of his own.

Perhaps it is just as well that I hadn't succeeded in getting a publisher earlier, since the book ended up the stronger for it, as I added and subtracted material. But years of rejection had taken their toll, and even now with my new success, I told myself, "I will not be consoled." However, the recognition did make life easier. And I did enjoy all the attention.

One result was that making a living was much easier now, and I never had to work in offices again. I was asked to translate a book

Neil Derrick (left) and Alfred Chester, Morocco, 1963

Field in Morocco, 1965

of Inuit poems for a fifth-grade teaching program about the Eskimos that was being developed in Boston. The editors of the program said they chose me because I was the only poet they found whose poetry could be understood by ten-year-olds. The project was suddenly terminated when it was revealed that the CIA was the real source of the funds behind it. But my translations were later published as a children's book, *Eskimo Songs and Stories* (1973).

I next was hired to write the narration for a documentary film, *To Be Alive*, which was shown at the Johnson's Wax Pavilion of the New York World's Fair in 1965 and won many prizes including an Academy Award.

But my main source of income for the next decade was giving poetry readings at colleges. Using my experience as an actor when I had sent out my resumé to producers and agents, I wrote to English Department chairmen, who I knew had budgets for visiting writers, and managed to set up small reading tours for myself two or three times a year. I'm a good reader, but it was a surprise when audiences laughed at my poems. I hadn't thought of them as funny. People laughed in surprise at the unexpected, at my use of a kind of language that was more informal than usual. They also laughed in recognition of the truths about human nature in the poems. They never expected to be entertained at a poetry reading. For that reason, it was always more fun to have an audience of ordinary people than the campus literary set, who would sit back listening critically.

During an interview recently, I was asked why my poetry was especially popular in Long Beach. The interviewer said she thought that this was somewhat strange since I'm very much a New York poet, and the West Coast doesn't usually think much of New York, where poetry is determinedly literary. Long Beach poetry, especially, represents "the movement towards the spoken idiom," as Gerald Locklin wrote. This connection with southern California began when Charles Stetler and Gerald Locklin, English professors at California State College, Long Beach, wrote an article about me for the *Minnesota Review*. I have a scattering of fans around the country, but along with Charles Bukowski, Gerry says I'm considered one of the "fathers" of Long Beach poetry, one of the originators of what Charles Webb calls "Stand Up Poetry." After my second book, *Variety Photoplays*, with its "old movie" poems was published in 1967, a number of the poets in Long Beach, Stetler and Locklin among them, started writing their own movie poems. In 1978, Sheep Meadow Press brought out *Stars in My Eyes*, a collection of my movie poems illustrated with appropriate stills from the movies.

If one way of poetry is to be superior, elitist, snobbish, the other, exemplified by Long Beach poetry, is to explore the clichés, the banal, and rescue everything that is vigorous in popular culture. I see our national myths in the offerings of pop culture, especially the movies, and like everyone raised in America, understand their metaphorical meanings, identify with their style and tone and language. With the failure of schools and universities to deliver an education that makes sense of our national experience, pop culture is practically all we have, though it is richer than pop artists present it. Hopefully, we can reclaim it and transform it into the genuine.

In the mid-sixties, through the poet May Swenson, Neil and I got to know a remarkable couple, Betty Deran, an economist, and Alma Routsong, a novelist, who were students of astrology, the ouija board, and Gurdjieff. On the ouija board we spoke with Jack Kennedy, who confirmed that his "killer roams free," with Katherine Mansfield, whose intriguing advice to gay men was to develop their feminine side, and my "guide," Jack London, who was irritated with me. Betty and Alma cast our horoscopes, and mine forecast correctly "trouble with publishers," and "not spiritual, but arriving at spirituality by his own hard work." Under these women's influence Neil and I read books on Buddhism, Gurdjieff, and other spiritual subjects. This was another break from my atheist father. I felt sure that, although I would always be an atheist, there was something else that atheism didn't quite cover.

Prayer came into my life. My favorite poem, especially in those terrible pre-dawn hours, is the Twenty-third Psalm. I'd like my own poetry to be healing like that. Or even just one of my poems.

Buddhism is without gods, and I found it a good antidote to Freudian therapy, since you are led to see what happens to you, even the worst things, as helpful to your development, obstacles to be overcome. The idea that I chose my parents seemed to liberate me from the Freudian rut of blaming my parents, though that had formerly been an improvement over blaming myself! Betty had been a Christian Science nurse and gave me a pamphlet that contained the healing principle in a nutshell, but without the Christ part, for which it was withdrawn from distribution. The conviction that the body is self-healing and there is no error in the universe liberated me eventually from hypochondria and doctors.

Yoga became a discipline which I've done ever since. I also took lessons in Alexander technique, with its reeducation of the body, which I incorporated into yoga. And I started another cycle of therapies, these more body-oriented, as opposed to the talk therapy I'd had, from Bio-Energetic to Primal, where insights were gained from falling apart in fits of screaming or helpless sobbing.

Perhaps these explorations were a preparation for what happened one night in the late sixties, when my life was jolted in a new direction, unforeseen by horoscope or ouija board, and as crucial as my discovery of poetry on the troop train. Neil and I were living on Perry Street in Greenwich Village, and I awoke to find him having an epileptic seizure in bed beside me. I knew it was the end of something and the beginning of something else. We had been together for eight years.

After much discussion, we both agreed that our close relationship might have been too con-stricting for him, and three years later we separated.

To try to recover my balance I went on a long overland trip to Afghanistan, a country I had been drawn to since seeing photos in *National Geographic*. My experiences in the heartland of Asia confirmed me in my new spiritual direction, and also helped me accept myself as a man. In Afghanistan, unlike the United States, men were allowed to be affectionate and there were no categories for the varieties of male sexuality. I started to see that my homosexuality was simply one of the possibilities, and that, too, I had chosen. Well, maybe my sexuality had been distorted by my bringing up, but what I did with it was my own choice, and okay.

After living together for more than ten years, it was not easy for Neil and me to separate, especially with the tight housing situation in New York. When I returned from Central Asia, we took turns in the apartment for several months, and then I applied for a studio in the Westbeth Artists' Housing Project in the West Village. I told the director I'd have to move out of the city if he couldn't give me a studio, and by some miracle, in spite of a long waiting list, he replied that that's what Westbeth was there for, to keep artists in the city, and assigned me a studio immediately. This turned out to be a long slice of a room with windows facing the Empire State Building. I could lie in my Yucatan hammock strung across the walls, looking at the changing light on the towers of Manhattan. May Swenson, when she sublet from me one winter, wrote a poem about it, called "Staying at Ed's Place."

Though Neil's seizures were being controlled by medication, he now started having visual blackouts and a brain tumor was diagnosed. The surgery took eight hours and he came out of it remarkably well, but over the following weeks lost most of his sight. Luckily, I was in Primal Therapy at the time, and would lie on the floor of the sound-proofed studio and scream. I found myself crying not just for Neil, but for myself; not for my current grief, but for my whole life, and I discovered some significant things about my lifelong depressions.

Neil was in the hospital for three months, since the staff was afraid to let him go home where there was no family to look after him and I didn't qualify. But I managed to convince them to release him weekends in my care, and that's when I started learning to look af-

Giving a poetry reading, about 1969

ter a blind man, as he was learning how to live like a blind man. In spite of our having broken up two years before, there was no question in my mind of walking away from this situation, and the decision to stick with him has shaped the rest of my life. Perhaps some people are born to be care-givers. My horoscope puts me in the "devotional" decan of Gemini. It might be a coincidence, but another person born the day before me is remarkably like me in this regard, Sylvia Winner, married to the poet Robert Winner who was a quadriplegic.

While Neil went off to a Veterans Administration blind-training school, I headed south in my Volkswagen van for a term as poet-in-residence at Eckerd College in St. Petersburg, Florida. Though I had taught poetry workshops in colleges around New York City, Eckerd was my only real experience living on a college campus and confirmed for me that that was not the life I wanted to lead. One of the chief rewards of teaching was that a few students became lasting friends. But for me, poetry did not belong to academia. Before the poetry workshop and

the MFA program became dominant, poets were self-taught. True, I had the luck to meet Robert Friend, but I doubt that any class could have given me what he gave me.

Neil had been to Europe many times, starting with a bicycle tour of England and France after high school, and a college year abroad. He had lived for those trips, but now with his blindness there seemed little point in him travelling any more. But a year after his operation, when friends Shami and Joseph Chaikin went with the Open Theatre to London, we took a chance and followed them, renting a bed-sit for a month. Neil quickly discovered that, even with his diminished sight, foreign travel was still satisfying. And I found I could cope with the extra burdens of leading him around and handling all the arrangements, though I continue to have nightmares about missing trains and planes and, worst of all, losing him.

Thus began a new chapter in my life. Since *Stand Up, Friend, with Me* came out in 1963, I'd had exactly the kind of career I wanted. It was a small but very satisfying one, where I could do everything by myself, with a classy publisher, good reception around the country on my reading tours, reviews, fan mail—all the attention I needed. I even earned my living at it. But taking care of Neil after he went blind became more important. It was the first time in my life I could feel useful in this way, and with the responsibility, not wanting to leave him alone for long, and dislike of the visiting-poet routine at colleges, I cut way down on giving poetry readings. When Grove Press was sold in the mid-seventies and I lost my publisher, it seemed that a cycle had finished. That feeling was intensified when my next book, *A Full Heart*, published in 1977 by Sheep Meadow Press, founded by my friend Stanley Moss, was badly mauled in the *New York Times*.

Neil could manage much of the business of life on his own, and even went around the city bravely with his white cane. But he wasn't much good in the kitchen and there were other things a pair of eyes was useful for. When he was sighted, he had published half a dozen soft-porn novels, and though he could now write a first draft on the typewriter, he couldn't read back what he wrote, which led to my working with him on his fiction.

I'd been invited for another stay at Yaddo, so, before leaving, I helped him plot a novel chapter by chapter that he could write in first

"As a bearded guru in my hippy period," about 1972

draft. When I got back from Yaddo I helped him revise it, resulting in *The Potency Clinic*, a comic coming-out novel, by Bruce Elliot, one of Neil's pseudonyms from his soft-porn days. But though I sent it on the rounds of publishers, none was ready for its sassy humor, so in 1978 we published it ourselves in a small edition under the imprint of Bleecker Street Press. I found this experience as a publisher a lot of fun—finding a cheap printer, sending copies to literary people, publications, and bookstores, filling orders, getting reviewed, and hearing from readers.

It was especially satisfying when a trio of young Germans who were setting up a gay publishing house, Albino Verlag, wrote that they wanted to buy the German-language rights of *Potency Clinic* for their first season's list, which included Jean Cocteau and James Purdy. They were attracted to the novel especially because it was humorous, a rare quality in gay novels at that time.

I'd always resisted doing anything but poetry, but I was loosening up. I had been all over the country, except the Deep South, on my reading tours, and now got the idea of editing an anthology of contemporary poetry that would present what poets were doing in each region. Ted Solotaroff, who was an editor at Bantam Books at the time, liked the idea and got me a contract for *A Geography of Poets* (1979). In order to get a different perspective of American poetry, Neil and I went to live in San Francisco for several months, to try to escape the usual New York-centered view of what was going on "out there" in the country and present a balanced selection of poets for once.

But that turned out to be just the trouble. The book wasn't reviewed in the *New York Times,* because, as the editor of the book review supplement told me, it was an anti-New York anthology. But though it only remained in print for several years, I keep running into people, especially on the West Coast, who studied it in their literature classes.

Wherever we were or whatever we were doing, Neil and I were always inventing plots for novels. We had so many ideas we talked of going into the plots business. So we were more than ready for another project to work on together, when, out of the blue, Bob Wyatt, an editor at Avon Books who specialized in original paperback novels, gave us the chance to write a big, popular "generations" novel about Greenwich Village. *Village* (1982) by Bruce Elliot, Neil's pseudonym which now became ours, followed a New York family over the years from 1845 when it moved into a house on Perry Street in Greenwich Village until the end of the Vietnam War in 1975. Though we researched Village and New York history, Neil was adamant that everything we used had to be integral to the plot, and much of the story grew out of historical events. We had a lot of fun with the plot, some of it borrowed from our favorite movies, but much of it quite original, incorporating themes of race and religion that have been significant in American life.

Every bit of it was written together. Neil would be at the typewriter while I would sit next to him scrawling revisions on the manuscript. Perhaps it was due to our laborious method, but we worked far longer hours than I ever had at poetry. For me, writing prose is a more "literary" exercise than poetry, and we settled on every sentence only after many, often fierce, struggles. All was miraculously forgiven when a chapter was done. My feeling about collaborating is that you can only succeed if nothing will break you up.

We finished a chunk of the novel during a winter in my brother-in-law Ack Van Rooyen's house in The Hague. It was the first of numerous stays in Holland and the beginning of our love affair with the Dutch. We lived in the attic room where the North Sea squalls beat on the tiled roof, but a little gas stove kept us warm. We would walk in the pale light of midday to the nearby boardwalk at Scheveningen and eat herrings from the fish store. I could only struggle with the Dutch language and its impossible gutterals, but somehow made myself understood in the shops.

We turned out *Village* in eighteen months, and for the first time I experienced the full treatment from a publisher, so different from having a book of poems published. After conferences, our editor even walked us to the elevator! No expense was spared to give the book popular appeal. An artist was commissioned to paint original scenes from the book for the end papers, and there were three different colored covers for the bookstore racks. It made

the B. Dalton best-seller list, and there was a window devoted to it at the store's Village branch, placards in the subways, full-page ads in women's magazines. It was astounding how much money we earned. With 220,000 copies sold, it was exhilarating to get those large royalty checks after the chicken feed from poetry.

But then I started hearing people say that I had given up poetry. True, devoting myself to Neil as I do, and writing together which takes up so much time, I've had to remove myself from poetry activities, readings, etc., but I continued to write poetry as always. It's just that now I was writing prose as well. No matter what else I'm involved in, deep down I've never deserted my commitment to poetry.

We have also been out of the country a great deal, especially after I was given the Rome Prize by the American Academy of Arts and Letters. We left for the year in Rome feeling that from then on we would be able to spend longer periods of time abroad. But our experience at the American Academy in Rome was not a happy one. Neil hated the dormitory living arrangements, with the bathroom down the hall and graduate student mateyness between the fellows. So we decided to leave and rent our own apartment, which caused a crisis in the head office. "This is an educational institution with rules," I was told by the director, and if I moved out, I would relinquish my fellowship.

The director ultimately backed down, and we escaped to our own apartment, though I continued to work in my studio in the Academy garden. But Rome, beautiful as it was, was impenetrable, and leaving it for good in May 1982 was a relief. We were heading for Berlin where in June *Die Potenz Klinik* by Bruce Elliot, translated into German by Gerhard Hoffmann, was coming out. We stopped off in Athens, where I still remembered some Greek from my stay in 1949, and then spent a few days in iron-curtain Sofia before flying on to Germany.

One of the publishing team at Albino Verlag, Peter Schmittinger, who has since died of AIDS, showed us West Berlin in his car, and there was a book signing in Prinz Eisenherz, the gay bookstore, where I signed for Neil. And throughout the entire week the singing of blackbirds outside the window of our room in a pension.

On our previous visit to Berlin, when we stayed with my sister and brother-in-law, I'd felt slightly repelled, but now I succumbed to the

Neil Derrick, about 1985

drama of being in Germany, where there is plenty to remind one that *It happened here.* Everywhere the twelve years of Nazism remain vivid, and the eye even puts together the remnants of the heavy, ornate Wilhelminian city destroyed in the bombing. And overlaying that, the divided city of the cold war, the two sides so different, each with its own qualities. The austereness of East Berlin, when we went over, seemed a relief from the glitzy, hyped-up West. In fact, every visit to Germany from then on, has been a welcome change from the messiness of life in New York.

After the success of *Village*, it looked like Neil and I were set up to continue writing novels together and we'd be able to live off them. Our editor even called us in for a discussion of another idea he had, a novel set in a Manhattan office. Unfortunately, though we threw in drug dealing, suicide, wife beating, a sexy rat of a boss who leads our heroine-typist a merry chase for years, *The Office* (1987) by Bruce Elliott (another "t" was added) did not sell. Suddenly, we were box office poison and that ended Bruce Elliot(t)'s career.

Still, we've held to our determination to live abroad as much as possible, even with our minimal income. I love speaking other languages. Whenever I'm in a place where a different language is spoken, I feel a wonderful sense of possibility. In addition, it's good for my ego, especially in the Arab world, where the old are not scorned as in the United States—they don't even notice you're old. In France, too, a man of my age is treated with considerable respect.

Though we've made numerous trips to Tunisia, Morocco, Turkey, Egypt, and various Eastern European countries, as well as throughout Europe, it is most satisfying to rent an apartment and actually live there. We've done that for months at a time in Berlin, Amsterdam, Tangier, Rome, but most often in London, where we stay in the remarkably lively, cosmopolitan neighborhood of Queensway. Wherever we are, we go on working, at the moment on screenplays, whether or not they will ever be produced.

My generation had the romantic idea—no, the imperative—that you must destroy yourself for your art, as Hart Crane did, and Rimbaud. Being an artist, like being a communist, meant working for posterity, not the present. Somehow I survived this illusion, though my friend Alfred Chester destroyed himself, and in 1971, died miserable and insane in Jerusalem. With all the attention he had received in his short life and publishing career, by the time of his death he was completely forgotten. Ten years later in the early eighties, I began my Alfred Chester Project, to get him back into print and revive his reputation. This led to our becoming friends with Alfred's English editor, Diana Athill, a remarkable writer herself, whom Neil and I visit whenever we are in London.

But editors kept telling me that they couldn't publish Alfred Chester because he was forgotten, which, I replied, was exactly why I wanted him to be republished! It took several years, but I finally connected with Kent Carroll of Carroll & Graf, who reissued Alfred Chester's last novel, *The Exquisite Corpse*, in 1986 with an introduction by Diana Athill. A few years later, Black Sparrow Press published two volumes, his selected stories and then the selected essays, which I edited. To help the revival, I persuaded old friends to write about him, and Cynthia Ozick published a memoir in *The New Yorker* about their friendship and rivalry at NYU. I published my own essays about him in the *New*

York Times Book Review, Boston Review, and *The Dictionary of Literary Biography,* as well as sending out a number of issues of an *Alfred Chester Newsletter.* Also ready for publication is the collection of his Moroccan letters. Recently I've deposited my archive of Chester books, correspondence, and other materials in the library of the University of Delaware, along with my own papers.

One inescapable fact about putting together a poetry anthology is that you have to read a lot of poetry. So when Gerald Locklin suggested that we do a sequel to *A Geography of Poets,* I started catching up on what had been going on in the poetry world since that last poetry-reading binge. I always advise young poets that you can't write poetry unless you read it, and read it closely, but I myself am not what could be called an omnivorous reader of poetry. I never went through an adolescent phase of reading through Byron and Shelley and Keats, or even Shakespeare, like many of the poets I know. It is true that certain poems are thrilling, but the rest seems largely irrelevant and boring, except to scholars, so I've always been out to make my poems *not* boring. Writing poetry, of course, is far more fun than reading it, and I sometimes think that my dissatisfaction with reading poetry is that I'm looking for the poems I would write myself. So, in a way, I was grateful for being forced to do all that reading for the anthology and find out what was happening.

If *A Geography of Poets* was a view of America from San Francisco and New York, its sequel *A New Geography of Poets* (1992), co-edited with my Long Beach buddies Charles Stetler and Gerald Locklin, was a view of America from southern California and New York. It was meant to celebrate the fact that, while no one was looking, a new kind of American poetry has been springing up in every corner of the country, a kind of poetry that is completely indigenous, emerging from the populist spirit, as opposed to the intellectual elitism of the Northeast. This nativist poetry accepts the limited education that we Americans generally get in school but sharpens it with the specialized education of the streets, and lets into poetry like air the informality, humor, quirkiness, vulgarity, in short the slanginess, that Americans have always had. These poems are related to tall tales at bull sessions, porn fantasies, stand-up comedy, conversations across bar stools. Strange in the usually arty-farty poetry world, here the sleaze in American life is accepted as normal. It is no accident that this demotic poetry movement should arise in southern California in the proximity of Hollywood, for it is most of all influenced by the sentimentality and tough-guy corniness of old movies. It puzzles me that this movement, the liveliest thing happening in American poetry today, which I called Neo-Pop in an article in *Poets & Writers* magazine, has still not been recognized, much less defined, and the major literary critics are not even interested!

After more than fifty years, it seems strange that I continue to be very much involved with poetry. Old friends like Stanley Moss still call up and read me their new poems over the phone. But I must confess that I send out my poems less, and usually to off-beat little magazines like *Exquisite Corpse* and *Chiron Review.* The process of writing has been considerably changed by a computer. With its help I also find myself writing prose these days, and other than the Alfred Chester pieces, I've had essays in the *Nation, Raritan, Michigan Quarterly, Parnassus,* and the *Harvard Gay and Lesbian Review,* among others. I'm even writing my memoirs.

As I write this, my world is on the verge of extinction. Everything is different now and I may be an anomaly, but I still feel that the Left, whatever its errors and ideological faults, generally has the best orientation for a livable society. The major theme in my poetry has been speaking up for the poor, the unwanted, the underdog, and by extension, the "lower" functions of the body. True to my Jewish traditions, I write from the heart, though that is unfashionable in our increasingly selfish, market-oriented universe.

When I started writing, I wanted my poetry to save the world. I saw myself standing up in the marketplace and speaking to the people. Later, I desperately believed, against the world, that poetry could save me. In spite of the evident truth that poetry can change nothing, I trust the instincts of the young and why they are attracted to poetry, as if it actually could overcome injustice. It has to do with an idealism that gets lost as you get older, especially as you get involved in the poetry world with its factions and power struggles. It has to do with poetry as magic, the magic of words.

I still believe it's a kind of magic.

BIBLIOGRAPHY

Poetry:

Stand Up, Friend, with Me, Grove, 1963.

Variety Photoplays, Grove, 1967.

(Translator) *Eskimo Songs and Stories* (for children), Delacorte, 1973.

A Full Heart, Sheep Meadow Press, 1977.

Stars in My Eyes, Sheep Meadow Press, 1978.

The Lost, Dancing, Watershed Tapes, 1984.

New and Selected Poems from the Book of My Life, Sheep Meadow Press, 1987.

Counting Myself Lucky: Selected Poems 1963–1992, Black Sparrow, 1992.

Fiction; under pseudonym Bruce Elliot, with Neil Derrick:

The Potency Clinic, Bleecker Street, 1978; German translation published as *Die Potenz Klinik,* Albino Verlag, 1982.

Village, Avon, 1982.

The Office (under modified pseudonym Bruce Elliott), Ballantine, 1987.

Editor:

A Geography of Poets, Bantam, 1979.

(With Charles Stetler and Gerald Locklin) *A New Geography of Poets,* University of Arkansas Press, 1992.

Head of a Sad Angel: Stories by Alfred Chester (introduction by Gore Vidal), Black Sparrow, 1990.

Looking for Genet: Essays by Alfred Chester, Black Sparrow, 1992.

Other:

Narration for documentary film, *To Be Alive,* 1965.

Contributor to numerous periodicals, including *Botteghe Oscure, Harvard Gay and Lesbian Review, Michigan Quarterly, Nation, Parnassus,* and *Raritan.* Editor of the *Alfred Chester Society Newsletter,* dedicated to studies of the late American writer, as well as a collection of letters from the author entitled *Voyage to Destruction.*

Fanny Howe

1940-

SEEING IS BELIEVING

Fanny Howe, Cambridge, Massachusetts, August 1967

My children and I grew up together in Jamaica Plain—a section of Boston that lies between Jamaica Pond and Franklin Park. The children went to the local public schools, then in the process of desegregation, and I went to school as a low-level instructor of creative writing. My life with my children began when I met their father in late 1967, only a few months after my father died of a heart attack. I had been working for CORE (the Congress on Racial Equality) in Roxbury. At first I traveled south with a friend to re-

port on goings-on down there; we went through Mississippi and Selma, Natchez, and the Carolinas. Later I returned to Boston to continue working for CORE. My partner in seeking out housing violations and reporting them was Jonathan Kozol, who later introduced me to Carl Senna with the warning, "Don't fall in love with him."

Carl was a writer, and I was also writing and editing with Bill Corbett the small magazine called *Fire Exit*. We accepted a good story written by Carl, who lived on Massachusetts

Avenue near Columbus Avenue in a building occupied mostly by prostitutes. His apartment was shrouded in blackness with hardly enough light available to see the few political posters on the wall. His front door wore his name on a card: *Carlos Francisco Jose Senna.* His father had been a boxer, Mexican, sent back to Sierra Leone under Nixon's Wetback Laws. His mother, African-American, moved to Boston from the South, where she was a schoolteacher and piano player.

Carl had almost finished Boston University but was now working as an attendant in a mental hospital, where he witnessed terrible abuse of the patients. His mother lived in the Whittier Street projects with his sister and brother, both of them grown and en route to independent lives. It didn't take me long to become involved with Carl and his family, but it was a couple of months before our relationship changed into romance. We were married a year after Kozol's warning, and had our first child exactly nine months later. We would have three children within four years, and I would spend the seven years of our tumultuous marriage in

"My father"

a skewed relationship to many old friends and family members. No one of them was rude or overtly racist. But the media and the environs around Boston were so charged with those exact possibilities that any personal exchange on the subject of home life would be fraught with symbolic value.

Both of us were needy and uprooted when we met. I was even worse than that: crippled by claustrophobia, riddled with terror attacks, paralyzed by shyness, morbidly afraid of human beings—especially any in a position of authority. Carl had no direction as far as a career went, and so we grabbed onto each other in an effort at stabilizing ourselves. It had always been my immersion in the political chaos of those days (and in earlier days, side by side, with my father) that had awakened me to the possibility that I was feeling justifiable despair, not depression; social outrage, not personal anxiety. I was liberated from my own personality to talk and think and walk politics. Carl's and my shared interest in political philosophies (Paulo Freire, Ivan Illich, Frantz Fanon) drew us together as much as anything else, and his experience with race and class issues became my education. My father had been a civil rights activist and my personal ally as well. I missed him. It was always like "one of the comforts of home" to immerse myself in politics.

There were many women like me—born into white privilege but with no financial security; given a good education but no training for survival. Some of us ended up in cults, some in jail, some in far-out marriages. The daughters of white activists tended to become more engaged than even their fathers were, and like certain Greek heroines, they drove themselves to madness and incarceration in carrying to the nth degree their fathers' progressive positions. Because my family (academic, artistic) had no extra money, there was no cushion for the crash from a comfortable home into the literal cold streets. Somehow Carl and I did manage to carve a niche for ourselves—through marriage and new jobs luckily acquired—just off the streets. We were both somewhat conservative in our habits. No drugs, no rock-and-roll. Crossing the racial divide was the only radical ingredient in what we were doing. Basically we were in hiding when we weren't working.

Carl was Catholic and his mother, who lived with us, was devoutly Catholic, attending daily mass on her way to work at the courthouse downtown. We had the children baptized, and I began attending mass with my mother-in-law hovering at the back of the church, and feeling myself excluded and estranged from the rituals. I read Simone Weil, the Boff brothers, Gustavo Gutierrez, and a variety of contemporary liberation theologians who incorporated socialist ideals with a Christian preferential option for the poor. And as the children grew older, each took catechism classes and First Communion. I grew increasingly comfortable sitting at mass and participating in everything but the Eucharist, for many years. The skepticism that was like a splash of iodine in the milk of my childhood home began to work its way out of my system.

Encircling this rather quiet and interiorized quest was the city of Boston and its racist and violent rejection of progress, desegregation, dialogue. Louise Day Hicks and the vociferous Boston Irish were like the dogs and hoses in the South. No difference. Boston, always segregated into pockets of furious chauvinism—from the North End to the South, from rich white sections of Cambridge to poor working-class areas there—did not know how to separate issues of race and class. The poor were set against the poor, while the rich continued to glide around the periphery dispensing moral judgments.

King was assassinated during the same season I met Carl. Parts of the city were cordoned off. James Brown was called in. We went to his concert that had been organized to ward off riots, and it succeeded. Although Boston never exploded to the same extent as other cities, the surge of Black Power was unlike anything that had happened there or in the country before. Blackness became the club that many whites longed to join. The raised fists, the street signals, the attitude, the rhetoric, the music—all these produced a change in white consciousness that had the effect of making whites defensive and aggressive on the one hand, or yearning for conciliation on the other.

Black Power forced individual whites to see themselves as unstable and isolated social products, people who had come to the end of the line, and not the transcendent and eternal beings that they were raised to believe themselves to be. It was a terrible blow to a mass ego. Without even knowing it, whites had been getting away with murder. The fundamental assumption that they deserved everything that they

Carl Senna, 1968

had, or didn't yet have, simply because they were white had to be rethought. Any knowledge of the history of civil rights in this country would quickly expose race as a national obsession from day one. Race as the way to measure intellectual superiority, that is. Mountains of documents argued to support this belief in white superiority; the very size of the heap revealed the desperate anxiety behind the claims. Black Power was its moral opposer, and it was powerful. It showed how quickly and thoroughly a change of self-image can produce a radical reappraisal by one's neighbors; this is a good thing to remember.

Boston, recalcitrant and class-divided, was a poor choice of a place to live as a mixed couple. Even the most enlightened white academics had no black friends, or tokens only, and fled quickly to the suburbs for the schools. Those who stayed and struggled in the inner city were few and far between, and were both self-interested and heroic. They renovated houses in the South End and Jamaica Plain and involved themselves in school committees and busing and clinics, doing so with the social optimism of an earlier, prewar generation. Yet many of them had no black friends at the end of the day, only colleagues in the battles for better schools for their children. In the black community there was very little agreement on anything, and be-

The author's daughters, Annlucien (left) and Danzy

cause it was a small and old community, hatreds that take time to thrive had taken root, and the disagreements on social action were irreconcilable.

Boston's white upper class is divided between the Republican core group, who are in business, banking, law, and who own property in the suburbs, and Democrats, who don't own much of anything and have stayed in the realms of "letters" and political policy, social justice and academics. Both come from Old Money, but the Democrats only have snuffboxes, teacups, and dusty portraits to show for it, while the Republicans have long driveways through trees and country clubs at which blacks and Jews have been for years unwelcome. These two types don't speak, and even they are divided into small mutually interested groups. Stockbrokers see stockbrokers; academics see other academics. Doctors talk to doctors; and teachers are too tired at the end of the day to talk to anyone but their families. There is very little cross-cultural exchange even at the most privileged level in Boston. From that point down, the divisions enlarged and darkened, and still do.

Boston is a parochial and paranoid city; it doesn't admit its own defects, and it belittles its own children as a result. It is a difficult city for African-Americans. In Boston, as in much of America, there has always been more interracial interaction among the poor, among working people, churchgoing people, and criminals, including the Mafia, than among the rich and privileged. When self-interest includes racial

crossings in order to sustain certain vital social transactions, then there is more intermarriage too. In Boston, in the early and mid-seventies, there was a group of young disenfranchised flower children who also intermarried; they were street poets and musicians. They took drugs; they crossed over. But most of them were drifting already apart and going in other directions around the time Nixon was impeached.

My children grew up with other racially mixed children who came out of that period. *Sesame Street* was their Cuba—an urban utopia that surely influenced their values for life. By 1980 almost all of their parents had divorced; their single white mothers ran their lives. Until those divorces it was as if we occupied a fleet of little arks that rose with the flood and tossed and sank; and inside our windowless habitats we blamed all the chaos on our marriages. Race war was enacted inside the tight little houseboats: violent language, violent action, intimidation, insult, accusations that made no sense, based as they were in an absolute lack of understanding of each other's cultures— all this in order to create a New World. We went so far out, we passed, on the way, insights and possibilities that were good as well as bad. "I am the Way," said Jesus, for following him would mean taking a path to the farthest reaches of understanding. There are worldly journeys that also travel to the end of the possible; they are hellish passions; you learn everything from them.

After a few months of marriage and pregnancy, we moved to a small town on the Salem harbor, north of Boston. We lived at the top of a very sheer short hill, called Sunset Road, that looked down onto the harbor. Carl's mother moved in with us, commuted by bus to her job in Boston, and we both had teaching jobs at Tufts University. Our decision to leave Boston was based in a certain self-consciousness about our marriage; our home was a hide-out. But we had friends who visited us there—the African novelist Ayi Kwei Armah, his then wife Fatima Mernissi, two friends, Joe and Lynn Long (also a mixed marriage), whom we had met in New Mexico, Robert Creeley, and other new and old friends from Boston and New York. The talk steered invariably towards politics and race.

Carl got more work in Boston, now as an editor at Beacon Press, so—much to my mother-in-law's sorrow—we returned to the city. In Jamaica Plain we lived in a large white house on a street called Robeson Street, which ran up Sumner Hill to Franklin Park, one of Olmsted's most glorious landscapes. Trees from this parkland spread huge branches over our house and the pudding-stone juttings that supported the enormous and shabby Victorian houses on this one street. Roxbury's Hill District has a similar quality, and there are probably five streets in Jamaica Plain that remain in this condition. We loved the house and filled it with Carl's family and various drifting Jamaican, Irish, and African people who needed temporary housing. I helped establish the neighborhood health clinic and became close to the people on the streets around. We started a day care in our basement, with two teachers and twelve little children, two of them mine; my third was still a baby beside me. In larger Boston, following Arthur Garrity's court order to the city schools, the black community was developing Operation Exodus, Metropolitan Educational Opportunities Council, Inc., the Bridge, Catholic Bridge—programs designed to lift black children out of the inner city and place them in suburban, private, and parochial schools. Blacks and whites together were also organizing magnet schools in certain deprived districts of the city.

At night I would leave a monumental pot of rice on the stove for those people passing through, who used rice as the staple of all their meals. Beans, vegetables, and Motown blasting. The children had a nursery in the attic where they developed intense fantasy lives around their dolls and stuffed animals, and my mother-in-law had a bedroom between ours and theirs, where two cribs sat side by side and the baby girls conversed in coos and whispers. My mother-in-law, a small dark-skinned woman with sloe eyes and a large mischievous smile, continued to work all day at the courthouse and then returned to help me (like a husband!) in the evenings; but a cancer she had treated with a mastectomy began returning and she became increasingly crippled with pain in the following years. She died two months before I gave birth to my third child. Her illness—and finally her dying—profoundly affected our family. We were never the same without her, and the whole fertile operation disintegrated in terrible ways. It was as if things outdoors began to grow inside the house, under the tables and in the sinks.

"My mother-in-law"

My book called *Robeson Street* was written during those years, as were my two short novels, *First Marriage* and *Bronte Wilde*. I wrote in a little room that adjoined our bedroom, but only in starts and fits—highly concentrated moments that transformed the style I had used in prose before, one that was conventionally narrative according to nineteenth-century standards. My new approach to storytelling was in this sense determined by my habits and duties at home (nursing, cooking, cleaning, walking children to the park, and so on). Multilevelled short narrative outbursts, a near heuristic version of fiction, were certainly influenced by my involvement since early childhood with poetry. I wrote poems in bed while I was nursing, or when the sated child was sleeping on my arm. Or I wrote them during potty-training sessions, or while cooking. The focus was always the sentence itself, which comes to me as a long word, a single sound and content unit. The less time I had to concentrate on prolonged prose sections, the more intense each single sentence became. There would be an outburst, then the product would travel around with me, being reduced and amended.

Before my marriage I had published two books and had an agent, and I seemed on the way to becoming a recognized member of my generation as a writer. My books came out with Houghton Mifflin, and I was well reviewed. All this radically changed during the course of my marriage and the change in my aesthetic practice. No one wanted to publish my new fiction, or my poetry. Certainly not Houghton Mifflin. The somewhat eccentric style reflected queer content. I was rejected again and again until I returned—rather timidly—to Avon Books, where I had worked as a reader years before and where Robert Wyatt was now the editor of a new series of experimental novels (Avon Equinox). Without much ado he published in paper my two novels; he was supportive. And I began my career as a paperback writer.

This was a fertile but lonely time. While I was involved in neighborhood politics and my true colleagues were other mothers, racial tensions in the city subtly invaded the household. More frequently than not, I found my point of view no longer fit that of my friends, even though we were committed to the same issues. Some world view was inexorably shifting in me, and I felt sidelined by conversations and remarks that would have slid by unnoticed before. Many whites were demonstrating against Vietnam, and much of the hot talk around that topic spilled into defenses and condemnations of underground organizations that believed in violent resistance. The four assassinations had changed the entire atmosphere of political debate in the country from polite reasoning to justifications for revenge. The Cuban Revolution and the liberation of African nations had already indicated to many of us that the only way to produce radical social change was to push the discourse to a criminal-inclusive language.

An example of this: white people are obsessed with race, and the subject comes up at least once in any three- or four-hour gathering. One night I went to a small town in Massachusetts to give a reading, and when I entered the room where all white people had gathered afterwards, they were saying, "If the lines ever get drawn, and the situation gets seriously violent, I know which side I will be on." And then they began to speak (liberals all of them) about their fear of blacks, their judgments of blacks, and I had to announce to them that my husband and children were black before hastily departing.

This event has been repeated so many times, in multiple forms, that by now I make some kind of giveaway statement after entering a white-only room, one way or the other, that will warn the people there "which side I am on." The situation most recently repeated itself about a hundred times in my presence over the subject of O. J. Simpson. His name was like the whistle of a train coming down the line; I knew what was coming—vindictive racialized remarks, coming from otherwise socially progressive white people. Louis Farrakhan is the only other public person who produces the same reaction. You would think that he had organized mass murders and guerilla warfare on American streets. On these occasions, more than any others, I feel that my skin is white, but my soul is not, and that I am in camouflage. It is clear to me that black men are in a no-win situation in relation to whites, including liberals who perceive them (but never say so) as sell-outs from their "own people" (not revolutionary enough) if they live with a white woman, and who then judge them as dangerous and anti-integrationist if they live with a black woman. It is the white dread of (and fetishization of) black men that has sustained the institution of racism. Integration is not a word that is heard anymore; incarceration has replaced it.

Only white women historically in this country have been condemned to a lower status than black men, and that was when they crossed over and married black men. Then they were officially, legally, relegated to the lowest social caste. Many times people stopped me, with my children, to ask, "Are they yours?" with an expression of disgust and disbelief on their faces. These were white people. In neighborhoods where there were Puerto Rican families with a wide range of colors and hair types among them, I felt safe; I was addressed in Spanish.

When they were very young, my children decided that they were black despite their fair skin and mestizo features. They decided this, with the help of their father, me, and the city of Boston at the height of the busing crisis when the school system divided families according to each child's physical appearance. We decided that it was a tribal more than an individual choice, and we shared our views on this score with the children.

After my third child was in my arms I had begun to feel that I contained in my body a fourth child, and sometimes I would hallucinate, hearing the sound of this missing child crying. In some way this sensation began to correspond to the experience of "covering," and soon I could honestly and deeply feel myself to contain an other self, a shadow. I have never felt empty physically since the birth of my son, Maceo.

There were at this time in Boston "women's groups," where small gatherings of friends would meet to talk about the condition of being female, of mothering and marrying. These groups often revealed economic differences between us more than ties that bound us, and they often wound up (disappointingly) as discussions of fat, breast size, and hormones. Yet something important happened in those gatherings anyway; feelings of intimacy and respect for each other emerged—feelings that women rarely had for each other before in their scramble to catch men. It was in these funky meetings that some insight was gained into the assumptions being made about our gender, by ourselves as much as by men, and so a refusal to collaborate was begun in living rooms and kitchens after dark.

At that time survival of my children and myself as their only caretaker was all that drove me after their father and I broke up. I learned how to bend the rules, to prevaricate, to be crooked, to get something for as little as nothing, to take now and pay later, fake facts in exchange for safety, to live by smoke alone, to feel grateful to cheap wine at night, to find the free clinics, the kind people, the food-stamp outlet, and to exchange free child care with other mothers. The potential for corruption, which is in all of us, is certainly triggered by the feeling of being absolutely alone with a desperate situation. I would do anything for my children. The emotion was not heroic or tough even. It was reactive. When this kind of situation lasts for awhile, your adaptation to crookedness can alter your personality unless you watch out. There is a point when you realize you are spending more time covering the traces of your dishonesty than you spent plotting it. I know women now, I recognize them, who are powerful and lively spirits, who have nonetheless become permanently dishonest in response to several difficult years caring for their children alone. I know that they would lie to their own best friend to get an extra buck, years after the need for that was over.

Some years after, I wrote *Holy Smoke*—a story about ethical chaos—as an experiment to see if my life would begin to imitate that story about a desperate woman in search of her child, a sort of modern Ceres looking for Persephone. But in the novel she went north instead of down. (We had, the children and I, fled to Canada for safety at one point; it became the setting for the high point of the plot.) And so my life did in many ways begin to imitate it.

When I finally did have to strike close to the streets (we lost our house, we had no money and nowhere to go, and made daily visits to dismal welfare and food-stamp offices), it was a stretch that nearly broke me, but there were several women who helped me out. One of these women was a young black psychiatrist, Daryl Utz, who worked at the neighborhood clinic. She was a brilliant and gentle counselor through this bad time, seated in a dismal office adjacent to the giant hospitals off the Riverway in Boston, wet snow falling outside. We shared champagne at New Year's; we became friends; she told me: "You married your mother!" I started commuting to New York to work two days a week, and on one of the days at home, she called me to say, "I am going to reverse roles and cancel our appointment for today," and then she committed suicide. It was this tragedy that gave me the impetus to leave Boston and settle in a shack in the woods in Connecticut. I saw Boston as a prison then, a race nightmare. Her isolated home in a white suburban tract where she had died seemed to be a metaphor for no-place-to-run-no-place-to-hide.

Nevertheless I, like her, chose the country, a wood by the sea, to recover in: a small town with a kind day-care staff and sliding scale; my sister; a very good public school in a huge green field; and a train to New York where I was then teaching at Columbia. The poet Maureen Owen was living in the same town and also working in New York, and we helped each other with child care when we had to spend nights away. She published two of my books of poems written at that time; we mimeoed and stapled them out in her barn. Simultaneously I wrote, during this time, *Poem from a Single Pallet* and *In the Middle of Nowhere*. The smell of the sea and bird songs in many ways worked as a tonic. But the race issue was a plague and a problem for the children, who had no friends of color to speak of, in that

"Maceo, Annlucien, me, and Danzy"

small privileged town. And we were not used to living alone. We always lived with other people.

Not for the first or last time, we were asked to leave the shack after a year (too many children; I had lied and said I only had two), and we moved into a house near the village green called the Welfare House by the neighbors. There we lived over a single mother, a Korean woman named Kyong, with her son Michael, and we happily became an extended family. It was the mid-seventies. We were then a family of four living on six thousand dollars a year, my income from Columbia. A small town is far preferable on a daily basis to a city, when you are poor, but the catch-22 is that there are few opportunities for work, for changing your situation. You can comfortably squat in the same economic position there for many years. I felt stagnant and lacking in hope there.

With my return, then, to Boston, in search of more opportunity, I began to play the school system along with many other single mothers, moving from one part of the city to the other, following the zoning. Racialization of our chil-

dren began immediately—they were coded by hair and skin tone to travel to one or another school, sometimes different ones. I remember fighting out this issue with an official over a table in some school in West Roxbury, until we found a school all three children could attend together. This perverse operation taught me to use race in our children's favor, calling them black in one district and white in another, in order to get the good school. I wrote an article for the *Boston Globe* at that time called "The Nouveau Pauvre," describing my own situation, as someone middle class who had fallen below the poverty line with droves of others, mostly women, and how we coped with it. We formed food co-ops and community gardens in abandoned lots running along the tracks to downtown Boston. And we also learned how to entangle the issues of economics and race in ways that served our children's interests.

Having determined that our children would get the kind of education that we had, but having no money to support that determination, we not only taught them at home, we also tracked them for Boston Latin, the city's best public school, or Brookline High School, as soon as we had steered them through the maze of Boston's elementary school system during the busing crisis. Whites were abandoning Boston for the suburbs, where the busing order was not enforced, in order to avoid sending their children to school with black children, and they left behind a trail of scrawled messages: *Nigger Go Home*. And some of those same whites worked in the city and often liberally encouraged poor whites and blacks to continue their struggle for integrated schools. It was the well-known American story: at all costs, don't mention economic injustice. Increasingly race was a red herring, a way to avoid seeing the ever-widening gap between rich and poor.

By the time my children were approaching sixth grade, one thing was clear: elementary school accomplishes eighty percent of the task of educating children for their entire lives. In the Boston public schools, between first and fifth grades, my children got all the basic learning they needed from excellent and committed teachers. Anything extra was my responsibility at home. From sixth grade on, the issues changed, and the school day was more of a social than an educational reality. The main lesson: learn your place in the pecking order through sports and clubs. The kids got a little history, English, bad language instruction, and small science. I could be of less and less actual help, because their attention was drawn elsewhere, towards the purely social. The truth is, from middle school to graduation, the public school system is cousin to the penal system, a way of keeping kids off the streets so they won't disturb the grownups.

I had returned to Boston with a feeble hope of reconstructing our marriage, but our struggles continued after we returned to live in Jamaica Plain. We moved when once again I was asked to leave an apartment, after Kyong and Michael moved in with us, putting six people in a two-bedroom space. It was then that my cousin Quincy gave me a down payment on a big old house and we could rent out sections of the house and this way pay the mortgage. I also began work on the project that would take eighteen months—*The White Slave*—a novel based on the true story of a white boy raised as a slave before, during, and after the Civil War. My agent at the time, Phyllis Seidel, believed I was the obvious person to write about "crossing over" from white to black, and I was paid enough by Avon to live for those months, while

I looked for another teaching job and rented out rooms in the house.

This novel—carefully written about imperilled people and set in Missouri—was cheapened in the marketing of it. The sexualized title, the vulgar cover. It was just one more debilitating experience for me, in relation to publishing. Somehow over that difficult decade I had fallen into a peculiar niche, which I occupied alone. Writing for money (three more paperback novels written about a biracial teenager), but for pathetic little sums of money, the same amount people got for pornography and Harlequin romance—and always about race—I existed in a nowhere land. The fact that I was not black did not help the marketing of my work for a popular audience; neither did my own continual voluntary withdrawal from the commercial publishing world.

I think for that time my involvement in the domestic scene permanently determined my position in relation to feminism. Those household ideals—which are of course social ideals, too—of an extended family who live together, sharing and helping and not competing with each other, were incompatible with an individualist approach to the social and professional arena. Between my domestic socialism and the outside world's social realism, I could only construct a narrow and weak psychological bridge, one that I was finally too suspicious to cross. I still wrote poetry frantically and continually. But I began to notice other friends, once my compatriots in literature, publishing like me with the Fiction Collective and Avon Equinox, had now moved to New York and were being given huge advances for hardback novels that would be well reviewed. I didn't really absorb what this might mean for me and continued to function in continual reaction to the necessities of each day. When James Wolcott in the *Village Voice* attacked my book *Holy Smoke*, using it as an example for all that he despised about the Fiction Collective, I felt as if I had stepped out to inspect the weather and was smashed by a fist in the face. His words haunted me. His judgments were like a negative mantra I would repeat at daybreak. I vowed never to read another review of my work again (and haven't) and withdrew even further away from the arena.

During these school choice crises, people used false addresses, moved, and begged in order to get their kids into decent places. We kept three such students, friends of my children, listed under our address and several times had to rush around to round them up before they were caught not living there. My daughters remained in Boston public schools until they went to college, and their education became the motivating force behind where we could live. My son went to a private school that generously paid almost his entire fee; I sent him there so that he could have more attention than I could give him, now that I was working more hours and he had no father at home. And by the time he was six I had figured out that he was a school hater (as I had been) and that I could place him in safe custody among generous liberals who were comfortable with his combination of good manners and color. The kindness of many liberals during this period was paramount in making it possible for numbers of children to escape the public school system, and I believe that my children's generation will increase the numbers of minority people in power through friendships made in their school years. They will bring others along with them, even if they are "only racially mixed" themselves.

Schools, clinics, housing. This triad dominated fifteen years of our waking lives. Yet in the midst of it all I was thinking intensely and reading voraciously. When I finally got a job at MIT, and my income went up to $26,000 per annum, I felt a certain degree of stability that would last for eight years—from 1978 on. At MIT I met Ilona Karmel, the writer, who would become my close friend and teacher; we shared readings in philosophy, theology, fiction. She bought my children—and me!—winter and spring clothes when the money was low, and she and her husband became a reference point for ethical affection in our lives. I read Hans Jonas's book on Gnosticism, Gershom Scholem's *Major Trends in Jewish Mysticism,* more and more Simone Weil, and I read books on the nature of time and theology. I audited a course given by Henri Nouwen at Harvard—on the Gospel of John; that was my first experience with supernatural teaching.

For several years, when we had fled Boston, I learned tarot cards and spent evenings, while the children slept, examining their kabbalistic roots and numerologies. This was definitely a pre-Catholic time for me, but I became very adept at reading people's fortunes—

Ilona Karmel

frighteningly so—and it was only recently (having given up cards over a decade ago) that I realized that this training was fundamental to my teaching practice. I read my students' work as if it were a spread, and see in their struggles with words the signs of Queens, Kings, Fools, Hanging Men, cups, and so on. I read them intuitively, closely, with the same concentration and predictiveness ajar. This revelation was only one more confirmation of the intensity of daily life, for those hours that seem meaningless—and even wasted—leave their mark.

It wasn't until five years after my divorce, when I joined those ranks of single white mothers, that I knew I would convert to Catholicism. By then I had had all the experience I would ever need to live in this world. I didn't want any more. My psyche could not include any more. Maybe there was no more experience that follows mortal fear and loss of all possessions. In Pauline terms, my worldly hope was transforming into theological hope. It seemed to me that Catholicism was the first choice I ever made and that it included many of the contradictions that by that time I saw as the actual shape of reality. Of course, I fell on the feminine side of church history, the side that favored monastic and communal living and mystical thought, and sharing of possessions until stripped of them entirely.

While I looked for a way into the church I immersed myself in the Hag Hammadi texts, and Gnosticism in general; it only helped to catapult me closer to Catholicism. My most significant teachers (after my mother-in-law) were Jews: Edward Dahlberg, Simone Weil, Ilona Karmel. And the Scholem book on Jewish mysticism was a blaze in the trail towards the church. But Gnosticism nearly drove me to a breakdown; it was so like the existentialism of my childhood and youth, and steeped in the poison of a skepticism I had witnessed for as long as I could remember. While gnostic thought at least faces the "disappeared God" and takes It on without flinching or faking, and while, in this way, it gives that God back Its wildness and our uncertainty, the terror that results and generates this story converts into a cynicism that can then spread into easy violence. I got scared by it. And my fear led me to dash around Boston looking for a priest. There were many false leads and rejections.

When I finally found the Paulist priest Father Moran at the top of a long flight of stairs at MIT, I was, I think, like a functional maniac. Exhausted generally, I was fighting my way through the days with love alone as my motivator. Within a few months and on a pouring rainy day, after much conversation with him, reading books he assigned, and a day on retreat, he welcomed me into the church. I was bursting with happiness when I took the Eucharist for the first time. This has remained the case.

I had by then vowed never to marry again, to live alone, to devote myself to my family and my work, but I had never dreamed how hard that would become: when the children left home, when I had to leave Boston to work across the country, when my work became increasingly obscure and teaching was my only value on a daily basis.

The years from 1968 to 1988 represented a Second Life for me—the one that followed childhood, the life when I processed and developed my emotions and my ideas about society, children, and work. In the middle of that time, my heart was broken—first by the violent end of my marriage and then by a three-year affair with a white male writer who grew sick of my hesitations. I had, since childhood, known people who shoved you out of their path, crying, "Sorry, but I am suffering!" on their way to get what they wanted. I had also known people who shoved you with the shout, "Sorry, I was only joking!" The first type, driven with ambition, felt guilty for getting everything they wanted; and horrifying themselves with their own murderous impulses, they complained of the unbearable pain they were feeling even as they pushed you back. The second type, less focused, more confused, but still ego-driven, would try to charm the very person they were pushing out of the way. There were also some people who apologized for shoving you even before they did it! By now, I preferred being alone to almost anything.

Yet I have always had good friends, and they have been my real family, and this was the case for many of them, too. It was, I began to notice, as if a group of us were born in a little tide pool by the edge of the ocean, and we swirled in circles, around and around, for our whole lives, encountering each other, affecting each other from youth on. Our destinies were deeply entwined. If this was the law of karma, then it was both profound and practical. In an ideal world one could construct a model community out of such a pool of friendships: the very same community that the poet Coleridge had hoped to create on the banks of the Susquehanna.

My written fiction during those years included *First Marriage, Bronte Wilde, Holy Smoke, In the Middle of Nowhere, The White Slave, The Deep North,* and three young adult novels. I wrote a few small collections of poetry, too: *The Amerindian Coastline Poem, Poem from a Single Pallet, Alsace-Lorraine, For Erato: The Meaning of Life, Introduction to the World, Robeson Street, The Lives of a Spirit,* and—my farewell to Boston book—*The Vineyard.* In my fiction I often tackled the issues of coincidence and determinism, not just in terms of plot, but in the actual process of constructing narrative. Discovering the trajectory for a story is exactly the same as understanding a set of choices you make in a day, a month, a year.

My muse was the body of work produced by the Italian neo-realists. This has stayed true. Since adolescence nothing has seemed to meet my yearning more fully than the films of Fellini,

Rosselini, Visconti, Pasolini. Seeing and believing: on screen the long word, a sentence, became populated in black and white, the people moving out of the shadows of the other world (the mind?) to act as visible language, language in action, transparent beings whose faces were illuminated circles. I liked the subtitles being where they were, sometimes even succumbing to the whiteness of the image and disappearing into it. I have always loved the tone of the translated poem: here it was, as a sounded voice, a writing. And here was my belief on film: in socialism, in the beatitudes. Without these films the world outside the windowpane would have lost a dimension; there would be greater social misery on the streets; this century would make no sense.

I keep going back to those films as I do to certain books, and certain people.

In those years my friends who were poets were mostly in New York and San Francisco. I was not part of any school or group, and when I was invited to speak—by the Language poets—and read at Langton Street in San Francisco, it was a high point in my writing life. Being essentially frightened of performance, it was not easy to go and stand up in front of a kind of "club" where everyone knew each other. Nonetheless—after it was over—I felt I had had my first experience as a writer outside my domestic site. This engagement with the Language poets has been the closest I ever came to participating in a movement, and it has been pretty minimal. My admiration for them has always been based in their commitment to stopping the sentimental flow of bourgeois associations in poetry and prose: a languor and vanity that have made "a good poem" a product that anyone educated can construct. A body of work is what interests me, almost in a literal slain and sacrificial sense, the body of the poet and her work as one long, complex, and cumulative shape over years.

Every city has its poetry "clubs" and Boston was no exception. For some reason—and sometimes by choice—I was never part of one there, but lived in relative isolation from the Boston literary scene. Both my identification with my children and my interest in Catholicism put me in a skewed position in relation to a public site. For many years I felt as if I was in hiding—with my family, with my writing, my thoughts, my books, with my close friends. The household was always filled with cousins and

friends, people who rented space or hung out there. I never wanted to leave home. It was hard to go to work even, and teaching, which was an agony for me—because of shyness—was a kind of testing site for me, and only the students themselves could charm me out of my self-judgment. The students have always saved me from the problem of teaching. And in the end, ironically, my time as a teacher was the only work I could defend before a court of law or God. It was the work I found the least easy to do and yet the work I was somehow fated to do for thirty years.

For all these years I have only taught workshops. I have never been tempted by literary history or criticism, or a kind of reading that converts the written material later into a personal work. I find it difficult to dissect novels and poems, although I can talk to a student about the potential and the difficulties in his or her own work. Contemporary poetics all but require that poets write essays about other poets and about literary theory. Primarily I read philosophy (Weil, Emmanuel Levinas, Edith Stein, Giorgio Agamben) and theology, mystical literature (Brahmayogin Upanishad, "The Cloud of Unknowing," Meister Eckhart and poems—often in translation—and books about race and class. Film is the narrative element I am most drawn to: my dream of a language from "the other side" is realized in certain movies. Film is the language of the gone. In certain writers I see that same look (in Proust, in some of Eudora Welty's short stories, for instance), but I rarely read new fiction, except in order to teach it, and have very little knowledge of American literary movements and their classifications. The whole movement of my mind goes out on tracks that have nothing to do—ostensibly—with my life as a poet and fiction writer. This (along with my hesitation at giving readings) has not helped me become firmly installed in contemporary literary life.

The people who published my poetry in volumes—Maureen Owen (Telephone Books), the Alice James Books group, Forrest Gander and C. D. Wright (Lost Roads Books), Lyn Hejinian (Tuumba), Patricia Dienstfrey (Kelsey Street Books), and Geoff Young (The Figures)—were all struggling themselves as publishers, yet each one of them represents a separate "school," ranging from New York to Boston to feminist to San Francisco Language. This disparity in publishers shows maybe more than anything how unsettled my position has been. It was not until I was leaving Boston that Douglas Messerli at Sun and Moon Books took me on (*The Lives of a Spirit*) and became my committed publisher. And this has been a blessing for a number of reasons, but mainly because I can now fulfill my ideas without fear of their having nowhere to go. His books fit my first dreams when I hoped—as a beginning writer—to sit on a certain kind of well-made shelf in a bookstore.

My relationship to the Catholic church remains central to me, and I would have to say that becoming a Catholic—second to having children—was the most significant choice of my life. But I would also have to say that even though this church works well with my form of belief, it is really about belief that I am talking when I talk about being Catholic. The recognition that only a percentage of ourselves is visible to the world is one aspect of such belief. And so the difficulties that I have with the church's opinions on several subjects, the limp liturgy at many parishes and boring homilies—none of these can kill the belief that gets fired in me at mass. I have come to Catholicism at a lively moment in its history, when the effects of Vatican II are still flying around in disarray. The liturgy is a mess and only just beginning to brush off the dust of Western Christendom—now defunct as an imperialist dream. In the early church, and in its hidden histories, new entrances into Catholicism—ones that are beautifully tucked in there already—include Ganges philosophies, Jewish and Islamic mystical poetry, and Buddhist practices, and these enlarge the meanings of the traditional ritual and reading, and of the word "catholic."

In my last year at MIT, when I was teaching one class for an experimental study group of supposed techy misfits, I took a course in avant-garde film taught by Ricky Leacock and John Gianvito. My friendship with John grew along with my interest in finally working with film. He taught me certain techniques, and then we made a short film together—*What Nobody Saw*—shot on the grounds of a mental hospital in Mattapan, near Jamaica Plain. John became my teacher, as far as film-making and film-going are concerned, and this remains one of my major preoccupations. I have made three videos since then, using equipment at the University of California, in San Diego, where I was invited to teach for the rest of my teaching life. But during my last year in Boston, when we were living on air, Bernard Campbell, the Catholic chaplain, invited me to be associate chaplain, and so I received a monthly check from the diocese of Boston. It was a happy time. I didn't have to teach and could hide away instead, up at the top of those stairs at MIT, looking down over the Charles River through three seasons, during which time I learned the backstage life of the church rituals and worked with students from a new perspective.

By this time my family had moved to Brookline for the good high school there, and we shared a house with an educator and masseuse, Joeritta de Almeida, and her daughter Adjoa, two of our oldest and best friends. The house was located just around the corner from the high school so that it became a center for lunch and after-school hours. Every weekend morning I would come down to the kitchen and step over large sneakers and legs lying all over the floors. I didn't know how happy I was with all of this chaos and company until it came time for me to head west to make money for the next round of their education—college.

For the first seven years of my time in southern California, where I was teaching, I worked on a series of monologues that have come together as a collaborative performance work—with actors and musicians—called *Tis of Thee*. This one work, more than any other, attempts to express the ideas I have about race and religion, to bind them and illuminate their relationship in our history. It is really the only piece of work of my own that I can talk about in an objective way. For the rest, I don't like to analyze my own material. In the case of *Tis of Thee*, I can say exactly what the process was and what I intended by it.

I began the story as a screenplay one spring when I was staying at the MacDowell Colony, during my first sabbatical from UCSD. This was after one of my daughter's friends had been killed by stabbing in Boston—only the first among droves more boys of their generation who would die like that—and I wrote a sort of treatment for a screenplay, in blocks, about the relationship between a young black man and his father, a cynical teacher. The young man feels responsible for the stabbing of his friend, because he was drugged when it happened and nonfunctional, and he ends up committing suicide when society, including his father, misunderstands his suffering. The young man is part of a group of mixed kids who have grown up together in Boston, part of the so-called *Sesame Street* generation. The parents are skeptics, exhausted by their own struggles, people who have failed to follow through adequately on the new social structures they have created.

This treatment, which has ended up in a drawer at home, was really an indictment of myself and my own generation, as people who broke everything down and then walked away. The failures of school committees, health services, community centers—these to me seemed to follow from our ultimate hysterical rebellion. We should have hung in longer, become more professional in our assaults on the corrupt institutions around the city. As parents we should have met together in groups and formed squadrons of caring involved neighborhood watches. What we learned—what I experienced and attempted—was how to live without money, how to share housing and food with other women, so that babysitting was unnecessary, and how to create day-care centers in people's houses. These were domestic revolutions. But we never took it to the next step (many of us were single mothers) onto the streets, and our children were an endangered species slipping from project to renovated town house and back again, without any protection. They were sent out daily to put into practice the theories of their parents.

One of the books that generated this piece of writing from me was the story of Eddie Perry, the Exeter student whose short and tragic life demonstrates the stranglehold tension between murder and suicide in this country. There is a point at which they become the same thing— in war certainly, but also in countries like ours seemingly at peace. Between 1978 and 1987, there were 20,315 black males murdered in America; in 1995 alone, there were 7,913. Many of these were black-on-black murder/suicides. Somebody's children.

At MacDowell (where I was living in the cabin dedicated to the writers of *Porgy and Bess*), I sat in the little living room looking out at a field silvered with frost and sank into a depression. The realities of what was happening to all of our children slammed me there. Why there? Maybe because I was away from home and my children and felt the distance as a lack of protection. But the reality was that they had many friends living imperilled lives around Boston. When some of these guys signed up for the Gulf War, they did so saying they lived in a war zone already, with helicopters buzzing above their houses and guns going off night and day, so why not get paid for that? When I finally began to do some writing, it was the contemporary treatment that I wrote, before I could begin to think in historical terms. I completed the treatment at MacDowell with the dull feeling that nothing more would come of it; and nothing did.

After some time, however, I began to write a more forgiving poetic text about miscegenation, one that was set between the end of the Civil War and the beginning of the civil rights movement. This was the section that would then preoccupy me for another seven years, although it is only twenty-one pages long. I wanted to understand where the histories of religion and race intersect, because much prejudice and social opinion is founded in a dread of creation itself. Racism—like Gnosticism—might be viewed as a quarrel with God, with the world as it has been given to us. I had written several books already that grazed against this subject in a few cases, and tackled it below the waist in another. But I wanted to carry the manuscript around with me and slowly but surely use it as a way to really pierce into the heart of both miscegenation and ontology. I had no idea that it would end up as a stage piece with music. It was simply random voices and observations for the first three years. It always began, however, with one voice, a woman:

In the days when I was still drawn to
   romance—like
gravity calling an arrow to a bleeding
   target's red center—
I experienced myself as a small child—
   always waiting.
I lived with my father who taught me
   these facts—that people are
like animals who always herd with their
   own kind—that
the cost of cruelty in one life is the debt
   you pay in the next one
—and that certain women have
   collaborated in the
failures of their times by remaining
   silent—and that these
women only enter history when they want
   to further their own cause.

Extended family: (from left) Adjoa, Joeritta, Michael, Maceo, Joy, Shelley, Annlucien, and Danzy

His opinions terrorized me and drove me
  to the beach
to find another father. Miscegenation was
  still a crime. It was
illegal then that I should burrow my way
  through sleet and hail
to the grey doors of the oyster shed. I
  did it anyway.
I had always been disobedient.

And then there was always a man's voice
saying:

I believed that she, being white and
  privileged, knew what she was doing.
She lay near me with her eyes closed
  listening to stories from a world
so alien, they might have been legends.
  Her passivity peaked as her rebellion
  weakened.
For a brief time, in such a state of
  abandonment, the situation seemed
  harmless.

I didn't condescend to her, although it
  was the time when women did not have
the vote and should have been treated
  with justifiable contempt—
given the fact that former slaves who had
  been denied education and training
in the running of the nation—were sent
  into a hostile society, and few of these
women—who should have been their
  allies—did anything to help them.
I knew I could be killed by one slip of
  her tongue—to the wrong man.
And pregnancy was a guarantee of my
  being lynched or imprisoned. . . .

And then these voices became part of a story
told, and the ghost of my first treatment, written at the MacDowell Colony, returned as their
child, given up for adoption after the Civil War.
The story was beautifully performed, with music, in San Diego, and through the long work
done on it, I came to a new understanding of
race as an arena where the deepest human
contradictions are exposed. The boy realizes that
race is nothing but the description of a face.

And the absurdity of a whole people having to defend their being based on their looks is existentially insane—would drive anyone insane.

The boy says:

Race is the most absurd quality assigned
    to a soul.
And maybe it's the very absurdity of it
that turns it into an obsession.
I mean, when you are forced to spend
    your life thinking about
something that means nothing,
you're living out the basic human
    condition.
You're living at the level of faith all day
    every day.
It's incredible. . . . A life of pure
    contradiction.

Racism in this way becomes the most extreme expression of anxiety. Other forms include nationalism, sexism, chauvinism—each of these being responses to the experience of the spirit stuck in history. The face, the accent, the trappings of physical shape—these are viewed as evidence of some fatal flaw in the intentions of the universe. The sight of the other person, rather than calling out friendship and empathy, calls out fear. And I think that this fear is huge and measures itself against an ultimate emptiness. It needs to be addressed in those terms.

In the meanwhile, it is women, continuing to give birth in a world that by its nature kills its children, who should be the ones Saint Paul described to the Hebrews:

They did not obtain what had been promised but saw and saluted it from afar. By acknowledging themselves to be strangers and foreigners on earth they showed that they were seeking a homeland. If they had been thinking back to the place from which they had come, they would have had the opportunity of returning there. But they were searching for a better, a heavenly home.

The importance of women in the revolutionary promise of a society on earth "as it is in heaven" has its origins in childbirth.

There is no greater contradiction inherent in any action than there is in childbirth. I learned everything I ever hoped to learn—and much more—from having children, from raising them, from saying goodbye to them. That is why my most fertile years began with them and ended with their becoming adults. No matter what work I have done since, it always has that experience for its motivating fire; and all the illuminations that lighted those years from 1968 to 1988 are the same ones I see by now.

BIBLIOGRAPHY

Poetry:

Eggs, Houghton, 1970.

The Amerindian Coastline Poem, Telephone Books, 1976.

Poem from a Single Pallet, illustrated by Colleen McCallion, Kelsey Street Press, 1980.

Alsace-Lorraine, Telephone Books, 1982.

For Erato: The Meaning of Life, Tuumba Press, 1984.

Robeson Street, Alice James Books, 1985.

Introduction to the World, photographs by Ben Watkins, The Figures, 1986.

The Vineyard, Lost Roads, 1988.

The Quietist, O Books, 1992.

The End, Littoral Books, 1992.

O'Clock, Reality Street Editions (London), 1995.

One Crossed Out, Graywolf, 1997.

Fiction:

Forty Whacks (short stories; contains "Forty Whacks," "Rosy Cheeks," "The Last Virgin," "Plug Body," "The Other Side of Lethe," and "Dump Gull"), Houghton, 1969.

First Marriage, self-illustrated, Avon, 1974.

Bronte Wilde, Avon, 1976.

Holy Smoke, illustrated by Colleen McCallion, Fiction Collective, 1979.

The White Slave, Avon, 1980.

In the Middle of Nowhere, Fiction Collective, 1984.

The Lives of a Spirit, Sun & Moon, 1987.

The Deep North, Sun & Moon, 1988.

Famous Questions, Ballantine, 1989.

Saving History, Sun & Moon, 1992.

Nod, Sun & Moon, 1997.

Fiction for young adults; published by Avon:

The Blue Hills, 1981.

Yeah, But, 1982.

Radio City, 1984.

Taking Care, 1985.

Other:

The Race of the Radical (children's book), Viking, 1985.

Also author of collaborative performance piece entitled *Tis of Thee,* and (with John Gianvito) a short film, *What Nobody Saw.*

Arthur Winfield Knight

1937-

I lived in a tent the summer before I entered the ninth grade. My mother and father were taking care of his parents—moving into the house where my father had been born and raised in Petaluma, California—because my grandfather had a series of strokes and my grandmother was confined to a wheelchair with rheumatoid arthritis.

I almost never invited anyone home because it was like living in a sanitarium. My grandfather's coughs seemed to shake the house, which always smelled of bananas and baby food—that was all my grandfather could eat—and I remember him trying to read the newspaper upside down.

When I moved into the house that fall, I tended to stay in my room upstairs, or I spent as much time in Petaluma as possible. I got a provisional driver's license, since we—technically—lived on a farm. I was fourteen and one of two ninth-grade students to have a license that fall of 1952. My parents bought me a new Chevy.

I thought my father was too quick to criticize people who were different than he was. Different was frightening to him. Different, to him, meant wrong. I think his fear was exacerbated by the fact that he'd had a nervous breakdown when he worked for Pacific Fruit and Produce in his twenties; it was during the Depression. I can remember when he wouldn't drive across the Golden Gate Bridge due to his nervousness.

I felt like a misfit and loved it. When I was a child, playing cowboys and Indians, I always wanted to be an outlaw, wanted to be the one who rode with Jesse James.

My parents sent me to the Baptist church as a child, because it was the one closest to our house. But I never understood why it was wrong to go to the movies—I loved them—or listen to the radio, and one day during recess at summer Bible school, I walked home, leaving my little friends in the park across from the church. I was probably six or seven, and it was the end of my religious training.

Arthur Winfield Knight

I spent most of my time photographing writers. I'd taken photography in the eighth grade, and by the time I was in high school my father and I had installed a darkroom upstairs. I owned a Leica, a Rolleiflex, and a 4 x 5 Linhof.

A woman in a bookstore in Santa Rosa told me there was a local Western writer named Thomas Thompson, and I phoned Tommy, asking if I could take his picture, after I'd read one of his books.

By the time I got out of high school I'd photographed more than a hundred writers, and pictures I'd taken had appeared on numerous dust jackets as well as in such magazines as the *Saturday Evening Post, Saturday Review, Playboy,* and *Mademoiselle.* I thought I wanted to be a still photographer, although I should have known better. (I wasn't photographing movie stars or athletes for a reason.) I wanted to be a writer.

Because I spent so much time with adults and because so many of them said I was an "artist," I tended to be disdainful of my peers. I'd heard my grandmother say things such as, "You're as good as the next person and probably better," and I believed it.

Henry Miller, when I met him, said being an artist meant being "a god," and I understood that. When I read *Some Came Running* by James Jones in college, I loved it because Jones portrayed artists as special, privileged people—privileged because they could feel things others couldn't.

I'd been a lifetime member of the honor society through junior high, but my grades went down in high school. I was bored.

"Real" learning took place in the homes of the writers I met—Irving Shulman, Kenneth Rexroth, Patchen, Ferlinghetti, and Huxley—and I cut classes when I could.

The only good teacher I had was Myrtle Brown. She taught senior English. She'd had my parents as students, and it pleased me when she said I was a better student than my father, probably because he wanted everyone to believe he was "perfect." It was a word he often used to describe himself.

Miss Brown got me to read *Ulysses,* and she kept telling me what a nice, intelligent girl Margaret Fisher was. We both loved literature and movies, and Margaret—almost inevitably—became my first girlfriend. Margaret was serious about her studies, an A student, but I was serious about other things.

I wrote and directed my first—and last—film, which ran about fifteen minutes, when I was in the eleventh or twelfth grade, and I wrote my first novel, which I later burned, between my freshman and sophomore years at Santa Rosa Junior College.

The novel was titled *Vacation from Youth,* and it was semiautobiographical. I wrote five typed, double-spaced pages a day, seven days a week, until it was completed.

By the time I was in my early twenties, I knew what a terrible book it was, although Finlay McDermid, the story editor at Warner Bros.,

told me he'd have purchased it if James Dean were still alive. One afternoon I walked out to the large pile where we burned the garbage and set the manuscript on fire, along with a second novel I'd written—a Western titled *Outcast*—the following summer.

I didn't like junior college, partly because I never had an inspiring teacher and partly because I had to learn how to study. I'd always had a hard time doing things I didn't like. But I'd completed all of my non-major courses before I transferred to San Francisco State College.

By the time I moved to what we all called The City in the fall of 1958, Margaret and I had broken up. We'd talked about getting married someday, but she was determined to get a Ph.D., even though she didn't know what she wanted to do, and I was determined to be a writer. But it was more than that. I think most sensitive people in the late fifties or early sixties suffered from the James Dean Syndrome. It was fashionable for artists—or for people who wanted to be artists—to suffer. The more angst

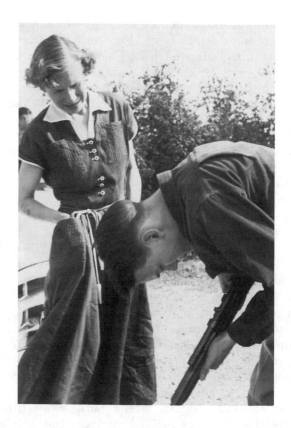

With his mother, Irja Knight, 1953

Arthur and his father, Walter Knight, 1953

one experienced, the more sensitive one must be. But it was even more than that.

I don't think many people falling in love for the first time live happily ever after. I probably had as good a chance of writing a bestseller when I set out to create that first novel as we did at putting together a lasting relationship.

Margaret went to Seattle when I went to San Francisco.

Probably a lot of young men from that time could have told you whether they wanted a "good" girl, sex, companionship, or someone who'd take away their loneliness for a night.

I wanted someone I could make love with, laugh with, talk about books and movies with, someone I wouldn't want to send home in a taxi in the middle of the night because, suddenly, I didn't have anything to say to her. I wanted it all.

But I settled for sex, dating a girl Paul Elmore had gone out with.

I met Paul in the cafeteria at San Francisco State College. We discovered we'd both grown up in Petaluma. When I told him I was

a writer, he asked if I'd look at a paper he'd written, and I said, "I never read unpublished manuscripts."

I could be arrogant.

The next time I saw Paul we were at a truck stop at the south end of Petaluma, and we ended up having dinner together. Then we went to the Washoe House, a bar a few miles outside of town. I always thought I was a pretty good drinker, but Paul went off to another bar when we left the Washoe House, and I went home to pass out. Some writer I was, Paul probably thought.

I didn't like Jan when Paul was dating her. About the time they broke up, she was going to Los Angeles to visit her mother and I was going there to spend part of the Christmas break with friends, so she rode along with me. Six months later, we were still riding along together, but our time was almost up.

We went to the movies so we didn't have to talk, and I made martinis for us in the afternoons. We walked around San Francisco at night, and I remember she got angry with me when I wouldn't buy her a flower. "Why would I want to do that?" I asked when we passed all the florists' stands on Powell Street.

I told all my troubles to a woman who headed the graduate program in liberal arts. She had her doctorate from Stanford and was the first to encourage me to be a college professor. Eleanore was probably in her midforties.

We'd cross the Golden Gate Bridge with the top down on my Ford convertible, the wind blowing our hair. We'd have lunch in Tiburon or Belvedere and sit out on the wharf drinking imported beer.

Eleanore had been engaged a couple of times, first to a child prodigy who was killed in a car wreck, then to an Italian who was blown up during the Second World War, then there was someone, I think, from one of the Scandinavian countries. When I knew her, Eleanore lived with her mother in an apartment on Arguello, and I think she'd given up. Maybe not, though. When I photographed her, she cupped her chin in her hands, her eyes young. I should have loved her.

When I'd moved to San Francisco, a friend and I lived in a drab rooming house— the only window in my room faced a dirty brick wall a foot or two away—on Sacramento Street. We were served communal breakfasts and dinners, and I think Bob and I were the only college students in the place. Most of the people there were blue-collar workers, uneducated, and they tended to be morose, even sullen. The walls were colored with cigarette smoke, and the dark carpets were worn, dirty. Nelson Algren would have loved it.

In the evenings Bob and I would walk down Van Ness Avenue to Turk Street. Bill, the bald-headed bartender at the Scottish Tavern, had a high, squeaky voice, and he didn't think college kids should have to buy drinks.

One night a couple of agents from the Liquor Control Board came into the bar, sitting at the other end of it. Bob and I could see them look our way, then we heard Bill say, "Hell, those boys are all right, they've been coming in here for years," and we weren't questioned.

We were twenty.

When Art Bland and I rented a small apartment on the corner of Frederick and Clayton, in the Haight-Ashbury District, the hippie thing hadn't happened yet—it was the fall of 1959—and the Haight was just a cheap, pleasant place to live. I think we paid ninety bucks a month.

Art had a brown belt in judo, and he could move quickly even though he was a big guy; he was a couple of inches over six feet, and he probably weighed two-fifty. He was also from Petaluma and, like Elmore, was attending college on the GI Bill.

By the time the fall term ended I was ready to quit school, even though I'd graduate in another semester. Probably it had something to do with the season. Christmas always bummed me out, probably because everything seemed so artificial, because people tried so desperately to be happy.

I wrote to Irving Shulman, asking if he could get me a job in Hollywood as a scriptwriter, even though I hadn't published anything other than a few newspaper articles.

Irving wrote back, saying he'd talked to Frank Gruber, a writer I'd photographed, who was one of the producers of *Tales of Wells Fargo,* a weekly television show starring Dale Robertson. Frank was willing to hire me as an entry-level writer. Salaries were set by the Screen Writers Guild, and, as I recall, I would have started at $375 a week—a lot of money in 1960.

I thought about accepting the offer, but I could hear Gruber telling people, "I made that kid," and I didn't think I could write many

The author in 1956

lines such as, "Shucks, ma'am, it was nothin'" without throwing up, so I decided I'd better finish college.

I think my parents imagined I'd get a job when I completed my B.A. in English, but Eleanore had encouraged me to get an M.A. in creative writing, and I liked the idea. My parents didn't; they wanted me to get a job for the summer. I got one at a collection agency on lower Market Street, and I spent most of my time typing threatening letters to people, including one to John Barrymore, Jr.

If I needed any proof that work was terrible and demeaning, I found it at the collection agency. After about three weeks, I went out for lunch one day, drank several martinis and decided I'd never go back, not even to collect the money I was owed. (Elmore remembers the experience differently; he says I quit the first day, so perhaps it just seemed like three weeks.) San Francisco had never looked better as I walked up Market to catch a streetcar.

My parents were unhappy and said I'd have to commute to San Francisco State if I wanted to go to graduate school.

That summer I finished *The Fires of Time,* the novel that became my master's thesis. The title came from a poem titled "The Man against the Sky" by Edwin Arlington Robinson, and the lines I quoted give some indication of my confusion at the time: "Or with an even likelihood, / He may have met with atrabilious eyes / The fires of time on equal terms and passed / Indifferently down, until at last / His only kind of grandeur would have been, / Apparently, in being seen."

The novel ends with Robert Lynch, my alter ego, driving his car off the road when he's drunk. When he looks at the car, two of its wheels stuck in a ditch, he slips on the edge of the bank, falling into the weeds. He lies on his back, staring at the stars, and the last sentence reads, "Finally, he began to cry."

Late that summer—1960—I met Veronica Joyce when I went to see Lu Watters in Cotati. Lu had played Dixieland trumpet in the late thirties in San Francisco and was credited with "reviving" traditional jazz. But he'd retired from music in 1950, moving to Cotati, and when I

met him he was a cook at the county hospital in Santa Rosa.

My father had been a great fan of Lu's, but Lu and I spent most of our time talking about literature. We were both interested in Henry Miller's work, and we both liked to drink.

Veronica was Patsy Watters's youngest sister.

Veronica and I began to go out, spending the weekends together. Generally, I'd pick her up late Friday afternoon in Oakland, where she lived with her mother and one of her brothers, and take her back there on Sunday evening. She'd been a blackjack dealer in Nevada and had come back to California after an affair ended.

Our relationship was fueled by sex and alcohol; I think we had genuine affection for one another, but getting married was a catastrophe. I think I asked her because she said she'd get a job in The City, working to support us. I'd be able to leave my parents', and she could leave her mother's.

We were going to get married at the courthouse in Carson City, Nevada, but we ran out

With Henry Miller, Big Sur, California, about 1957

of gas on the freeway near Davis, less than two hours from San Francisco. We hitchhiked to a service station.

It was an omen.

The next day, walking down the courthouse steps in Carson City, I had the only epiphany of my life. I think it was early October. It was bright out, sunny. The yellow aspens trembled in the wind, and you could tell winter wasn't far away.

Oh shit, I thought, this was a mistake.

I was right.

I'd seen Veronica change when she was drinking, but I don't think I wanted to realize how destructive she could be. Sometimes she'd yell so loudly the woman who lived below us—on Ashbury Street—would pound on her ceiling with a broom, asking Veronica to be quiet. Veronica would lean out one of our windows, almost falling into the courtyard, and yell, "Why don't you mind your own business and shove that broom up your twat?"

She swore more than anyone I knew.

Veronica worked at a bank on Haight Street—she could walk to work—and I was always surprised when she managed to get up and leave our place in the mornings, ruined by hangovers. Most days, both of us were ruined.

I'd go to school and take walks in Golden Gate Park—it was only a few blocks away—and I began to work on a novel about a married couple on the verge of a divorce.

By December, Veronica and I knew we were going to split up, but we waited to tell our families until the holidays were over, living through the agony of the holidays and my twenty-third birthday, December 29.

Veronica's oldest brother wanted her to get an annulment. After consulting a couple of attorneys who said it was impossible, we went to an associate of Mel Belli, who got us one with no problem.

When Veronica moved out, I asked Paul Elmore if he wanted to room with me, and he did. By that time, I'd finished the first semester of graduate school and I'd taught two courses. I was walking down the hall at San Francisco State wearing Levi's and cowboy boots when Eleanore stopped me and asked if I'd like to teach. One of the faculty members was going to be out for the term due to illness.

"When would I start?" I asked.

"In five minutes."

"Why not?"

I could use the money, and maybe it would be an interesting experience. I'd never seriously considered teaching. My average student was older than I was.

Not long after my marriage ended, I stopped by Margaret Fisher's place in Penngrove, and her mother told me Margaret was a graduate student at Stanford. I got Margaret's address and phone number, and we started going out again. We went to movies and played Scrabble, then Margaret and a friend of hers got an apartment in The City, even though she'd have to commute to Stanford; it was probably an hour away.

Then Margaret got her own apartment.

We didn't fight the way we had in the past, but one night, holding her, I realized how tense she was, and I left her place, going down the dark stairs. Something inside of me broke, and I never went back.

Maybe you really can't go home again. Maybe there's no such thing as a second chance.

I don't know.

Margaret went on to get her Ph.D.; I became a writer.

Success stories.

We do what's important, I guess.

Bland had graduated but couldn't find the kind of job he'd hoped for—he talked more and more about giving up, about becoming a carpenter—so Paul and I said he could move in with us. I had the only bed; Paul had the couch that made into a bed, and Art put his sleeping bag on the floor.

Paul and I shared what food we had with Art—we were all broke—and gave him enough money for the streetcar so he could look for a "good" job. I wasn't convinced there was such a thing.

We ate a lot of soup, bought a lot of cheap hamburger. I think we paid thirty-nine cents a pound, three pounds for a buck. Sometimes we'd invite girlfriends and have dinner by candlelight. Paul stole the candles from a candle factory he worked for in San Rafael. He told people, "I'm always dipping my wick."

About that time a friend, Walter May, said, "It's hell to feel something big inside you and not be able to do anything about it. I'm not close to anything anymore, not even myself. I never have the feeling that I've read something great, or seen or done something great, or even conceived something great. No woman at close range, only the dead ones past, and sometimes the strange, swift, colorful passers on the street. Sometimes I wonder if I'm a squashed genius, or a crushed dreamer."

Walt spoke for a lot of us.

Art and his girlfriend were ready to break up; a girl Paul was dating had an abortion—Paul mortgaged his Volkswagen to pay for it—and I was ready to go to work for the second time. When the spring term ended, I needed three more classes to get my M.A. I took two of them during the summer but had to take the final one that fall.

My thesis had been accepted, and I'd provisionally passed my orals—provisionally because Herb Wilner, who'd been on my committee, said I had the worst attitude of anyone he'd ever met.

When the oral exam was over, Wilner walked down the hall with me, putting a hand on my shoulder. "You can't say fuck the system and expect to graduate," he said, but that wasn't entirely true. I didn't have to repeat the orals, but I had to read twelve novels for Wilner and write thirteen papers, twelve dealing with the individual books and the thirteenth with all of them.

Art, Paul, and I moved into a second-story flat on Vicksburg Street in Noe Valley. Art had found a job by then.

I had to find one, too.

I even went to employment agencies where you paid a fee if they found you a job. At one of them, after my interview, the woman who'd asked what I thought I might like to do, said, "You don't want a job."

"Of course I do. I'm here, trying." But she was right.

After I'd filled out a few forms or had an interview, I'd stop for a beer or two or something to eat.

I'd sit in those dingy restaurants on Market where the waitresses all seemed hard, tired, the lines cut into their faces as if someone had put them there with an X-acto knife. They always seemed to have fingernails with chipped polish, and the cooks were overweight men who wore dirty aprons. The calendars shone with grease.

No one wanted to hire me because I was 1-A in the draft—no one but the State of California. It would hire anyone.

Actually, I could type a hundred words a minute, and I knew my ABCs, and those were about the only requirements for the job. I worked as a clerk-typist for the Division of Highways' Legal Department.

My boss was an old Irish lady with a hunched back, and the guy at the desk next to me was a homosexual biker who liked foreign films and James Michener novels. I always expected him to hang up his whips and chains along with his leather jacket in the morning, but he hid them somewhere.

I could have driven to work in fifteen minutes, but I couldn't afford to park my car in the financial district where I worked, so I caught a trolley on Church Street in the early morning. Then I caught another trolley on Market. Finally, I walked the last three or four blocks. The commute took me an hour.

I could do the work in three or four hours, but I had to pretend to be busy the rest of the time. I hid in the toilet whenever possible, reading—reading—but I couldn't be gone from my desk for long.

The only "fun" I had was going to a bar called The Town Pump for a couple of beers with Art each night. It was a long semester. I always seemed to be standing on Market Street in the near darkness waiting for a trolley. When the one I needed to catch finally arrived, it would be full, rushing by me, and I'd stand there, my raincoat wrapped around me, in the cold wind, cursing the people who streaked by. Cursing the trolley system, my job, Wilner.

The day I finished my course work, I quit my job, moving back to Petaluma with my parents. I told them Walt May and I planned to go to Europe later in the year, and they wondered if I'd ever get a job.

Meanwhile, I had my physical at the Oakland Induction Center. I was so sure I wouldn't be drafted, I took my car rather than taking the bus the army provided, because I believed I'd be coming home early.

I'd had nephritis in the seventh grade and had been on a salt-free diet through most of high school. But I was lucky; I'd outgrown the disease. I also checked a box saying I'd tried to commit suicide.

A friend who'd tried to kill himself told me the army had dismissed him when they found out, and I concocted my story. If it had worked for him, why wouldn't it work for me?

It did, and I ran down the steps of the induction center, clutching the notice that proclaimed me 4-F, while everyone else marched down the street for the free lunch the army was providing.

For the moment, I was the freest man alive.

I finished the novel based on my marriage to Veronica, using a quote from William James about people who lived on the dark side of their misery lines for an epigraph. I called the book *Threshold of Pain,* and the writing was deliberately flat, like James T. Farrell's or John O'Hara's or like Burrough's in *Junky.*

During the summer of 1962, I worked as the publicity director for the Sonoma-Marin Fair in Petaluma, then I sold the Ford convertible my parents had given me and went to Europe with Walt May. We bought one-way tickets but were only there two or three months. I saw *Mr. Ed,* the TV series about the talking horse, for the first time in England. We came back to the states on a freighter that docked at Norfolk.

When I returned to Petaluma, my parents told me I couldn't smoke in the house because my father had pneumonia—fair enough—and I remember going outside, leaning against the used Chrysler I'd bought in Ventura, smoking . . . wondering.

I got a job writing, selling ads, and helping with the layout for the *Redwood Rancher,* a magazine in transition. The new owner wanted to create something that would be of interest to anyone who lived in the Redwood Empire, an area that probably began in Petaluma and stretched to Eureka, five hours north. I lived in an apartment built above a barn on Petrified Forest Road, outside Calistoga, in the Napa Valley.

Then I began to date Carole.

She was Chinese, and her first marriage had been arranged, although she'd been born in America. I'd known her casually in high school. She was a couple of years ahead of me, and she'd worked in the produce department at the Petaluma Market, which was co-owned by her stepfather. Most people in Petaluma referred to it as the Chinese Market.

Carole had a son by her first husband, and he got custody of the boy when she divorced him. Then she'd met a man whose last name was Smith, and, she said, they got married and had a daughter, Sandra. (Carole named her after the actress, Sandra Dee.)

When Carole married me, the name Smith appeared on the wedding certificate, but a cousin of hers later told me Sandra was illegitimate; Smith, if that was his name, didn't want "no Chink kid," and he drove off in a Cadillac convertible when Carole said she was pregnant.

I quit my job at the *Redwood Rancher* and got one teaching high school English in Anderson, California. Carole, Sandra, and I moved there late in the summer of 1963. It was a small Central Valley town between Red Bluff and Redding, and most of the people there worked for the Kimberly Clark plant. Their sons and daughters were my students, and most of them were apathetic; their lives seemed unimaginably drab.

Mine wasn't much better, although I saw a lot of Lu Watters that year. He and a redheaded woman who taught English with me had an affair that year. She believed all redheads were descended from the lost continent of Mu.

Kennedy was assassinated that November. I remember sitting on the front steps, listening to the television—"The President has been killed; the President has been killed"—and drinking iced tea because we were too poor to afford beer. I could see the snow on top of Mt. Shasta in the distance. I'd been one of the most promising students in the creative writing department, and now I was correcting the poor grammar of students who didn't care.

I also adopted Sandra that year—she would have been three or four—and I remember Carole wouldn't let me read the papers her attorney had prepared. (Later, I realized she didn't want me to know Sandra was illegitimate.) I suppose someone more stable, more sensible, would have called the whole thing off. I should have but didn't, probably because I didn't want to admit—yet—I'd made another huge mistake.

I quit my job teaching English at the end of the year, even though I didn't have another. We moved into the large house on Magnolia Avenue with my parents while I looked for work. I was hired as a journalism instructor at Riverside City College in southern California.

Carole had gone to Riverside with me, but she'd stayed at the motel while I was being interviewed. I thought she was being paranoid when she said I wouldn't be hired because she was Chinese, but we were invited to a faculty barbecue at my boss's house early that fall, and, when we arrived, I could tell he wondered, "Who's the Chink?" We were never invited to another party.

Carole was the guiltiest person I'd ever known. Years later, I became friends with someone who'd written an autobiography titled *Guilty of Everything*, but Herbert Huncke was able to laugh about his "guilt." Carole was tormented by hers.

She'd flown to Carmel one weekend, trying to put her life into perspective. On the way back to the airport in a taxi, she suddenly felt hot and she heard a voice saying, "You're going to hell, you're going to hell." She pounded on the window separating her from the driver as the voice got louder, "You're going to hell," and she told him to take her to the nearest church. She'd been raised Catholic.

Carole said, "He told me I'd miss my plane, but I didn't care. I would have died in that backseat. The taxi wasn't really taking me to the airport, it was carrying me off to hell. I told the driver he had to take me to see a priest. At the church . . . there was a woman with red hair . . . on the steps. She was a whore. Or something. She was waiting. At dusk. I told the priest . . . a lot of things . . . I haven't told anyone . . . In confession." She could only get the words out in short, frightening bursts. Carole was sure the devil was real.

I told myself she'd get better. I almost felt like Salinger's Franny, reciting the Jesus Prayer over and over, but I didn't believe in Jesus.

Carole began to read Swedenborg and asked if I thought there were angels in trees. I didn't think there were angels anywhere.

I remembered the girl Carole had been, working in the produce department. That was before she'd married Norman. Before she'd given her son up. Before she'd become the mistress of a man named Smith or worked, she claimed, as a high fashion model at I. Magnin's in San Francisco. Who could be sure?

At the end of the school year my boss shook my hand, wishing me well, and said he hoped I'd find a job I liked—elsewhere.

I got one teaching freshman English at Delta (Junior) College in Michigan.

We bought a used six-cylinder Ford with no backseat before leaving Riverside. The Chrysler had stopped running a few months earlier, and I'd been walking to my classes; happily, we only lived a few blocks from the campus.

We put the few possessions we had into a U-Haul I pulled behind the Ford, and Sandra rode in back, propped up by pillows.

In 1964

When we got to Petaluma, where we were going to say goodbye to our families, we checked into a motel because Carole didn't want to stay with my father, and I didn't blame her. He liked to bully people, and he had temper tantrums. I'd seen him lie on the floor, kicking his feet, when he didn't get his way.

He was predictably angry when we didn't stay with him. He and my mother had lots of room; it was silly to pay for a motel, blah, blah, blah. He ranted.

In his anger, my father called me an "educated bum" before inviting us to dinner the next night. His mood shifts could be extraordinary. I accepted because I didn't want to be yelled at any longer, but I left a note on my parents' door the following afternoon saying we wouldn't be able to make it. Then Carole, Sandra, and I moved to a run-down motel at the south side of Santa Rosa, less than half an hour away. We were there a week.

Years later, my mother said my father cried when he read I'd left town in the local paper, but I don't know why he would have.

Carole became more and more puritanical, saying I should give up teaching literature because it was "dirty." That I should give up being a writer. By then we'd made it to Michigan somehow, pulling the U-Haul over the Sierra Nevada Mountains and the Rockies. It was late fall, and we'd lived on too little for too long.

It all ended in the large two-story house we'd rented in an old residential neighborhood in Bay City. I came home from my classes one afternoon, and Carole told me she'd given my Wellington boots to someone who'd come to the door from the Salvation Army or the Goodwill. I was tired and angry and I remember thinking, "So this is how it ends—absurdly—with Wellingtons." We agreed I'd file for a divorce, since Carole didn't want to go to court.

Carole got a job cooking and cleaning for some nuns in Saginaw, and I flew to Chicago with Sandra, putting her on a plane to San Francisco. Carole's mother and stepfather had agreed to take her.

The next morning I was back at Delta College, walking down the hall, when a girl in one of my freshman English classes spoke to me. She said, "You look like you could use a friend." She was wearing a blue jumper, and she looked too young to be smoking a cigarette. She was seventeen.

I said, "Go away, little girl," but she didn't.

She was in my class, and we'd see each other in the cafeteria or in the hall. Glee seemed to be everywhere I was, and we began to talk.

I don't think I said anything stupid about how I thought the glee had gone out of my life, then she'd appeared, but I don't remember specific conversations, just their intensity. Sometimes we'd be so caught up in what we were saying that one or both of us would forget to go to our classes.

I felt old at twenty-seven.

I was getting a second divorce, and I lived in a state where the warmest temperature one month was two degrees above zero.

What had gone wrong?

I'd written four books no one wanted to publish and was working on a fifth, *All Together, Shift,* about my marriage to Carole. Maybe I had a neurotic need to be unhappy. Walt May wasn't the only one who thought he was a crushed dreamer. "Three thousand miles of broken ass, that's me," he'd said in one of his letters. That was me, too, I told Glee.

She and I had been seeing each other a couple of times a week, sitting in her parents' parlor because they didn't approve of our relationship, even though there was a ten-year age gap between them, and Glee's mother had been excommunicated from the Catholic church for marrying a divorced man.

Glee moved out of her parents' home when she turned eighteen, ostensibly rooming with a girlfriend, but she was always at my place after that.

Glee had contracted rheumatoid arthritis when she was two, and she took cortisone on a daily basis to keep the swelling in her joints down. Her doctors told her they didn't know what they were doing to her—they might be killing her—but she had to take steroids if she wanted to walk. Ten years later we'd find out what the doctors had done to her, but we didn't talk about her disease very often when she moved in with me.

By the time summer came Glee and I knew we were going to be married, and she closed out her savings account, giving me the money so I could look for a new job.

I had interviews in Virginia, Pennsylvania, West Virginia, and Indiana and was offered three of the four positions I'd applied for, but I accepted the one at California State College in California, Pennsylvania. It was a small town in northern Appalachia, about an hour south of Pittsburgh and an hour north of Morgantown, West Virginia.

Glee and I were married by a justice of the peace in Michigan that September—the day after my divorce from Carole was final—then we drove to Pennsylvania, pulling a U-Haul behind the used Chevy I'd bought from Hertz. All of my possessions—and Glee's—were hitched behind us. It didn't seem like much to show for twenty-eight years, and I felt the way the Joads must have, but I was headed for a different California.

We rented our house from the ex-chairman of the English department, who'd moved to New England. He was a strange old fellow with one arm, and he reminded me of Ahab. He wrote to us, saying we might hear some field mice in the attic at night, but they turned out to be sewer rats. We could see their eyes gleaming in the darkness when we went up the stairs to our bedroom, and we could hear their claws scratch at the insulation above us. Our landlord had never paneled the ceiling.

I'd talked about starting a literary magazine since I'd met Glee, and she finally told me we ought to do it. I think she got tired of listening to my drunken plans.

We called it *the unspeakable visions of the individual,* and the title came from Jack Kerouac. I believed he was the greatest prose writer America had produced, and he and I had exchanged a couple of brief notes before he died in October 1969.

Glee and I had published eight issues by the end of 1973, then we decided to produce a book-length volume dealing with the Beat Generation. It would have more than a hundred photographs and more than sixty thousand words, and it would cost us more than five thousand dollars to produce two thousand copies. We thought they'd end up, unsold, under our bed, but it was a project we believed in—something we could share.

By 1973 Glee was dying.

She'd gained a lot of weight, partly because the cortisone made her body retain water, and it was difficult for her to walk; even going from our bed to the bathroom, perhaps fifteen feet, had become difficult for her by the time *The Beat Book* was published in 1974. (I was also publishing some short fiction and poems by that time.)

Allen Ginsberg phoned, obviously excited about our achievement. He'd never seen the photo of Kerouac we used on the cover, and he suggested reviewers we should send copies to. In the next year *The Beat Book* received favorable reviews in the *Los Angeles Times,* the *New Republic,* the *Village Voice,* and *American Poetry Review,* but they came too late for us to enjoy them.

The cortisone kept doing its job, internally destroying Glee. By the time the spring term ended in 1975, I knew we had to get help. I knew Glee needed to go into the hospital.

She was afraid of hospitals, probably because she'd experienced so much pain in them. I don't think she saw them the way most people do: as a place to get well. She saw them as a place where you went to die, and they terrified her.

I phoned Glee's sister, Joy, explaining our situation, and she said she and her husband could put me up when I got to Michigan and checked Glee into the hospital.

I got Glee to the emergency entrance at the hospital in Bay City, a day's drive from

where we lived, and they admitted her immediately. I gave them her medical history, my Blue Cross and Blue Shield numbers, my place of employment. It was insane. Glee was dying, and I stood there filling out forms.

Glee was in and out of three hospitals that summer. I'd spend hours with her each day; it was one of the most difficult jobs I ever had. I remember standing at the end of a long hall at a hospital in Lansing, listening to Glee scream while doctors performed a bone marrow test on her. I remember her crying, telling her doctor she knew she was going to die. He said she wasn't—but she was right. I remember she said she was going to divorce me if I didn't check her out of the hospital on the Fourth of July, even though she couldn't walk, but she changed her mind the following day.

When I returned to Pennsylvania to teach my classes that fall, Glee was too sick to go with me. When she lapsed into a coma, I flew back to Michigan because the doctors thought my presence might bring her out of it, but it didn't work.

Glee looked at me, wide-eyed, but it was obvious she didn't see me. I thought I knew what Nick Adams meant when he said he was afraid his soul would leave him if he went to sleep in the dark.

I flew home again—and waited for another phone call.

It came from my mother-in-law in late October.

Glee had wanted to be cremated, so I had to hurry back to Michigan, signing the necessary papers within twenty-four hours.

There wasn't any funeral service.

I stayed with Glee's mother for a week or so. I guess it helped both of us get used to the fact that Glee wasn't there anymore, that she wasn't coming back. (Glee's father had died while we'd been living in Pennsylvania.) I wasn't in a hurry to go back to work because a lot of people who knew Glee casually or who knew her and didn't like her would tell me how sorry they were, and I didn't want to deal with that.

When I did go back to Pennsylvania, I spent most of my time with the colleague I felt closest to, Karl Kiralis. He was probably fifteen years older than me, married for the third time, and a member of Alcoholics Anonymous.

I'd been annulled, divorced, and widowed at thirty-seven, and I asked Karl, "What do I do now?"

"Now you live happily ever after," he said, and I liked that idea.

The wife of another colleague had died, and he hadn't been "right" since. Five or six years had passed, but Gene still had Helen's name on his checks, and her clothes still hung in his bedroom closet. When you asked how he was doing, he said, "I'm as well as the Lord allows," and you knew the Lord wasn't allowing much.

Glee didn't want me to end up like that. She'd told me to find a blonde and take her to the Riviera. I found the blonde, all right, but we flew to the real California that Christmas.

Kit had taken creative writing from me during the second semester of her freshman year, and she was going to marry someone named Mark. She was nineteen that spring of 1972, but she moved slowly; I remember watching her come up the steps of Old Science, where my class was held. (The English department was the largest on campus, but, for some inexplicable reason, we were the only major de-partment not to have our own building. Classes were held everywhere.)

Kit had been hit by a car when she was seventeen; it had thrown her more than forty feet, and she'd been in a coma for nine weeks. When she'd come out of it, she'd had to learn how to walk and talk again, and she spoke with an accent no one could pinpoint.

She'd attended schools in Pennsylvania, Ohio, and southern California, absorbing various dia-lects, and the speech therapist she'd worked with had come from Maryland. People would guess she'd come from Canada or the Deep South. Her father had been a career navy man.

When Kit turned in an autobiographical short story based on her relationship with Mark that spring I told Glee, "That marriage is never going to work." I considered myself an authority on bad marriages.

By the time Kit took another creative writing class from me, three years later, Glee had died and Kit was ready to get a divorce.

She'd never met Glee, but she sent me a sympathy note because she claimed I was the only professor she'd had who'd talked about

The author and his wife Kit, with Allen Ginsberg, California State College campus, 1980

his wife as if he'd actually liked her. In fact, she said, I talked about all three wives as if I'd liked them.

Other professors, Kit said, pretended they didn't have wives or talked about them disparagingly; in either case, that meant they were on the make.

I couldn't find a phone listing for her, but Kit had put her return address on the envelope that contained the sympathy card, so I knocked on her door. It was late afternoon, and I asked if she'd like to drive over to Brownsville—across the river—with me. I was going to pick up a case of Heineken at the beer distributor there. (Pennsylvania has an archaic liquor system.)

Kit began to cry, saying she wouldn't be very good company. Her husband was in the air force, and he was coming back from a "remote" mission in Turkey in six or seven weeks. All he wanted to do was drink Pepsi and watch Tarzan movies on television, and she said he "fumbled" in bed.

Going out with her helped me to forget about my pain. In a way, my life was better than Kit's. I knew, somehow, I was going to go on, but she didn't know what she was going to do. I tried to get her to eat at least one meal a day and to get some rest, but she was afraid to go to sleep because fuzzy green monsters ripped her throat out in her dreams.

I stayed at her apartment the night before her husband came back. She was going to Oklahoma with him. I hated saying goodbye in the morning; I'd just lost Glee and now Kit was going away and it didn't seem fair. I knew that was absurd, but I didn't like it.

In the morning I got a phone call from Kit, and she asked if I'd still like her to move in with me. She'd "given" her husband one hour for each month he'd been gone, and the marriage "broke" after fifteen hours. It had broken a long time ago, but she didn't need to hear that.

She moved in with me on a Monday morning.

We were watching television in the bedroom on Tuesday night when someone knocked on the front door. When I opened it, Mark and Kit's mother, whom I'd met, and her brother were there. I asked them to come into the house, which was a huge mistake, and they paraded into the bedroom. Kit's mother insisted I'd "drugged" Kit, and they were going to force

Arthur and Kit Knight, 1980

her to go with them. I tried to stay out of it, but Kit was equally insistent: she was staying with me.

I called the cops, and they arrived in less than five minutes. There was a lot of yelling and crying, and I stood there drinking beer. I'd always said it didn't pay to mess around with married women. I didn't know I could like cops so much.

Kit's mother was red-faced. She kept yelling, "Is this what we pay the cops for? Huh? Is it?" when they told her Kit could stay with me if she wanted to. She was twenty-three.

We flew to San Francisco a few days before Christmas. My parents picked us up at the airport, then took us to their home in Livermore. I'd told Kit we might be leaving abruptly, warning her about my father. He'd taken a job working for the East Bay Regional Park District shortly after I'd left California, and it was good for him; it forced him to pretend he was "normal." My mother was fond of saying he could "fool" people.

It was a strange time. After not seeing each other for more than ten years, my father and I shared a hospital room. We were scheduled to check into the Livermore hospital on New Year's Day 1976 and to have hernia operations the following morning. His went a lot more smoothly than mine, which had been postponed due to Glee's health.

My father checked out of the hospital in three or four days, but my operation had to

Lu Watters and Kit Knight, Cotati, California, 1983

be redone, and I was hospitalized for more than a week. I teased Kit, "I bet you'll never run off to California with anyone again."

We visited Petaluma several times once I was able to drive. The town was probably twice the size it had been when I'd left, but Kit loved it. She said she'd like to live there someday, and I told her, "I've already done that," although I thought I'd like to write a book about day-to-day life in northern California—what it had been like, what it was like now. Since I'd been born there, I could see it as a native; since I'd been gone so long, I could also see it as someone new to the area.

Kit and I spent the Bicentennial summer on the road. We went to New England, visiting John Clellon Holmes, who'd been a friend of Kerouac, then we visited Herbert Huncke and Carl Solomon in New York City. It was a Beat odyssey, but we also met James Drought, who'd written *The Gypsy Moths,* and his wife in Connecticut.

We were home long enough to do our laundry, then we drove cross-country, discovering America, discovering each other. Kit brought a white wedding dress with us, hanging it in the backseat; we planned to get married wherever we were when her divorce was final, but we were back in Pennsylvania and the summer had ended before that happened.

We were in Abilene, Kansas, on the Bicentennial Fourth when Kit had a tooth abscess. We went to the emergency room at the local hospital, and a dentist they phoned prescribed

codeine and an antibiotic and said he'd see Kit in the morning. Later I wrote a short story, "What It Means to Be an American," which will be out this year in an anthology called *Heartlands,* edited by Peter Crowther and Edward E. Kramer, published by White Wolf.

We met Allen Ginsberg and William Burroughs, Jr., in Boulder, and we visited Fred Harman, who'd created Red Ryder, when we were in Pagosa Springs. Later, we met Michael and Joanna McClure in San Francisco, and we saw Carolyn Cassady, whom we'd met on our earlier trip west, in Los Gatos. We also visited Irving Shulman and his wife in Sherman Oaks.

By the time summer had ended we'd visited the Grand Canyon, Mono Lake, and we'd driven through small Southern towns where the locals stared at us as we passed by, Kit's white dress flapping on its hanger above the rear seat.

We were married in August, and our daughter, Tiffany, was born the following April. Kit had wanted a daughter, and she'd had her name picked out for years. A daughter was fine with me, too; I told people I knew what it was like to be a boy. Raising a girl would be interesting.

Kit and I both kept a daily journal during the last months of her pregnancy. I thought it would make an interesting book, and John

Kit Knight with Herbert Huncke, 1984

With his daughter, Tiffany, 1994

Clellon Holmes agreed with me; he wrote a preface for the manuscript, calling it *Coming to Term,* but it was never published. However, Kit and I coedited a Beat anthology, which we titled *The Beat Diary.*

Kit's parents had told us they'd never accept our marriage, and they meant it. They didn't accept our daughter, either. We lived in Pennsylvania for the first sixteen years of Tiffany's life, and we were never invited to Kit's parents' house for Christmas, even though we lived less than an hour and a half from each other. I was sure we'd be invited the last year we were there, but I was wrong.

Kit believed her parents had planned to relive their lives via her marriage to Mark, and she "screwed things up." I wondered why anyone would want to relive lives that were as drab as theirs; it was a mystery.

By 1984 we had enough poems to make up a collection, which we titled *A Marriage of Poets,* and—this time—we found a publisher. Poems by us alternated, and James Drought wrote a preface for the manuscript; Bill Katz, in *Library Journal,* called it one of the best small press books of the year.

That was also the year I wrote my first play, *King of the Beatniks.* As I said in a preface I wrote for it later, "I had no reason to believe I could write a successful play, but when Tennessee Williams died there weren't many people left who were writing the kind of plays I wanted to see. Williams's work interested me because he was able to create characters with dimension, not just stock figures who exchanged glib dialogue, and while his work was realistic, it also had a poetic ambience . . . People who'd read my fiction said I wrote convincing dialogue, but dialogue was only one aspect of playwriting, and I kept telling myself I ought to stick with what I knew: writing poems." (By that time I'd probably published more than a thousand.) But as I went on to say, "The idea of writing a play based on Kerouac haunted me." I completed it in less than two weeks, even though I was teaching at the time.

King of the Beatniks was published in a Beat anthology in Belgium, then it was published as a book by Water Row Press in Massachusetts. The play had three acts, and the first act was performed at a playwriting festival held in Shropshire, England, where it won an award for its "poetic language." Subsequently, it was banned in Wales for its "lavatorial language." Later, it was produced in its entirety in Split, Yugoslavia, where it had been translated into Serbo-Croatian.

I received a sabbatical for the spring term of 1988, and we rented a cabin in Rio Nido, California. People referred to it as "the slums of Guerneville," which was a couple of miles away. Both towns were built along the Russian River, and Guerneville was noted for its large gay population; because of it, Sonoma County had one of the highest death rates from AIDS in the nation.

Tiffany attended the fifth grade in Guerneville, and Kit got a job working for the *Russian River News.* The editor had written a feature piece about us, then Kit began writing a weekly poem-column (each column consisted of a poem), which ran for more than four years. From what we could gather, it was the only column of its kind to appear regularly in a newspaper in America.

I wrote articles and poems and began researching a novel about Jesse James. Jesse had written a number of letters—most of them pro-claiming his innocence—to newspaper editors, and that gave me the idea for what would become *The Secret Life of Jesse James.* I adopted Jesse's persona and wrote the novel as a series of letters he sent to friends and family members; people told me it was the first epistolary novel to be set in the Old West.

Kit's job at the *Russian River News* added dimension to our lives. She'd become a celebrity in Guerneville by the summer of 1991 when I wrote a review of *Thelma and Louise* in response to a comment the gossip columnist Liz Smith made: she said teenaged girls shouldn't be allowed to see the film because Thelma and Louise were bad role models, and I thought that was idiotic.

I went to see the film a second time, taking Tiffany (the nearest teenaged girl I could grab), then I gave the review to Kit's editor, Julia Koch. It was the first film review I'd ever written, and I told Julia to use her judgment: run it or throw it away. She ran the review, and when we had lunch with her the following week, she asked if I'd like a job as a film critic. I didn't like the idea of seeing dozens

Kit, Julia Koch, and Arthur, Guerneville, California, 1991

of bad films on a regular basis, but I told Julia I'd think about it for a week.

I took the job.

I was lucky. I received another sabbatical for the spring of 1992, and I planned to take an early retirement at the end of the spring term in 1993. (By that time I would have taught thirty years, and I'd be fifty-five.)

We rented an apartment in Cotati, about ten minutes from Petaluma. My parents had returned there in 1985, moving into a mobile home park for senior citizens, because my father was convinced no one liked "old people." No one liked him, but that didn't have anything to do with age.

Tiffany attended Petaluma High School; Kit wrote a novel about Mrs. Jesse James, and I began to review films for the *Anderson Valley Advertiser,* which, despite its title, is probably the most radical newspaper (and one of the most literary) in America. The publisher, Bruce Anderson, quotes Joseph Pulitzer ("Newspapers should have no friends") and Lenin ("Be as radical as reality") on the front page each week. There's also a motto, "Fanning the Flames of Discontent," which appears below the paper's masthead.

On our way back to Pennsylvania late that summer, we stopped in Tombstone, Arizona, then spent a night in Lincoln, New Mexico, because I wanted to write a novel about Billy the Kid's erotic life, although I hadn't found a publisher for the Jesse James novel at that time.

I wrote the Billy the Kid book, teaching my final year, and we left Pennsylvania permanently in 1993. We made an offer on a home in Petaluma on June third and moved into it on July third, and two years later Tiffany graduated from Petaluma High School, my alma mater; she was the fourth generation to do so in the Knight family.

Because she'd never made a final grade that was lower than an A on either coast, Tiffany received a full scholarship to the University of Arkansas in Fayetteville, where she's majoring in English and physical therapy.

Nat Sobel, one of the best agents in New York, is representing my Billy the Kid novel, and I've just completed one about John Dillinger. The fact that the three novels I've written in my fifties all deal with outlaws probably says something about me.

I'd like to write a novel about Sam Peckinpah because his film, *The Wild Bunch,* changed my life in ways I'm not able—precisely—to define. I first saw it in 1969, the year it was released—the year Kerouac died—and I believe it's the best film ever made. It moves me enormously each time I see it. A group of aging outlaws go to Mexico in 1913 because there's no longer a place for them in America.

I understand Willie Nelson and Waylon Jennings and Kris Kristofferson when they talk about being "outlaws." It's a mind-set.

At one point I'd thought about editing a collection of short stories dealing with the closing of the Old West. I still like the idea—because the people from that time were going through the enormous changes many of us are experiencing as we head into a new century. I told the president of the university, who had hired me when he headed the English department in Pennsylvania, "We're the old outlaws." It might have seemed cryptic, but John just puffed on his pipe, nodding.

My novel about Jesse James was published in 1996, along with another one, *The Darkness Starts up Where You Stand,* which takes place in southwestern Pennsylvania during the Vietnam era; it deals with a young woman who's a heroin addict, a bisexual biker, and an arsonist. I wrote it when I was thirty.

*

Kit and I take things one day at a time now. My retirement doesn't give us enough money to live on, but we earn a few dollars writing, and I began to teach part-time at the University of San Francisco, a Jesuit institution, in 1995.

My students are reentering juniors, ranging in age from their midtwenties to sixty. As I like to tell people, "They know a lot, but they want to know more."

Not long ago, a teller at the bank asked how I liked teaching at the University of San Francisco, and I said, "I love it."

The students I'd taught in Pennsylvania had become dumber, more sullen, more prone to make excuses each year, and I didn't envision myself teaching again.

Kit and I go on.

Paul Elmore, after all these years, is still one of our closest friends, and we see Art Bland, now a retired building inspector in Fresno, and his wife when we can. We have a circle of

Arthur and Kit Knight

interesting and supportive friends, and a young woman, Maura Gage, who was a student of mine in Pennsylvania, has begun researching my life for a critical biography she plans to write.

Almost every day here is good, although there have been hitches. When Kit and I attended a Western Writers of America convention in Albuquerque during the summer of 1996, we asked my father to water our lawn, and, against our explicit wishes, he cut down the magnolia tree in our front yard.

We haven't spoken to him since then, although I told him I'd accept an apology. But he not only prides himself on being perfect, he likes to say he's "never regretted a thing, never apologized."

At eighty-two I don't think he's going to change.

I can't say I miss him, but I feel sorry for my mother.

Maybe we'll be able to stay in Sonoma County, maybe we won't. As I like to tell Kit, "If worse comes to worst we can always live in a trailer in Tonopah." Given my retirement income, we'd have enough money for typing

paper, an occasional hamburger, and plenty of cheap wine.

Kit says, "No trailers, trailers are tombs with awnings. I'm not living in a trailer."

BIBLIOGRAPHY

Poetry:

What You Do with Your Aloneness, New York Culture Review (Brooklyn), 1977.

Forty, Tailings, 1979.

Angst, Wolfsong, 1980.

The Mushroom Nightshirt, Quick Books, 1984.

(With Kit Knight) *A Marriage of Poets,* Spoon River Poetry, 1984.

Wanted, Trout Creek, 1988.

Tell Me an Erotic Story, Tempus Fugit, 1988.

Twenty-one Notches, Muggwart, 1991.

Basically Tender, Esoterica, 1991.

Outlaws, Lawmen and Bad Women, Potpourri, 1993.

Anthologies, edited with Kit Knight except as noted:

(With Glee Knight) *The Beat Book,* the unspeakable visions of the individual (California), 1974.

The Beat Diary, the unspeakable visions of the individual, 1977.

The Beat Journey, the unspeakable visions of the individual, 1978.

the unspeakable visions of the individual: Tenth Anniversary Issue, the unspeakable visions of the individual, 1980.

Beat Angels, the unspeakable visions of the individual, 1982.

Jack Kerouac, *Dear Carolyn* (letters to Carolyn Casssady), the unspeakable visions of the individual, 1983.

The Beat Road, the unspeakable visions of the individual, 1984.

The Beat Vision, Paragon House, 1987.

Kerouac and the Beats, Paragon House, 1988.

Fiction:

All Together, Shift (novella), Horizon, 1972.

Who Moved among the Others as They Walked, Hilltop (England), 1974.

Our Summer Made Her Light Escape, Realit, 1974.

The Secret Life of Jesse James, BurnhillWolf, 1996.

The Darkness Starts up Where You Stand, Depth Charge, 1996.

Nonfiction:

(With Kit Knight) *Interior Geographies: An Interview with John Clellon Holmes*, Literary Denim, 1981.

The First Time (autobiography), Dramatika, 1982.

The Golden Land (memoir), Ellis, 1985.

Plays:

King of the Beatniks (three-act), Water Row, 1986.

The Abused (one-act), Norton Coker, 1988.

Contributor of more than two thousand poems to periodicals, including *College English*, *Cottonwood*, *The Massachusetts Review*, *The New York Quarterly*, and *Poet Lore*. Knight's short fiction has appeared in the anthologies *Christmas Out West*, edited by Bill Pronzini and Martin H. Greenberg, Doubleday, 1990; *New Frontiers Volume II*, edited by Pronzini and Greenberg, 1990; *The Montanans*, edited by Pronzini and Greenberg, Fawcett Gold Medal, 1991; *Cat Crimes III*, edited by Greenberg and Ed Gorman, Donald I. Fine, 1992; and *New Trails*, edited by John Jakes and Greenberg, Doubleday, 1994.

Guest editor with Kit Knight of *The Beats*, a review journal. Film critic for *Anderson Valley Advertiser*, Boonville, California, 1992—.

Hank Lazer

1950-

Lazer at approximately one year old with his father, Chuck Lazer, on McDaniel Street in 1951

Henry Alan Lazer: born July 4, 1950, in San Jose, California, supposedly as the parade went by.

A memorable declaration of independence.

Father: Charles Lazer, age twenty-three, a native of San Jose, a superb athlete.

Mother: Wendy Goodman Lazer, age nineteen; fine pianist; after growing up in Brooklyn, moved to California.

Sister: Terri Lazer, born August 24, 1954.

*

She would push the child up and down the block. He would sit up in the stroller and talk to passersby.

She told me I became known as the talking baby. This was in San Jose, then still a small but rapidly growing city. She would walk with me on the edge of the Rose Garden area. We lived on McDaniel Street; we walked up and down Park Avenue, past the first Merry Mart—the clothing store that my father and great-uncle would take over from my great-aunt. They would expand it, and it would become a large children's department store. Dad, with Uncle Leon, had the Merry Mart; Mom's parents, Manya and Charlie, owned the Style Mart; Uncle Ben owned the Mayfair.

We lived on McDaniel Street in a house that was nine hundred square feet. Instead of a car, my parents bought my mother a piano first. I would go to sleep listening to mother practicing. I remain familiar with a standard romantic repertoire for piano. From the little Merry Mart to the grocery store to the Rosicrucian Museum and back. That was our walk. Or up the block, McDaniel Street, the other way from home to the Rose Garden.

> . . . so I return here
> a block from the house
> where I was born.
> . . . .
> I would like to say
> some kind of god
> lingers here, can be found
> in a dark, perfect rose,
> that a spirit has watched
> me here since infancy,
> as I lay in the shade
> unable to lift my head,
> or now, as I look
> from rose to rose
> for a clue, some
> shape or presence
> I can call "you" and sing to.
>
> (From "The Rose Garden,"
> *Doublespace*)

(From left) Lazer's maternal grandmother Manya Goodman, Lazer at age two-and-a-half, Lazer's mother, Wendy Lazer, on Hanchett Avenue, December 1952

as they aged and as they died, an exotic Russian Jewish story, the aftermath of pogroms and migration, being played out in unlikely San Jose.

> When Rudóy went on
> he told about being thrown
> from the train onto a pile
> of bodies and being shot.

> (From "The Story of
> Rudóy's Life," *Doublespace*)

> We asked
> about Russia and the journey out,
> Manchuria and Japan, the hick-

> town San Jose which she left
> after a year and then returned to
> never to leave again.

> (From "Kerensky," *Doublespace*)

> At age twelve
> she held the flashlight
> while border guards
> gangbanged her best friend.
> This was in Russia.

> (From "Stories," *Doublespace*)

*

The baby talked a lot. He used big words; he spoke clearly and amazed grown-ups. My first word, or so the story goes, after the blurted first "ma-ma" and subsequent "da-da," the first noteworthy word surprised my mother. I kept pointing to it, up on the wall. And though I may have gotten the syllables a little twisted, I pointed at it and said, clearly, "cockoo cloock."

A poet's autobiography, *that* version of the story, begins (of necessity) with specific words.

And whole phrases: *vahne pischt de ganz*; *a mushel kabak*; *shlug kopf*. My grandparents all had fairly heavy accents. They spoke Yiddish, but not as a first language. Though my father mostly defined himself by an American (assimilationist) distance from his immigrant parents, even he would sometimes say those Yiddish words, surprisingly, with considerable pleasure. They say he had a bit of a gift for languages, but mostly I think of him as a gifted athlete and a reasonably quiet man.

I could go on and on about my childhood in San Jose. Actually, I would tell you very little about *my* childhood. As I did in *Facts and Figures* (Book One of *Doublespace*), I would tell you what I remember and *how* I remember and what I have been told about *their* lives. In poetry, my first task was to tell *their* stories, to put language to use, to record their stories

I graduated from Pioneer High School, a public school in San Jose, in 1967. I had skipped a grade in elementary school; I graduated with a 4.0 grade average as valedictorian of a class of approximately four hundred. I played golf and basketball in high school. Oddly, English was always my worst subject. I received plenty of awards for achievement in mathematics and the sciences. In the summer of 1965, I attended a National Science Foundation summer institute in mathematics at University of California, Berkeley. I lived in International House. I learned, among other things, that I was not a genius in mathematics. The study of mathematics was sufficiently precise that one could tell, as with gunslingers, who was the quickest. I was very good at mathematics; I was not in the category of exceptional genius. And that knowledge ate away inside me for several years. That summer at Berkeley, I did not take my classes very seriously. I began to enjoy Berkeley. I played Ping-Pong in the basement of International House, and I got good enough to hang in there in games with some of the top Asian players in the house. I also went to lots of used bookstores—Moe's and Shakespeare's especially—and I did lots of reading (mainly of European short stories—not poetry). I took part in political protests. I remember taking part in a "celebration" of the dropping of the atomic bomb. And I took part in the folk music scene. In exchange for setting up seats and working on the stage at the Greek Theater, I gained free admission to the Berkeley Folk Festival, and I got to meet Mike Seeger and Mississippi Fred McDowell.

When I began to consider colleges, my mom took me on a trip to southern California. I interviewed at Cal Tech, Harvey Mudd, and Occidental. At Cal Tech, the admissions officer asked me the first question: "Research or applied?" The fact that I didn't know what he was talking about gave me a big clue that I was not a good candidate for a technical/science college. I ended up going to Stanford, figuring that if my interest in mathematics waned, it might be nice to be at a school with lots of other strengths.

At Stanford, again I struggled a bit in English. I have a vague memory of one of my English classes being canceled my first year due to the death of Yvor Winters. I didn't have the slightest idea who Winters was or what he represented. I do remember hearing that he was eccentric, that in his later years he had begun to give away the prose books in his library as he claimed that only poetry was worth saving. In mathematics, I advanced fairly quickly. I placed out of the early calculus sequence and soon found myself in an advanced number theory course. The professor had recently won the Fields Medal (mathematics' equivalent of the Nobel Prize); allegedly there were only two people in the world who could understand his work. I was not one of them. I experienced a serious internal resistance to any further study in mathematics. I suppose that I could foresee the limitations of my intelligence in mathematics, and that sense of limitation was unacceptable. By contrast, one of the joys and torments of poetry is the utter imprecision of accomplishment. In poetry, you never really know how you're doing. There is not some mode of knowledge that acts as a barrier or limitation. The directions of discovery are unpredictable and, seemingly, infinite. So I dropped the math class, thinking to myself that if I were to engage in a realm of study that was so abstract, I might

as well study something like philosophy, which had an ostensibly more direct relationship to human beings. I continued to take science classes—biology, chemistry—as part of a pre-med curriculum, but I also began to take more and more literature classes.

I began Stanford young and immature (emotionally, physically, and experientially). My parents were not wealthy. I was on partial scholarship. At Stanford, I encountered levels of wealth that astonished and revolted me. One student didn't like her dorm room, so her parents also rented her a house off campus. (She was a Rockefeller.) Another student in my Western civ class would refer to Uncle Bomb. (Her uncle was the Secretary of Defense.) Another student in the dorm had a serious debate over whether or not to cut his hair for Thanksgiving. (His family—owners of Dean Witter—threatened to cut him off if he showed up with long hair.) Another student was upset because his parents hadn't made the proper arrangements to reserve a train car to ship his new Jaguar XKE. (He had to endure nearly a month without his Jag.) And many of the East Coast preppies were steeped in irony and disappointment, having preferred Harvard or Yale and settled (with proper poise and disdain) for Stanford. They

Lazer's grandparents: (from left) Manya and Charles Goodman and Chaim and Fanya Lazer, Mother's Day, 1973

"Manya Goodman (my mother's mother) and Sonia Poe (Manya's sister, my great-aunt); collectively, Manya, Sonia, and Fanya were referred to as the 'nya-nya-nya's'"

had read everything we were about to read the entire first year.

I became friends with the less affluent. I, like many others, got a good education in drugs, music, and radical politics. During my four years at Stanford, the campus was shut down by demonstrations the last three years. The drugs—mainly pot, LSD, and mescaline—were about vision, continuous with an interest in Zen Buddhism (I learned zazen and sat occasionally with a formal sitting group), William Blake, and jazz and blues. My hall advisor my freshman year had a great collection of jazz and blues records; I began my education in John Coltrane, Miles Davis, Eric Clapton, B. B. King, and Bob Dylan (whom I had already been listening to quite carefully for several years). And I learned more and more about a loosely socialist leftist politics.

And poetry? By about 1965, my cousin Ben (who was my age and who lived next door to me) had introduced me to the writing of his current favorite: Allen Ginsberg. The poems in *Howl,* especially the title poem and "America," were so different from the dull crap we were reading in high school. My cousin had begun writing his own poetry, and he had also written a fairly lengthy manifesto for a new religion. I still didn't really read much poetry, but I began to be interested.

At Stanford, I have a clear memory of the first poetry reading I ever attended. I was tak-

ing a course in early American literature from Albert Gelpi. He arranged for Denise Levertov and Robert Duncan to give a reading. I remember quite clearly being knocked out by Duncan's "Poem beginning with a line by Pindar." Eventually, I found that poetry was ideally suited to my quest for moments of intensity. The highly focused act of reading (and writing) required in poetry was a perfect match for my own developing intelligence. I began to read and write poetry. I also began a fairly serious interest in black-and-white photography, and thus I began to learn to see, to focus, to frame, and to work. I had a beat-up car, a 35mm camera, and access to a darkroom. And I took more and more courses in English, though I already began my practice of reserving contemporary poetry as an area of self-instruction. I was most drawn to the English romantics, especially William Blake. I wrote my honors thesis on Blake, though my post-college trip to Europe, beginning with a couple of weeks in England, convinced me that I had little or no connection to English culture. When I returned from that trip, I never again took a serious interest in English literature.

The most provocative and lasting teaching I received at Stanford was political in nature. I took a great course from Bruce Franklin, a

Hank Lazer, end of freshman year, seventeen years old, May 1968

course on Hawthorne and Melville (with a substantial component on Marx). Franklin's Marxist reading of Melville remains with me to this day. In many classes, he would offer us challenging alternatives: Should we meet class today, or should we blockade the recruitment center where the CIA will be? Do you want to train with rifles with the Venceremos Brigade this afternoon? Do you want to go to Oakland to film the FBI's invasion of the Black Panther headquarters? Would the class prefer it if I graded you on a collective rather than an individual basis? In another class, oddly enough with William Chace (who would later be identified as a conservative in Stanford's debate over Western civ), we read Mao Tse-Tung on literature and art. I gave serious thought to going to Cuba one summer with friends who were going to work on the sugar cane crop. Instead, I worked one summer as a business intern with Litton Industries traveling to Japan; Beverly Hills; Springfield, Missouri; East Orange, New Jersey; Washington D.C. (where, to the amusement and approval of my boss, I fell asleep during a meeting with State Department officials). I worked for a year and a half as a shoe salesman in the Merry Mart, the children's department store that had been owned previously by my dad and great-uncle and had been purchased by a man who had begun as the shoe salesman when he was in college.

I took only one poetry writing class, and I never really made contact with the emerging "creative" writers. I took an advanced poetry writing class from Thom Gunn my final quarter at Stanford. I remember submitting a group of dense, allusive, somewhat inscrutable poems (I remember one called "Cardinal Noumenon") in order to be considered for admission into the class. As a teacher, Gunn was extremely accepting. He tried to determine what kind of poem we were trying to write; a key part of his commentary always included some recommended reading. He began the course with a careful reading of Pound's "The River-Merchant's Wife: A Letter," a poem which has remained a favorite of mine. I continued, though, to work principally in isolation as a poet. I did not make any particularly close friendships in the course. I began to read and write on a more daily basis, and I began to attend poetry readings. During the winter of 1971, I remember attending readings by Robert Bly and Gary Snyder, and I became quite interested in

*Lazer's paternal grandmother Fanya Lazer,
eighty-three years old, July 1982*

W. S. Merwin's writing. Through the example of Bly's magazine, *The Sixties*, I began to revive my fluency in Spanish so that I could read the poetry of Pablo Neruda, Federico García Lorca, César Vallejo, Rafael Alberti, Vicente Aleixandre, and others. The most valuable lesson I learned from Gunn was the thoroughly overlapping activity of reading and writing.

The learning environment at Stanford was an unusual one. I had excellent teachers—Bruce Franklin, William Chace, Martin Evans, Bliss Carnochan, Anne Mellor, Larry Friedlander, Albert Gelpi, Thom Gunn. But the greater part of our education took place out of the classroom. Demonstrations, rallies, and teach-ins offered a hands-on political education. I had been raised in an activist (Jewish liberal Democratic) family. My Uncle Leon, who had been a Young Socialist, warned my cousin Ben and me about the dangers of joining any radical organization. By the early 1960s, Ben and I had worked on many Democratic campaigns in central California. By the time I was thirteen, I had become fairly effective at voter registration drives. So the political climate of the late 1960s was an extension of an activism I had already learned at home. My parents, for example, had been staunch integrationists, an unusual position among realtors.

At Stanford, political activism was part of the ongoing education. There was also a newly developing drug and music and religious consciousness scene. The emergence of Bob Dylan's music, the Beatles, Cream, B. B. King, the Grateful Dead, the Jefferson Airplane, Jimi Hendrix, Otis Redding, Miles Davis, and so on, were events and words of seemingly personal importance and urgency. Pot was smoked openly all over campus, and many of us were experimenting with LSD, psilocybin, and mescaline. A friend's father owned a beach cabin south of Santa Cruz, and a group of us would often spend weekends in splendid psychedelic isolation. Our quest in drugs was for vision and enlightenment. The drug use, for me, went hand in hand with a study of Zen Buddhism and, through visionary poetries and poetry of the deep image, with a study of alternative modes of consciousness. The music, too—as Hendrix, and Miles, and Coltrane, and Dylan, and the Dead explored modes of expression that left beyond traditional melody or traditional lyrics—reenforced a life based on exploration and an art-making that was investigative and heuristic. Some sense of the chaos, casualness, and intensity of those years comes through in "Not My Own Life":

> Richard ate great
> quantities of ice cream,
> grew fat, dabbled in heroin,
> and did poorly in school.
> In the egg-shaped depressions
> inside our refrigerator door
> you could usually find
> psilocybin or acid.

(From *Doublespace*)

The innocence of that drug world, though, faded quickly. One good friend, who had become involved with heroin, was arrested for receiving a substantial shipment of hashish. And the finances of dealing dope became a bit staggering. One year, as summer vacation approached, a friend was trying to put together a deal to represent our entire dormitory so that he could purchase a bale of marijuana so that we would all be well-supplied during the traditionally dry summer months. Another friend eventually became a partner in a drug cartel. He would fly down to South America. His Bay Area investors included doctors, dentists, and lawyers who would buy shares in speed boats used to deliver the pot. And then cocaine became part of the scene. The financial stakes changed, and weapons became part of the business. The marijuana business had always been fairly gentle by comparison.

After the 1971 winter quarter at Stanford, I traveled for two months in Europe. I was in the process of breaking up with the woman I had been living with my senior year, but we began the Europe trip together, only to break up again after the first couple of weeks in England. I had studied Blake (and had written a senior honors thesis on Blake), so I was eager to spend time visiting various British museums, galleries, and libraries. My experience in England, however, confirmed for me, immediately and seemingly permanently, a sense of my own Americanness and my discomfort (or disconnection and distance) from British culture. When I entered graduate school the next fall, I had no interest at all in studying British literature. I spent much of the two months traveling on my own. I did lots of reading and writing, extending my growing interest in Gaston Bachelard's phenomenological writings and beginning a fairly thorough reading of Kierkegaard.

I had decided to go to graduate school in English not because I envisioned a career in teaching nor because I understood anything of the politics of the institutionalized study of literature. Though I already thought of myself as a writer, I didn't even consider applying to programs in creative writing. My own simple assumption was that I had spent many years studying mathematics; if I wanted to be a decent writer, I needed to do much more reading. For me, a Ph.D. program would be a (funded) means to do that reading. I ended up choosing between Virginia and Harvard. Both offered decent fellowships, but I chose Virginia for a couple of reasons. First, I figured that my approach to a graduate program (combining critical writing and poetry) might cause some problems. Virginia's program was on the rise, and they had recruited me. I figured that they would be more tolerant of my efforts to stretch or alter their program. And second, I wanted to try living in a more rural locale, and the descriptions of the Virginia farmland appealed to me. I had also decided that graduate school was my best opportunity to leave the San Francisco Bay Area if I was ever going to know a part of the country other than California. I had just turned twenty-one; I had broken up with my girlfriend; I knew nothing (firsthand) about the South; I knew no one at Virginia. I packed up my 1967 Corvair and drove to Charlottesville.

The University of Virginia was considerably different than I had imagined. In comparison to the Bay Area of the late 1960s, Mr. Jefferson's university presented what I perceived to be a shocking conservatism. Women had been at the university for only a couple of years and still were, in many quarters, resented. My roommate, whom I had not met, was (quietly) gay and openly concerned about space in the closet for his collection of ties. The predominant poetic tastes had little to do with the holistic deep image nature poetry I had been reading in California. My first reaction to Charlottesville was quite negative; I left town immediately and went to visit my cousins outside of D.C. I returned and gave graduate school a try.

I was not prepared for the pace or the intensity of graduate school. We were always reading too much too quickly. My advisor explained that we were not reading to savor and enjoy but to decide what we would go back to read later. (He said graduate school reading was like going through a cafeteria line: pick the dishes you like the most and plan to go back for seconds.) My first semester, I took a course from Alan Williamson on contemporary American poetry. Williamson was a young, insecure assistant professor. Even in our seminar, he sat at the head of the table, hid behind his briefcase, and called us Mr. and Miss, and seemed never really to learn most of our first names. The fifteen-week semester consisted of nearly half the course devoted to the study of Williamson's teacher, Robert Lowell. At the end of the seventh week, as we finished our study of Lowell, Williamson looked up from behind his briefcase and asked us how we had enjoyed reading Lowell. I immediately volunteered that we had spent too much time on Lowell, that Lowell was vastly overrated, and that only a little bit of the poetry had been particularly interesting.

During that first semester at Virginia, in 1971, several things of importance took place: I continued to write poetry; I cemented my determination to keep my distance from a professionalized literary education (even while I pursued a Ph.D.); my interest in American literature developed; I began my systematic read-

ing of Thoreau's *Journal* (an activity that I have continued, on and off, for the past twenty-five years); I learned that of the 165 first-year graduate students in English at Virginia only about twenty of us would survive and receive a Ph.D.; I developed a serious case of mononucleosis; I began a relationship with the woman whom I would marry a few years later. In the spring, I took a poetry-writing class from Alan Williamson. In spite of our serious differences, I did learn a great deal from him. He was a truly fine teacher for the relatively narrow range of poets whose work he admired: Lowell, Plath, Jarrell, Berryman, Frank Bidart. His passion for Rilke's poetry got me reading Rilke with considerable intensity. I learned as much from the cultural politics of the class as from any specific readings. In a class of about fifteen students, as a heterosexual male I was in a distinct minority. My introduction to and comfort in an emerging gay culture began with this group of students. The other major commonality among the students was an intensely psychoanalytical orientation. In keeping with our devotion to confessional and familial poetry (with Lowell's *Life Studies* and Plath's *Ariel* being our models), it was best to write poems about nervous breakdowns, near breakdowns, and the pathology of family neuroses. My relatively harmonious and principally loving upbringing left me ill-suited for what seemed to me to be psychological scab picking. Even so, a good bit of that confessional aesthetic would emerge, though altered, with little of the attention directed back at my own psychological state, in my writing of family lyric-narrative poems.

By the middle of my first year at Virginia, I had moved twenty miles from campus. I lived with my girlfriend in a tenant farmer's two-hundred-year-old house. We had walking rights to several thousand acres, and I spent most afternoons hiking, reading, and writing. I also began to read extensively Spanish and South American poetry as well as a range of European poetries (including Rilke and Trakl). To some degree, this (self-taught) curriculum came from Robert Bly's many translation projects: Neruda, Vallejo, Lorca, Hernández, Alberti, Aleixandre, Tranströmer, and others. Somehow, my interest in Rilke also led me into sustained reading in Heidegger, especially the newly translated collection *Poetry, Language, Thought*. Not without considerable worry and some significant hazing, I survived Virginia's notorious permission-to-proceed (i.e., the hurdle of faculty judgment between the M.A. and the Ph.D. programs), though nearly all of the students who were writing poetry were washed out of the program. I had also begun to view the Ph.D. program as a credentialing process that might allow me to earn a living while I continued to read and write. My goal was to earn a Ph.D. without confusing that institutional certification program with my own designs for an education in poetry. Of course there would be some overlap, but the university education would always be only a subset of a more comprehensive, stubborn, idiosyncratic, self-directed curriculum.

Over the next several years, I continued, often at a substantial physical and psychological distance from campus, to develop my reading and writing interests. I developed a strong (and continuing) interest in mid-nineteenth-century American literature, especially Poe, Melville, Emerson, Whitman, and Thoreau (and later Douglass). In 1972, Diane Wakoski taught at Virginia and introduced us to a range of poetries that Williamson had not covered: Jerome Rothenberg, Clayton Eshleman, Armand Schwerner, and David Ignatow. I began to publish poems; my first "major" magazine publication in *The Virginia Quarterly Review* in 1973 included the poem "Point Sur," a poem for my father. I began to learn about the quickly changing world of poetry magazines and small presses. In 1973, I taught my first course, an introduction to poetry writing. I found that I loved teaching. And at Virginia, in part because the department had run off nearly all of the poets in the program, as an odd survivor I began to have some impact on the poetry offerings. I played a role in recommending Robert Hass's hire (for one year). The fact that I had been teaching Gregory Orr's poetry in my classes may have played a small role in his being hired. Orr and I worked together very well. My final year at Virginia, when I worked as a lecturer after completing the Ph.D., he and I co-taught a graduate course in modern European poetry. I also began to publish brief reviews of poetry in *The Virginia Quarterly Review,* first working with Charlotte Kohler and then with Staige Blackford. I gave my first few poetry readings, and in 1976 I organized a reading series that included many of the writers who had gravitated to Charlottesville: Ann Beattie, Mark Strand, Peter Taylor, Gregory Orr, Mary Lee Settle, Philip

Graham, and John Casey. We also had bilingual poetry readings from Spanish and from Italian poetry. By the time I left Charlottesville in 1976, there was a very active scene for fiction writers, and there was even a reasonably congenial environment for poets. In addition to the local readings, various "stars" visited and read: John Ashbery (who read from his new book, *Three Poems*), Gary Snyder (who visited my farmhouse and took us on a hike), and even Robert Lowell (who was introduced by his old friend Peter Taylor and who gave a truly delightful reading).

At Virginia, I did receive a part of an education in poetry. Alan Williamson's introduction to the confessional poets (especially Lowell and Plath) and to Rilke proved helpful. The year that Robert Hass spent at Virginia was also extremely beneficial. Bob has both a photographic memory and the gift of mimicry (as well as a lively sense of humor). I learned a great deal by listening to Bob read or recite poetry. His gift for mimicry was so exact that many times after Bob's stay in Charlottesville, I would hear a poet read only to find that the poet's reading sounded like a pretty good imitation of Bob's version of the way the poet reads. What Bob emphasized was two-fold—a precision (and condensation) of visual description; a precision of musicality (usually a delicately but insistently recurring assonance and consonance). Bob's delighted readings of highly musical poems such as John Logan's "Three Moves" remain with me to this day.

The other major friendship/influence during my stay in Charlottesville was the poet Gregory Orr. In Greg's case, the emphasis was on a very precise visual imagery. One of Greg's key mentors was Stanley Kunitz. Through Greg's example, and through his advocacies as a reader, I learned a great deal about the integrity and demands of a particularly condensed, concentrated lyric poetry, where the lyricism resides principally in the possibilities of the precisely written visual image. For Greg, that orientation gave him a way to narrate and explore, over many years and many books, both a personal history (principally the accidental shooting of his brother, but also a range of broader familial concerns) and the roots of a kind of obsessive lyricism. With Greg, I would read and discuss a range of European poetries. For my own early poetry, he was a generous and well-focused reader.

*

I knew next to nothing about Alabama. When I told my grandma Fanya that I was moving to Alabama, all she could say was, "with a banjo on your knee?" (This is the same woman who, when my mother told her that my sister had mononucleosis said, after a long pause, "Is it good for the Jews?") I was eager to go to Alabama—I was eager to go anywhere—as a means of marking the end of my first marriage and as a way of starting over. Jobs, especially tenure track jobs, were very hard to come by. Even though I was offered another year as a lecturer at Virginia, everyone, including the department chair at Virginia, advised me to take the job at Alabama.

It took me a little over two years at Alabama to understand the political situation I had been put in. I had been hired by a chair who told me (and wrote in my letter of offer) one thing, but the head of creative writing had been told something else. I thought I would be teaching American literature and creative writing. When I went to the head of creative writing's farm for a social visit, he told me, immediately, that he had opposed my hiring and that he would make my life miserable. He tried, intensely, for many years. And there was additional intense factionalism in the department, the net effect of which was that I was cordoned off from any substantial involvement with creative writing. After nearly twenty years, that freeze is just beginning to thaw slightly. Initially, what this institutional politics meant was that I would have no visible public role as a poet and no institutional support in my capacity as a publishing poet. I continued to write, both poetry and criticism (as I always have), and I continued to publish my poetry in magazines. But I was in my mid-twenties; I did not have a book of poetry published, and the withdrawal of any public role as a poet was painful, initially. I suppose, too, that being a young writer I had some fear that without a public role as a poet I might stop writing or fall prey to an increasing and recurrent sense of the futility of my efforts as a poet. What I soon discovered, though, was that this bitter local politics actually had a liberating effect on my writing. I had, not through my own efforts, been freed of many of the perils of professionalism. My job would have nothing to do with what I published of poetry. So, I did not

have to force out a forty-eight-to-sixty-four-page first book of poems, and I did not have to subscribe to the assembly line of the workshop. I was given the freedom, at the price of losing institutional support for my activities as a poet, to proceed in whatever manner I wished. A good friend told me that if he were I, he would never again mention within the English Department that I wrote poetry. Another good friend would kid me, saying that my poetic license was only valid when I crossed the state line heading outward.

I was in the midst of some fairly substantial changes in my poetry. After arriving in Alabama, I began a series of poems called Day-Poems. I had grown increasingly uncomfortable with the deep image and sincerely plainspoken modes of writing. What bothered me about nearly all of the poetry being written within academia was that the model for the poet and the poem involved an unspoken validation of the institutionally sanctioned split between creative and critical faculties, or, to state that split in the context of its history via Plato, a split between poetry and philosophy. My own thinking and writing had, from the very beginning, been simultaneously "poetic" and "critical," or "poetic" and "philosophical." But within the university of the 1970s and early 1980s, with the rise of the creative writing industry and the mass replication of the workshop model for poetry, these faculties (in both senses of the word) were segregated. For me as a poet, such segregation felt, eventually, like a frontal lobotomy. Many of the resources I began to wish to bring to poetry were "forbidden."

In the Day-Poems, I deliberately set out to write in directions that contradicted the rules I had been taught in my limited exposure to creative writing: show don't tell; no ideas but in things; avoid abstractions; a poem is the brief speech of an individual in a dramatic situation. For several years, I wrote Day-Poems, trying to discover interesting and engaging modes of writing that did not depend on sharp visual images or on a plainspoken sincerity. I sought a poetry that could accommodate my interests in philosophy. In other words, I sought a poetry that could be a site for my full intelligence, my full being, such as it was, such as it would turn out to be.

I also began to realize the necessity of travel and correspondence to my vitality as a poet. After being cordoned off from any institutionally or publicly sanctioned activity as a poet at Alabama, I wrote for several years rather quietly, publishing poems in magazines, but virtually lacking in any public presence or public identity as a poet. In 1982, a former student of mine from Virginia, Richard Jones, wrote me about a poetry conference he had organized. He invited me to attend. It was the first time I had left Alabama for such an event. It proved to be immensely important. When I arrived, I was treated as a poet. Richard immediately put me on a panel discussion, and I was not only allowed but encouraged to hang out with the other poets. Most importantly, I met Louis Simpson at that conference, and I roomed with David Ignatow. Those two friendships proved to be extremely important and nourishing. By chance, when his introducer failed to show up, I ended up giving an impromptu introduction for Louis Simpson's reading in the Rotunda. I had been reading Louis's poetry for several years and had found it to be the closest (in spirit and technique) to my own family narratives. I had developed a deep respect for the particulars of Louis's quiet narrative poetry, and we immediately became close friends. I visited him at his home on Long Island, and we corresponded regularly. Louis proved to be very helpful to me as I sharpened my skills in fusing elements of lyric and narrative poetry. For a number of years, we exchanged poems and essays, and Louis was a crucial reader and critic for my early work. One result of this friendship was my editing *On Louis Simpson: Depths Beyond Happiness* for the University of Michigan Press's Under Discussion series.

My friendship with David Ignatow proved to be equally crucial and sustaining. David and I spent a lot of time talking together during the conference. The only poems I had carried with me were the Day-Poems, and though they were not at all representative of my more accomplished earlier work, I read many of these newer poems to David. He prescribed "George Oppen," a recommendation which still sustains me. David and I continue to correspond, and I continue to be inspired by his dedication as a poet, as well as his willingness to read and consider new poetries.

As another means of my learning about this division between poets and critics, I organized a symposium at the University of Alabama. The symposium, "What Is a Poet?," held in Octo-

ber 1984, included Charlie Altieri, Charles Bernstein, Kenneth Burke, David Ignatow, Denise Levertov, Marjorie Perloff, Louis Simpson, Gerald Stern, and Helen Vendler. For me, the entire event proved to be an immense learning experience. Naively, I had thought that I simply had a bright idea: bring a range of poets *and* critics together to discuss the nature of poetry. It had struck me that poets and critics did not talk to each other and that poets with different views tended to avoid one another and to describe one another in unchallenged caricatures. What I had not counted on was the depth (and history) of antagonism that my symposium would uncover. In *What Is a Poet?*, the book which was published after the symposium, there is a picture of the concluding panel discussion. Nearly all nine of the participants are leaning forward to speak into the nearest microphone.

During one of the presentations, one of the poets from my own university led a small walkout; she kept muttering, "Who can understand what he's saying?" Czeslaw Milosz had originally been scheduled to participate, but he pulled out. John Ashbery, after some negotiations, declined because he did not want to fulfill the requirement of giving a lecture since, as he put it, he did not write criticism. (I could not persuade him that virtually all of his long poems included plenty of passages that could qualify as criticism; and, of course, he had earned a living for many years as an art critic.) It was Marjorie Perloff, whom I first met in 1983, who asked me if I had ever heard of the language poets and would I consider inviting Charles Bernstein. I had not heard of the language poets; I had not heard of Charles Bernstein. But I did know that I wanted at least one younger poet to be involved, and I wanted someone (similar to Ashbery) whose own writing would challenge the more plainspoken and lyrical poetics of Simpson, Levertov, Stern, and Ignatow. I arranged to meet Charles Bernstein in New York City, and my subsequent contact with many of Charles's friends helped to shape my own work. More importantly, my friendship with Charles Bernstein (and subsequently with Ron Silliman, Douglas Messerli, Lyn Hejinian, Susan Howe, Rachel Blau DuPlessis, and others) gave me my first sense of a viable poetry community that was not alienated from readings in philosophy and theory.

From the symposium, I began to get a clearer sense of the depth and passion of differences

Panel discussion at "What Is a Poet?" symposium, University of Alabama, October 1984;
(from left to right around the table) Lazer, Denise Levertov, Charlie Altieri, David Ignatow,
Marjorie Perloff, Gerald Stern, Helen Vendler, Charles Bernstein, and Gregory Jay

among poets and critics. Because poetry as an activity is so undervalued in America (except for a relatively safe chosen few who receive considerable financial reward for the work), there is a compensatory hypersensitivity over differences of viewpoint. As a friend has said: "The lower the stakes, the higher the infighting." I have sustained active friendships and correspondences with Ignatow, Bernstein, and Perloff. The latter has been particularly generous in putting me in touch with many poets and critics. But the narrative of my friendship with Louis Simpson perhaps typifies the difficulties and instabilities of many literary alliances. After six or seven years of correspondence and friendship, I sent Louis several poems and an article I had published in *The Nation* (on the poetry and poetics of Charles Bernstein and Ron Silliman) that indicated the changing nature of my own readings and writings. The book (*On Louis Simpson: Depths Beyond Happiness*) that I edited had just been published. As a gift—a token of thanks for Louis's generosity and help in editing the book—I sent Louis a smoked salmon. Before the gift reached his house, Louis, in response to my poems and article, had sent me a blistering letter attacking my new interests. In effect, his letter accused me of consorting with the party of the devil, and Louis

made it quite clear that we could no longer remain friends. I was hurt and shocked by his letter. He had also refused delivery of the salmon (which was returned by UPS to our house in Tuscaloosa). The returned salmon arrived during my son Alan's first week of life. Alan's birth had been a dangerous one with the potential for a life-threatening viral infection. He spent his first week of life in the intensive-care unit, and day by day we rode an emotional roller coaster (as, with various test results, we faced the possibility of serious brain injury or death). Alan's situation helped me to put the falling out with Louis in perspective. I waited a month or so, and then I wrote Louis a very carefully worded reply. I claimed that, yes, the range of my poetic affinities had undergone a significant change, but that change did not negate my previous interests, including my interest in his poetry. I remember citing Pound's line, "what thou lovest well remains." And that has actually been somewhat true for me. I continue to read and enjoy the work of Robert Frost, for example, and the work of a number of other poets whose writing would, on the surface, seem to be incompatible with a number of my other enthusiasms. Louis and I did not speak to or correspond with each other for the next eight years. I saw him recently (June 1996) at a poetry conference at the University of Maine. We shook hands cordially, but there really was no substantive friendship to resume.

In the meantime, in a pre-e-mail world, my travels allowed me to meet a number of writers whose work meant a great deal to me. I remained in contact with Charles Bernstein and Marjorie Perloff; I met Ron Silliman, Lyn Hejinian, James Sherry, Leland Hickman, Stephen-Paul Martin, Douglas Messerli, Susan Howe, Jack Foley, Jake Berry, David Antin, and Jerry Rothenberg, and I entered into a number of important correspondences, including an ongoing exchange with John Taggart. By this time, my lack of institutional support for my work as a poet had become irrelevant. I had plenty of people from whom I could learn, and there were enough readers, editors, and poets taking some interest in my writing.

In a very concrete sense, the form of my first big collection of poems, *Doublespace: Poems 1971–1989,* enacts my sense of the cultural politics in American poetry. David Ignatow described the book as "a noble attempt to bridge the chasm between Language poetry and the traditional anecdotal and meditative poetry of the 'free form' mode." George Starbuck wrote about *Doublespace*: "I was handed this as a finest, newest specimen of 'Language' Poetry, which it is, which it is. And I had been wondering if 'Language' 'Poetry' would be getting over its Molierian amazement at itself. And so I trudged, clambered, sauntered, stooped, for a long ways, tracking H Lazer's ingenuities and discoveries, a long way into it all before I woke up to where (and how) I had been taken. What a lovely, capacious, populous poem-of-America surrounded me. Hailed me, corralled me, jargoned at me. Jazzy and matter-of-factly apocalyptic. I stood rebuked I stood entranced."

Doublespace consists of two books (under one cover), Book One: *Facts and Figures* and Book Two: *Made from Concentrate.* The two books open from opposite directions (thus *Made from Concentrate* opens from the back of a standard book and moves inward) and end in a blank page in the middle of the overall book. The first book consists principally of family narrative poems and lyric poems, with some fusion of the narrative and lyric tendencies. The second book consists of three series of poems: Law-Poems (which collages "original" sections of writing with lineated sections taken verbatim from the Ala-

bama legal code); Compositions (twenty-four phrasal poems, with stanzas based on various numerical relationships); and Placements (nine poems in an invented form that includes a recurring "seed" phrase; these nine poems are sandwiched between poems "Zero" and "Ten," each of which involves a particular visual design).

After entering the usual first-book contests that nearly all beginning poets attempt, and after having some courteous near-misses with a few different publishing houses, I began to think of the book as potentially something other than the standard book-format of forty-eight to sixty-four pages of one's best available poems at the time. My failure to publish a first book quickly, oddly enough, liberated me from a convention of the book that I had not yet questioned. After many years of writing, I designed *Doublespace* as a way to embrace the conflicting, seemingly discontinuous, mutually challenging modes of writing that I had engaged in. David Antin suggested that *Doublespace* "appears to present two ways of thinking and work-

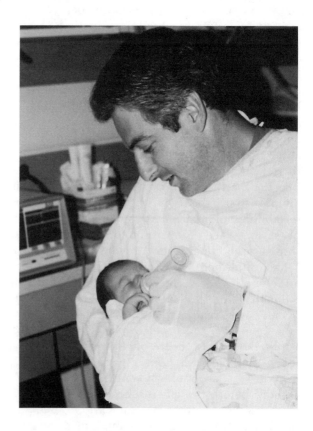

Hank Lazer feeding son Alan Dabney Lazer, less than one week old, August 1988

ing that contend for the same (doubled space): a modernist way the way of collage that fragments and assembles language registers and styles in a junkyard of mediated texts, and an older narrative way that tracks its meaning through life experience under the fitful lights of memory and desire; moving from right to left like Hebrew or left to right like English, the two ways refuse to blend, each exhibiting its own excellences and insufficiencies." The blank portion in the middle of the book, for me, represented those several years of writing Day-Poems, a way out of and away from the modes of poem making I had learned, but a series of poems that in and of themselves found a home in my attic. By the time I was able to persuade James Sherry (editor/publisher of Roof Books and Segue Books) to publish *Doublespace*, I already had a very definite design in mind. The layout of the book, including its movement in two directions toward a blank middle and the design for the cover, I had already established (in a manner that was stubborn and nonnegotiable).

I designed the cover of *Doublespace* with two paintings side by side. To the left is a portrait (by Phyllis Herfield, *Portrait of a Young Man,* 1981–1982) done in a realistic mode with a suggestion of an earlier mode of Flemish paintings with a fragment of an exterior scene visible through a window. I had seen this painting for several years at my aunt and uncle's house. The young man strikes me as a somewhat exaggerated version of the artist, a bit oversensitive, a bit posed. He wears a red beret, a black long-sleeved shirt; draped about his shoulder (in a kind of studied casualness) a white sweater. His hands are placed on an open book. In my memory of the book, I had imagined something along the lines of the illustrations to Maurice Sendak's *Where the Wild Things Are.* For me, the painting provides a somewhat ironized relationship toward my own earlier work, a kind of sincerity and sensitivity, a somewhat one-dimensional youthful seriousness, that I mocked, though with exactness and tenderness, by choosing this painting as a frontispiece for Book One. The right-hand painting, *Evasive Vases* (by Susan Bee, 1988), is more abstract, though it is still figural in nature. I was drawn to this particular painting because, with a partially pulled back drape on the left border, it acknowledges the theatrical and artificial nature of the work of art. A bluish-purple

Cover for Doublespace: Poems 1971–1989

hand extends from a white vase toward a somewhat human figure in the background. The human figure has a set of branches emerging from its head. Clearly, this is not a "natural" setting; it is a staged setting, a *made* scene in a work of art. Though Susan's painting, for me, emphasizes a certain constructedness, there is an important residue of the figural. The hand gesture actually echoes the hands of the more realistic painting by Herfield.

The overall book *Doublespace* asks, as do the two paintings side-by-side, what is the relationship between these two modes of writing which abut one another? Are the modes of reading for Book One at all compatible with Book Two? How might a reader circumvent the segregation, particularly aesthetically, that seems to govern the American poetry world? And what becomes of the personal, the figure of the person, in a more abstract and artificial artistic practice? Once sincerity has been understood as a trick of rhetoric, what contexts remain available for personal expressiveness?

Susan Howe suggests that my writing in *Doublespace* "returns to unsettle American cultural inheritance." In the Law-Poems, the obsessive rationality and the dream of a finalized clarity of the law is subjected to the peculiar scrutiny that we bring to the reading of lineated poetry. As George Starbuck noted, "The Law is his [Lazer's] test case of the too-muchness all around. . . . He is showing us the ineluctable welter from which Justice is made and justice done." What I learned through the composition of the Law-Poems is that in collage work, in the work of juxtaposition, ridicule and flat irony are rather easily achieved. But I began to experiment with a more sympathetic residency with the law. The issues taken on by the law—definitions of personhood and of identity; rules governing imitation and counterfeit; concepts of ownership; attempts to govern professionalism; the treatment of venerated objects; the treatment of the dead; regulations for education; attempts to clarify agency and personal responsibility; and so forth—were, in fact, issues of importance in the poetry.

14-5-3 It shall be unlawful to work any convict,
state or county, in any coal mine of Alabama.
in darkened rooms alone or in groups
they like to sit still and watch images
of their kind moving about talking and
especially cracking jokes   by the time
the average child graduates from high school
he or she will have spent more time with
the tv than in school   it can be ward june
wally and beaver   or frank faye mick henry
  and joyce
but think just think over all those hours
what must be taken to heart

14-3-44 All convicts must be clothed during the
  term of
their imprisonment in a comfortable manner in
  coarse and cheap
clothing made in a uniform and peculiar style so
as to distinguish them from other persons.

                     (From "Law-Poems," *Doublespace*)

I began, at times, to write deliberately flat poetry in "my" sections of the Law-Poems in an effort to shift my own ventriloquist's sympathies and those of the reader to the law. I also became intrigued with the fact that these laws, of the state of Alabama where I have lived since 1977, were, in some crucial sense, "mine." I was entitled, I thought, as a citizen of the state, to use the laws in my work without requesting permission. These laws struck me as one of the few written expressions that, exactly as written, I had a perfect right to steal and recirculate in another context.

By the time I had completed Book Two of *Doublespace*, I had settled on a way of proceeding with my writing of poetry. My reading of Ron Silliman's *Ketjak* and *Tjanting* had been a particularly formative experience in arriving at my rather mathematical constructivist approach to writing. Specifically, I responded to the humor and inclusiveness of Ron's work. And the mathematician in me responded to the formulas that constituted a spine or design for Ron's work, especially his use of the Fibonacci sequence as a means for determining the number of sentences in the accumulating paragraphs of *Tjanting*. I also loved the puns and the sports trivia present throughout Ron's work, a kind of inclusiveness that, for me, put to rest the caricature of the avant-garde as humorless and as housed only in the realm of high art. I also had become fascinated with Charles Bernstein's construction of his large books based on a principle of difference: each poem differed markedly from the poem which preceded it and from the poem which followed it. I began to think of Charles's books as based on a guiding principle of self-differing writing. He seemed to me determined not to produce a writing characterized by *a* voice (versus the workshop dictum that the poet must find his voice). As opposed to the commodity fetish of the commercial art world, where the galleries typically encourage an artist to produce an idiosyncratic and recognizable signature/style, Bernstein seemed determined to evade such a personal distinctiveness. Similarly, I had been reading a good bit of John Cage's work, and his chance-generated texts and his mesostics became attractive models for a writing that was not first and foremost a foregrounding of personal expressiveness.

I began to think of my writing as a serial enterprise, a kind of serial heuristics, where I inhabited a particular mode of composition for a fixed period of time. I was determined to avoid a kind of perfectionism or craft that led to self-imitation and to repetition. Often the most difficult phase of writing for me became that period when I tried to design a new mode of investigation that might sustain my interest and be of value for a year or so of writing.

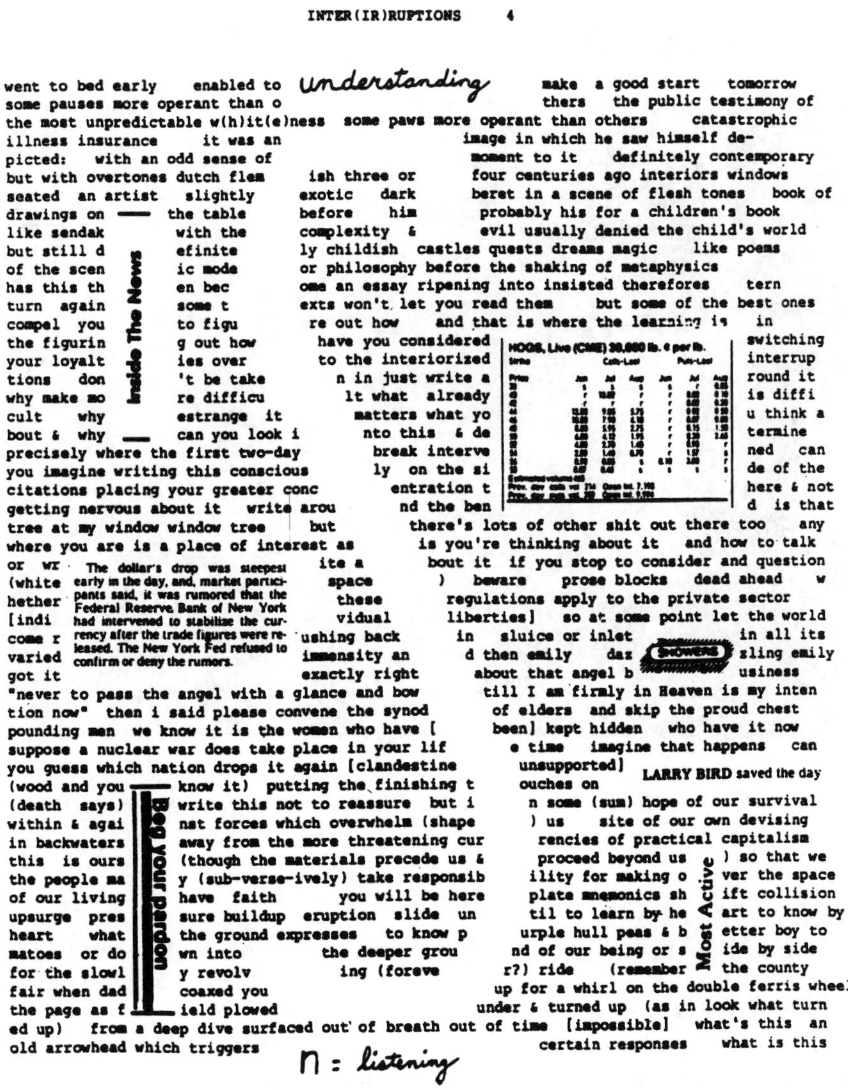

INTER(IR)RUPTIONS　4

went to bed early　enabled to　*understanding*　make a good start　tomorrow
some pauses more operant than o　　　thers　the public testimony of
the most unpredictable w(h)it(e)ness　some paws　more operant than others　catastrophic
illness insurance　it was an　　image in which he saw himself de-
picted:　with an odd sense of　　moment to it　definitely contemporary
but with overtones dutch flem　ish three or　four centuries ago interiors windows
seated an artist　slightly　exotic dark　beret in a scene of flesh tones　book of
drawings on ——— the table　before him　probably his for a children's book
like sendak　with the　complexity &　evil usually denied the child's world
but still d　efinite　ly childish castles quests dreams magic　like poems
of the scen　ic mode　or philosophy before the shaking of metaphysics
has this th　en bec　ome an essay ripening into insisted therefores　tern
turn again　some t　exts won't let you read them　but some of the best ones　in
compel you　to figu　re out how　and that is where the learning is　switching
the figurin　g out how　have you considered　interrup
your loyalt　ies over　to the interiorized　round it
tions don　't be take　n in just write a　is diffi
why make mo　re difficu　lt what already　u think a
cult　why　estrange it　matters what yo　termine
bout & why ——— can you look i　nto this & de　ned can
precisely where the first two-day　break interve　de of the
you imagine writing this conscious　ly on the si　here & not
citations placing your greater conc　entration t　d is that
getting nervous about it　write arou　nd the ben　any
tree at my window window tree　but　there's lots of other shit out there too　any
where you are is a place of interest as　is you're thinking about it　and how to talk
or wr　ite a　bout it if you stop to consider and question　w
(white　space　)　beware　prose blocks　dead ahead
hether　these　regulations apply to the private sector
[indi　vidual　liberties]　so at some point let the world
come r　ushing back　in　sluice or inlet　in all its
varied　immensity an　d then emily　das ~~skowers~~ zling emily
got it　exactly right　about that angel b　usiness
"never to pass the angel with a glance and bow　till I am firmly in Heaven is my inten
tion now" then i said please convene the synod　of elders and skip the proud chest
pounding man　we know it is the women who have [　been] kept hidden　who have it now
suppose a nuclear war does take place in your lif　e time　imagine that happens　can
you guess which nation drops it again [clandestine　unsupported]
(wood and you ——— know it) putting the finishing t　ouches on　**LARRY BIRD** saved the day
(death says)　write this not to reassure　but i　n some (sum) hope of our survival
within & agai　nst forces which overwhelm (shape　) us　site of our own devising
in backwaters　away from the more threatening cur　rencies of practical capitalism
this is ours　(though the materials precede us &　proceed beyond us　) so that we
the people ma　y (sub-verse-ively) take responsib　ility for making o　ver the space
of our living　have faith　you will be here　plate mnemonics sh　ift collision
upsurge pres　sure buildup eruption slide un　til to learn by he　art to know by
heart　what　the ground expresses　to know p　urple hull peas & b　etter boy to
matoes　or do　wn into　the deeper grou　nd of our being or s　ide by side
for the slowl　y revolv　ing (foreve　r?) ride　(remember　the county
fair when dad　coaxed you　up for a whirl on the double ferris wheel)
the page as f　ield plowed　under & turned up (as in look what turn
ed up)　from a deep dive surfaced out of breath out of time [impossible]　what's this　an
old arrowhead which triggers　certain responses　what is this

n = listening

(vertical text in left column: Inside The News / Beg your pardon)

(vertical text in right column: Most Active)

HOGS, Live (CME) 30,000 lb. 4 per lb.

The dollar's drop was steepest early in the day, and, market participants said, it was rumored that the Federal Reserve Bank of New York
had intervened to stabilize the cur-
rency after the trade figures were released. The New York Fed refused to
confirm or deny the rumors.

A page from INTER(IR)RUPTIONS

I had also become intrigued with Ron Silliman's long-term project: The Alphabet—his ongoing series of twenty-six books. I had been drawn to other long-term writings, Pound's *Cantos*, Williams's *Paterson*, Duncan's *Passages* and *Structure of Rime*, and others. I began to map out something that I might call *10 X 10*, which would be a series of ten books, each including ten poems in a particular compositional mode. The first of these works to be completed was *INTER(IR)RUPTIONS*, published in 1992 by John Byrum's Generator Press. *INTER(IR)RUPTIONS* is a series of ten collage-poems that incorporate a wide range of materials, from stock-market quotations to batting averages, from a typed over printing error in a literary introduction to passages from literary theory, from hog futures to fashion and personal advice columns from *Seventeen* magazine, from Emerson's journals to a Valentine's Day listing of children's names in *the Tuscaloosa News*, from neurophysiological research to decorating and restaurant trends reported in *Metropolitan Living* to a solicitation from a literary agent. I had been giving serious thought to the place and possibilities of collage-composition, partly as a result of my reading David Antin's groundbreaking essay, "Modernism and Post-modernism: Approach-

(From left to right) Jane Lazer, Alan Lazer, Hank Lazer, and Julie Sexton, November 1996

ing the Present in American Poetry" in *Boundary 2* (fall 1972, pp. 98–133).

In *INTER(IR)RUPTIONS*, I was involved in several projects that remain central to my preoccupations as a poet. I was devising a kind of hybrid form of expression seeking to incorporate more and more kinds of discourses within the terrain of the poem. Once I had become aware of the segregationist practice of the workshop-personal-lyric—a "naturalness" (of rhetoric and vocabulary and voice and address) dependent upon a repression of serious consideration of the origins, history, and limitations of its "natural" modes of production—I immediately sought ways to include many different kinds of writing in my poetry. The Law-Poems represent one obvious effort to do so, as do the various incorporated materials of *INTER(IR)-RUPTIONS*. As that latter title indicates, there is also a kind of competition for attention, a conflict—one discourse interrupting another or irrupting from within the other. As in the Law-Poems, I often would try to speak most intensely through the "other" discourse, enacting

within the poem Rimbaud's observation "*je est un autre.*" I had also experienced (in Placements in *Doublespace*) an exhilarating sense of moving words and phrases around on the page. These linguistic units, by virtue of the unlimited options for their placement on the page (options which were being reenforced by the rapidly changing computer technologies), began to take on a more material and tangible feel in the process of composition.

But before such a discussion of poetics begins to sound too abstract, I would also point out a significant personal dimension to my practice of collage-composition. In the family-lyric-narratives of Book One of *Doublespace*, one figure in particular is slighted: my mother. I had wondered for quite some time why I could not tell her story and why I could not adopt her language. At one level, there was a certain redundancy. My father—hardly a person one would call academic or philosophical in his interests—and his side of the family represented a certain stability and practicality, his own father's bookishness notwithstanding. From my father's father, a man who knew biblical Hebrew as well as most rabbis, I learned that it *did* make some kind of sense to know twelve languages and to be the owner/operator of a small neighborhood grocery store. My mother's side of the family provided me with a certain flair, an unstable quality of genius (which in my grandparents and great-aunt manifested itself in a kind of disabling paranoia and bitterness late in their lives), a passionate interest in the intricacies and humor of language (particularly Yiddish but also English), and the chutzpah to consider doing something unusual. On that side of the family, there were intellectual legends to consider. My uncle became a neurosurgeon (but one who studied biblical Hebrew, offered detailed readings of my poetry that were as insightful as those of any professional critic/poet, and climbed serious [physical] mountains as well); for a year of his medical training, he slept on a lab floor to save up money to buy a sailboat. One cousin became a theoretical physicist, though his studies at Cal Tech also led him to go to England to study Shakespeare, to become at University of California, San Diego, an ally of Marcuse, and to become fluent in Yiddish so he could read Isaac Bashevis Singer. The fact that I was writing poetry was already, in one sense, an affirmation of my mother's tongue and her artistic passion. She had been a concert-level pianist, studying piano at San Jose State after moving from Brooklyn to California. My father, after he could no longer stand the business of co-owning the Merry Mart with my great-uncle (a man my dad would describe as someone full of great ideas but who could never function before ten in the morning), teamed up with his old tennis doubles partner and went into the real estate and insurance businesses. He then teamed up with a golf buddy to open his own real estate business; then, after being blackballed (in part, by supposed friends and members of the Jewish community) for trying to sell a home in a predominantly white neighborhood (in fact, in our own neighborhood) to a black family, he bought a liquor store near Fort Ord and moved to the Monterey Peninsula in 1971. In the meantime, after honing her golf game, my mother went to work in real estate. She proved to be very skilled at selling and advertising. Eventually, my parents formed their own real estate business in Carmel.

Thus, a section such as

> this new development features large plots
> of land   one to five acres for each house
> no two alike of course   with several distinctive
> styles tudor mansion victorian gingerbread
> california modern   and southern plantation
> overall the eight hundred acre estate proudly
> preserves one of the area's last stands of virgin
>   pine
> rolling hills afford each home a spectacular
> undisturbed view   some from a specially
> projected dining room   others from a redwood
>   deck
> ideal for a first estate   family investment   or
>   retirement

(From "Law-Poems," *Doublespace*)

might be described abstractly as representing my efforts toward an inclusiveness in poetry. But on an autobiographical or personal level, such language is for me an entry into one aspect of a mother tongue: advertising. And such language, with its manipulativeness, its effort to sell something to a reader, does, for me, have obvious off-rhymes with poetry. David Antin once described poetry, in a TV discussion of his second sky-poem, as "an advertisement for nothing." Perhaps ideally. But a poem *is* an advertisement for itself; a poem, at a minimum, seeks to entice a reader to pay attention to it. A poem is also an advertisement for its author, for the poet. The Law-Poems also enact a family joke. My parents have often told me that they thought, with my annoying skills for stubborn argument, I would have made a good lawyer (which I have always taken as a simultaneous compliment and insult). So, the discourses of real estate, advertising, the law (my uncle Leon was a lawyer), as with the familial narratives of the lyricized old country, take on an aspect (albeit somewhat displaced and recontextualized) of the personal as well.

Similarly, a number of the collage-sources for *INTER(IR)RUPTIONS* have a personal dimension to them. My stepdaughter, Julie, was an avid reader of *Seventeen*, so I began to read her magazines and sought a way to incorporate (and the key is to do so without falling into the trap of a glib one-dimensional mockery) her reading and thinking. My wife, Jane, not an academic and not interested in poetry, is very talented in interior design; so, I began to read her back issues of *Metropolitan Home*

ideologized bodies	:	bearing scars
baring stars	:	venom mouse
unreckoned	:	unrecognized
stick to the subject	:	socially expected taxidermy
off at my place	:	strained through a painful
face	:	nostrils flared
extracranial perception	:	book(land)speculator
crafty lefty	:	serves up
frozen rope	:	dozen roses
hymn big lyric	:	when describing stop

Page 143 from 3 of 10

(where, as chance would have it, I stumbled across a feature story about a couple from Demopolis, Alabama, who, after moving to the big city, learned to make use of their small-town heritage). Similarly, the research in neurophysiology was sent to me by my uncle and, as the two key research labs are located in Berkeley and Palo Alto, involves some personal humor and Bay Area cultural politics in the description of rat-environments at (UC) Berkeley and (Stanford) Palo Alto.

*

I have deliberately been constructing *a* kind of autobiography: a story of my life *in* poetry. I believe that such an autobiography is of value—the life of the writing. It is, I suspect, only of interest to someone who is already interested in the writing. Such an autobiography demonstrates why movies about the lives of poets inevitably focus on something other than the writing. Hollywood will focus on the turbulence, drama, and extremism of a crazy personal life. The poetry, the endless writing itself, the petty struggles for recognition and/or a public existence for the work, the slow correspondence, the late-night or early-morning moment of insight; the slow imper-

ceptible gradations of aesthetic and philosophical change; the gradual understanding of a once-enigmatic passage—none of these have a place in the movie version of the life. But in a written document, in a reference autobiography, here, attention will be given to that life-in-writing.

Having made my case for the life-in-writing, let me then contradict myself. Poetry, for me, is *a* passion among other passions. Intellectually, I began with a passion for mathematics.

> I studied the secrets
> of n-factorial, imaginary numbers,
> the graceful curve of the integral,
> and the solution to the quadratic equation.
> A language stripped of language.
> I lived in a room on Cambridge Drive
> lying on a red corduroy bedspread, book open,
> working on an extra problem or two.
> I would scratch down a sign
> and its exact consequences,
> the secret language, world
> without mother or father or sister,
> equations with coordinates for n-dimensions.

(From "Number Theory," *Doublespace*)

I believe that poetry—writing, reading, thinking—poetry as David Antin defines it: the language art—is and has been my most comprehensive passion and my most enduring passion. (As I write this passage, I would estimate my devotion to poetry as a nearly thirty-year activity.) My involvement with poetry is a daily one. I am, nearly every day, either writing poetry, writing essays on poetry, reading poetry, and/or thinking about issues related to poetry.

The writing of a new poem is much more exciting than the publication of a book. The latter inevitably involves a disconcerting time warp. The poems were written years ago; the concerns in the poems are often not one's precise concerns in the present. As one reads one's own books, one encounters a previous self. I am not arguing for some sense of development and progress. Indeed, that earlier self may have been more intelligent, more on the mark. But it is a prior self. When I published *Doublespace,* for example, my greatest fear was wondering how I would react to the earlier lyric/narrative poetry. The book itself had been a gesture *not* to disavow my earlier work; the book had been an effort to give the earlier work a different context by contrast and conflict with the more innovative work in Book Two. I found that I continued to feel a great fondness for the earlier writing—"what thou lovest well remains." I was aware that I would not and could not write in that manner now, but I respected and enjoyed and stood behind the earlier work. I found that I enjoyed reading it aloud. At poetry readings, whether at the Ear Inn (to an audience of avant-gardists) or at a conservative university, I took pleasure in reading these poems. A book publication, or at least my experience of it, puts one through such a test. The exercise of reading aloud from one's earlier work is akin to a seance or to a momentary possession, with a mixture of moderate discomfort and immense familiarity.

What then are my other passions? Several important loving human relationships, including an ongoing (seventeen years as of 1996) second marriage, a stepdaughter (now twenty-five years old), and a son (now eight years old). I have a passion for teaching, an activity I began (without ever really intending it to be a career) in 1973. I have—here is my father's

influence coming through—been serially devoted to various sports. I have played tournament tennis, AAU volleyball, tournament Ping-Pong, basketball (in high school and in many leagues after that), diving (in high school), and I swam competitively in Masters swimming in my late thirties. But my most sustained passion in sports has been golf. My father was an extraordinary athlete. Growing up in San Jose, he was one of the state's top golfers and one of the state's top tennis players. He had a golf club in my hands when I was two years old, and I played golf through high school. As a socialist in college, golf seemed like "bad faith," so I quit the sport for approximately twenty years. I returned to playing seven or eight years ago, and when the weather and my job permit, I try to play or practice nearly every day. In the past year or two, I have, on occasion been able to play par or sub-par golf, and this past summer I managed to lead a local tournament after the first round. Golf for me is essentially a spiritual discipline. On the golf course, both literally and metaphorically, I am in contact with my father (who died at age sixty-nine of

Cover for 3 *of 10 (cover by Jess)*

(From left to right) Chuck Lazer, Alan Lazer, Hank Lazer, and nephew Matthew Schmale, November 1990

leukemia on February 16, 1996). I suppose that it helps that I am wearing his shoes, his shirt, using a set of his clubs. The course is a site where I feel his presence. As I recognized many years ago, I can feel his face, his particular mode of concentration, when I address the ball:

> As I stare down
> at the ball,
> bring it into
> precise
> focus,
> each shadow
> in the well
> of each dimple,
> stare down
> in a kind of focused
> anger,
> and start
> the club back
> on its slow
> full
> inward arc,
> I wear
> his face.

(From "Tricks," *Doublespace*)

He was not (until the last year of his life) an especially verbal person. My interest in poetry was, in many ways, antithetical to his being; the poetry comes much more from my mother's side of the family. But in physical activity, in the precise labor and discipline, and in the camaraderie and jockish way of being together that a sport allows, one could come to know my father. In golf, oddly, I feel a continuity of spirit with my father that I imagine to be very much akin to what a son would feel if his father were a rabbi and the son chose, at some point, to follow a similar path.

In the midst of this fundamentally literary autobiography, I dwell on golf for a number of reasons. There are many ways to live a life in poetry. I have chosen a life of variety and contradiction. I have many different interests, and I follow those interests with passion, devotion, and energy. In George Oppen's words, "we [I] have chosen the meaning of being numerous." My wife is not a poet, not an academic, not much interested in high literature.

I am a Jew; I live in the Deep South; I teach courses in literature; I am an academic administrator (since 1991, assistant dean for humanities and fine arts); I am an avid golfer; I spend nearly every day listening to jazz and blues; I am a father with a young son; I live in a racially mixed, upper-middle-class neighborhood, which means yard work and a large mortgage; I am an avid sports fan; I have followed dance for many years, and this past year I began working as a choreographer.

What I'm describing is my rejection of the virtues of singularity. I know many artists/poets who are married to or live with fellow artists/poets. They go, on occasion, to writers' colonies so that they can have the isolation and focus that is crucial to the pursuit of their craft. They do not like to be interrupted. I suppose that one of my book titles, *INTER(IR)-RUPTIONS*, speaks to my own choice. John Cage talks about telephone calls and their relationship to his writing. One might view such things as an intrusion, as something that interrupts one's concentration. Like Cage, I have learned to embrace those interruptions, not as interruptions but as the content of the life being lived, as a gift. (Of course, not all interruptions are fruitful!) I have found my life and my writing to be enriched by contradiction and multiplicity. I write best when there are other time pressures, when I know that I have only the early morning before I get my son's breakfast and go to administrative meetings at my office. Or during the quieter time of the summer, when I am juggling my writing with my golf-addiction and my desire to cook a good pasta dish while the acidic tomatoes from my father-in-law Harold Dabney Duncan's farm in Pickens County are in season.

Since the completion of Book One of *Doublespace*, my poetry has increasingly reflected the range of my interests and experiences. At times, I have worried that I could get more done if I focused more exclusively on my literary projects. Clearly, there are certain literary projects that I can not do under my current time constraints. For example, I would love to write a book on Thoreau's *Journal*, and I would love to devote a book-length essay to a meditation on Stein's *The Making of Americans*. Professionally, I may even choose to continue in academic administration, and the next job in that career path would be considerably more time-consuming.

But this is not a story of someone who thinks he is "captain of his fate." Much of what I do depends on chance, circumstance, and opportunity. In the late 1960s, when I "chose" to devote myself to poetry, America was in the midst of an economic boom. At Stanford, a school of less than six thousand undergraduates, there were six hundred English majors. A few years later, as the United States entered a recession, 95 percent of Stanford's freshman class anticipated a career in medicine or law. Today, no doubt, if I were beginning college again I might study literature, but I would probably choose to become a doctor (due to the extreme financial pressures that today's students face). I came to Alabama because, in the tight job market of the mid-1970s, it was the only tenure-track job offer I had. And I have stayed here, in part, because of a continuing tight job market and because of the unaffordable housing in many more desirable locations. I am in academic administration because the opportunity presented itself, because it pays better, because I enjoy the activity, and because it got me out of an at times unpleasant and claustrophobic English Department. In keeping with my affinity for multiplicity, my current job requires me to work with ten different departments and thus demands that I consider the interests and activities of a range of fine and performing arts. Similarly, I spent this past year working as a co-choreographer with Cornelius Carter because we were good friends and because the opportunity presented itself. I stay in administration, even with the starched white shirts and ties and the endless long meetings, because of the money and because I do not want to return to the more narrow identification with *an* academic department.

Similarly, my poetry is about a conflict, or a chorus, of voices, the juxtaposition of different (sometimes conflicting, sometimes reenforcing, sometimes interacting in ways that are unpredictable and unknowable) discourses. I have begun to consider the rapidity of shift in voice or discourse as constituting a kind of metric. In my earlier innovative work—Law-Poems or *INTER(IR)RUPTIONS*—the shifts are rather blockish and sharply delineated. In my most recent work, *Days*, those shifts can occur in the span of two or three words. I have not wanted to go to a writers' colony. Why would I retreat? From what? To what? In the demanding rhythm of the juggling act I have been living,

I have been able to write a fair amount. It is a writing consistent with that contradictory living.

*

In the spring of 1993, I traveled to China. The occasion for the trip was the publication of *Selected Language Poems.* The book includes substantial bilingual poetry selections by me, Charles Bernstein, and James Sherry, as well as essays by me and Jeff Twitchell on the poetics of contemporary experimental American poetries (translated into Chinese by Yunte Huang and Zhang Ziqing), and a preface by Zhang Ziqing, a leading Chinese scholar of twentieth-century American poetry. Yunte Huang and I traveled to Chengdu, Guiyang, Beijing, Nanjing,

"Page 33 of Selected Language Poems, *the biographical introduction to my section of poems"*

and Suzhou, giving lectures, readings, and discussions. James Sherry joined us in Beijing, Nanjing, and Suzhou. The trip began with an event organized by our publisher to celebrate the publication of our bilingual poetry book. That event, in Chengdu, was covered by eighteen newspapers and four TV stations. There were theatrical and dance presentations and poetry recitations by college and university student groups. A group of medical students did a wonderfully intelligent modernist presentation of one of my poems; their presentation had a self-conscious artificiality to it that offered a perceptive reading of the poem's structure. Another group had set one of James's poems to a Peking opera format, and his poem was sung to us. Immediately after the event, one TV reporter (who was wearing a Toronto Blue Jays cap) asked me, "Isn't it true that in a market economy such as that of the United States that only a very few people read 'pure' literature? Might not China's movement into a market economy result in a great deal of damage to the production of 'pure' literature? And, please, our news spot will be brief, so speak slowly and confine your answer to about two minutes."

In Beijing, we spoke at Peking University, and we met with a group of poets, critics, editors, and artists at September Gallery, the first modern-art gallery in China. For that latter discussion, we were joined by Fredric Jameson who was in Beijing to deliver a lecture. The most inspiring part of the trip was getting to meet and spend several days with the poets Che Qianzi and Zhou Yaping in the city of Suzhou. We spent many hours in conversation, and, as a group, we wrote some poems. Yunte Huang is currently finishing a Ph.D. in poetics (at State University of New York at Buffalo), and he will soon publish the first translation into Chinese of Pound's *Pisan Cantos.* During our travels, I wrote in the early mornings and was able to complete a long poem, *Early Days of the Lang Dynasty,* a poem which draws its structure from the architecture of the Round Altar in the Temple of Heaven in Beijing.

*

As I am completing this autobiography, a culmination of sorts is taking place. In the past few months, I have published four books:

(From left to right) Yunte Huang, Che Qianzi, Hank Lazer, James Sherry,
Zhou Yaping in Suzhou, May 1993

the two volumes of *Opposing Poetries* (essays on contemporary poetry, Volume 1: *Issues and Institutions,* Volume 2: *Readings*); *Early Days of the Lang Dynasty* (a twenty-seven-page poem written during my cultural exchange trip to China in spring 1993); and *3 of 10,* a big collection of poetry (163 pages, three extended series of poems, with a cover by the artist Jess). These books represent a decade's worth of writing in criticism and in poetry. It is too early to tell what attention the books will receive. These books have presented me an opportunity to give readings and talks—at Shippensburg University, State University of New York at Buffalo, Stanford, University of California at San Diego, even at my own campus where on October 24, 1996, I gave my second reading in twenty years. Where possible, I have used the readings as an occasion to introduce multivoice presentations of several of the poems from the series Displayspace (in *3 of 10*). I have also made use of slides and computer-scanned images of a number of the poems I'm reading so that the audience

can see (as well as hear) the poems, viewing the layout and design of the poem-on-page while listening to an oral version of the poem. Audience members thus have an opportunity to experience the poems as instances of a conflicting intersection of textuality and orality.

At present, I have completed one new manuscript of poetry, *Days,* a series of poems written over the period of a year-and-a-day. Many of the poems include some handwritten elements (including cross-outs, variants, marginal notes, and the date of composition), thus placing the poems in a space that shows allegiances both to manuscript and digital cultures. The poems themselves are highly lyrical, paying homage to a wide range of poets of the short line: Robert Creeley, Louis Zukofsky, George Oppen, Emily Dickinson, Sylvia Plath, and others. Many of the poems explore affinities—particularly in quick shifts in direction—to the music of Thelonious Monk and John Coltrane, as I enact rather than thematize a jazz poetics. I am also currently completing a collection of ten longer poems tentatively called *Tenor*. And in my critical writing, I have been exploring new modes of lyrical poetry and a re-evaluation of the relationship of myth and poetry.

As I have tried to tell my students, the mail is a more important site for education than the classroom. At present, my own community of correspondents includes Ted Enslin, John Taggart, Lyn Hejinian (who was in residence at the University of Alabama for spring 1996), and the choreographer Cornelius Carter. There is a steady conversation and a sharing of work with Jack Foley and Jake Berry. To put it quite simply, these friendships sustain my writing. Over the past several years, I have had opportunities that have truly surprised me. In 1995, I worked with an advanced choreography class at the Harvard Summer Dance Program and saw young choreographers improvise multivoice dance versions of several of my poems from *Days*. Jake Berry and I were instrumental in publishing a special issue of the *New Orleans Review* (edited by William Lavender) called "The Other South: Experimental Writing in the South," a collection of poems and an essay. (See "Toward a New Southern Poetry," *New Orleans Review*, summer 1995, pp. 39–41.) Perhaps this collection will begin to counteract the narrowly defined stereotype of Southern writing. I have had the opportunity to return to the San Francisco Bay Area to read at Cody's in Berkeley; Jack Foley interviewed me for a radio program on KPFA; and in February 1997 I read with Lou Harrison, Michael Tilson Thomas, and Jack and Adelle Foley at the San Francisco Conservatory of Music in a celebration of composer Lou Harrison's eightieth birthday. Currently, along with clarinetist Scott Bridges, I am teaching a course in arts collaborations to a group of dancers, poets, musicians, photographers, and composers.

As for what's next, I don't know. Growing up in California, I knew nothing of Alabama; I have lived in Tuscaloosa for twenty years. I did not foresee myself doing administrative work, and I have been doing it for nearly ten years. And there is the sustained and miraculous joy of my relationship with my eight-year-old son Alan. Just the other day we were riding around in the country listening to bp Nichol's "Ear Rational" and chanting back our own incantations. Alan's words often find their way into my poems. As for the poems I am writing, I remain pulled in two different directions: to-ward a more performance-oriented approach (which tends toward oral performance and toward collaborative, multi-arts works) and toward a further exploration of the principally visual possibilities of the page (particularly as the page is made electronic). As a poet, I remain committed to a project of serial heuristics, of cycles of work that are intentionally self-differing. No doubt, my reading, listening, living, and corresponding will take my writing in directions that I cannot foresee.

BIBLIOGRAPHY

Poetry:

Mouth to Mouth, Alderman Press, 1977.

INTER(IR)RUPTIONS, Generator Press, 1992.

Doublespace: Poems 1971–1989, Segue Books, 1992.

Negation, Ink-A! Press, 1994.

Early Days of the Lang Dynasty, Meow Press, 1996.

3 of 10: H's Journal, Negation, and Displayspace, Chax Press, 1996.

More than one hundred publications of poems in various magazines, including *Central Park, The Nation, San Jose Studies, Southern Review, Temblor*, and *Virginia Quarterly Review*, 1973–1997. Poetry appeared in the following anthologies: *Anthology of Magazine Verse and Yearbook of American Poetry*, 1985 and 1986; *The Art of Practice: Forty-Five Contemporary Poets*, Potes & Poets Press, 1994; and *For David Ignatow: An Anthology*, Guild Hall/Canio's Editions, 1994. Also contributed to electronic chapbooks, including ten poems from *Days* (RIF/T #5: http://wings.buffalo.edu/epc/rift/rift 05/) and six poems from *Days*, with an introduction and commentary (*Experioddicist*, Chapbook #1: NinthLab@aol.com). Works in translation, include: *Selected Language Poems: Charles Bernstein, Hank Lazer, and James Sherry*, translated by Yunte Huang and Zhang Ziqing, Sichuan Art and Literature Publishing House [Chengdu, China], 1993.

See also "China, Innovative Poetries, and Translation," co-authored with Yunte Huang, in *Central Park* 24, spring 1995, pp. 231–241.

Criticism:

Opposing Poetries, Volume 1: Issues and Institutions, Northwestern University Press, 1996.

Opposing Poetries, Volume 2: Readings, Northwestern University Press, 1996.

More than thirty essays and reviews published in various magazines and journals, including *American Book Review, The American Poetry Review, American Literary History, Contemporary Literature, ELH, Modern Poetry Studies, The Nation, Temblor,* and *The Virginia Quarterly Review,* 1980–1997.

Editor:

On Equal Terms, Symposium Press, 1984.

What Is a Poet?, University of Alabama Press, 1987.

On Louis Simpson: Depths Beyond Happiness, University of Michigan Press, 1988.

Performances and collaborations include "Garden-Works" (collaborative installation—sculpture, video, photography, sound with six other artists), performed in Birmingham, September 27–October 18, 1991; "Certain Shirts, Uncertain Pants" (performance piece with Richard Giles and Karen Graffeo), performed in April 1992; and "Cantus in Memory" (co-choreography, with Cornelius Carter; dance piece for eight dancers), performed at University of Alabama, February 29–March 3, 1996.

Mary Mackey

1945-

I date my understanding that I have been amazingly lucky from a hot summer afternoon in 1966 when, at the age of twenty-one, recently graduated from Harvard and recently married, I stood on the edge of the Inter-American Highway looking out toward the Pacific. I was perhaps five miles north of San Salvador, and between me and the water lay a vast garbage dump, smoking and reeking in the muggy Central American air. Overhead, vultures were circling in that slow, relentless rhythm that comes over them when they know a feast has been laid. There were shapes moving through the garbage, but glare coming off of the ocean was so intense that it took me a while to realize that the stumbling shadows were human. Old men, women, and small children—desperately poor and probably starving—were sifting through orange rinds, chicken guts, plastic bags, and human excrement trying to find something to eat. Dizzy with horror and heatstroke, I sat down on the hot asphalt, put my head between my knees, and made myself a promise: no matter what happened to me, for the rest of my life, I would never allow myself to forget that I had been given food and clothing and a good education in a world where there were people who considered finding half a loaf of moldy bread a piece of incredible luck.

I came into the world on a cold, overcast January day in 1945 when V-2 rockets were falling on Britain, our planes were bombing Tokyo, and Hitler's suicide and Hiroshima were only months away. At the time of my birth, my father's father was a barber in Marion, Kentucky, a town so small that there was no lock on the jail door. At the age of eighteen, my father, John Mackey, had migrated north to Evansville, Indiana, the local land of opportunity, where he had put himself through Evansville College, working nights as a bellhop and studying in the hotel's freight elevator. Not long after Pearl Harbor, he had joined the U.S. Army which had sent him to medical school. By the time I

Mary Mackey

was born he had his M.D. thanks to an accelerated wartime course of study that had included only one day off a year (Christmas).

My mother, Jean McGinness, came from a solidly middle-class Irish-German family. Her mother was a devout Methodist who divided her time between home and church, and her father worked as an engineer at Servel designing refrigerators and airplane motors. Before her marriage, my mother had played the viola, read voraciously, and at the age of sixteen had won herself a full scholarship to Smith. Unfortunately my grandmother had been scandalized by the idea of a young girl living where her parents couldn't keep an eye on her; so she had forced my mother to give up her scholarship. Determined to get an education, my mother had enrolled in Evansville College and majored in chemistry with the intention of going on to medical school, but although she graduated at the top of her class with glowing recommendations from her professors, she was not able to find a medical school willing to admit a woman. Some of the schools told her quite frankly that if she had been a man they would have accepted her on the spot.

Unable to become a doctor herself, she met and fell in love with my father who was already enrolled in pre-med courses. They married in the spring of 1942. While my father was in medical school, she was the wage-earner for the family, working as a chemist for Mead Johnson—a job she held until a few months before my birth (she was one of the first women Mead Johnson had ever hired).

I was the first of my parents' three children, healthy except for a slightly deformed foot that made it necessary for me to wear corrective shoes until I was five or six, but my health was short-lived. For reasons no one could figure out, I soon developed a tendency to come down with serious strep infections. For several years after the war, my father remained in the army, serving as a military doctor in charge of inductions. We moved from base to base, and—between learning to crawl at Camp Polk, Louisiana, and learning to talk at Tinker Field, Oklahoma—I battled one strep throat after another. The worst of my childhood bouts with strep took place in Worcester, Massachusetts, during a blizzard when I contracted pneumonia, ran a fever of over 106 degrees, and (so I am told) stopped breathing long enough to turn blue. My mother and father rushed me to an Army hospital through the storm, where my father injected me with penicillin—a new drug which at the time was only available to the military. If I had been born a year or two earlier, I probably would have died.

Hearing about the debt I owed to antibiotics has given me a life-long respect for (and interest in) science which often appears in my poetry. At the same time, the high fevers of my childhood (which lasted until I had my tonsils out at thirteen) left me with an ongoing interest in altered states of consciousness—surrealism, insanity, and hallucination—since every time my temperature spiked over 104 or 105 degrees, I would start seeing strange things. Years later, combining the two influences, I wrote

my doctoral dissertation on the relationship between mysticism and science in the nineteenth-century novel ("The Human Position: Hudson and the Darwinian Revolution"); and I have incorporated my fever-visions into numerous poems (such as "Breaking the Fever"), and into several of my novels, most particularly the prophetic scenes in *The Last Warrior Queen* (1983), *The Year the Horses Came* (1993), *The Horses at the Gate* (1995), and *The Fires of Spring* (1998).

Since my father was a doctor, hospitals continued to play a major role in my childhood. For the most part, I saw them as friendly places where I was fussed over by the nurses, fed candy, and shown bassinets filled with newborn babies. One of my earliest memories is of dancing for the wounded soldiers. I am two or three: a small, chubby, brown-eyed blonde dressed in a white party dress, twirling and prancing between beds of bandaged men, some of whom lack arms and legs. When I finish, the soldiers applaud me, and I am hooked forever on the desire to make sad people happy.

In 1948 my father completed his military service, and set up his first medical practice in Rockport, Indiana, a small river town on the Ohio that had a distinctly southern flavor. Within weeks everyone from the riverboat captain to the minister's wife knew me by name. I could get strawberry ice cream cones on credit at the drugstore or pick up the phone and tell the operator to "let me talk to my Daddy," and she would recognize my voice and connect me to his office. I loved Rockport, and perhaps if I had grown up there, I would have become the kind of writer who chronicles the Gothic eccentricities of life in a small southern town; but my father was getting paid in chickens and bushels of corn, and my mother was feeling trapped in a place that didn't even have a movie theater to recommend it, so in August of 1949 we moved to Indianapolis, where my life settled into a predictable pattern that was to last the rest of my childhood.

We lived downtown on the corner of Thirty-second and Broadway in a quiet neighborhood where the streets were shaded by buckeyes and maples and all the houses had big front porches. In the early fifties, before everyone had television and air-conditioning, most people spent the hot summer nights rocking in porch swings and watching the children play under the street lamps. When it grew too hot

Mackey's parents, John and Jean, shortly after their marriage, 1942

to sleep inside, my parents made my friends and me pallets on the front lawn, and we'd go to sleep to the humming of locusts. During the day, when we weren't in school, we were allowed to run more or less wild as long as we came home before dark.

My brother John was born in 1950, my sister Jane in 1955. Although I helped change their diapers and sterilize their bottles, they were both too young to play with. Still, I never lacked for friends. Thanks to the post-war baby boom, our neighborhood was filled with children, but by some strange statistical anomaly there were no girls my age within ten blocks in either direction. So I grew up in a gang of boys, playing baseball and football, wrestling, throwing knives, roping phantom cattle, and refighting the great battles of World War II with cap guns and paper bags full of dirt and nails. Despite the fact that I insisted on running around without a shirt (until I was forced into one at the age of seven) and excelled in boyish activities like shooting sling shots and jumping off garage roofs, I never tolerated anyone calling me a "tomboy." I had several

fistfights with boys who dared suggest that I should go back to my dolls and won at least half of them.

Although I was very short and only weighed half what the boys weighed, I soon won a reputation for being stubborn and slightly crazy. My favorite technique was to move in close, hold on, and keep on punching no matter how much the boy I was fighting with knocked me around. My parents had read me Kipling's story "Rikki-tikki-tavi," and I suspect that I was the only kid in my neighborhood who regularly imagined that she was a mongoose.

Because of the years I spent playing with boys, I never learned that females were supposed to be passive. On more than one occasion, this has come in handy. About a year after we moved to Indianapolis, when I was no more than five, I encountered a man named Bill. Bill rented a room from the middle-aged widow whose fish pond often served my gang as the beaches of Normandy, and he used to regale me and my friends with stories of how he had knocked out the teeth of enemy soldiers to steal their gold fillings. One day, when my friends were nowhere in sight, Bill grabbed me and shoved his hand up under my dress. True to my reputation as the human mongoose of Thirty-second street, I instantly bit through his thumb, and he threw me to the ground with a howl. He never tried to molest me again.

From first through sixth grade I attended P.S. 76, a huge, gloomy brick building with marble floors and a picture of George Washington prominently displayed on the wall of every classroom. Both McCarthyism and the Cold War were in full swing, so our teachers spent a lot of time teaching us about the godless communists and their plan to blow Indianapolis off the map with nuclear weapons. In my second novel, *McCarthy's List* (1979), I have described how the air-raid sirens periodically would go off and we would be herded into the halls to wait for the flash of light that would turn our little bodies into piles of ash. Around 1953, just to make the identification of our remains easier, the powers-that-be issued every child in Indianapolis dog tags which we were ordered to wear at all times. I promptly exchanged my tags with my best friend, Tommy Weaver, so if the Russians had bombed us, that's the name I would have died under.

At P.S. 76 opinion about me was divided. Mrs. Walton, my fifth-grade teacher, told my parents that I was the most gifted student she had ever taught, while my sixth-grade teacher (who could never forgive me for publicly correcting her when she claimed that Prague was the capital of Bulgaria) complained to the principal that I was a smart aleck and a born troublemaker.

My sixth-grade teacher had a point. My parents read to me almost every night before bedtime; and during the day, I read everything I could get my hands on from the Oz Books (which I adored) to my father's medical texts (which included horrendous accounts of fetal deformities). Because I read so much, I came to school armed with a huge vocabulary of words I could barely pronounce. I did well enough in every subject (except math) to be branded a teacher's pet; but at the same time I talked out in class, interrupted the other students, and argued with the teacher. I can remember stubbornly holding to the proposition that the shortest distance between two points was *not* a straight line if there happened to be a mountain in the way, and no amount of reasoning or threatening could persuade me otherwise.

As a result, I was punished frequently. Sometimes when I talked out of turn, the teachers would stuff my mouth with tissue and tape it shut; pick me up by the hair and shake me; make me stand for an hour on my tiptoes with my nose in a chalk circle; lob erasers at me; smack me with a ruler; or shut me up in a dark cloakroom—which was actually a treat because I got to eat the library paste and other peoples' lunches. Oddly enough, despite the punishments I received, I loved school. I had a vivid imagination that needed to be fed with books and ideas and public debate. By the time I was in the third grade I had convinced my entire class to pretend that they were a hive of bees (I was their Queen, of course); and in my spare time, I was already starting to write poems and short stories.

Probably one reason that I survived the Indianapolis public school system in relatively good shape was that every summer, I escaped to another world where I was petted, praised, and adored. During the month of July, I often spent a few weeks in Evansville with my mother's parents. My grandmother McGinness (whom I

Young Mackey, 1947

called "Nana") was an ardent bird-watcher and a dedicated catcher, filleter, and fryer of fish. She and my grandfather owned a lot on a small lake. On summer mornings, before the sun rose too high, Nana and I would row out to the deep end, bait our hooks with the doomed worms and cast our lines. We had our lucky bobbers and our superstitions, and we always caught three or four times as many fish as my father or grandfather caught with their fancy hand-tied flies.

After we had pulled in our limit of blue-gills and crappies, we would spend the rest of the day hiking in the woods. Nana knew every flower and tree by name; she could point out fox dens and poison mushrooms and teach a small child how to walk silently through knee-high brush. I owe my love of wild things to my maternal grandmother, and the lyrical vision of nature that she gave to me appears in many of my poems (such as "Wild Woman" and "Skin Diver").

After my brother and I had visited the Yankee branch of the family for a few weeks, we were usually sent south to Marion to spend part of August with our father's people, which (when all our cousins and relatives of lesser degree were totaled up) seemed to include virtually everyone in Crittenden County. Marion was the county seat, and my grandmother, Alice Mackey—a registered Democrat—had managed to get herself elected county clerk, which was not a small accomplishment since Republicans had dominated the county for decades. Allie was a short, round, friendly, warm-hearted woman with a spine of steel who had conducted a curious election campaign: riding back into the hills where the moonshiners hid their stills, she had dismounted from her mule, stood in the middle of the path, and yelled that she was "one of the Wathen girls." (The Wathens—her father's people—had come across the Cumberland gap with Daniel Boone, intermarrying with the Clemens who ultimately produced another writer named Mark Twain who was a distant cousin of mine). When the moonshiners emerged from the bushes, double-barreled muzzle-loading shotguns in hand, to welcome her as kin, she told them she was running for county clerk and asked for their vote. At election time whole wagonloads of backcountry people showed up to scratch their ballots and vote her into office.

Mackey with her best friends, Larry Sherman (left) and Tommy Weaver (right), in her front yard on Thirty-second Street, 1952

For a few days my grandmother would feed us on cream cake, fried chicken, and beaten biscuits; and take us around town to show us off. Then, when she judged the time was right, she would call the mailman and arrange for him to take my brother and me out to the family farm in the back of his beat-up Ford pickup. Dressed in jeans and straw hats, my brother and I would jolt along the rutted roads through clouds of red dust which came from the richest bottom land in the western part of the state. My family owned 140 acres of it tucked into a bend of the Ohio River right across from Cave-In-Rock where the river pirates used to hide and divide up their loot after they had attacked the flat boats.

Shortly after the river appeared, winding muddily beyond the willows, my brother and I would spot Uncle Wid waiting for us in his mule-drawn wagon. Uncle Wid was a tall, lean, mild-mannered man who loved his mules as if they were members of his own family. He could roll a cigarette with one hand (holding the tobacco pouch in his teeth) while he plowed behind the team, and he worked harder than any human being I have ever met before or since. Wid had once been a cook on the big riverboats that plied the Ohio, and when he

*Maternal grandparents, Clem and Mabel McGinness,
in the 1940s*

married my Great Aunt Ebbie (over the strenuous objections of my great-grandfather), great-grandfather had forbidden Wid to set foot on the farm since riverboat cooks were known for their cussing and low-class ways. For the first ten years of their married life, Ebbie and Wid had lived apart. She had tended to great-grandfather (who suffered from Parkinsonism) and sneaked away on weekends to spend time with her husband.

Great-grandfather had been famous for his learning and his tyrannical nature. He had worn a white suit and a large white hat when he limped out to oversee the hired hands, and for many years he had presided over the farm like a minor god. On their wedding night, he had ordered my great-grandmother to give him boys, and when she stubbornly persisted in giving birth to girls, he retaliated by giving all of them, except my grandmother, boy's names. Aunt Ebbie's actual name was Ebenezer Gabriel; Aunt Kittie, a widow who also lived on the farm, was named Christopher; and Aunt Fen—who lived in Nashville—was named Fenwick. But by the time my brother and I started visiting the farm, great-grandfather had been dead for many years, and Wid, for whom he had had so much contempt, was comfortably settled into great-grandfather's big walnut bed next to Aunt Ebbie.

Getting into Uncle Wid's wagon was like climbing into a time machine and going back a hundred years. As you drove toward the farm everything modern disappeared, and even the words Wid spoke had a Shakespearean tinge that gave our conversations a strange formality. At the farm itself there was no plumbing and no electricity. The water came from a cistern hauled up by a bucket on a rope. Light came from coal oil lamps. Food was kept cool in the root cellar or the springhouse. Aunt Ebbie and Aunt Kittie collected wood ashes and fat and made soap in the front yard in a huge iron kettle. They both could card, spin, and weave (although since feed had started coming in calico sacks the spinning wheel had been gathering dust in the attic).

Wid plowed with his mules, hoed and harvested his crops by hand (with the help of five or six men hired on for the busiest part of the season), slaughtered his own pigs, and salted down his hams in the same huge wooden trough that had been sitting in the smokehouse since 1792. Since I was a guest, my chores were light. I fed the chickens, brought in the eggs (which seemed like a daily Easter-egg hunt), and churned the butter in an old wooden churn whose handle had been worn thin by generations of women. During the day, if I wanted to go out, I had to wear a sunbonnet since my great aunts held with the nineteenth-century notion that a "lady" never allowed herself to get a tan.

After the dinner dishes had been cleared away and washed in boiling water and homemade brown soap harsh enough to take the skin off your hands, the whole family adjourned to the front porch and amused themselves by telling stories. The stories my Kentucky kin told were part of a rich oral heritage that went back several hundred years, and some of them, in the great Scotch-Irish tradition, were rather gruesome. No allowances were made for the presence of children. I heard of the little boy who had hidden in the field to surprise his daddy and been bailed by a mechanical hay bailer; of the massacres that took place in 1775 when my ancestors were helping Daniel Boone blaze the Wilderness Road. My relatives chatted about the milk-fever epidemic that killed so many women and children in the early 1800s as if it had happened last Tuesday and bragged about my god-knows-how-many-times great-aunt, a midwife who had discovered a cure for it.

One night I even heard a terrifying story about a neighbor who had found his wife in bed with another man and taken an axe to both of them, chopping them into "little skittering bits." For several days I was too frightened to go into the henhouse by myself. Then I discovered that all this had happened when Teddy Roosevelt was president, which news calmed me considerably.

I have used quite a bit of this material in my poetry (see, for example, "Wild Woman," "Betony," and "My Grandmother's Bed"); but in a more subtle way, the summers I spent with my Uncle Wid, Aunt Ebbie, and Aunt Kittie are the source of my lifelong interest in writing historical fiction. Having lived a nineteenth-century childhood for a few weeks every summer, I feel more like a former resident of the past than a tourist. When I wrote *A Grand Passion,* which is set in Russia at the turn of the century, or *The Kindness of Strangers,* which recreates the radical theater of Berlin in the 1920s, I was able to work on a deep, emotional level, integrating historical research with a living sense of how people, now long dead, might have perceived their world.

This is also true of *The Last Warrior Queen* and the entire *Earthsong Trilogy,* for although I make no claim to have reproduced the world of six thousand years ago with perfect accuracy, I believe that having lived outside of the modern world with people who were still bound to the land and directly dependent on nature for every bite of food that went onto their table has helped me imagine what it might have been like to live in a Neolithic village better than any amount of library research.

Combined with my mother's history and example, these Kentucky summers also helped make me into a feminist—which might seem strange at first glance since in the early 1950s the rural south was still a patriarchal culture where the women scurried around fetching the men glasses of water and fresh socks. But there was a tribal aspect to women's lives that gave them a certain status. They worked hard, and the work they did was important and valued.

The Wathen Women, 1920s: (from left) Mackey's great-grandmother, grandmother Alice Mackey, two cousins, Aunt Ebbie, Aunt Fen, and Aunt Kittie, on the family farm in Marion, Kentucky

If they were abused, the code permitted them to take revenge (with or without the help of their male relatives). It was clear to me, even from an early age, that if Uncle Wid had ever laid a hand on Aunt Ebbie, she would have waited until he was asleep, brained him with a skillet, and gotten off scot-free since not a jury in Crittenden County would have convicted her. In short, these women were tough, competent, and took no shit.

Since I believe that most of the basic themes and imaginative material that later appeared in my poems and novels came out of my childhood, I have spent quite a bit of time describing my early years. I will now move at a brisker pace. In 1955, when I was ten, I entered the sixth grade. Some time in the following spring, my teacher attacked me in the middle of class, hitting me so hard with a ruler that she broke it over my hands, leaving them badly bruised. No doubt if this happened today, there would be a lawsuit and the incident would make the front page of the *Indianapolis Star.* Instead, my parents waited until the end of the semester and then, at considerable sacrifice to themselves, they quietly pulled me out of the public school system and enrolled me in Tudor Hall, a private girls' school.

Suddenly, instead of being in a class of fifty children who share twenty-five desks and twenty-five books, I was in a class of fifteen girls who had never in their lives been hit by a teacher. Suddenly, instead of being bored to the point of insanity, I was being taught French (by a real French woman), advanced math, ancient history, Latin, music, drama, and English by someone who knew the difference between James Joyce and Joyce Kilmer. In public school I had been making C's and B's with an occasional D. In private school within a month, I was making A's with only an occasional B. Best of all, I was finally in a place where my love of reading was considered an asset rather than a troublesome affectation. Tudor Hall was by no means a perfect place. The other girls' families were for the most part richer than mine, and sometimes they could be snobbish and cruel, but Tudor opened up a new world to me— one that extended far beyond Indiana.

In October of 1957, a little more than one year after I first crossed the threshold, I had a revelation of sorts in the middle of geometry class. The teacher was lecturing on tri-angles, and I became entranced by the pure beauty of form and proportion. At that moment, I decided that I wanted to be a poet. That evening I sat down and wrote six poems. By Christmas, I had written an entire book of poetry. I still have this book and the poems look amateurish to me now, but they were a beginning. On that day, I started to write in earnest.

I stayed at Tudor through my freshman year in high school, doing well but growing increasingly unhappy. In the summer of 1959, I begged my parents to let me transfer to North Central, one of the best public high schools in the state. I was now living in the North Central district because, by that time, my father had passed his boards in Ob/Gyn and gone into private practice, and my parents had moved us to a four-bedroom, two-story, colonial-style brick house in the suburbs.

In the fall of 1959 I entered North Central where I was placed in advanced classes in everything but algebra. Almost immediately, I acquired a boyfriend—a very tall senior named Steve who taught me about jazz, beatniks, and atheism. Steve asked me to go steady and gave me his ring to wear around my neck, which worried my parents since they were terrified that I would get pregnant, a fear exacerbated by my poetry which had taken such a passionate turn that my English teacher hurriedly called my mother in for a conference.

They need not have worried. I knew a lot about sex, but at that point almost all of it was coming from Ovid's *Art of Love* (which I had found in the library), the poems of Shelley, and my father's medical texts. All through high school various boys tried to seduce me (some in most ingenious ways—one, as I recall, let me win at chess and then read me an essay on free love), but I made it to graduation (and beyond) a virgin. I had a plan that was not compatible with unplanned pregnancy or early marriage: I intended to escape from Indianapolis by going east to school where I would learn some skill that would permit me to spend my life in Paris smoking cigarettes with the Existentialists and writing poetry.

In my junior year, I underwent a political flowering. At the beginning of the semester I had vaguely liberal tendencies that centered around a belief in racial and gender equality and a staunch opposition to any government policy that might provoke nuclear war. By the end of December, I had worked for the Kennedy

The Mackey family, 1957: Mary, age twelve, on the right;
sister Jane, eighteen months, and brother John, seven

campaign, become an ardent supporter of the Civil Rights movement, decided I was a socialist, and was sporting a "Ban the Bomb" button that got me in no end of trouble with my conservative American history teacher. I owed this conversion to leftist politics to three people: Voltaire, Bertrand Russell, and Gordon.

Voltaire had spoken to me across the centuries, informing me once and for all in no uncertain terms that the Bible was not, as I had always been taught, historical truth. Bertrand Russell (to whom I wrote an ardent fan letter and from whom I received a polite reply) had written about nuclear disarmament in a way that had moved me deeply. Gordon was my new boyfriend, son of the town socialist; a short, articulate, fiercely intellectual boy with tightly curled brown hair who affected Brooks Brothers suits, smoked a pipe, went to the Unitarian church, and who had actually shaken JFK's hand (Gordon's father was a big contributor to Kennedy's campaign).

Gordon introduced me to his friends, all of whom were eccentrics; and, deciding that

they were kindred souls, I took to them immediately. Besides staying up late at night to discuss art, Armageddon, and desegregation, we started an informal spelunking club. On weekends we would drive to southern Indiana to map hitherto unexplored caves for the Indiana Speleological Society. While my parents were worried about Gordon getting me pregnant, the two of us were making forty-five-minute crawls through tunnels so narrow we couldn't lift up our heads and walking around the rims of shafts that fell away hundreds of feet into the black depths of the earth.

On one memorable occasion, five of us tried to swim out of a cave by plunging into an underground river. The darkness was black, cold, and complete, and when I tried to surface I found myself clawing at stone. There was no air above me. As my mind turned into a high-pitched jibbering thing at the back of my skull, I instinctively swam on and by luck came out into the sunlight alive (as did all the rest of the spelunking party). I still think that jumping into that underground river was both the stupidest thing I have ever done and the closest I have ever come to death.

In the spring of 1961, I wrote a musical play which was performed on stage at North Central and one of my sonnets won an honorable mention in the *Atlantic Monthly* poetry-writing contest. That June, Gordon graduated from North Central and left Indianapolis for New York to become a freshman at Columbia. A year later, having reviewed my grade-point average, SAT scores, my Merit Scholarship, and a list of extracurricular activities that made it look as if a group of clones named "Mary Mackey" had been busily at work, Radcliffe College informed me that I had been accepted into the class of 1966.

I have dealt extensively with my years as a 'Cliffe in my novel *Season of Shadows* (1991). As several critics have noted, I have a love-hate relationship with Harvard. To this day, I never know whether I should revise my will to leave the University everything I own or tear up their pleas for contributions without opening the envelope. The reason is quite simple: I got an excellent education in Cambridge; but in 1962, when at the age of seventeen I arrived to begin my studies, Harvard was probably one of the most sexist universities in America.

On the plus side, I took Shakespeare from Harry Levin and Medieval History from Giles Constable; audited Erik Erikson's course on human development; drank tea with David Riesman, and worked in the Harvard Ethnobotanical Museum under the watchful eye of botanist Richard Schultes, one of the most inspiring researchers I have ever encountered. James Watson once deigned to pause in his unraveling of DNA to argue with me about the relative value of the humanities versus the sciences (he felt that no one majoring in the humanities should ever be accepted into Phi Beta Kappa junior year because it was "too easy for them to make good grades").

In my own junior year, when I qualified for an honors tutorial, I had the good fortune to be assigned to William Nestrick who became my tutor and mentor. For the next twenty-four months (Mr. Nestrick was not one to recognize summer vacations), he made it his job to educate me thoroughly in English, American, and French literature, working me so hard that graduate school later seemed like a lark in contrast. Mr. Nestrick immersed me in the works

of Proust and Joyce, both of whom later exercised a significant influence in my writing. To these, he added large doses of medieval philosophy (centered primarily around the writings of St. Thomas Aquinas) coupled with an extensive analysis of the French symbolist poets, the iconography of the stained-glass windows of European cathedrals, and a running commentary on innumerable novels and manuscripts, some so obscure that Harvard apparently owned the only existing copies.

But as fine as it might be to listen to Mr. Nestrick discourse on Dickens's rough drafts, or have Robert Frost show up in your humanities class, or discover that the book you had just checked out of the graduate library had also been checked out by John Kennedy when he was an undergraduate, it was always clear to me and my Radcliffe classmates that, while females were tolerated at Harvard, they did not have the same rights and opportunities as the male students.

There were, for example, no female professors (as I recall, in the first 350-some years of its existence Harvard never gave tenure to a woman). Although Harvard and Radcliffe students took classes together and were assigned the same books, no Radcliffe student was allowed to use—or even enter—Lamont, the undergraduate library. ("That's all right, dear," one Radcliffe dean informed me. "There are so many more men than women here that you'll always be able to find a boyfriend to check the books out for you.") This meant that during the time I was at Harvard struggling to become a poet, I was never permitted into the Lamont Library Poetry Room, nor was I permitted to attend the poetry readings which were given there by Alan Ginsberg, Robert Lowell, and other well-known poets.

Harvard offered only one creative-writing class, which was filled by competition. In my sophomore year I was the only Radcliffe student to win one of the coveted slots (although I personally knew several fine women writers who submitted manuscripts). Thus for two semesters I sat with fourteen male students, feeling uncomfortable and somewhat out of place as I tried to figure out what it meant to be both a poet and the only female at Harvard officially permitted to study creative writing. Many years later, when I myself became a teacher of creative writing, I created two special classes designed to meet the needs of women.

Having been raised among boys, I was used to being in the minority, so I stuck it out and fought for my right to create a different kind of poetry. After a while, the men began to treat me with wary regard instead of condescension, and at least one decided that I was worth asking out for coffee and conversation. Robert Colwell was a biology major. Over our cups of espresso he announced that poetry was only a hobby for him. He planned to become an "ecologist"—a term I had never heard anyone use before and which struck me as mildly eccentric. Rob came from Colorado. His father was the principal of a large public high school in Denver, but the family had inherited money that went far beyond a principal's salary, and they owned a ranch in the mountains where they bred Herefords.

One cup of coffee led to another, and Rob and I gradually began to spend more time together. In the summer of 1964, I reluctantly said goodbye to him and went off to tour Europe with a Radcliffe classmate. When I returned, I headed out to Colorado to meet Rob's family. Rob was a handy guy who looked better in jeans than in a coat and tie. He taught me how to saddle a horse and herd cattle, and before the visit was over, he presented me with a small silver ring he had made himself. That fall the *Harvard Advocate* published my first poem ("The Death of Mabel Donahue"), and I appeared on stage at the Loeb theater with John Lithgow (he had starring roles in *King Lear* and *Julius Caesar,* and I was "woman-crushed-in-the-crowd"). In November, Rob asked me to marry him, and I accepted.

We were married a year later in December of 1965. Six weeks after the wedding, as I was studying for finals, my Aunt Ebbie stumbled over a baby pig while walking through the barnyard and was attacked by an enraged sow who knocked her down and chewed off one of her legs and most of her left arm before Aunt Kittie beat the beast off of her with a broom. I found it difficult to explain to people at Harvard that down in Kentucky my great-aunt had nearly been eaten alive by a pig, and I think that I spent most of my last semester in Cambridge walking around in a daze.

In June of 1966, I graduated from Radcliffe and Harvard simultaneously (Radcliffe women received a dual diploma), having written an honors thesis on serial publication in the nov-

els of Charles Dickens. A few days later, Rob and I flew to Costa Rica so that Rob could take a course in tropical ecology. Instead, tropical ecology decided to take a course in him. On the night we arrived in San José, he developed a high fever from what later proved to be recurring typhoid, and I realized that the Spanish I had learned at Harvard had been curiously lacking in words like "help," "delirium," and "dying." Later, when we traveled to less civilized parts of Latin America, I also discovered the first two words you should memorize when you learn any language are "don't shoot."

In August, Rob and I moved to Ann Arbor to begin graduate school at the University of Michigan. Rob planned to get a Ph.D. in population ecology, and I intended to get one in Comparative Literature. (I would have studied for a doctorate in English Literature, but I was informed by the chair of the University of Michigan English Department that he "did not like women graduate students" and would give me no financial support.)

From the very beginning Rob and I had a troubled marriage. Now, some thirty years later,

*Herding cattle at Echo Valley Ranch,
owned by Rob Colwell's family, 1969*

I have no desire to rehash the details of our problems (the curious can consult my first collection of poetry, *Split Ends,* the most autobiographical of my works). Despite our differences—which began about eight hours after the wedding ceremony and ran on more or less continually for the next six years—he and I had some memorably good times together, particularly when we were living in the jungles of Costa Rica.

The jungle (which had not yet been renamed "the rain forest") was dangerous and beautiful in roughly equal proportion. Huge flocks of green and yellow parrots flew over the research station screaming like a hundred rusty hinges; purple orchids bloomed in knee-high mud; timid deer-like agoutis peered out of the brush; any leaf could turn out to be an insect, any vine a snake. During those hot, mosquito-bitten months, I often felt that I was being given a glimpse of the world as it might have been thousands of years ago; but at the same time, all around me, I saw a delicate balance that was relentlessly being destroyed as the great trees were logged for wood and charcoal.

For the rest of my life, I was to be haunted by the destruction of the Costa Rican rain forest (90 percent of which has been cut down as of 1997). The jungle became the setting for my first novel, *Immersion* (1972), the central theme of which was the plundering of nature which goes hand-in-hand with violence and the breakdown of harmonious relationships between men and women. I was to continue to explore these same themes in many of my subsequent novels, most notably *The Earthsong Trilogy.*

Meanwhile, I could hardly complain of a lack of adventure. In 1967, I stepped over a nine-foot pit viper and lived to tell about it; was attacked by a rabid bat; found a jungle rat swimming around in my coffee pot; nearly swallowed a poison centipede while brushing my teeth, and made a near crash-landing in a small plane that ran out of gas. In 1968, while driving the Inter-American Highway back to the United States, Rob and I were caught in the eruption of Mount Arenal, survived a major earthquake in Nicaragua, and were caught up in the Olympic rioting in Mexico City. More than once we ended up with illiterate fifteen-year-old peasants holding machine guns to our chests while they tried to read our passports upside down; and I began to get quite blasé about danger, as if I were some sort of female

*In the Costa Rican jungle,
at Peninsula de Osa, 1968*

Hemingway who had been issued a god-given guarantee of immortality.

Even so, there were terrifying moments. The most frightening came in 1969 in central Mexico, in a town which shall go unnamed. Rob and I were invited to a party by two of our fellow Americans who had no idea we spoke fluent Spanish. In fact they didn't know we spoke Spanish at all, so when three men in white ties and black shirts arrived (Mexican Mafia, perhaps? I never knew), they began to do business. Their business, it turned out, was running drugs and guns between Mexico and Guatemala. Rob and I got out of there fast, terrified that we might say something that indicated that we'd understood them. We never learned their names, but I can still remember the pale, junky face of our host; his preppie accent; his firm, young-man-on-the-way-up handshake, and his cordial Dale Carnegie smile.

As long as Rob and I were living in Latin America, our relationship was tolerable; but every time we returned to the U.S., our marriage began to spin out of control. In 1969, I fell in love with another man and decided the time had come to leave; but no one in my family had ever been divorced, and I couldn't bring myself to be the first, so instead I broke things off with my lover and applied for a National Defense Education Act Scholarship to study Russian in the Soviet Union where, among other things, I took in much of the material which I later used in *A Grand Passion*.

After two months of eating black bread and drinking vodka, I returned to Ann Arbor with a good grasp of Russian prepositions and a renewed conviction that it really was time to call it quits with Rob. If I had acted on this decision immediately, I might have saved myself a great deal of pain, but once again I hesitated. A week or so later, in the middle of a party, I suddenly began to choke and gasp for breath. I had been taking birth control pills for four years and the hormones had caused a blood clot to form in my legs. The clot had broken loose and lodged in my lungs (which was fortunate because, had it lodged in my brain, my budding career as a writer would have been over). For the next three months, I lay flat on my back in a dark room unable to bear noise or light. It seemed like a poor moment to speak of divorce. That fall, when Rob was offered a post-doc at the University of Chicago, we decided to move to Chicago together and give our marriage one more try.

In the nine months I lived in Hyde Park, I finished my doctoral dissertation, wrote my novel *Immersion*, and helped in the formation of what was just beginning to be called the Women's Movement, producing a number of essays, poems, and critical articles for the new feminist publications that seemed to be springing up on all sides. For example, when I was at Radcliffe, I had found a copy of Kate Chopin's novel *The Awakening* in Harvard's graduate library. Since almost no one except a few scholars had heard of Chopin in 1970, I spent a few weeks writing an essay on her life and work. When the essay was published, it helped reintroduce Chopin's novels and short stories to a new generation.

As my interest in feminism grew, I began to make sketches for a novel which would explore the relationship between the way men treated women and the way the male scientists I had met in Costa Rica had treated nature. I wrote *Immersion* out in longhand in the stacks of the library of the University of Chicago in a half-trance-like state. In part I was indebted to Robbe-Grillet for the hyperattention to detail and the odd manipulations of time that became the stylistic core of the book; but I was also indebted to something deeper and more personal. *Immersion* is a prose work that is balanced on the edge of poetry. Using the Costa Rican rain forest as a background, I explored multiple images of deception, illusion, and transformation. Sitting at a wooden table with my eyes closed, I probed my unconscious and felt a great grief coming toward me. At the time, I thought that this grief was coming from the past, from the rain forest whose destruction I had witnessed. I was right about the grief but wrong about its origins. I was moving toward it, not it toward me. It was coming from the future and in the spring of 1970, it was very close indeed.

That May, shortly after President Nixon appeared on TV to admit to the American people that we had troops in Cambodia, I returned to Ann Arbor, defended my dissertation and received a Ph.D. in Comparative Literature. With half the college campuses in the country paralyzed by student strikes, Rob and I were not optimistic about our prospects for finding academic jobs for the fall term; but ecologists proved to be in high demand that year, and in June, U.C. Berkeley offered Rob a position as an assistant professor. That August we piled all our possessions into a yellow Ryder truck and headed for California to begin what I would later think of as the worst two years of my life. In less than fourteen months, I would be sleeping on a mattress on the floor in an apartment full of crazy artists: divorced, unemployed, ill, alone, nearly penniless, and bleakly depressed.

When you write about great pain, it is hard to know where to begin. Suffer long enough, and a kind of blankness spreads over everything. You may remember that you were in bad shape; you may remember that bad things happened; you may even remember an entire day when you lay flat on your back watching a spider build a web in the corner of the room; but often you cannot quite remember the sequence of events. Fortunately if you are a writer, you leave a trail of words behind you. The trail I now follow comes from my first collection of poetry, *Split Ends*, which I published myself in 1973, selling my stereo to pay the printer.

As soon as Rob and I arrived in Berkeley, we moved into a household composed of the two of us, Rob's former college roommate, Jeffrey, and Jeffrey's wife, Leslie, who had graduated from Radcliffe the year after I had. Four ambitious, high-strung, competitive, Harvard graduates with marital problems do not make for a harmonious living situation, and the strains soon began to surface.

By mid-September Rob had retreated to the university where he was working himself into a state of total exhaustion trying to set up his lab and write his lectures. At home, I shut myself in my study and wrote one futile job-search letter after another to every educational institution within commuting distance of Berkeley. If I had been willing to leave California (and Rob) to take an academic position, I could have found one; but not having left my husband for my lover, I couldn't see leaving him for a regular paycheck—a decision which in retrospect was to prove shortsighted.

Sometime during that first Berkeley fall, a great fire swept through the hills, Rob found a new girlfriend, and I fell in love again. I had first met Mark in 1967 when I made a short trip to San Francisco to participate (albeit briefly) in the Summer of Love, and he and I had corresponded a few times over the intervening years. In the fall of 1970, we ran into each other again and, since I was unemployed and Mark was doing freelance film sound, we both had a lot of time on our hands. On the weekends when Rob was off with his lover, Mark and I would drive to the Sierra to help his friends build a geodesic dome. On other occasions we steamed ourselves in remote hot springs, or went to the beach, or lay around Mark's listening to music. On more than one night, Mark came over to my house to have dinner and the six of us—me, Mark, Jeffrey, Leslie, Rob, and Rob's lover—would all sit around drinking cheap wine and making civilized small talk.

In December, Rob and I packed up and headed down to Costa Rica for another stint in the jungle. After two months of living in a remote field station on the Peninsula de Osa, I flew from San José to Bogotá to join Mark who wanted to revisit his old Peace Corps haunts, while Rob remained behind to teach a course in tropical studies.

In the four months Mark and I spent traveling through Colombia, Ecuador, and Peru, we grew very close. For a while we lived in a small village on the Caribbean coast of Colombia, snorkeling, swinging in our hammocks, and occasionally driving stray burros out of our open-air kitchen. When we grew bored with the sun and the sand, we took a plane to Leticia—one of the backwaters of the planet, a squalid settlement of weather-beaten huts where the Amazon flowed past the desolate remains of Indian villages.

In Leticia I saw what life was like when all the normal rules of law and order were suspended. The town was so corrupt that it gave me a new understanding of the novels of Joseph Conrad; and I began to reexamine the possibility—which I had long ago rejected—that human nature was deeply flawed. This was to exert a strong influence on the poetry which I was to write over the next two decades.

As far as I could tell, Leticia was run by one man: a "game warden" who poached rare birds and alligator hides and flew in rich European tourists to hunt down the last of the jaguars. The great illegal trafficking in cocaine which was to devastate the region in the late seventies had not yet begun, but already there were rumors that the Colombian Air Force was flying drugs to Bogotá hidden inside fish to foil the dogs.

Latin America is a school whose main curriculum is tragedy, supplemented by brief courses in beauty, danger, and corruption. Before Mark and I finished our journey, we had been through a major civil insurrection in Cali (where we lay face down on the tiled floor of our hotel room listening to machine gun fire and tanks rattling through the streets); flown into Cuzco in a plane that nearly merged with a mountain; and climbed the perilous trail to Huayna Picchu (where—terrified of heights—I froze in panic on a slick stone step half as big as my foot, looked down at the 2,500-foot drop-off in front of me, and refused to move until Mark coaxed me down).

By the time we headed north again, I had lost that feeling of invulnerability that had made it possible for me to look down the barrel of a machine gun without blinking. I had come to believe that domestic tranquility is the exception, not the rule; that civilization is only a thin veneer over chaos, and that life itself is perilously fragile. The poetry I wrote in my journals during those months, was brooding and dark; and I began to fear that the United States, which seemed so divided over Vietnam, might some day go the way of Colombia, Peru, and Honduras.

When Mark and I finally returned to Berkeley, I went back to Rob and made one last half-hearted attempt to patch up our marriage, but he and I had both changed so much that there was little left to patch. A few weeks later, I left him, moved in with Mark, and began to study film sound through a union program for women and minorities. Free of the distractions that had haunted me for most of my marriage, I also began to write short prose sketches, several of which later formed the basis for my second novel, *McCarthy's List*.

This should have been the beginning of a happy, productive period, but in the fall of 1971 a series of tragic events occurred which plunged me into a deep depression. I was particularly distressed by the death of my cousin-in-law from leukemia. Gail was a few years younger than I, and I had gone camping with her only a few weeks before she was hospitalized. Several other terrible things happened in quick succession, but since these events involve other people's lives as well as my own, I do not feel free to describe them in detail even though a good quarter of a century has passed. Once again, the curious can consult *Split Ends* where I have been more forthcoming.

Grieving and distraught, I fell into a melancholy that grew deeper by the day. Gradually, I stopped eating, lost weight, and started to have horrible nightmares. Each morning I woke with a sense of dread and panic. My body felt as if it were made out of lead. Sometimes I could hardly remember who I was or where I was. Nothing gave me pleasure: not food, not sunlight, not sex.

During that fall, I lost interest in everything except writing. In some way which I still do not completely understand, my pain became a source of feverish creativity. In the first weeks of depression and the long months that followed, I ate, drank, and breathed poetry. The poetry did not cure my grief, but it gave me a voice when silence would have been intolerable. The pain I experienced during those terrible days has never been fully resolved, but it taught me compassion, and it still survives as a dark undercurrent in my work and the source of some of my most powerful poetry.

By mid-November, I had come to a decision: my life could not go on as if nothing

Mackey reading her poetry at the founding benefit for the Feminist Writers Guild, Berkeley, 1977

had happened. Within a month, I had left Mark and was trying to remake my life from scratch. I wanted a decent job, monogamy, and a good night's sleep. I wanted to go on writing poetry. I wanted to stop defining myself by the men I lived with. I wanted to stop grieving; I wanted to stop wanting to die.

But instead of getting better, things just went on getting worse. Since I had almost no money, I rented a room in an apartment with two women artists. One was given to fits of rage—she used to slash up her paintings with a butcher knife and on at least two occasions she destroyed our telephone. The other woman used to go down to Telegraph Avenue every night and bring home a different lover, half of whom were speed freaks with rotten teeth and yellow-tinged faces. It was a crazy place to live, and I was lonely, confused, and nearly without friends; but the worse my life got, the better my writing seemed to go. I wrote most of *Split Ends* in that apartment and revised *Immersion* there, sitting on the floor with my portable electric typewriter between my knees

Mackey (right) with novelist Valerie Miner (left) and poet Jana Harris, Berkeley, 1977

since I owned neither a desk nor a chair. After a while I became so depressed that it took me nearly an hour every morning to put on my socks, but no matter how desperate I became, I went on looking for a job. I managed to hustle up a number of gigs doing 16mm film sound or writing short scripts, but I was running low on grocery money until I found a fairly good-looking winter coat and a pair of heels in a Salvation Army store. Thus equipped, I went to an interview at Sonoma State University and convinced them to hire me for the spring semester to teach several lower-division literature classes.

By April my poetry was being widely published—mostly in women's magazines—and I had met Alta, the editor of Shameless Hussy Press, who read *Immersion*, told me it was brilliant, and announced that she wanted to publish it. I will always be indebted to Alta for taking my work seriously. Her encouragement was the first I had ever received from an editor, and it couldn't have come at a better time.

The press, which was located in Alta's garage, was old and dangerous (you had to tie your hair back so it wouldn't get caught in the gears and ripped from your skull), but on it Alta had published some of the first works of Ntozake Shange, Susan Griffin, Pat Parker, and Paul Mariah. I can still remember the din the motor made, the smell of wet ink, and the satisfaction I felt when I held the first damp pages in my hands. As far as Alta and I can tell, *Immersion*—which came out in 1972—was the first feminist novel published on a feminist press to appear since the 1930s.

Little by little, in the most mundane ways, I began to pull myself together. Thanks to my job at Sonoma State, I acquired enough money to move out of the apartment of crazy artists. I had long suspected that my depression was due—at least in part—to some physical imbalance (a theory which at the time was not widely accepted by the medical profession since depression was believed to spring from childhood traumas). In the early summer of 1972, I insisted on, and received, a complete physical which confirmed that I was suffering from hypoglycemia—a condition which could be treated by diet and exercise.

That August the chair of the English Department at California State University, Sacramento, called to offer me a full-time position as an assistant professor in English and Women's Studies. Two weeks later, I met my first classes and never again had the leisure to spend an hour brooding about which sock to put on first. The Women's Studies Program at CSUS, one of the first in the country, was new, highly politicized, and all-consuming. The governing board met for four hours a week, inventing a new academic discipline, thrashing out political differences, fighting for survival, and doing it all by consensus.

Over the span of a few months, working both within the university and within the community, we created a number of new resources for women: nontraditional courses which concentrated on women's contributions to various academic disciplines; support and counseling for abused women and victims of rape; help for the growing number of mothers who were having to raise their children alone; and reentry programs for older women returning to college. Our program attracted writers like Kate Millet (who taught for us for a semester) and feminist scholars like Robin Morgan and Phyllis Chesler who lectured at the Women's Studies conferences we hosted. Thanks to Women's Studies, I also made the acquaintance of Marge Piercy. Marge and I have kept up a correspondence ever since, reading each others manuscripts and giving each other critical advice.

Since I held a joint appointment in Women's Studies and English, I also had obligations to the English Department. During my first two years at CSUS, English assigned me to the New

College Program and informed me that I would be teaching literature courses to a mixed group of eighteen-year-old freshmen and recently released convicts who had been admitted into the state university system as a condition of their parole.

This made for an interesting situation. In the spring of 1973 alone, three of my students were arrested for knocking change out of parking meters, two were arrested just before mid-terms as accessories to a murder, and one nearly overdosed on heroin while I was explaining the niceties of *Hamlet.* Working with people who had problems so much more serious than my own helped me put my past into perspective, and my depression continued to lift.

In 1973 with the help of poet Lynda Koolish, I founded Ariel Press and self-published *Split Ends,* my first collection of poems, with artwork by Ruth Weisberg and Mady Sklar (Sklar's drawings had also appeared in the original edition of *Immersion*). Although I continued to teach at CSUS, assistant professors did not receive much more than a living wage in those days, so I was hard-pressed to pay the printer, but ironically—a few months after *Split Ends* appeared in the bookstores—I made the first serious money I had ever made by selling an original screenplay about a deaf child to an independent film company. As I mentioned earlier, before I got the job at Sonoma State, I had freelanced by doing sound for short commercial and educational films, and by writing an occasional script. But *Silence* was of a different magnitude altogether. Directed by John Korty and starring Will Geer (who had become famous by playing Grandpa Walton on the popular TV series), it was a full-length feature film shown both in the U.S. and abroad. Although no artistic masterpiece, it won several awards for its sensitive handling of the world of a disabled child. Subsequently I wrote a number of screenplays including a science fiction version of *Moby Dick* for another independent producer and an adaptation of my novel *McCarthy's List* for Warner Brothers.

With my financial problems solved for the moment, I spent the summer of 1974 living in a tree house at Black Bear Ranch, a commune near the Oregon border. There I ate roasted goat, wandered around the woods, learned the names of the major constellations, and wrote most of the poems that appear in *One Night Stand.* There were many things about Black Bear

that reminded me of my childhood visits to Kentucky—the lack of plumbing and electricity, for example—but I don't think either Aunt Kittie or Aunt Ebbie would have known what to make of the women's house, the moon rituals, and the communal child rearing.

In January of 1975 I returned to Indiana to teach for a semester at Indiana University. This was International Women's Year, and in February the U.S. State Department suddenly discovered that it needed a female poet with a Ph.D. and an academic position who had a comprehensive knowledge of the American cinema and spoke fluent Spanish. I have no idea how many women in America fit this description in 1975, but they settled on me, and by May, I was on my way to the Dominican Republic to spend two weeks teaching courses on film and poetry.

Another member of the delegation was a young writer from Atlanta named Pat Conroy. I had long been interested in writing a second novel, and as Pat and I sat around drinking rum and eating fiery snacks, we talked about various ways I might go about writing something more accessible and less experimental than *Immersion.* Pat had a way of cutting straight to the core of the craft, and inspired by his advice, I returned to Bloomington and began to draft the first chapters of what would become *McCarthy's List,* a comic novel about McCarthyism, paranoia, revenge, and Indianapolis in the fifties, all written in a style which I dubbed "first person insane."

Pat had put me on the right track. *McCarthy's List* was published by Doubleday and did exceptionally well. To my amazement there was not only a British edition but one in Swedish.

No doubt I would have enjoyed my literary success more if I had not made the mistake of getting married for a second time in 1976. My marriage to Paul lasted a little less than two years before we decided that it was impossible for the two of us to go on living under the same roof. About the time *McCarthy's List* came out, we separated.

Many years later, Paul returned to apologize for his part in the debacle; but he need not have bothered. Except for wounding my pride, he had done me no great harm, and I bore him no ill will. On the contrary, I was grateful to him for introducing me to a meditation technique which I have continued to practice daily for the last twenty years. Meditation helped me to get rid of the last remnants of my depression and was the inspiration for a very effective system of creative visualization which I invented for myself several years later. This system, which allows me to access my unconscious at will without having to resort to the usual writerly crutches of drugs, drink, and disaster, has proved an inexhaustible resource for fiction and poetry.

In 1978—shortly after Valerie Miner, Susan Griffin, and I banded together with a group of West Coast women writers to found the Feminist Writers Guild—Gallimaufry Press published *Skin Deep,* my third collection of poetry, most of which I had written while I was in Indiana. Over the next two years I wrote more poetry and a sequel to *McCarthy's List* entitled *Rose La Rose* (which was never published).

In 1981, discouraged by the constant infighting in Women's Studies, I went to the chair of the English Department and asked him to "buy" the half of my appointment that Women's Studies owned so I could teach exclusively in English. I had always been a gender equality feminist, and over the intervening nine years the English Department at CSUS had made great strides in this direction. Women writers from a wide range of ethnic backgrounds were now regularly included in our literature courses, there were half a dozen full-time female faculty members in English, and the department had recently invited Maya Angelou to come to Sacramento to teach for a semester.

Although I was relieved to be teaching full-time in the English Department, I did not stop being interested in the roles women have played in history and society. In the early 1980s, inspired by Merlin Stone's *When God Was a Woman,* Charlene Spretnak's *Lost Goddesses of Early Greece,* Mary Renault's *Persian Boy,* and Samuel Noah Kramer's masterpiece, *History Begins at Summer,* I wrote *The Last Warrior Queen,* the first of my novels to deal with prehistory. Crafted in prose that once again is balanced on the edge of poetry, the novel is a fictional recreation of the myth of the descent of the Sumerian goddess Inanna into Hell. Among other things, it chronicles the transition from matristic to patristic concepts of God which may have taken place in Mesopotamia some six thousand years ago.

In retrospect, it is clear that *The Last Warrior Queen* was a good fifteen years ahead of its time. The publishing house that bought the novel was swallowed up by a bigger house during one of the corporate take-overs of the eighties; and although Marge Piercy praised it as "audacious and amazing" and Tillie Olsen called it "superb storytelling," no one knew what to do with it. In the end, this feminist, utopian, mythic, poetic, philosophical novel was marketed as science fiction.

In the spring of 1984 my agent, Barbara Lowenstein, suggested that I write something that would appeal to a wider audience. I agreed that this was a good idea and began to cast about for a subject that would let me explore topics that were of serious interest to me. After a few false starts, I settled on ballet. The history of ballet, I discovered, revolved around issues of female power and exploitation. Ballerinas had been the rock stars of the last century (their fans had done things like make their toe shoes into soup and eat them laces and all); yet at the same time they were often plagued with difficult choices between work and love, career and family life, art and sheer physical survival. Through meditating, I had also become interested in mind-body coordination, and this too was an essential aspect of ballet.

For nearly three years, I read every book on ballet I could get my hands on, saw dozens of performances, and interviewed dancers, impresarios, and choreographers. The result was *A Grand Passion,* my most commercially successful novel to date. Translated into eleven languages (including Finnish and Japanese), it sold well over a million copies.

Meanwhile, I continued to write poetry. In 1987 Fjord Press published my fourth collection, *The Dear Dance of Eros.* A year or two earlier, I had begun to write a regular column entitled "Eros, Void, and Earth" for *Yellow Silk,* a literary journal. In more than a dozen essays, I had examined the connection between pornography and violence, and explored the separation of holy from erotic which had led to what I termed the "thanatotic prejudice": the conviction that only death and suffering were topics worthy of serious attention. *The Dear Dance of Eros* was both a highly personal account of eros in my own life as well as an attempt to reconnect the powers of sex and creation on a mythic level.

While researching *A Grand Passion,* I had stumbled on several compelling accounts of the radical theater in Berlin in the 1920s. These

Mackey (left) with Steve Murray and Tiina Nunnally, editors of Fjord Press, Seattle, 1987

were the starting point for my fifth novel, *The Kindness of Strangers* (1988). In this work, which chronicles three generations of women actors, I examined the rise of fascism, the conflict between mothers and daughters, and the high price women must pay when they are forced to choose between work and family.

Nineteen eighty-eight was also the year I began my four-year term as chair of the West Coast branch of PEN. Besides setting up literary events and becoming a kind of one-woman welcoming committee for writers who were visiting the Bay Area, I concentrated on building a strong Freedom-to-Write program (PEN Freedom-to-Write works on behalf of writers in all countries who have been imprisoned because of their writing). This was a particularly busy (and very public) period for me since I continued to write occasional nonfiction pieces, serve on the poetry committee of the Bay Area Book Reviewers Association (BABRA), and review books for the *San Francisco Chronicle*.

After the publication of *The Kindness of Strangers*, I turned once again to my own life for material. The result was *Season of Shadows*, the

tale of a thirty-year friendship between two Radcliffe roommates. Although, as I noted earlier, the novel draws heavily on my years at Harvard, it is not autobiographical (one of the main characters is a terrorist and a fugitive). *Season of Shadows* touches on the Civil Rights Movement, the Vietnam War, and the impoverished (and hence unstable) condition of third-world countries in the mid-twentieth century. Set in Massachusetts, Michigan, California, and Nepal, it is a chronicle of mixed loyalties, personal and political seductions, and bad choices made for good reasons.

By the time *Season of Shadows* was published in 1991, my personal life had changed so much as to be almost unrecognizable. In 1986, I had begun a relationship with Angus Wright, a professor of Environmental Studies at CSUS whom I had known as a colleague since 1972. Angus was the first even-tempered man I had been with since the early seventies, and I found his company an unspeakable relief.

Angus and I had a great deal in common. He also had gone to graduate school at the University of Michigan, had a Ph.D. in Latin

Mackey with Angus Wright, Sacramento, 1986

American history, spoke Spanish and Portuguese, and had lived in South and Central America during the same years I had. He had two children—Jessica and Joseph—whom I took to immediately. The third time we had lunch together (ostensibly to practice our Spanish), he promised me that he and I would be *"muy felizes conjuntos"*—very happy together—and so we have been for the last eleven years.

I suspect that it is rare to find a perfect companion at the age of forty-one, but I was fortunate enough to do so. Angus combines a brilliant mind with a warm heart. His love and loyalty have been my mainstay for over a decade now, and his writing on environmental issues—particularly his *Death of Ramon Gonzalez*—has inspired a great deal of my poetry and forms much of the philosophical underpinnings of *The Earthsong Trilogy* which I have dedicated to him.

Writing the Trilogy was a project that took me over five years to complete. In 1991, before *Season of Shadows* was in the bookstores, I was already immersed in research on Neolithic Europe. Guided by archaeologist Marija Gimbutas's two powerful studies, *The Language of the Goddess* and *The Culture of the Goddess*, I gradually began to construct a multilayered story that

centered on one of the most important—and most neglected—transitions in world history: the nomad invasion of Europe which took place in the latter half of the fifth millennium.

Before I encountered Gimbutas's works, I had assumed that Neolithic Europe had been populated by tribes of hunting and gathering people who lived in caves or rude shelters and made stone tools. As a novelist, I was intrigued by Gimbutas's vision of an era when Europe was at peace, united by trade and a spiritual tradition that stretched from Brittany to the Black Sea.

Gimbutas theorized that the people who lived in Europe some six thousand years ago worshipped the Earth itself, which they saw as a living being who gave birth to all life. They represented the living spirit of the planet as female, as a goddess or Great Mother, and they made thousands of images of her, some of which have survived to our own time. Gimbutas noted that the worship of the earth was an old religion, stretching back tens of thousands of years.

I found it encouraging to imagine that there actually might have been a time when women were respected, children were treasured, men and women got along, the earth was honored, and warfare was virtually unknown. Here, in one place, were many of the themes I had been pursuing in my work for the past two decades. Here were the important questions and, perhaps, even a few of the answers; but Gimbutas had presented them in a highly technical form almost inaccessible to the public at large.

I was convinced that I could reintroduce the human element into prehistory by weaving together fact and fiction. By filling in the blanks—by inventing the poetry, prayers, music, and customs of the people of Old Europe, I could transform something dry and academic into something human and compelling.

With this goal in mind, I set out to write three novels linked by common characters: *The Year the Horses Came, The Horses at the Gate,* and *The Fires of Spring.* Since I had vowed to be as true to the scientific and archaeological record as possible, this became a massive research project which required me to study archaeology, meteorology, ethnobotany, geology, and comparative mythology. Among other things, I had to learn (at least in theory) how to weave, throw pots, track animals, chip arrowheads, milk goats, ride horses, fight with a spear, and survive for five days in a blizzard.

Writing is a strange road: you travel it blindly, never knowing where it is going to take you. In 1992 Angus and I lived in Brazil in a small coastal town near the site of one of the last remnants of the Atlantic rain forest. There, using a child's notebook and indelible ink to foil the tropical damp, I wrote of a priestess named Marrah who had lived in Brittany three hundred generations ago. Two years later, in the summer of 1994, Angus and I found ourselves in Rumania and Bulgaria with Gimbutas's biographer, Joan Marler, searching for bird goddesses and nomad gold in dusty museums while outside uniformed men with machine guns (who seem to have haunted so much of my life) stood on the roofs of buildings looking for signs of trouble.

In November of 1996, I finished *The Fires of Spring.* This summer I have been invited to Washington to present portions of it and the other two novels in the *Earthsong Trilogy* at the Smithsonian. In the interim, I plan to continue writing in the journals I have kept for the last twenty years. No doubt soon I will read something or hear something that will cause a new novel or a new series of poems to begin to grow somewhere deep in my unconscious. Perhaps they are there already. Hiding at the point

where the past meets the present. Waiting to be revealed.

BIBLIOGRAPHY

Novels:

Immersion, Shameless Hussy Press, 1972.

McCarthy's List, Doubleday, 1979.

The Last Warrior Queen, Putnam, 1983.

A Grand Passion, Simon & Schuster, 1986.

The Kindness of Strangers, Simon & Schuster, 1988.

Season of Shadows, Bantam, 1991.

The Year the Horses Came (Book I of *The Earthsong Trilogy*), Harper, 1993.

The Horses at the Gate (Book II of *The Earthsong Trilogy*), Harper, 1995.

The Fires of Spring (Book III of *The Earthsong Trilogy*), Penguin, 1998.

Poetry:

Split Ends, Ariel Press, 1974.

One Night Stand, Effie's Press, 1976.

Skin Deep, Gallimaufry, 1978.

The Dear Dance of Eros, Fjord, 1987.

Screenplays—feature length:

Silence, CFA, 1974.

Eloise, Hargrove Productions, 1975.

Dark Oceans, Lawrence Levy Productions, 1980.

McCarthy's List (adaptation of her novel), Warner Brothers, 1980.

Screenplays—television documentary:

As Old as You Feel, Columbia Broadcasting System, 1978.

The Restoration, Public Broadcasting System, 1982.

Editor:

(With Mary MacArthur) *These Women,* Gallimaufry, 1978.

(With Mary MacArthur and Janis Agee) *Secrets,* Gallimaufry, 1979.

Work also represented in anthologies, including *She Rises Like the Sun,* Crossing Press, *American Visions,* Mayfield Publishing, *The Book of Eros,* Harmony Books, and *Life Prayers,* Harper. Contributor of poetry and nonfiction to numerous publications, including *Fireweed, Harvard Advocate, New American Review, Poetry Now, Poetry USA,* and *Yellow Silk.*

Alice Notley

1945-

As I seem to keep saying, most of my earliest memories concern a house on an alley in Needles, California in which I lived between the ages of four and seven, from 1949 until 1952. What I've not yet successfully described is something that happened in my memory, during the '80s, after I'd been shocked by the deaths of several people. That is, that the alley house (which had long since been torn down) changed from being near in time to far in time, and in doing so changed from being real to being art. Suddenly and upsettingly in my mind it looked like "the Fifties," and it looked both golden and frozen. The house, on a small dirt road behind the Desert Inn Motel, was flimsy and white-boarded with a fenced-in yard in front, a chinaberry tree and some poisonous oleanders, a dirt driveway next to the house in which sat the current car: a brown Chevy and then a two-toned Olds. Until the '80s I dreamed of that house as if it were still standing and a vital setting of my struggles, but after my brother's death in 1988 I stopped dreaming of it almost entirely and when I pictured it it was always in a painterly morning light with the car next to it a gleaming curving museum-piece. I recently wrote a book of poems trying to break through the frozenness of that vision and make the house and my childish self come alive again. I have a horror of living in sociology; and I didn't even like the car when I was small: it was never beautiful or artistic or necessary but was always un-nature to me.

I was born in Bisbee, Arizona on November 8, 1945, in the Copper Queen Hospital. I remember almost nothing of Bisbee where we lived for two years, or of Prescott where we lived subsequently for one year. My father, Albert Notley, worked for a Prescott man, Wilmer Webb, who was called Webb by nearly everyone including my infantine self. Webb owned a small chain of auto parts stores. My father began by sweeping the floor of Prescott Auto Supply. Sometime after he married my mother he took

Alice Notley, 1950

a job at Bisbee Auto, then returned to Prescott and Prescott Auto, and was finally offered the job of manager of Needles Auto. My father had grown up in Prescott. My mother, born Beulah Oliver, grew up in Phoenix. They both came from large Depression-poor families of Southern origin, the exception being my English grandfather, who died when my father was four. Education was hard to come by because of the pressure to help support others. My father left school after the tenth grade; my mother managed a few months at Abilene Christian College in Texas and then some courses at a Phoenix college. She steered her three daughters, though not her son, towards a college education. He couldn't have sat still long enough to have gotten one, I guess. We were in many respects luckier than he was, though I've become increasingly ambivalent about the value of "an education." Mine was my ticket out of town, for when I was young my greatest fear was of having to stay in the desert. Now I sometimes think I'd like to go back to Needles and live, but I can't drive a car and I'm still unwilling to learn. My education in schools, including the New York School of Poetry, much as I love it, wasn't my real education. I gave the real one to myself and continue to do so, unlearning so much.

Needles is plain and hot and beautiful. No one of worldly consequence lives there, so it's full of interesting people. Well I can't tell their stories, I wouldn't have the right. When we lived down on the alley, we were in a no-status land, but after we moved up on the hill we seemed to be more involved in not being tacky, not that we succeeded. I hope not. My parents became implicated in town politics and concomitant feuds, which I later recognized as being similar to those in the poetry world. Needles and the poetry world are composed of tiny turfs. All of those fights I think have faded for my mother, who considers Needles her larger family, the people she's always known and couldn't leave. I look to her increasingly for clues to survival, survival being one of the great talents of the Olivers. The Notleys all died off with some dispatch, and I sometimes wonder if the English half of their inheritance wasn't too complicating, since they were prone to conditions like mental illness and alcoholism. The Olivers are more monolithic. The clue to my mother's survival and élan seems a combination of energy and laziness: you go out and gamble (in Nevada), gambol, but at a certain point you lie down on the bed and do the crossword.

I was educated first in the Needles public schools: the D Street Elementary School, Vista Colorado Elementary School, the Needles Junior High, and then Needles Union High School. I think the "Union" comes from the fact that students were bused in from various tiny desert communities like Essex, Amboy, and Iron Mountain. Needles has a large (percentage-wise) Mexican-American population, as well as a large (percentage-wise) Mohave population from the adjacent reservation: Needles has now grown to a size of five thousand. Some local family names: McCord, Medrano, Garcia, Mejia, Chavez, Calderon, Edmonds, Greenwood, Beauchamp, Notley of course, Lyon and Lyons, Acuña, Claypool—Claypool being the owner of Claypool's Department Store, about which I still dream, since its "departments" remain resonantly metaphorical entities: Basement, Hardware, Toys, Appliances, Ladies Wear, Groceries. All of these names and words have been useful to me, but nonverbal Needles is extraordinary. Partly it's the Colorado River, which creates in 120-degree heat a deliciously icy contrast, so that life is replete with extreme sensation. In this landscape oneself doesn't amount to much. The river is deep green and blue, and the surrounding purple-brown mountains are changeably shadowed; the land is rocky and full of gullies; there is a lily which blooms in the spring, the desert lily for which Lily Hill was named, once famous among boys and now covered with houses. The cactuses themselves don't ever seem to bloom—I've always considered the rumored brief desert spring a myth. Creosote contributes pungency to everything, though when I was young I thought I never wanted to see another creosote bush again. As I say in Paris, where I live now, that I'd just as soon be dead as hear another accordionist. I've sometimes written that Needles is all dust and pallor. It's very windy in winter but never cold. I never owned an overcoat or winter jacket until I moved to New York to go to college.

I read books and played the piano and listened to records: Broadway, classical, and folk. I disdained rock but secretly listened to it too when other people played it, but I refused to buy it because it seemed so childish. It had no capacity to reach beyond its tiny social moment, and it had no interest in making its tiny moment expand. I preferred the way that nineteenth-century symphonies, by Brahms say, played across our landscape and the way that folk music seemed to call me into my own future as haunting as anyone's past in a ballad or blues. As for the show tunes and standards, I just liked the wit of the lyrics, the way that lines and rhymes fit together; I memorized without trying great swatches of such lyrics and that was undoubtedly my first poetry education. I was sort of an impossible kid for the other kids: I worked at it. I didn't want to be pulled into the emotional field of similitude to them and so the danger of staying, staying in Needles. They were forming earnest little couples at the

Playing the piano in Needles, Arizona, about 1962

age of twelve, thirteen, the boys not as tall as the girls yet, slow-dancing to those imbecilic songs. I couldn't bear it. I began to work at getting out and when my senior year came applied almost exclusively to faraway schools. I had never heard of the one I finally attended, Barnard College, before I applied. I won a pretentious-sounding scholarship and so took off.

I don't think I was at all shocked by the transition to New York when I was seventeen going on eighteen. I had trained myself to think I didn't know what anything in life was like, coming from Needles; so I couldn't be shocked. I flew to New York in the company of a girl from Los Angeles, who was also going to Barnard, and her parents. They rented a car and we drove from Idlewild Airport (this was a few months before Kennedy's assassination) through endless brick-walled streets to Morningside Heights and the five buildings of Barnard College. There, various girls instructed me to buy certain clothes, the things one needed to live in the East, coat, boots, sweaters, certain kinds of dresses and shoes. I was quite dressed up for about one term after which I grew my hair long again (I'd cut it off because I'd heard everyone at Barnard had long hair) and settled into a uniform of stretch jeans and maroon or green or black turtleneck jer-

sey. I also started to write stories for creative writing courses I took; most of the stories were about Needles and I suppose if I'd continued to write prose I might have become a "minor regional novelist," a phrase, so I've read, printed on a tee shirt once given to Larry McMurtry. McMurtry of course is not that though I might have been. Of the more important of my stories, I wrote two from a male point of view and two from the point of view of a young girl. I pretended to be, variously, my friend Tony Garcia, caught in a circumstance of violence; a married man named Stillwater, who learns something important from the Mohaves (I can't remember what) about how to be himself; myself as a little-girl Meursault, in the inescapable desert heat capable of something like murder; and finally myself as almost myself, absorbing the reality of a favored aunt's—a Notley's—death from brain cancer. It would be the latter story for which I was accepted into The Writers Workshop in Iowa. I remember wishing I had more willpower just to write and not be so drawn towards sex and love; but I seemed to know that if I could keep getting a story out periodically, the reflex to write would finally become built into my will. I was certain that I didn't know how to write and so wrote painfully, always wondering if this might be the way it was done.

I gradually realized I liked New York because of what the people there were like, in that combination of tolerance, communality, and aggression (which I took to be interest in what's going on) which makes New Yorkers different. I had never been anonymous before, and I declared to anyone what a pleasure that was, using that word "anonymous." I had also never been anywhere where it was okay to freak out publicly, where misery wasn't kept secret and in fact no issues seemed to be under wraps. Then there was all the music and all the art, both of which were of comfort the year I had my first death-dread depression, 1964–65. Of course New York was so cold, standing on a corner, waiting for a cab, December 19th oh 1965, in *nylons* and a dress, having been to the Playboy Club with friends one of whom had a Club key. I was open to most experience; I spent a lot of time in my jeans at the Bleeker Street Cinema and the Thalia Theater, viewing "foreign films." I also had friends who were jocks from a couple of the Columbia fraternities. These boys always included the fact

Notley in New York, 1971

that they were "screwed-up" in their self-presentation: this screwed-upness being evident from their belonging to fraternities at Columbia. I also went to SDS meetings to hear folksongs sung by Phil Ochs or hear Timothy Leary lecture on the properties of LSD. The Vietnam War had begun and began gradually to matter to me, finally becoming embedded in my next-to-deepest self when my brother wound up in the war in 1970. I didn't realize that till he died in '88 and I found out I'd been tricked, all along in my life, into believing that a woman mattered like a man politically, when in reality she was nothing, not a participant in the formation of policy, not a voice, not even a soldier, not even dead, just nothing, a storyless mourner, a receptacle of the consequences of men's actions. In the '60s it never occurred to me that I was a woman in that way; I didn't want a woman's things or a woman's situation, but I didn't feel doors were closed to me, because my ambitions though huge were non-materialistic. I simply wanted to find out the Truth. My first year at Barnard I was required to take the supposedly antiquated

hygiene course and to read for it *The Feminine Mystique* by Betty Friedan. I discovered that my fellow students were hostile to the book because it told them not to waste a privileged education just to marry and have children. That was exactly what most Barnard students wanted to do, but I had no idea why.

I graduated from Barnard in 1967 and went immediately to Iowa, fearful that if I took a full-time job I would stop writing before I knew what writing was. I became a poet of sorts the first month there, having met some student poets, read a few poems by living poets, and attended my first two poetry readings. I do mean this happened instantaneously, something clicked, though I still didn't know how to write or what to write about. Literary writing isn't instinctive: if you don't know about it, you don't do it. If you find out about it and see that you want to do it, you will be imitating whatever first comes along. I imitated poets like James Wright and Sylvia Plath because everyone in Iowa was reading them; I didn't imitate other Iowa possibilities like Donald Justice and William Stafford, I think because they wrote exactly like men. I also imitated Robert Creeley, who has remained important for me and is a friend, though at the time I failed to notice that there were hardly any nouns in his poems. I looked for an etched-on-the-page quality and, it seems to me now, some sort of transsexual quality. My favorite poets in high school and college had been Blake, Dickinson, and Yeats, visionaries rather than writers articulating from ordinary life roles, sex-based. But in Iowa I couldn't become unmuddled as to what my artistic purposes might be, and I was tired of school. Meanwhile there was the war in Vietnam, and Martin Luther King, Jr., had been assassinated. I'd begun to save money from modeling for art classes. I decided I would emigrate to Canada like all the boys who refused to go to war; I thought I should have to make some sort of hard choice too. So I left Iowa after one year and flew to Toronto but I stayed for only one day, went back out to the airport and bought a ticket for San Francisco. Virtually the day I arrived Bobby Kennedy was assassinated there: I seemed to have joined up with moral chaos after all. I stayed in San Francisco a few months working in an office, traveled to Spain and Morocco with hippyish people, rapidly became bored with that and wound up back in Iowa the following February. That was 1969. Ted

Berrigan had been in Iowa City for a semester and had just separated from his wife, Sandy. We became lovers; and further, he and my teacher Anselm Hollo, the Finnish-English-American poet, introduced me to another poetry, that of the New York School and the Beats, the rest of Black Mountain, and so forth. It seemed to become clear, again instantaneously, what kind of poet I would be. What was not immediately clear was that I would later turn to the lessons of Dickinson and Blake when I began writing my own visionary work of the '80s and '90s.

These are places where I lived within a few years after I received my MFA degree at the end of 1969: Manhattan, Buffalo, Southampton, Queens, Manhattan, San Francisco, Bolinas, Providence, Bolinas, Chicago, London, Wivenhoe in Essex, England. Ted and I were married in Chicago in 1972 and I gave birth to our two sons, Anselm (named after Anselm Hollo) and Edmund, in Chicago and Colchester, Essex, respectively, in 1972 and 1974. But in 1973 I also met Doug Oliver—yes Oliver—the British poet to whom I am now married. Ted and I were friends with Doug and his first wife Jan when Ted was poet-in-residence at Essex University, and Doug and I remained geographically distant friends for many years, through the time of Ted's death and Doug's separation from Jan, and afterwards. I'm struck by the non-linearity, the simultaneity or braidedness of the events in my life. As Ted used to say Whitehead had said somewhere, everything that's going to happen is already happening. During these few years I also met such people as Anne Waldman, Joanne Kyger, Allen Ginsberg, Johnny Stanton, Ron and Patty Padgett, George and Katie Schneeman, Lorenzo Thomas, Edwin Denby, Rudy Burckhardt and Yvonne Jacquette, Joe Brainard, Simon Pettet, and other people important as colleagues and/or friends. I suffered a severe postpartum depression; learned how to write poetry in two or three styles, becoming one of the first American poets to treat as subject childbirth and motherhood. I also began a close association with Ted's other children, David and Kate; and I met for the first time Doug's daughters, Kate and Bonny. It's all back there happening in various houses. I'm young and thin and troubled, and resilient—as tough as my mother perhaps. But also I'm suddenly myself as I am now, fullblown writer.

Having written my first "unexpected" works, the sonnet sequence *165 Meeting House Lane*, and my first substantial poems, the ones I had to write for what they said, such as the poem "Dear Dark Continent." In 1973 I wrote the poem "Your Dailiness," which until about 1977 was the single work I was most proud of and which is possibly the most "inspired" poem I've ever written, in that it came to me whole—I saw its several dense pages all at once as a unit and then spent a day leisurely remembering what I had "seen" and writing that down in a proselike line dominated by the sentence:

Your Dailiness,

       I guess I must address you begin and progress somewhat peculiarly, wanting not afraid to be anonymous, to love what's at hand I put out a hand, it's sewn & pasted hingewise & enclosed in cover. I'm 27 and booked, and my grandfather

My grandfather, I begin with, played dominoes called them "bones". Bones is a doctor on Star Trek.[1]

Chicago, where I spent some three years, is an interesting city, partly because it *is* The Second City; its feeling of constant putdown by the existence of New York adds a chip-on-the-shoulder touch to its self-conscious toughness and meanness and openheartedness. I associate Chicago with severe winters, feeling down, learning to live with my radiant boys; the genesis of important friendships from among Ted's students at Northeastern Illinois University and students at other local universities; and my continuing poetic education through books and also the Chicago Art Institute, its considerable collection of modern paintings and its library. Chicago's poetic life was sparse; we were dependent for information and stimulation on the people who happened to come through. We couldn't afford to be cliquish: in that circumstance every poet counts and all poets are equal; and so it was in that one way a superior situation to that in New York or San Francisco. One can quickly become cliquish and opinionated in those cities; and again now in Paris one can't be. In Chicago I began editing the mimeographed magazine *CHICAGO,* a legal-sized somewhat illegible journal which concentrated on largish selections of poems by a recurring group of people: Anselm Hollo, Ron Padgett, Lorenzo Thomas, Tom Clark, Anne Waldman,

Bernadette Mayer, and myself and Ted, plus others who appeared not quite as frequently. I was in the process of making esthetic choices; I've been pleased to discover in the process of writing essays recently, largely about second-generation New York School poets, that those poets still hold up for me. The poets I first chose for *CHICAGO* each endured and carved a unique space around themselves, are poets I count on. There's a pleasure in my loyalty to them, and their poetry is loyal to me.

In the middle of our time in Chicago we happened into England, as I've indicated, for a year and half. My parents came to visit us, my father bringing along the banner of the Needles Rotary Club to exchange with the Colchester Rotary Club. He didn't seem as well as he had before. Ted noticed his decline more than I did and was proud of him for the gesture of the banner, the seeking out of the other nation's club. I must have told my father about the two hospitals in Colchester that bear our name, the Black Notley Hospital and the White Notley Hospital. Essex was the county from which my father's father and his siblings had emigrated earlier in the century. We didn't look up any records and no family history was articulated, but we were in touch with something primary concerning us. My father died about a year later, after we'd moved back to Chicago, of cirrhosis of the liver. Ted and I and the boys flew to Needles a week or two before his death, and I had my final conversation with him and helped watch over him in the hospital as he entered a coma. In his hospital room I wrote in my notebook for comfort:

> lilaceous bus of the Missouri
> or an injury, lights and darks reversed
> tend to attract affection, the
> shaft of a column constricted part-
> tooth to caress in love
> a body useful in combination
> how could you? and durability
> of its figure or timbre or
> profane the pardon with
> cosmetics over rocks out-
> guessing outside the rings,
> an act of shocking outskirts[2]

My sister Margaret was unable to come say goodbye because she was giving birth to her oldest son. My sister Becky was part of the group surrounding his bed for several days. My father, being closest to my mother and my brother Albert of all of us, seemed to turn away from them. This upset my brother terribly; he'd come back from Vietnam feeling so guilty that he couldn't extricate what he'd done in the war from what had transpired between himself and my father in his teens, simply a hard but not untraditional confrontational saga. I didn't know how guilty he felt at the time. He had married Kathy, my sisterlike sister-in-law, and they'd begun a family across the river from Needles on a nice piece of land with, at various times, dogs, cats, pigs, cockatoos, a horse, a burro, a goat.

Not long after Ted and I had returned to Chicago, Ted himself became ill and was diagnosed as having alcohol hepatitis. He too was fated to die of cirrhosis of the liver, though not for another eight years. Ted was really, by his own account, a "pillhead" but quite a bit of drinking had gone on in Chicago and England; after he died the doctor who'd performed the autopsy assured me the marks on the liver were consistent with those made by alcohol. That again is the future which is now the past. I was shocked to find out that my father's death was in store for Ted; since Ted never went to a doctor again for his liver, I never had to take the fact in frontally after my initial discovery. I found out Ted's prognosis only by watching television, not by being told by him: on educational TV a man saying that in the majority of cases, alcohol hepatitis leads to cirrhosis. While he was still ill, actually feverish, we left Chicago for New York, left the last of our easier situations in which there was a teaching job, a steady income, and a house. We had enjoyed a financially "normal" life for three years but never would afterwards.

I have a fear of making people's deaths and flaws and seeming fates more important than their actual existences. In being oneself there is no story. A story's imposed from the outside, constructed in relation to the outside. But just two or three people together isn't a story, it's living. I have no judgments to make except in the moment. I feel that I have no special character, that I know what I know, that I'm essentially a poet. Also that the people I've loved and who died are still free inside themselves, uncharacterized and unchronologized by me or anyone.

In March of 1976 Ted, myself, and the boys came to live at 101 St. Mark's Place in New

(From left) George Schneeman, Ted Berrigan, and Franco Beltrametti, "in George's New York studio," about 1979

York, on the Lower East Side according to Ted, in the East Village according to the trendier. Our apartment at 101 was a doorless railroad flat (later when Doug lived there with me and the boys one door was installed), supposedly a two-bedroom walk-through but those two rooms were tiny cubicles; the perfunctory tub in the kitchen; toys, plants, paintings, and dust. I lived there altogether for sixteen years and it was always full, of voices and bodies and objects, sometimes seemingly haunted by the dead. In the '70s Ted and I invented a way of living there in which it was our offices and a thriving salon as well as our home. We raised the kids together, both of us being live-in parents; they were part of everything we did, like when peasants take their kids into the fields with them. I can hardly remember anymore how we made a living: since we were a continuous open salon/workshop, we managed to extract bits of money and teensy loans in exchange for the reading of people's work, advice on next steps

to take in poetry, and general character analysis, Ted being a skilled consultant and myself a fast-learning apprentice in this business. This business was not at all formalized. Also we sold books after we read them; considered all reading fees to be income not superfluity; Ted got a few one-term poet-in-residence gigs; I wrote some pamphlets for the Franklin Library; we led workshops at The Poetry Project of St. Mark's Church, a focal point for poetry community activities; sometimes a reading was actually lucrative; one year we both got NEA grants. It was an arduous life, stimulating, dangerous, and very social. Some of our significant co-conspirators and just plain friends were Steve Carey and Marion Farrier, Tom Carey, Eileen Myles, Simon and Rose Pettet, Harris Schiff, Elinor Nauen, the Schneemans and of course Peggy DeCoursey, but there were a host of people who trailed through. We didn't have a telephone from 1974 (Chicago) until 1980 so in order to contact us at all you had to come over.

My work from the '70s and early '80s reflects the apartment's doorlessness and polyphonic voicefulness. I invented poetic forms to incorporate all those presences but most especially the children and Ted, large fugal sometimes prose-seeming poems in which both daytime and dreamtime are allowed to talk. I also wrote quasi-normal lyrics; also became a collagist as a sideline (another source of income). I had begun to publish books with small presses in the early '70s. *165 Meeting House Lane,* my sonnet sequence, was heavily influenced by Edwin Denby's as yet unpublished later sonnets; *Phoebe Light,* published after *165 Meeting House Lane,* contained both earlier and more recent poems; *Incidentals in the Day World,* which Anselm Hollo called "a friendly giant," collected so-called baby poems and others; and *For Frank O'Hara's Birthday* contained "Your Dailiness" plus poems titled from a list of possible titles sent to me by Ron Padgett ("How Green Was My Hairbrush," "She's a Friend of Shirley Niebank's," etc.). My next book, my first perfect-bound book, *Alice Ordered Me To Be Made,* is a product of living in Chicago, of being involved with painting and making my own collages, and of the shock of my father's death. After I moved to New York I seemed to write more and more. *When I Was Alive* is a book of imitations of long-dead male poets; *How Spring Comes* and *Waltzing Matilda* contain the poems in the new forms I was inventing, the former being the more streamlined and classical of the two collections, the latter being the more experimental and daffy:

I remember so much that I generally don't ever
want to talk about it But first will you answer if I
ask, I said something like, he was as good as the
best, And she looked at me between loyalty & me
All right you dumb broad ex cathedra infallible bullshit in ex domine & the rest of it forget it, 100
   degrees and
Yes she admitted, he's a real one, he's a great as
   I'm glaring at you
& this jackass was already falling on the floor
   talking about
parataxis and parthenogenesis, he lost his hardon
   for the
scene &
        be generous. It's all
yours.[3]

On a typical day in the late '70s. The alarm goes off and we coax the kids to get up, without moving ourselves since we'll have been up late writing, Ted up later than I. They fix themselves cold cereal and go off to school, sometimes, I find out later, not washing their faces, big deal. We fall back asleep. I get up around eleven, sit drinking coffee and reading, begin writing in one of those blackbound art notebooks with nice paper no lines: I use the second-to-largest size, nine by twelve inches, and either a black felt tip or Schaeffer cartridge pen. As for the books I'm reading, I methodically keep both a prose book and book of poetry going, as well as a trashy prose book, something readable; aside from the stack of books by peers that's always on my desk. At a certain point Ted gets up and we begin to worry about where the day's money will come from. It's possible that at this point Eileen or Steve will show up with the same problem, and there will be other kinds of deals going down, not to be mentioned now in the real present. Often a package of sellable books gets made up by Ted and I go off to, say, the Phoenix Bookstore, Bob Wilson's reliable decades-old (but now gone) poetry bookshop institution where small-press books can be found and rare signed editions, Gertrude Stein or Lewis Carroll or W. H. Auden. I enjoy my dealings with Bob, I come home with some cash, the kids come home, some television gets watched, some more people come over, books get read, anecdotes exchanged: Anselm or Edmund is no longer friends or again

friends with Laurence or Michael or Johnny or someone at school, Yung Ho or Tahir or Luz; I make dinner, pasta, or hamburgers, or maybe porkchops with pasta, or cube steaks with pasta. Cigarettes get smoked, beers get drunk, other substances partaken of. Possibly more people come over, possibly one of us goes out to a poetry reading. The boys do their homework and watch television and go to bed in their bunkbeds talking to each other like birds from nests. Everything happens simultaneously in each's consciousness because of the doorlessness so we are limpid complexes as individuals and my poems are too. We are all equal, though Ted gets to talk the most. We get along well: you have to to live in such a space. At about nine o'clock or sometimes later Ted and I begin the serious work of writing, he on the bed in our so-called bedroom really a cubicle, myself around the corner in a chair. I hope to get a poem; he hopes to get a poem; and often we do. Then bed and dreams, which are also a form of work, since they must be kept track of and interpreted, which requires, while asleep, a certain mildly strenuous engagement different from the process of just sleeping: you have to observe and remember the dream. At least I do anyway. Ted often takes a very-early morning walk and comes back with the *New York Post* and a Pepsi before falling asleep after the sun's come up, an ancient habit of his. He has to write when people aren't there because when they're there he talks, because that is what he does. He doesn't like to think, he likes to talk his thoughts, or read, or write. He's probably the best talker I'll ever meet. His style of talk is based on several important skills and components: barroom and streetcorner storytelling, Jesuitical and Socratic method involving detached questioning and examining of subject, use of much anecdotal and comparative information from the world of sports, the ability to read the mind of the person he's speaking to so he can represent that person's point of view as he himself continues to talk, much extrapolation of information from the heroic art worlds, those who came before, the Abstract Expressionists, the Cubists, the Impressionists. He is a very strenuous husband; he implies I am a strenuous wife. But—and this will be clearer after his death—he is pressed for time; he doesn't have enough time to listen to other people. He has to do all of his thinking, i.e., talking, now.

New York in the '70s, the New York poetry and art world of the '70s, had a feeling about it of being *after* the Truly Greats, a feeling of *after*. Could one ever be as great as the giants of the first half of the century, Williams and Stein say, or for that matter as great as some of the poets of the '50s and '60s, people like O'Hara and Schuyler, who'd chosen to write in seemingly more minor modes but whose poetry was nonetheless extraordinary? Could one be as funny as Kenneth Koch? Or as humane as Allen Ginsberg? I've never thought of myself, to myself, as any of the terms I've been labeled: postmodern, experimental, second-generation New York School, even feminist. I use the latter two of these terms when I must call myself something before other people. The former two I have more trouble with. Postmodern feels like a critics' pomposity not just a sorting label and I don't like most critical writing. To that extent I'm surely not postmodern, postmodernism being so entangled with criticism and philosophy. The reason I have trouble with the word experimental is that I consider myself to be the future mainstream; my technique isn't different from ordinary on principle but concerns itself with what must be done next as poetry requires. I think I've always thus been not quite of my generation; certainly in the '70s I didn't feel I was doing '70s things, punk, consciousness-raising, and so on; I didn't at all disapprove of them but I couldn't raise children, raise money, write poems *and* deliberately be of my times like that. New York itself seemed to be tiring out in the '70s but that's one of its ongoing illusions. Painting was important to me throughout the '70s. I grew distant from it in the '80s, in the context of '80s art money and fads and the '80s galleries which contributed to the perfidious upscaling of my neighborhood. Among painters I was always most involved with the work of George Schneeman, his mysterious esthetic of translucent paint, Platonic space, and Siennese facial nuance, an esthetic which also included the famous "unhandling of paint": the point was not to look like a virtuoso, the point was to get all the relationships of the painting right, sometimes sublimely, sometimes wittily or both.

I suppose I solved the problem of *after* by being part of one *first*: part of the first really strong and numerous generation of American women poets. With Anne Waldman and Bernadette Mayer, I was creating a certain female

(From left) Notley, with Anne Waldman, "in a photobooth," Rome, August 1979

voice, which as I say somewhere else we seemed to pass around among us as it picked up its initial characteristics from each of us: a love for the sentence from Bernadette, a brave forthrightness from Anne, a feminized traditional lyric sound from myself. Those are the qualities I first perceived in us. But the voice then seemed to pass around more, as we assimilated tricks from each other, adding, changing, becoming more complex. We weren't terribly conscious of doing this; self-conscious movements are more a male phenomenon. And other women were obviously part of what we were doing, e.g., Maureen Owen and then Eileen Myles, and perhaps a little further away stylistically, women such as Lyn Hejinian, Leslie Scalapino, Susan Howe, Fanny Howe. But how did Ted solve the problem of coming *after*? Partly by caring for poetry much more than he cared for himself: this left him free to do as he pleased. He liked for his folder to contain a lot of poems which looked completely different from each other, each of which was unique though it might seem small. He worked on new forms which were both lucid and enigmatic, rune-like cognitions, etchings, by someone trying to be ordinary and also trying to make everything he did count.

Poetry readings became more and more important to Ted's and my practice. It was perhaps our most important form of publication, the most constant, dependable one we enjoyed. It was also the best way of testing the poem itself, of seeing how good it really was. This practice was tied in with the existence of a receptive audience, which was primarily that rigorous audience which assembled every Wednesday at eight o'clock at The Poetry Project; that core audience, though, spread across the country to include an ideal listening space one might find oneself in really sometimes, in several other cities and even other countries. When I wrote my poems I imagined myself reading them in the Parish Hall at St. Mark's or in a certain room in San Francisco; if they sounded right in that room-in-the-air then, chances were, they were right. So in a certain way we wrote our poems for our friends, but we were also creating an orally conceived poetry, if you will a people's poetry, whose shapes and sounds must be pleasing to the audience on any hearing of them, even the first. Of course no good poem can be gotten on the first hearing. Our community centered around St. Mark's— spreading outward and importantly relating to The Naropa Institute and, say, The Poetry Center in San Francisco—and was also the focus of our political knowledge and struggle. Thus all the poets I knew fought with each other at various times in various configurations. Because we were serious.

Around 1981 the tone of my life began to change. The chanciness of our financial arrangements, a sense of deterioration in Ted's health, the fact that his mother was dying of lung cancer, not to mention the bizarre national politics and economics just stepping into place, all these together resulted in a feeling that everything was strained. I felt it in my poetry too; the warmth and openness of it could be a little forced now and the lines didn't come

as fluidly. Strangely Ted and I were invited to attend the Bisbee Poetry Festival in '81; we were asked to read our poetry in the city of my birth and my mother joined us there. She hadn't been back to Bisbee since she'd left it in the late '40s. At the same time in Prescott Webb was dying, so her mood was elegaic and likewise strained. After my father's death, she'd assumed the management of Needles Auto with my brother alongside and had decided to buy the store from Webb, my father having bought a fraction of it while he was alive. Auto supplies and the world of Webb were still her world but it was changing. In Bisbee we stayed in the Copper Queen Hotel and visited the building where I had been born, the former Copper Queen Hospital; my mother saw me perform on a public stage for the first time. I read my long serio-comic poem "The Prophet" for her:

At one beginning, when you are a baby you are or there are two, but
    your mother
Is so hard for you to see, that she is simply the other in airy
    heaven. If
Your mother is now say an auto-parts salesman who eats tacos with
    you in dreams. If
She finds you a bit of a wastrel. It's important—well you
    are each
Flawed, specific, & idiosyncratic in the eyes of the other,
    yet you once
Shared a heavenly space, where you were the newborn, she the mother
And neither had characteristics to the other except for
    love & there & ever.
There is another beginning without her where there is no you.
    And where
Is the father in all this? the innocent pained beloved guy.
He's given you his face.[4]

I also read for her the untitled poem about Needles weather that she of all people living understands best:

    Clouds, big ones oh it's
    blowing up wild outside.
    Be something for me
    this time. Change me,
    wind. Change me, rain.[5]

After our return to New York Webb died, and my mother attended his funeral, which was the sort where people stand up unasked and eulogize the deceased. She called me afterwards to say that men usually did such eulogizing but that she had resolved to speak at Webb's funeral after hearing me read my poetry at Bisbee; she had made a speech quoting from Ted's poem "Things To Do In Providence" and felt really good about it. In Bisbee I had also met Dawn Kolokithas, now Baude, who is my friend here in Paris. I'm using Webb's name as a symbol of all spinning and intrication in life. The web my parents worked in. And part of the one I'm partly caught in and partly spin.

I don't seem to remember 1982 very well. Perhaps I wrote nothing successful that year; I usually remember times by what I wrote in them. Ted's mother Peggy died in July of that year. Two weeks after her death, while visiting in Needles, I watched with my brother on his video player the John Ford cavalry trilogy, something we did for many successive summers thereafter. The movies drew us together without conversation, reminding us of our childhood, making our landscape feel heroic, making us sad too for war. In 1983, on July 4th Ted died, almost exactly a year after his mother's death. He actually did ask me what day it was a little before he died, and I actually did say Independence Day, though I didn't consciously know he was dying until the moment it happened. I also, the previous evening, lightly administered a last rite, sprinkling him with a bit of gin and tonic and saying "May the 14 pieces of Osiris now be joined together." We had experienced a terrible year of poverty and inter-poet feuding; his health, obviously, hadn't been good and he'd been mentally agitated sometimes almost delirious, all this happening without doctors, diagnoses, hospitals so the death, which was to be expected, was nonetheless sudden-seeming. We had twenty-two dollars the day he died, twenty of it being what was left of a forty-dollar loan from John Godfrey to take our kitten Wystan to the vet. Financial help quickly flowed in from our generous community, and the boys and I had a sufficient financial cushion to grieve against. Kate and David had both made plans to come to the East Coast, to be near Ted; we all bolstered each other during the ensuing difficult time. Kate attended SUNY Stonybrook awhile and then lived in the city; David, now an entymologist, studied water fleas in Philadelphia and in the Poconos, later going off to the University of California at Davis to concentrate on fruit flies.

I'm not sure how I would have gotten through my first year of widowhood if I hadn't

At the Bisbee (Arizona) Poetry Festival, 1981

simultaneous to my suffering become fascinated with the process of it. That year was for me dense with education. I learned that I'd been living on the surface of life and assuming too much the complacencies of my culture, that existence is not mysterious or that its mysteries will always be hidden from us, that the only truth lies in daily life and in the possibility of humane social interaction. But grief is neither a social form nor a superficiality, it's one of the most mysterious processes I know of: it eats at you while you sleep, literally devouring all your excess body weight: you lose weight sleeping. I used to feel it like that, wake up and feel my body being got at—I wouldn't be thinking or remembering anything at all, it would just be *doing it* by itself. A literal darkness got into me as well and into my eyesight, and that symptom, the seeing of the world as darker in hue than it had been before, didn't lift for four years. I also had fleeting visionary experiences; the barrier between waking and dreaming life occasionally broke down. Under the weight of this process I seemed to have to examine all my assumptions about what I was and how to live. The style of my poetry changed; it wasn't funny for a long time. I was barely conscious of writing poems that first year, rather I scrawled things to keep on going and later realized they worked as poems.

> Towards him your dreams are
> Without their powers
> Towards you they seem to deliver
> His love as if from where.
> There is no Where.
> There is no his.[6]

Our life, mine and Anselm's and Edmund's, changed a lot of its forms, since we had to stop being a salon. It was necessary for us to be more alone in order to concentrate on getting through and then making something new.

New York was now '80s New York, one of the silliest things I've ever seen. The yuppy mode of life was clearly moronic, but I guess it wasn't just a fad since it's still at the core of what's going on now in the '90s, an insistence on the primacy of money and business and the boiling down of ethical questions to one simplicity or its opposite: family values or the notion that everything is accidental and contextual. Along with other people in the '80s I became obsessed with the fact that the world had shrunk to something compassable and without much piquancy, everything was too comprehensible, too known. I'm sure this is one reason why people believe in UFO's, to be able to entertain the possibility of an unknown world or species, way of thinking or behaving, geography of planet or spirit. Poetry and art are now about the invention of meaning, just as so much of life takes place in computerland, because all that seems left to explore is the air between things, the imagination, which is presumably infinite, but very wearying when it becomes minutiae of one sort or another: endless words or ideas or scenarios.

In the '80s, after 1983, I published *Margaret & Dusty* and *At Night The States.* The former consists mostly of poems I'd written before Ted's death, poems which now seem inevitably to track a progress toward that event: *they* knew what was coming. *At Night The States* consists of small poems I wrote in 1983 and 1984 and of the title elegy written in 1985:

Notley and her son Edmund Berrigan, New York, 1984

> At night the states
> making life, not explaining anything
> but all the popular songs say call
>   my name
> oh call my name, and if I call
>   it out myself to
> you, call mine out instead as our
>   poets do
> will you still walk on by? I have
>   have
> loved you for so long. You
>   died
> and on the wind they sang
>   your name to me
> but you said nothing. Yet you
>   said once before
> and there it is, there, but it is
>   so still.
> Oh being alone I call out my
>   name
> and once you did and do still in
>   a way
> you do call out your name
> to these states whose way is to walk
> on by that's why I write too much[7]

I also wrote a three-act play about Ted's death called *Anne's White Glove,* for Ada Katz's Eye & Ear Theater, which ran for a week at LaMama Annex in 1985. As for my financial life, I received a small monthly allowance of survivor's benefits, I did some typing and filing for Allen Ginsberg enterprises, I continued with the usual teaching of workshops, giving of poetry readings, etc. The rent at 101 remained low and the material desires of the three of us never seemed to grow out of bounds; we wore our jeans and ate our pasta and watched the neighborhood and participated in our friendships for entertainment. Anselm and then later Eddie became obsessed with the New York Yankees—not an expensive hobby. Eddie had actually become a poet, had been one since he was six; Anselm didn't write his first poems until later in college but has since made up for this previous deficiency of output.

In 1987 I went to a poetry festival in Luxembourg organized by Pierre Joris, who had been a friend since my year in Wivenhoe, and became "involved with" my friend Doug Oliver who was also performing at the festival. My English year and a half which had provided me with so many friends—Marion Farrier, Helena Hughes, Simon Pettet, and others—had gently re-enclosed me in its strange force field. I visited Paris for the first time that same week in May, staying in Doug's apartment and wearing to dinner at La Coupole and Louis XIV a lovely dress, a dark sheath with flamelike insets, that Kate had lent me for my trip. Doug decided to spend the summer in New York and Kate and her husband David Morrison made their apartment available to him while they visited Sandy in California. He then met my sons and our household opened to him. And now for the hard part: when Kate and David had returned from California, Kate crossing Houston Street on the way, with David, to take Anselm and Edmund to the movies, was hit by a motorcycle and died that same night in Bellevue Hospital where she had also been born. She was twenty-two. Like Ted's her funeral was held at St. Mark's Church, in the parish hall where poetry readings take place. Sandy conducted the funeral with the help of friends and a rabbi, then carried Kate's ashes back home and buried them in the garden in Albion. Another bleak time of mourning began, with Doug returning to Paris to teach a final term there and myself staying on with the boys at St. Mark's Place.

For me the poet's job consists of writing poems; that's how I've always approached it and I've tried not to do much else. It's a form of service, a cultural necessity of which society now

seems to have only the smallest inkling. It still prophesies, it still praises and celebrates, it still performs, in understated ways, rites of resolution, transition, mourning—deals with marriages and deaths, as well as observes and satirizes and tells stories about the broader outlines of what's transpiring in a city or country. From about 1986 I had been interested in writing an epic, but the necessity of mourning Kate and at the same time of welcoming my marriage to Doug temporarily overrode that particular intention. I had personal rites to perform and so I wrote the sequence called *Beginning With A Stain*, which is about the inextricable tangle of loss and love:

Call her the warmth of the breath that we all breathe
Breathe that love, breathe its unforeseen transformation
to transform with the final going out of, the
    giving back of it—
Descend into the commonplace, speak as to think,
employment of breath, of her, as delicate foliage
    as hours
Talk a future derived, this is that new life—
The metamorphosis also is boiling out of our
    sockets—[8]

I write about my life because I understand the world best from its vantage, though I don't always write about it directly now. In the late '80s I became interested in story and character as possibilities in poetry and began frequently to transform my experience into fictional poems.

In February of 1988 Doug moved to New York and we were married. I had undertaken for a second time a marriage which was a partnership of poets, even an aesthetic conspiracy. Doug's and my conspiracy contained more of overt politics than Ted's and mine had; also we shared an interest in narrative poetry and in medieval storytellers like Dante and Chaucer. Our Englishes were different and that was and is exciting and stimulating. In the meantime in Needles in that same year, my brother Albert was careening towards his death. His life seemed to have become quite insupportable to him, full of guilt and terrifying nightmares, physical pain from a torn-up shoulder and a drug addiction consequent from both of those factors. He entered a series of hospitals and treatments which seemed unable to deal with his problems. In August of 1988 he was admitted to a

"Albert Notley Jr. in Quang Tri, Vietnam,
January 17, 1971. 'Me and our dog "Skeeter"'
is written on the back."

rehab in Pennsylvania where he was finally treated
for both drug addiction and post-traumatic stress
disorder. With my sister Margaret I visited him
at the rehab, and he recounted to us lucidly
and powerfully everything that had happened
to him in Vietnam. He said he was returning
home soon, though the staff had recommended
a further stay, but he had a longing to see his
children. A few days after he returned to Needles,
on September 6, he died of an accidental
morphine overdose; the nightmares had returned
immediately and he obviously felt he could still
rely only on the one way to deal with them. I
of course flew to Needles for his funeral. He
is buried next to my father in the Needles
Cemetery; my father's gravestone has carved on
it "Hasta La Vista," my brother's gravestone has
carved on it "I've finally come home." At the
graveside service, at my mother's request, the
same lines of Ted's were read by my brother's
fellow vet, Dicky Roten, as she had read at
Webb's funeral:

The heart stops briefly when someone dies,
a quick pain as you hear the news, & someone
    passes
from your outside life to inside. Slowly the
    heart adjusts
to its new weight, & slowly everything continues,
    sanely.[9]

My mother professed to feel glad for my brother.
The day before the funeral she lay on the bed
drinking Bloody Marys and saying, "I just feel
good for him." That feeling didn't last super-
ficially but stayed meaningful in some deeper
way.

My brother's death has been one of the
most pivotal events of my life, crystallizing so
much for me about politics, sexual politics, war,
and poetry. After his death I became determined to write an epic poem, to create a female protagonist, and to come to terms with
the issue of the relation of women to heroic
action. I had already spent some two years doing
research, reading, thinking, trying things out.
In 1988, actually before my brother's death, I
began an elegy for him entitled "White Phosphorus."

"Whose heart" "might be lost?" "Whose mask is
    this?" "Who has a mask,
& a heart?" "Has your money" "been published,
    been shown?" "Who can &
can't breathe?" "Who went" "to Vietnam?" ("We
    know who died *there*")
"This was then" "Is now."[10]

Early in 1989, using the measure I had worked
out in both *Beginning With A Stain* and "White
Phosphorus," I started writing the long poem
which would eventually be entitled *The Descent
of Alette*. The poem took two years of continuous work to complete; it involved as always
material from both my waking and sleeping
existences. I observed my dreams all night and
in the daytime rode the subway, since most of
the action of *Alette* takes place underground.
The New York subway seemed a much bleaker
place than formerly, filled as it was with the
homeless dispossessed during the real-estate frenzy
spurred by Reaganomics. Everyone "under the
ground" looked unhappy: the homeless, the
ordinary workers, and certainly myself, who now
stood for both my own misery and my brother's.
We were all the same entity, and so my poem
came to be about the liberation of "us" from

the tyranny of those who live above the ground, the de facto elite with their excessive material ambitions and their morally ambiguous involvements in the arts and sciences: the *superficial.* Another kind of thing I noticed, as I walked about the subway system observing things, was that I was finally old enough not to have to be a woman in the sense that men didn't stare at me much any more. I was free. It was a pleasure to be a sexless artist in process, an allowed observer, even if I was still dealing, in poetry and in the poetry world, with issues of the sexes and sexism. I finished the poem exactly at the end of 1990. In that same year Doug and I began editing and publishing together a magazine called *SCARLET,* whose first editorial celebrated the end of the '80s. For me the '80s had been awful both personally and as a member of the larger community; I was glad to see the economy crash somewhat and with it some of the vacuity of those times, although the Gulf War in early '91, as the first instant war, didn't predict a much more sensible future.

Doug and I spent the early '90s writing narratives and editing *SCARLET,* which was elegant and political and, however briefly, influential, and working in part-time ways. Doug worked first as a word processor, then was hired through Ed Foster to teach various things at Stevens Institute, in Hoboken, where Ed gently subverts the way of the engineer with a taste of literature. But we both taught at the Maryland Institute, College of Art, having been hired by dear, now-dead Joe Cardarelli to teach art students creative writing and literature; we would take the train to Baltimore together once a week and teach a class each, then take the train back and eat a late-night Indian meal at our favorite Indian restaurant, the Haveli, at Second Avenue and Sixth Street. I grew fond of this arduous day trip; it was while looking out the window of the train to Baltimore that I began to meditate on the nature of my most interior self as I was just being there looking, no one and exactly me. I also taught private workshops, had ad hoc teaching and reading links to various institutions, and continued to maintain a long-

"With Doug Oliver at 101 St. Mark's Place," New York, 1990

standing summer connection with The Naropa Institute in Boulder, Colorado. Meanwhile first Anselm and then Edmund left for college, SUNY Buffalo and SUNY Purchase respectively.

In the spring of 1992 Doug and I decided to move to Paris, after he had been asked to return to his previous place of employment, the British Institute in Paris. I had wanted to leave New York for a long time. The succession of deaths in the '80s—another was the death of my close friend, the poet Steve Carey, in 1989—had deadened me to the city; Anselm complained of the same frozenness before he left for college. This imaginative freeze was allied to the changes in my memory of childhood I've spoken of: as my childhood became "art," New York became opaque, dark, unchanging. It was as if I couldn't see anything anymore, couldn't take in changes properly, was incapable of being stimulated by the gaiety or agitation of strangers on the street, their color and movement, all that had delighted me in the '70s and much earlier when a college student in the '60s. New York as a community had been so important to me, and obviously it still was, since it was New York I wrote about in *The Descent of Alette* but in a so-called surreal way. I couldn't make raw contact with it in my work. The little book I wrote in the winter of 1991–92, *Close to me & Closer . . . (The Language of Heaven)*, has very little of urban life in it. It's a conversation with my father about what it's like to be dead, in alternate prose passages: his, and verse passages: mine. I would wake up each morning and hear something like his voice in my head, speaking with his hesitations and intensities and stresses as I remembered them. He had become important to my poetry over the years, delivering instructions to me in dreams and finally becoming the figure of the owl in *The Descent of Alette*. Now I wanted him to speak as himself, an ordinary intelligent man capable of deep insight, capable of philosophical discussion but only in his own language:

> Well, anyway, I thought I'd try to tell you—
> since you're a poet—about <u>here.</u> A little
> about how we <u>think</u> here. It's not with . . .
> we don't think in words—or pictures—necessarily. Not the way you're, translating <u>me</u>
> on your page. Translating me into <u>you,</u> which
> . . . but sounding like me since, you're my
> <u>daughter.</u> But thinking . . . is a fluid here—
> a . . . connection—or <u>light.</u>[11]

In September of 1992 we gave up the apartment on St. Mark's Place though everyone advised us to keep it and sublet it and somehow manage it from three thousand miles away. As Rose Pettet said, "You can't give up a cheap New York apartment. That's like a Normandy peasant giving up his bit of land." Allen Ginsberg advised us to sublet it to Peter Orlovsky and criticized us to others for not keeping it for our sons. Everyone had an opinion; this was all funny and lovely. George and Katie Schneeman hosted a going-away party for us; we gave a farewell reading at The Poets Cafe; had farewell dinners with everyone and flew off to France. I've missed my New York friends a lot, though perhaps still not New York itself. I've sometimes desperately missed the Southwest, and Needles, as if I've not only lost them through space but through time. However, the French landscape is spicy and poignant and often rugged and soothes in me some of those sensations of loss.

Our first Paris apartment was on the rue Lepic in Montmartre, above the pollution but haunted by tourists; a street noisier in summer than even St. Mark's Place. I was shocked by what I'd done, moved into a new culture. From the outside foreign cultures had previously seemed uninteresting to me in that I wasn't in them; they knew nothing of my struggle and situation. The French were short and fine-boned and well-dressed, compact, made-up. The first thing I found out really about the French was that although they have well-organized *looking* bodies they are scandalously inefficient at moving those bodies about; they are haphazard, they don't look where they're going, one bumps into them all the time. Also their cars. I was fascinated. My French friend, Nadia Barontini, told me this is because one is *"toujours pressé,"* always in a hurry. The next thing that happens is that you're in the new culture and your old culture seems embarrassing and stupid. On Montmartre we would pick out the tourists and guess their nationalities: Doug blushed at the English, I blushed at the Americans, though both looked not aggressive but lost here. The English always seem as if they'd really rather not be travelling; the Americans move so differently from Europeans, without tension in, or retraction of, their limbs, or tension about their mouths when speaking: I can always spot an American across a *métro* car by the slack mouth. Well that is all vaguely racist

The author's sons, (from left) Anselm Berrigan and Edmund Berrigan, San Francisco, 1996

but if one didn't speak of such things, nothing worth talking about might get said. What will we do with our delicious differences in the new multinational world? which my move here had suddenly made realer to me. What will we breathe for air? There are more cars in Paris than anywhere I've ever lived, and more of honking, under a brown-blue sky. Oh yes it's a very beautiful city, if you like monuments. I find them obnoxious. I like Parisian shop people and I like the way people talk and interact here, though it's harder to see it than in New York, there are no stoops. My first book written in Paris was *Désamère;* its characters are the dead French poet Robert Desnos, myself fictionalized as Amère/Désamère, and my brother and others in a desertified landscape after drastic environmental change. The book asks is there a future, the question being intertwined with a discussion of the recent past and a terrible, seemingly uncontrollable present:

. . . Everyone has denied the angel so it's left them
Or is it, Amère, that you're naked with
Guilt, or old sorrow?'
'What I'm guilty of,' Amère says,
'Is being in a human culture—
But how can we have life without that?
Desnos, I want to be free like you'[12]

After a numb first year, I found workshops to teach and started a routine of returning to the United States once or twice yearly to visit and give readings. My sons come to Paris regularly, both now practicing poets. Other friends pass through often. Doug and I frequently visit England. In 1994 and '95 I broke my pattern of writing fictional narrative poems and composed a book called *Mysteries Of Small Houses,* made up of poems written in the first person singular. It was an attempt to locate the self, the darkly crystalline heart of one and the more enduring of its accruements, and to investigate the constancy of the self over time. The book, when it finally found its straightforward chro-

Alice Notley in France, 1994

nological shape, became as well an autobiography in poems. Since its completion, I've been working on a long libertarian-feminist insouciant work called *Disobedience.* A few years ago I began writing essays on poets of my generation who more or less share my poetics, since we've been written about very little. Our attitude as a generation tends to the "It's all in the poems" variety, which has not served us in a world where criticism has become more important than literature, certainly than poetry, off which it leeches.

Last year Doug and I moved into a different apartment, the small apartment in the 10th arrondissement on which he'd been paying a mortgage for some years. It's even smaller than the one on St. Mark's was but it looks rather the same, the same paintings on the wall, the same cat lolling, the same two people sitting at desks, litter of papers and books, fine dust. Ron Padgett came to visit last month and said so, "It looks just like your other apartment!" I write, I jog, I workshop people, I write a lot of letters. I dream all night about the geography of Needles. What does Broadway mean?

What does Front Street mean? I don't ever seem to dream about either of the houses I lived in there. Broadway's divided into several parts: near the old Episcopal Church, maybe because behind it was a special desert path of mine; the first Needles Auto, and, further down Broadway, the second and more major Needles Auto; the street that runs off of Broadway alongside Claypool's; also the place where Broadway and Front Street intersect to form the highway out of town, the east end of town, which leads to nighttime desolation. Then there's the old Civic Center, in which I recently appeared in a dream on some balcony that never existed, with my two sisters, all of us in hats. We had to go to the graduation tea at the Ladies Club, as I did do once and hated doing. Margaret is now a musicologist and Becky a computer engineer, but in my dream we were little girls prissy in our hats. I never dream about my brother. Sometimes I dream about Ted: he'd written some new poems recently which were very clear but would twist into an unexpected ending.

Lives, though obviously pleasurable and all there is to do, are rather stupid, being utter invention and yet so dependent on how others think they ought to be lived. One's own options are few. I despise how current ways of thinking try to affirm this fact as both the only metaphysical truth and something potentially positive. I don't think it's either. My life is for poetry and for wholehearted passive resistance to the way things are. I would like to give the future something more than a desert of data, of myriad new meanings, and unbreathable air. I hate meaning . . . that's a funny thing to say! But I'm not interested in meaning, I'm interested in being right here, no veils. That's why at the end of *The Descent of Alette,* when the tyrant dies the sky turns bright blue:

"The sky was jeweled blue, rich blue"
"'What we can have now,'" "a woman said," "'is
   infinity" "in our lives"

"moment by moment," "any moment" "He no
   longer lies" "between us & it"
"The light is new now," "isn't it?" "The light has
   been made new'"[13]

I wait for that moment but I can only have it *for* moments, so I kind of wait for those moments. I'd like to become self-effaced enough, being a mere speck in the vast ancient realm of poetry, that I would disappear into an explosion of some new morning-star self or non-self. Self-effacement is especially difficult when it is of no service to an important political cause, for instance feminism. So I quietly meander between the one and the other. Some choices shouldn't be made.

Alice Notley
January 1997
Paris

NOTES

All titles, except where otherwise noted, are by the author.

1. *Selected Poems of Alice Notley* (Hoboken: Talisman House, 1993), p. 2.
2. *Ibid.*, p. 8.
3. *Ibid.*, p. 69.
4. *Ibid.*, p. 56.
5. *Waltzing Matilda* (New York: The Kulchur Foundation, 1981), p. 29.
6. *At Night The States* (Chicago: Yellow Press, 1987), p. 26.
7. *Ibid.*, p. 74. (Also in *Selected Poems of Alice Notley* [Hoboken: Talisman House, 1993].)
8. Alice Notley and Douglas Oliver, *The Scarlet Cabinet* (New York: Scarlet Editions, 1992), p. 354. The poem is from Alice Notley's sequence, *Beginning With A Stain*.
9. Ted Berrigan, *Selected Poems* (New York: Penguin Books, 1994), p. 65.
10. *Selected Poems of Alice Notley*, p. 115.
11. *Close to me & Closer . . . (The Language of Heaven)* [and] *Désamère* (Oakland: O Books, 1995), p. 7.
12. *Ibid.*, p. 86.
13. *The Descent of Alette* (New York: Penguin Books, 1996), p. 147.

BIBLIOGRAPHY

Poetry:

165 Meeting House Lane, "C" Press (New York), 1972.

Incidentals In The Day World, Angel Hair Books (New York), 1973.

Phoebe Light, Big Sky Books (Bolinas, California), 1973.

Out There 4: Featuring The Poems Of Alice Notley, Out There Press (Chicago), 1974.

For Frank O'Hara's Birthday, Street Editions (Cambridge, England), 1976.

Alice Ordered Me To Be Made: Poems 1975, The Yellow Press (Chicago), 1976.

A Diamond Necklace, Frontward Books (New York), 1977.

Songs For The Unborn Second Baby, United Artists (Lenox, Massachusetts), 1979.

When I Was Alive, Vehicle Editions (New York), 1980.

Waltzing Matilda, Kulchur Foundation (New York), 1981.

How Spring Comes, Toothpaste Press (West Branch, Iowa), 1981.

Sorrento, Sherwood Press (Los Angeles), 1984.

Margaret & Dusty: Poems, Coffee House Press (St. Paul, Minnesota), 1985.

Parts Of A Wedding, Unimproved Editions Press (New York), 1986.

At Night The States, Yellow Press, 1987.

From A Work In Progress, Dia Chapbook Series (New York), 1989.

Homer's Art, The Institute of Further Studies (Canton, New York), 1990.

(With Douglas Oliver) *The Scarlet Cabinet: A Compendium of Books* (contains the following by Alice Notley: *The Descent of Alette; Beginning With A Stain; Twelve Poems Without Mask; Homer's Art*), Scarlet Editions (New York), 1992.

Selected Poems of Alice Notley, Talisman House (Hoboken, New Jersey), 1993.

To Say You, Pyramid Atlantic (Riverdale, Maryland), 1994.

Close to me & Closer . . . (The Language of Heaven)/ [and] *Désamère,* O Books (Oakland, California), 1995.

The Descent of Alette, Penguin Poets (New York), 1996.

Mysteries Of Small Houses, Penguin Poets, 1998.

Autobiography:

Tell Me Again, Instant Editions (Santa Barbara, California), 1981.

Criticism:

Dr. Williams' Heiresses, Tuumba Books (Berkeley, California), 1980.

Publisher and editor of *CHICAGO,* and with Douglas Oliver of *SCARLET,* both poetry journals. *Anne's White Glove,* a three-act play, was produced by Eye & Ear Theater at LaMama Annex in 1985.

Douglas Oliver

1937-

Some writers are like Petrarch, Wordsworth, Dickinson: of austere consciousness and strong spirit. Others are more malleable in their artistic practice: Boccaccio, Coleridge, Poe, inventors of forms. I fall into the Boccaccio-Coleridge category: insecure and changeable, trying constantly to reform myself. I name the great only to make sure I'm doing my job right, within my category.

When I look far back into my past, dioramas light up. I am moving in them, never quite the same, as if bewildered to be observed, bigoted, purer. And then ready to change again so as to reappear in windows always further from my starting point.

At age fourteen I bought my first pair of good binoculars. The diorama this time shows not myself, exactly, but some things I'm looking at in the luminous greying of the lenscircle.

They are dunlins, brownish little wading birds with black tummy patches, and they're running about on the deserted Stanpit Marsh, their reflections following along the watery mud. Enlarged in the lens, they become fictional, running in another world, and this is what fascinates me. I draw nearer but set the redshanks piping: their white underbellies flock up and the whole flight of them turns over like a lace underside with a dark cover as they bank across the estuary. A heron has its neck out, and its body decides to shunt off, reluctantly enclosing air in its mesmerizing wing-beat.

My binoculars fall on their neck cord. I enter this diorama myself, a boy short for his age, heading back to retrieve his bike from the brambles. Stanpit Marsh occupies the middle of Christchurch harbor, and the path home has an exit squeezing between shops on the mainland road. Four miles to the left is Boscombe, a Bournemouth suburb on England's south coast where I grew up. The London Assurance moved my father's branch office there in case the Germans bombed the docks in my birth-town, Southampton, twenty-five miles to the right.

Douglas Oliver, 1994

In that fifteenth year, I built a cloth birdwatching hide which I never used and I began keeping a supposedly scientific card index for species identified: "Nesting Habits Observed" (usually none); "Distribution" (ink-blotched maps); "Literary Quotations" (*"That's the wise thrush . . . ,"* etc.). But I did not become an expert birder. My interest wasn't scientific, wasn't natural history. Partly I was escaping the middle-class houses of Boscombe's clifftops. The land for them had been sold by Shelley's son, so all the roads bore poet or lake names: I lived in Browning Avenue; other roads were Byron, Shelley, Coleridge, Wordsworth, Penrith. . . . Behind box hedges the solid houses secreted retired

"My mother, Marjorie Oliver, with her mother, probably in Southampton in the 1930s"

colonels, wireworm-thin old ladies on fixed incomes, well-to-do shop owners, and a couple of boys next door who went to expensive Catholic schools. It was all conservative and restricting, mind your manners. In watching birds I discovered a beauty my boyhood life apparently had no room for; it was my way to "unangrify" myself and gain a peacefulness among wide horizons. American writers say to me: "You British poets, with your birds!" In fact, I am better known for political poems, but here is one about those marshes:

The Heron

I talk of voices either real or virtual in my ear;
of shadows, only those that pass over islands'
    sunny turf
vivid to my eye. But when I come to all my birds,
all I've ever seen, they are too many. I talk of
    things unseen.

Together, they would pack the sky like moving
    embroidery
in the white silks, browns and blacks of their
    great tribe,
like endless litters of puppies writhing,
a heavenly roof alive but no progress of flight in it.

Every memory adds to this intricate plot;
starting up redshanks first, and they bank, flashing
    white,
across a sepia estuary where I felt freedom
in watching their undulating patterns on the air.

They flight down but hold at mid-height: horizontal
stick puppets of the Styx. The black light whitens
with the harmonious wings of swan formations,
the day cast over with their bright feathering.

Behind the swans the sky absolutely fills with starlings
homing to roost as once I saw them over Stonehenge;
gulls flock up and hold there, and brown passeriformes
spring between airspaces and stop on invisible branches.

Millions of birds, crows and daws, teal,
quicker wing-beated than wigeon, among mallard
    hordes;
swifts print arrows on the pulsating featheriness;
the sky is covered over with the puppy litters.

I can't tell you all the names; I'm worried
about the birds rabbling the sky. D'you suppose
I can avoid even the dusty body of every sparrow,
or every sparrow hawk flipping over a thicket?

Unseen, this nature crowds my mind. If there's
    pulsation,
it's disturbing; if stasis it's a painting
and all the life goes out; but any sudden switch
between pulse and the static is schizophrenic.

In the foreground of the multifarious flights
one talismanic bird, a heron, lifts to the top
of its single leg and takes off like an umbrella.
Fluff in a corner of the past becomes grey flame.

Its shoulders unshackle and heave, legs become
    the addendum,
the beak stabs out purposefully from the sunken
    neck.
It sails. In this flight's brevity
I find what lives for me among all the dead songs.[1]

This comes from an autobiographical sequence, *An Island that Is All the World*, in a 1990 selected works. The sequence is a mixed poetry-prose form adapted out of Dante's *Convivio*. The prose accompanying "The Heron" says that in bird-flight my adolescent self found the freedom and rhythmic grace that were to lead me to the mystery of poetry's stresses or beats:

In a poem, each stress is held in memory and perceived as a unity of sound, meaning, and special poetic emotion. All durational things on either side of the stroke (the wing-beat) of stress—the length of its syllable, all its sound qualities, what words come im-

---

[1]In *Three Variations on the Theme of Harm,* London: Paladin, 1990, pp. 58-9.

mediately before and after it in the poetic line, the whole movement of the line—make us think how weighty or light the individual stress is. The stress centres a tiny island in memory. The centre of the island is occluded; it is the moment when we think the stress actually happened. We can even strike its instant, a little late, by tapping a finger. If we could bring all those instants fully into consciousness, the poem would become vivid.[2]

Trying to recapture these memories is like that: their centre is occluded like a fog in the diorama window, and yet within them is some kind of wing-stroke that would suddenly lift the heron again, as the poem says.

I was a late child to Scottish parents who grew up before the First World War. My sister, Mona, was the best painter at her art school, and became a devoted village art mistress, lonely in a churchy way of service to others. My brother didn't quite make dentistry and adapted to a business life; like Mona, he has made success out of being a good person. When I think of kindness, an important word in my writing, I sometimes think of both of them. Don't tell me it's sentimental to talk about goodness.

My parents' middle-class Tory generation were staggered when Britain turfed out the hero, Churchill, after the Second War so that the Labour Party could install the Welfare State. Taking tax money for social welfare was property theft from the industrious: socialism was criminal. They would have felt happier with today's swing to conservative-liberal economics. Conflict with children growing up in a socialist society was inevitable; the term "generation gap" was invented then.

It was my father's sense of the righteous that I had to wrestle with—he a Church of Scotland son of the manse from Glasgow. A man of absolutes, he could spend his whole life puzzling with equal passion over why sinners benefit from good people's prayers or why "indict" is so often pronounced "indite." He'd say that if he found sixpence (fifty cents) in the road he'd take it to the police station.

My mother, a hard-hitting tennis player and golfer, was prone to spoonerisms; she'd run indoors from our garden henhouse calling: "Quick, there's a hat feeding with the wrens!"

[2]Ibid, p. 57.

During my childhood I thought her fun but scatty; in adult life I remember her with deep admiration for her shrewdness, bravery in facing adversity, and cheeriness.

We had a family tree, which my preacher-grandfather drew up by riding round cemeteries in Ayrshire, Scotland, in pony and trap. My father updated it according to an intricate scheme that no-one could understand. We were family-proud, that is, snobbish, and had legends. The family tree claims that a descendant of Robin Hood married into the family and that an ancestor from Tarbolton, Ayrshire, introduced Rabbie Burns to Highland Mary. Of more substance, my great-uncle Thomas was knighted for pioneer research into occupational diseases such as miner's lung; another great-uncle was a Harley Street doctor; my grandfather won the gold medal for elocution at Glasgow University; my mother's grandfather was editor of the *Glasgow Herald* newspaper and interviewed the notorious Lily Langtry at his home; my uncle Mark Morrison captained Great Britain at rugby football; while my maternal grandfather's obscure business failure was due to alcoholism.

These were stories of grey and mostly grand forebears. As if in proof of grandness, the only survivor, my grandmother, who lived with us until I was about seven, was so fearsome that when she taught me to read at the age of three I dared not do otherwise. After her death, we left her bedroom forever ghosted.

Occasionally, my father, whom business worries had made irascible, would revert to his 1920s personality, when he would wear yellow spats and sing at young ladies' soirées. He was elaborately literary, rounding on my argument with, "As my old Latin master used to say, 'Boy, you are erecting an aery castle on a foundation of rotten planks.'" But amazingly he could suddenly clown. One snowy New Year's night, the doorbell rang; my father and a neighbour were outside looking enigmatic. They turned abruptly and mooned us in their underpants, for they had taken off their trousers but had held them dangling in front as if they were still wearing them. I could hardly believe he'd done it: neither would anyone who had seen this burly, bald, neat-moustached freemason dressed up in white tie and tails to go to the Mayor's Ball. At his funeral, one of London Assurance's tough bosses told us that as a young inspector he had been scared of my father's disapproval. He was Father rather than Dad.

Yet I used to carry in my wallet an alarming letter written for my daughter Kate's seventh birthday, in which he hopes she won't play "'Annie Laurie' with one finger" (on the piano), an astonishing dirty joke for one so intimidating to young children.

Our family mostly had the dry Scottish humour: turns of phrase applied to the understanding of human characteristics. My mother's uncle Crawford, a choleric lawyer, became white-knuckled with rage one well-soused Christmas when the maid dropped the turkey off its silver salver. Crawford glowered at the bird quivering on the carpet and muttered, "It's all right, Maggie. It's deid and it'll stay deid." That was the kind of anecdote we liked. So I was brought up to use a sharp tongue, to judge character, to play lots of sport, and to ready myself for a business or professional career.

Bird-watching seems in hindsight the first inkling of poetry to come. In my thirteenth-fourteenth year—1951—a schoolmaster took ten minutes out from construing Virgil to explain the rules of Latin prosody. The rules are utterly banal: for example, a short vowel is "short" if followed by a single consonant, whereas long or short vowels followed by either two or more consonants or a "double" consonant are "long." Strangely fascinated, I asked him afterwards if we could do more about prosody. Knowing I spent his lesson drawing cartoons, he suspiciously replied, "No." I went back to drawing cartoons. In my thirties, I was to begin research into prosody, putting electrodes on people's throats as they read poems so as to record traces of the vocal music. While the resulting book was in the press, I acquired an old Bournemouth street directory. That Classics master really was called Percy Cushion (Persecution).

In 1952, an English master read to us sarcastically "A Grief Ago" by Dylan Thomas, to show how obscure the New Apocalypse poets were. Astonished that a mere poet might baffle me—I was set to become a veterinary surgeon—I bought a grubby anthology containing Thomas's "Poem in October," which has herons in it priesting the shore. I sold most of my bird library, bought Thomas's new *Collected Poems,* then bought more poetry books.

Developing here was an adolescent desperation about lack of personal freedom, an interest in the music of poetry (wing-beat), a nascent distaste for right-wing social forms, and a retreat into an isolated world of imagination. Not that this has made me in middle-age a better person than either of my parents, but in certain respects I have better views.

Last night I had one of my recurrent nightmares in which totalitarian hordes invade my "nation." Sometimes the nation is like the road circuit round an English town, Colchester, where I lived in the 1970s with my first wife, Jan, and our two daughters, Kate and Bonamy. Sometimes the nation is a Bournemouth hotel but with labyrinthine stairways and soldier-thugs chasing me. Sometimes it's a miniature suggestion of Haiti with an airport on a shallow hillcrest, sugarcane fields down central slopes, and a wooded road with voodooed shadows forming a perimeter where you can buy fried fish from stalls.

Why Haiti? To slip out of dream into real life a moment, I possess a photo of myself alongside Haiti's dictator, Jean-Claude Duvalier, taken in the mid-1980s. I was helping Greg Chamberlain, Haitian expert and Great Eccentric, investigate press repression. We gate-crashed the president's launch of a flagship medical centre in the hills outside Port au Prince and drank his champagne while the cocky Home Minister Roger Lafontant, who had personally rubber-hose-whipped a journalist a few days before, strolled around dangling an Uzi. A Haitian woman opposition journalist was to be pistol-whipped by police the day after we visited her (Reagan's policies, not our visit, being the excuse). Still bleeding, Jocelyne Claude took a taxi to the Catholic Radio Soleil to broadcast what had happened. Her father, Sylvio, withstood the regime's torture eight or nine times. For this kind of reason Haiti acts as a symbolic nation in my nightmares.

In dreams and poems you can have "the personal and the political" united, because they are visions, and visions are pure. The dreamer acts either bravely or not and that changes the whole scene. What a poem or dream can do real politics couldn't, not unless the dreamer-poet-legislator was pure and so was every citizen. Self-righteousness and totalitarianism are two great motivators of cruelty. So any writers who, like me, occupy themselves with quite wide-ranging politics should first explore their personal flaws.

In last night's dream the nation was just a classroom. I wandered among desks at which cowed citizens pored over fascist propaganda and torturers lined the walls, watching for the merest eye-flicker of dissent. As I debated how to take a stand against this, everyone rushed towards a vertical mouth in a wire-mesh curtain. Curfew: you had to get through before the jagged mouth closed. I wiggled inside and found myself in the familiar labyrinthine hotel, plotting escape. Unusually, I found a way out down some steps to a cove with the night sea coming in over sand. I must already have been writing this autobiography in my sleep.

For the dream flips me back to adolescence. Now I'm sixteen and walking by Bournemouth Bay at night watching white frills ride the inky tide as it creeps over shadowy sand. This is 1954, winter on the south coast, and the great hotels up the cliff are blank-windowed, empty. The town council has, I think, repaired the two town piers blown up in 1940 in case the Germans sailed their destroyers thirty miles across the Channel from France. (I watched those explosions from the cliffs with my mother when I was about three.)

As I walk seaside with an adolescent mood on, I believe myself a failure: At school, wanting too late to change from science to arts, I flunked key university-track exams and, under family pressure, left school when turning sixteen. Now, my father has got me a job as an insurance filing clerk, a fate which I find hilarious and defeating. That afternoon, I have been snogging in a cinema with an office secretary, my volatile Jewish girlfriend, Sheila, who seems more in love with William Holden than with me. It's almost an illicit relationship for both of us: she won't take a "goy" home; my suburbs are quietly anti-Semitic and rabidly anti-Black.

A gull flashes white in the promenade lamps and down the sea rails fishermen have looped their lines far out into the night waiting for some fish stupid enough to take their bait. I feel as if I have taken the bait of a business career. I only want to be a poet. Birds, personal frustration, prosody again.

In those days, I was trying to give myself the university education that I'd missed. I would read until 4 a.m., crawl into my insurance office the following morning and sleep it off in the chilly filing room upstairs. I had cut my job in half. Instead of filing and refiling correspondence relating to new insurance policies, I piled it all a metre high in an office corner: when asked for a document I would rifle through

the heap; only when a policy was finally issued would I take it upstairs. No-one said anything because I was a cricketer and the office team's victories were free business publicity in the *Daily Echo*.

That year, still sixteen, I was waiting for Sheila in Bournemouth's first expresso bar one day when I began to wonder what poetry's great secret was. Why was I so drunk with it?

She was late as usual. A few nights previously, I had just managed to wean her back from a glib boy we met at a dance. He'd chatted briskly about how our minds were always too late to experience time's "instant"—I suppose he'd been reading St. Augustine's *Confessions*. I grumbled to Sheila afterwards that he was being shallow; but actually I couldn't see why. So it was sexual jealousy that energized me as, in the cafe, I began jotting down the names of poems which, by giving me that peculiarly artistic thrill, seemed, somehow, to answer the question about time.

For years I kept that piece of paper. I remember looking at one title, *The Ancient Mariner*, and having a Descartes-by-his-stove illumination: it was as if a *truthfulness* hovered just in front of my nose. To put it into my adult terminology: a poem's music models the passage of time. The meaning and emotional significance of the words are taken along in that flow. Agreed, we can't bring "instants of time" into consciousness. But a poem is, through its music, repeatable in its performance, or at least nearly so, depending on the stability of our interpretation. Consequently, we can keep travelling through a poem's "instants" almost in the same ways, as it were eternally. Also, poems transform the real into the imaginary. Every time we perform a poem by writing or reading, the passage of time through it reawakens. The imaginary comes to life because its time has. The dunlins run again in the binocular lens. So poems can make the imaginary in its many aspects seem real.

You may think this a commonplace; but at sixteen it was a wonderful realisation whose fuller significance I have not, even today, exhausted.

Since I had no instructor, I elected to study under Coleridge. The great polymath became my lost university: he was almost my only teacher in my teen age, speaking to me across the centuries. Lowes's *The Road to Xanadu* has lists of Coleridge's library borrowings: I tried to read whatever the poet had read, even though the hunt took years. So I encountered not only the great but also the slightly more recherché— not just Milton or Spenser but also Samuel Daniel, not just Galileo but also Giordano Bruno (who led to Frances Yates rather than, as usual these days, the other way round); or Thomas Maurice's *A History of Hindoostan*, Psellus's angels, Marco Polo's *Travels*, Bartram's *America*, and so on, following from book to book, still working in isolation.

Not, I suppose, utter isolation. I was brought up without contact with girls of my own age. I'd look for them in a Bournemouth jazz club. One day the club doors opened and in trooped a brigade of blonde-haired Scandinavian girls— as if, that very day, Bournemouth began its modern language school industry. I was still only sixteen, looked younger, and these girls would say, "Have you got an older brother?"

At the club I made friends with an older man, John Barker, a former merchant seaman turned jazz expert who taught me to read writers like James Baldwin (*Go Tell It on the Mountain*). He eventually became a designer of fast-lay aircraft runways for jungle warfare, I think. A mutual friend, Brian Dicker, a budding physicist and Dixieland trumpeter, had a pact with me: he'd teach me science if I told him about the arts. And so I progressed my education my own way, shopping among secondhand bookstalls. If I didn't like a famous author I'd tell myself it must be my narrowness; and I still tell myself that. Lack of received booklists is the advantage the autodidact has over the university educated.

I walked into John's house one time and he put on a shellac 78. "Listen to this." It was Bessie Smith's "Careless Love." I froze in the middle of the room. The record confirmed everything I'd begun to think about art as a performance that recreates time. She sings that song so simply that even a couple of errors become part of its perfection. I'd play "Careless Love" at home over and over, lying on the floor with my ear two inches from the speaker, trying to guess its secret. Why is it mainly teenagers who do this? Each time, in some shuddery way across the decades, across the Atlantic, across the cultures and genders, I became part of her flesh.

Still at that crucial age of sixteen, I got near a poet. John was staying with friends: a large house, seemingly deserted, and with a driveway full of packing cases. No-one would answer my knocking but two hysterical children besieged me when I penetrated the side door. John appeared, plus a vet, plus a woman whose crotch-tight striped jeans, then, in Bournemouth, made me gape. The vet kept talking about her "brother Gerald," his brown mice, pet fox, a chimpanzee which had got loose in J. J. Allan's, a local department store. . . . The story kept multiplying into a menagerie. "Of course, I remember Gerald chasing his pelican round the garage, trying to feed it sardines. . . ." They left John and me alone, and he told me I was in the Durrell family house—Gerald, the zoologist, Lawrence, the poet and novelist, and Margot (striped pants), the sister, married to the Dixie trombonist Mac Duncan. I inspected a book Lawrence had annotated, awed that I couldn't understand the marginal comments.

So even a dropout like me *might* meet poets. I was very naive: two private schools, an all-boys' state school, hot Christianity, an insurance office, getting drunk, playing poker with an adult cricket team, keeping on the fringes of the new Teddy Boy gangs with their crepe-soled shoes, long-lapeled jackets, and bike chain weaponry, plus midnight hotel dances with Sheila, hot shit.

And then national military service. The Royal Air Force bored and shocked me. I mean, I was a complete prig. I'd never had to share my life with, for example, a psychotic blue with dirt, who tried to chop his hand off so he could get discharged as unfit; or with another who, in the service of obscure desires, laid turds in the communal baths; or others who plotted to smear boot polish all over a lazy, obnoxious eighteen-year-old. Fortunately, I could talk fast enough to stop the boot polish plan and plenty of jokes won friends but no intimates.

I learnt how to type and dash off a bit of shorthand (taught in exactly the same manner as dismantling the Bren gun), acted a little, did the camp radio broadcasts, and was demobbed at nineteen without a clue how to become a writer.

The usual "writer's jobs" followed: hotel dishwasher, porter, coach tour clerk, ice-cream seller, amid spells of unemployment. I got deeply depressed, and, thanks to my despairing father, ended up as a legman, unpaid, for a free-lance journalist. Ashley Brown had a fantastic press cuttings collection stored down ceiling-high alleys in his garage. He made a living partly with hard news, partly with trade journalism,

Family portrait, taken at the back of the Cambridge house, 1969: (from left, standing) the author holding Tom, Marjorie Oliver, Jessie and Jack Hughes (in-laws), and (in front) the author's first wife, Janet, next to Kate Oliver (on tricycle)

partly with stories assembled from his cuttings and headed: "Sultan Was the World's Record Lover." He let me go round women's dress shops for *Drapery and Fashion Weekly*, then said, "You've got some cuttings yourself now: if you compose a reference, I'll sign it."

This landed me a job on a peculiar farm machinery monthly in London run from a flat you could only reach by fire escape. Eventually it was sold and we moved to the Strand. Trade journalists lived high on the hog then, handing in shabby macs at the Savoy or Dorchester vestiaries, or travelling round Europe on freebies with John Deere tractors or fuel injection firms. I learnt little about farming but acquired a taste for St. Emilion, Pouilly Fuisse, and Chambertin and, strangely, discovered how to write better prose. Roger Wilding, the original proprietor, was an old *Sunday Times* sports editor, and would give me a pound extra if he liked a headline. I'd earn it like this: the man-

aging director of Ford (Tractors) Europe was driving a harrow along a country lane when a tine caught a passerby, hurling him to the ground. He found that the victim was his rival, the managing director of Massey-Ferguson (Britain). "Cultivating an acquaintance."

I married my first wife, Janet Hughes, a school teacher, in 1962 when I was twenty-four, she twenty-six. This would be a long story, how such a solid marriage fell apart after twenty years. I neither chose wrongly, nor was I not in love, nor have I ever relinquished my original admiration. I was a journalist who had only published four inconsequential poems. She couldn't have anticipated the depth of my commitment to poetry.

The only way into general news was to sign on as agricultural specialist on the *Cambridge Evening News*, sliding into news reporting as soon as I could. That took me out of intellectual isolation at last: journalism itself is an education and I had close contact with the university. I stayed for nearly six years, and ended up running my own book page and writing in-depth news features and the leaders.

For some years, Jan gave up teaching for motherhood. She taught me how to live sensibly in a house, how to handle our newborn children and guide them as they grew up. We lived beside windy Cambridge farming land and I'd drive about the countryside on stories all day, write up court stories and theatre reviews at night. Things were very stable between us. Once a year, I'd maroon myself in an anonymous hotel room and for a week produce source material for the next year of poetry. We took sailing holidays, spent time with her extended London family, and I joined her father's village cricket team of farmers and farm laborers playing under the oak trees; our most celebrated batsman was aged seventy.

Provincial journalism lands you day by day in surprises. Let's say some factory chimneys are discharging white dust. You go with a photographer down a line of tawdry municipal housing. "Good afternoon, I'm from the *Cambridge Evening News*. I suppose you are surprised, disgusted, and furious at the white dust that has settled on your car outside there." "Er... yes, I am." "Fine. Now if you'd just give me your name and address and wait while my friend here takes a snap." On to next door. By the time we'd got to the last house down the row, we were wanting to go home, but an eighty-year-old albino man with pale eyes answered the bell. "Good afternoon, I'm from—." "Come in, come in," he said eagerly. He seated us on a hard settee and said he'd make some tea. His footsteps echoed up the stairs behind the flimsy walls. Twenty minutes went by. The door was flung open and in came the albino dressed as Carmen Miranda in a rhinestoned ball gown and an immense hat covered with artificial fruit.

Even in local journalism you meet cabinet ministers, MPs, archbishops, bishops, lords, a prime minister perhaps; and also criminals, con artists, and beauty queens. It's an eye-opener. The Italian premier, Aldo Moro, visited Cambridge (some years later, he was found assassinated in a car trunk in the middle of Rome). We were entering Trinity College chapel and I stopped by a statue of Francis Bacon, who was ousted as Queen Elizabeth's chancellor for taking bribes. Bacon sits with a thoughtful finger to his forehead but looks unbalanced, as if falling out of his stone chair. My jacket was tugged behind. I turned to find the foreign secretary, Amintore Fanfani, grinning at me—Fanfani also took turns at Italy's main jobs, prime minister and president included. He thumbed towards Bacon: "'E is thiinking: 'ow can I diddle ze Briitish goverrrnment!'"

There is another side to local journalism. You meet mothers whose children are lost to drugs or have died; you walk into tearful inquests held in farmhouses where a husband has shot himself; and eventually—*too slowly*—you realise the harm that journalism does to dysfunctional families. Usually, your "human interest" stories will come from the poorer part of town; you steal those private troubles, sell them, and in England some noble press lord pockets the proceeds. Much journalism lards over its doings with the savorous grease of "public interest"; otherwise they'd stick in your throat. Swallowing the grease along with the word "professionalism," I long thought my good intentions meant I was acting well.

Sometimes, I would scribble "Village Chase Ups" in the office news diary and disappear into Cambridge University library, emerging about 4 p.m. to speed round some of the villages to find a quick story. I could also use journalism to meet writers: I interviewed W. H. Auden, Stephen Spender, Philip Larkin (later), and various others. And in Cambridge I acquired my first poet friends, learnt how to perform with a folk-jazz band, read in the university clubs, was part of a backup to the Incredible String Band, and so on.

Alan Ross at the *London Magazine* had already taken some poems and, in an act of editorial encouragement that I never repaid, Nigel Dennis printed a four-page poem from me, a complete unknown, in the top international monthly, *Encounter*. It was just after *Encounter* had been exposed as receiving CIA money; Stephen Spender had resigned in outrage, and Nigel Dennis was honorably trying to clean up the mess. Perhaps I should have, but I didn't send Dennis anything else because I had begun to scrutinize closely the reviews I was willing to publish in.

Robert L. Peters was a visiting poet-professor from California with whom I had a memorable visit to the Lake District. I mostly went out at nights with the "New Cambridge" poets, as they were later called: J. H. Prynne, John James, Wendy Mulford, Andrew Crozier, Anthony Barnett, and the wider circle including Denise Riley, Peter Riley . . . well, it was a whole network which had strong links to American poets and a few links to France. If I now have so many poet friends, it began then. Prynne gave me one or two free tutorials, and the first "booklist" I'd ever had. I never wrote in any "New Cambridge" style—there never was one; there were to be many imitators of Prynne himself. But I retain a personal loyalty to those poets, despite all the changes in my own writing.

They were sharp, aggressive times. John James had such spontaneity he could spin an evening round on his finger. Jeremy Prynne was already a Cambridge legend for his fast poetic intelligence and wit. Wendy Mulford had quick judgment and entertaining expression of it. Andrew Crozier's taciturnity would break into speedy insights and his steady care for literature through his Ferry Press is now a matter of record. In 1969 he published my first book, *Oppo Hectic*, a mimeo with cover by the sculptor Barry Flanagan. This group showed me that my adolescent obsessions with prosody really led towards truthfulness of spirit. They understood those particular questions better than most mainstream or "experimental" poets I've met, and only a few American writers of my own acquaintance—Ed Dorn, Ted Berrigan, Kenneth Koch, Alice Notley, some others—have matched that understanding.

To take a representative evening, we started in the Eagle pub, centre-town; went on to another pub to meet James Gordon; and ended up in a farm cottage miles out in the flat Fenlands, where his mother, a superannuated Anglo-Saxon scholar, let us set up three typewriters round her dank living room. We wrote collaborations while her formidable Old English sheepdog, Byrhtnoth, bounded all over everywhere. In one collaboration, John James and Andrew Crozier satirized my reformist sense of politics—we'd been having an argument, I suppose. A sequel came in Paris, where I was living a few years later, and the two of them were giving a reading which featured the old collaborations. When they reached the Byrhtnoth poem, Andrew said, "Why not ask Doug to read this one?" Why not?

I recount this to illustrate that my politics were "town," not "gown." Leaving John and Andrew aside, I didn't trust the university politics of the 1968 period: the student Left had a mouthful of democracy but they didn't have a democratic tone; so I didn't think them socialist. At the height of the '68 sit-ins, I became exasperated with a bunch of them: "But how on earth is a whole nation's consciousness going to change just because you've changed the ownership of the means of production?" "Haven't you read Hegel, page xxx," snarled a particularly well-bred student.

The worst death I've been close to came near the end of our time in Cambridge when our Down's syndrome baby, Tom, died in his cot in 1969. He was nearly two. The premonitions and guilts that flew around the event were winged by his mental handicap: surely he above all should have been protected. Thirty years later, my finding him seems as horrible as ever. Tom had been our middle baby, between my daughters Kate and Bonny, and his death cut right through all the heartless university-driven political questions.

My 1973 novel, *The Harmless Building,* begins:

> For the moment the truth is hiding in obstreperous fiction. I can, however, say that a real mongol baby died and that his memory affects my life. In his mongolism I find an analogy for my own stupidity. He and I are united at that primitive level of thought where our ideas are fairly random, not ambitious, only half out of thought-chaos itself. . . .

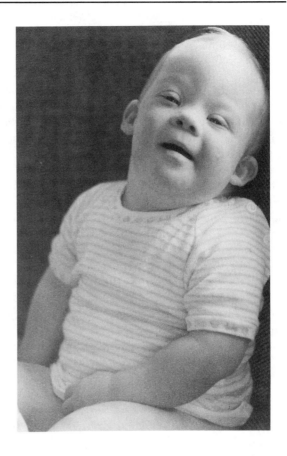

Tom Oliver, age one, "shortly before he died in 1969. Of the figure who represents Tom in The Harmless Building *I was to write: he 'had the true blessedness allowed only to the really low in IQ'"*

> This fiction may at times pose as clever, but you will bring the moral to it if you succeed in tracking my stupidity.[3]

You don't call it "mongolism" any more. But I can't think of Tom without intensely believing in an utter democracy of soul, whatever the level of our intelligence. It makes me ashamed of our modern ambitions, of our intellectual or financial elitism, of our trickle down economics, as if the heart had a mostly closed tap on its underside.

> See my baby lay his head on a down pillow,
> pigeons flurrying on the boulevards.
> Lay my bird in down.
> Well, Tom's long in his coffin, inside his altar,

---

[3]*The Harmless Building,* London: Ferry and Grosseteste Presses, 1973, p. 5.

in some cathedral I've made for him
lit by summer photographic flashes.
I scarcely dare cross those cracked flags.[4]

Soon after our baby's death we gladly moved to Paris, where I'd taken an editing-translating job on the English desk of Agence France-Presse, France's equivalent of UPI. Those were romantic times at AFP, when lines of typewriters clattered between teleprinters in a huge room inhabited by French, Spanish, Latin American, German, American, and English journalists. Almost everyone had a colourful life-story. Recently, in a Kenneth Koch-style poem, I commemorated those days, twenty-five years ago now—AFP's English desk posted the poem on their bulletin board. Young Jon Swain went out to make his name in Vietnam and Cambodia; Maurice Chanteloup had a weak chest after imprisonment in North Korea: he spoke five or six languages; Finlay Campbell had covered the Seven Day War and turned alcoholic as a result; a desk chief had a Maoist son in the *maquis*; Bill Smith was a well-known novelist; Dirk Kinane was an in-law of Ted Hughes; Greg Chamberlain was already a Haiti freak, a motor mouth with extraordinary stories; others were flamboyant womanizers; one genius had memorized great chunks of Spinoza, had large divorce debts which inhibited return to America, and eventually disappeared from view in, I think, Guatemala.

On a quiet night, you'd go in for an 11 p.m. start, type a quick story, and start a series of forays down to the all-night prostitutes-and-drifters bar, Les Finances, on the corner of Place Bourse. If some world leader had a heart attack the desk chief would ring the hard-bitten barmaid, Marianette, and she'd tell you to go back up to the newsroom. At 3 a.m., you'd go out with your genial mate, Colin Shaw, for a three-course meal in La Rotunde—frog's legs, two bottles of wine—he was later a big wheel on the *Guardian*'s foreign desk before retiring to become a lay parson. By 5 a.m. the first Cambodian war copy was coming in upstairs, sobering you up instantly.

In this period, 1970–1971, I was in touch with a group of post-structuralist French poets. Claude Royet-Journoud and his wife Anne-Marie

Albiach had just finished publishing *Siècle à Mains*, with Michel Couturier. That review, a showcase for postmodern poetic experiments, antedated the American L=A=N=G=U=A=G=E magazine, a front-runner for American "language poetry," and Claude has had great influence on that side of the scene. I had already read Derrida, Foucault, Lacan, Althusser, Debord, etc., because in Cambridge during the late sixties I used to buy whatever books the university lecturers had ordered in the shops.

George and Chris Tysh were in Paris and arranged most of the readings by visiting American poets; I organised one or two British ones. I met briefly several poets who were later friends, Lee Harwood, Barry MacSweeney, Ron Padgett, Dick Gallup, can't remember them all. At one reading, an American poet irritated me by claiming the Charles Manson murders were incredibly significant politically (the 1990s have seen so many cult suicides that perhaps he was right). So when after a reading of my own I was asked what most interested me as a writer, I replied: "The difference between good and bad emotions." "*Emotion, c'est de la merde,*" another poet commented. I have always thought that kind of remark is the real shit.

In Paris, because of Tom's life and death, I had become obsessed with the career of the education secretary, Margaret Thatcher, whose politics in my view threatened disadvantaged people. By 1971, shortly before we returned to England, I was writing the first draft of *The Harmless Building*, a novel whose black comedy is governed by malignant presences, but whose *raison d'être* was certainly Tom's death. It was jointly published in 1973 by two small presses, and reprinted by Paladin in 1990. As a 1980s article at the height of Thatcherism reminded me, it contains this ironic exchange:

"Mr. Edward Heath has potential greatness," said McFarlane.
"So has Mrs. Margaret Thatcher," said Masterson, betraying a surprising interest in education.[5]

But if I was the first novelist or poet—or journalist perhaps—to anticipate Thatcher's *fullest* potential, this was because Tom's death had made my nerves raw.

---

[4]"Well of Sorrows in Purple Tinctures," *Douglas Oliver: Selected Poems,* New Jersey: Talisman House, p. 132.

[5]*The Harmless Building,* p. 80.

The Harmless Building, which only Peter Ackroyd among reviewers picked up on at the time, satirized both French deconstruction and American fragmented prose styles. The story dutifully deconstructs itself in the middle, so that its second movement is a different "text" transforming the first half; there is decoherence, absurdist metaphor, much about writing and body image, a parody of Jacques Lacan in the text, and a Derridean refusal of unity and closure. But feeding into the black comedy is Tom's death and what it meant for my beliefs, like a tributary of the River Styx spreading its sooty mists everywhere. The book implies: deconstruct what you like—that's always an open game—but you cannot deconstruct *this*, the performance of our lives in their anguish, pleasure, and belief.

All of my books since then have followed a planned development from the purely personal, broadening to the social and political. I once described the books as propagating like strawberries, as by tendrils leading from *The Harmless Building*, the mother plant. In a more mobile image, it is like the swimming of a jellyfish, expansion and contraction.

Meanwhile, Jan was struggling with the dullness of Asnières, a Parisian suburb. Sometimes we'd manage a good break, a trip to the Loire or dinner at the ancient Procope restaurant in Paris, a woozy stroll by the Seine afterwards. But there was no doubt I was having the better time of it. Our two daughters were turning bilingual but seemed spaced-out, and since I was on the AFP night shift, I was changing night-day rhythms twice a week to be with the family.

Because the family wasn't too happy with all of this, we returned to England after nearly two years. London journalism was going through a depression, but the editor of the *Coventry Evening Telegraph* knew me and we went there. After two months, my disquiet at modern journalism had come to a head: the paper turned out to be too right wing; there was freemasonry about; I hated doing the human interest stuff. I wrote some stories deliberately against the newspaper's politics but they were still pub-

The author with his parents, Athole and Marjorie Oliver, on a visit to Paris during the Agence France-Presse days, 1971

lished. I quickly went off to Essex University to fill in holes in my education.

I was thirty-three, Jan was supportive, and we took a small fisherman's cottage about 300 yards from the estuary in Brightlingsea, a small sailing town on England's east coast. A fair-weather sailor at best, I bought a frail dinghy with a mended mast and we could sail down-estuary any free afternoon. Beside the mud flats, shining pink under November sun, I'd watch herons, brent geese, greenshanks, and redshanks pick about, while a short-eared owl quartered the reeds behind. Across the water was a bird sanctuary where Jan and I would sleep overnight in a musty caravan and listen to four or more nightingales singing from the woods.

Essex University, which is near Colchester, was in those days a spitfire campus with a reputation for sit-ins—but also for poetry. Poets who have been associated with the campus or who have lived in Brightlingsea would include: Donald Davie, Elaine Feinstein, Robert Lowell, Ed Dorn, Andrew Crozier, Ted Berrigan, Alice Notley, Tom Raworth, Anthony Barnett, Tom Clark, Ralph Hawkins, Simon Pettet, Helena Hughes, David Trotter, and Jeremy Reed.

As a mature student, I had time to read for the first time in my life. The pseudo-radical idea that poetry is elitist was very fashionable on campus. I created an anti-elitist poetry service called *Aiken Jacks,* which printed anyone's poems at all; once a week, I'd set up a table in a quadrangle and give the mimeos away, take what you want.

The following year, 1973–1974, Ted Berrigan and Alice Notley arrived, Ted to take up the poet-in-residence post that Ed Dorn had vacated two years before. Ted didn't know about *Aiken Jacks,* and later he was to blarney that he had reawakened campus poetry. In fact, I was wary when we met because I didn't want him bossing the show: the wariness lasted five minutes because of Ted's genius for generosity. No-one in my adult life has taught me more about how to *use* emotion wisely. Ralph Hawkins, Simon Pettet, Charlie Ingham, and I started *The Human Handkerchief*—"Do you need the word 'Human' in it?" asked a contributor. Ted provided the American contacts; I provided most of the British ones. A friendship with Anne Waldman began at this time and, most significantly it now seems, I gave a reading with Alice in which there was electricity between our styles.

However, my family was struggling on my student income, so Ted huckstered money out of the Poetry Society for us both to read in someone's sitting room—we played it tailgate like two jazz bands trying to outblast each other. I expect he won but he handed his own fee to me, a favour I wasn't able to return until eight years later when he was skint in New York.

In 1974, Wendy Mulford, with her fine little press Street Editions, published a poem of mine written entirely during a series of night visits to a Derbyshire cave. It was a burlesque oracle, a retreat into myself to find a truer origin for spreading my poetry outwards—that jellyfish movement in a contracting phase.

My father died that year, playing a round of golf at the age of eighty—his ideal death. We felt he had left a large space. I had to drop summer work to be with my mother, so we ran up more debts. But the family was enjoying life by the sea; our daughters had turned out bright and funny and Jan was running a

"Identically dressed for a Brightlingsea theatrical event in the 1980s, Kate and Bonny Oliver, my two daughters, find it amusing to pose at home"

private playgroup. In 1975, Essex University Literature Department gave me a tenure track job directly after my bachelor's, something that I suppose would be impossible these days. Jan had also taken a full-time schoolteaching post by then and we didn't see each other much. After two years of sweatshop existence, we felt it better for me to go part-time.

In fact, I find the next four years difficult to write about. I was awarded an Arts Council grant to study boxing in Milan but the resulting novel was dreadful. I spent most days feeling pallid and talentless, rewriting that wretched novel with the curtains tight shut. I'd do the shopping and clean house and acted as press officer for a campaign which saved the town from the worst effects of a commercial wharf development. Jan, whose talent is to work within a particular environment, felt more fulfilled than I did in Brightlingsea, a town of unusual local loyalty—whereas I am restless, urban, and like a lot of action. The only wider conversation was in pubs, where the student-style politics left me crazy-headed. I got near a clinical frustration and felt my creative energy at a low ebb.

I went on tour with the poet and percussionist Anthony Barnett and some noted free jazz musicians; I published a curious book of cartoons and matching poems about Uruguayan politics called *The Diagram Poems*, and, with Margaret Thatcher's accession to the British premiership in 1979, started an anti-Thatcherite poem, *The Infant and the Pearl*, which took years to finish. In 1981 I spent a winter teaching at the University of L'Aquila, a hill capital in Italy's Abruzzi. The following year, after I took a master's in applied linguistics, London University's British Institute, back in my heart's home, Paris, offered me a lecturing job. At first, Jan was going to come but then she decided not to. She has recently taken early retirement from schoolteaching in Brightlingsea where she has become a prominent local personality.

The one who moves agrees to be the villain: that's the best way to work it for those who stay. So be it. Our life ambitions had diverged too greatly: the separation eventually became complete. Half of my life seemed to fall away. Lacking the habitual close contact with my daughters, I became unmoored.

A future had to be created out of what I did like. I like living in Paris because struggling with another culture keeps me awake. I like the French version of punctilious kindness.

Outside Haiti's famous Olaffson Hotel: (from left) Greg Chamberlain, journalist and Haiti expert; Aubelin Jolicoeur, immortalized as "Petit Pierre" in Graham Greene's The Comedians*); Douglas Oliver; and Bernie Diederich, former* Time Magazine *Caribbean correspondent, author of* Papa Doc, *and Greene's principal informant for* The Comedians. *"This is during my second Paris period," 1984.*

In Paris I can get a better perspective on world politics than in Britain or America; and I never know who I'm going to meet next.

On my forty-second birthday, I had a sidewalk dinner in Montmartre with Greg Chamberlain, his wife Laurie, and members of Grenada's New Jewel revolutionary government who were in town seeking Mitterrand's support against Reagan's hostility—the United States hadn't yet invaded. Two days later I dined with a British economics adviser who sneered, "Who cares about little Grenada?" Shortly, everyone did. The Americans swept in after the Grenadan prime minister, Maurice Bishop, and governmental colleagues were assassinated by a rival

New Jewel faction led by Bernard Coard. Some months afterwards, I went to Grenada, again with Greg, and at Mama's, a two-table restaurant outside St. George's, ate mongoose and armadillo with Bishop's closest surviving friend, Kendrick Radix. By chance, dining with us was Errol Coard, who was over from New York to visit his brother Bernard in prison. The conversation kept safely to skin diving.

I sometimes study small, contained countries—Uruguay, Haiti, Grenada, the Cape Verde Islands off Africa—to see more clearly why purist left-wing regimes always fail. Of course, they are immediately destabilised economically by the world power groups, as Grenada was. But—going back to that Cambridge student and his page of Hegel—ordinary people won't accept for long any elite definition of what their "change of consciousness" should be. The Grenadans preferred their lives free of politics, free of international opprobrium, and who can blame them? They weren't the ones getting their rocks off; the elite were.

You'll say that's obvious. But my anxiety here is to keep a socialist conscience alive despite the hopelessness of socialist policies. I was finishing my anti-Thatcher poem, *The Infant and the Pearl*, in Paris at this time, 1983–1984, and the poem attacks monetarism for its harsh social effects while lamenting socialism's inability to control financial liquidity or to create economic energy. With the fall of the Soviet Union and the rapaciousness of global free trade, these issues are even more urgent today. I wrote in *The Infant and the Pearl* that it is unthinkable

> to pretend that the poor will profit from
>   policies
> whose mercy has greyed in the pearly mirror
> of the nation's identity.[6]

As a "townie," I have always thought that ordinary life, and not literary or political philosophy, provides my poetry's true subject matter. Yet I am on a particular "side" of poetry—one that opposes mainstream trends that conform to government arts policies. A key event in Britain for my "side" was a classic series of "collected poems" published by Anthony Barnett from Allardyce, Barnett in the 1980s. My own

"Meeting Alice Notley again at the Luxembourg International Poetry Festival," 1987

collected volume, *Kind*, republished *The Infant and the Pearl*, so it's a moment to talk about it.

"Infant" in the poem's title means, essentially, a Down's syndrome child as symbol for all the socially disadvantaged. "Pearl" requires a longer explanation. First, I'd decided that I'd need an elaborate prosody to avoid political rant and to create something enduring. John Hall had remarked once that *The Harmless Building* reminded him of the medieval *Pearl* poem because of the role a child plays in it. That struck home: on a snowy January night in Cambridge when my elder daughter, Kate, was about to be born, our front door was flung open and an immense midwife stood amid the flakes. "I'm Pearl," she said in a low, thundery voice.

And "Margaret" of Margaret Thatcher is Greek for pearl.

The fourteenth-century *Pearl* has more complex metrics than perhaps any other English poem. Its 101 twelve-line stanzas (100 for perfection, 1 for unity), are each rhymed as closely as an Italian sonnet. Their first lines contain a key word, their last line is a refrain, and these change at five-stanza intervals. The four-stress lines all alliterate up to four times. I had long been interested in the timing of consonants and the alliteration spoke to these interests. So the *Pearl* poem's title linked my life experience to an elaborate prosody capable of passing from grand political statement to the raciest satire without loss of stateliness.

---

[6]*The Infant and the Pearl*, London: Silver Hounds for Ferry Press, 1985, Section XX.

As in the medieval poem, a lost child re-appears as a maiden who talks of relinquished ideals. She comes to the ideal shore of a river under crystal cliffs and instructs the dreamer who is marooned on the time-laden shore. She is Rosine (a figure from *The Harmless Building*):

The windows of that world shone as they
    opened
at her passing; her compeers in the sans-
    pareil
surely hid in the cliffs, their heightened
purity transparent; Rosine's apparel
was royal red, a red brightened
by the crystal country which, like Campari
running through ice, her progress reddened
as she turned and re-entered my reverie.
Like the lost lioness—not the Tory
roary British lion but a better emblem,
a more lithe, love-like beast—she
walked shoreward in that unworldly kingdom.[7]

---

[7]Ibid., Section XIII.

Performing The Diagram Poems on the Luxembourg stage, 1987 (the diagrams are displayed on a stand to the left)

Shortly after I'd returned to Paris in 1982, my mother died and about a year later my sister phoned to say she had liver cancer. Mona died with a courage that has greatly affected me, for it matched the courage in her lonely life of service: six hundred people crowded the church at her funeral. These two deaths intensified the desperation and vivacity which characterised the 1980s for me in Paris, as I worried about the effect of separation on my family. I holed up in a studio above the raucous Avenue de Clichy, had short-lived affairs, and told my friends that during my long summer break they could ring me any time and I would get out of bed and join them in some cafe. Three a.m., I'd jump up and go down the street to Le Havane, then an exotic cafe used by Pigalle's Brazilian transvestites.

I'd write through the night, too, for that would keep away sleeplessness. In the summer of 1985, for example, I wrote the technical book on prosody that I've mentioned. It took just two months. I'd start at 7 p.m. with a bottle of wine beside me and continue till 3 a.m. until the wine was finished. If someone rang, I'd drop it all and go out. One night I blearily erased a whole chapter while trying to save it on the computer at 3 a.m.; after a mentally blitzed ten seconds I began again, finished a fresh version at 7 a.m., and went out to Le Havane for an early morning coffee. The book, *Poetry and Narrative in Performance,* is a difficult read because I was asserting difficult new ideas about poetic music and writing so hastily: one day I'll write a more accessible version.

In the book I insist that poems are not "texts." Critics, linguists, and "theory" schools prefer, most of the time, to treat them as inter-textual entities, so that form remains without closure but lies open to the wider social and historical influences upon the poem. That way, left-wing poetics can get to work. There's a role for that kind of analysis providing it doesn't get bookish and pretentious. But individual "voice" in a poem became for a while unfashionable among the academy-influenced poets, though I imagine with the growing influence of "pragmatics" in linguistics the pendulum may swing back again from "text" to "performance" and "voice," which is where my own interests lie.

Our lives can be seen as a text, too: I am deadening my life down into a text as I write. But it's the shoddy performance of our lives that we need to cure, not just the way we talk about them. If the owner of a muzzled dog has a bandaged hand, trust neither dog nor owner. Performance makes our lives real and it makes art come alive. Good writing, coming from the flawed heart, should be so clear a performance that it willingly opens itself out to hostile criticism.

This thought has since the late 1980s turned my writing away from "difficulty" and towards accessibility. I am not doctrinaire about this; it's just what I'm currently doing. As for my flawed heart, towards the end of this second period in Paris, I had two deeper relationships which convinced me, at last, that I was an emotional and moral mess.

But I had a stroke of luck. An old friend, the poet and translator Pierre Joris, was living near République and in 1987 he organised a poetry festival in his native Luxembourg. He invited British, American, French, Italian, and Luxembourgish poets. One New York invitee, Alice Notley, who had been a widow for some

years, wrote asking if I could arrange a week or so in Paris for her after the festival.

I don't like exaggerating friendships: I had known Ted for only a year, though the relationship stood me in good stead for the rest of my life. He would have that effect on people. After Ted and Alice had left Essex in 1974, I had seen them as a couple only once more, at a 1982 New York festival of British poetry a year before his death. During the intervening years, Ted and I had hardly ever written. I think we didn't need to. When Ted's major lifetime collection, *So Going around Cities*, was published, it was dedicated to Alice, Anselm Hollo, and myself.

After we had performed at the Luxembourg festival, Alice and I got together. That summer, I went to New York to meet the boys, Anselm and Edmund Berrigan, then twelve and fourteen, at the home of Kate Berrigan and David Morrison. On the plane going over, I studied baseball in *USA Today*. About the second thing I said in my plummy English voice was something like: "Hey! What do you think

Two close American friends, Anselm Hollo and Jane Dalrymple-Hollo

of that Tommy John, still pitching away at his age!" Satisfactory remark. So I had to become a Yankee fan, a Steinbrenner enemy, and all that. Now that the boys are men we can still manage a nostalgic reference to the old pitcher.

Kate Berrigan, Ted's daughter by Sandy (Kate's brother, David, and his wife, Sarah, remain close to us), was killed by a motorcycle that same summer, just after Alice and I had agreed to get married. The following year, our first year of marriage, Alice's brother, Albert, who had never really recovered from being a sniper in Vietnam, overdosed, probably accidentally, after a stay at a rehab. The brunt of this was borne by Al's family and Alice's mother, Beulah, a smart desert woman everyone immediately warms to. Alice's poetry still contains a rage at the politics that led to this waste. These two tragedies are not my story to tell but I lived through them intensely because my near ones were doing so.

My five years in New York were lively. I'd joined Alice and the boys in the same cramped railroad apartment on St. Mark's Place where I'd last seen Ted—the address had been famous to me for years. Anselm and Eddie became sons to add to my two daughters, and I sentimentalize to myself sometimes that anything done for them is also done for Ted.

We began poor enough for me to have to tap St. George's Charity, an old foundation which helps the British settle in New York. For years afterwards they'd send us a sugared Christmas cake, and that always touched me. I became a part-time word processor at Sloan-Kettering Cancer Centre in midtown New York. I would weep sometimes as I transcribed HIV-positive interviews from tape. Two good patrons, Ed Foster at Stevens Institute in Hoboken and the late Joe Carderelli down in Baltimore, arranged better-paid teaching—I'd worked for New York University's extramural program but quit because of the low pay.

Across two avenues was the St. Mark's Poetry Project, a centre for many American poets I either knew personally or through their work. It was clear from the first reading Ed Friedman gave me at the Project that my poetry was "British" and different from prevailing U.S. tendencies; it could run up against the attack on Eurocentrism. Given the world dominance of American culture, that's something I've had to struggle with. I could be treated as ignorant of ideas I'd been thinking about

"*Stepsons Anselm (left) and Edmund Berrigan, on a visit to the first Paris apartment—in Montmartre—after Alice Notley and I settled there in 1992*"

for thirty years, or accused of being "orphic" or less kindly as writing "a stream of bat's piss."

When there's an orphic quality in my work it is always there in a burlesque and I'll take a moment to explain why. Postmodern philosophies do not speak well to me about certain metaphysical aspects of our speculations. To list just a few: the incomprehensibility of space-time at utterly extreme macro- or micro-levels; the strong possibility that we have premonitions, the apparent immediacy ("presence") of genuine visions given as "complete"; time-slowing or speeding during unusual mental states; virtuoso violin playing or mathematical calculation among the very young; the gravity of perhaps telepathic communication on death-beds; and so on. I don't claim any special insight into these phenomena but my old interest in prosody is involved even here.

Once I encouraged a group mostly of critical theorists to identify *for themselves* features of poetic stress that suggest we operate a sort of mental time-bending (when we "hear" a poetic stress we actually seem to model its ineffable "presence" or "instant" in our immediate memory by a sort of time-bending). They couldn't deny their own findings but dismissed the whole discussion as "British empiricism." The argument might validate "presence" and "voice"; and that wouldn't do. But I am being neither reactionary nor religious—I have a fairly good lay person's knowledge of astrophysics and quantum science and am as well educated in linguistics as the average critical theorist. But I include the more orphic aspects of poetry so as not to become untruthful in the sense of willfully unmystical; and I burlesque the orphic so as not to become untruthful in the sense of willfully mystical.

Ted's great personality had left a broad mark on the Lower East Side and I became most friendly with those who didn't try to see whether I was a replacement for him. Fortunately, it was Ted and Alice's inner circle that accepted me most frankly, and who are among my closest American friends. They are nearly all poets, writers, or artists, or spouses of the former. Johnny Stanton and Eleanor Nauen, George and Katie Schneeman, Marion Farrier and her late husband, Steve Carey, his brother Tom, Simon Pettet, Eileen Myles, Harris Schiff, John Godfrey, and Tom Savage lived nearby, while Peggy DeCoursey would be a chapter on her own for her unselfishness. One or two lived out their AIDS tragedies, most notably Ted's collaborator, Joe Brainard, the artist, who had been generous to us. Well, it was a poetic village with too many to list. Phil Whalen came up for a memorable visit and we've been down once or twice to San Francisco to see him. Allen Ginsberg, who died two nights ago as I write this, was a family friend, but how many will remember his greatness of soul! Anne Waldman would busy in and be considerably grand, and a couple of summers she invited me to teach at the Naropa Institute, one of life's better gigs. Ron Padgett was around; Lorenzo Thomas came up a couple of times; Lita Hornick would take us out to dinner at the Caravelle or the Côte Basque; I have only really got to know Kenneth and Karen Koch here in Paris. You can learn much from such people.

I have always liked mixed neighborhoods but St. Mark's Place was special: not just ethnically, though that is always a bonus, but in terms of how people lived. So there we were with riots protesting the expulsion of the homeless from Tompkins Square Park, Molotov cocktails flaring in the night under TV lights, the police one notorious night making cavalry charges outside our windows, or the protesters scattering down our street overturning garbage cans to prevent pursuit.

If there have to be homeless, let yours be a neighbourhood where they live; let there be ancient citizens on fixed incomes, others with mild Mafia or pornography pasts, young writers doing shit jobs, middle European supers,

Korean or Hispanic bodegas, Polish breakfast places, Jewish delis, errant punks, hardworking plumbers, kids about to go right or wrong, drifters, a plump, wise African-American shopkeeper next door, commenting on it all in monosyllables. Oh, if we have to, add slim young women running trendy dress shops or Italian-style cafes and one or two suits with briefcases hurrying off to work. Better, let there be poets—a plaque on W. H. Auden's old apartment, and memories of Frank O'Hara on Second Avenue. If it could just have held there, in its social mix, without developers wanting to pretty it up for profits and, worse, so that the social classes become separated.

The Tompkins Square Park riots had a corresponding mix of causes. Few locals could bear to see the homeless ousted from their "tent city" in the park, yet knew the tents were an impossible policing and sanitary problem. Developers and the newly arrived yuppies wanted a clean neighbourhood for their money. This tension led to some genuine pro-homeless leftist activism plus that more vicious activism, hooliganism really, that goes looking for trouble. I began to write about the gap between New Yorkers' terrific private idealism and their cynicism about political solutions.

In poems, as I say, you can make happen whatever you want to: visions are "pure." Spurred by the park riots, I began a long, narrative poem, a satire which assembled disadvantaged characters into what I called *Penniless Politics*. Their party, Spirit, gains power in a brief mirage, before the vision dissolves. The personal, the political, and prosody; these are my recurrent themes here. The poem contained a parodied, politicized version of the life lived round me. It needed a narrative prosody. I took Tasso's *ottava rima*, klutzed its smooth lines to yield a squawking New York effect, and altered the rhyme scheme for street rap tonality.

Penniless Politics had a curious history. It was unforgivable cheek for a white Scotsman-emigré to write about African-American, Hispanic, and related issues. But while I've had various African Americans and Hispanics applaud my poem or say they find it funny, only a couple of white poets, one of them British, have so far objected to its themes, at least to my face.

In fact, I deliberately performed excerpts from the poem before multiethnic audiences so that they would have a chance to catcall. About this time, Bob Holman, poet, theatre

Douglas Oliver "in a favourite Paris restaurant, 'Le Thoumieux,' with Alice Notley and visiting British poet Andrew Crozier, whose Ferry Press published several of my early books," about 1994

director, and arts entrepreneur, got together with Miguel Algerin and restarted the famous Nuyorrican Poet's Cafe on the Lower East Side. The big feature was a poetry slam, a competition which was judged like Olympic skating and had originated, I think, in Chicago. I got in at about slam evening number three, where I was one of the judges, and saw that the café was a perfect mixed audience. In their tolerance, they even let me win one night—the first series was eventually won by the brilliant Paul Beatty with his fast-spiel poems, and Bob's showmanship eventually made the slam an international hit. My definition of a good poetry venue is a place where some homeless zany can walk in off the street and create a few problems. That cafe was such a venue.

Alice had been working on several poem sequences, including her now-celebrated *The Descent of Alette*. I had a Robert Louis Stevenson pastiche ready—*Sophia Scarlett*, a feminist version of a novel Stevenson had projected before his death. And we had begun a newspaper-style poetry magazine, *Scarlet*. It was Gulf War time, so we had plenty to editorialize—and agonize—about; Alice ran a "Dream Gossip" column, which printed everyone's scandalous dreams; Anselm Hollo had a regular filler feature of aperçus called Hollograms; and we were called one of the brightest new small poetry reviews for a while. We serialized *The Descent of Alette* and *Penniless Politics* and our final issue was a fat book, called, to continue our scarlet thematics, *The Scarlet Cabinet*.

The *Cabinet* was like a collection of disparate medieval manuscripts. It collected four poem sequences by Alice, including *Alette*, my Stevenson novel, *Penniless Politics*, and a set of sutras. The idea of the last item was that I would *first* write a half-serious "bible" in sutras, and then create in a novel the heroine who would believe in that bible—she turned out to be a comic goddess. (The novel's theme was New York's urban problems; I've recently paired it with a partner story, entitling the result *The Second-Rate Deity*.)

While this was going on, the cultural historian Patrick Wright came to New York to interview me for the *Guardian* about *Penniless Politics*. Iain Sinclair published a mimeo edition in London, quite like the old days. That edition suddenly received an extravagant review from the playwright Howard Brenton, went into rapid reprint, and a Bloodaxe trade edition resulted.

The great work of this New York period was becoming a substitute father to Anselm and Edmund, and helping them to go to college. Anselm, after some college journalism at Buffalo, is taking a poetry master of fine arts at Brooklyn. Eddie, who had published three mimeo books by the time he was fourteen, is writing poetry in San Francisco. So there's a five-poet family dynasty—their real father, Ted Berrigan, their mother, Alice Notley, the two sons, and the Brit stepfather. The boys are getting good readings and early publication.

Just because my new marriage was so fortunate, my past beforehand seemed an unapproachable topic to write about, lest I say anything to upset my daughters and first wife. Memories had formed into precious mental islands. I took that as theme for the prose-poetry autobiographical sequence that I previously cited in connection with the heron poem. The sequence, *An Island that Is All the World*, was published in my selected fiction and poetry, *Three Variations on the Theme of Harm*, by Paladin in 1990.

At fifty-five years old, I was offered my old lecturing job back at the British Institute in Paris. I had to earn a more secure income and it was important to get back in closer contact with my daughters. Since Alice also needed a change after about twenty years in New York, and the boys were in college and giving us the green light, we took the opportunity.

Nowadays, I can see Kate and Bonny regularly. Kate is an English teacher in the inner London schools and Bonny is project director for the Institute of Psychiatry on a major study of twins; I don't need to worry about lack of contact any more. Instead, we spend all our money phoning the boys in the States, or on plane tickets in either direction.

Alice and I live in a tiny apartment in Paris's Jewish crystal quarter; we write at computers back-to-back, and field calls from streams of overseas visitors. We keep going off to Britain or the United States to perform, and we run a creative writing group which produces its own magazine. Pretty much, we keep in touch with our craft-colleagues, not least with younger poets. I get about a book a year written, though it's stressful to do that sometimes. We find dining out on our own our best entertainment.

Recently, I've turned my writing towards Paris itself: not to find romance in its river bridges but to search out its ethnic diversity and social tensions. Modern Paris, still somewhat a city "of asylum," looks outwards to the world: that's the exciting thing about living here. It will be a tragedy if the fascist National Front manage to blind any more French people to this excitement. Living near the Barbès-Rochouart and Stalingrad areas, for example, encouraged me to write a book of poems about the travails of Africa. Again, I tried to lay that work open as much as possible to criticism of my limited, white viewpoint. Parts of the book appeared in *Penguin Modern Poets 10*, a volume I shared in 1996 with Iain Sinclair and Denise Riley. Iain, who nowadays is a prominent British novelist, has often been helpful to my poetry.

To continue this multicultural theme, in the 1980s I'd been friendly with Paul Celan's widow, the pastel artist Gisèle Celan-Lestrange; her death just before my 1992 rearrival in Paris was a great shock. Living in our current apartment in the crystal quarter led to a group of poems about two great Jewish exiles, Heinrich Heine and Paul Celan.

Other poems explore the extraordinary expansion of Chinatown in the thirteenth *arrondissement*—the expatriate Chinese, whose European distribution of goods is centered on Paris, constitute throughout the world a whole nation in exile. Another long poem goes into the video arcades of the tourist areas, haunted by unemployed young men. Representing the city of Paris could evidently be a work for the rest of a life.

In assembling an American *Selected Poems* for Talisman House in 1996, I presented my poetry much along the lines I have described in this essay. For me, the question of which genre to write in lies constantly open.

Those who limit poetry to their own definitions of it, even if those definitions seem the most modern and progressive available, limit our view of the human species. Surely an artist has to struggle constantly with any restricted view of human possibility imposed by political leaders at world, national, regional, and local levels. Well, that includes leaders within his or her own art, too. Wasn't I dreaming about totalitarian hordes the other night? If I ever get a quotation into the human memory may it be this from the opening of *Penniless Politics*:

All politics the same crux: to define humankind richly.[8]

And the same would be true of poetry.

BIBLIOGRAPHY

Poetry:

Oppo Hectic, Ferry Press (London), 1969.

In the Cave of Suicession, Street Editions (Cambridge), 1974.

The Diagram Poems, Ferry Press, 1979.

The Infant and the Pearl, Silver Hounds Press (London), 1985.

Kind (collected poems), Allardyce, Barnett (Sussex), 1987.

Three Variations on the Theme of Harm (selected fiction and poetry), Paladin (London), 1990.

Penniless Politics, Hoarse Commerce (London), 1991, Bloodaxe (Newcastle), 1994.

(With Alice Notley) *The Scarlet Cabinet* (a compendium of books including Oliver's poems *Penniless Politics* and *Nava Sutra*, and his novel *Sophia Scarlett*), Scarlet Editions (New York), 1992.

(With Iain Sinclair and Denise Riley) *Penguin Modern Poets 10*, Penguin (London), 1996.

Selected Poems, Talisman House (Jersey City, New Jersey), 1996.

Novels:

The Harmless Building, Ferry Press, 1973, revised edition published in *Three Variations on the Theme of Harm*, 1990.

Sophia Scarlett, published in *The Scarlet Cabinet*, 1992.

Criticism and research:

Poetry and Narrative in Performance, Macmillan (London), 1989, St. Martin's (New York), 1989.

---

[8]*Penniless Politics* in Douglas Oliver and Alice Notley, The Scarlet Cabinet, New York: Scarlet Editions, 1991, p. 3. (Also Newcastle: Bloodaxe, 1994).

Len Roberts

1947-

Len Roberts, 1995

I did not write a poem until I was twenty-eight years old, 1975, when I found myself alone in an old farmhouse in Germansville, Pennsylvania, recently separated from my first wife, unsure of who I was or where I was going. So I wrote what I thought then were "letters": to my father, Raymond Richard Roberts, who had been dead six years, having died of a heart attack at the age of forty-seven in 1969; to my older brother, Nicholas Donald Roberts, who was at that time institutionalized at the Albany Veterans' Hospital for another one of his "nervous breakdowns," an ailment which began when he entered the Marines in 1959 and which was to eventuate in his death, also at forty-seven, in 1989; to my younger brother,

Raymond Richard Roberts, who had been raped at the age of eight in 1956 and had turned "queer," as we called it in those days, and who, in 1975, was living what I considered to be a riotous life of homosexuality in Boston; and, finally, letters to my mother, whom I blamed, justly or unjustly, for the downfall of my family, Margery Elizabeth Roberts, the waitress supreme of that time at the Holiday Inn, Watervliet, New York.

Loss, loss, loss filled those letters, and I felt exuberant writing them, thinking then they would never be mailed, the typewriter's keys hot with rhythms and poppings that I know now mark those fortunate times when one truly writes.

I took those letters to Ken Fifer, my office mate in the English Department at Northampton Community College, Bethlehem, Pennsylvania, where I still teach to this day, and showed them to him because for the first time in my life I *liked* what I had written, and because he was the only writer I knew, having published several articles and poems in journals. Kindly, Ken informed me that these were not letters at all, but poems, long-lined poems, and he patiently began to show me the craft of poetry. He spent hours a week with someone he must have thought a complete dunce, but grateful, I think, to at least have someone to talk with about poetry.

We argued, we shaped, we stopped talking, but those letters took form as poems and, at the first public, open reading I had ever attended and participated in, I stood up, thirty years old in 1977, and read two of them aloud to an audience for the first time. I was trembling, more nervous than the day I was married. And, as fate would have it, Allen Ginsberg, my hero of poetry, was in the audience that day at Lafayette College's Roethke Festival. Astonishingly, he came up to me after the reading, said my poems were "authentic, original," and that I should send them to his friend, David Cope, an editor in California. I did, and David passed them on to Bill Mohr of Momentum Press in Los Angeles, who liked them and published my first book of poems, *Cohoes Theater*, in 1981, a slim, fifty-five-page volume of three hundred and fifty copies. And so it began.

My father, mother, and two brothers were the principal characters in those first poems, and they have continued to appear in various guises in many of the poems I've written these past twenty years. By rolling their lives over and over in my mind, so to speak, I think I hope to make some sense of their troubled lives and thus make more sense of my own, which brings me to the beginning.

I was born at 2:15 A.M., March 13, 1947, in the Cohoes Hospital to hardworking, lower-class parents, who lived for the first five years of my life in a third-floor flat at 27 White Street and then moved to 31 Olmstead Street, one row house in a long line of row houses built for the Cohoes Textile Mill workers a hundred or so years before.

I do not remember much about those first five years, but a dominant, recurring image is that of my mother weaving in and out of shadows cast by venetian blinds opening and closing. She had had two nervous breakdowns during that time for which she had been hospitalized and had been diagnosed as having agoraphobia, a fear which caused her, I gather, to drift to and away from the windows, staring out at the streets where she desperately wanted to walk and talk like the other neighborhood women. Ultimately, however, she turned away due to her great fear of what lay in wait for her *out there*. So she imprisoned herself, with her two young sons, to do nothing but keep everything, clothes, floors, our faces, immaculately clean, as though that cleanliness might in itself bring some order and meaning to her life. Two poems which try to capture her fear (and mine) at this time are "Trying to Tell My Mother about Her Guardian Angel" and "She Goes Out to Buy Groceries."

My older brother, Nick, who had been born in 1942 and who, I was to find out years later, was my stepbrother, was in grade school by then. That left my younger brother, Ray, born just fourteen months after me, on May 13, 1948, to be my sole companion as our mother thumped the iron on yet another shirt or held yet another glass to that dim kitchen light to make sure it had no swirls left after she had stuffed it with the drying cloth. If we dropped crumbs or spilled milk, she would slap and scream for hours, and I remember well waiting to hear the sound of my father's boots on the stairs, knowing at least she would probably yell at him, not us, and we might sneak off to our rooms.

My major sense of those years is that of terror, of a hand coming from out of nowhere to slap and pound me for doing something I had no idea was wrong. I may have left a glass ring on the countertop, or dropped a piece of toast from the breakfast table, or perhaps my hair was not parted correctly, or my socks mismatched; the occasion mattered little, for the end result was usually the same, and I would clamber to my room, if I was lucky, to lie on the bed and beg God to let me be strong and last another day.

She must have been in her own kind of hell, too, I see now, for she was terrified of leaving those small rooms where she had to spend day after day with two young children she did not know how to raise. The only way she seemed able to deal with her fear was to

Len (right) with his older brother, Nicholas, and younger brother, Raymond, 1951

clean, clean, clean, and then clean again. She refused to let us go out to play in the backyard because we would get ourselves and our clothes dirty, and yet she would *still* give us three baths a day, her hands rough in our hair as she yanked and rubbed, our tears rolling with the suds down the drain. Everything had to be perfect, the kitchen chairs tucked under the table, not a speck of dust on the dressers, not a hint of a smudge on the linoleum. She had the same "clean-crazy" attitude, as my father would call it, about herself, spending hours trying to get her fingernails clean and polished, trying to give her hair an exact, straight part.

I can remember looking at a cylinder box of Lincoln Logs and wanting to build a cabin, but I was afraid to take the logs out of the box for fear they would scatter on the floor, making her angry. I can see her now, towering above me, making me want to run but knowing there was nowhere I could escape her in those rooms. Some poems which present this atmosphere of terror are "The Roof on White Street," "Little Lives," "The Power of Numbers," and "The Cowboy."

The few moments of freedom I do remember back then on White Street occurred when she would bring us to the rooftop where she would hang out the laundry, three stories up, with those old, brown, curved ceramic tiles edging the border that felt so cool to the touch no matter how hot the tarred roof was. I was amazed

then, as now, that I could actually hang my head over those tiles and look straight down, my first sense of freedom, without her hands suddenly pulling me back. I could escape her sight, I realized, as well as her sudden eruptions of anger and screaming, her swinging hands that left my brother and me, all too often, cowering in some corner or closet.

I do not remember much about my father those first several years on White Street, but I know he worked as a draftman's apprentice at the Cohoes Envelope factory, and that he attended Hudson Valley Community College in Troy, New York, at night to take drafting courses. Many nights I would watch him with his pencil, ruler, and compass, drawing houses and garages on dark blue gridded paper. He seemed happy then, whistling to Tommy Edwards' "The Other Side of the Mountain" and "Please Love Me Forever," but he would eventually quit the courses and the dream, and by the time we moved to Olmstead Street he had become a truck delivery man for White Eagle bakery, the kind of job he would have until the last years of his life.

My freedom increased greatly when we moved to Olmstead Street, for I had turned five and was about to enter school, a fact which thrilled and terrified me, for I had had little contact those first years with other children except for occasional visits from aunts and uncles who brought my cousins to play.

Unfortunately, though, I had not spoken a word until I was nearly three years old, because, as my mother still innocently recalls, the doctor had said there was something in my environment I did not want to communicate with. Thus I had a tremendous lisp which, especially when I was nervous or excited, made the words that came out of my mouth an incomprehensible jumble. Added to that, my parents sent me to St. Joseph's kindergarten, where the nuns and the children spoke, for the most part, French, a language I had never heard before except for a few short exchanges between my father and his mother or father, Selena and Leonard Roberts, who were first-generation French-Canadian immigrants.

So I found myself doubly lost as I sat in that rigid seat, never daring to ask a question or to even attempt answering one, knowing I would not be understood. The dominant image of that classroom experience is of flickering shadows also, like my mother's back on White Street. They flitted against walls and, often it seemed, a hand or ruler would descend with a whack across my head or hands for something I once again had done, unknowingly, wrong.

I am sure, today, that inability to speak back in that classroom, and, to a lesser extent, for the subsequent several years, was one of the determining factors for my love of words. To find the right word, to say it, to be understood, was and still is a miracle that everyone else then seemed to take for granted.

My difficulties with language were not limited to school, however, for my father, by nature a quiet man, under the heavy influence of my mother's domestic fury, withdrew so greatly into himself at night when he came home from peddling bread that he would just sit at the kitchen table for entire hours without uttering a single word. Like a statue, I often thought, except for his hand which now and then lifted a glass of Schaefers or a Lucky Strike to his thin lips, the silent chug or drag, the hand lowered to the table again to lie there completely still.

But I would be remiss if this were the only picture I painted of him, for there would be some nights that he would play his harmonica and sing country-western songs, nights when he would tap dance on the star-speckled linoleum and, sometimes, even get my mother to whirl with him. He could pull a nickel from my ear, a marble from my brother's cuff, and I have never known anyone who could build a higher house of cards, five, six stories up, which, before the lights went out, he would let one of his lucky sons blow down.

I loved watching him dress for a night out on the town, too, putting on his white shirt with French cuffs, gold cuff links with three gold R's glittering across their ivory faces, and the tiepin he would pierce his paisley ties with, the arrow tip pointing toward his heart. He had been an amateur boxer before the war and, although he weighed only about a hundred and fifty pounds, he was physically fit, trim, ready to drop to the floor and do fifty push-ups on a whim.

Those few times I saw him at relatives' parties, he was the one telling the jokes, the one to start the game of horseshoes, the one to pass the beers around. That was when I was very young, though, and by the time we

The author's parents, Raymond Roberts and Margery Lizak, with her son, Nicholas, a year before their marriage, about 1945

were on Olmstead Street a few years he grew more and more silent at that kitchen table, until, at the end, it was hard to tell if he was even breathing. A few poems about these happier times, which were even then tinged with his growing despair, are "The Coin Trick," "Learning to Dance," and "Without Taking Off His Coat."

My mother, on the other hand, made up for my father's increasing silence with her steadily increasing verbal and physical abuse. She had her reasons to be unhappy, too, condemned, it must have seemed to her, to a life of poverty she could not escape, trying to balance a budget that at its best allotted a meal of meat once a week and a daily ration of a glass of milk per son. Added to the continual grind of such penny-watching was her own nervous, easily agitated, fear-ridden personality. She felt that everyone was watching her, in and out of the house, that her hair was always parted wrong, her imitation pearl earrings and necklace glaringly false.

She must have felt, I realize now, that she was a child of St. John's Alley (where she had been raised), probably the poorest street in Cohoes, and that every day of her life was an impossible struggle not to feel inferior to everyone else. Those few times when she took my brother and me out, I could see her literally flinch if any passerby made a sudden movement, terror crossing her face even as her hands clenched ours. As I grew older, I could only imagine what had brought her to such a state, but I do know my father never, not once, hit her.

She, however, did not mind hitting us, and I can still remember the flurry of her hands slapping my face and the five flames her fingers would leave on my cheeks. I would try as hard as I could not to cry but sooner or later the tears would come and I would feel humiliated, completely defeated, ashamed. To this day I will not allow anyone to even give my cheeks a gentle tap.

She would go into fits of rage, screaming, kicking, striking out in any way she could. When we had done something that she considered to be *really* bad, like ripping a pair of pants or dropping and breaking a glass, the belt would appear. One afternoon, after committing some forgotten heinous act, my brother and I were made to strip naked and get on the bed, where she whipped us with the buckle-end of the belt. I can still see that belt whizzing toward my head; I ducked and then heard the dull thwack that it made as it hit my brother full in one eye. He bled quite a bit, which made her stop immediately, realizing for once exactly what she was doing, I think. For a long time we sat on that bed, my brother and me naked, my mother pressing a wet washcloth to his eye, all of us sobbing. This experience appears in my poem, "The Angel on the Wall."

I now attribute her frenzied behavior to lapses into states that bordered, and sometimes edged over into, insanity. Her mother, Helen, who had been married to Horace Trudeau when she was fourteen, also used to go into such fits. I imagine my mother was passing down what she had undergone. These rages were, in her family, part of a larger problem of mental instability, as evidenced by the fact that four of the five sisters of her family had multiple nervous breakdowns. Oddly, none of her four brothers had these mental traumas. (The one sister who didn't have such breakdowns had

"escaped" to Massachusetts with a healthy, intelligent young man; she was about seventeen when she left, and she never returned except to visit.) I have often thought that if my mother had had a better childhood, as well as a better education, she would not have done the things she did.

Another manifestation of her lot in life was and is her inability to speak correctly, a fact which, I am sure, led me to excel in English as a child and which probably led me down the path of poetry. Although she had completed tenth grade at St. Bernard's in Cohoes, my mother continually confused words and phrases to the point that, to this day, I find myself saying "for all intensive purposes" instead of "for all intents and purposes," or I will mix my tenses because she made little or no distinction between past, present, and future, as though time were one big blur to her.

An example of her misuse of language which has stayed with me occurred when she had come home the first night from her job of waitressing at the Holiday Inn and proudly clinked coins onto the tabletop, announcing that these were her "guities." Even at eight or nine years of age, I thought the word did not sound right, but I used it for a few years until I realized one day that she had meant "gratuities."

Like so many others of their generation, my mother and father had reasons for not continuing their education, the major ones being poverty and World War II. One of nine children, my mother quit school and went to work in the textile mills of Cohoes when she was sixteen, thus helping her parents to support her brothers and sisters.

Two stories my mother used to tell us when we were young typify, I think, her younger years. The first one went like this: On a typically cold, upstate New York winter night, she had gone to bed with her sisters. It was freezing, as usual, she would tell us, so cold that she sometimes felt numb. Well, early the next morning, while it was still dark, she woke to her sister screaming and thrashing in the bed beside her. When the light was turned on, she saw a large muskrat in the corner of the room and then, at the foot of their bed, blood. The muskrat, which had evidently crawled up from the canal in front of their row house, had bitten her sister's foot while she slept. My mother could never sleep soundly in that bed again, she would tell us, and we, as children, knew exactly what she meant.

The second story was less dramatic but still shed a good deal of light upon her youth. One night when she was almost asleep she heard some movement downstairs. Her parents were asleep, she thought, so she crept down the stairs to see what was making the noise. There, at the kitchen table, she would whisper to us, were her mother and father eating cake. *Cake,* she would hiss, that they would not share with their children, and which her wages had helped to buy. Whether or not my grandparents were such people, I never knew, but my mother often held up that incident as one she felt most represented her early life: poor, naive, and betrayed.

Shortly after quitting school, my mother became pregnant with Nick in 1941, when she had just turned seventeen. She married Nicholas Lizak, Nick's father, that same year. Lizak, the son of Russian immigrants, supposedly abused

"My mother-to-be, in WAC uniform,"
about 1944

her to the point that she left him to enter the Women's Army Corps (WACS) in 1942, leaving Nick to be raised by her parents. She served two years as a nurse's assistant and was given a medical discharge for a nervous disorder in 1944.

Within a few months of her discharge, she met my father, who had been medically discharged from the Army for malaria and jungle rot. My father helped her to get a divorce from Lizak and also to have the marriage annulled by the Catholic church, since my mother was so young at the time she wedded. After dating for a couple of years, the first of which my father had to spend mostly in bed to recover from his illness, my mother and father married on June 30, 1946, and, from what I have heard from friends and relatives, they had a couple of years of happiness.

My father, too, seems to have been swept up by the events of those times, and he also managed to complete only the tenth grade. When he was seventeen, in 1939, he joined the National Guard and went to work in the Conservation Corps (CC) camps, sending home to his mother and father twenty-five of the thirty dollars he made each month. His father, Leonard Roberts, after whom I am named, was a truck driver and had been in a serious accident. He had broken twenty-two bones and was bedridden for more than a year at that time, so the money was greatly needed. My father worked in the camps until World War II began, when he and many of his friends who made up Company B, 105th Infantry were sent overseas, first to Saipan and then to Guam and Guadalcanal. About half the company was to return.

Although I never once heard him talk about the war, my father bore its effects every day of his life that I knew him. He went in weighing about a hundred and fifty pounds and came out weighing about a hundred pounds, due to severe malaria and jungle rot. He had seen three years of active duty and returned home with a Commendation for Valor and a Purple Heart, neither of which he ever spoke about.

I would sneak into his bedroom to take out the set of big black books with W.W. II embossed in gold letters on their covers, four in the box, to read the pages he had earmarked. The glossy black-and-white pictures of Japanese soldiers buried in sand up to their heads, with bare-breasted native women kneeling next to them doing God knows what, still

"My father in army uniform," about 1941

glares in my head at times. Once I found an old newspaper clipping about three American soldiers who had shot a high-ranking Japanese officer and then eluded search parties for months in the jungle. I never dared to ask my father if he was one of the three, but I often imagined him there, alone, running scared. Several of my poems refer to his war experiences and their aftermath: "The Coin Trick," "The Seven Steps," and "First Rooms," among others.

My parents' plight was not uncommon, I know, but with little education and no skills they became part of our country's massive lower class. Those nights I watched them struggle over a budget which never could be met convinced me at an early age that I would need an education to escape the wheel of poverty they had been born to. Not that our lack of money bothered me greatly then: perhaps a bit ashamed of the hand-me-down clothes, a bit angry because I could not have the ten cents for the Saturday movie all the other kids were going to, a bit desirous of more than that one glass of milk served at the dinner

table. Yet, even though I never articulated the thought until years later, I sensed strongly that I wanted to live a better life than my parents and that education was the way to get it.

My parents knew this, too, and they somehow were able to afford sending their three sons to the Catholic grade school of St. Bernard's in Cohoes even though at that time the tuition was a whopping seventy or eighty dollars a year, or, in our world, two and a half months of rent money. St. Bernard's required a shirt and tie be worn and, if possible, a sport coat, and this dress code mirrored a much fiercer moral and educational code which the good nuns were more than happy to enforce.

So, with a bad lisp and an even worse "command" of English, with no social skills whatsoever due to the virtual confinement of my younger brother and myself with my mother for the previous six years, in 1953 I entered that first grade with its wall of windows and screwed-down desks to begin an education which I believe has literally saved my life. The first thing that struck me was that my teacher *spoke* to me; no yelling, no commanding, just words spoken in a mild voice. I was amazed, and I was determined to do just as the voice said. Unfortunately, I was more ill-prepared than even I had feared, for I could barely be understood when I spoke. This was a situation which the school's third-grade teacher, Sister Ann Zita, who was also a speech specialist, was about to remedy.

When I first met the good Sister, she promptly, without any explanation whatsoever that I recall, brought me to the auditorium stage, where she positioned me at its center and placed a children's version of the Bible, replete with pictures, into my hands. After selecting a verse and repeating the words several times, she would place three marbles into my mouth and ask me to read the passage as clearly as I could. In addition to not knowing exactly what I was reading, I was also terrified of swallowing one or more of those marbles.

I remember *trying* to say "I can't," but nearly choking with the effort. I think I tried to pop the marbles out and I think Sister gently asked me to put them in again; of the process involved I remain unsure, but of the end I am certain—for an hour that morning I attempted to read passages from that children's version of the Bible with three marbles in my mouth. This ritual would continue for three years, an hour each morning before school began, until my memory had been honed razor-sharp and most of my lisp had disappeared or, as I used to joke, had been swallowed with at least a dozen marbles.

Sister Ann Zita also taught me where the letters were formed in my mouth, how to blow out breath to form the "w" of wind, the catch at the back of the mouth that the "q" of quick requires, the mushing of lips to form the "m" of moon and so on and so on and so on. Where would I be today if she had not devoted herself to that young boy trying to form words? I can only imagine the blur the years in school might have become, with my inability to speak clearly, and the resultant failures.

I hated every second of every minute of every hour in that seemingly always-dark auditorium, with Sister's black-winged form moving further and further back until, those last days, she stood in the open doorway with its promise of light. Yet I can think of no greater gift anyone has ever given me, one for which I have been thankful many, many days of my life. I have written several poems about these mornings and the attempts to form words correctly, as in "Correcting the Lisp," "Cursive," and others.

But as the speech program was underway, I had other battles to fight, too, and the war metaphor is not used idly here, for I sensed even then that I was heartily struggling to be the person I could be. Reading was the next hill to be taken, and it was, and still is, a joyous ascent. When I entered that first grade class I was, for the first time in my life, surrounded by books, books, and more books. They were neatly stacked on shelves against an *entire* wall, higher than my head, with even more books piled on top. An incredible sight for someone who came from a house which had *no* books whatsoever, except for the mounds of comic books which my older brother, Nick, would greedily devour instead of doing his homework. He would leave his school books, as he liked to quip, in school, where they belonged. I do not remember once seeing either my mother or father ever reading a book, nor do I ever remember either of them reading to me, at any age.

Books were, however, to become my salvation. I took to them and they took to me, for I did not have to speak, just listen, to commu-

nicate, to connect with someone "out there," and I threw myself into the task the way a swimmer who loves the sea will throw himself into the waves: headfirst, holding my breath, and ready to go.

Because we could not afford to buy books, and because I did not comprehend until about third grade that I could borrow books from the library, I found myself reading my brother's comic books at home, *Superman, Batman, GI Joe, Turok,* and *Lash Larue.* When they were exhausted, I stacked them neatly in a cardboard box which I hefted onto my shoulder and brought to one of my friends' houses to "trade": ah, the wealth of those nights, when we would flip through the other's piles, carefully selecting our favorites. Then the bartering would begin, a crisp, new 10-cent comic for two older ones, or three 10-centers for the 25-cent Giant, until, the bargaining over, I would hoist the box to my shoulder again and walk home, happy with such treasure that I would immediately devour!

I progressed eventually to the *Comic Book Classics* of "Moby-Dick," "The Last of the Mohicans," and "The Tale of Two Cities," among others, the kind of comics not many of my friends would read, so I branched out to George Roberts, who has been a lifelong friend. George is two years older and was a bit set apart from the other kids on the block, more studious, and an athlete, too. So I continued my ritual of trading with him, learning new titles, talking about the meaning of the tales, sometimes even reading away an afternoon together on his screened-in porch.

It was about this time, when I was in third or fourth grade, that I discovered the Cohoes Library, a beautiful, old Victorian mansion situated on top of a wooded hill which had been converted into the town library. I don't know how I found out about it, being sure only that my mother or father did not bring me there. I remember the long windows of sunlight, the gleaming wood floors, and the shelves of books which seemed endless as they glittered across entire walls. I would walk from our row house up Big John's Hill, cross the abandoned Erie Canal blocks which were usually a muddy swamp, then climb the forested hill which was about a half-mile long to get to the library. It never seemed a long walk, then, and I made that trek hundreds and hundreds of times in all seasons, including upstate New York winter days when the snow would be up to my waist and the wind whipping the cap right off my head.

A few years ago I returned to Cohoes with a friend and we made that walk on a pleasant summer afternoon, at the end of which I had to lie down in the grass for a good half hour just to get my breath back! But then it was pure excitement, for I was on my way to another adventure, perhaps with Ivanhoe or the Count of Monte Christo, perhaps with the Hardy Boys or the Wright Brothers. I was not at all interested in poetry then, only in the stories in which I could be brave, ingenious, and free.

One of my most pleasant memories of those times is a sunny summer morning, lying on the floor beside a window, flipping the pages of some book and suddenly being hungry. There, outside, was a big, old pear tree with fruit glistening. I was soon in its branches, my head filled with words, my hands reaching out for what I can still picture as one of the most beautiful red-yellow pears I had ever seen. I can even feel the slightly dangerous leap I had to make to get it, my feet leaving the branch a good twenty feet up in the air, my hand snatching it and my feet landing safely. Then the walk back to the library and the book, my stomach filled with that delicious, plucked fruit.

Reading put me in a realm where I could become who I thought I *really* was, beneath the hand-me-down clothes and the bowl haircut: not the son of just another family on Olmstead Street, but a quick-thinking, heroic young man who was just waiting for an opportunity to prove himself. Although I had no direction for my reading, I managed to read the book *Ivanhoe,* one of my favorites at the time, and I *became* Ivanhoe for hours at a time; or I would become Chingachgook, the Great Serpent in *The Last of the Mohicans,* knowing that my grandfather Roberts's Mohawk blood flowed through me; or I would be my father in one of the *G.I. Joe* series, lost in the jungle of the woods behind my home, starving, dying of thirst, but still searching for the enemy with my BB gun.

Davy Crockett, Admiral Perry, Ahab, they all allowed me to leave my average existence behind and be transported to a more exciting life, the very same kind of transport I feel to-day when I am writing a poem, entering another life, traveling God knows where, but fully alive and raring to go.

Reading became so serious a matter that I began to carry a book around with me wherever I went. I don't think I read those books much in public places, but I remember the safe, secure feeling I'd get from feeling their weight in my back pocket or in my hand, secure enough even when the wealthier citizens of Cohoes would drive by in their large, shining Buicks and Oldsmobiles, never seeming to see me as I sat on that row house porch or stood on a corner, my future unwinding even as they blindly drove by. Maybe I was just a kid from Olmstead Street, but I was a kid with a book.

The attitudes of my parents and neighbors also changed toward me about this time, for the more I read, the more they seemed to respect me. "Respect" may be too strong a word here, but they certainly saw reading as what Andrew Hudgins calls an "unalloyed good." They saw it as self-improvement, a way perhaps to enter the middle class they so desperately wanted to become members of, and so they encouraged me.

My reading also created a kind of distance, though, a separation from my family members and, gradually, from most of the other kids on the block. I was leaving them behind, and ironically I felt that my departure was a kind of betrayal. The more I read, the more I knew, the more distant I grew from them. A bittersweet victory for me, one I've written about in "The Cellar."

My father, when he saw my growing interest in learning, took an active role in teaching me what he could, remaining mostly silent, still, but when he spoke it was usually about something I could learn. Many nights when he'd come home from peddling bread, at that time for White Eagle bakery, he'd empty his breadman's leather purse on the table and have me count the coins and stack them in piles. As I counted, he'd ask me mid-count how much change I'd give if a woman ordered a box of doughnuts at twenty-four cents and a loaf of bread at eighteen cents and handed me a five-dollar bill. For hours, it seemed, he would drill me on math, honing my responses to the point that in eighth grade I took a senior course in Advanced Algebra and Solid Geometry, a subject which I passed with honors at the high school and passed with a seventy-three on the New York State Regent's exam.

His drills were not limited to math, however, for he'd ask me the names of plate, spoon, and knife in French, pay me a penny apiece for memorizing the names of the presidents and their dates of office, show me the countries behind the Iron Curtain on a large, blue faded map. Perhaps my memory magnifies exactly how many nights we'd spend like that, but for a few years it seems he devoted what energy he had left to prompting me in such ways, always staring intently at me through the haze of his Lucky Strike smoke, making me feel as though there were nothing more important that either of us could be doing at that point in our lives. It is that attitude, that caring for knowledge, more than any facts I might possibly have learned, that I carry with me to this day. I have written several poems about those nights of learning, including "Learning on Olmstead Street," "The Equation," and "The Names of the Presidents."

Still, I was your average student in most subjects at St. Bernard's up to seventh grade when, by good fortune and God's grace, I came face to face with the most feared and infamously merciless nun in the entire history of St. Bernard's, Sister James. Stone-faced, as square as a block of stone and just as craggy, Sister James seemed then to be at least eighty but had the power of ten men when she wielded her notorious three-edged brass ruler and let it fall upon some unfortunate wrongdoer's shoulder or head.

Now my brother Nick, who was not a model student, had gone before me into all of the classes at St. Bernard's. Although he was a well-liked, basically good-hearted boy, he consistently refused to do any kind of studying or homework and somehow usually found himself in some kind of trouble that the good nuns, with the help of Father Flannigan, took great pains to straighten out. My reputation as a Roberts-boy, then, preceded me, and Sister James seemed to lift her scraggly eyebrows an inch higher when she first called off my name, her owl-eyes piercing me where I sat with the unworded warning that I had best behave or she would have my head. Or so I thought. But it was Sister James, whom I place as my second "guardian" beside Sister Ann Zita, who created one of those moments of recognition

in my life which has stayed with me more than forty years, one of those moments which swings your life in a definite direction, so that you are never the same again.

I was giving a report on some topic that has escaped into the blankness of time, standing there before my peers, still gangly and awkward, the tallest boy in the class, when my lisp, as it would in such moments of crisis, suddenly snatched a few words from my mouth and brought them out in an incomprehensible jumble. This, of course, created a murmur of laughter, which I tried to escape by laughing with it. It was then that Sister James, who had never, to my memory, given me a single word of encouragement, stood as straight as her blocky frame would allow and began to blast those callous classmates of mine for their derision, saying in no uncertain terms, in words I will never forget, that I would amount to far more than anyone of them could imagine.

In the astonished silence that followed her reprimand, I was left standing as though with the mark of God stamped deeply on my forehead, a mark that left me no recourse but to try to live up to what she had said. I continued with my report, without another lisp or stutter, and sat down to a quiet applause, but in my heart I had been scorched, branded, because Sister James, the Feared One of St. Bernard's, had gone on record as saying that I was important and would actually amount to something. And I began to believe her, such is the power of words!

Things, both good and bad, come to me in threes: three brothers; living at 31 Olmstead Street; my birth date 3/13; my brother Ray's 5/13; my parents married on 6/30; my mother's birth date on 12/30; my son's birth date on 2/13, and so on and so on. ("The Power of Numbers," a poem in my most recent book, *Counting the Black Angels,* is based on this recurrence of threes in my life.) Well, it was no different during my eight years at St. Bernard's, for I had three "guardian" nuns attending me there, two of whom have already been noted, Sister Ann Zita and Sister James; the third, Sister Sylvia, descended upon me when I entered her eighth-grade class.

As I have said earlier, my brother Nick's reputation prepared the way for me at St. Bernard's, and Sister Sylvia's class was no exception. However, I think she was at least mildly surprised that I actually behaved in class and studied. (Several of my report cards from fifth through eighth grades reveal that I consistently received mostly "U's," for Unsatisfactory Behavior, but I attribute that to a misinterpretation of my youthful energies which were so constrained at home. However, the onslaught of sexuality certainly did make me feel that I was "bad," and I have written several poems about the "sinner" I thought I was, as in "Learning Natural Instincts" and "The Way of the Cross.")

Be that as it may, Sister Sylvia, without ever saying so, took me on as her "project" for the year, and with her guidance I actually became valedictorian, much to everybody's surprise, not least my own. Even my attempts at playing basketball were going well, with Father Flannigan himself handing me the MVP trophy when our CYO team won our league's championship. Small peanuts, I know, looking back, but proofs that I might lay claim to a life better than my parents'; that I might own a house and a nice car, not have to worry about spending a dollar.

Well, what a turnaround! And most of it due to Sister Sylvia, who tutored me after school, not only in our class subjects, but on topics she thought would help me to excel in area high school scholarship exams. Not only did she prepare me for such exams, she filled out the applications for me, drove me to them, and waited as anxiously as I did for the results: one four-year scholarship to Keveny Academy in Cohoes; one two-year scholarship to LaSalle Institute, a military school, in Troy; and a two-year scholarship to Christian Brothers Academy in Albany. I selected LaSalle Institute, a school taught by the Christian Brothers of the order of St. Jean-Baptiste de LaSalle; in my sophomore year they extended my two-year scholarship to four years.

I knew then and I know now that I was not any smarter than many of my fellow classmates in that eighth-grade class, but I was blessed because I was selected by that good Sister, and that selection helped to determine the course of my life.

At this point in my life, I had seemed to "arrive." I was getting good grades and could look forward to attending a fine high school. I no longer stuttered, either, except in cases of extreme agitation, and the lisp had nearly disappeared with the warts that had flourished on my hands and arms. The world seemed to stretch out before me except that my mother's

abuse was growing worse and my father's silence was deepening as he sank into his bottles of Schaefers; except that I had in effect lost my younger brother and was about to lose my older brother, two situations I will discuss shortly.

A sense of doom hung over me then; although I never articulated it, I *felt* it, *sensed* it, and it would not go away no matter how many awards I received or how many baskets I made. It was as though a hand hovered above me, not unlike my mother's hand when I was a small child, I know now, and that it would descend with a whack or slap whenever it chose. And there was nothing I could do about it. I tried to capture this sense of impending, arbitrary punishment in poems such as "The Black Hammer," "We Sat, So Patient," and "Joshua's Tent."

I suppose that's why so many of my poems are brooding and dark, with a lightness entering them only since the birth of my son. With his entry into the world I began to shake, at least occasionally, that sense of imminent and arbitrary suffering I had learned so well when young. I acknowledge my gratefulness to Joshua for this release, albeit temporary, in the poem "The Moment."

If there was a punishing hand waiting to descend, however, there was also a helping hand ready to lift me up. Several hands, actually, and they usually belonged to members of religious groups: nuns, brothers, and friars. Such intercession occurred primarily during my grade school, high school, and college years. Later, the same kind of help would come from poets.

But before leaving my younger years behind, I need to recount two painfully important episodes of that period of my life: my younger brother's rape when he was eight, in 1956, and my older brother's initial nervous breakdown in the Marines in 1962. I was, so to speak, my younger brother's keeper for a number of years. One year older, I often had to endure, as older brothers must, his tagging along wherever I went, a particularly resentful practice when I was with my friends. This was especially true those long days of summer when we all went swimming in the Mohawk or Hudson River, or, as it happened one fateful day in 1956, at Carlson's swimming pool in Cohoes.

A young man, about twenty, who had a tattoo and smoked a cigarette a minute, and who was thus very exotic and interesting to

Ray and me, took what seemed a friendly interest in us, to the point of buying us candy and letting us sprawl on the grass beside his and his girlfriend's towels. It was a hot day, with dandelion fluff flying everywhere, the water clear, and our bellies full.

As the time to go home drew near, though, Ray balked and would not leave. He demanded to stay with his new friends. Being the older brother, I was responsible for making sure he was home for supper, so I put him in a headlock and dragged him out of Carlson's and halfway up Mohawk Street, until he broke free and ran back despite my threats. Disgusted, I walked home and told my mother what had happened, and we both spent the next few hours waiting for his return.

When he did show up, he was sobbing at the door, scratched, bruised, trying to say what had happened, mumbling even as my mother made him stand, naked, on top of the kitchen table, presumably so she could see him better beneath the kitchen light. I remember her head bent to examine his penis and balls, and, with a sense of discovery, the bite marks on his thigh. Even more clearly I remember her saying, as she held his private in her hands, "Now he'll be queer," repeating it over and over until my till-then silent father dragged her out into the hallway where their voices rose and fell to the rhythm, it seemed, of my brother's crying. He had, with a knife to his throat, been raped and then made to suck on our new friend's penis for hours along the bank of the Mohawk River.

The police were called, the man picked up and imprisoned, eventually for ten years since this had been his third conviction for such charges, but I was left to blame myself for years for what had happened to my brother. It was I who should have brought him home. It was I who should have known what the young man wanted. Or so I thought because no one *ever* talked about the incident afterward, even those nights I'd wake screaming from a nightmare in which the tattooed man was coming to get me with his knife because I testified against him.

Ray, as my mother had prophesied, did become "queer" a few years later. The first I'd heard about it was from a friend who told me he was blowing boys for a dollar a head, down in the front-left side of the Cohoes Theater during matinees. Stunned, I was too afraid to

Brother Nick in Marine uniform, about 1960

tell my mother and father, and I was too ashamed to ask Ray if it were true. So I did what I had learned to do from my family: kept silent. When he was about twelve or thirteen, he had bisexual relations, I know, because he would bring young girls to our flat when our parents were out working. But the girls turned to boys by the time he was fourteen or so and he fully asserted his homosexuality, an assertion which was to cause him great pain and castigation in the small, conservative town of Cohoes.

To my shame, I shunned him, too, calling him "fruitcake" and "homo," or telling him to go put on one of his dresses, just as the other boys did when he tried to tag along. Since we shared a double bed, I grew afraid that he would try to touch me and so I drew an imaginary line down the middle and forbade him to cross it. If his leg or arm fell on my side, even in sleep, I would thrust it back, an action which often ended up in a battle royal which he, as the younger and weaker brother, was fated to lose. I can't imagine what must have raced through his mind those nights when

I, who was his only companion for so many years, not only rejected him but physically beat him for what I homophobically considered a transgression. He must have felt so completely alone. . . . The thought of it today weighs my head down.

At this point in his life, Ray started using drugs that many of us were to experiment with only several years later, and he made "friends" with older boys from nearby colleges who would come to pick him up in their cars. My parents were so lost in their own private hells that they didn't seem to notice what was happening to him, or they didn't care.

When my mother left my father in 1962, Ray went with her to Troy, where he became more anonymous and could drift more freely, a drifting which took him eventually to San Francisco, Miami, and many other cities. He finally ended up in Boston where he now works as a nurse's aide and lives a quiet life with his longtime lover, Paul. I have written several poems about Ray's rape and its subsequent effects on his life, most specifically in "Brothers" and "In the Kitchen."

This was the first event in a series of what I consider to be a stripping away of my family members, leaving me, finally, without a family at the age of twenty-one. The second of these events was to occur in 1959, when I was in

The author's brother Ray, California, about 1971

seventh grade. My older brother, Nick, on his seventeenth birthday, had an argument with my mother about some lost topic, but its effects were to be disastrous. The next day, February 11, 1959, he joined the Marines, left within a few weeks, and I never saw my brother again as I had known him those first twelve years of my life. Nick had served in the Marines for three years, stationed on Okinawa since 1960, before he came home with what the doctors later called a nervous breakdown, that generic term I knew all too well from my mother's breakdowns.

I did find out, years later, that Nick had been given seven electro-shock treatments that first year of his illness, and that one of his recurring diagnoses would continue to be "disorder of brainwave patterns." No wonder. When he did return home in 1962, he would seem normal for weeks at a time but then would suddenly disappear, as I would learn, to the Albany Veterans' Hospital for therapy.

He became a chain-smoker and, for a long time, a heavy drinker. He also would have severe mood swings, occasioned, I'm sure, as much by the drugs he was taking as by his illness. Nick, who had always been a cheerful, kind brother, could suddenly turn into a threatening, angry young man. He never once hurt me, or any member of my family, but he was very strong and I grew afraid of him, keeping my distance as much as I could. This situation only lasted for about a year, though, for when my mother left with Ray in tow, Nick rented his own apartment where he would live when he wasn't in the V.A. Hospital.

Once again, true to my family's pattern, no one spoke about what had happened to Nick, or why, or how. Rumors would float to me now and then from his friends who had been with him in the Marines or who had kept in touch with him, rumors of three men raping Nick during basic training, of his parachute straps entangling during a night jump, of his girlfriend, Bunny, writing him a Dear John letter . . . but nothing that was ever confirmed, so that part of Nick's past seems as mysterious to me as the ever-present hand I felt hovering above my head in those days. It had fallen on my brother Ray, and now on my brother Nick. It seemed only a matter of time till it fell on me.

Many times those first years, and in subsequent years, I visited Nick, sometimes when he was "out" (he had managed to get married twice and to have three children during these periods), sometimes when he was "in." Visits at the hospital were especially painful, watching him take those drug-induced tiny steps, his lack of recognition sometimes when he saw me, fellow patients stealing his cigarettes while we talked, once, even, an old-timer crapping on the floor just beside Nick's bunk. At forty-seven, Nick's age when he finally died of emphysema, he looked and acted seventy-five. I was glad he died, as I know he was, too. I have referred to Nick's breakdown and his subsequent twenty-seven years of hell in many poems, most fully in "Talking to the Poison Sumac," "Building the Barn Door," and "While the Tractor Idled."

So by the time I entered high school I had virtually lost my two brothers and was about to lose my mother to divorce and my father to a steadily worsening alcoholism. Fortunately, I was doing well in school and sports, and I was able to turn my energies outward.

During seventh and eighth grades I had developed a love for basketball, a love fostered by my friend, George, who lived on Van Vecten Street, and whose backyard faced my backyard across an alley. Just about every Saturday morning, in all seasons, George would be tapping on my bedroom window at about 8 A.M., getting me out of bed to play ball. In winter, we would shovel snow from the macadam, wear boots and gloves, slide on our drives, and fall on our jumpshots; in summer, we would be washed with sweat several times a day—for we would play *all* day—as our feet burned and our bodies browned, and we loved every second of it. George, two years older, was the high scorer for Keveny Academy's varsity, and he taught everything he could to a stumbling beginner.

I vividly remember those Sunday afternoons in the late '50s and early '60s when we watched the Celtics demolish any team they went up against: Cousy with his no-look passes, Russell with his stuffs, Casey Jones kissing the ball off the glass from twenty feet out, and the youngster, John Havlichek, eternally diving for the ball to make the clutch save. Then, when the game ended, I'd run down to the gym to play our weekly CYO game, pivoting like Big Bill, tipping the rim, now and then even putting a jump shot in. Our team was undefeated, I was its center and high scorer—such fame that my

grandmother Roberts would cut out the two-inch notice at the bottom of the Cohoes Section of the *Troy Record News* that would have my name and points scored in five-pica type! To this day I have that scrapbook she so dutifully gathered together for me and, when my children reach the appropriate cocky age, I like to take it out and show them I was not always an old, slow man.

Books, basketball, and, shortly, girls were to take my life over completely, and I would leave my first family behind (or so I thought) for the rest of my life.

The high school I chose to attend, LaSalle Institute in Troy, was an all-boys' military academy with strict academic requirements and a reputable sports program, so I was able to throw myself wholeheartedly into that life and forget, relatively, the turmoil my family members were caught up in. I could not escape their unrest for long, though, as I was made to realize dramatically in my sophomore year, when I discovered that my mother had a lover where she worked, at Marshall Ray's Coat Factory in Troy.

I met her new man, Jim Terry, one late, rainy afternoon in the fall of 1962. I had been studying at the kitchen table when someone started banging on the door—loud, insistent banging. When I opened it, a big man, about six feet tall and weighing well over two hundred pounds, was standing on our porch. He asked if "Marge" was home and I said no, at which point he began to sob, repeating over and over "I love her, I love her."

It took me a few seconds to realize he was drunk and the "her" he was referring to was my mother. The rain was pouring down on him as he stood there without a jacket or umbrella, and I could not take my eyes off the drops as they hit his face and mixed, I suppose, with the tears. Then I saw the black car idling behind him on the cobblestones of Olmstead Street, and I heard another man's voice yelling, "C'mon Jim, he's just a kid."

It was then, and only then, that I realized I had grabbed a baseball bat, which I always kept in the corner of the hallway, and was trying to lift it to get a good swing at Terry. He held my arm down though and was about to hit me with his free hand when the other man's voice blurted out. Terry threw me back, slammed the door, and hopped into the car to drive away. I can still see the fumes of the exhaust rising in clouds a lighter gray than the rainy afternoon, as I stood on that porch with the new knowledge sinking in.

That day marks my final separation from my mother and her troubled life. It turned out that she had told my father she would be leaving him, but he had begged her to stay for a few months to see if they could work things out. An insane arrangement, I thought then and now, one which I did not help any by insulting her whenever I got the chance; for instance, when I walked up the stairs I would yell "tramp, tramp, tramp" as loud as I could, hoping that she would come out into the hallway to say something to me. She never did.

I was glad she was leaving, especially after I'd learned that she and Terry had been lovers for the previous two years. Terry, a member of what was then called the "Irish Mafia" of Troy, was a petty thief and troublemaker, and it seemed right to me that she would be with him. My attitude did not help my father's cause, of course, but I don't think anything could have.

They were a tense few months, for Ray had sided with my mother, and I with my father; the battlelines had been drawn, the children recruited, and the war raged, ending only on the day she left. I was hurt, although I didn't know it then, thinking my anger was just that, pure anger. It took me years to realize my mother had been formed by her past, as we all are to some extent, and that she was as much a victim as a victimizer. That knowledge helped me to forgive some, if not all, of what she did.

Nothing could help my father at this point, though, for when she left he stared longer and harder at his glasses of beer, beginning his long decline in earnest, managing to kill himself by drink within seven years.

I turned outward, to school, sports, and lovely girls, mostly, unfortunately, the former two, although I tried desperately for the latter, sometimes with success. I caught the 6:30 A.M. bus from Cohoes to Troy, returning home on the same bus about 8 P.M. each night to go directly to my room where I would study until about midnight and sleep, repeating the cycle every school day of the week. I would spend the weekends working, practising a sport, or dating, so I was rarely at home.

Despite the family troubles, especially my father deteriorating before my very eyes, my overall impression of those four years of high school is of freedom and fun. I was able to keep my grades on the honor roll for each term and thus keep my scholarship, and I played basketball, football, and a year of tennis and a year of track, with a good deal of marching and dating in between. As a military academy, LaSalle required we wear uniforms, march in formations, learn to use rifles and read maps, the whole shebang.

That spring of my sophomore year, 1962, I borrowed George Roberts's license (he was then eighteen) and applied for a lifeguard position at Thompson's Lake Campsite in the Hedelberg Mountains just north of Albany. It was a state-run campground and I had to be eighteen to get the job, so when the interviewer asked to see some proof of age, I showed him George's license, keeping my thumb over the "George." Unbelievably it worked and I half ran from that government building and hopped into George's car—he was waiting anxiously to see if we could pull it off, too—and we duly celebrated, lying about my age again at a nearby bar.

It was an incredible summer, my first experience of complete freedom with, incredulously, droves of nursing students from St. Peter's Nursing College of Albany camping there throughout the season. And I was, albeit under false pretenses, eighteen! Able to drink, to stay out as late as I wanted for I had my own lifeguard's cabin, and to do just about whatever I cared to do. I enjoyed it so much I returned there as lifeguard the next summer, and spent the following three summers lifeguarding at other beaches and pools.

When I returned home in late August, my father and I set up our living relationship which was to last until his death seven years later in 1969. Although my social life was as full as a young man could want, those seven years were scarred with watching my father sink deeper into his death, a sinking neither I nor anyone else could keep him from. Over those seven years he lost job after job, twice for embezzling money, his last being a salesman for suntan lighting fixtures that the company sent men to pick up the day after his death. He drank more and more and ate less and less, weighing only a hundred and five pounds at his death.

He would pick up odd jobs now and then, hanging wallpaper or painting, but then he'd

*"Me, a junior in high school, wearing
LaSalle Institute uniform,"* 1964

drink the money away in a binge or throw it
away at the Saratoga Race Track with the hope
of somehow winning his life back. The truth
was, though, that he loved my mother and he
simply did not care about living anymore after
she'd left. I think he hung on as long as he
did, with those occasional spurts of ambition
and work, because he felt obligated to provide
me with a place to live and eat, but he was
not even able to give that after the first few
years. This phase of my father's life left a deep
imprint on me and I've probably written more
poems about his last years than any other topic,
including such poems as "When the Dead Speak,"
"He's Alone," "Pissing in the Wind," "Easy to
Say, Easy to Say," "Burning the City," "The Million
Branches," "Clear January, zero degrees, my last,"
and "The Sparrow and *the Winter's Nest of Snow."*

So I worked every weekend at whatever I
could get, a mainstay being an usher at the
Cohoes Theater, the title of my first book of
poems. Later I would be promoted to Assistant
Manager, which meant I got to lock up at night
after the manager had gone home early. If I

wanted to eat, I worked, and I had a huge
appetite then. I remember Saturday afternoons,
standing in the shadows near the storage room
of the theater, wolfing a big bag of popcorn
between my walks along the aisles, washing it
down with gulps of water because I had not
eaten since the previous afternoon.

And I remember Mary, who ran the Bar-B-Q
Chicken Palace catty-corner to the theater, waving
me over about noontime on Saturdays, when
the little kids were all lined up outside the
ticket booth. She would hand me a white bag
with half a barbecued chicken and dressing in
it, with thick slices of sweet cornbread, and a
little, plastic covered container of gravy I would
pour over it all when I had a break and could
sit and eat in the projectionist's room.

Mary knew, as did just about everyone from
that part of Cohoes, that I was on my own,
and I was continually surprised by wonderful,
thoughtful gifts on our row house doorstep,
like Mrs. Brown's (believe it or not) pans of
baked beans, and Mrs. Tremblay's smoked sau-
sage. Gifts appeared in other forms, too. Mr.
Bisaillon, for whom I worked blacktop whenever I could, once stopped his car and handed
me a ten-dollar bill "to go out with a pretty
girl." These were people who could barely pay
their own bills, who rarely ate meat because it
was too expensive, and yet found something
to share with me.

My grandmother and grandfather Roberts
helped, too. Nearly every morning on my way
to school my grandmother's head would pop
from their second-storey window to toss down
a piece of fruit or a candy bar, even in those
blue-black upstate New York winter dawns when
ice threatened to form on the tip of your nose
with every breath. One poem I've written recently about this daily ritual is "Anointing Her
Five Senses."

Those summer evenings, after a full twelve-
hour day of working blacktop with my grandfather—my feet burning, my skin on fire from
the oily fumes of that 360-degree blacktop shooting from the truck's chute into my wheelbarrow—my grandmother would have dinner waiting for "her men," as she would call us: fried
chicken, corn on the cob, thick homemade bread,
and quarts of lemonade which we'd sit on the
front porch to eat and drink. Neighbors would
stop to talk, the streetlights would come on
with their mellow buzz, and there I was, a young
man in a community of workers. God, how I

miss that feeling of being part of something bigger than myself. So, when I finally came to write at twenty-eight, how could I not people my poems with these kind souls? "The Block," "Working Blacktop," "Pushing Cars Out of the Snow," "Telling the Girl Story While Shoveling Snow," and other poems attempt to describe these days.

My father left 31 Olmstead Street, on and off, beginning my junior year in high school, to live with a woman who sold women's clothes at Cohoes Manufacturing, and who could drink at least as much as he could. I would see him from time to time. Once, I came across him with three other men, sleeping a drunk off in a huge, blue Cadillac convertible parked behind Desormau's parking lot. The top was down, whiskey and beer bottles were strewn all over the seats, and the sun shone on four heavily bearded, close-eyed faces. It must have been quite a binge, I remember thinking as I walked quietly past.

I paid the rent when he didn't, and I provided my own clothes, food, whatever I needed, from sixteen onward, and I learned the necessity and value of work as well as an ingrained sense that I can only rely on myself, an attitude which can be extremely frustrating for those who love me. This value of work shows up in several of my poems but can be seen most clearly in the previously mentioned blacktop poems of *From the Dark* and in "Shoveling While the Snow Keeps Falling."

In my senior year of high school I was faced with the fact that nearly all of my classmates were going to college, but I had no resources and little knowledge of how to go about it. Most of my friends were from families with parents who themselves had gone to college, so the step was as natural and inevitable as breathing. No one from my family, on the other hand, had graduated even from high school. We were expected to go to work, or to enter the service, two options I was seriously considering when Brother Michael, my English teacher for the sophomore and junior years, came to my rescue, giving me books to help me prepare for New York State's Regents Exams, which everyone had to take. I studied hard, he'd check my work, and, when the results came in, I was granted a full four-year Regents Scholarship which I could use to attend any school in the state. Luck? I don't think so, and I place Brother Michael, gentle and caring soul that he was,

with the triad of Sisters from St. Bernard's: Sister Ann Zita, Sister James, and Sister Sylvia.

In determining what college to attend, I once again turned to my friend George Roberts as a model; he was attending Siena College in Loudonville, just seven miles from Cohoes, and he liked it. So that's where I went, to be taught this time by yet another religious group: the Franciscans.

Although I entered Siena in 1965, in advanced placement in all subjects except math and Spanish, my freshman year was incredibly mediocre, with "C" being the usual grade, or variations thereof. I knew I was busy and did not have too much time to study, but only when I went to the school counselor for help— for if I fell below the "C" average I would lose my scholarship—did I realize how many things I was doing wrong. He had a list of ten things that could hurt a freshman student's academic performance, and I was doing all of them, from having a steady girlfriend, owning my own car, and working more than twenty hours a week to playing a sport.

I was, however, unwilling to give any of those things up, and my sophomore year was just as undistinguished as my freshman year, but I managed to get through it *with* the Regents intact. During these two years my father's state worsened, I had not talked with either my mother or younger brother, and my visits to Nick in the V.A. Hospital were close to intolerable. I lifeguarded during the summers, worked as assistant manager at the Cohoes Theater on weekends the other three seasons, and did as many odd jobs, such as painting and small blacktop repairs, as I could get. I was dating a girl seriously and thought I was in love, an idea easy to live with then because a group of my friends, whom I played ball with, dated many of this girl's friends, and we all had a good time when we went out. My life, again, seemed to be straightening out.

But the Vietnam War was raging in that autumn of 1968 when I returned to Siena to sit in a class where, one day, I found two of my classmates gone, drafted into the Marines, leaving the rest of us wondering who would be next. That afternoon I went to the Coast Guard Reserve recruiting station and put my name on the list, and, a month later, in mid-October, I was called for basic training. I dropped from my classes, with Father Amadeus Fiore, the English Department Chair, assuring me I would not lose the semester from my Regents Scholarship, and I went to Cape May, New Jersey, to begin what turned out to be nearly a full year's active (boring) duty and three years of reserve (boring) duty.

After seeing what had happened to my father as a result of World War II and to my brother as a result of his being in the Marines, I was, to say the least, wary about entering the service. Three of my friends had already died in Vietnam by that time, and I was determined that I would not be added to the list.

Not that I was smart enough to see that we should not have been fighting that war in the first place. To tell the truth, I didn't give it all that much thought then, for I was too busy working and studying. I wasn't fearful, either, although that probably would have changed immediately had I been sent overseas. In fact, several of the guys I had played football and basketball with were in Vietnam and, at times, I half thought I might go, too. What kept me from making that mistake, though, were the memories of my father's malaria-ridden and jungle-rotted skin at the kitchen table, and Nick's drooling lips that moved incoherently when he struggled so desperately to say something that made sense. There was no way in the world that I was going to end up like them. No way.

I think I flitted along the edge of a breakdown, though, or whatever it might be called, while I was in basic training. Because of my military training at LaSalle and during my two years of ROTC at Siena, I was made master-at-arms for our company, Company C, which basically meant that I was responsible for teaching my fellow recruits the manual of arms. If, on the drill field, our bolts did not click shut simultaneously (and they rarely did, at least at the beginning), then I was reamed out by Chief Turner and, in turn, I was to ream out my fellows.

One of the tricks then was to put the unsynchronized recruit's thumb into the chamber and let the bolt slam back on it, thus teaching him the necessity of remaining alert to all commands. The drawback was that the thumb might be broken; at the very least it would swell tremendously and give its bearer a most difficult time on the training field. A tried and proven method, I was told by Turner one night when he was nearly incoherently drunk,

one I had to use on a recruit, Tommy Rivers, who kept screwing up. Tommy was *just* seventeen, and as my luck would have it, he slept in the bunk above me. Every night he would sob, quietly, but for hours at a time. And I was supposed to smash his thumb.

Well, the upshot of all this is that I refused and Turner had his way with me for several nights, once even marching me into the Atlantic, with full pack, on a cold Cape May November night. He did give me an about face, though, as the waves got to my chest. One of those nights, when I had gotten about two hours of sleep, the guard whom I was supposed to relieve of duty came to wake me. I don't know exactly what happened next, but when I "came to," I was on top of this poor fellow, smashing him in the face again and again. There was blood everywhere. The first thing I remember is being held by four or five other members of the company, and looking down to see the guard's body and blood.

The next morning Turner called me into his office and, for the first time in the eight weeks I had known him, spoke with a calm, almost kind voice. He informed me that I had apparently acted in my sleep, taking my frustrations out on the man I was supposed to

Len Roberts (top row, second from left), with fellow Coast Guard recruits at Port Security School, Yorktown, Virginia, 1968

relieve of guard duty. Then he slid a sheet of paper toward me and said, if I signed it, I would probably get a medical discharge from the service. I could go home! No more marching, lousy food, womanless nights. But then my father's, mother's, and brother's discharges flashed before me and I knew I couldn't accept it, regardless of the possible effects of my decision. Turner accepted my decision but told me I would be gone if another incident occurred. It didn't. In fact, I was designated marksman for the company, a member of its four-man swimming team, as well as its master-at-arms when we received Honor Company Award upon graduation.

I've spent some time telling this because it was one of the few times when I felt that I actually skirted around a nervous breakdown, thus giving me an insight into my mother's and brother's worlds. It was terrifying, knowing I couldn't control myself like that, and it helped me to understand their fears better. It also taught me something about myself. Before Turner offered me that discharge, I thought I would have done just about anything to get out of there. Almost anything. But I refused to get out the way my mother and brother had. I needed to know I *could* deal with similar pressures and come through. A poem of mine which connects my time in the service with my father's is "First Rooms."

I spent most of the following year with easy duty as a Port Security Guard, standing watch over foreign ships, inspecting cargo, and running a forty-footer up and down the Delaware River looking for oil spills.

After my stint in the Coast Guard I returned to Siena with a new attitude and made Dean's List my last two years, with just about straight A's my final year. I even took the one creative writing course I've had in my entire life, a fiction writing seminar that was taught by one of the few women professors on campus, Ms. Ann Barker. Ms. Barker was "older," a good twenty-five years of age, and she was absolutely gorgeous.

I had been reading and loving Hemingway's short stories, one of the few authors I liked during those four years of college, and so I tried writing my own "war" stories, although the closest I had come to a war was driving that patrol boat up the Delaware River. "The staccato of machine gun fire," and "lying wounded in the dust" and so on and so on

filled those pages I would gladly read aloud during class because *she* was listening! I realized shortly thereafter just how horrible those first attempts were, and I did not even try to write "creatively" again for eight years, not until I had finished my doctoral program.

But, again, I was at a crossroads. I was about to graduate from college and was unsure of what to do with the rest of my life. Should I accept a job in New York State government which was waiting for me when I graduated, get married, play ball in the Cohoes men's league, and live happily ever after? Should I attend Albany Law School, which had a place for me and do all of the above, but with more money? I was leaning toward the latter when, one hot summer afternoon of 1969, another one of my "guardians" showed up once again to change the direction of my life. I was relaxing during a break from my maintenance job at Siena, my feet on the maintenance desk, when Father Vianney Devlin, a Franciscan with whom I had taken several English courses, walked abruptly in and snapped a white envelope down in front of me. "Consider it seriously," he said, and then as abruptly walked out.

In the envelope was a two-year assistantship to the graduate English Department of the University of Dayton, if I wanted it, and a note from Father Vianney telling me, in short, that I would make a much better English teacher than lawyer or government worker. Was this, again, my angel? Or was this the devil in disguise, for I had my eyes set on making money, buying a nice house, nice car, the whole pie, and here was an offer to get a master's degree in English?

No tough decision, I thought, but by this time I had learned not to ignore these messengers; I could not dismiss Father Vianney that easily. I thought and I thought and I thought, and eventually decided that, in truth, I was not ready to be married, and that, in truth, I did not want to work in an office the rest of my life. The teaching life, at a college level, *did* appeal to me, and so I decided to accept the white envelope's and Father Vianney's offer. I would leave for Dayton in January 1970, since I had to finish an extra semester at Siena to make up for the time I'd spent in the reserves.

My life in Cohoes was coming quickly to an end, with all of the familiar friends and streets, as well as with my family, but how much of an end I was to find out only a few months later, on November 2, 1969, when my father died of a heart attack. Actually of alcoholism, which literally and slowly killed him during those seven years after my mother had left.

I received the call while at the Coast Guard station, and it was my duty to inform my mother, whom I had not seen those seven years, of his death. I clearly remember walking into the Holiday Inn in Watervliet, still dressed in my uniform, soaking wet from a rainstorm, and seeing her walk toward me with a pot of coffee in her hands. Such a domestic scene, I thought, but even irony escaped me when she finally recognized me and nearly fainted on the ugly red carpet. When I told her, she actually wept, but as I left I felt that I had been talking with a complete stranger.

The break was complete, then, that January of 1970 when I packed my old Plymouth with everything I owned and headed for the great Midwest, in search of something I could not even put a name to.

For the previous nine years of my life, I had attended an all-boys military academy taught by Christian Brothers, an all-men's college taught by Franciscans, with about a year of military service thrown in for good measure, so when I got to the University of Dayton, which in 1970 was listed in *Playboy* as one of the top ten "most partying" schools in the nation, I felt like I had entered paradise. Knowing no one, with no one knowing me, I was completely anonymous for the first time in my life, and I devoted myself totally to partying, first, and studying, second, with breathing spaces for a few games of basketball in between.

Those two years are a blur of parties, papers, and some very good intramural basketball games, for I was still trying to play, although my knees were weak and my breath going. I was also teaching two freshman composition courses, which I greatly enjoyed, confirming Father Vianney's hunch that I would be at home in the classroom. My life seemed to be righting itself again, with no clouds on the horizon, which could be seen a long way off in Dayton, Ohio.

I took as many courses as I could in modern American literature, loving especially Hemingway, Faulkner, and O'Neill (especially *Long Day's Journey into Night*) as well as Thomas Wolfe, who at that time of my life seemed to be the most poetic of fiction writers! Still, I had little interest in poetry, although I liked well enough T. S. Eliot's shorter poems such as "The Hollow Men," "Gerontion," and "The Gift of the Magi," and I appreciated Frost's and Auden's work, although I was not overwhelmed by any of it. I never dreamt of attempting to write a poem even then, consigning myself to the role of teacher of literature without any regret.

Until I met Herbert Martin, an African American who was poet-in-residence at the University and, who, as it happens, just retired this past year, in 1996. Herb is twelve years older than I, which made him about thirty-five then, and he was quite a character, singing in the corridors, dancing ballet although one leg is two inches shorter than the other, performing star roles in local plays, and, to top it all off, a *poet*. Now I had never met a writer before, and so I was fascinated to see what the creature was like. At some party or other I introduced myself to Herb and we became fast friends, as we are to this day, with me tagging along as he sailed through those days with published poems and, by that time, two published books.

Herb introduced me to contemporary American poetry, giving me books by such poets as James Wright and Galway Kinnell, Adrienne Rich and Allen Ginsberg, John Logan and Anne Sexton. Where had I been the previous twenty-three years of my life? I was overwhelmed, delighted with what I read and came back for more and more, which Herb smilingly piled into my hands, knowing, I think now, that I was handling the red coal and might very well one day pop it into my mouth, being changed evermore.

The thought of writing a poem still never occurred to me, for I placed poets in another, much higher realm than the one I lived in, but I gathered their riches and, by the time I left Dayton, had a good-sized box full of books by my favorites, much like that prized box of comics I used to hoist onto my shoulders those cold upstate New York winter nights to bring to my friends for trading.

In August 1972, I also left Dayton with a master's degree in English, two years of teaching assistant experience, and an engagement to Denise Geiger, who, on November 12 of that year, was to become my wife. Denise was a junior when I first met her, and by the end of her senior year we had decided to marry. I had been offered a fellowship to the English doctoral program at Lehigh University, Bethlehem, Pennsylvania, and we rented a small farmhouse in Whitehall, about ten miles from the University.

I thought it was time for me to settle down and Denise represented the stability I'd longed for. Her family was well-to-do, as we used to say back in Cohoes; her father was vice president in charge of national sales for Dunn and Bradstreet. Very nice house, cars, clothes, just about everything I had always considered to make up the "good life." (Our wedding, which was the fanciest one I'd ever attended, had nearly five hundred guests.) To top it all off, Denise was very pretty, kind, smart, and honest. What more could I have asked for? It seemed perfect.

From the start, however, I singlehandedly demolished our marriage, which lasted three years, a period of my life which shames me most.

Denise worked as an assistant buyer at Hess' Department Store in Allentown, virtually supporting us, while I studied, cheated, lied, and did just about everything a decent person would not do. I found myself *bound* to another person, and I could not live with it, or, as I remember shouting during one of our arguments, "I did not *want* to be loved by anyone." Fear of commitment? Memory of my mother leaving? Pure self-indulgence? I went round and round with such thoughts until, with the complex fatigue such circlings bring, I gave up and ran out. I haven't written much about our failed marriage and divorce, but one very early poem, "Ritual," does present those awful times fully.

The year before we finally separated, we had bought an old farmhouse in Germansville, Pennsylvania. It was completely run down, needing all new plumbing and wiring as well as a new roof and interior walls. The land was seven acres, with a forty-by-sixty barn and a hundred-and-twenty-foot long lumber shed that was twenty feet wide. I threw myself into that house the way I should have thrown myself into my marriage—wholeheartedly—and by the end of the year it was just about done.

Although I hired a plumber to do most of the pipe work, I managed to learn how to do the rest by trial and error and by asking at the local hardware store for tips. I learned to hook up and run wire, put up walls (even getting the spackling right!), sand floors, and replace rotten rafters before putting new plywood and shingles on the roof.

I loved doing the work and, since then, I have rebuilt or remodeled, depending on who you talk to, three houses, the last being the one my family and I presently live in.

During the years since then I have often thought of how similar building a poem is to building a wall, a room, a house. The same attention to detail is needed, the same patience, the same understanding that some days I couldn't drive a nail straight to save my life nor put down one good word. I imagine that's why I have so many poems about building things, such as "Building the Barn Door," sections of "Pathways," "The Tools," and "Considering the House," among others.

That last year of our marriage, 1975, in addition to working on our house, I was teaching a five-course composition load at Northampton Community College, with two extra courses per semester for additonal pay, as well as advising the school newspaper and literary magazine, activities I would continue for the next ten years. I was also finishing my dissertation, ironically titled "The Wound of Love: An Analysis of Allen Tate's 'Seasons of the Soul,'" which had become a heavy rock about my neck.

My life was so busy that I had to allocate two hours a week just for myself, Sunday afternoons, so I could watch the NBA game of the week. That didn't leave much time for Denise and me, and I see now that I was running from her with that flurry of activities, running from marriage itself.

I was at the bottom of something dark and dank, and it had an awfully familiar stink to it, a stink I stirred up even more by writing those "letters" which turned out to be my first poems. Perhaps I had to hit bottom before attempting to understand who I was and what I had been doing, but 1975 and 1976 were dark years where the only light appeared in the form of scribblings on legal-sized yellow paper. My father came back, my mother and brothers, with a vengeance that was bittersweet, like picking a scab or scratching a welt of poison ivy, the picking and scratching leading to more of the same.

I don't know what I would have done if I had not started writing poems. Perhaps continued my downward spiral? Perhaps turned to indifference for relief? It's impossible to tell, but I see those poems as heaven-sent, and I am thankful.

Allen Ginsberg's "Howl," "Kaddish," "A Supermarket in California," "Sunflower Sutra," and "In the Baggage Room at Greyhound," Philip Levine's *1933* and *The Names of the Lost,* and James Wright of nearly all the poems in *Saint Judas, The Branch Will Not Break,* and *Shall We Gather at the River* swept me away again as they had in my Dayton years, but this time I yearned to be able to write such powerful poems. Then James Dickey, Kenneth Rexroth, Randall Jarrell, Robert Lowell, John Logan, Anne Sexton, Sylvia Plath, and Theodore Roethke took over my days and nights, and the ink flowed and the binders filled with poems which, mercifully, have never seen the light of publication. I was hooked and diving, and I have been ever since.

It was Ginsberg who influenced me most in those beginning days. My first poems, which, as I've mentioned earlier, would appear in *Cohoes Theater* in 1981, were mostly long-lined, modeled after his lines in "Howl" and "Kaddish," and I tried for the same bold, personal mode of his early poems. I loved his outrageous honesty and gutsiness, no subject being off-limits, no word being too crude. I read "Kaddish" with wave after wave of recognition, from the nervous breakdowns to the menstrual blood. Here was a poet I felt in my gut, and I devoured everything he wrote, hoping someday to be able to write *half* as well as he could.

After separating from Denise in 1975 (we were legally divorced in 1978), I drifted for a couple of years on the social scene, dating, traveling when I could, but mostly studying for my doctoral exams in modern American literature and working on the dissertation which was approved in 1976 and found its proper place in the bottom drawer of a desk in the attic. In the summer of that year I received the doctorate and ended the period of study which had begun six years before in 1970. Then, in 1977, one summer night while teaching an American literature survey course, the topic that evening being Anne Bradstreet, I saw Nancy Crane, the woman who was to become my present wife.

I had just rushed back from playing a softball game at the Lehigh Fields, with a few beers in my belly and sweat and dust covering my skin, and I was a bit into Anne's dialogue between the Flesh and the Spirit when Nancy, in

a yellow halter top and cut-off jean shorts, walked by. Even I was bored with the curriculum-required dialogue, and when she smiled and waved at me through the huge picture window I was absentmindedly staring out of, something struck me in my chest that still strikes me some mornings when I lie in bed staring at her face. Another gift, I've realized since, but at that time I just thought *beautiful.*

I had my class, my text, we were only about half an hour into a three-hour session . . . but I could not resist. "Ten-minute break," I abruptly said, and rushed to the door so I wouldn't miss her. No need, though, for she was waiting for me, knowing, she has reminded me many times since, that I would be out of that classroom shortly. The first words out of her mouth were "I'm divorced and have two kids." "Okay," I remember responding dumbly, then managing to ask her for a date later that night; she accepted and we've been together ever since.

Nancy had two children, Tamara and Bradford Day II, from her previous marriage, and the four of us needed more living space than the one room I had in a house rented with two other bachelors. (The house in Germansville had been sold in 1976 so Denise could have some money to start her life over again in

"Nancy Crane the year I met her with her two children, Bradford (left) and Tamara Day," 1977

New York City.) So I bought a condemned garage in a back alley of Bethlehem for fifteen thousand dollars and immediately went to work, once again, rebuilding it. I spent all of my spare time in 1978 and 1979 posting the floors, studding new walls, putting on an entirely new roof from the rafters out, new electricity and plumbing throughout, and on and on until, still amidst spackle dust and rusty nails, we moved into 1537 Mercury Street where we would spend the next four years. Brad was nearly three and Tammy was seven when they came to live with me, and the four of us made a family, something I had not had for many years.

Oh, those were some banner days, in love, playing ball, going on camping vacations with Nancy and the kids, trying to write poems, teaching. And they just kept getting better and better as some of the poems were eventually accepted. I still vividly remember my first acceptance; *Mr. Cogito,* a long, slim, green-covered journal took a poem titled "Crayfish." I was so excited, almost shocked, as I sat in a lawn chair in our backyard, letting the glory soak in. It was a wonderful moment that's been hard to beat.

Nancy and I lived together for four years, both of us still smarting, I think, from our failed marriages, and were married at St. Stephen's Church in Allentown, Pennsylvania, on New Year's Eve, December 31, 1981. It was a small celebration, with her mother serving as her maid of honor and my friend David Musselman being my best man. Nancy's dad and two children, Tammy and Brad, served as witnesses and the congregation.

At this point in my life my "guardians" started to take the guise of poets, and they, too, showed up just when I needed them. Fred Closs, an English professor at Lafayette College, Easton, Pennsylvania, started the Roethke Festival about this time, 1977, and he annually invited major American poets to come for a weekend of readings, workshops, and parties to which the community at large was invited. These spring weekends were the highlight of my years then, for I was able to hear the poets I had been reading, able to sit across from them at a dinner table and, a few times, to get drunk with them afterwards.

It was at the Roethke Festival that I dared to read two of my poems aloud to an audience—the point where I began this tale. Allen Ginsberg gave the main reading and then there

Len and Nancy's wedding picture,
New Year's Eve, 1981

was an open reading; mostly college-age poets got up and read, so I was doubly shy, feeling so much older than they, and so much worse, too. But my idol, Ginsberg, was in the audience, and so I forced myself to get up and just do it.

Well, it was a nerve-wracking experience but the results were far better than I could ever have dreamed. Allen came up to me after the readings were over and said he liked the poems I'd read very much and asked to see them! Well, here I was again, being lucky, so I handed them over and held my breath. He read them there, right on the spot, emitting a generosity and kindness I've rarely seen matched in the years since. Then he suggested that I send these two, and any others that I had, to the editor David Cope, with a note saying that he, Allen, had suggested I do so.

Imagine my excitement and joy, to have Allen Ginsberg himself like my work! Too much for words.

I did send a batch of poems to David Cope, who responded kindly, too, and suggested that I send the manuscript to Bill Mohr with his recommendation. I did, and Mohr published my first book of poems, *Cohoes Theater,* in 1981, as I've mentioned earlier. It was a wonderful turn of events, one which I had never dreamed might happen.

It was at the Roethke Festival that I also met Gerry Stern for the first time, who was in fact a "neighbor" of mine, living just six miles away from me, in Raubsville, along the Delaware River.

Gerry was then, as he is now, a "wild man" of sorts, bounding with energy, ideas, inspirations, and as I got to know him better I would visit him in Raubsville sometimes on weekends, helping him with work around his house often, talking as we worked. He would critique my poems, tell me to be less logical, more musical, encouraging me in ways I knew even then I did not deserve.

That was the year Gerry was to win the Lamont Award (1977) and his life was to be changed forever. He, too, was teaching at a community college, Somerset CC in New Jersey, and we would commiserate about the impossible workload of five courses each semester that left so little time for writing poems. That was one of my most meaningful early years as an aspiring poet, for here was a poet I admired with whom I could talk about poetry. That's all I needed, and, between what Gerry and Ken Fifer told me, I began to piece together my own practicing aesthetic which was, at best, some notions on specificity and the overriding importance of the right image, the absolute *need* for strong music/rhythm in the long line, and, in my case, a narrative form that would help me to tell my "stories."

When Gerry started winning his awards I was ecstatic for him but also sad, for I knew he would not be around long. I was right, too, for within a few years he was off to be a poet-in-residence at various schools, including the University of Alabama, and, ultimately, the Writers Workshop at the University of Iowa. Although we kept in touch, I had lost steady personal contact with a good friend and wonderful poet. Ironically, though, the wheel has come full circle, and Gerry has just recently returned to live in Easton, twenty years later, and the good talks have returned with him.

Hungry for any feedback at that time, I also attended a poetry workshop at Lehigh University, which was composed of four professors and myself. The poems they were writing were still very formal, more like the poems of Ransom and Tate of the forties and fifties, and I found myself at odds with them as they were with me. Then one day, about 1979 or 1980, C. K. Williams, who was giving a reading at Lehigh, sat in on the workshop as part of his "duties." He listened quietly for an hour as we discussed each other's poems, and he said very little, as I remember it. But on the way out, when he and I were down the corridor a bit from the others, he put his arm around my shoulder, leaned down and whispered, "Don't listen to a word they tell you. You're doing fine." Another messenger from out of the blue? No doubt about it in my mind.

It was a couple of years later, about 1982, when C.K. wrote to me and asked me if I had a manuscript of poems I might send to a series he and Paul Zweig were editing for the State University of New York Press (SUNY) at the time. I was surprised and flattered, of course, for C.K. had become another one of my poetry models, with those long, winding narrative lines of *With Ignorance* and *Tar,* lines which could incorporate the entire world *and* the mind of the poet! I thought then and still think that those long-lined poems of Charlie's are one of the major breakthroughs for American poetry in the twentieth century, both for their "breadth of conception," as Paul Zweig put it, and for their deep range of emotional power.

I was so happy that he liked *my* poetry enough to actually consider it for book publication, that the fact of publication was truly secondary. But he did like the manuscript and he did publish it with SUNY in 1984: my second book of poems, *From the Dark.* Before publication, though, Charlie went through the poems with a very fine-tooth comb, making several comments on just about every poem, from suggestions about line breaks and musical endings to narrative control. I have never had an editor pay such close attention to my poetry, and I learned as much from those comments as I have in all the workshops I've ever attended in my lifetime.

These poems, like those of the earlier *Cohoes Theater,* were filled with my past: my father, mother, and two brothers again, but by this time I felt that they were haunting me. I wanted to move on to other subjects, other concerns, and life came to my assistance by giving Nancy and me a beautiful baby boy in 1984, thus

With Gerry Stern, about 1977

adding a powerful new character to my poetry and changing my life for the good, completely.

Nineteen eighty-four was an eventful year, for not only did *From the Dark* come out, but so did my son, Joshua Leonard Roberts, on February 13, after hanging on an extra two weeks in his mother's womb. It was his birth, and the subsequent thousands of hours I spent raising him, that finally inspired me to write poems about something other than my first family and their loss. *Sweet Ones,* my third book, which was published in 1987 by Milkweed Editions, having won their Great Lakes & Prairies Contest, contained poems about my *present* as well as my past family, and I felt as though a new dimension of possibilities had opened for me in my writing. I did not always have to look backward; I could look around, and ahead, too.

My poetry is always about people. I am incapable of writing a good poem about an animal or a scene from nature. What propels my poetry is a concern, a connection with people, and Joshua was just what I needed to connect with at that time in my life. He was so small, so vulnerable, and here I was, his father, the man responsible for his well-being, and I was determined to do a better job with him than my parents had done with me. I began to see in him parts of myself and parts of my father, my shyness and stubbornness, my father's physical quickness and daring, and, without knowing it, by raising Josh correctly, I was also re-raising

myself and my father, giving us both, so to speak, another chance at missed opportunities.

That's why, in poems like "The Drivers," I compare Josh to my Dad, both of them madly swerving their vehicles out of sheer exhilaration, and why, when I'm raking leaves with Josh in a poem like "More Walnuts, Late October," he becomes, in a sense, my father, and so the three of us are together in that field. There is a sweetness in being able to bring my father back like that, so he can be happy with his son and grandson, and live, through the poems at least, some of the good moments he did not have in his own life.

Joshua, then, was and is a blessing in both my life and poetry, and, especially for the latter, he arrived just at the right time. He quickly became the main topic of my poems, teaching me how to look at the world afresh, which I have written about in poems like "The Moment" and "Learning the Leaves."

Things come to me in threes, as I've mentioned, and 1984 was another proof of this, for not only was my son born, and *From the Dark* published, but I also received a National Endowment for the Arts award in poetry, twelve thousand and five hundred dollars, which bought me a semester off to write as well as some peace of mind. Throughout my career of teaching at Northampton Community College, I have taught five courses, mostly of composition, per semester, often with overloads for extra money, with an average of twenty-five students per course.

With Nancy and their son Joshua, 1984

When those papers rolled in, any inkling of inspiration rolled out, and writing poems was left for midnight hours (which I've never been very good at) or for summer mornings, the afternoons reserved for other part-time work I did for more cash.

So the NEA grant was a godsend, one which gave me the time to write many of the poems which would go into my next two books, *Sweet Ones* and *Black Wings.* Not only did I have more time to write these poems, but I also had a different inspiration, for I had met two poets who were to become fast friends and greatly influence my life and work, Sharon Olds and Hayden Carruth.

In the spring of 1984, just a few months after Joshua's birth, Sharon came to read at the Roethke Festival at Lafayette College. Because I was a fledgling local poet, I was asked to bring her around to the reading, introduce her to colleagues, and generally make sure she was okay. Well, she was so kind and gentle, so fragile, or so it seemed, and yet so powerful a poet, that I was immediately drawn to her and became her friend. I can remember, just be-

fore her reading, that one of the members of the English Department had said something to her that was on the border of discourtesy, and, seeing her body physically withdraw from the harshness, I leaned over and merely said something to the effect that she should not let it bother her, he was just like that. She took my hand and squeezed it hard, said I was very kind, and we've been friends ever since.

Hearing her poems, and, later, reading them, for she was kind enough to *ask me,* a poet not even well known in the Lehigh Valley, if I would exchange books *with her,* I knew I was in the presence of a force I needed for my own life and poems. In both *Satan Says* and *The Dead and the Living,* I heard a new voice, one that could talk about present domestic scenes as well as past ones, a voice that could contain love as well as hate, all of the ambiguities inherent in familial relationships. My son Josh had just been born and I had been spending countless hours with him, since Nancy worked full-time and I could arrange my schedule to be at home when she wasn't, and here were Sharon's wonderful poems about her son and daughter, about

their vulnerability, and here was Sharon drawing connections through the generations, from
her father, through her, to her children.

She, too, was a gift, another guardian, I
realized, who had arrived at the perfect time
to show me a new way to go in my poems.
Sweet Ones and *Black Wings* demonstrate this influence in content; it was to be Hayden Carruth's
influence that would further affect both the
content and form of those and later poems.

Several months later, in November of 1984,
I was standing in a circle in one of the
fancy dining rooms at Bucknell University, one
of ten invited poets and fiction writers to give
readings and workshops at their annual Writers Festival. A group of us were talking about
this and that, when an older man, about sixty-
five, in dungaree jeans and dungaree vest, fe-
rociously smoking a pipe, came and stood about
a foot behind me. I stepped back so he could
enter the circle, but he didn't, just stayed where
he was. Strange, I thought at the time, and in
a few minutes he just walked back to his table

where he was sitting with a very pretty, dark-
haired woman about half his age.

At that point, Karl Patten, who was then
the unofficial "poet-in-residence" at Bucknell,
and had been for about thirty years, sidled up
to me and whispered that Hayden Carruth
wondered if he could talk with me. I was astonished first of all that Hayden Carruth was
even in the room without me knowing it, and
second of all that he wanted to talk with *me*. I
suspected a hoax and I told Karl as much, but
he then pointed to the fellow in the jeans
and said *that* was Hayden Carruth, and he *did*
want to talk with me.

I'd read and loved Hayden's *Brothers, I Loved
You All,* so it took me about three seconds to
get to his table. He stood up and introduced
his lover, Cynthia Roberts, and himself, asked
me to sit down, and thus began a deep and
fiery friendship of twelve years. It turned out
that Cindy had read my book, *From the Dark,*
had liked it and given it to Hayden to read,
who in turn also had liked it. Very much, he
said, and I was on top of the world for the

*"With Hayden Carruth at our house on Wassergass Street,
Hellertown, Pennsylvania," about 1980*

"Bradford and Tamara, on Brad's graduation day from high school," 1991

rest of the night and for months afterward. We talked, we laughed, they came to my reading the next afternoon and, when we parted, we exchanged addresses and telephone numbers, although I fully expected Hayden to be too busy to keep in touch.

I was dead wrong. From that weekend on, he and I began an exchange of letters which has filled a drawer of my filing cabinet, long letters about craft, about the poetry scene, about life, growing old, about trees and plants and just about anything that could come from his incredible mind and heart. I listened and I learned, making lists of questions to ask him when he would come to visit, as he did about four times a year, spending from four days to two weeks at a time.

We would take walks through the fields and woods surrounding my new house on Wassergass, which we had bought in 1983 as a handyman's special, and which I was slowly, once again, rebuilding: house, barn, chicken coop, small barn that served as a garage, pond, and seven mostly untamed acres. (Hayden liked the fact that I

could work with my hands, and sometimes we'd talk "shop" for hours, beams, trusses, what weight shingle on the roof. . . . I think such talk brought him back to his Vermont days, which seem to have been the happiest of his life.)

There was a forty-acre tract above our land which a doctor in town owned and, in return for being able to pick raspberries there and clearing dead trees for firewood, I would keep it "civilized" by mowing walking paths every now and then. Hayden and I and Josh, either in my arms or toddling behind us, would take long walks there in any season, Hayden telling me I would have to learn the names of the plants and trees, I would have to stop writing in the faddish "eternal present," I would have to start experimenting with my line breaks more, I would have to expand beyond the topic of my first family—"Christ," he would say, "there's your living son right in front of you. Write a poem for *him!*" Hayden has written a good poem about one of his solitary walks here, "Folk Song: On the Road Again," which is in *Scrambled Eggs and Whiskey.* I, too, have written several poems about Hayden's visits at this time, including "Cold," "In the Field," "The Yellow of Mulberry," and "Midwinter."

These were wonderful days of poetry talk, work talk, and silence, days when I felt that I had been given a "father in poetry," someone I could talk to about anything, someone who could show me the way.

I am a slow learner, and awfully stubborn at times, to boot, but Hayden's advice slowly sank in and I tried to expand my cast of characters beyond my father, mother, and two brothers. This starts happening in *Sweet Ones,* with the appearance of my son and wife in the poems, and it continues in *Black Wings,* where I begin to branch out into my Catholic school experiences, into "religion." Because of Hayden's influence, I dedicated *Sweet Ones* to him.

Our friendship continued, deep and strong, right up through August 3, 1995, when my wife and I drove to his home in Munnsville, New York, to celebrate his seventy-fifth birthday. Unfortunately, Hayden had started to drink early that morning and by midnight, when we were leaving, some very unpleasant words were said and we parted yelling. We have not spoken to each other since.

However, I am grateful for the precise, deeply intelligent advice he's given me, and I realize he's helped my poetry more than anyone else.

My magic number of three appeared once again in another good year, 1988–89, when *Black Wings* was selected for the National Poetry Series Award, I received my second National Endowment for the Arts award, and I was awarded a Fulbright Scholar award to teach American literature at Janus Pannonius University in Pécs, Hungary. Northampton granted me a full-year sabbatical at half-pay and Nancy, Brad, Josh, and I were off to spend fourteen months in Europe, our first prolonged trip there, although we had visited for a couple of months in 1981 and 1984. (Tammy was in college and did not want to disrupt her education, so she remained at Lafayette.) Using Hungary as our base, we managed to spend time in Spain, France, Yugoslavia, Germany, and Italy, creating the finest trip of our lives thus far.

While teaching in Pécs, I became interested in the work of one of Hungary's great living poets, Sándor Csoóri, and with the help of students and colleagues who provided me with literal drafts, I began translating his work into English. This task met with unexpected success and, in addition to many of the poems being published in journals such as *Partisan Review* and the *American Poetry Review,* Copper Canyon published a volume of my translations of Csoóri's work, *Selected Poems of Sándor Csoóri,* in 1992. I enjoy Csoóri's poems so much, I am still translating them today.

Once again I felt as though I had "arrived." Not all of my poems were being rejected by editors, an anonymous NEA committee had liked my work enough to give me money to take a year off to write, and I was living in Europe! Not bad for a kid from Olmstead Street, I thought, wishing my father could be alive to enjoy my success.

During our fourteen months in Europe, we spent two weeks in Spain, a month in Italy, a month in Greece, and about six weeks in Yugoslavia, which is our favorite place on this earth. In both 1981 and 1984, when Nancy and I were able to travel, we had visited the island of Hvar, off the Adriatic Coast of Yugoslavia. At the unsettled end of the island, near Sucarej, lies a beautiful cove where Vide Ivan Kovic has a pension of five rooms. The cove has a town address of Bogomolje with a total of about twenty people living there. To us, however, it's Paradise.

Joshua Roberts, about 1991

The first time we went to Europe, as a belated honeymoon in 1981, we had discovered the island of Hvar by a marvelous stroke of luck. After spending about a month in France and Italy, we found ourselves one night in a taverna in Venice, where we met some Austrians. They noticed we were "obvious lovers," as they put it, and they sent a bottle of wine to our table. We joined them and, when the talk came round to where we were going next, we said we thought we'd try Greece for the sun and swimming. They demurred, insisting that we go to Hvar, which had no tourists and was much more beautiful. Drunk, we acquiesced.

The next morning the spirit moved us and we went, driving to Bari where we caught the ferry to Split; from there we caught another ferry to Hvar. Fortunately for us, we ended up on the "wrong," unsettled end of the island and began the sixty-three kilometer drive on a bumpy dirt road to the other end. About fifteen kilometers down that road we saw a donkey path leading to a gorgeous cove, so we parked, changed into our swimming suits, and began our descent to what we would soon find to be "Vide's Pension."

We loved it so much we stayed for a full month, paying fifteen dollars a day for our room and board, with homemade fruit brandy thrown in as an extra, as much as we could drink! We swam, we read, we took long, slow walks through the lavender hillsides. I grew more in love each day, a feeling I had resisted most of my life, and I was actually growing comfortable with it. I've tried to capture some of these days and nights in the last section, titled "Partisan," of my second book, *From the Dark.*

We returned to Vide's Pension, with Bradford and our newborn, Joshua, in 1984, to spend another wonderful month, this time interspersed with short trips into the Yugoslavian mainland. And so, when we returned to Europe via the Fulbright to Hungary in 1989, it was a given that we would return to Vide's for a month. Again, our stay was completely refreshing, but there was a change in the atmosphere already, as though the island itself had a presentiment of what was to come. A Russian couple came to stay for two weeks, a first for Vide, and they were rumored to be working for the "government." Then Vide's brother, who was a colonel for the then-Yugoslavian Free Army, suddenly appeared and stayed until a day after the Russian couple left. I vividly remember nights of playing a Yugoslavian form of pinochle on the balcony overlooking the Adriatic, Vide pouring another round of slivovitz, the full moon rising above the limestone cliffs of the mainland. . . . My heart grows heavy to think of what has happened to that country since.

All good things come to an end, though, and we eventually had to return to Hungary so I could finish my teaching work. That in itself was saddening, for we hated to leave what we had come to consider our "second home." When we arrived back in Pécs, though, I was to receive worse news.

On April 6, 1989, I was sitting on the patio of our flat in Pécs, the spring sun warming my face, when Nancy suddenly appeared and said my mother was on the telephone from the States. Now my mother does not call me unless there is some dire emergency, and she had not called once during our stay in Hungary, so I knew even before I picked up the receiver that someone was dying or was dead. It was Nick. He had died two days before of emphysema, ending the twenty-six years of his life which he had spent drifting in and out of Veterans' Hospitals and relationships. My mother had tried to reach me but we had been traveling back from Yugoslavia. Nick was buried that very morning. I sobbed but, just as I had felt at the news of my father's death at the same age of forty-seven, I was glad his suffering had ended. I know he was too.

Returning home with Csoóri's surreal poetry ringing in my head, I began writing the poems which would eventually appear in *Dangerous Angels* and in *Counting the Black Angels.* Both those books contain poems about my Catholic school background and, because they are about religion, are able to leave the naturalistic settings of my earlier poems behind and become, I think, more surreal, more imaginative. I'm sure that Csoóri's magnificently surreal touches in his poetry greatly influenced this change in mine, a change which I hope continues. I was glad of this, for I'd begun, as I've said earlier, to feel hemmed in by my first family, trapped in that kitchen where my mother reeled with anger and my father sat smoking and drinking.

The classroom setting gave me the opportunity to move into other subject areas, too, such as astrology ("Learning the Planets" and "Learning the Stars"), mathematics ("The Power of Numbers" and "Angels in the Experimental Catechism/Math Class"), science ("Learning about the Heart" and "Learning the Leaves"), sex ("Emma in the Class on Reproduction" and "Learning Natural Instincts"), and religion ("Second-Grade Angel," "Counting the Black Angels," and "On Hearing That We Were All Boundless, Unimaginable Energy").

I had moved beyond my first and second families, even though I was still writing many poems about those characters, and had entered a larger realm where the imagination felt freer and rangier.

As I was roving in these new fields of poetic material, I received a letter out of the blue from a poet whose work I feel has been a very important model for my own—Phil Levine. Phil had been at Gerry Stern's house in Iowa, I learned, when Gerry gave him a copy of my book, *Sweet Ones,* and suggested he read it. Phil really liked the poems and then wrote me a letter to say so! Again, I was grateful and ecstatically happy that this poet, whom I had long admired, liked my poems! I immediately wrote back, telling Phil how greatly I admired his work, and how, often, it would serve me as a model, an inspiration for my own, and we began a distance-friendship that still results in three or four letters a year.

The fact that has given me the most satisfaction about my poetry writing, other than the poems themselves, is that poets I admire have extended themselves to tell me they like my words. No grant or publication could ever replace this feeling of acceptance and camarade-

"Chris Thompson, Hayden Carruth, Steve Berg, and Bill Kulik at our house," 1994

rie. When I feel that I am completely dry, that I will never write another poem for the rest of my life (which is about six months of every year), I fall back upon their trust and it keeps me afloat.

To put this in better perspective, I have been teaching at a community college for twenty-three years, have never taken a creative writing course except my junior-year excursion into Ms. Ann Barker's fiction workshop, and I am not in any of the "loops" of poets of my generation, such as Bread Loaf or Warren Wilson or any of the other popular writing programs. I was, and am, in other words, cut off from the poetry world that buzzes all around me. Not that I wanted or want to be part of it. I didn't and I don't. But I did long for a connection, and the approval I received from such poets as Allen, Gerry, Sharon, Hayden, C.K., and Phil gave me that. It has helped me to keep writing.

In 1991 I received another incentive, a John Simon Guggenheim Memorial Award in poetry, replete with twenty-eight thousand dollars I used to buy a full year from teaching and thus devote to my writing. It was during 1991 and 1992 that I completed most of the poems for *Dangerous Angels* and *Counting the Black Angels,* as well as finishing the selected volume of Sándor Csoóri's poems.

The Fulbright Committee also gave me a translation grant that year so I could continue my work on Sándor Csoóri and Sándor Kanyadi, the latter being an ethnic Hungarian living in Transylvania. The grant was for three months so I packed my bag and laptop and headed for, first, Hungary, where I worked on some Csoóri poems, and then for Transylvania where I worked on the Kanyadi poems. The fifty or so days I spent traveling through Transylvania in 1991 are among the most memorable I have ever had because of the severe austerity and wildness of many of the places (camping out in the Carpathians is one that stands out!) and because of the wonderful simplicity and kindness of the people I met.

One incident that encapsulates my feelings of that trip occurred on a late afternoon when Tibor, my traveling companion, and I arrived at a small village in our two-cylinder Travant which, with a wind behind us, could speed up to thirty miles an hour! A group of men, women, and children had gathered on one of the muddy streets of the village, as though waiting for someone. When we stopped, we learned that they were gathered to say farewell to a young mother and father and their six-year-old son who was very ill.

The parents, dressed in their best clothes and carrying a small dufflebag each, were waiting for a friend of a friend from a neighboring village to come with his cousin's car so they could travel the more than fifteen hundred miles back to Budapest where their son could get proper medical treatment. (It was common knowledge that, under Ceauşescu, the Romanian hospitals did not pay particular attention to Hungarian patients. I don't know what the policies are today.)

We also learned, through one of Tibor's friends, that the parents had no money and no place to stay in Budapest; they were just going to trust that they would make it there and their son would be helped. Tibor gave them the key to his flat in Budapest and I gave them a hundred dollars, the equivalent of a month's salary for an established factory worker then, both of us struck by their incredible love and courage. The sun was setting and the cold Carpathian air was settling on us all when the friend of a friend finally drove up and took them away. I never did learn what became of the boy, but I often think of him and hope he is alive and well.

In 1992 Copper Canyon Press published *Selected Poems of Sándor Csoóri* and, as mentioned earlier, in 1993 Copper Beech published my fifth book of poems, *Dangerous Angels*. Many of these poems, as the title suggests, deal with my Catholic grade school and high school experiences, just as the poems in my next volume, *Counting the Black Angels,* do. It was during these years, 1992–94, that I met two other poets who were to become fast friends, brothers-in-poetry, if you will: Larry Lieberman and Steve Berg.

I had met Larry back in 1991, when I had interviewed for a creative writing position at the University of Illinois at Urbana-Champaign, a job which they did offer me but which I eventually and regretfully had to decline accepting for several reasons. Our daughter was to be a senior in a college just eight miles

"With Nancy and Joshua," 1995

from our house, our son Brad was to be a senior in high school, and our youngest boy, Joshua, had just entered first grade and, for the first time in his life, had made friends. These were situations we knew of and could deal with if we were to move, but, as fate would have it, Nancy's mother became seriously ill with cancer just at that time, and Nancy felt obligated to stay near her (we live twenty miles away). It was one of my toughest decisions ever, one which I sweated over for a full week, but the end result was that I would be staying on Wassergass.

My friendship with Larry was revived in 1993 when I sent a manuscript of poems for the University Press's February reading and he accepted *Counting the Black Angels* for publication. I was thrilled, knowing full well the high quality poetry they published. Even back in 1991, when I first met him, I had felt an instant friendship forming, a brotherly bond, and when we communicated in 1993, it came back even stronger. What struck me about Larry when he took the manuscript was that he, unlike previous editors, did not want me to cut poems, but *add* them, so much so that the book grew from about seventy to over a hundred pages by the time it was published. And throughout the entire process I could rely upon and trust entirely Larry's judgement; he knows my work better than I do, and that's no exaggeration.

Through Larry I met Steve Berg, who had accepted a couple of my poems previously for the *American Poetry Review*, but whom I had never met. Now I'd loved Steve's work for years, dating as far back as the early '70s when I first began reading contemporary American poems. His books, *The Daughters* and *Grief*, had bowled me over with their personal voice and deep emotion, and I had read every book of his that had come out since. I also thought his anthology, *Naked Poetry*, was a great collection of contemporary American poems. (I was sure then and am still sure that he is one of our most undervalued poets writing today.) So I was anxious to meet the man, and this is how it happened.

Larry was giving a reading at Lehigh University in the spring of 1994 and I invited Gerry Stern, who by then was living in nearby Easton much of the time, to come over to our house for some drinks afterwards. Hayden was visiting at the time, and other local poets were invited, too, so Gerry asked if he could bring a couple of other poets. I said sure, so Gerry called Steve, who, with his friend Bill Kulik, the wonderful translator of Robert Desnos's poems, drove up from Philadelphia.

We had a roaring night of it, reading poems, diving into the pool, drinking just about till dawn. I can still see Steve and Hayden leaning their heads toward each other, about three o'clock in the morning, talking, talking, talking, smoking Cuban cigars, Steve sipping brandy, Hayden downing Bushmill's, and I thought, "If only I could take all of this brain/poetry power and bottle it . . . ," but then I had another whiskey and drowsed off on one of the chaise lounges.

I have been fortunate throughout my life to have good friends and what I have called "guardians," those who have appeared just when I needed them, but I feel these past few years have graced me far beyond my deserts. Gerry, Larry, Steve, Bill, Hayden, Phil, Sharon, C.K., and so many others have blessed me with hours, days, years of such wonderful talk and friendship that it would be hard for me to create a better scenario for the path my life has taken.

My daughter, Tammy, is married and has a son of her own, Lucas, and my oldest son, Brad, is roaming around Virginia Beach, having completed nearly three years of college and now trying to "find himself," a worthy enterprise. My youngest son, Joshua, who threatens to usurp my father's position as the most-written-about character in my poems, is now thirteen (turned, in fact, on the day I am writing this!) and is just about a young man. My wife, Nancy, will have her doctorate in nursing this summer, after many years of labor. I have outlived my father and older brother by nearly three years so far, my fiftieth birthday arriving in two months as of this writing, on March 13. I have a family, a house, and at least a few poems I can be proud of, as well as wonderful friends. I'd never expected to come this far, and I am grateful.

BIBLIOGRAPHY

Poetry:

Cohoes Theater, Momentum, 1981.

From the Dark, State University of New York Press, 1984.

Sweet Ones, Milkweed Editions, 1988.

Black Wings, Persea Books, 1989.

Learning about the Heart (chapbook), Silverfish Review, 1992.

The Million Branches: Selected Poems and Interview (chapbook), Yarrow, 1993.

Dangerous Angels, Copper Beech, 1993.

Counting the Black Angels, University of Illinois Press, 1994.

Acupuncture and Cleansing at Fifty, University of Illinois Press, 1998.

Translator:

Sándor Csoóri, *Call to Me in My Mother Tongue* (chapbook), Mid-American Review, 1990.

Selected Poems of Sándor Csoóri, Copper Canyon, 1992.

Other:

Nutcracker (one-act play), first produced in Bethlehem, Pennsylvania, at Northampton Community College Theater, 1978.

Work represented in many anthologies, including *Anthology of Magazine Verse and Yearbook of American Poetry,* 1983–89; *The Best American Poetry,* 1992; and *Pushcart Prize XVI.* Contributor of several hundred poems to magazines, including *American Poetry Review, Boulevard, Georgia Review, Hudson Review, New England Review, Ohio Review, Paris Review,* and *Poetry.* Translations represented in many magazines, including *American Poetry Review, Delos, Denver Quarterly, Field, Northwest Review, Partisan Review,* and *Translation.*

Floyd Salas

1931-

ON THE LAM:
A Writerbiography

My autobiography is my writerbiography. I am only my writing. There is no life without my writing. There is no reason for living without my writing. I *am* my writing, all of me.

I'm a writer because I grew up in a house full of books. My father had a library of history and geography books, as well as *Dante's Inferno* and the *Police Gazette* and pulp fiction detective novels. My older sister, Dorothy, read volumes of Book of the Month Club bestsellers and *True Confession* magazines. And my brother Eddy had a Renaissance man's library which included everything from Baudelaire to Marcus Aurelius to Plato to Dostoyevsky to Bennet Cerf to books of literary criticism and biographies to American history. All of which I read. I read from the libraries of all three all my life. That's why I'm a writer.

My family on both sides came to this country from Spain with Coronado and Ponce de León. I am supposedly descended from Coronado himself, according to a female scholar cousin of my mother's, Eileen Sanchez de Bankson, who is a curator of a small Colorado museum in the Spanish Peaks mountain town of La Veta and who is writing a book on the family. She says it's possible that Ponce de León, too, is an ancestor. I told her she had better document those claims exactly since it's not politically correct in Hispanic circles to claim to be descended from the imperialistic Spanish conquerors. I can claim my Navajo Indian blood from five generations back, but I better keep quiet about my aristocratic Spanish lineage and my Irish and Belgium blood and the bastard line which comes from a redheaded Catholic priest, who bribed a bureaucrat with $500.00— a grand sum then—to be allowed to stay in this country when all the Spanish Catholic priests were being deported after the Mexican repub-

Floyd Salas with Trixie,
Oakland Hills, California, 1944

lic drove out the Spanish monarchy around 1823. In a family geneaology, his daughters and granddaughters said he was French, though his name was Castro. I have read of Frenchmen in boxing circles called Rodriguez and Fernandez. So, it's all true, sort of.

I was given the last rites when I was born and immediately caught the whooping cough during a national epidemic in 1931. I was given goat's milk instead of my mother's milk because my mother was too ill herself to breast-feed me. My diet was closely watched because I was so scrawny, and after that I never caught any childhood diseases except for a three-day bout with the measles at six, and I didn't catch colds then either. I was deceptively strong and healthy all my life, in spite of that debilitating first illness.

My father taught me to read from the comic strips when I was five. I went to Ebert Elementary School in Denver, Colorado, starting the kindergarten in the fall of 1936. Denver schools always produce students who are among those who get the highest scores in the SAT college tests. When I was in the second grade, my teachers realized I had a very superior intelligence and could already read far beyond my grade level and gave me my own individual curriculum: academic subjects with higher grades, an hour alone in the library by myself every day, and gym and art classes with the kids my own age. I was receiving a rich boy's education in a public school. Then they skipped me ahead a grade in June 1939, but my family moved to Central Valley, California (called Boomtown by the inhabitants), in the summer and I went to a mountain school in the fall of the year by the Shasta Dam where my father had found work at the end of the Depression. Though I was now in the fourth grade and only eight years old, I was no longer the star student and had to make this shift for myself. I did okay, though small for my age. I didn't know how to play games like softball and basketball and was so tiny the teachers put me with fat kids and skinny kids and other outcasts and, except for one female teacher who once picked me for the class team in a softball game against the fifth grade boys, never gave me a chance to get picked by the bigger guys for their teams. That only reinforced a tendency toward solitude that all bookworms have.

Yet, I come from a family of boxers as well as scholars. One brother, Eddy, eleven years older than me, was an intellectual prodigy and the other, Al, nine years older, an outstanding athlete and Golden Gloves boxer. I won every schoolyard fight I ever had all through the nine public schools I went to in twelve years, and on the very first day of school in the mountain community of Boomtown, I won three fights and the respect of every kid in the school. I also would chase kids home from school, even if they were on the school athletic teams, if it came to that.

Boys asked me to be in their clubs and I always said yes. But I was still a bookworm. So, all my school life, I always had two entirely different types of friends: scholars, artists, poets, musicians, and other cerebral outcast egghead types and jock athletes. I've spent my writing life telling stories about tough guys and brainy guys. Every one of my books is about a brain who is a boxer, no matter what the locale or the subject matter, and every book is different.

In the fall of 1940 we moved to Oakland, California, and for a time, my family had a very happy life and a lovely home there. We had a lot of money for anything I wanted. Christmas was a wonderland of presents piled under a magnificent tree in a huge front room. Then my mother died in 1943 when I was twelve and my brothers went to fight in World War II. When my oldest brother committed suicide in 1950, I wrote this poem:

> Kids born in 'thirty-one
> wore shoes had lunch on relief
> Adolescent years
> shipyards
> fears
> Ma worked
> bright coin
> and grief

My mother's death caught me and held me all my life, and when my brilliant brother Eddy killed himself in the early years of his incredibly successful life, when I was only nineteen, I knew for sure there was no benevolent God. Though I loved Jesus and wanted to be like him, I saw how he died and heard his last words, "My God! My God! Why hast thou forsaken me?" and knew that a caring God was all a sentimental lie. God always was, still is, and always will be for me, an empty circle of infinity. The essence of being is an incomprehensible and unrelenting circling force of life and death. There is no eternal paradise or Hell and only mortal fear and self-centered narcissism project the human lie that God looks like us or cares for us. The only sure future we truly face is death and absolute nothingness. God loves us, but not the animals we eat? What a sentimental fallacy! Most dogs have a greater capacity for selfless love than we humans do. Incomprehensible force there is. Understanding of it there isn't. True benevolence is a lie. We live by murder. We kill other beings, ani-

*Mother, Anita Sanchez Salas,
wedding photo, Colorado, 1915*

mal and vegetable, to stay alive for a short time. Then we die and there's nothing. This is existential reality and I am an existentialist. Whatever force created this unhappy mess has no pity or concern for any of the individual objects, human or otherwise, that exist within it.

So, if there is no heaven and no benevolent divinity and no future happiness after death and only nothing after this brief light of suffering and, yes, love and joy, too, according to what I can perceive, then I must make the most of it. There are only two priceless things in existence and these are love and time and so I must spend my *time* doing what I *love*, appreciating and making beauty with words out of suffering and joy so that my perceptions might live on, however fleetingly, past this so brief respite of consciousness called living. This is why I write. Because there's nothing better to do.

In spite of the good fortune of growing up in a house full of books and getting a really sound beginning to my education, the death of my mother, Anita Sanchez Salas, from heart disease plunged my family into sadness and tragedy that, in spite of the heroic efforts of my sister Dorothy to keep the family together, nearly ruined all our lives. It was in the middle of the war and my father owned rental property and we had lots of money and a big house, but it was no longer a *home*. Everybody in the family was unwittingly broken by my mother's death. Dorothy got divorced after having four kids, and eventually had four husbands, finally marrying the first one, Frank Golubin, over again when he was dying from heart disease. She is now starting to write her first fictional stories built upon her love of family. She's a natural mother and loves everybody but has spent most of her life struggling for individual expression and happiness after our mother died. I always told her that her life is a Book of the Month Club bestseller like all the stories she's already read, and she's starting to write it now, if slowly.

Eddy got a four-year scholarship to attend any university in the state of Colorado when he graduated from high school in 1938, was a pre-med Cal graduate, who passed the California state board in pharmacology in 1943 so he'd have a profession when he came back from the war, studied post-graduate history at Harvard, and was a naval officer in the war. He taught at a naval academy, but after our mother died, he volunteered for active duty and fought in the Pacific and was in the invasion of Japan. After the war he worked in naval intelligence and was stationed as a cultural attaché at the U.S. Embassy in Paris. Then he was seduced by a rich Catholic monsignor in New York and became a practicing bisexual. He started his own successful professional pharmacy in downtown San Francisco at the age of twenty-nine and committed suicide in it at the age of thirty. I found him dead there when I came to work in the morning. This experience convinced me to be a writer, though I'd already written stories, poems, and a play that was produced in summer school when I was fifteen.

Al, two years younger than Eddy and nine years older than me, became a dopefiend after Eddy killed himself, and went on a twenty-five-year heroin run that put him in two prisons, half a dozen jails, and on welfare. All of his nine children but the very oldest and very youngest of his daughters have had an addiction to drugs. Four of his children that he helped get hooked committed suicide while very young adults. Two of their mates also killed themselves. All of his sons, including the two still alive and three that are dead, have been hooked and in jail for it. One has been in prison for stabbing a security guard. None of his children—and there are two sons and three daughters still living—are at this time hooked and Al was clean the last fifteen years of his life, I'm happy to say. A son and daughter of his hate me for the material I write (like what I'm relating now). Another son and a daughter of his do not. Al's oldest daughter both loves and hates me.

My youngest sister, Annabelle, is married to a plumbers union board officer who looks like a Mafia don. We do not speak because I feel that I saved the life of their youngest son—by weening him off drugs and tutoring him and letting him live with me while he went to college for a year until he was able to support himself and graduate with a bachelor's degree. Her husband has never thanked me, though before I helped their son, Floyd (who is named after me), the father would not even allow his son's name to be mentioned in his upper middle-class house, because the son had burglarized it when he was on crack. Now the son is the apple of his eye.

Such is the price paid by my family for losing the moral core of the family—my mother—and the price paid by myself for daring to write about it all. So much for my family.

Now for my writer self.

From being the class counselor and one of the two boys that my junior high school homeroom teacher predicted would be school president by the ninth grade, I came back from summer vacation and the death of my mother into the eighth grade and got suspended three times and finally kicked out of the school in the ninth grade and sent to a high school with the reputation as one of the roughest around (though even it would be considered wimpy by today's standards). It was a melting pot of a school and had only one stabbing in all the years I've known about it, before, during, and after I left it, when there are shootings all the time in urban high schools now.

I went blind when my mother died. Instead of getting ulcers in my stomach, I got ulcers in my eyes from the sight of my dead mother in the coffin with a sore on her lip. I became hysterical and threw myself into the coffin and they had to drag me out of it and send me off to an aunt's house for a few days to recover. But I still went blind in one eye at a time right after her funeral. This was the second time I'd felt grief over death. My Irish grandmother had died only a year before and though I cried, I never suffered the great despair that the death of my mother plunged me into. I'd go to school and could only see my sad father sitting by the big front-room window, in the dark, grieving. I grieved all day. I couldn't concentrate very long before I'd get sad again and couldn't read intensely like I could before. It seemed that I'd try to do the homework, but a dark cloud hung over me, and even if I did the homework, I'd lose it by the next day. There didn't seem to be any reason to do anything, except try to escape the sadness inside me by having some kind of excitement and fun.

I was arrested five times in fifteen months for cutting school, staying out late at night, fighting in the streets, and, finally, joyriding in a car stolen by an acquaintance. I remember I couldn't figure out why things were so different, why I was so different than I used to be only a few months before, from the class star—"an angel," as one old friend said—to a bad, naughty boy. I still went to church every week, saved all my money, bought defense stamps, was polite to everyone, joined the Boy Scouts and became a patrol leader and passed more tests than any other boy in the city in the week at Boy Scout camp when I was thirteen. But I got into a fight at camp and so didn't win the outstanding medal. And that's been the story of my life ever since, if a medal can be construed as gaining the spoils of victory, of superior achievement. (When my play was put on in summer school when I was fifteen, the drama teacher never announced to the audience that a student had written it, though he produced it along with a professionally written play.)

But I had the good fortune, because I had intellectual friends, to get my third job after high school at age seventeen as a page in the Oakland Public Library. It was a grand old Victorian slate-gray granite building, with huge walls and high ceilings and windows that could have been in a cathedral, and Roman columns and glass floors that you could see through in the stacks, like looking up through the bottom of a Coke bottle. Thick and beautiful as frozen ice. Beautiful the upper stacks where only the employees went, pages like myself, to get reference materials by a buzzer. Beautiful the sense in my teenager's head of the quiet and seriousness that hung like a light mist over the readers' bent brows, as if they were bending to prayer. Beautiful to sit down on a stool when I stacked the books on the public shelves and read passages out of book after book after book, for a year. Beautiful to take these books home when I really got interested. I'd work real hard and get my eight hours of work done in four hours, then make myself scarce in the public stacks and read by the hour, everything from *Black Boy* and *Native Son* to *This Is My Beloved* by Walter Benton to *The La Guardia Reports on Marijuana*, 1937, to *Mother India* to books on black magic and the psychology of dreams and the life of Soapy Smith, conman extraordinaire in Alaska, and Joaquin Murieta, the California bandit. Life was rich. My head was full of words and stories and great ideas on how my mind worked and made visions at night. I'd dream of the bookshelves at night. Wandering among them. Lost and happy and a little bewildered by the magnitude of the journey of the mind that stretched ahead of me, if I wanted to learn all that there was possible to learn in a lifetime, as soon as possible.

I first heard of a modern long narrative poem when a fellow page wanted to show me something sexy in the book room, where we loaded up our trucks to go out and shelve. "Why should I say your thighs are like lilies. / Lilies are neither quick nor scented / They can neither fire love nor quench it." I fell in love with *This Is My Beloved* and stole the book for months at a time. There were other copies so I wasn't a total thief. But I returned it like I returned all the books that I borrowed for periods at a time. If I'd been in college, doing graduate work, they would have granted me the same privilege. I took it. I returned the books and I became a writer and won a few awards and got good critical reception and thanked God I got to work in a public library where education was free.

It saved my life. For that reason a public library is the first bastion against tyranny. The first thing the reactionaires do is cut off education so people won't be smart enough to see through them. The battle over the NEA, which publishes the works of protest by writers

Floyd's older sister, Dorothy Salas, 1942

like me, when the corporate publishers won't touch us, came out of right-wing Republican think tanks like the Hoover Institute, whose members know that the control of consciousness is the key to control of the country and command of profit. The library is the most socially important structure that can be built. Without libraries we will become ignorant and enslaved. President Kennedy quoting Lincoln said, "Whoever wants an uneducated society to be free, wants something that never was and never will be."

I'll go on. But first I must say something. I became a writer against all odds, oppression, suppression, and social ostracism, ranging from the police to the universities I attended, to my next-door neighbors, close friends, and my family. And here is that story, book by book.

I was a brilliant student at Cal, the University of California at Berkeley, with an A minus grade-point average. Josephine Miles, the reigning poet laureate of the campus, and the only truly famous poet there, read my poems when I was a sophomore and said that I was a natural

Ensign John Edward Salas,
Floyd's oldest brother, 1944

poet. But on Saturday nights, I would smoke a joint with my artist buddies and make sculptures for my sculpture class, though I was an English major. Two of those painter buddies, one, Norman, an African American, crippled from polio, and the other, Peter, an Italian American, a brilliant nonconformist, got involved with dealing pot and got busted and everyone who hung around with them in the artistic community of Berkeley was guilty by association when, in 1955 and 1956, smoking pot was a felony punishable by prison time. Peter had once been sent away as a teenager for dealing pot by a state narcotics agent, who was himself later sent to federal prison for trading heroin to junkies for stolen goods. And the agent had sworn to send Peter to prison if he ever got involved in dealing again.

One night I had the misfortune to be outside Peter's liquor store when he was closing up shop. I didn't know that he had been set up by a mutual friend. When I saw a strange car keep circling around as if the guy was either a crook or cop, I jumped out of the car where I was sitting and raced the guy to the door of the liquor store and slammed it shut and locked it in his face. In two seconds, two great big narcs in blue suits hit the door and tried to knock it open. I ran to the back and flushed Peter's pound of pot down the toilet. Then when the set-up man got Peter to open the door for him and then stood in the door so it would stay open, I guessed what he'd done, called him a fink, and blasted him. I then pounded him on the back. This was strike one against me. (See *Buffalo Nickel* for more on this incident.)

Then, studying for a U.S. History final until late one night, another African American buddy, Fred, and I decided to go get a couple of joints to relax with after beating our brains out for six hours or so. We went down into West Oakland to buy them. Fred took so long that I went down Seventh Street looking for him, found him, but when we jumped in my car and got to the intersection, a plainclothes narc car swerved in front of us. I spun by it and up the wrong side of Adeline Street and got far enough ahead of them for my buddy to throw the pot away. Then I slowed down. They cruised by us a couple of blocks further away, but they didn't try to stop us.

After that, I gradually noticed that I was being tailed around the campus and did a little research at the law library and saw that there was no charge that they could stick me with. But they did take away my boxing scholarship, one of the first two boxing scholarships Cal ever gave, and also took away my will to continue pursuing my education there, but not my will to become a great writer, which I was sure I could become. It was an incomprehensible feeling based upon the profound spiritual feelings of love which would overcome me and transfix me when I wrote. Some grand illumination would grip me and hold me until I wrote the feeling away. It was beginning poetry and often clumsy, but not always, like the poem I wrote as a freshman at Oakland Junior College, when I was twenty-four years old, my third college already after changing my major from fine art to education to English, and after dropping out of the commercial world executive career track I was on so I could find something worth living for besides just making money and gaining power.

On the way to the library one day, I saw a tree stripped of its leaves and wrote:

Fall

A dog's muddy footprints
among the star-specking leaves
Evanescent factors
Summer is done
The trees stand shred-dry
with the breeze

One other day I saw a beautiful Persian girl in a classroom at Cal that students used to study in. She was gorgeous, a tawny blonde, and I wrote:

For Beauty

Oh see how the green wind blows
the banjo strings of humming grass
and the bumblebee wipes his sword
on a copper leaf

Then I stood up, walked by the small desk chair she was sitting at near the window, dropped the poem in front of her and rushed out of the classroom without looking back. I never saw her again.

I loved those two poems. I wrote a dozen more like that, with varying degrees of skill. I had the gift of language, but most were a little romantic in the nineteenth-century sense, and Josephine Miles said I should keep writing, but that I needed to read more. She didn't say why, but I know now that she felt it would take me out of an archaic romantic sort of style I had, like that of the classics I'd read. There were no Beat poets then. I gushed with corny feeling, like all young poets.

Oh, I am a winter rose lover
dancing to the worried winds

This was me, the poet, at Cal. I believed in love everlasting and the songs that sang in me. I smashed IQ tests. I was a bonafide genius in the brain-power department. But it was the feeling that prodded me to write, the desire to assuage the need to express my emotions. In addition to my mother's death, my brother Eddy's suicide, and my brother Al becoming a dopefiend, my father eventually remarried a woman who disliked his children.

I was trying to make something out of myself. I worked at the library fifteen hours a week, trained with the boxing team for two hours each weekday, now had a wife and wonderful son in the first grade, took care of my brother Al's kids, since he didn't, and managed the apartment house my father had bought my brother and me, as well as carried a full load of units. I caught colds all the time. In the fall of '56, I had about ten doctor appointments to receive anticold medicines, and complained that the pills would get me a little whoozy at times. I still got great grades, but I was driven to the edge of my endurance by my schedule and it was only the poems erupting that saved me from a breakdown. But they kept me joyous. Life was beautiful. I had a beautiful wife and a very handsome son. I was handsome. Girls swirled around me all the time. I loved the girls, too.

When I used to show up at Josephine Miles's office, she would let me walk right in, to the annoyance of one female grad student who told me that she and other grad students were working on big papers and had made appointments. I listened to the student. It did make sense. But I was a sophomore in English, and two professors, one a poet, had said my work was beyond their help and that I should go see Josephine Miles—only she could help me. The Spanish teacher, a sexy twenty-two-year-old, who later got a reputation in poetic circles as a teacher and critic, said, "Now, don't expect her to tell you that you're a poet!" "Okay," I said and walked up to Josephine Miles's office and knocked on the door and went in and handed her a poem. She told me what day to come back, and when I did, she asked if I'd written any more poems in the couple of days since I'd seen her and then said that I was a *natural poet.* All the time she talked to me, she smiled. She told me that she was taking a year off but gave me her home address so I could send her my poems. What a gift!

But in the meantime, the surveillance was hot and heavy. A guy who resembled Jack Dempsey, tough like a crook or a cop, and who in no way looked like either a professor or a student, used to follow me around the library. I decided to leave town. The night before my last exam in Spanish, I made love to my young Spanish teacher, told her I was not looking for a sweetheart, and said that I was taking off for L.A. to write, whether I succeeded or not, and she said, "You'll succeed. Because you're whole." And I did, in my way.

I hitched a ride with my brother-in-law Frank in a truck, leaving about five o'clock in the morning—I'd already slipped out of my apartment house the day before—and left for L.A. from my sister and brother-in-law's house. My wife took circuitous routes by car from our place and kissed me goodbye, saying she was sure nobody had followed her.

My first day in downtown Los Angeles, I went to Pershing Square to watch all the sky pilots try to preach all the people into heaven, and later wrote my first short story about them in modern prose on and sent it to Josephine Miles. She said, first of all, that it was very powerful and she might be wrong, but she thought it might be a dramatic poem.

But I had seen a man that day in Pershing Square who was in one of the many groups that congregated and debated the problems of society and existence in the park, in the midst of the city's skyscrapers. He was a middle-aged, gray-haired man, with light eyes behind wire-rimmed glasses, who looked like an intellectual and sat on a garden ledge and swung his feet back and forth, and never once raised his

Floyd Salas, while a student at the University of California at Berkeley, June 1956

voice. He said on this sunny winter day in January 1957 that the youth of the country would rise up in revolt against the militaristic, authoritarian society of the McCarthy-Eisenhower years. I was a student on the lam, just driven away from the campus by the police for illegal, antisocial behavior, and I said, "I come from the campus and it's a rigid conventional society without any kind of revolutionary mood. The students are conformist." And he said, "But they will revolt." And they did. I was one of them. In 1961, just four years later, I started the Student Peace Union at San Francisco State University to oppose the very military-industrial complex he was talking about. This was the year that Kennedy became president and the school put up a speaking forum on the campus for the first time.

I went to Long Beach from Los Angeles the next day and stayed with my wife's aunt and uncle for three days until I got a job and moved into a rooming house near the Douglas Aircraft company. I scored a perfect 100 in the IQ test and was hired as a timekeeper immediately.

I spent my days in poetic solitude. I lived a quarter mile or so from the aircraft plant entrance in a room I was to share with another worker in another aircraft plant. He was a Southern boy, mid-thirtyish, heavy, but not really fat. Uneducated but a nice guy who took me to an Okie nightclub where I met a beautiful brunette, who looked like a movie star and came over to sit by me at the bar and asked me why I didn't come over to her table when she stared at me. I didn't tell her I was shy. She went out in the car to kiss me, but I never saw her again. My roommate moved out because I would come in from the swingshift at 1 A.M., switch on my lamplight, turn on the radio low to classical music, drop down on my bed, and start writing. He had to get up in the morning for the day shift. He never complained to me, just moved out in a few days. I was sorry, but I had to write at night when I got off work and I had the time for it. I had been training for the intercollegiate boxing season at Cal and was in good shape and full of energy. After I finished the story, I'd write poems until I fell asleep around three or four or five, sometimes six in the morning. When I woke up, I'd eat a breakfast of two raw eggs stirred up in Ovaltine or orange juice, then shower and shave. Then I'd go to the library,

Father, Ed Salas, and stepmother, Dolores, outside Salas' Place, one of their restaurants, Oakland, 1955

which was a half a block away from the rooming house, and read books of criticism on Dylan Thomas and any other poets I found to be interesting. He was my favorite at the time. I'd study and sometimes memorize one of his poems that day. Then I'd go back to my place and sometimes, though not always, smoke a joint, then go to work as a timekeeper at the airplane factory. I could do all the work there in two and a half hours if I pushed it, which I did when I wanted to write a poem that night at work, or, if not, still go to work with Dylan Thomas's poetry ringing in my head.

I'd be checking time cards on a rack in this factory aircraft plant (which was surprisingly quiet) and through my head would be raging: "The force that through the green fuse drives the flower / drives my green age / that blasts the roots of trees is my destroyer. / And I am dumb to tell the crooked rose / my youth is bent by the same wintry fever." Or "As I was young and easy under the apple boughs, / about the lilting house and happy as the

grass was green / In the sun that was young once only / Time let me play and be / happy in the mercy of his means."

It was a beautiful existence. I missed my wife. I was lonely, but I was also rich in creative mental energy. I reveled in my loneliness like a solitary poet drunk on his own feeling. I'd get off work after midnight and buy a hamburger for dinner at a fast-stop joint, then eat my burger and walk the dark streets of residential Long Beach reciting my poems aloud to myself, exulting in the beautiful feeling of love that gripped me. I'd walk for hours in poetic happiness, in love with my solitude, exulting in the huge feelings of ecstasy that wanted to burst from my chest. I made joy out of my sadness. I felt like a cross between Dylan Thomas and Poe, Baudelaire and De Quincey. The great feeling that transfixed me seemed the stuff of the immortal spirit, that my words held my uplifted soul and rang with the universal song.

That was the young poet I was. But having read the lives of conmen and great bankrobbers from the *Police Gazette* in my father's library and the Oakland Public Library where I had my first real, steady job at seventeen, I had learned that the great masters of crime knew how to live in solitude and escape detection. So I did, too, and never got busted, ever again, once I made up my mind that I was going to make the police persecution pay for me, that I was going to use the enforced solitude to become a poet, a humanitarian writer, an asset to his society, not a criminal in any sense of the word. And I'd keep smoking pot, too, a victimless crime, and much less a vice than booze, the most harmful drug on earth, and the one sanctioned by this hypocritical society.

I stayed at Douglas Aircraft for about three months, then went back and got my wife and child and left again for Long Beach. This time, I took bus boy and bar boy and kitchen helper jobs until I found myself a good job. I took a test for the job of a Remington Rand salesman on Wilshire Boulevard in Los Angeles. I got the highest grade on the I.Q. test that they'd ever had. It was a naval officers' test of seventy-five questions, with a time of twenty minutes. Nobody had ever finished it. I finished it in sixteen minutes and got two answers wrong. I was hired immediately, and picked, with two other high scorers, to be sent back East for three months of special training.

I was to spend one month studying in Long Beach before being sent East to the main factory. But in two weeks my boss called me into his office and showed me a telegram that said simply: "Fire Floyd Salas immediately." And so I was out of a job. Two days later, I got a job as a bar boy at the Wilton Hotel in Long Beach and was asked to fill in as a bartender when the night bartender at the basement beach bar had to skip town for locking the cops out when they tried to bust one of his whores for solicitation. I did well there. They wanted to keep me. But I dropped one of my joints on the floor of my wife's uncle's apartment and her mother, who had come to Long Beach with us, called the Long Beach police and they set a trap for me. I found this out from the manager of the hotel, who told me about it when I told him that I didn't want to get anybody in trouble but the cash that I was given by the office to open the bar with every morning was off every day but on this day there was too much money. When I told the manager this, he nodded his head, then told me a few minutes later that I was a good boy and that I'd better watch out because the Long Beach police had me under surveillance and were setting a trap for me.

I quit the next day and spent the next several months bouncing around from bus boy job to apprentice waiter to bar boy in town after southern California town, always moving when I felt the heat getting too close again, but writing, always writing short stories and poem after poem after poem. Finally, when a customer in the bar of a resort called the Antelope Valley Inn in the town of Lancaster in the Mojave Desert made friends with me and asked me to help him with some cement work he wanted to do at his home, I knew it was another trap and quit the next day.

I went back to Oakland with my wife and child, moved into another of my father's houses to house-sit while he was in southern California for a few months. I collected an unemployment check of $22.00 a week, and wrote all day, every day while my wife worked as the assistant manager of the credit office in a downtown women's store.

The narcs were still in Oakland waiting for me. They had chased me out of Cal, so I drew unemployment and wrote. I lived, though I didn't know it at the time, one block from where Jack London had written his early stories. He had been one of my idols since boyhood. I'd read his books and his biography, and I thought of him as my spiritual progenitor. I would try to live up to his example.

I sent my stories to Lowney Handy, who had helped James Jones, the author of *From Here to Eternity,* and she wrote back that I was a very promising writer and she would continue to help me by mail because she had heart trouble and had no more room at her writers' colony in Ohio. She gave me instructions on how to develop as a writer. So every day, I'd continue my habit of eating two raw eggs in a glass of Ovaltine, shower and shave and then sit down and copy great works of literature, word for word, letter for letter, period for period just as she had told me to do. I must have copied fifty short stories ranging from Steinbeck to James Purdy and John Updike, Faulkner, Hemingway, and novels, too. I copied all of *The Great Gatsby, As I Lay Dying,* huge sections of *Ulysses* and *The Sun Also Rises,* the beginnings and ends of every chapter in *From Here to Eternity,* large portions of *A Portrait of the Artist as a Young Man,* and, a couple of years later, two-thirds of *Rabbit Run.* I quit at what I considered the true end of the book, though Updike kept going for another hundred pages or so. After I'd copy for two or three hours or until lunch, I'd then start writing one of my stories, either reworking, continuing, or starting a new one. I'd write all afternoon until dinner time. Then I'd eat and return to the back sun porch where my writing room was, lined with my brother Eddy's and my own books, and study poetry. I'd read and translate Lorca and Vallejo. There was no Neruda, the commy, around to read in the U.S. then. Then finally around ten or eleven, I'd quit and get ready for bed.

This was my normal pattern. All the time that I spent in the back porch office, a small foreign car, with a big antennae sticking up from the back bumper to attract my attention, would circle the block, riding through the alley behind me, letting me know that I was being watched. This is called hostile surveillance. Plainclothes cops would come up behind me in the unemployment line and stare at me and try to un-nerve me, or knock on the front door and suddenly flash a badge in my face to scare me and disrupt my writing. But I kept writing. All of this for supposedly smoking a joint on Saturday nights, but really for daring

The author's first wife, Velva (Harris) Salas, with their son, Gregory, and a nurse in the Salas Pharmacy, owned and operated by Floyd's brother John Edward ("Eddy") Salas, 1950

to outwit the cops for a friend's sake. But I was determined that if they were going to try to capture me, I was going to make it pay off for me. If I had to withdraw from all society in order to save myself, then I would make it a creative solitude, and I did.

A maitre d' immigrant from Mexico, a handsome white man and his mate, an anglo real estate woman who sometimes did business with my father, had become friends with my father and his wife, and he wanted to read my palm one day. He said that I had the hand of a person who could forge his own destiny, that I could shape my own fate. This happened to me the spring of 1958, after my father returned from southern California. This was what I was sure I could do, but his words strengthened me. I remember my younger sister Annabelle at the kitchen table in my father's house being resentful. She never did like my bohemian lifestyle and thought I should go to work and support my wife and kid just like any other married man. Why should I be so superior? Who did I think I was, anyway?

I won the Rockefeller Foundation scholarship to the El Centro Mexicano de Escritores in Mexico City in July 1958, with the short stories that I had written and worked on during the months since I had been driven out of Cal in January 1957. I won my escape from the local narcs with the talent that they had forced me to develop by driving me out of the university and what would have been an academic future for me as a professor somewhere. (I'm leaving out at least a hundred more entrapment tries that would take more than a book-length volume to relate.)

One acquaintance, now dead, who tried to set me up a couple times in 1958 said, "You're so driven to be a writer, Floyd, because there's no other way you can make it in society." And he was right. I worked in an Oakland cannery for ninety twelve-hour days in a row the summer of 1958, with only one day off after forty-five of those days, and saved a thousand dollars to keep me alive when I was gone for the promised year on the Rockefeller. I was exhausted, but determined. I left in October just before Halloween by myself since my wife had been promised a job in Mexico City, if she stayed with her women's department store job through Christmas, which she did and they got her a job as a private part-time secretary for a millionaire owner of the only American style motel—at that time—in Mexico City when she joined me in January 1959.

I paid some dues though. And though I got away from the local narcs, the same kind of game started in Mexico City a couple of days after I got there and before I could retire to creative solitude again.

I had only been awarded a scholarship. Two other guys from the U.S. who never reached a professional level in their writing, let alone achieved any fame, also got fellowships in 1958, the year I applied. They received a couple of thousand dollars for the year. I had to pay my own living expenses. I was suspect, not respectable. I had a bad rep. I also wrote about criminals as if they were human beings. But I made the year pay off and completely wrote and rewrote seventeen new and old stories, and came back from Mexico City never having been helped with a cent from the center, except for a part-time job they gave me for a couple of weeks. Other writers from Mexico who had received fellowships asked me if I got any money and I said no, but I would have liked to. Then I gave the director, who was a well-known successful writer, my stories to read when she came back to the States for a while. She skimmed them and wrote, "These look all right to me," and sent me on my way. So I went away, unhappy, but not bitter or defeated. But I'll never forget that not one person in that center ever asked me or my wife and child to any social function of any kind except for one single time when my wife came back with me to Mexico City in January 1959 and the director took us to a play put on by a group of drama fellowship winners, actors, and playwrights. She did not smile once the whole night.

When I first arrived in Mexico City in October 1958, a tall dark man in a brown suit used to stand outside my door in the small hotel I was staying in, and I'd see him every time I left or entered my room. Finally, I asked, "What are you watching me for?" And he smiled and, very slowly, said, "Com-u-nista!" I could tell you more, but that's enough. My wife was a blonde of Mormon, now agnostic, stock, who had the face of Elizabeth Taylor, very beauti-

ful. When she joined me in Mexico City, we sent my son to a private school in the ritziest section of town, Chapultepec, like all the other Americans who had children. The principal of the school was so impressed with my wife, she hired her to teach my son's fourth-grade class in both Spanish and English, and when Teacher's Day came around, she got more presents from her students than any other teacher in the school. My wife is the only person I ever knew who learned how to speak Spanish by taking it in high school. Still, my son didn't have one friend there. He only received one invitation from another student and it was withdrawn without explanation. I'm sorry my wife and child had to pay my dues for me. The sins of the fathers shall fall upon the sons, if smoking pot can be considered a sin. Such is the price of nonconformity and artistic rebellion in any society.

When I came back to the United States in July 1959, I found I needed help getting a true editorial perspective on my work. Josephine Miles couldn't criticize fiction and I had stopped sending my poems to her. But first I had to earn some money. I worked in the cannery for three months, again to save money and get back in the black, which I did, though I got fired for breaking a guy's jaw because he had threatened me. The narcs were at the cannery, too, and my brother had blabbed that I had brought a pound of pot back from Mexico with me, so when another guy accused me of selling an ounce to his cousin-in-law, which was a lie, I blasted him hard in the stomach with a left hook, folded him up like a jackknife, and told him not to fight or he'd lose. He groaned, "I'm hip!" and never talked pot to me again. A few years later, he was found in an orchard outside San Jose with a bullet in his head. He had become a well-known fink. But then another guy, a tough Puerto Rican who didn't like me being his straw-boss, the assistant to the foreman, wouldn't turn off the machines at lunchtime because the year before he had made fifteen minutes overtime washing them off after everybody went to lunch for a half hour. This went on for two months or so. Finally, we fought and I broke his jaw with two quick left hooks and got fired, which forced me to look for another job. So I got a job as a bus boy in a first-class restaurant, but didn't like it, though the maitre d' told me if I stuck in that racket I'd be as good a waiter as Lou, the best waiter there. I then applied for a job as a shoe salesman when I didn't even know how to measure a foot size. I fibbed about my experience, got hired, and then told the manager, who was an excellent shoe dog, that I'd rather watch him as he sold a pair first. I watched carefully as he used the foot scale to measure width and length size, then took over on the next one and became his top salesman the six months I was there.

Then I called up Walter Van Tilburg Clark, author of *The Oxbow Incident,* in January 1960, at his office at San Francisco State University, where he was head of the Creative Writing Department, got him on the phone, said I wanted to work personally with him, told him I didn't want to enter the Creative Writing Department, that I already was a writer, and he said, "There will be a card waiting for you at registration." And it was the most important thing that had happened to me in my writing life since Josephine Miles took me under her wing, somewhat, three and a half years before.

I had wanted a shoe salesman's job so I could work nights and weekends and use all the days of the work week to write. So I quit my full-time job to take the directed writing course with Walter Van Tilburg Clark, who had written a truly great book, and planned to find another part-time job. But I was such a good salesman, the company hired me back to work in another location, a warehouse type store on weekends and two nights, twenty-four hours a week, which gave me the time to write during the day. I *had* brought a pound of pot back from Mexico with me, so I wouldn't have to go out on the street to buy it and take my chances on getting busted. I used the pot to write. It lasted me two years and was a creative tool that allowed me to use both my day mind simultaneously with my dreaming mind, letting the day mind follow and support the dreaming mind into the world of imagination and metaphor. I didn't use pot to play. I used it to work. But it was work I loved.

I now wrote in the daytime and worked nights and weekends and began to rewrite all the stories I had written in Mexico City. Walter Van Tilburg Clark said I had some talent when he first talked to me about a couple of my stories and then told me how to rewrite, what to aim for, what was wrong with these drafts, mainly that there was no deeper meaning to the action of the stories. I asked him for his

note pad and insisted on taking notes when he didn't want me to because he felt it was stifling, but I convinced him to allow me to do it and to also give me his notepad with his criticisms on it, which he reluctantly did. Then I went and studied in the library, reading books on symbol, theme, and metaphor, as well as everything I could find on Rimbaud. I always studied poetry after I studied fiction, because fiction was harder for me than poetry, and I wanted to learn both. Then I rewrote the Pershing Square story and sent it to Clark when I was running a trampoline center in Russian River, up the coast a hundred miles, for which I quit the shoe salesman's job. When I went to see him in late spring, he was very excited about the story and sent me away with a thousand-word new beginning to my story written by him in his tiny handwriting. It was great. I both loved and resented it. I feared that he was taking over my story, yet, I recognized what the great act of giving it entailed as well as the map laid out right there in front of me of how to make my tale—of a red-headed devil berating a tiny black woman preacher in the park, with skyscrapers and the pigeons flying all around—succeed. I broke the whole section he'd written down into parts so I could understand exactly what he did. He told me the story was quite well-written and urged me to keep writing and to enter the creative writing program he had founded at State because he was retiring to go into Nevada and write himself. It was wonderful. One of the best experiences of my life. I'd seen him twice and he had illuminated metaphor for me. And he'd loved my story so much he'd written his own beginning to it. He helped shape my life. And that fall, I entered the Creative Writing Department at SF State. It turned out to be one of the most important forces in my writing life, as important as Cal and Josephine Miles. I was forging my way.

San Francisco State was a conservative commuter's school with a blonde, pink-complexioned homecoming queen and sororities and fraternities. Fraternity bullies would come and harass us when we demonstrated for "Peace" and "Hands Off Cuba." I didn't care about them. I was there to talk, read, write, and breathe writing, both poetry and fiction, and knew with the heat that was on me that I could never ever even think about being a teacher. I was an outcast, a pariah. There was only one way I could make it in America and that was by becoming an important writer. So I had no intention of using a degree to get success, which included teaching. In fact, the worst grade I ever got was a D in Mental Health in 1963, a required course for public school teaching, which I could substitute for a science class. I got the D because I challenged the professor—who was always using me as a guinea pig in the class—to quit talking about being creative and let me go home and create my sculpture and I'd bring it back to him at the end of the summer session to prove what I'd done. For some reason, though I never told anyone, he knew I got up every morning and wrote before I came to school. He gave me a D because I wouldn't give him the sculpture I'd carved out of sandstone, therefore proving I hadn't learned how to play the game. The one thing the authorities wanted to teach me was to learn how to play the game and prove that I was rehabilitated and thereby break my stubborn idealistic attitude.

I did great at State. Herb Wilner, the new head of the department wrote in his note on my brilliant term paper in "The Craft of Fiction" class, studying the construction of the novel, that he paid me tribute for my ideas and my writing. I got A's in everything but fiction writing because I was too clumsy and didn't polish the manuscripts. My poems were published in *Transfer,* the best college literary magazine in the country. I was on the editorial staff. (It wasn't until I won the Joseph Henry Jackson Award in 1964, for an unfinished work of fiction, worth a thousand dollars and contact by agents and publishers, Harper, that is, that I began to get A's in fiction, when I was already a graduate student.) Creative writing departments grade on neat clean styles. I was struggling to gain control of a tragic subject matter, crime and murder, that was huge, novel size, not neat little short stories about minor personal hassles, and I didn't sweat style. Everybody who read my stories would say, "Great. Powerful. But they're not short stories. They could never be published as short stories. They'd have to be published in hardcover, if at all." Finally, after one year at State, I said to myself: If these stories aren't short stories, I'll make them into long stories, novels. And I did. My first three novels were originally three of the very first short stories I wrote when I applied for the Rockefeller.

Character sketch by Floyd Salas, from his series of line drawings "A Rogues Gallery of the Insane," 1957

But in the meantime, since I wasn't going to be able to teach anywhere, I figured I had to be able to earn a living doing something, so I took a journalism course writing for the daily paper, the *Golden Gater* in the fall of 1961, but told the instructor that I was working on a novel in the mornings and wouldn't be able to come to class, though I'd write for the paper. Well, he didn't like that very much, but I then wrote an article on SF State students picketing the AEC building in Berkeley, a block from Cal, and took pictures of them, too. The editors put it on the front page with my by-line, and nobody ever bothered me about attending class again. Also, the media picked it up and whammo! Now, the movement got some press and TV, and the authorities decided to bust them. Then when they got busted, a troop of reporters showed up at the court hearing and they got more publicity. I didn't realize what I'd done until a Quaker named Cecil, a big middle-aged preacher, who worked with the small band of pacifists at school, told me I was doing a wonderful job publicizing the movement like that. I also was the primary organizer of a demonstration in Union Square in downtown San Francisco in which I tried to get all the dissenting groups in the Bay Area to object to the atomic bomb military industrial complex in order to save the world. And I also organized an all-night vigil that hit the front pages when the Russians set off the hydrogen bomb. But it wasn't until the Vietnam War had started and the whole country started demonstrating that I realized what I'd done, that I'd actually been in the vanguard of the student movement, just as that intellectual in Pershing Square that January day in 1957 had predicted.

But I learned all about radical politics when I went from school to school, SF State to Cal to socialist and communist and anarchist and pacifist groups in San Francisco and Berkeley, trying to rally everyone together for the cause. I didn't know that you weren't supposed to tell the truth, that repeating publicly what people said wasn't good politics. Once, I spoke out at a socialist club dinner party meeting that I got to address for the proposed rally in Union Square in San Francisco. The chairman of the party told everybody to go to the rally because it would be good for them, for their political group, and for that reason, only, to do it. I got up and spoke in this anarchist restaurant—anarchists were the only ones beside the students who cared or did anything about the war machine then—and told the socialist club that that was exactly the wrong reason to do it. I wanted them to join the rally because they loved us and the country and the world, not because it would pay off for them. When I finished only one woman clapped, but hard, and in the rest of the big restaurant, where a group of anarchists were sitting, one young man said, "Good speaker!" as I walked out.

Then when another student and I organized the Student Peace Union in the early spring semester of 1962, everybody started jockeying for political power, since I seemed to get all the publicity. I was already writing the second draft of my novel *Tattoo the Wicked Cross* and was only carrying 11 units in school so I could devote most of my day to it. When I showed up at school one afternoon and saw the table set up on the commons by the student activists and people were acting cool to me in an attempt to keep me from being president of

the peace union, I shook my head and said, "I pass. You can keep this presidency," and went home and wrote on my novel. In two years it would be the novel that would win the Joseph Henry Jackson Award and bring me attention and fame. And the Student Peace Union would not commit another act without my leadership that attracted any attention from either the school or the public media.

But it wasn't over for me. An undercover CIA agent, posing as a student on the campus, asked me to work with the "company" in order to keep the student peace movement democratic—though he wouldn't positively identify the agency until I met with his supervisor. He told me that smoking pot would get me in trouble if I didn't cooperate. I said it sounded like a blackmail threat. When I then backed off from the Student Peace Union, he put my name up for the presidency in my absence, but it wasn't accepted since I wouldn't attend the election meeting. Then when I still wouldn't attend any of the meetings and stayed away from school to write my novel, the *heat* now infiltrated my family through my new brother-in-law.

But even though I stayed home to work on my novel, I still got embroiled in politics at school. I'd written a poem called "The Professor and the Lumberjack" and submitted it to *Transfer* magazine. It was accepted, but because I was then being ostracized for some unknown reason, it was stuck on the last page of a play by one of the editors and overlooked when the magazine was attacked and held up from distribution and sales by the right wing student body president for the word "arty-farty" used in a short story about a musician who breaks up with his girl. The story was written by Clancy Carlile, who would later write the novel, *Honkytonk Man*, which would be made into a movie produced by and acted in by Clint Eastwood. A student judge ordered the magazine released, but when it was, everybody read the magazine and discovered my poem about a homosexual orgy which ends in murder and I became famous on the campus, though the student newspaper, which had followed my political organizing, reported the furor which followed by hardly mentioning my name, even though right wing forces on the campus, including a couple of professors, tried to have the magazine banned for good and took the issue to the college council meeting of professors and student body officers, where both mine and Clancy's school records were examined. One history professor then complained because students like Clancy and I were almost straight A students, which meant that writers of obscene material were being rewarded by the Creative Writing Department. All they did was fan the flames and sell the magazine out and make me famous on campus now for my outrageous poem as well as my political acts of dissent.

That spring of 1962, on May Day, the first black nationalist appeared on campus and created a scandal with his attacks on the white power structure and his demand for a separate black country within the United States. He preached hate and I took him on. One African American poet, Welton Smith, whom I knew and befriended, put his arm around my shoulder and said, "I claim Floyd as a friend." But I was so disturbed by the demand for separation when I and all my friends worked hard for integration of all peoples in the United States, especially the African American element, I went home and wrote a poem and called it into the student newspaper office where the main editor, John Burkes, who later wrote for *Newsweek,* took my call and typed up "May Day 1962" and put it into the next newspaper that week. That, too, raised a stink, but I found that a couple of the right wing professors now even said hello to me.

It was a prophetic poem. Because that was what indeed did happen. The black power movement became violent and created a backlash and all the blacks and liberals and student activists suffered. But I got such a reaction from black poets and the few black people that were then in The Movement, who wanted me to sympathize with and understand them, I wrote another poem the next week and it was even more prophetic.

To a Black Messiah

You seek a promised land?
with the fence posts planted by your own hand?
You wish to sow black seed with black topsoil?
pocket the bright fruit
that glitters on the branch
like coins?

bend your knee to a black God in a burnoose?
with a broadsword?

show the small of your back to that apostle
with the bleeding rib
and the pale brow?

Then there must be a messiah!
A black man
crowned in the kink of his own thorns
while seeking the timber of black truth
for that silver nail
that blood clot
in his pink palm

There must be a messiah!
if anti-Christ and the white man's lie:
the fang in the lamb's bleat
the rape in Georgia cotton
that is veiled
in the lace of scripture

There must be a Messiah!
willing to paint the blackened ulcer
of his race
with the iodine of his own veins
willing to stitch the bruises of his own skin
on the patches of discolor
in the white pigment
of a pale skinned pride

If you deny the Christ
there must be a Messiah!
to shoulder the lynch tree
and hang from its branch

like a flag

"To a Black Messiah" unwittingly prophecized the deaths of Malcolm X and Martin Luther King six years later. But now, though the black poets were pleased, the professors who spoke to me the week before ignored me again. But I called it as I saw it and it came true.

All the time that I had called in both the poems on the phone, because I had written them at home, the phone kept clicking as if someone was trying to distract and interrupt the phone calls that would then give me more publicity for my outrageous acts of dissent. That was in the spring. I used to see guys following me around campus all the time, even when I played around with a couple of girls. I felt I had to get published in some way, so I decided to go see Lawrence Ferlinghetti, who had not spoken at the demonstration I organized at Union Square, but did attend it. He was the publisher of *Howl,* after all, and seemed the logical choice for my biblical poems, which I called *Prayers of Heresy.* He remembered me and read a couple of the poems, then called them psychopathic and sent me on my way. And this is the guy who published *Howl?* Who had to fight a criminal charge for publishing sexually psychopathic poetry? Here are two of the poems.

Scarecrow

Out of a tent of wind
came a tuxedoed scarecrow
dancing for me
with hinged limbs of broom
whistling a dirge
through the bearded straw of his chin

His tongue was laughing black
His eye the shadow of crow
The silken knot at his throat
the strangled heart of a bow

Still he danced
His cane steps tapped their song
until I cried that I could not dance
with the murmur and shiver of silk
'till my toes had nails of bone
my eyes
the curdle
of milk

Black-lipped Bird

A black-lipped bird
hunting from a wind
snatched the yellow stalk of my tongue
from the belly of a rain cloud
and spit it on the peak
of a climbing mountain

No odor of mint pine there
only dogwood
and bat screech
poison leaf
and goat pellet
and the numbed pond
of a rock spring
stiff
with the peelings
of August snow

I was still desperate and went to the left-wing radio station KPFA and left some poems there, asking if I could read them on the radio. A couple of days later I got a call from a guy named John Leonard, who asked me to come in and read them. He was a personable blond guy who would later become the editor of the *New York Times Book Review* section. I was so excited that when he put me in a room by myself with a mike and closed the door, I started reading right away in a rushed, excited voice, mumbling and slurring my words. I'd gotten through about three long poems when he came to the door and said to get ready and watch the red light above the door. When it went off I was supposed to begin reading. I'd been reading to myself all this time but had unwittingly warmed up for the reading and now could read calmly and strongly for a good half hour, poem after poem. Then when the KPFA folio came out with the programs listed for the next month or two, I wrote to my hero, Norman Mailer, who had been clipped hard by a *Time* magazine reviewer for his first book of poems, written in a poetic form and style of his book. I told him I sympathized with him and liked the poem he had written to the editor and printed in the letter section and told him that my reading would be broadcast over WBAI in New York City, since it and KPFK in Los Angeles and KPFA in Berkeley were all three members of Pacifica Radio. He wrote back saying that he was too busy writing to listen to my poems and that I was trying to cash in on his fame. Well, I lost that one, but I still didn't quit.

I wrote to Lowney Handy again, sent her some stories, and asked for her help with my writing. She wrote back and said she still had a bad heart condition and couldn't help me but that she didn't know how or when, but she was sure that someday I would be a well-known, well thought of writer. Well, that was two strikes, though the last one might have been called a foul ball. She died a year or two after that letter.

I then saw a poster announcing that Nelson Algren was going to appear at San Francisco State and I showed up. After his speech, I went to the back stage door of the auditorium and introduced myself and said that I wrote the same kind of material he wrote and asked him if he could help me. We were walking away from the auditorium and he suddenly asked me if I was a boxer. When I asked him how he could tell, he said by my walk, my movements. Then he gave me the address of his agent Candida Donadio and told me to write to her. I was writing the third draft of my novel *Tattoo* then in the fall of 1962 and it wasn't quite ready to send yet, and I didn't want to strike out with a few short stories, so I held off writing right away.

Then the next thing that happened was my wife began to act strangely and make bizarre comments. One time—after I had gone to review a Beckett play at the Actors Workshop at the Marines Theater in San Francisco for the school newspaper, we were leaving a crowded bar in Jack London Square in Oakland and she called out, "Floyd! These guys are bothering me!" When I stepped up to protect her, one of them leaped at me and when I threw a punch at him, she stepped in front of me and blocked my punch with her hip so I couldn't get him good. We wrestled out the front door and I got him down, but I still didn't hit him, just pocketed my review notes as I sat on him while a pickup truck pulled up to us and kept its headlights on us so everyone could see what was happening. Then he did the strangest thing I ever saw in my life. He threw his arm across his face and when he pulled it away, there were cuts on his eyes. Still, I didn't hit him and the fight ended.

Then a couple of weeks later, when some woman who drove a Cadillac and belonged to the business crowd my wife belonged to leaned all over me in a bar and tried to kiss me and I held her off, my wife surprised me by saying it was okay I should have kissed her. I finally pinned her down about both acts among others and when she admitted she was put up to it by the police, I said call the DA right now and tell them they can bust me walking down the street with a joint and put me in prison. If they can get to you, I quit. She said she'd go talk to the police the next day and I should hold off. That next evening she said I only had to do 90 to 120 days and I was pleased that it wasn't San Quentin. The following morning a police wagon came, but instead of taking me to jail, took me to the psychiatric ward at Highland Hospital. The jolly redfaced cop driving the wagon said that a colleague of mine had died that day, Robert Frost. Then he showed me the arrest warrant at the hospital which said, ". . . is writing a social protest novel and believes the police are after him." When I told a doctor the narcs were after me and I, like Raskolnikov, who thought he was above the law in *Crime and Punishment,* had brought suffering to my family, another doctor came in and acted as if I was crazy. So, I stayed up all night the night before court, lying in my bed, figuring out what to do, and the next day in court, after my wife testified against me, saying I was

acting crazy, never mentioning all the weird phone calls and the cars that followed us everywhere we went or her cooperation with the police, which she had admitted to me. I told the judge that I had been smoking pot and was just imagining the police were after me, which meant I wasn't crazy. I saw the head doctor spin around and stare at me. But now I had out-finessed him, and the judge said, "You seem tense. Go spend a couple of weeks on the funny farm anyway, so you can rest." And I did, and took no medication the whole time I was there, at Napa Hospital, telling the doctor I didn't want to become an emotional cripple. I was probably the only person in the nuthouse, including the doctors and nurses, who didn't take tranquilizers. When the doctor asked me what my IQ was and I said 150 plus, he guffawed and proceeded to give me an IQ test right then. By the time he was finished, his eyes were wide with surprise, but the love of my wife for me was ruined.

I got out of the nuthouse three weeks later but they wouldn't release me completely because I hesitated when I was asked if I would stop smoking pot completely. I had to spend seven more half weeks there before I was finally allowed to leave for good. When I first got to Napa, an Oakland narc was in the receiving room. He said hello to me and put his arm around my shoulder because I had been willing to give up. Then when I was received, the head of the State Bureau of Mental Health, who looked like Alfred Hitchcock, came in, took my statement and immediately left. A group of psychiatrists had an interview meeting with me, the only person that whole day of maybe fifty people who had arrived at Napa Hospital to be interviewed by them. One of them asked me why I smoked pot and I answered, "Because it makes me love everybody."

When I was finally released under the conservatorship of my wife after ten weeks, on the grounds that I would now get a job as a reporter at the *Oakland Tribune,* where a cousin's husband was copyeditor, I put a rifle in my mouth to see if I could kill myself, then stood up and started writing the fourth draft of *Tattoo.* I wouldn't ask my cousin for the reporter job. I was too idealistic and wanted to get it myself, so I was hired as a copy boy. I quit after a couple of months to take a reporter's job with a suburban newspaper, then went back to school to get my M.A. and finish my novel.

I finished the fourth draft and sent it to Candida Donadio, who read it and then sent me a rejection letter. I wrote to Nelson Algren again and told him that she'd rejected it, but that it was a powerful story and I still wanted to get it published even though I was now working as a reporter for a suburban newspaper. He wrote back to me that it was my own hope talking about it being powerful because Candida would have taken it if it were. Nevertheless, he told me to send it to him and be prepared to have red marks all over it and don't think about jumping off the bridge either. I felt he had misjudged me and didn't send him the book, which I regret to this day.

But I then read that Allen Ginsberg was in town after a year in India and I called up Ferlinghetti's City Lights bookstore. I got Ginsberg on the phone, told him I'd like to show him my poetry, that I was an outcast writer and made him say, "Hey! Don't scare me!" though he agreed to meet me there. I told him I'd drive right over. I lived at that time in the Montclair upper middle-class district of Oakland with my wife. She was making a lot of money as a head bookkeeper.

There he was still dressed in the flowing robes of an Indian fakir waiting in the bookstore for me. We went across the street to a café that would later become the famous restaurant Tosca, and I showed him some of my *Prayers of Heresy*. A blond man sat at the table right next to us by himself and listened to everything we said. Ginsberg turned the poems down, too. I was right where I started, only worse.

I decided then to send *Tattoo* to the Joseph Henry Jackson Award competition, which had been won the year before by Leonard Gardner for *Fat City*. The prize was only a couple of years old at that time. If I didn't win it, I was going to jump off the Golden Gate Bridge. It was my last hope. But in June 1964, a telegram was delivered to me by a guy in a sport coat who looked like a plainclothes cop. When I called the number, I was told I had won the award, but couldn't tell anybody about it. I had to keep it a secret. I couldn't understand that. Herb Gold, Tom Parkinson, and some other man were the judges. I was so excited, I went to see my father in his restaurant and told him and talked excitedly about it. When I called the person I had talked to at the San Francisco Foundation which administered the award about what to do next, the man said, "Don't bother," in a real cold voice. It turned out that I was the only person who won the award who was never given an award luncheon for it, to this day, over thirty years later, though I myself was one of the judges two years in a row, for 1978 and '79 and attended the luncheons. Still, I didn't have to kill myself and my life did change for the better.

The award brought me fame and the novel earned me much more fame when it was published in 1967. It was called a work of genius, a classic first novel, and the best first novel in ten years in the *Saturday Review of Literature,* among other rave reviews, including the *New York Times*. It was also picked for the Evergreen Book Club as a dual selection with Norman Mailer's *Why Are We in Vietnam?*

I was no longer considered crazy by my friends and family, but eccentric. Such is the benefit of being accepted by society. I then wrote to Nelson Algren and sent him a copy of the article about the award and said, "I'm not gloating, Nelson. I've got a long way to go. I just wanted you to know that it was a powerful book like I said it was, no matter what Candida Donadio's opinion was."

But I'd lost the love of my wife and within two years, in 1966, a year before the book was published, my wife and I broke up for good. I'd played around with a couple of girls at San Francisco State in 1961 and '62, and that was how the FBI got to my wife, with the help of my brother-in-law and sister Annabelle, of course. But I'd been true to my wife since, though she didn't love me anymore after the humiliation and subjugation of my time in the nuthouse. I had started going to church again and was going to get remarried in it so I could go to confession, but when I asked her if she still loved me, she said she didn't know and I called the marriage off and quit going to church. I completely broke with my family after that and didn't talk to any of them again until they started showing up after I won the Jackson Award and I got all the publicity after *Tattoo* was published. But it was over. I no longer had a marriage nor a family of any kind. I was totally alienated from all close human contact. The only good thing, to me, that came out of the nuthouse was that the state department of vocational rehabilitation gave me a monthly stipend to get my two degrees, a B.A. and an M.A. from San Francisco State.

I applied as a teaching assistant to a creative writing instructor, George Price, at State and did so well they gave me a job. I started teaching creative writing at San Francisco State the summer of 1966 and moved out of an upper middle-class neighborhood of Oakland, Montclair, and into the Castro district of San Francisco with a young writing student, Juliet Calabi, before that district was a gay enclave. It was a sad, yet beautiful life. I was free now and could flirt with any woman I wanted and there was no guilt. Still, I loved my wife and yet knew that it was over between us forever. She wanted me to come back a few months after I left, but it was too late. I did go back once, but as soon as I was there, I felt the pressure of the police again and told my son, when I drove him to Skyline High School, where he was now going, that it was being watched by cops. Within two weeks after I moved out of the house because I felt I was being set up, one hundred students were busted at the school for pot and many of them were asked if I had furnished pot to them. One particular incident, in which I took my son and a couple of his buddies over to the Haight-Ashbury district and stopped to buy a six pack of beer, was used as an example of my supplying him and his buddies with pot. But it wasn't true and there were no charges made against me. But my life as a family man was over forever.

But I had spent four and a half years writing *Tattoo* and had lost my wife and my life and I didn't want to go through that again. So I wrote a novella, *What Now My Love*, in twenty-three days in February 1968, when I had the flu and rewrote it four more times in five months and sold it to Grove Press. I'd been working on my second novel, *Gin for Xmas*, during the fall of 1966 and up to the fall of 1967. I sent it to Grove and when they didn't answer right away, I wrote and told them that the book was as great as *Tattoo* and whoever didn't think so didn't know nothin' and I didn't care who he was. They sent me a contract for $2,000.00 and the book back to rewrite. When I reread it, I felt it was too sentimental and wrote the other book, *What Now My Love*, and sent that to them instead and they snatched it up. I would try to rewrite *Gin for Xmas*, an autobiographical novel about my brother Al and me four more times over a total of thirty-five years, counting the time I wrote it as a short story in 1957, before I'd make it a pure mem-

Juliet Calabi, 1967

oir and write it three times in two and half months on a computer in 1991 and sell it immediately. But that was my fourth published book and I am getting a little ahead of myself again.

I was living in Capitola below Long Beach at the southern tip of the San Francisco peninsula when Martin Luther King got killed the spring of 1968, and I went back to Berkeley to fight for freedom again. I'd signed a separate peace with myself about fighting the establishment after my disillusionment with the Student Peace Union so I could write and do my thing and not get mixed up in any more political power stuff. But now I felt I had to do something. Malcolm X and the Black Panthers were getting shot down, too. It was a crisis. So I went back to Berkeley, wrote an article on the killing of a teenage Panther, Bobby Hutton, by the Oakland cops that was printed in the *Berkeley Barb*, then moved to San Francisco and joined the sit-in occupation of the San Francisco State administration building. It lasted one week and we won 14 out of 15 of the points we sat-in for including a new black studies department, a La Raza department, and the lowering of admission standards to allow 1,000 minority students into the college. The only thing we didn't get was ROTC, pronounced rot-sy, off campus. We beat everybody but the Pentagon. Undercover cops were everywhere. I challenged one when he walked upon the banner we were making in the basement of the Ad building, pretending he was drunk, and jerked him outside where no one could see us and told him that if he kept molesting us, I was going to blast him and he split. But that didn't help me with the FBI, the CIA, and the SF police department. The phone in the house we were staying in—my new lady and I, Ginny Staley, with another couple, Steve Wiesinger and Barbara Schatan—got tapped. The ignition of my MG got jammed when I tried to drive home one night. But the greatest irony of all was when I got accused of being an undercover cop. I believe it was because I took on the central committee when they tried to run things without consulting the mass of students sitting in. When I tried to get the mike to speak about it, one of the ruling members of the committee running the sit-in took over the mike and kept it away from me. I was really hurt and didn't come back. And in a couple of days, I got letters from students, all girls, in the sit-in, telling me to come back and join them and I did. Then everybody knew that I was a wild novelist former teacher there who had helped start all this seven years before, and the students welcomed me back and kept referring to me over the mike. It made the whole battle worth it.

Also, in 1968, I took on Saul Bellow when he appeared about two or three weeks before we staged the sit-in of the administration building at San Francisco State and said the university should be a haven from vulgarity for the writer. I asked him to confirm that he'd said that since I'd come into the auditorium late. He said he was sorry I had to sit in the aisle so far back because it was so crowded but he wasn't going to answer that question. Then a young woman near the front asked how much of his work was autobiographical and he said it was none of her business. The English and Creative Writing faculty members who were sitting on the stage behind him smugly clapped with each of his answers. Then another young writer,

Frank Olson, sitting near me in the aisle, asked him why he called his last book *Herzog* instead of Bellow, and there was an uproar at the impudence of these young people. I jumped up and said, "Do you realize what you're doing worshipping that effete man down there in that expensive suit. I bet he can't even come!" An even greater uproar followed. All the faculty people on the stage were fit to be tied, and people stood up and some clapped and others cheered, and I hurried out. When I got outside, I saw a beautiful student I knew standing with some other students. I thought I was going to be attacked when one woman standing a few feet away from her said, "You should be ashamed of yourself. He's a great man." But a student with a motorcycle helmet in his hand, standing next to the beautiful girl I knew, said, "Bellow asked for that. You stood up for all of us." And a couple of weeks or so later, I joined the sit-in at the Ad building.

After the sit-in, Ginny and I, Steve and Barbara, and Vic and Mary Roerich, spent three months in the Siskiyou mountains of northern California on an old homestead still owned by the original family of Vic's wife Mary. Vic was an artist buddy who lived next door to us in San Francisco on the hill with a view of the Golden Gate. Then in September we left for Europe, my lady and I, Steve and Barbara. On the plane, *my* seats were sold twice. So they had to unsnarl the mess first. It turned out the guy who was given my seat was a dope dealer who was retiring on the proceeds of his business and going off to Europe for a while, where he bought a fairly new Mercedes and took me for a ride in it in Mallorca. But there was also a couple who sat behind Barbara and Steve, and the guy was the only man on the plane in a suit with a white shirt and tie. The plump woman in a blue-skirted uniform with him looked like she went to a catholic college. She took my picture as soon as I stepped off the plane. I wrote all about this in *State of Emergency*. But in Europe, I planned to write a novel about the seizure of the Ad building and my days as a student radical. It turned out that though I managed to write it, called *Lay My Body on the Line*, in four years from 1968 to 1972, I didn't get it published until 1978 by Ishmael Reed and Al Young, two great African American writers, as a Y'Bird Press project, funded by the NEA. That year I also got an NEA grant of $7,500.00, which I put down on a four-unit apartment complex, in which I still live very cheaply now. (I bought out two of my original partners and now own the property with my son, Greg. Without that NEA, I wouldn't be able to afford to even live in Berkeley, let alone in a private cottage behind the tri-plex, in which I have written six books already.)

But all my time in Europe was ruined by the machinations of the CIA and Interpol. I was tailed everywhere. Every contact I had with every publisher in England and France was controlled by the same two agencies working together and every police department in every city or village I lived in, whether in England, Spain, Morocco, or France. It made life there a constant trial. In Spain we were harassed so much that I finally fought a six-foot-four, red-haired Spaniard who stuck his camera in my face and snapped my picture for the tenth time that morning. Then when I finally knocked him out after being down three times myself, and went to a doctor to set my misplaced knuckle, the doctors broke my thumb and mis-set my knuckle, bent my finger over, so that if I hadn't torn the cast off after three weeks, I would have had a permanently crippled claw for a hand. I had to have the hand operated on after I got back to America, thanks to the Writers Guild, who paid for it on the grounds that I was an impoverished writer. The CIA made life itself a living death in Hell. I moved from country to country trying to get away, but only moved myself into another police jurisdiction. I was treated like a political pariah, and had to come back to the U.S., New York City, to get *What Now My Love* published. I wrote all about this in *State of Emergency*, which wasn't published until twenty years after I finished it by Arte Publico Press on *April Fool's Day*, 1996. Every day while I was in Europe, I was worked on in an attempt to control my writing and my activities. It was *1984* on an international level. What should have been a great happy creative trip became a sinister unhappy nightmare.

Tony Brown, Mailer's publisher of *Armies of the Night*, wouldn't publish either of my novels, *Tattoo* or *Love*, in England, though I got to meet Mailer for the first time and we had a great conversation in which he told me I was going to have to become a performer if I wanted to make it in America, then told me to call him when I got to New York. Spain broke my bones. Morocco threatened me with the hospital, if I persisted in my writing about my radical life and harassed me and my girl all the time. When I went back through Spain to Paris, five men in black raincoats tried to bust me on the ferry from Tangier to Algeciras and a CIA agent tried to ride in the van I was riding in to Paris, though I refused to allow him to do it. In the café next to the Algeciras dock, he talked about smuggling dope and making big money. All these dope dealers were making big bucks, people kept telling me. It just so happened that the owner of the van I was riding in had thirty pounds of kif hidden in the vehicle and my lady was carrying about a half a pound hidden on her body. The nephew of a Grove Press sales manager came over with us carrying hash cookies and loose kif in his pockets. I was the only one who came in clean, yet I was the only one that was surrounded on the ferry by the men in black raincoats. But I was clean and they couldn't bust me. France had published my first novel *Tattoo*, but wouldn't publicize it or me or allow me to attend any book functions, nor would they attend my reading at the Shakespeare Book Store by the Notre Dame in Paris because I didn't play the game and didn't call up James Jones again when he didn't call me back after they'd given me his private number. One night, when I was being followed down the street by some big American agents in trenchcoats, I stopped and wrote this down, but was interrupted before I could finish it by a woman walking with my lady, Ginny, and I.

Down Wet Paris Streets

I'm with you baby!
Yeah Eldridge
you and me and Leroy
and every other crazy motherfucker!
Kiss my ass!
Those fucking bulls tail me in trench coats
down wet Paris streets!

Shiver!
and write these words down on a damp car top
Raindrops on my palm
follow this heat in my hand till I get this down
and leave some blood on their hands
All these paddy poets
And I mean Ginsberg too
Cop-outs all of them . . .

After three months or so in Paris, I gave up and headed back for the U.S. on July 3,

1969 and arrived in New York on the Fourth of July, Independence Day. When I went into Washington Square in Greenwich Village to play my drums, only I received a citation to appear in court for creating a public disturbance though there were ten other drummers. In New York, I did get my book *Love* edited and a publication date set for January 1970, but I was not invited to a single social function by any of the Grove Press staff, except for one business luncheon, in which my food was burned in a posh restaurant, exactly as it had been burned in a fine restaurant in Marrakesh. I participated in every protest demonstration I could that hot summer, including picketing Rockefeller's apartment next to Central Park. It was a great but bitter experience and merely capped the whole year of turmoil and the fight to keep writing my novel of political dissent.

I didn't finish the book, *Lay My Body on the Line* until election day 1972, three years later. I was then told by Luther Nichols, the West Coast editor of Doubleday, that it was the book they were all looking for about student radicals, but it was too late. He then invited me to lunch, which I refused since the protest movement was still very strong at that time, and it was hardly too late. It took me six more years and a Democratic president, Carter, to get the book published in 1978 with NEA money. The National Endowment for the Arts has supplied the funding for the publishing of all my work since 1970. This includes the book published by Arte Publico Press in 1992, my memoir, *Buffalo Nickel,* the republication of *What Now My Love,* 1995, *State of Emergency,* 1996, and my first book of poems, *Color of My Living Heart,* 1996. With the new restrictions Congress has passed, I cannot ever again apply for an NEA fellowship and I have never received a Guggenheim.

After I came back to Berkeley in September 1969, I had been nominated for a Guggenheim by Harry T. Moore, the renowned biographer and critic of D. H. Lawrence and his work. I was invited by the writer Kay Boyle to a reception for him at her home in the Haight-Ashbury district of San Francisco. With the publication of *Tattoo,* he had compared me to Susan Sontag and Robert Stone in an important review in 1967. Half the Creative Writing Department at State was there, also Lew Welch the Beat poet. I gave Kay Boyle a copy of *Love.* Everybody was supposed to go to dinner

With his son Gregory Salas, at Ocean Beach, San Francisco, 1969

together, but I didn't have any money. So Harry took my lady and I to the St. Francis Hotel for a drink. We had a great talk and he mentioned that the giver of the Guggenheims was going to be in San Francisco the next week, but I didn't have the social, opportunistic bent to seize upon the chance to meet him, though I knew I had been nominated. I was so used to not being included in social functions, I assumed I was not invited, and though Harry called from the St. Francis and said that my lady, Ginny Staley, had left her purse there, I still didn't get the hint. And I didn't get a Guggenheim. I remember the night I found out. I lay in bed in the dark and cried quietly to myself. It wasn't how good I wrote. It was how well I played the game. I didn't even know when there was a game! As soon as I saw subterfuge, I backed away and so never learned to play. Subterfuge always meant trouble. It always meant cops. It always *was* cops in one form or another. I didn't back away when I sensed them primarily out of principle but to keep from

*Ginny Staley, the author's second wife, Berkeley
brickyard, next to San Francisco Bay, 1979*

being manipulated and all that entailed, meaning
finally being corrupted and coerced into a willingness to play so bad you had no values left
to write with (like screwing the right person,
letting your lady get screwed by the right person) which is why nearly all American novelists never again reach the promise of their first
books. They learn how to *make it* and forget
how to create. They become power driven and
ambitious, rather than loving and creative. I
did not trust the cops. The cops don't trust
each other. Each runs on a power principle
that is total. They get paid to look for trouble,
so they can stop it any way they can. They
enjoy wielding the power. That's why they're
cops. So they create trouble through entrapment so they can bust somebody and earn their
bucks. I back away. Instinct rules me. Thought
follows.

But thought, thinking the problem of entrapment through, works. Thought crystallizes.
Thought reveals the pattern of the subterfuge.
The pattern is in the action. The pattern reveals itself, if I look at it. Maybe the whole

world runs on this subterfuge, but it still smacks
of deceit. And deceit is harmful to the de-
ceived, even if they don't realize it, or if they
do, it hurts, too, to see the deceiver hide himself
from you. No friendship exists at that moment,
nor can it ever if the attitude remains the same.
Maybe everybody lies like this, but the cops
do it, too, and the cops hunt people who break
marijuana laws. So that makes me always an
object of attention, which coupled with the
weapon of my words, my talent, a threat, if I
write about the patterns, meaning write about
the cops. Also, in spite of a humanitarian impulse, when someone manipulates you, me, we,
you struggle to escape their power and you
don't like being subjected to unpleasantness.
Because it is unpleasant. So you, me, we don't
like the unpleasanter. Not for personality reasons, but for self-protective reasons. I stay away
from the subterfuge and unpleasantness, stay
away from people who employ it, which keeps
me out of the literary business because this
business is based on the power principle, get
the advantage, do the other dude in, which
makes me, because I shy away, a monk. Which
makes me think and write because I am in an
intuitive, subconscious state of emotion, which
is creative solitude. The supreme irony of being eternally hunted is that it forces me into
a personal privacy which is so intense that I
have to write to relieve it. Fun, huh?

Then, after I cried over not getting a
Guggenheim, I hung around the Cal campus
in Sproul Plaza in 1972 for a few months. I'd
get up in the morning and read for about
four to six hours, then walk or bike down to
the campus. I'd been coming down like that
through the two and half years I'd been back
in Berkeley. But now I did it every day and
became one of the Telegraph Avenue regulars.
I'd come home for dinner, then write in my
journal, then go back to the campus. Soon, I
belonged to the ever-changing crowd. It was a
great summer. We'd decide to have a party in
the early evening and then send black guys
and girls down the street to beg change because people would give to them. The streets
weren't filled with beggars in those days. One
young girl used to work a corner on Haste
and Telly, but that's all. So, the crew of guys
and girls would come back with handfuls of
change and I'd drive down to a liquor store,
buy some gallons of cheap wine, and we'd go
to somebody's house and have a party. We did

it several times a week. It was great fun. One day, crossing the campus with my long-haired shepherd Sergie, a cop car pulled up next to me and the cop in the passenger seat asked me for my ID. When he looked at it, he was so surprised because I looked so young he said, "Oh! A forty-year-old hippy!"

"Novelist," I said, and he said, "You're the guy who's been putting on all these parties."

I said, "Yeah! And if I had more money, I'd get my picture in the papers for it."

He looked away, thought a moment, then nodded his head, and gave me back my ID.

I didn't have a hot thing going with my lady Ginny anymore. Too much suffering had cooled our romance. She flirted with guys and I had a couple of girls I liked to look at and be around, but that's all. A seventeen-year-old little blonde beauty and I fell for each other though. Her father was a teacher and she was just hanging out at the campus with her Catholic school girlfriend during the summer before college. It never got further than a couple of kisses because I did still have a girl and didn't want to get entangled. There was a certain loyalty between us after the horror of Europe, and we got along well together, Ginny and I. I used our adventures in San Francisco and Europe for my two political novels, *Lay My Body on the Line* and *State of Emergency*.

My lady Ginny Staley helped organize with another girlfriend at the California Public Health Agency the first political demonstration by state employees ever to protest the bombing of Cambodia and/or the Vietnam War. For that reason, she was chosen by Emerson Dagget, the liberal head of the public health magazine, as a journalism intern for the magazine and her future was secured. She ended up being the only original person of that staff left after Reagan closed it down at the end of 1972 because it was so liberal and made one small office out of it in Sacramento. So I moved to Sacramento with her in January 1973, with my son so he could go to Sacramento junior college.

I was trying to sell *Lay My Body on the Line* still and sent it off to Scribners. In the meantime, in that Sacramento house on the edge of the Oak Parks, mainly African American, neighborhood, I read 71 books on revolution from a list compiled by Professor Solomon at San Francisco State. It had everything from Camus's *The Rebel* to Tolstoy's *Resurrection*, a haunting tale of idealistic students, which is never read in American campus literature classes. I discovered *The Brothers Ashkenazi,* and many I had already read, like *The Possessed*. It was like a grand survey literature class or two in graduate study. I was demoralized though. I had never received payment for *Tattoo* being published in France or Spain or *What Now My Love* being published in Japan. The publisher in England gave me $75 only for *Love*'s publication there. I went to a lawyer in Sacramento named Brown. He and his partner turned the case down because there wouldn't be enough money in it for them. To this day, I have never been paid. Though I've had other lawyers write letters about it to agents like Robert Lescher, and all the publishers, all of which say they already paid an agent, including Lescher. One lawyer Moore, the famous African American lawyer who had defended Eldridge Cleaver at one time, sent for my FBI files under the Freedom of Information Act. There I found about half of it blacked out, but enough to confirm my suspicions about a teacher in San Francisco since I had written in my journal when he called me and tried to get me to shut up. These pages disappeared from the file when I checked for them before putting the file in my safe deposit box, along with the pirated copy of *Tattoo* put out by Studio Books, the pornographic subsidiary of Grove Press.

I had a friend then, Stan Rice, assistant director of the poetry center, who told me to appear for an interview for a new state coordinator of Poetry in the Schools, an NEA sponsored organization, with him and the director. The director didn't want me. He did. He'd taught with me on a week-long gig in Point Arena, up on the California coast. He thought I was great. And I thought he was. He held out and I got hired as one of the two state coordinators of PITS. I was there three years and my poetry bloomed.

I had to develop the program in the whole state and Nina Serrano, the other coordinator, had San Francisco. It was the best thing that could have happened to me and my poetry. It brought me out of my now habitually paranoid personality by making me use my naturally extroverted social personality. I love people. They're fun to me. Fun to be around. Fun to love. Fun to dance with and have fun with. Fun to teach. The job made me leave my solitary room and go out and deal with teachers, superintendents, professors, students of all ages, and pretty girls. After I'd gone up and down the state in the fall of '73, I wrote forty long poems in about six weeks. I suddenly burst out into long declamatory poems like "The Politics of Poetry," "Steve Nash," and "Hail to the Poet Laureate."

I'd written long poems before, "The Prophecy of Jonas," "Kaleidoscope of an Assassination in Black and White," and "Trip to the County Fair," "Elegy to a Betrayer by an Outlaw Prophet.'" But now I wrote as if writing for a huge audience of 2,000 people like the readings that I'd been going to. I also wrote a poem called, "Pussy, Pussy Everywhere," a comic poem on the secret police. "The Politics of Poetry" was a tragic poem on the secret police. I wrote long love poems and the poems poured out like a gush of hot feelings. Day after day, even though I had to travel, when I came back home, they'd pour out again. It was a sad, but rich poetic life again. I thank Stan Rice for that opportunity. I built that program up across the whole state. And it brought me out of my monk's cell. It was another of those important stages in my writing life.

But when 1976 began I was still trying to sell my political novel *Lay My Body on the Line* and finish my other political novel *State of Emergency*. I got a flyer in the mail from the Scott Meredith Agency and read an article on Norman Mailer founding The Fifth Estate and decided to write to him, since I'd met him and he'd been my hero since I first started to write. In fact, it was after I read *The Naked and the Dead* that I tried to write my first short story when I was twenty-one years old. Here's the letter I wrote:

Dear Norman,
I read in the paper that you founded The Fifth Estate on your fiftieth birthday as a muckraking operation on the intelligence community and that it had published the names of CIA agents in its paper or had passed the info on to the Greek papers who published them and the head of the CIA in Athens was offed. I am sorry for him, Welch, as I am for any man who dies to perpetuate the military-industrial system that now oppresses us. But I then remembered that the topic of your lecture here in Berkeley last year was "Poetry and Espionage" and that you had asked me in a private conversation later if I had an agent. I

then received a flyer from the Scott Meredith Literary Agency requesting submissions of my work on the terms of $150 apiece per novel, of which I have two, per reading by them. Since I haven't sold anything to a major publisher within the last year, I decided to write to you and ask your help in getting a sympathetic reader for one finished novel I have called *Lay My Body on the Line* and a second unfinished one called *State of Emergency* which are both about poetry and espionage.

I have been trying to get *Lay My Body on the Line* published for three long years. I started it on Election Day 1968 and finished it on Election Day 1972. It is about the corruption of the radical movement by the FBI and the CIA, plus local police. It is about the collusion between the Movement and the secret police, how *They* get to the very leaders of our most radical groups and get them to cooperate against other radicals, which they would call—if they dared speak of it at all—as realpolitik. The basic plot movement is the seizure of an administration building by campus revolutionaries

Leslie Woodd, a close friend, poet, and companion of the author, with her dog Miki

which the protagonist joins because he believes that both Martin Luther King and Bobby Kennedy were assassinated in a coup d'etat pulled off by the Military-Industrial Complex secret police. The time span is roughly encompassed by the deaths of King and Kennedy.

The novel is not some James Bond bullshit thriller but about real espionage on the streets and universities of Berkeley and San Francisco. Agents and editors have read the book. Some have called it great, the best book on student revolution yet, the book we were all waiting for, then have rejected it for *subjective* reasons or—if I have been able to corner them in person—because it is too late for books on student revolution and too early for material on the CIA. All have said the level of the writing is of the highest calibre. I myself believe it is the best book I have ever written and that there are no political novelists writing today because the Establishment, that is the Republican Administration, pressures the big houses to perpetuate the lie that nobody is interested in student revolution, period, while the revolution continues unabated—witness the SLA, the New World Liberation Front, and the constant bombings all over the country, in spite of the fact that they have assassinated our leaders: Malcolm, King, and the two Kennedys.

I have revised and tightened *Body* these last three years. It moves quickly and dramatically, graphically, yet the viewpoint is third-person subjective. It is original in concept, form, and style, not to say content. I am a political novelist who writes from a revolutionary viewpoint. My hero begins as a peace demonstrator and ends as a violent revolutionary. That is what the establishment readers object to. It could be all about student revolutionaries as long as the formula that supports the system was inherent in the attitude of the writer. This writer wants to change society by producing socially relevant art on the level of *The Naked and the Dead*, *Barbary Shore*, and *Deer Park*.

All of my novels are about the individual fighting the police. In the first book, *Tattoo the Wicked Cross*, Grove Press, 1967, which was offered as a dual choice with *Why Are We In Vietnam?* by the Evergreen Book Club, a boy fights the authorities as represented by the superintendent of the reform school (I have never been in a reform school) and an inmate cadet captain. In my second novel, *Gin for Xmas*, which I still have to finish, two boxer brothers turn bunco men and

The boxing coach, University of California at Berkeley, 1984

end in jail. My third novel, *What Now My Love*, is about three young people hunted down by the American and Mexican police for smoking grass and dropping acid (Grove Press, 1970). My fourth novel is *Lay My Body on the Line*. My fifth novel, of which I just finished the third draft, is about a radical writer who is pursued and harassed from America to London, to Spain, to Morocco, to Paris, and finally to New York City by the secret police. It is called *State of Emergency*. It moves on the themes of loyalty and treason and what constitutes a true patriot: the policeman as witless soldier doing his military duty or the idealistic rebel who fights to make his country as great as its constitution.

I doubt if you are familiar with my reputation but *Tattoo* is considered a reform school classic. I won the Joseph Henry Jackson Award in 1964 for it and a Eugene F. Saxton Fellowship in 1965. It is included in a bibliography of great novels called *Good Reading, 1969*, which also includes *The Naked and the Dead*, just above J. D. Salinger's *Catcher in the Rye*. But I have starved since Nixon took office. I am a serious writer who is being pirated by a pornographic subsidiary of Grove Press called Studio Books, which publishes *Tattoo* without a copyright page. My books are sold in France, England, Spain, and Japan but I do not receive a penny in royalties and though I have tried to sue, the lawyers stalled me for six months, then dropped out of the case. Officially, my books are out of print in the U.S. I am a political prisoner in my own country who is not in jail. I cannot publish. I am blackballed just like the Hollywood Ten of the Fifties but without the fanfare, without the publicity which gives power.

When you gave your lecture here in Berkeley last year, I asked you on the open mike when you were on stage if it wasn't true that the Establishment Critics had broken you as a revolutionary political novelist of great social import in the Fifties by putting you down as a craftsman and thereby forced you into journalism by taking your confidence from you. You have agreed with that. In fact, I was talking about McCarthyism or, in truth, Republicanism, getting to you, too, and diverting you from your artistic path to a documentary one and thereby lessening your impact on the society. The great social protest works of *The Naked and the Dead, Deer Park,* and *Barbary Shore,* which fought fascism as it oppressed us were no more. The revolutionary soldier had been beaten by the hostility of a conservative administration. The pigs won another battle. You did not write the great political documents *Miami and the Siege of Chicago* and *The Armies of the Night* until deep into a Democratic administration, books which I love and which have influenced me as a writer and I am talking about *The Novel as History*.

I continue to be influenced by you. I try to use the novel to capture the most significant struggle of our time, the political one between the people and the police state. But I need some help, man. A long time ago, in 1963, when I was being hunted down by the narcs for smoking grass and run out of school for radical activities and finally put in the nuthouse for three weeks full-time, seven weeks part-time, I wrote to you and asked you to listen to my antiwar poems on WBAI. You wrote back and said that you were too busy and that I was trying to cash in on your fame. That hurt. You were my idol. I did need support but you must have been—and probably still are—swamped with requests for help and were

probably justified in your answer. I'm a published novelist now but I'm in the same fix as I was then. But now, you yourself have a stake in my struggle: poetry and espionage. I appeal to you to help me and I know that you are impossibly busy. Yet, I am a practicing agent of all the things you taught about the artist and the rebel, both political and social, and I am paying big, big dues for it. Give me a hand, man, please.

Yours hopefully, Floyd Salas

Mailer never answered. I sent it registered mail, February 9, 1976, to the Scott Meredith Literary Agency and got it signed by a woman named Ellyn Reeymen on February 11, 1976. I keep it in my safe deposit box, since the single copy I had of the pornographic copy of *Tattoo* that was being sold without a copyright page by Grove Press was stolen out of my basement, but not until I had photocopied the cover and put that in my safe deposit box. The lawyer, Ellen Levine, who wrote to me from New York about it has since died. I never wrote to Mailer to ask him about my letter nor asked Mailer for a thing again, until *State of Emergency* finally got published in 1996, and when he came to San Francisco on a tour for his book *Picasso, A Portrait of the Artist as a Young Man.* He treated me like an old buddy, insisted I sit at the table with him for the whole night and offered to look at it when I told him that he was a character in it. He wrote back to me:

Dear, Floyd,
    You're not going to be happy with my reaction but I like you enough to know that our relations have to be honest. I just didn't take to the new book. I only read about fifty pages but it didn't turn me on enough to continue. [He quit after the section about him.] Understand that my eyes are not too good anymore and so I can't read a great deal and I get irritable easily. Not liking your new novel could easily be my fault, but there it is. I just couldn't get interested in the main character. It may be that I've known too many guys like that. None of this takes away from what we talked about at Tosca's. I enjoyed drinking and rapping with you, and will look forward to going with you and Chequi Torres [former light heavyweight champion of the world and an author, too] whenever you get to New York. Let me know in advance, however. I spend most of my time these years up on

Cape Cod in Massachusetts trying to get work done.

Yours and best, Norman

Nevertheless, I really liked his Picasso book and nominated it for a PEN Oakland literary award for 1995, which it won, and he wrote me a thank-you letter, calling me a great guy. But though he called me at home in Berkeley afterwards to tell he he'd called me at my hotel, he never did show up in New York.

In 1976, I read my poem "Pussy, Pussy Everywhere" at Ken Kesey's Hoo Hah in Eugene, Oregon, and almost caused a riot. The poem is a comic satire on the secret police, and when one thousand women wanted to kill me, one thousand people, both men and women, clapped for me. I thought it was just a comic poem meant for a sophisticated audience. I'd read it in Berkeley and didn't have a problem, only caused lots of laughter. But it caused a huge uproar, my usual thing, in my naivete. Two women poet editors, Laura Beausolei and Susan Hopkins wanted to put it in the *Haight Ashbury Journal*, but a couple of other editors convinced them not to print it, so Ishmael Reed published it in *Quilts IV* with an essay by me about it.

When the local Eugene, Oregon, newspaper wrote about the Hoo Hah, Ginsberg and Kesey were the big names, of course, but they gave the lead to my poem and the reaction to it, saying that poetry often disturbs (as did *Howl* and *One Flew Over the Cuckoo's Nest*). I'd say that all my work falls into that category of disturbance. I'm still there; nothing has changed since I began writing.

I must say that I think Kesey, Ginsberg, Bellow, and Mailer have all written great works. Kesey's *One Flew Over the Cuckoo's Nest* and *Sometimes a Great Notion;* Ginsberg's *Howl* and *Kaddish;* Bellow's *The Adventures of Augie March* and *Henderson the Rain King;* Mailer's *The Naked and the Dead* and *The Executioner's Song* are terrific. This is not to mention the other memorable books that Mailer has produced, including his great political works like *Miami and the Siege of Chicago* and *Armies of the Night*. Mailer's genius in particular is his theoretical conception of the novel, which sets him head and shoulders above most writers even when the works themselves don't reach the level of the greatest work.

My only hope, it seems, is to live long enough for the work not to be controversial anymore. In 1977, I won the Joseph P. Lynch Memorial Fellowship for Outstanding Teachers and got hired to teach at Cal. It was ironic since they'd taken away my boxing scholarship years earlier in an attempt to stop my education, but had only succeeded in postponing it. It took a Democratic administration to loosen up the media and the populace again. I'd already come back to the campus and had been helping with the boxing team for two years. The first year I was given a free hand, 1976, I turned out three intercollegiate national boxing champions, at 112, 126, and 132 weight classes. In 1984, I turned out two more national champions in the heavyweight and featherweight divisions.

I am now president of PEN Oakland, the only multi-cultural chapter in the world of the international PEN writers organization, founded in 1922 by John Kenneth Galbraith, whose main purpose is to help downtrodden American writers. Ishmael Reed who is chairman of the board, Reggie Lockett, Claire Ortalda, Jack Foley, John Curl, and I were the founding members.

I work at part-time college teaching jobs to stay alive, and have four polished, unpublished novels. Two of them are historical novels about early Spanish California, *La Favorita*, about the romance between Count Rezanov, the high chamberlain of Russia; *Day of the Dead*, about an aristocratic Spanish woman who was the richest woman in California during the Yankee Conquest and Gold Rush, who had seventeen men die fighting over her fortune; *Heat of the Hunt*, about a poet rapist who preys on the literary community of Berkeley and is never caught; and *The Dirty Boogie*, a Romeo and Juliet, "West Side Story" about a young Hispanic who falls in love with a girl from a Mexican ghetto and fights for and finally loses her. The historical novels are about Spanish aristocrats and so are politically incorrect, and my rapist in *Heat of the Hunt* is half Spanish and half Irish and also politically incorrect so my Hispanic publisher Arte Publico won't touch them.

I have won five literary awards for outstanding fiction: the Rockefeller in 1958, the Jackson Award in 1964, the Saxton Fellowship in 1965, an NEA in 1977, and a California Arts Council Literary Fellowship, 1993, and two outstanding teaching fellowships from the University of California Education Department, 1977 and 1984.

Floyd Salas and Claire Ortalda, 1987

At the time of this writing, October 1996, my last novel *State of Emergency,* which is about the hunting down and suppression of a radical writer by the CIA has not been sent out for reviews, neither prepublication nor otherwise, by my publisher Arte Publico. I have also been informed by the managing editor that they do not plan to publicize my first book of poems, *Color of My Living Heart,* October 1996, nor set up any readings because poetry doesn't sell either. Furthermore, they will only have an autographing session in the Arte Publico booth for my poetry book of my *two books* published in one year, 1996, at the 1996 San Francisco Book Festival, though I am on the advisory board of the festival. My second wife, Ginny Staley, the person the heroine of *State of Emergency* was based on, has married a CIA agent who travels from post to foreign post for the State Department wherever he's needed doing maintenance program management. This confirms the sound basis of the protaganist's paranoia and mistrust of the heroine in the book when she breaks with him at the end of the book

though she still loves him and now believes in his political persecution. I am her ex-husband and I am the only person who knows her intimately who has not been interviewed by the FBI about her character.

At this moment, I have sent out *The Dirty Boogie* and *La Favorita* to yet another agent who might like them, I hope, and find a publisher for me, who would pay me a decent advance and advertise my books, maybe even publish the other two polished novels. I am as blackballed now as any screenwriter or director ever was in the McCarthy years. My only hope is to live long enough to outlive the problems I write about.

But every day, the writing pours out of me. Fiction, novels and short stories, and poems. The creative act at the age of sixty-five is undiminished. But a work of literature is not finished until it is read. So the work remains undone.

Such is the price of artistic rebellion against the literary establishment and the power structure in any modern society.

The Politics of Poetry
Dedicated to Norman Mailer[1]

After a while
they disconnected the wire from my finger
and connected it to my ear.
They immediately gave a high dose of electricity
My whole body shook in a terrible way
My front teeth started breaking
At the same time
my torturers would hold a mirror to my face
and say:
Look what is happening to your lovely green eyes
Soon
you will not be able to see at all
You will lose your mind
You see
you have already started bleeding in your mouth

Torture tactics in Turkey
an urgent appeal
on behalf of hundreds of thousands of innocent
   victims
now suffering the tortures of the damned
Amnesty International
USA

---

[1]Author takes the liberty of changing specific names in different publications.

But there is more to torture than the cell
There is a different kind of Hell

Secret hush of the police sighing
over the snail trails of bookworms
sticking
to the leaves of the library
Those fakes in pipe and tweeds
just as hard as the street dudes
only wearing a sheepskin over the weeds

or the lines of your smiling face
the sense of the lie
behind your grinning teeth

Take them out and dip them in a glass
swimming with solvent
murky clouds of lime
that will dissolve them in time
Dark sores on the calcium
Can't you see it?

Think
of never being able to say a word
for fear it will be heard
and transmuted and computed
and filed in the appropriate place
deep underground
with leaden walls to shrink your balls
catch even your cocktail chatter
or the privacy of your bedroom
where you grimace at the mirror
and cry in your secret heart

Caught in the web
gossamer traces of it brush your face
when you enter a doorway
whispers
that still hang in the air
faint fluttering of skirts
and hum of static
the pretty girls with robes on
beckoning
beckoning

You
like the animal come home from the hunt in a
    heat
the battle fought
needing love
and the musky smell of sex
carrying your offering
wrapped in puffs of cotton
with a red silk ribbon and a bow
the selfish beast
caged down inside
and the angel
let loose with beating wings so hard
it makes you thirst.

. . . .

But she doesn't love you
Secret Agent of the Police State
set out to warm your heart

Listen
There is more to torture than the coffin of the
    cell
of that Hell
There is more to torture than the blow
the kick in the nuts
the knee in the groin
the smash in the face
the broken nose
the blood in the pee
the stiff bones and the puffing muscles
the cattle prod and the bottle up the snatch

Dear Norman
how would you like to wake up in your own
    windowless room
with your heart's blood wetting the bed around
    you?
the mattress seeping through to the springs
with your guts?
blank wall above you?
stone brick around you?
sunk in a concrete hole to keep the worms out?
with only the dampness to decompose you?
skin a dull yellow in the cold air?

Waxy odor
The Ghoul has a painted face
with powder and rouge like an actor
he lays in the bed without flowers
without sniffling mothers
and suffering fathers with hands on their hearts

Without family the poet lies
The Holy Days click by
Soon his time will be up
Fold him into a drawer
some marks of his name and number
the day he died
just his scratch on the wall
and the unread poem under the bed

There is more to torture than a cell
There is a worse kind of Hell

Still
a brown horse shivers his glossy sides!
twitches his mane!
swishes his tail!

Look!
I can see my shadow!
It gathers at my feet!
moves when I do!
jumps! steps! stops!
trots a little!
turns with me!
as if my toe were the axis of the sun!
and all things good!
and all things fun!
turned with it!

BIBLIOGRAPHY

Fiction:

Tattoo the Wicked Cross, Grove Press, 1967, Second Chance Press, 1981.

What Now My Love, Grove Press, 1970, Calder and Boyars, 1971, Arte Publico, 1994.

Lay My Body on the Line, Y'Bird Press, 1978.

Buffalo Nickel, Arte Publico, 1992.

State of Emergency, Arte Publico, 1996.

Color of My Living Heart, Arte Publico, 1996.

Editor:

Stories and Poems from Close to Home (includes "The Politics of Poetry" [poem], "Dead Lion or Live Dog: The Artist in American Society— Some Reflections on the Suicide of Richard Brautigan" [essay], "Steve Nash" [poem], "Kid Victory" [short story]), Ortalda & Associates (Berkeley, California), 1986.

Contributor:

"Buddies and Bad Actors," *Forgotten Pages of American Literature,* edited by Gerald Haslam, Houghton Mifflin, 1971.

"Dead Time," *Chicano Voices,* edited by Carlota Cardenas de Dwyer, Houghton Mifflin, 1975.

"Steve Nash" (poem), *Calafia: The California Poetry,* edited by Ishmael Reed, Y'Bird Books (Berkeley), 1979.

"Brothers Keepers: Buckeye and Boomtown," *California Childhood,* edited by Gary Soto, Creative Arts (Berkeley), 1988.

"Buffalo Nickel" (chapters 1 and 9), *Short Fiction by Hispanic Writers of the United States,* edited by Nicolas Kanellos, Arte Publico (Houston, Texas), 1993.

"To Sergie My Sweet Old Dog Who Died in Old Age" (poem) and "Wyoming Is an Indian Name" (poem), *Many Californias: Literature from the Golden State,* edited by Gerald W. Haslam, University of Nevada Press, 1994.

"Once I Was Blind and Now I Can See" (essay), *Perspectives on Raging Bull,* edited by Steven G. Kellman, G. K. Hall, 1994.

Other:

President and founding member, PEN Oakland, Oakland, California, the only multicultural chapter of the international writer's organization, 1989—. Judge of literary competitions: Joseph Henry Jackson and James M. Phelan Awards, 1977–78; PEN Center USA West Fiction Awards, 1989–90; Marin Arts Council, 1993. Boxing coach, University of California at Berkeley, 1975–91.

Contributor of poetry, essays, and reviews to numerous periodicals, including *The Americas Review, Berkeley Barb, Evergreen Review, Konch, Library Journal, Quilt 4, Transfer Fifty, The Writer,* and *Y'Bird Magazine.* Salas's novels, manuscripts, letters, and notes are held in a collection in the Bancroft Library, University of California at Berkeley.

Tattoo the Wicked Cross has been translated into French and Spanish and *What Now My Love* has been translated into Japanese.

Cumulative Author List

CUMULATIVE AUTHOR LIST
Volumes 1-27

List is alphabetical, followed by the volume number in which autobiographical entries appear.

Abse, Dannie 1923- 1
Ackerman, Diane 1948- 20
Acosta, Juvenal 1961- 27
Adcock, Fleur 1934- 23
Ai 1947- 13
Aldiss, Brian W. 1925- 2
Alegría, Claribel 1924- 15
Allen, Dick 1939- 11
Allen, Walter 1911- 6
Allman, John 1935- 15
Anaya, Rudolfo A. 1937- 4
Anderson, Poul 1926- 2
Andre, Michael 1946- 13
Anthony, Michael 1930- 18
Appleman, Philip 1926- 18
Arden, John 1930- 4
Argüelles, Ivan 1939- 24
Armantrout, Rae 1947- 25
Arnold, Bob 1952- 25
Ashby, Cliff 1919- 6
Atkins, Russell 1926- 16
Aubert, Alvin 1930- 20
Awoonor, Kofi Nyidevu 1935- ... 13
Banks, Russell 1940- 15
Barnes, Peter 1931- 12
Barnstone, Willis 1927- 15
Barrio, Raymond 1921- 15
Baumbach, Jonathan 1933- 5
Bausch, Richard 1945- 14
Bausch, Robert 1945- 14
Becker, Stephen 1927- 1
Belitt, Ben 1911- 4
Bell, Charles G. 1916- 12
Bell, Marvin 1937- 14
Beltrametti, Franco 1937- 13
Benford, Gregory 1941- 27
Bennett, Hal 1930- 13
Bennett, John M. 1942- 25
Bergé, Carol 1928- 10
Bernstein, Charles 1950- 24
Berrigan, Daniel 1921- 1
Berry, Jake 1959- 24
Bishop, Michael 1945- 26
bissett, bill 1939- 19
Blais, Marie-Claire 1939- 4
Blaise, Clark 1940- 3
Bloch, Robert A. 1917-(94) 20
Block, Lawrence 1938- 11
Blotner, Joseph 1923- 25
Booth, Martin 1944- 2
Booth, Wayne C. 1921- 5
Bourjaily, Vance 1922- 1
Bova, Ben 1932- 18
Bowering, George 1935- 16

Bowles, Paul 1910- 1
Boyd, Malcolm 1923- 11
Boyle, Kay 1902-(92) 1
Bradley, Marion Zimmer 1930-. 10
Brée, Germaine 1907- 15
Brewster, Elizabeth 1922- 15
Bromige, David Mansfield 1933-.. 26
Brophy, Brigid 1929- 4
Brossard, Chandler 1922-(93) 2
Brossard, Nicole 1943- 16
Broughton, James 1913- 12
Brown, Dee 1908- 6
Brown, George Mackay 1921-(96) .. 6
Brown, Rosellen 1939- 10
Browne, Michael Dennis 1940- 20
Bruce, Lennart 1919- 27
Bruce-Novoa 1944- 18
Brunner, John 1934- 8
Brutus, Dennis 1924- 14
Bryant, Dorothy 1930- 26
Budrys, Algis 1931- 14
Bullins, Ed 1935- 16
Burke, James Lee 1936- 19
Burroway, Janet 1936- 6
Busch, Frederick 1941- 1
Caldwell, Erskine 1903-(87) 1
Cartland, Barbara 1901- 8
Cassill, Ronald Verlin 1919- 1
Cassity, Turner 1929- 8
Caulfield, Carlota 1953- 25
Caute, David 1936- 4
Cela, Camilo José 1916- 10
Chappell, Fred 1936- 4
Charyn, Jerome 1937- 1
Cherkovski, Neeli 1945- 24
Choudhury, Malay Roy 1939-.... 14
Ciardi, John 1916-(86) 2
Clark, Tom 1941- 22
Clarke, Austin C. 1934- 16
Clement, Hal 1922- 16
Codrescu, Andrei 1946- 19
Cohen, Matt 1942- 18
Colombo, John Robert 1936- 22
Condon, Richard 1915- 1
Connell, Evan S. 1924- 2
Cook, Albert 1925- 27
Coppel, Alfred 1921- 9
Corcoran, Barbara 1911- 2
Corman, Cid 1924- 2
Corn, Alfred 1943- 25
Creeley, Robert 1926- 10
Crews, Judson 1917- 14
Cruz, Victor Hernández 1949-.. 17
Dacey, Philip 1939- 17

Daigon, Ruth 1923- 25
Dann, Jack 1945- 20
Davey, Frank 1940- 27
Davie, Donald 1922- 3
Davis, Christopher 1928- 20
Davison, Peter 1928- 4
Delbanco, Nicholas 1942- 2
Delgado, Abelardo B. 1931- 15
DeMarinis, Rick 1934- 24
Dennison, George 1925-(87) 6
Dillard, R.H.W. 1937- 7
Dillon, Eilís 1920- 3
Disch, Thomas M. 1940- 4
di Suvero, Victor 1927- 26
Djerassi, Carl 1923- 26
Dove, Rita 1952- 19
Dudek, Louis 1918- 14
Duncan, Robert L. 1927- 2
Dworkin, Andrea 1946- 21
Eastlake, William 1917- 1
Easton, Robert 1915- 14
Eaton, Charles Edward 1916- 20
Eigner, Larry 1927-96 23
El Saadawi, Nawal 1931- 11
Elkins, Aaron 1935- 18
Elman, Richard 1934- 3
Emanuel, James A. 1921- 18
Enslin, Theodore 1925- 3
Epstein, Leslie 1938- 12
Eshleman, Clayton 1935- 6
Fast, Howard 1914- 18
Federman, Raymond 1928- 8
Feinstein, Elaine 1930- 1
Feirstein, Frederick 1940- 11
Ferrini, Vincent 1913- 24
Field, Edward 1924- 27
Fisher, Roy 1930- 10
Fitzgerald, Penelope 1916- 10
Flanagan, Robert 1941- 17
Foley, Jack 1940- 24
Forbes, Calvin 1945- 16
Ford, Jesse Hill 1928- 21
Forrest, Leon 1937- 7
Foster, Edward (Halsey) 1942-..... 26
Fox, William Price 1926- 19
Freeling, Nicolas 1927- 12
Fry, Christopher 1907- 23
Fuchs, Daniel 1909-(93) 5
Fuller, Roy 1912-(91) 10
Furman, Laura 1945- 18
Galvin, Brendan 1938- 13
Garrett, George Palmer, Jr. 1929-.. 5
Geduld, Harry M. 1931- 21
Gerber, Merrill Joan 1938- 20

331

Cumulative Index

CUMULATIVE INDEX

The names of essayists who appear in the series are in boldface type. Subject references are followed by volume and page number(s). When a subject reference appears in more than one essay, names of the essayists are also provided.

INDEX

INDEX

INDEX